Society and Thought in Early America

A SOCIAL
AND INTELLECTUAL HISTORY
OF THE AMERICAN PEOPLE
THROUGH 1865

by Harvey Wish
WESTERN RESERVE UNIVERSITY

LONGMANS, GREEN AND CO.

NEW YORK   LONDON   TORONTO

1950

LONGMANS, GREEN AND CO., INC.
55 FIFTH AVENUE, NEW YORK 3

LONGMANS, GREEN AND CO. LTD.
6 & 7 CLIFFORD STREET, LONDON W I

LONGMANS, GREEN AND CO.
215 VICTORIA STREET, TORONTO I

SOCIETY AND THOUGHT IN EARLY AMERICA

Printed in the United States of America
VAN REES PRESS • NEW YORK

Society and Thought
in Early America

To

Anne and Dorothy

Preface

The present unique position of America in world affairs and its aspiration to moral leadership lend high relevance to serious inquiries regarding its social and intellectual inheritance. Hundreds of Europeans, some as gifted as Tocqueville, Crèvecœur, and Bryce, have left ambitious explanations of what an American is and have attempted to probe beneath the surface effects of local color. Unfortunately, too many of these observers came with ready-made formulas that made accurate reporting impossible and they built mountains of myths that obstruct the path of social historians. Natives, too, have added to the American myth. The South is too often seen by Europeans and even by Americans through the nostalgic tunes of Stephen Foster or the characters of Harriet Beecher Stowe's *Uncle Tom's Cabin;* neither of these Northerners spent much time below the Ohio River. A generation of historians of the frontier, while adding their indispensable knowledge and fertile syntheses to the story of westward expansion, has perhaps inadvertently left the impression that the American experience was entirely unique and hence Americans are a people apart from all others. Too many have neglected the fact that continual cultural borrowings from Europe took place at practically all times in American history. The extent to which this cultural interaction resulted in distinctive American institutions and ideas is, of course, the chief problem of the social historian. Too often the complex strands of institutional and intellectual history have been kept apart artificially because it seemed hazardous to integrate them. Because of all these considerations, an early book on American social and intellectual history has to steer a difficult course among the innumerable reefs of conflicting interpretations, bias, and long-respected facts which revisionists have dissolved into myths. Broad incursions into economic history are necessary despite the multiplicity of subject matter. But the urgency of general interpretive works of social and intellectual history requires no defense today.

The author feels renewed gratitude to the hundreds of co-workers in the writing of history whose books and articles have illuminated so many significant facets of our past. The bibliography in this book can indicate only a portion of this basic indebtedness. The author has profited from the opinions of many specialists, some of whom read chapters dealing with their research fields: Marshall Knappen of the University of Michigan, Samuel H. Brockunier of Wesleyan University, Louis B. Wright of the Folger Shakespeare Library in Washington, Charles A. Barker of the Johns Hopkins University, Max H. Savelle of the University of Washington, Carl Bridenbaugh of the Institute of Early American History and Culture in Williamsburg, Richard B. Morris of Columbia University, Thomas C. Cochran of the University of Pennsylvania, Richard Hofstadter of Columbia University, Louis Filler of Antioch College, Ray A. Billington of Northwestern University, Joseph Dorfman of Columbia University, Carl Wittke of Western Reserve University, Aaron I. Abell of the University of Notre Dame, Avery O. Craven of the University of Chicago, Clement Eaton of the University of Kentucky, and Bell I. Wiley of Emory University.

HARVEY WISH

Cleveland, Ohio
January, 1950

Contents

Illustrations

17th Century
between pages 20 and 21

The Royal Exchange, London
Cheapside, the handsomest street in London
Stone Street, New Amsterdam
The Water Stairs on the Thames
New Amsterdam, 1660
The John Ward house, 1684
The John Ward house kitchen
Mission San Xavier del Bac
St. Luke's Church, Isle of Wight County, Virginia
Sioux Scalp Dance
The College of William and Mary
"Penn's Treaty with the Indians," by Benjamin West
Harvard College
The Swedish Lutheran Gloria Dei Church, 1700

18th Century
between pages 116 and 117

"Benjamin Franklin," by Benjamin West
The Newport, Rhode Island, Synagogue
Bedroom of the Shaw house
Chamber of the House of Burgesses, Williamsburg
Hall of the Van Rensselaer manor house
"The Artist in His Museum," by Charles Willson Peale
"Professor John Winthrop of Harvard," by John Singleton Copley
"The Peale Family Group," by Charles Willson Peale
New York City Hall
"The Artist Showing a Picture from Hamlet to His Parents," by
    William Dunlap
"Tontine Coffee House," by Francis Guy
"At the Loom," artist unknown
"George Whitefield," by Joseph Badger

xi

· 1 ·

The England of
Roger Williams

I

THE London in which James I began his reign in 1603 was a crowded, half-medieval city of perhaps 200,000 persons. Farmers, artisans, and even sons of country squires were drawn to London by its bustling trade, its crafts, and its overseas commerce. Cargoes of Chinese silks, Indian spices, Persian and Turkish rugs, Russian furs, and Venetian glassware were unloaded at its vast wharves to fill the shops with exotic goods from distant lands. Its wealthy merchants, founders of hospitals and schools, had almost come to over-shadow in prestige the long-entrenched landed aristocracy, and now challenged the power of the absolute monarchy and the Established Church of England. Many a former tradesman had added to his property an old monastic estate seized from the Catholic Church, and had thus won rank as one of the gentry. In this London Roger Williams was born about 1603.

His father, James Williams, had risen from the ranks of the apprentices to become a shopkeeper and a member of the influential Merchant Taylors' guild, a survival of the medieval craft system. The guild principle, long in decay, had arisen in a world of economic scarcity and painfully slow production, when the Christian canonist had tried, by imposing a "just price" in the interest of producer and consumer, to guarantee the fair distribution of limited supplies. "To leave the prices of goods at the discretion of the sellers," wrote a fourteenth-century cleric, "is to give rein to the cupidity which goads almost all of them to seek excessive gain." From the same ethical standpoint, churchmen had outlawed interest on loans as sinful usury, had forbidden monopolistic and dishonest practices, and had condemned advertising and soliciting as unfair trade methods. Thus Christian guildsmen had hoped to keep economic life, with its besetting sin of greed, under the control of Christian ethics, though they had accepted the existence of fixed class lines between wealthy nobles, merchants, craftsmen, and ordinary laborers. Such economic control would insure each man "the necessaries of life suitable to his station."

In England, as on the Continent, the growth of cities and of a large middle class had been fostered by several factors—by the commercial consequences of the Crusades, which opened Europe's window to the southeast; by the Commercial Revolution, which pushed the frontiers of trade around the globe; and by the Renaissance, which not only rediscovered the civilizations of Greece and Rome but also stimulated economic life through the revival of the classical scientific spirit.

From the Italian states of the Medici bankers and the Venetian merchants, especially in the great commercial age of the fifteenth century, had come a highly developed form of double-entry bookkeeping which made possible efficient business planning and modern capitalist theory. Venice, whose merchants had been exchanging expensive goods between the Orient and Western Europe for centuries, had never been under the spell of the anti-competitive philosophy of the medieval church. Venetians taught the lessons of capitalistic enterprise to such world banking houses as those of the sixteenth-century German Catholic family of Fuggers in Augsburg and their neighbor competitors, the Welsers and Hochstetters. In this century of the rising English *bourgeoisie*, the Fuggers had declined to a mere shadow, wasted by the religious wars and by the extravagance of their clients, the Spanish and German Habsburgs.

While the Fuggers had engaged talented canonist lawyers to prove that interest on loans could be reconciled with church law, England sought to retain the medieval ban on usury. But in 1571 Elizabeth yielded to commercial pressure and allowed interest up to 10

per cent. Churchmen who lamented the rising spirit of avarice failed
to comprehend the new economic forces of business and speculative
expansion. Statesmen trying to regulate national economic life, as
medieval communities had sought to control local wages and prices,
clashed with the increasingly competitive and individualistic businessmen of the seventeenth century.

Merchant capitalists, allied with profit-minded noblemen, were
now able to invest their wealth to great advantage in the relatively
new joint-stock company, the prototype of the modern corporation.
They saw dazzling opportunities for dividends in such overseas
enterprises as the Levant Company, the Virginia companies and,
largest of all, the East India Company. Private enterprise, organized
into joint-stock companies, was capable of financing and administering projects of colonization and development that had overtaxed
national treasuries and ruined smaller pocketbooks. Between 1620
and 1643 the colonizing companies for New England alone spent
£200,000 and employed two hundred ships in carrying 20,000 emigrants. The East India Company, destined to become a "state within
a state," was conducted on so large a scale that it attracted for one
voyage (1617) £150,000 subscribed by one thousand shareholders,
including fifteen earls and dukes. James I, who revived the crown
policy of selling to his favorites profitable monopolies on everyday
needs, thus angered the Puritan merchant class who then demanded
a freer commercial policy in their own interest. They overthrew this
monopolist system in 1624, and after the Civil War the regulation
of trade ceased to be a royal prerogative.

Despite commercial restrictions, the merchant capitalist had ample
opportunity as a middleman to market goods made by the craftsman who no longer dealt directly with the consumer, as he did in
medieval times. By European standards, English industry was relatively free from government control, although the statute books carried detailed regulations of wages and prices. In the country,
new towns arose that had never known the restrictive guild system.
The road toward economic liberalism, stretching into the present
century, was partly traversed in the days of the Stuarts. As the
merchants of London, the seaports, and the commercial inland

towns gained in economic strength, they moved on, logically enough, to make a bid for political power. This was the path to the Puritan Revolution. Before the seventeenth century ended, they were to sweep away the absolute state of the Tudors and the Stuarts for "a government of laws rather than of men" in which Parliament reigned supreme. From this successful merchant and lawyer class, bent on recasting the social order in their own image, emerged a revolutionary individualism that clashed with the arbitrary business and religious policies of the monarchy. Outspoken Puritans in Parliament fought the trade monopolies of the king and resisted the forced loans.

2

Roger Williams as a youth shared the intellectual excitement of religious radicalism that had infected the middle classes of eastern England as well as their brethren across the Channel, the French Huguenots and the Dutch Calvinists. Puritan leaders and many of the rank and file, too, were largely recruited from the urban business and professional classes, though many valuable allies came from the squirearchy and some from the plainer folk. "Freeholders and tradesmen are the strength of Religion and Civility in the Land," asserted a leading Puritan scholar, "and Gentlemen and Beggars and Servile Tenants are the Strength of Iniquity." Puritanism, encouraged under Elizabeth by the return of those once exiled to John Calvin's Geneva by Catholic Queen Mary, was the genuine if belated English Reformation. Henry VIII had separated the Church of England from Catholic Rome largely for dynastic and personal reasons and was content with a state-supported Anglican Church that retained most of the medieval doctrines and practices, except for allegiance to the Pope. The bourgeois Puritan Revolution was to change all this. Before its strength was spent, it would modify England's whole religious system, as well as her economic and social structure.

Throughout the Stuart period, the Puritans feared the rising strength of the Catholic Counter Reformation, the missionary victories of the militant Jesuits, and the decisive Catholic gains in the early phases of the Thirty Years' War, which had begun in 1618 with disasters for the Bohemian and German Protestants. Although the Calvinist King Frederick of Bohemia was the son-in-law of James I, the Puritans had nothing to hope for at home from their monarch. James I, son of the tragic Mary Stuart, Queen of Scots, had been rather easily reconciled to the execution of his Catholic mother and had been reared a Protestant, but he had received more than his fill of Calvinism from the Scottish Presbyterian clergy who had challenged his power and that of his nobility. Heir of Tudor absolutism as well as of Stuart divine-right aspirations, he had sensed that revolutionary Puritanism, because of its conflict with the Anglican Church of which he was supreme head, was incompatible with monarchy. When at his accession the Puritans in the so-called Millenary Petition requested certain changes in the church ceremonials, as too reminiscent of Rome—such changes as the elimination of the sign of the Cross in baptism—he had bluntly insisted on rigid conformity to "one doctrine and one discipline" or he would "harry them out of the land." This decision, made at the Hampton Conference, meant a declaration of war between the monarchy and the Puritans, presaging the era of civil war from 1640 to 1660.

With a keen eye upon dynastic safeguards, James I had warmly embraced an alliance with the Anglican hierarchy of bishops who claimed a divine-right succession from early apostolic authority. Alarmed Puritan critics saw in this claim another manifestation of the process that had made a pope of the ancient bishop of Rome. "No bishop, no king," ran the Stuart argument, and the cause for ecclesiastical conformity was championed in 1628 by William Laud, the zealous new Bishop of London.

One doctrinal aspect of the High Church movement away from Puritanism was the disquieting advance of Arminianism into the Anglican fold. Followers of the influential Dutch theologian, Arminius, had insisted on the continuity of the Church of England with the pre-Reformation English Church, thus lopping off the rigid Calvinist dogmas, such as absolute predestination, and leaving the door ajar for a reconciliation with Rome. The Catholic peril itself had been widely publicized in the abortive Gunpowder Plot, which aimed at the destruction of the Parliament buildings as a preliminary to the Catholic seizure of power, even though few actually and openly avowed this faith and those who did were stigmatized as traitorous allies of Spain. The penal code forced Catholicism into underground channels and led many to follow Lord Baltimore to his haven for Catholics in Maryland.

Although the different branches of the sect interpreted the Puritan program variously, many of these groups aspired to capture the entire Anglican Church and to transform it on the basis of scriptural inspiration into a national federation of churches along lines suggested by Calvin's theocracy at Geneva. One wing sought the principles of Puritan church organization in the Presbyterianism of John Knox of Scotland, Calvin's friend during the sixteenth-century era of the Puritan martyrs. This meant a close association of congregations under the supervision of a central theocratic synod of elders after Old Testament models. One small dissenting group of Puritans, the Separatists or Brownists, because of its simple and democratic organization, won Roger Williams over completely. Separatist churches were each ruled by its parish members and each aimed directly at the Reformation ideal of "a priesthood of all believers," which entailed the removal of all high clerical intermediaries between God and man. A third Puritan form, the type transported to Massachusetts and Connecticut, was a non-Separatist kind of Congregationalism which was largely the product of the learned theologian, William Ames of Cambridge. The Congregationalists sought a less centralized national church that permitted a good deal of local autonomy.

All these Puritan groups shared the hope of abolishing the church hierarchy and the medieval ritual still surviving in the Church of England from Catholic days—hence the name "Puritans," signifying those who aspired to "purify" Protestantism. The simplicity and intimate communion with God associated with early apostolic days was the ideal. Puritanism was to have its Homeric epic in John Milton's *Paradise Lost*, which depicts man's first disobedience in the Garden of Eden through Satan's wiles. In a mighty conflict between good and evil, the angels of God expel the rebellious legions of Satan from heaven into hell. As Adam and Eve leave submissively "hand in hand with wandring steps and slow," they are comforted by the Angel Michael's promise of the Second Coming and a future redemption.

3

The Protestant Reformation, especially in its Puritan form, did not stifle interest in the classical culture of the Renaissance, but it redirected popular attention toward the primitive Christianity of the first century A.D. This meant a new asceticism, an otherworldliness derived from the martyr era of Christian Rome in which English, French, and Dutch merchants played the role of latter-day "Saincts." Business enterprise, as Calvin saw it, had the ascetic merits of a divine "calling" in which success attested to the salvation of the individual and his "predestination" for heaven. Both Protestants and Catholics—the latter recently through the militant Counter-Reformation—were infected by this reawakened spirit of self-denial, sobriety, and discipline. Labor, traditionally man's penance for original sin, was exalted to a new dignity.

Laborers were not too grateful when the innumerable Catholic saints' days with their pageantry and hilarity were abolished by the Puritan Parliament during the Commonwealth era, even if this saved them from the alleged evils of idleness and effectually increased national productivity. The substitution of a strict for a convivial Sabbath was just as discomforting. To the Puritan agitation for a strict Sabbath day of rest, James I replied in behalf of the humbler folk. In his *Book of Sports*, which ministers were compelled to read to their congregations, he demanded, "For when shall the common people have leave to exercise, if not upon the Sundayes and Holidayes, seeing they must apply their labour and winne their living in all working dayes?" Sabbatarianism did not stem from John Calvin, who dismissed this as a "Jewish notion." Actually, Anglican laws on the Sabbath were strictly "Puritanical," but few bothered to enforce them. The early Virginia colony was to borrow many such statutes. In Merry England, boisterous drinking, "wanton" dancing, and gross sensualism filled the Sabbath to the scandal of merchants as well as churchmen. Bearbaiting and bowling were common pastimes.

The theaters, which often ignored the Sabbath and were thought of as peopled by actors with corrupt morals, were partly closed during the Puritan Revolution. Louis Wright suggests that triumphant merchants thus satisfied their heaped-up resentments against being portrayed as usurers, cuckolds, and Puritan hypocrites. However, though the doors of the theaters were locked to the upper classes, the poorer classes were able to avoid the ban.

The victorious Puritans were to silence church organs and choir singing as papist "inventions," foreign to the simplicity of early Christianity. Puritans did not actually dislike music—many, like Cromwell, were intensely fond of it—but they fought its sensual influence over the churches. In an iconoclast frenzy, they smashed hundreds of stained-glass windows, ornate altars, and saintly images. Under Cromwell, the Puritans revived annoying sumptuary laws, punished profanity, discouraged dancing, outlawed Easter, and made Christmas a day of fasting instead of one of revelry. Even the Englishman's well-known capacity for austerity reached its limit, and he welcomed relief during the Stuart Restoration after 1660 despite its pagan excesses and moral holiday.

But the ascetic virtues of self-reliance, thrift, and hard work—diligence in one's calling, as the Calvinists phrased it—had taken root amongst the *bourgeoisie*. They became the shining gospel of success and effectively displaced the knightly code of romantic feudalism. In the American colonies, Benjamin Franklin, in his *Poor Richard's Almanack*, was to popularize the new bourgeois morality in the eighteenth century, as Samuel Smiles was to do for England in the nineteenth. Daniel Defoe's popular *Robinson Crusoe* (1719) exemplified the virtues of self-reliance and perseverance.

4

Roger Williams was a first-hand observer of the current constitutional revolution of the middle class against royal absolutism. As an able court reporter, familiar with shorthand, Williams attracted the attention of Sir Edward Coke, formerly Elizabeth's Attorney General, and became his protegé. As Chief Justice of the Court of

Common Pleas and later of King's Bench, Coke was the powerful champion of a revived common law against the divine right principles of James I. He was the brilliant formulator of the revolutionary legal attack of the merchants and lawyers against Stuart absolutism. The common law, a medieval English concept embracing traditional legal rules and practices, was based on precedents expressed in judicial decisions. It was interpreted by Coke as embodying reason and principle above the arbitrary whims of kings and their agents. In Anglo-American jurisprudence, this came to mean a "rule of law" rather than of men, a system binding upon all citizens and protecting the individual against the state by elaborate technicalities of procedure and rule. Thus the "natural-rights" philosophy of Puritanism, stressing the individual judgment and conscience, was substituted for the authority of the prince and his judges. The revival of the common law in the seventeenth century also meant more social prestige and jobs for a growing body of lawyers.

In typically English fashion, Coke, Selden, and their legal associates infused new life and meaning into moldy documents like the Magna Carta, which was created to protect baronial privileges, and made them bulwarks of natural rights standing above the king's prerogative. America was to borrow this legal system, so solicitous of individual rights, only after the English lawyers had begun to refashion the Magna Carta, the common law, trial by jury, habeas corpus, due process of law, and other personal and property safeguards into stout defenses of the rising merchant and professional classes. Coke's arguments were to serve American revolutionists like James Otis in their attack upon King George III.

While James I, who had united Scotland and England under his personal rule, interfered with the courts, and campaigned against the new political initiative taken by the semi-bourgeois House of Commons, Coke asserted the independence of the judiciary and denied that the king could change common law by proclamation or create new offenses or issue writs in common law courts to prevent the hearing of a case. Thereupon Coke was dismissed as Chief Justice of the King's Bench. He continued the struggle, however, under Charles I. In Parliament he initiated the famous Petition of Right in

1628, which condemned the monarch's extortion of gifts, loans, and taxes, the practice of arbitrary arrest, the compulsory billeting of soldiers in private homes, and the unrestricted issuance of orders for martial law. Here, indeed, was an influential precedent for the American quarrel of 1776.

Somewhat obscured by the triumphant advance of the bourgeois revolution were the more radical demands of many of the lower middle class and the less privileged; these demands looked toward social and economic as well as religious and constitutional reform. Some of these radicals, who were to influence Roger Williams profoundly, were stigmatized by Cromwell as Levellers. These revolutionary liberals even went beyond Coke and the moderates by searching for their principles in the laws of nature (the natural-rights philosophy), rather than in arid legal precedents. They endowed man with innate and inalienable rights that were to be defended by political institutions based on the free consent of the individual expressed through universal manhood suffrage. The generation that wrote the American Declaration of Independence and the French Declaration of the Rights of Man was to be indebted to the Levellers for this popular middle-class philosophy of natural rights. In their natural-law doctrines appeared the later American constitutional idea that there was a fundamental law that was superior to simple, repealable statutes. American abolitionists were to find comfort in the "higher-law" doctrine and to refuse to be bound even by the Constitution when that ran counter to what they conceived to be the higher authority of natural law. In economic affairs, the Levellers were more circumspect, although they attacked monopolies, the land enclosure acts, and burdensome taxes.

Still more radical were the True Levellers at the bottom layer of society. These Diggers, as they were called, wished to abolish private ownership of land and to establish a Utopian kind of Christian communism. Gerrard Winstanley, a London tradesman, and the Digger leader, asserted, "The Earth must be freed from entanglement of Lords and Landlords to become a Common Treasury for all." Such experiments in Christian communism were to find occasional imitators in the New World.

5

In a nation still overwhelmingly rural, with four-fifths of its people deriving an income from the soil, the ruling classes of nobles and country gentry could not be expected to yield the reins of power to the parvenu merchants. But the landlord group was being gradually stripped of its feudal authority. The House of Lords, composed of all the peers of the realm, was watered down by the Stuart policy of selling peerages wholesale, thus indirectly giving the wealthy middle class representation in that august body. James alone added sixty members and Charles I half that number. During the Civil War, the Puritans confiscated many noble estates, thus creating a new landed gentry with middle-class rather than feudal roots.

Below the peers were the lesser aristocracy and the country gentry—the squirearchy—upon whom rested the burdens of local government, particularly the duties of justices of the peace. Contemporaries found the squire an elusive figure for generalization: some were boorish, though others were highly cultivated in taste; many were only interested in breeding race horses and dogs, while others devoted themselves conscientiously to their tenants and neighbors. Cromwell and William Brewster, both from the squirearchy, represented a wing of the country gentry that supported the Puritan cause.

Just below the gentry was England's proud "yeomanry" of several hundred thousand independent small farmers, extolled in the national traditions of popular defense and hospitality. Although contemporary writers bemoaned their disappearance and the decline of hospitality before the advance of commercialism, many of the yeomanry apparently rose into the gentry as large-scale landlords in the new capitalist agriculture by marrying the daughters of the squires; others, however, sank into the laboring class. This traditional hierarchy of ruling classes was obviously split by the increasingly capitalist nature of farming, which required funds that only the *bourgeoisie* could provide. The rural gentry, therefore, saw a natural political ally in the urban middle class as against the displaced peasantry and the rootless city craftsmen. Thus, the Stuarts, for all their aristocratic supporters, were not lacking in substantial allies among the masses.

Emigration to the New World was due in large measure to the serious economic dislocation accompanying the early stages of large-scale commercial farming. An agrarian revolution, dating back to the fifteenth century, was gradually altering the traditional subsistence farms. As population increased and land values rose, inflated partly by Tudor currency debasement and partly by expanding foreign demands for English wool and grain, the new capitalist landowners raised their rents, turned to more scientific and more costly methods of cultivation, and evicted tenants who no longer fitted into the scheme of things. Village lands, held as commons, where all might pasture cattle and pigs or gather wood, were enclosed by influential landowners for sheep raising or crops; wastelands and fens, whose title was often communal or belonged to poor families who eked out a living by raising poultry or by fishing, were reclaimed at considerable expense by the newcomers. Scattered arable strips, held in medieval style by peasants who moved inefficiently from one strip to another, disappeared as the more scientific farmers, merchants, or thrifty artisans embarked on commercial farming. Draining of fens, manuring of lands, careful animal breeding in segregated pastures, and crop rotation, all of which required substantial capital, represented the new order in the seventeenth century. Stubborn tenants, wedded to the old order and resisting the loss of their lands, were often dealt with harshly in the courts.

Although the enclosure movement and related changes worked ultimately for the welfare of England by making it possible to support millions more at a higher standard of living on the crowded little island, too many evicted farmers and farmhands failed to find other types of work. "Sheep eat men," cried the evicted bitterly as they watched one or two shepherds take over the land on which perhaps twenty had gained a livelihood. Peasants rioted, slaughtered the sleek cattle of the wealthy farmers, and destroyed many of their recent improvements. Descendants of England's freed serfs wandered idly over the country as "sturdy beggars," arousing among

the propertied gentry fears grimly preserved in the ditty, "The beggars are coming to town."

To deal with this situation, the Tudors repressed begging, fought
vagrancy by restricting movement from one parish to another, and
regulated almsgiving. However, after Henry VIII dissolved the
monasteries, which had provided considerable poor relief, and gave
or sold their vast resources to favorites, the English state was compelled to take over relief on a national scale. Successive acts toward
this goal culminated in the famous Elizabethan Poor Law of 1601.
This made every parish responsible for its own poor with overseers appointed by the justice of the peace to collect a poor rate for
dependents. Work was to be provided for the able-bodied, and children were to be apprenticed to learn a trade. Sturdy beggars, some
of whom had burnt the barns of farmers who refused them alms,
were to be compelled to work at rates fixed by the local justice—
usually a well-to-do squire who tended to favor the lower rates. The
recalcitrant might be whipped, branded, and, if residents of another
parish, could be banished. Vagabonds and rogues stood in the pil-
lories or sat in the stocks, and boys were even permitted to throw
stones at them. Those who went to jail starved on the "county al-
lowance" of bread and very little else, or perhaps died of prison-
disease in a filthy, crowded room. Care was taken that the "impotent
poor" did not find public charity too attractive. Children, sent to
workhouses to learn trades, were delivered sermons on "Contented-
ness in a low condition, and the excellent Joyes of Heaven and the
Horror of Hell." Illiteracy was the usual fate of such children of the
poor. Altogether, the Poor Law of 1601 did not eradicate pauperism
and the government showed increasing alacrity in transporting
"divers idle young people" to the colonies.

This law was merely part of the Tudor system which made national those medieval regulations over wages, prices, and conditions
that were formerly of local scope. In Roger Williams' day, Elizabeth's Statute of Apprentices (1562) was still in effect, extending to
the nation the seven-year apprenticeship rule of early guild days for
all sixteen-year olds of the poorer classes, except those engaged in
farm work. Many years later, these apprentices rebelled against this

forced training, its long hours and hard work, and the master's control over their goings and comings. Little wonder that they resented the Puritan campaign to abolish the hilarious, if papist, saints' days and to set up a prim Sabbath.

Another method of aiding the poor, derived from feudal paternalism, was to require local authorities to store up wheat in times of plenty for famine periods and farmers to set aside one-fourth of their wheat for the poor at low prices. The squire, in the manor-house world where he busied himself with his dogs and horses and with his duties as justice of the peace, was expected to act paternalistically toward unfortunates. However, medieval methods worked worse than ever as more rural folk became tied to the uncertain wage system and lost the few cottage acres that had enabled them to supplement their small incomes.

London's poor were scarcely better off than their rural brethren. Not too far from the prosperous merchants' homes and the staid noble mansions were the antiquated tenements where the poorer classes were "heaped up together and in a sort smothered." The city's narrow and crooked medieval streets—mostly wiped away by the Great Fire of 1666—were littered with garbage thrown from the windows. Here were found, also, the debris of human society—thieves, vagrants, prostitutes, drunkards. Epidemics of devastating proportions broke out periodically. In 1603, when Williams was an infant, one-sixth of London's population was killed by the plague. While the well-to-do fled to the country, the laborers suffered severely and were reduced to beggary. When the plague death toll had fallen to a moderate thirty or forty a week, the government reopened the theaters and permitted the plain folk to return to their dogfights and bearbaiting.

6

The price revolution of Williams' day lessened real wages and added to the suffering of the English masses whose income was frequently regulated by law. This inflation was largely caused by a huge flow of precious metals from Spain's lands overseas and the new central European mines. In 1624, the Virginia Company gave is its colonial objective, "The removinge of the Surcharge of necessitous people, the matter or fewell of daungerous insurrections, and thereby leavinge the greater plentie to susteyne those remayninge within the Land." Thus economic pressures, including a keen hunger for land and enhanced social status, were entwined with religious motives as explanations of emigration. Religious factors were usually more influential with middle-class elements than with the very poor.

England's future, in the minds of seventeenth-century leaders, was threatened by the alarming disappearance of her ancient forests, so basic to the building of ships and to the needs of her growing mills and iron furnaces. The Baltic sources of wood were too uncertain, partly because of Sweden's monopoly, which kept prices high and sometimes cut off England's supply at critical times. Hopes of empire rested on the ability of new colonies like Virginia and later New England to provide the mother country with lumber, pitch, tar, rosin, cordage, and masts. The fuel shortage, which might have made the Industrial Revolution of the next century impossible, was to be solved eventually by the discovery of efficient methods for mining coal.

Beneath the factors dividing the country in the Puritan Civil War persisted a strong current of nationalism and imperialistic ambitions. The glory of the victory of 1588 over the Spanish Armada still exalted English sea power and trade at the expense of the Catholic Habsburgs. The Tudors, from Henry VII to Elizabeth, had put down the anarchic power of the feudal aristocracy, which had flared up in the War of the Roses, and had unified England under their banner. Now the nation was actively seeking its place in world trade against Spain, France, and Holland. English seamen of the Elizabethan Age penetrated Russia, Central Asia, and the New World; they fought the Barbary pirates and, with Francis Drake, circumnavigated the globe. English merchants of the Muscovy Company enjoyed in Russia the privilege of self-government, denied to the Czar's own subjects. The East India Company traded among the Hindus and the Moslems of India, advancing inexorably upon foreign competitors.

Mercantilist advisers, in the interest of "political arithmetic," argued that accumulating precious metals and stimulating exports was the economic key to empire. They made a fetish of the goal of a "favorable balance of trade," which was to be achieved through a planned excess of exports over imports. To do this, production through bounties must be stimulated, new colonies must be added to the empire as markets and sources of raw materials, and the carrying trade between the homeland and the colonies must be monopolized. Above all, the Empire must be kept self-sufficient in strategic military supplies and trained seamen. Such objectives meant a violent international contest for power such as the wars of Cromwell and Charles II against the commercial rivalry of Holland. From this struggle, English nationalism emerged stronger than ever. For the middle classes, the modern nation-state, which stressed the fraternity of all Englishmen, was the ideal instrument of power against the semi-feudal dynastic loyalties of subject to king.

7

Like many another Puritan, Williams studied theology at Cambridge, entering Pembroke Hall in 1623 as the protégé of Coke. This famous university, then in the ascendant over its older rival, Oxford, included among its students Cromwell, Milton, William Brewster, John Winthrop, John Harvard, Thomas Hooker, and John Cotton. Indeed, Cambridge became so popular with Puritans that its Emmanuel College, with its tutorial system, furnished the model for Harvard. Restricted though the University's medieval and theological studies seem from the modern standpoint, the college-cultivated man still gained something from the robust Elizabethan Renaissance. The great age of Shakespeare was scarcely over, for the bard had died in 1616 and such late plays as *The Winter's Tale, The Tempest,* and *Cymbeline* belonged to contemporary literature. Ben Jonson, author of *Volpone, The Alchemist,* and *Catiline,* was then in high favor with the extravagant court of James I, lending his talents to the elaborate masques, a kind of English opera celebrating a festive event. The literary tradition of Christopher Marlowe and his

Cambridge "University Group" was a fresh memory. Another Cambridge man was the creative John Fletcher, whose fruitful collaboration with Francis Beaumont of Oxford had given England scores of her most popular plays, such as *The Maid's Tragedy* and *Rule a Wife and Have a Wife.*

Williams was still at Cambridge when Dr. William Harvey published his epoch-making *De Motu Cordis* (1628), showing on the basis of experimentation that the blood is driven outward from the heart as the source of the circulatory motion and is returned to it. Scientists had already anticipated some of Harvey's observations, but his demonstration effectively ended the sway of Aristotle's idea that the blood is elaborated from food by the liver as the dynamic force. Lord Chancellor Francis Bacon, then in disgrace through the efforts of the parliamentary party, became the godfather of the age of experimental science and secularism through his inductive theories of logic and his pungent essays. His *Advancement of Learning* (1605) inspired many with the hope that a rational world of science was possible, as did his *Novum Organum* (1620), a new and disturbing book in Roger Williams' time. In 1614, John Napier of Scotland had published his first work on logarithms to simplify the mathematics of astronomy, but his tables were almost immediately applied to the practical science of navigation. Pioneer advances were being made in meteorology, optics, analytical geometry, and allied sciences.

Intellectually, the time was ripe for middle-class speculation on the nature of the state and its roots in popular consent. The century was to bring forth the liberal doctrines of John Locke and of James Harrington, author of *The Commonwealth of Oceana* (1656), as well as the liberal constitutional ideas of Coke and Selden. John Milton could write the Puritan epic and still pen a defense of divorce and attack the traditional censorship over faith and morals. "Lords and Commons of England," wrote Milton in *Areopagitica,* with the calm assurance of one stating an incontestable fact, "consider what Nation it is wherof ye are ... the governours; a Nation not slow and dull, but of a quick, ingenious, and piercing spirit, acute to invent, suttle and sinewy to discours, not beneath the reach of any

point the highest that human capacity can soar to. Therefore the
studies of learning in her deepest Sciences have been so ancient and
so eminent among us..." Thus, upon this premise in his noted
essay on the "liberty of unlicenc'd printing," he argued for the free
expression of opinion and learning without the need for a clerical
imprimatur or a state license. The Reformation doctrine of individual liberty became part of a crusade for liberalism in the Puritan
Revolution. Yet New World Puritans, who began with the medieval
belief in censorship and the ideal of an Old Testament theocracy,
were slow to adopt Milton's counsel. The fullest implications of the
liberal concept of freedom did not come overnight.

In spite of the advance of science and secularism, medieval attitudes persisted. When Oxford instituted the Savile professorships of
geometry and astronomy in 1619, many of the gentry refused to
send their sons to be "smutted with the black art." Sir Walter
Raleigh's interest in chemical experiments and applied science led
to accusations that he had set up a school of atheism. The medieval
Faust legend, expressed in Marlowe's moving play, incarnated the
folk belief that science could be acquired only by selling one's soul
to the devil. Most revealing of the vitality of anti-rationalism was the
witchcraft craze.

Puritans took far too prominent a part in the witchcraft frenzy
of the early seventeenth century, especially early in the reign of
James I when at least forty or fifty were hanged as witches and during the years 1645-47 of the Long Parliament when two hundred
witches were executed in the eastern Puritan counties. Witches and
devils were the staples of ancient and medieval societies; they became the object of successive crusades among Catholics and Protestants alike after a fifteenth-century pope and the sixteenth-century
Bible literalists insisted on the scriptural injunction, "Suffer not a
witch to live." Elderly and eccentric persons, fascinated by the personal power attributed to occult art, were often convinced that they
actually belonged to Satan's kingdom when they pricked the effigies
of their enemies to injure them or tried their hands at raising tem-
pests, haunting children, and industriously doing the devil's work.
French fanatics, not the least of whom was the Renaissance philos-

opher, Jean Bodin, destroyed thousands of lives in the last part of the sixteenth century. In Germany, thousands of suspects confessed under torture and were executed or imprisoned. Besides, Renaissance rationalism, with its roots in classical lore, left a wide gap for the magic of ancient Rome, the trusty love philters, and other charms and incantations.

James I, who left Scotland after a witchcraft craze had taken innumerable lives in forty years—one writer even claims the fantastic number of 8000!—found the English most receptive to his own brilliant campaign against Satan. Newsletters carried reports of stranded mermaids on the seashore and witchcraft was a prop to the best literature, including Shakespeare's. Intellectuals like Sir Thomas Browne and Francis Bacon were ready to prove the actuality of witches and to discuss their everyday habits. The king, whom the discerning had called "the wisest fool in Christendom," wrote, while still in Scotland, his own treatise, *Demonologie,* to silence the few outspoken rationalists on the Continent who questioned the existence of witches, and to enlighten his countrymen on the intricacies of the subject. His favorite formula for trapping witches was to bind and wrap the accused in a sheet and then to cast the body into the water. If the suspect was indeed guilty, the water, being an element of baptism, would reject the body and it would float. Under James I's Act of 1604 punishing witchcraft, a reign of terror began and was revived under Puritan sponsorship in later years. Hundreds of English folk—popular tradition inflated this to 70,000! —were executed. New England Puritans, whose hanging of witches stained the history of the colonies, were mild offenders by these standards, destroying not more than thirty-four as witches in the seventeenth century.

Cambridge, like Oxford, was touched only in part by Renaissance intellectualism, much to the sorrow of a critical student like Milton. Boisterousness and traditional college sports were in full evidence. One student recalled that the University of the 1620's was full of "swearing and drinking, rioting and hatred of all piety and virtue." Town-and-gown fights lost none of their medieval zest, to the discomfiture of sober townsmen. Students enjoyed dancing, vaulting, football, and—despite prohibitions—swimming, frequenting taverns and brothels, watching cockfights, and joining in bearbaiting. They acted—or overacted, as Milton claimed—in student comedies and interludes. Most distasteful to the Puritans was the trimming policy of the University on matters of religion. Cambridge could flirt with Calvinism and yet champion the Established Church and monarchial supremacy. Together with Oxford, the University was to become a royalist stronghold at the outbreak of the Civil War.

Very significant, however, was the influence of Cambridge in determining the unusual intellectual interests of the Puritans. Its gifted faculty united Renaissance and Reformation beliefs in Christian Platonism. The Cambridge Platonists, who made up a brilliant circle at the University, drew heavily upon Petrus Ramus, a French humanist who had embraced Calvinism and had attacked the decaying Catholic scholasticism of that day, which was dominated by Aristotle's logic and rhetoric. To denounce Aristotle, who was intimately bound up with Catholicism, was a recommendation to many Puritans, but the absence of Aristotle left them without a philosophic structure and might have forced them to turn to the "inner light" doctrines and "enthusiasms" of other Protestant sects. Ramus developed instead a Platonic system which made Puritanism a rational cult in a philosophic sense, suspicious of individual claims to divine revelation. This view was clearly expressed by one of the Cambridge Platonists, Benjamin Whichcote, tutor of Emmanuel College, who reconciled Platonism and Christianity upon the ground that "The Christian religion is intellectual, rational, and spiritual." Such a formula, consistently applied, insured the intellectual leadership of Puritan New England.

8

The visitor to Cambridge in Roger Williams' day was also struck by the outstanding examples of Renaissance architecture in its buildings, a development considerably in advance of most of urban England. The era of James I marked a transition from the typical Gothic style of the Middle Ages to the classicism of the Renaissance. Jaco-

17th Century

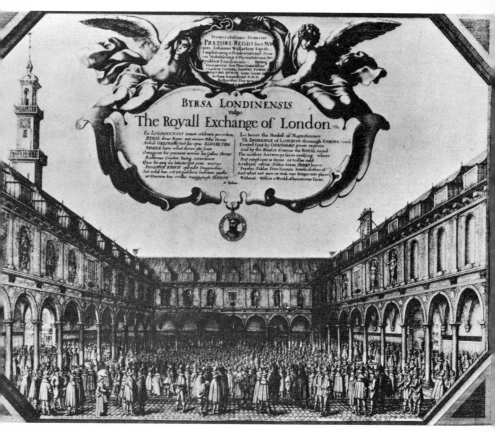

The Royal Exchange, London, financial center for many Puritan as well as non-Puritan merchants. (Engraving by Hollar, 1644; Folger Shakespeare Library)

Cheapside, the handsomest street in London, 1638, showing the royal entry of Marie de Medici. (From *Histoire de l'Entrée de la Regne mère du Roy tres-Chrestien*, London, 1639; Folger Shakespeare Library)

Stone Street, looking toward Whitehall, New Amsterdam, 1659. (Miniature group, Museum of the City of New York)

London in Roger Williams' day: The Water Stairs on the Thames. (From Visscher's *View of London*, 1616; Folger Shakespeare Library)

New Amsterdam, 1660. (Model by C. Capehart and J. E. Dougherty, Museum of the City of New York)

The John Ward house, built in 1684. This illustrates the seventeenth-century New England house with its many gables, overhangs, and diamond-paned casements. (Now on grounds of the Essex Institute, Salem, Massachusetts)

The John Ward house kitchen. (Essex Institute)

Mission San Xavier del Bac, near Tucson, **Arizona**, founded by the Jesuits in 1732. (Library of Congress)

St. Luke's Church, Isle of Wight County, Virginia, whose pointed windows and stepped-up gables illustrate its seventeenth-century origins. (Library of Congress)

Sioux Scalp Dance, upper Missouri, as sketched by George Catlin in 1832. These Sioux lived farther east in early colonial times. (Smithsonian Institution)

The College of William and Mary (now restored) was begun in 1695 and is believed to have been designed by Sir Christopher Wren himself. The statue honors Lord Botetourt, Virginia's royal governor, and was the work of a London sculptor, Francis Hayward. (Colonial Williamsburg, Inc.)

"Penn's Treaty with the Indians," by Benjamin West. (Pennsylvania Academy of the Fine Arts)

Harvard College. Harvard Hall at left was completed in 1675, Stoughton Hall in center during 1699, and Massachusetts Hall in 1720. (Library of Congress)

A Prospect of the Colledges in Cambridge in New England

The Swedish Lutheran Gloria Dei Church, dedicated in 1700, was one of the first colonial churches to install an organ. (Library of Congress)

bean styles favored old half-timbered buildings with the structural details, such as heavy-beamed ceilings, exposed. The medieval spirit of amateur and communal inspiration for architecture was passing in favor of the individualistic concept of a single expert architect.

This was the age of Inigo Jones, a former stage manager noted for his settings for Ben Jonson's masques. Jones had studied in Italy and had there fallen under the spell of the Italian classicism of Palladio, with its emphasis on the solid Doric orders. Palladian art proved to be "the gateway to the Renaissance," culminating in the pure classicism of Christopher Wren during the next generation. Wren, designer of St. Paul's Cathedral, was to replace the medieval half-timbered houses of London with the elegant multi-storied Renaissance brick buildings and fine-spired churches of the era following the Great Fire of 1666. He envisaged wide avenues, symmetrical streets, and impressive approaches in a broad pioneer conception of city planning, unfortunately never fully executed. Nevertheless, Wren was to influence city planning in the New World through William Penn's new city of Philadelphia, which followed the classical symmetrical pattern. The sophisticated Italian influence also affected the plan of the traditional manorial estates, whose uncultivated deer parks gave way in part to the graceful Italian style of rectangular gardens highly cultivated and crossed by broad walks.

While architecture advanced, painting made only mediocre progress, despite the court aid of the early Stuarts to a few distinguished continental portraitists. James I, though notably deficient in esthetic sense, did bring to England Anthony Van Dyck, the graceful colorist of the dominant Flemish school. Charles I, a zealous art collector and connoisseur, made valiant efforts to keep the great Flemish artist, Rubens, in England, but succeeded only in getting a few commissions executed, such as the Whitehall decorations. From Hans Holbein the Younger, court painter to Henry VIII, stemmed an English vogue for exquisite miniature portraits copied from large originals. As yet, however, the English artists of the early Stuart era offered little more than a tolerable competence, far overshadowed by the Flemish, German, and Italian masters.

The joyous Elizabethan spirit of song was somewhat muffled during the early Stuart period, hard pressed by Puritan suspicions of lustful intonations, particularly in the music of stage plays and court masques. From the Netherlands and Italy, a century before had come the intricate harmonies of the madrigals, unaccompanied lyrics sung in three or more parts. This age of the madrigal flourished particularly on upper-class sponsorship. Sacred music continued to thrive, offering composers, who were frequently organists, many opportunities for anthems, masses, and instrumental pieces, such as those for the virginal, the predecessor of the spinet. When the Puritans destroyed the organs during the Civil War, with the dual intention of eradicating these Romish survivals from the churches and of preventing the taverns from appropriating them for profane use, a serious blow was dealt to an entire phase of musical expression. Still, paradoxically enough, the beginnings of opera in England and a large and increasing output of musical publications coincided with Puritan rule. Cromwell himself was somewhat of an innovator in popularizing concerts, and Puritan psalm-singing took on a crusading fervor. On the farms and in the pastures of England, laborers and servant girls sang the ballads of old, many of them destined to cross the Atlantic and to survive in a newer land.

Besides these phases of the Renaissance spirit, there was also the popular interest in adventure and travel. That generation had a keen love for the stories of the daring Spanish explorers and the Elizabethan sea dogs who sacked the rich cities and treasure fleets of the Spanish Main. In their mind's eye, they followed Raleigh along the fabulous banks of the Orinoco, looking for the gold of El Dorado, or along the bleak shores of Newfoundland. At Oxford, Richard Hakluyt, outstanding geographer and lecturer, had recently published many English travel narratives in epic prose. His expansionist propaganda for the New World, and perhaps the enthusiastic references to America in the popular plays of the day, had inspired Sir Humphrey Gilbert and his half-brother, Walter Raleigh, to explore the North American coastline during the 1570's and 1580's in the vain hope of founding a profitable settlement with their limited private resources. John Smith had long ago given up his apprenticeship to a merchant to become a roving soldier of fortune, a hero of hair-raising adventures which lost nothing in the telling. As an honored founder of England's first permanent settlement at Jamestown in 1607, he published in London his fascinating accounts of New England, Virginia, and other distant lands.

In 1627, Williams took his bachelor's degree at Cambridge, but he did not persist long in his original intention to continue advanced studies. He may have been antagonized by the rising High Church tendencies at the University. Two years later he married Mary Barnard, a serving girl, after a frustrated attempt to marry a woman considerably above him in social station. Acting as a private chaplain, he, like many other Puritan divines, saw no future for clerical preferment in Stuart England where Puritanism was forced on the defensive. The bright New World beckoned and opportunity came to him when he met Thomas Hooker and John Cotton, the future Massachusetts leaders, and he became interested in the Massachusetts Bay Company. The Puritans looked upon their destination as a land of Canaan where they might set up an ideal theocratic state. Already a host of speculative writers of the Renaissance, like Thomas More and Francis Bacon, had portrayed ideal Platonic states, which men came to identify with some unspoiled land in the New World. Besides, the Reformation impulse of primitive Christianity with its apostolic communism and Old Testament ideas encouraged many sects to dream of a New Jerusalem across the Atlantic. So began the Great Puritan Migration of 1630.

· 2 ·

The New England of
Roger Williams

I

On February 5, 1631, Roger Williams entered the Puritan stronghold of Boston to accept a call as church teacher. Upon arrival, he
found himself unable to agree upon fundamental church principles
with the Puritan theocrats and he decided to look elsewhere for a
post. As a strict Separatist, he disliked the authoritarian rule of a
state church and demanded that the Bay Colony break its final ties
with the Church of England. He insisted upon the sectarian ideal
of a free church system deriving from the complete separation of
church and state.

These Separatist ideas seemed impolitic to the Boston leaders because, among other things, they would antagonize the Crown. The
newcomer made things worse by revealing the full implications of
his anti-authoritarian beliefs: he denied that any magistrate had the
right to use force in maintaining religious orthodoxy. Such an opinion
ran counter to the ideal of the Calvinistic theocracy which was
founded on the medieval and biblical theory of the union of church
and state. Freedom to the theocrats did not include the right to err
in doctrinal matters and Bay Colony leaders assumed the traditional
power to punish heretics and sinners of all sorts. Refusing to admit
that any theocracy had a monopoly over truth, Williams angered
the Bostonians and left to accept a position with the congregation
at Salem where Separatist principles had been lately established.
Before he could take up his new duties, he was dogged by the hostile

Bay Colony leaders who warned Salem of its calamitous error and deprived him of his church. Thereupon Williams left to go southward to the chief Separatist outpost—Plymouth.

Along Plymouth's little Leyden Street, reaching crookedly across a hill to the ocean, Williams found some three hundred Pilgrims who had arrived since 1620.* Their exodus from England and Holland was like that of the ancient Israelites whose Old Testament world and religious mission seemed very real to the "saving remnant" of Separatist followers of William Brewster and William Bradford. Actually, the crowded double-decked *Mayflower* on which the first colonists came and which furnished a proud patent of aristocracy for so many descendants carried far more "strangers," outsiders interested in the economic possibilities of fishing and hunting, than "saincts" devoted to Christian purity. Longfellow's romanticized trio, Captain Miles Standish, John Alden, and perhaps Priscilla Mullins, herself, was not at first among the Separatist saints.

Of the original Separatist congregation of famed Scrooby, which had emigrated to Amsterdam and Leyden during 1607-8 to escape religious persecution at home, only a few Pilgrims—notably Brewster and Bradford—arrived. The Dutch Calvinist churches, observed Bradford approvingly, "were shapen much neerer the primitive [Christian] patterne than England for they cashered the Bishops with al their courts, cannons, and ceremoneis, at the first." For, unlike other Puritan sects, the Pilgrims were radical Separatists who yielded no quarter to compromise with the Romish Church of England and held to the democratic congregational principle of independent church organization and self-government, excluding bishops as well as the rest of the clerical hierarchy that stood between man and God.

---

* Like other English immigrants, so Hrdlička, the anthropologist, later discovered, they were not the tall, blond, longheaded Nordic giants that so many American racialists assumed when they helped shape the National Origins Act of 1924 to restrict "inferior" Mediterranean and eastern European newcomers in favor of "Nordics." The Puritans were mostly of medium height, almost dark in complexion, and round-headed in type; the misapplied political term "roundhead," inspired by the relatively few Puritans who cut their hair in this distinctive style, had then some basis in anthropology, if not in the way originally intended.

Back in England, Robert Browne, founder of Separatism, had won the contempt of his sect by going over to the Anglicans, but the name of Brownist still clung to the Pilgrims. Yet, the Separatists, in their appeal to James I for support of their emigration plans, had promised in the Leyden Agreement of 1618 to recognize the authority of the Anglican bishops and the basic articles of the Church of England. Most of those who voyaged on the *Mayflower* were actually reared in the Anglican Church. Despite the fact that only about thirty-six of the one hundred and one passengers were definitely Separatists, this united minority had no intention of allowing religious "errour" in the form of complete tolerance to adulterate the purity of the sect.

In Holland the "saincts" had not prospered materially and had shown a centrifugal tendency to embark on novel sectarian speculations, even criticizing the truths of their Dutch brethren. Bradford bewailed the common distaste for "great labor and hard fare" among his people. "Yea," he wrote sadly, "some preferred and chose the prisons of England, rather than this libertie in Holland with these afflictions." Assimilation among the too easygoing Dutch with their relaxed Sabbath was taking its toll of impressionable youth and endangering orthodoxy. Besides, all knew that by 1621 the uneasy military truce between the Dutch and the Spanish would end with possibly disastrous results. Wars of religion were still engulfing the peace of Europe. Hardly had the French religious wars of the sixteenth century between Catholics and Huguenots ended before the devastating Thirty Years' War began in 1618. Sectarian bitterness raged, witchcraft manias infected most sects, and tolerance meant merely a truce until the exhausted partisans were prepared to resume the struggle.

The Pilgrims had planned to go to the milder clime of Virginia, despite the Anglicans there, and had secured a land patent from the Virginia Company, but instead they reached the shores of Massachusetts where the fishing was abundant and a sure resource against adversity. A new patent was later secured from the Council of New England. Their way had been smoothed, as in the case of the other colonial adventures, by the financial aid of the flourishing new type of joint-stock company whose corporate organizations made possible large collective capital for settlement and trading so lacking in the individual or partnership resources of the pre-capitalistic era. Upon arriving on November 11, 1620, off Cape Cod, where an unruly mob on board was eager to shake off the authority of the Virginia Company, the leaders managed to conclude the Mayflower Compact, destined to remain the Plymouth constitution because they failed to get another charter. In this historic covenant, modeled after the principles of congregationalism, they combined themselves "into a Civil Body Politick" and promised to obey the laws for the colony. The Mayflower Compact became in American tradition a social contract, the embodiment of government resting only upon the consent of the governed.

Government by consent, however, was only partly a fact, for Bradford's minority of saints consulted the settlers only when "we thinke good" and the theocratic ideal of a Bible Commonwealth meant the imposition of orthodoxy from above—when this was expedient. An annually elected governor and a Council of Assistants were selected by orthodox freemen; this represented, actually, a relatively narrow suffrage in favor of the original landowners and saints. As new towns were added, town deputies were elected to a General Council. By the time New Plymouth was absorbed by Massachusetts in 1691, both colonies were already practicing a similar system of local government although theocratic elements had been drastically reduced. Altogether the Pilgrims and their neighbors were far closer to the medieval union of church and state than to the modern Protestant separation of the two.

Unaware of the scrutiny they must bear before their remote descendants, the Pilgrims, who had pooled their wealth to purchase the *Mayflower*, began as communists, sharing their lands in the Biblical spirit of apostolic communism. To Governor Bradford this brief experiment was merely a "conceite of Plato's," the Utopian Greek communism suggested in the *Republic*. Young men soon objected to working for other men's families, and husbands denounced the "slaverie" of their wives in laboring for others. The able were dissatisfied at having equal rewards with the shiftless. A severe

winter and disease left hardly fifty survivors by the second year and
John Carver, the first governor, was among the dead. His successor,
Bradford, who eventually became the richest man in the colony with
an estate worth $45,000, hailed the collapse of the communistic ex-
periment in 1623 as proof of his contention that it ran contrary to
human nature. Thereafter, the leaders granted individual parcels of
land to each family usually according to size; and, as a result, production, even in the stony soil of eastern Massachusetts, sharply increased. The settlers even began to meet their debts abroad with
overseas shipments of corn, lumber, and beaver skins.

Fur trading with the Indians proved profitable, although Plymouth never became a rich colony. The people found relative peace
during the early years since a plague had providentially wiped out
the local Patuxet tribes on the eve of the arrival of the *Mayflower*.
Conveniently, a few friendly Indians like Samoset and Squanto,
"the tongue of the English," remained to teach some vital lessons in
cultivating corn. In 1636 Plymouth began to expand to include the
towns of Duxbury, founded by Standish and John Alden, and
Scituate, until by 1643 ten new towns became satellites of New
Plymouth. Large families thrived in that abundant land. John Alden
and Priscilla, for example, were to be blessed with eleven children.

Like their Leyden meeting house, the Pilgrim church—called
"meeting house" to avoid any concession to Rome—stood in stark
simplicity in the tradition of Christ born in the manger. A small unpainted clapboard house, poorly lighted and furnished with little
more than bare wooden benches, served the community until 1683
when a more esthetic building replaced it. The New England meeting house was modeled after the Elizabethan parish church, used at
various times as a place of worship, as a center for parish transactions, and as a school.

The pastor, here, as elsewhere among the Puritans, devoted several hours to a carefully prepared and plainly phrased sermon.
Elder William Brewster of Scrooby Manor, who had attended Cambridge and had taught English to the students at the University of
Leyden, frequently preached during the years that the colony
lacked a minister. He avoided lengthy sermons, except on special

occasions and "solemne days of humilliation." Bradford admired his public criticisms of evildoers and his gift of "ripping up the hart and conscience before God." Not one inclined to rest on his Greek and Latin learning or his background in English diplomacy and publishing, Brewster labored in the fields along with the farm workers. There were few doctrinal quarrels in the colony, although the meeting house witnessed scenes of tearful self-accusation and public confession. More than any other Puritan colony, the Pilgrims showed marked toleration, if not complete equality, toward Anglican settlers.

Theology apparently was a less exciting adventure for the Pilgrims than for their brethren of the Massachusetts Bay Colony. John Calvin, high priest of a Hebraic theocracy at Geneva, influenced both the Plymouth and the Massachusetts colonies, but he was far from being the sole religious mentor for the Puritans. Calvin's version of the crucial doctrine of predestination received more emphasis from Jonathan Edwards at the beginning of the eighteenth century than from the divines of the seventeenth. Still, the churches taught what Milton was expressing in *Paradise Lost:*

> Of Man's first disobedience, and the fruit
> Of that forbidden tree, whose mortal taste
> Brought death into the world, and all our woe,
> With loss of Eden, till one greater Man
> Restore us, and regain the blissful seat,
> Sing Heav'nly Muse . . .

In man's depraved state, fallen as he was from high estate by his original sin, the salvation of his soul could not be achieved through good deeds (works); in fact, it was gained solely through the unearned mercy (grace) of God, Who, being all-knowing, predestined the elect to heaven and others to "the deep tract of Hell." Membership in the church of the elect depended on a rigid examination into one's spiritual life, usually through the revelation of an inner redemption in a religious experience vouchsafed the fortunate ones. Children of such members shared the "covenant" of membership except for the communion service. This limited basis for church membership was extended in 1657 by the Half-way Covenant which allowed baptism to children of pious parents, even those lacking the "experience."

However, Calvinist determinism in an extreme anti-rational form was largely foreign to seventeenth-century Pilgrims and Puritans. New England sermons left considerable hope for salvation through good deeds and a man might hopefully seek proof that he belonged to the brotherhood of the elect because he tended toward the good life. When the sulfurous odors of hell-fire finally penetrated everyday life under the proddings of Jonathan Edwards' Great Awakening in the following century, they were accompanied by an emotional safety valve of systematically induced conversions that proved one's fellowship with the elect.

Still, if the Puritan sects were not undeviating Calvinists, they accepted the Scriptures in a most literal way. Unlike the Anglicans, who preached latitude in religion and believed that the Bible revealed only the broad outlines of Christian truths, the Puritans found in the Bible a guide to the most trivial as well as to the most important acts of everyday life and a complete constitution of church organization.

Church organs, even if this wilderness people could have afforded them, were "the devil's bag-pipes," reminiscent of Rome and banned in Plymouth as in all Puritan towns, although secular music was far from hateful to Puritans on either side of the ocean. But the Plymouth congregations lacked all musical instruments except for the deacon's pitch pipe and sang the psalms from memory, too often creating a squeaking dissonance. Tithingmen acted to still the noisy children's section with the birchrod. Eventually, as the Puritan communities grew, sharp class distinctions crept into the newly built pews where differences of rank were recognized in seating members.

Asceticism failed to win an impressive victory in the Plymouth Plantation as far as sin was concerned. During the "crime wave of 1642," Bradford complained of "drunkennes and unclainnes," adultery, and even sodomy. Satan had more power "in these heathen lands" than in Christian states. He theorized, "So wikednes being here more stopped by strict laws and the same more nerly looked into, so as it cannot rune in a common road of liberty as it would, and is inclined, it searches every wher, and at last breaks out wher it getts vente." Possibly, he finally hazarded, evil was not actually greater here than elsewhere, but more publicly exposed. Not least among the delinquents was the visiting Boston pastor, Cotton Mather, who fell into difficulties at Plymouth for "his Notorious Breaches of the Seventh Commandment" among his female parishioners. Somewhat hastily, the Pilgrims—and Puritans in other towns—assumed that premature births among recently wed couples necessarily signified premarital relations and therefore they reserved the public stocks for offenders on this score. Swearing and smoking were evils punished by fine.

Still, as Williston points out, the Pilgrims, unlike the Bay Colony, never hanged a witch and passed no laws against "gay apparel." Elder Brewster owned blue and violet coats and a green waistcoat; and Bradford was not much farther behind the rainbow in his choice of clothes. Dress was as elaborate as one's station permitted. In Puritan New England, as in Elizabethan and early Stuart England, the lower classes were discouraged, often by statute, from aping their betters in matters of dress. Nothing is so misleading in considering the nature of Puritan asceticism as to identify it with the extremely austere garb of Augustus Saint-Gaudens' statue of the gloomy Puritan.

Christmas, tainted by its pagan origins, was pointedly ignored by the Pilgrims and their neighbors, although the unconverted among them might observe this holiday "till they were better informed." However, when Governor Carver found these unregenerate playing in the street on Christmas Day "some pitching the barr and some at stoole-ball and shuch-like sports," he rebuked this playing while others worked and declared that if conscience required Christmas observance, they might do it at home. "Since which time," as Bradford noted approvingly, "nothing hath been atempted that way, at least openly. . . ." Much more important was Thanksgiving Day, set aside as a festal day by Bradford in 1623. A fruitful harvest had been wrested from a seven-week period of drought by the miraculous intervention of God following a "solemne day of humilliation" in which continued prayers for divine intercession had been made. Bradford noted proudly that the Indians, who had vainly prayed for rain, had been deeply impressed by the results achieved by Pilgrims.

High in the modern indictment of the Pilgrims, as witnessed three centuries later in Howard Hanson's successful opera, *Merrymount,* was their attack on Morton's Maypole. Merry Mount (now Quincy) was ruled by Thomas Morton, a fun-loving, aristocratic Anglican lawyer of some classical pretensions in poetry. Bradford thought him guilty of "athisme," lasciviousness, and selling arms and drink to the Indians—as did the French and English elsewhere. Morton employed the Indians to hunt for him and taught them the use of guns. His settlers, most of them male indentured servants who had fled from their masters—such escape was a doubly serious offense in that day of extreme labor shortages—offended the Pilgrims by "dancing and frisking together" with the Indian girls. Besides, Morton reduced their profits by shrewd dealings in the Indian fur trade, and, more seriously, threatened the security of the frontier by arming the Indians.

There was, therefore, more than a Freudian sense of sex frustration involved when John Endicott, who was then founding a Separatist colony at Salem, cut down the Maypole and warned Morton "to looke ther should be better walking." When the settlers persisted in their ways, Captain Miles Standish of Plymouth—"Captaine Shrimpe" his foes called him—arrested Morton for deportation to England. The Maypole, like Christmas observance, suggested a pagan past and was condemned by the Puritans, but the Merry Mount situation had in it genuine elements of danger to life at the hands of Indians with modern arms. Otherwise, forced uniformity was often dispensed with in that wilderness environment where men were so few and the conquest of nature so difficult. While England kept hundreds of capital crimes on its statute books, Plymouth recognized only seven and actually executed only for murder or sodomy.

Education did not thrive among the Brownists, who were recruited from the plainer folk and, for doctrinal reasons as well, held schooling in lower esteem than did their Bay Colony neighbors. Few university men like Brewster and Roger Williams came to humble Plymouth, and decades passed after the founding of Harvard College in 1636 before Plymouth youth entered it. However, the settlement was above the frontier average in literacy, for small home libraries were common, even though the books were heavily devotional in character. Brewster, who had attended Cambridge, led with some four hundred books, a collection in which Calvin and other theologians predominated, but it was leavened by Renaissance authors like Erasmus, Bacon, More, Machiavelli, Raleigh, Hakluyt, and even the English dramatist, Dekker. Bradford's eighty books revealed his historical as well as theological interests and the references in his own *History of Plymouth Plantations* show more than a nodding acquaintance with classical learning. Miles Standish's tastes were even more historical, his fifty books covering Turkish, English, and world history as well as Caesar and Homer. Altogether this was a creditable showing for the first Pilgrim generation in the wilderness.

In 1633, Plymouth lost Roger Williams, whom Bradford thought "a man godly and zealous, having many precious parts, but very unsettled in judgmente." The newcomer had offended Plymouth, long concerned about its defective land title, by suggesting that even the king had no right to grant lands without a previous agreement with the Indians. As his biographer, Brockunier, points out, Williams was one of the first Americans to attack the white man's imperialism toward primitive peoples—though Latin American history also has its early counterpart to Williams in such men as Las Casas. The newcomer was no model of tact, for he assailed James I for telling a "solemn public lie" in claiming to be the first to discover this land. Bradford was relieved therefore when Williams agreed to return to Salem. Here, in a town whose Hebrew name signified peace, was to ensue a fierce controversy between the Salem adherents of Williams and the Massachusetts Bay theocrats.

2

Within a decade of the Pilgrims' landing, a far greater Puritan
migration had come to Massachusetts, settling the coastal towns of
Salem, Boston, Charlestown, Dorchester, and finally moving along
the Maine coast. In 1630, John Winthrop had arrived with a company of 700 on the *Arabella* and its ten sister ships. By 1643 some
20,000 persons were living in the Massachusetts Bay Colony, thus
totally eclipsing the New Plymouth Plantation in importance. London "adventurers" (investors) had helped finance this exodus of
"choice seed" into the wilderness, including scores of university
men, innumerable well-to-do merchants and squires, as well as the
humbler artisans and farmers. Governor Winthrop, formerly lord of
Groton Manor and a prosperous Puritan lawyer who had graduated
from Cambridge University, was the founder of Boston. Amid the
early sufferings from disease and exposure, he had written resolutely
to his wife in England, "It is enough that we shall have heaven,
though we should pass through hell to it." The English Puritans
were deserting Middlesex and East Anglia, fleeing the counter-revo-
lutionary campaign of Archbishop Laud to stamp out dissenters to
the Church of England. That decade preceding the Puritan Revolution of 1640-60 was indeed a critical one for dissenters. For many
of the humbler emigrants, there was the goad of severe unemployment and disorderly conditions. To them New England's fishing,
farming, and fur trade offered almost certain economic salvation.

The Bay Colony's government, like that of Plymouth, was theocratic in the spirit of Calvin and Israel; though the Puritans followed lay leaders, the ministers had a powerful advisory role. In
the fashion of Stuart England and of the medieval state, the government was judged competent to regulate economic life, religion, and
customs, as well as politics. Suffrage was limited to church members,
as in Plymouth, and genuine power resided in the hands of an orthodox minority whose leaders acquired extensive land grants for
themselves. The elected magistrates and governor were the stewards
of a sovereign God, for the rule of the people lacked divine sanction.
Winthrop found no scriptural authority for a "meere Democratie"

and asserted that "a Democratie is, among most civill nations accounted the meanest & worst of all formes of Governm't—it hath been allwayes of least continuance & fullest of trouble."

Even closer to the Mosaic tradition of stewardship practiced by Calvin at Geneva was the very erudite and eloquent minister, John Cotton, who had been a Fellow and head lecturer at Emmanuel College, Cambridge. Many believed, according to his admiring grandson, Cotton Mather, "God would not suffer Mr. Cotton to err." This divine, though far from being the humorless fanatic portrayed by later generations, did not admit that the covenant idea of New England Congregationalism meant democracy:

Democracy, I do not conceyve that ever God did ordeyne as a fit government eyther for church or commonwealth. If the people be governors, who shall be governed? As for monarchy and aristocracy, they are both of them clearely approved, and directed in scripture, yet so as referreth the soveraigntie to himselfe, and setteth up Theocracy in both, as the best forme of government in the commonwealth, as well as in the church.

Cotton, Winthrop, and other Puritan leaders believed in maintaining class distinctions and had little sympathy for the concepts of social equality held by a few leveling sects of the time. They accepted with Calvin the medieval ideal of social stratification, holding that each person could serve God best by remaining in the station to which he had been divinely appointed. Although the Massachusetts churches came over to Congregationalism which stressed the freedom of each congregation, the Boston leaders perpetuated their oligarchy by adopting the Presbyterian principle of synodal control over the churches.

Against this church-state, with its undemocratic Court of Assistants and governor overriding by their veto power the sporadic outbursts of the freemen, there arose critics and rebels. John Cotton's talents were frequently needed to justify this state of things in a New World in which free lands and economic and social opportunity could be enjoyed by pioneers willing to break away from the closely knit settlements of the seaboard. Pastors seceded with their flocks to open new frontier communities. Thomas Hooker and his Newtown (Cambridge) congregation resented the oligarchic order and together with residents from Watertown, Roxbury, and Dorchester (all now part of metropolitan Boston) left the stony soil of the coast in 1635-36 for the fertile Connecticut River valley lands and founded Hartford, Windsor, and Wethersfield. Actually, the Connecticut leaders had no intention of embarking on the rudderless sea of democracy and broadened the suffrage only slightly more than the Bay Colony did. The rest of the Puritan structure was carried over intact.

More fundamental in his criticism of the oligarchy of "visible saints" than Hooker was Roger Williams. The Bay Colony had resented his Plymouth attack on the right of the king to give Indian lands away, but in 1635, while the Winthrop group were under fire from disfranchised settlers, they had to deal with a fresh challenge from Williams. He contended that the magistrate had no power to punish breaches of the Sabbath, idolatry, blasphemy, and heresy except in cases disturbing the civil peace. Here was an attack upon the very foundations of theocracy, for it denied to civil officers the power to enforce religious orthodoxy. Williams held that spirituality and regeneration were an inward matter of conscience beyond the pale of the state and that truth could not be established by force. From this flowed a positive doctrine of tolerance and freedom of thought far more profound to an earnest searcher for truth than mere expediency. A tolerance based on the dignity of the person was far more vital for the American tradition than one based on commercial advantage and indifference to moral and spiritual values. Secondly, Williams had clarified the notion of separation of church and state as even the Pilgrim Separatists had failed to do after the first years. From these doctrines, it was a short step to Williams' later teachings of a democratic social compact existing to protect the inalienable right of conscience.

The Boston leaders managed to exile Williams despite the resistance of the Salem congregation by threatening to challenge the town's land titles. He escaped deportation to England by fleeing in mid-winter to Plymouth and then to the friendly Narragansetts among whom he acted as a beloved missionary; later he extended his role to acting as a peacemaker between Puritans and New England Indians. From the Narragansetts, he and his followers obtained title to the future city of Providence and most of Rhode Island. Here he proclaimed "that grand cause of Truth and Freedom of Conscience." This meant to him not only constitutional guarantees for civil and religious liberty, but also majority rule and a land policy based on equality of economic opportunity. Easygoing Rhode Island thus became a liberal experiment and showed hospitality to dissenters of all types. No laws compelled church attendance and no religious tests existed for officeholders. Puritans attacked Rhode Island as Belial and with much worse epithets, but the colony went on its way undisturbed.

Meanwhile, in 1639, Williams became a Baptist, following the London Baptists who rejected infant baptism as meaningless and contrary to the Scriptures and early church tradition. The Baptists not only practiced adult immersion but denied the power of the state over matters of conscience and stood for the freedom of each congregation from external pressure. Within a few months, however, the restless Williams moved to an even more advanced position by joining the Seekers. This English sect had rationalist ideas culminating in their claim to have ended the long Reformation search for the true Christian church uncorrupted by "men's inventions." This followed from their belief that it was no longer possible to prove that any existing church was the genuine successor of the original church of Jesus.

In 1643-44, while Williams was in London on behalf of his colony, he had occasion to make a classical defense of tolerance and democracy against the Boston theocrats. John Cotton had just written a defense of the Boston church-state system in a tract, *The Keyes of the Kingdom of Heaven*. Williams replied vigorously in *The Bloudy Tenent of Persecution for Cause of Conscience*, developing his now familiar doctrines for the benefit of Englishmen on both sides of the ocean. All governments were merely the creatures of men, existing solely for their welfare, and resting only upon their consent. Therefore, he reasoned, rulers were the servants of the people and not empowered to decide on the truth of religion. In Puritan England,

Williams supported Cromwell in the new policy of welcoming Jews, excluded from the country since medieval times. And in Williams' Rhode Island, Spanish and Portuguese Jewish refugees found a secure home, though warned away elsewhere in New England. Williams was a severe critic of the Quakers, then beaten and even hanged in Puritan New England and abroad, but there was no question that Rhode Island was open to those who kept the peace. Puritan pressure did not alter the colony's offer of asylum to the oppressed of all lands.

By 1647, under its new charter, Rhode Island had swept away survivals of feudalism such as primogeniture, had set up a liberal bill of rights, had codified the laws, had provided for direct democracy along modern lines of legislative devices, and had passed a criminal code that was highly enlightened by the standards of the time. Only in public education did this amazing commonwealth lag seriously behind, despite remedial efforts of the well-intentioned, for the Baptists and the Quakers of that time were less than lukewarm on the subject of secular learning.

Second to Roger Williams as a "troubler in Israel" was the persuasive Anne Hutchinson, whose Antinomian ideas of a gospel of love involved no less than eighty-two heresies, in the minds of the Massachusetts synod of 1637. In her Boston home, encouraged at first by John Cotton himself, she had discussed certain inner-light doctrines which gave each Christian a share in God's divinity through personal revelation under a "covenant of grace" and made the ministry superfluous. By eliminating the ministry as the final authority on the meaning of the Scriptures, she endangered the whole theocratic structure. Puritan theologians, reared on the Ramean logic of Cambridge, rejected such claims of personal revelation as "enthusiasms" destroying the harmony of reason and faith and anti-intellectual in tendency. During the bitter controversy in which Cotton recanted and Mrs. Hutchinson was exiled, Antinomian partisans fled to new settlements. The Reverend John Wheelwright, brother-in-law and champion of Anne Hutchinson, founded Exeter, New Hampshire. Another, William Coddington, made Portsmouth, Rhode Island, an Antinomian fortress, where Mrs. Hutchinson was welcomed, and he also founded Newport in 1639. The "dictatorship of the regenerate," to use Dr. Perry Miller's apt phrase, had put down Anne Hutchinson as it did Roger Williams and other rebels.

Puritans paid only lip service to the ideal of a mass conversion of all Indian souls to Christianity. Even though the seal of the Bay Colony portrayed an Indian crying for salvation, "Come over and help us," they left a record in this respect far inferior to the French Canadians, the Spaniards, and the Portuguese. Instead, the Puritans, like other English colonists, came to regard the Indian as a pariah, if not as an eternal enemy. Few shared the lofty peacemaking ideal of Roger Williams, founded on an intimate knowledge and appreciation of the Indian as a human being. He had lived among the Narragansetts, whose chief, Canonicus, treated him as a son. Williams' demand for fair payment to the Indians for their lands and just treatment in trading and other matters met with severe criticism from the Boston leaders, except when they wished to use him as an intermediary in a pending Indian war.

The six linguistic Indian stocks within the present bounds of the United States and Canada were represented east of the Mississippi by less than 200,000 nomadic, primitively armed, and poorly supplied people. New England and Virginia knew particularly the tribes belonging to the Algonquian stock, famous for King Philip, Massasoit, and Pocahontas. Fur traders of New England came into contact with the warlike Iroquois stock, which included the powerful Five Nations of central New York, the main pivot of the fur trade. Iroquois leaders like Hiawatha found little idealization among New Englanders, although a descendant, Longfellow, seated in a comfortable Harvard library far away from the redskins, did undertake the task.

The Iroquois League of Mohawks, Senecas, Oneidas, Cayugas, and Onondagas had come into existence about 1570 dedicated originally to the achievement of universal peace through brotherhood. Their founders had been Deganawida, a chief believed to be of virgin birth, and Hiawatha, reputed to be a benevolent wizard and orator, who had been reincarnated to enjoy a second birth upon earth. Iroquois decisions rested upon the mothers of the tribes who selected the chiefs subject to popular ratification and used democratic controls similar to the modern initiative, referendum, and recall devices. Descent was reckoned through the mother's line. Their alliance with the Dutch, their involvement in the Anglo-Dutch and Anglo-French imperialist rivalries, particularly in connection with their pivotal influence in the fur trade, led to intertribal wars as the Indians were compelled to choose sides, thus extinguishing whatever peace mission the Iroquois may have once felt. Those who chose assimilation to English ways did not escape the violent pressure of the newcomers.

In New England, the Pequot War of 1637 broke the power of the local tribes and made them more receptive to a major experiment in race relations. This was a system of segregated communities of "praying Indians," embracing 1100 tribesmen in fourteen towns on the eve of King Philip's War of 1675. In that savage conflict, the Christian Indians remained loyal to the paternalistic Old Testament theocracy of their Puritan leaders who were financed by a London missionary society. Some of the more apt Indian neophytes acquired an astonishing knowledge of Calvinist theology, although strict Puritanism in sex matters proved a heavy strain on the tribesmen. Like the Jesuit theocracy of colonial Paraguay, the "praying Indian" towns practiced primitive communism in an isolated agrarian economy.

The champion of this system of Indian conversion was the saint-like John Eliot, "apostle to the Indians," a Cambridge-trained minister who stressed simplicity rather than fine doctrinal points. With considerable effort, he managed to learn enough of the local Indian tongues to publish the *Catechism* in 1653 through the Cambridge press at Harvard. This was followed in 1661-63 by an Indian Bible. Like Williams, Eliot was a humanitarian and protested the enslavement of Indians after the Pequot War.

Puritan mistreatment of the "pernicious creatures," as Cotton Mather called the Indians, led to the large-scale King Philip's War. From that conflict emerged a literary record of Indian savagery that set the model for later Indian tales. This was *The Narrative of the Captivity and Restoration of Mrs. Mary Rowlandson* (1682), an exciting autobiographical account of a preacher's wife who was cap-tured by King Philip's warriors; the book went through at least thirty printings. Indian relations, like Negro relations in the ensuing era, signified the racial limits of the colonial melting pot, outside of illicit unions.

3

No indictment against the Puritans has been more damning than the witchcraft hysteria of 1647-63 and 1688-93, yet this record pales alongside contemporary Catholic and Protestant witch hunts in the Old World. Popular belief in magic and witchcraft of course ante-dated Christianity and was never wholly displaced in the peasant mind. Contemporary scientists, even some in the Royal Society, cast horoscopes, practiced alchemy, and regarded witches as part of the natural order. Europe's skepticism of witches was combatted in 1484 by Pope Innocent VIII who asserted that Germany's witches were responsible for stillbirths and other calamities, and he issued instructions for torture to secure confessions. In the ensuing hys-teria, the Inquisition was kept busy stamping out the devil and his works. Protestants drew special inspiration from the biblical injunc-tion, "Thou shalt not suffer a witch to live." The great German witch mania of 1629 involved three hundred small children accused of intercourse with the devil. Calvinist Geneva alone, according to con-temporaries, executed five hundred witches in three months. In England, the Puritan era claimed innumerable victims. Old women, invalids, and demented persons were easy targets for charges of witchcraft and were tortured and burned or hanged.

When this delusion reached the New World, aided by zealous books and pamphlets on witches north and south, the colonies shared the contagion, although actual executions for witchcraft probably occurred only in New England. God's purpose had long been seen not only in the Bible but in omens like comets, two-headed calves, and stillborn children. Winthrop saw deep signif-icance in the discriminating mice in his son's library who ate only the pages of the Anglican prayer book, leaving all else untouched. Therefore, it was not difficult to believe that witches, too, had their place in this order of things. In 1647, a witch was hanged at Windsor, Connecticut, followed by another at Hartford the next year. The excitement increased until eight were hanged in that colony and six in Massachusetts. Only Rhode Island was content to allow the witchcraft law to remain a dead letter. In 1684, Increase Mather, Harvard's president, lit new fires of fear with an essay on the supernatural in New England. His pedantic son, Cotton, in another publication, added his own firsthand knowledge of the invisible kingdom of Satan.

These incendiary influences were fanned by voodoo tales brought by slaves from the West Indies to New England, and out of these grew the sensational Salem witch hunt of 1692. Hysterical children told how they were possessed by the devil and accused their neighbors of satanic plots. By September 1692, twenty persons and even two dogs had been executed as witches; the jails were overflowing with two hundred accused. When the most prominent citizens began to fall into the dragnet intended for the devil's own brood, the clerical inquisitors reversed their position. The next year, Increase Mather issued a pamphlet asserting that it was far better to allow ten suspected witches to escape than for one innocent person to be condemned. The influential magistrate, Samuel Sewall, rose remorsefully in church to beg public forgiveness for his part in the shedding of innocent blood. Others followed his example.

Thus ended the witchcraft craze in New England—though it continued in Old England. But a severe blow had been struck at the theocracy that had been so zealous in the witch hunt. After the Glorious Revolution of 1688 in England, a fresh breath of religious freedom came with the Massachusetts Charter of 1691, which extended the franchise to all propertied Protestants. Merchants in the flourishing seaboard towns pressed for tolerance as indispensable for business. Already the Half-way Covenant, as previously noted, had paved the way for broader church membership. The horrors of hell-fire, implied in the predestination doctrine, which limited the elect to a fortunate few chosen from the beginning by God, were dimmed until the Great Awakening.

The witchcraft episode reveals the link between theology and law among the Puritans. England's legal system, already modified by Coke, Selden, and their fellow lawyers in the revolutionary seventeenth century, was not wholly accepted in New England, as Professor Richard B. Morris has shown in his studies of American law. Firstly, Puritans like John Cotton held that the Bible was a complete law book and that this "higher law" of the Scriptures was ever superior to man-made "positive law." Secondly, the frontier created new economic and geographic conditions that often made common-law technicalities inapplicable. Finally, a provincial society bred few lawyers and possessed too few of the basic textbooks needed to perpetuate the traditions and precedents of the English law.

Although the Massachusetts Charter required that no laws might be passed "repugnant" to the laws of England, the General Court (legislature) asserted in its declaration of 1646: "Our allegiance binds us not to the laws of England any longer than while we live in England, for the laws of the Parliament of England reach no further, nor do the king's writs under the great seal go any further." The word "repugnant" was taken to mean no more than "contrary to the law of God and of right reason." Connecticut's legislature attempted a similar declaration of legal independence in 1665. By 1698, Rhode Islanders were reported by a royal official to hold that "no law of England ought to be in force and binding to them without their own consent for they foolishly say they have no representatives sent from themselves to the Parliament in England."

Puritan ministers, advisers of the magistrates, borrowed the "higher-law" concept from the Stoics and medieval schoolmen, equating it to the "law of nature" or "the law of God" as revealed in the Bible. The later abolitionist emphasis on the "higher law" existing above the Constitution, particularly as expressed by William Seward on slavery, was directly in this tradition. The idea of a "fundamental law" that made a conflicting statute null and void had been clearly expressed by the Levellers, among others, in England and became distinctive of American legal philosophy. Englishmen, with their emphasis on the supremacy of Parliament, did not allow the idea of "fundamental law" to develop beyond the rhetorical stage. Following Hebraic law, the New Englanders made capital offenses of idolatry, witchcraft, blasphemy, adultery, bestiality, and sodomy. Sex morality was stringently enforced. Essex County, for example, drew up 122 indictments for sex offenders between 1649 and 1660, far outrunning England's populous Middlesex County despite the English Puritan crusade.

The spread of the common law into the British colonies was re-sisted by the poorer classes during the formative seventeenth cen-tury until the final product was Anglo-American rather than English. Lawyers were discouraged by local laws forbidding legal fees, and laymen were scarcely equipped to apply common-law precedents. Frontier communities disregarded technical common-law rules that were intended to protect litigants, for delays and protracted appeals were too expensive. Pleading was reduced to a simple direct procedure in colonial courts and justice moved swiftly, even at the cost of dropping valuable rules of sound evidence. Frontier demands in New England that property law should pro-mote equal distribution of land led that section to abolish the aristocratic English rules of primogeniture by which almost every-thing was left to the eldest son. Besides, New England's rocky soil and broken-up terrain favored small farms.

The scarcity of women on the frontier and their vital economic role tended to raise their social status above that implied in the common law, which allowed husbands to hold their wives' prop-erty. As a result, married women enjoyed, in many instances, the right to make contracts and to sue in the courts; as heads of families, they sometimes even received land grants. Wives were protected by what Dr. Morris calls the "humane paternalism" of Puritan legisla-tors and judges who punished personal abuses against wives and their children, recalled deserting husbands, and even enforced the conjugal rights.

New England courts usually showed more clemency toward civil crimes than did those in England, where capital punishment was inflicted for a multitude of offenses. But where heresy was involved, as in the case of persistent Quaker missionaries, Massachusetts re-sorted to lashing and hanging. Early Quaker methods of winning converts shocked many a Puritan. Samuel Sewall noted in 1677 that a Quaker woman raised an uproar by breaking into a meeting house completely dishevelled, with "face as black as ink"; even more effective in stirring up congregations were the young Quakeresses who occasionally walked in wholly nude as a "sign" of God's judgment upon their rulers. At least four Quakers were hanged during the 1650's.

Mutilation for crimes was as common in the colonies as across the sea. Sewall's diary recorded in 1685, "An Indian was branded in court and had a piece of his ear cut off for burglary." A perjurer might be forced to wear a cleft stick on his tongue and to stand in the pillory for all to observe. Sometimes, the lawbreaker had to stand outside the church with his offense listed on his hat or had to exhibit himself in the public stocks. Sexual lapses were often punished by pitiless publicity. Hawthorne's suffering Hester Prynne, who wore the scarlet letter "A" for adultery on her dress, had her historical prototype alongside those who wore "D" for drunkenness or even "I" for incest. Ear-croppings and whippings apparently led as modes of punishment. Jails, like their English models, tended to be "graves of the living," for, as a resident of Boston observed in 1686, "Lice, Drink, and Tobacco are the Compound."

Later caricatures of Puritan justice ignored harsher English equivalents and borrowed much from the alleged Connecticut Blue Laws. These were actually forged by a hostile Anglican minister, Samuel Peters, who published in 1781 his popular and largely fictional, *General History of Connecticut by a Gentleman of the Province.* Among these imaginary "blue laws"—the phrase belongs to a later generation—were those forbidding women to kiss their children on the Sabbath or to "make minced pies, dance, play cards, or play on any instrument of music except the drum, trumpet, and jews-harp."

Actually, Puritan asceticism was limited in practice. It is true that Cotton Mather preached against stage plays, cards, Christmas observance, and dice. He criticized the popular reading of "vain Romances" as a "meer loss of time," but like many other Puritans he drank without troublesome inhibitions. Barrels of cider were piled up in Harvard's cellars for the convivial commencement affairs. New

England magistrates did try with limited success to outlaw gambling, tavern dancing, Sabbath-breaking, and Christmas observance tending to "Popish revelry" and disorders. However, laws against dice, card-playing, quoits, ninepins, bowling, and shuffleboard, "whereby much precious time is spent unprofitably" were evidently ill respected, being more honored in the breach than in the observance. Booksellers kept stocks of playing cards, for which presumably some demand existed, even if only from the benighted Anglicans. Smoking, formerly condemned by James I as well as by local laws, had its devotees. Taverns persisted as highly convivial centers where beer, cider, and rum flowed copiously amid dancing and music. Idleness was a grievous sin not only for Puritans but for other middle-class colonials who suffered from continued labor scarcity in a land blessed with economic resources.

As for dancing, Puritans on both sides of the Atlantic could agree only on the evil of "unchast Touches and Gesticulations" in mixed dancing. John Cotton, writing in 1625, showed a relatively tolerant view, "Dancing (yea though mixt) I would not simply condemn—Only lascivious dancing to wanton ditties and in amorous gestures and wanton dalliances, especially after great feasts, I would bear witness against." Percy Scholes, who has seriously modified the prevailing interpretation of Puritan asceticism, reminds us that the great Puritan poet, Milton, wrote in *L'Allegro*:

> Come and trip it as you go
> On the light fantastic toe.

The New Englanders did indeed enjoy a robust amount of "seasonable merriment" as the clerical complaints alone would suggest. Thanksgiving Day, Harvard Commencement Day, private festal events, "Training Day" with its feasts and sports for the militia, and other occasions enlivened everyday life. Games like soccer and target contests were popular. Children, like others of their breed before and since, were not usually preoccupied by inner torments over salvation; on the contrary, their section in church teemed with forbidden activities of all kinds and the discipline of the deacon's birchrod may have been required in self-defense for the adult community. By 1651, Boston and Salem shops supplied toys and dolls to the offspring of the saints. Boston had a fencing school in 1673 and for a brief period, a dancing school. Music was excluded from the churches, it is true, except for the "meerest unison singing of slow psalm tunes," but trumpets and drums served as church bells and the jew's-harp, at least, was a popular instrument. Some guitars, violoncellos, and virginals, judging from the inventories, apparently escaped any Puritan ban. More elaborate instruments, such as organs, were usually lacking in seventeenth-century colonial life and, in fact, were discouraged by other sects as well, notably by the Quakers.

Just as Puritan asceticism in recreational habits fell far short of the saintly hair shirt, so personal dress tended to approximate that of Elizabethan and Stuart England. Class lines, as in England, rather than religious orthodoxy, dictated styles. Drab simplicity was no virtue among the Bradfords, the Brewsters, the Winthrops, the Mathers, the Saltonstalls, and the Appletons. The clergy, it is true, complained of immodest styles that imitated court fashions and they fought a losing war at the end of the century upon silver ornamentation, ruffs, lace, long hair, and finally, on the adoption of periwigs. At no time, apparently, did the short-cropped haircut of the "Roundheads" dominate Puritan headdress.

As the decades rolled by, landed "gentlemen" and the merchant class "Misters" took to wearing satin doublets, full breeches, red drawers, slashed ornamented sleeves, gold-topped gloves, silver-headed canes, and beaver hats. Their wives preferred silk hoods and bonnets, fine gloves, shoes with silver buckles and French heels, and substantial amounts of jewelry. On the other hand, the small farmer "goodman" and his "goodwife," down to the indentured servants and the few slaves who had begun to trickle in, chose their clothes according to a much lower grade of social standing. Among the humble, deerskin breeches or long trousers and wooden-heeled shoes might be supplemented by colored stockings or knit caps. In general, homespun materials rather than imported stuffs were used in the farmer's wardrobe.

Puritan dwellings, after the primitive years of wigwam-style homes and thatched cottages, took on a distinctive style of architecture that was truly "functional" in its emphasis on plain harmonious lines adapted to local needs and expression. Even the Calvinist austerity of unpainted, simply furnished church buildings carried with it genuinely esthetic elements admired by later generations. Little was known in New England of the building that has become the typical American log cabin, for this originated in Scandinavia and parts of Germany and was apparently introduced in 1638 by Swedes and Finns along the Delaware. Like an organic thing, the two or three rooms, built around a huge central brick or stone chimney with its several fireplaces, grew by annexes as the family grew in size. The mid-century Ipswich, Massachusetts, house of John Whipple reflects the medieval English style of East Anglia, the leading Puritan area. The two stories, the second showing the distinctive overhang, were constructed in the stout half-timbered style and were connected by an interior staircase. The overhang provided protection for the lower wall from the driving New England rain and snow. A central brick chimney served fireplaces in each of four rooms. Warmth in that severe New England climate was retained by sheathing the half-timbered frame with clapboards split from logs. Characteristic of this and other colonial houses was the medieval tendency to reveal the inward details of structure without using any prettifying concealments. Hence, seventeenth-century architecture has been classified as "the medieval style in America," the finest example of honest functionalism before the day of Louis Sullivan and Frank Lloyd Wright.

"Here is good living for those who like good fires," wrote a visitor to New England. Despite few pictures and bare walls and but a few homemade articles of furniture, there was considerable cheer in Puritan homes. The wealthy managed to import elegant English furniture. After the first hard years, food was ample and varied, including fresh and salted meats, grains, vegetables, and fruit. Suspended from the chimney or ceiling were large hams and strings of dried apples and seed corn. New England's famous "hasty pudding" was made of cornmeal and milk. The equally famous boiled dinner consisted of boiled meat or fish, boiled vegetables, and sometimes baked beans and brown corn bread, usually served on a large wooden or pewter dish. Forks remained for some time a curiosity that one might gaze upon at Governor Winthrop's home. On cold nights, one had such resources as warming pans, heated bricks, patchwork quilts (whose making was a source of neighborly enjoyment), thick woolen bed rugs, and deep feather beds. The rural home tended to be self-sufficient as far as possible and contained spindles and hand looms.

The family was a strong patriarchal unit, strengthened by the economic role of both old and young as well as by religious, biological, and social needs. Endless toil aged the housewife before her time and shortened her years. Marriage, tied up with complex legal and property questions such as dowries and inheritances, was a civil ceremony even in the Puritan church-state. A high mortality, aggravated by sweeping smallpox epidemics, tuberculosis, childbed deaths, and infant mortality, was offset by a large birth rate made possible by early marriages, quick remarriages for the widowed, few divorces, and very few abiding bachelors.

The sick and ailing had recourse to various herbs or special home remedies or they might trust the dubious skill of a medical "chemist" or one of the few colonial "doctors," practically all of them trained only by apprenticeship. Still, if life seemed unbearable, the patient might try to cure his headache by the blood of a male cat's ear mixed with nurse's milk; for dropsy, a sovereign remedy was hog lice; toothaches were cured by opium and various infections were treated by animal dung. All sorts of ailments might respond to the lancet of a doctor who practiced the medieval art of Galen or who tried the uncertain chemical compounds of Paracelsus. The midwife, whose ignorance frequently went beyond the limited field of obstetrics, accounted for many a premature death. Despite these handicaps, New England's population reached 90,000 by 1700, mostly spread along the coast and along the banks of the Connecticut River.

Most families lived on subsistence farms, raising staples of wheat, rye, and Indian corn and planting garden plots of squash, pumpkin, and other vegetables. Cellars were crowded with barrels of cider and preserved foods. The commons, or unfenced village land, were shared by the community. Cattle raising expanded until horses were bred for export. The woods and streams were prolific in wild life. An attempt was made to divide the land proportionally, according to the size of families, although the ruling Winthrops and Salton-stalls held baronial estates.

All lived in essentially rural "townships" of some forty square miles, a local unit borrowed from pre-Restoration England when it had tremendous vitality, being entrusted with church taxation, poor laws, education, crime repression, and road building. These activities necessitated the famous institution of the town meeting, "an independent republic built around a church," a form of direct democracy wherever membership restrictions remained few. In-formal weekly or monthly meetings, distinguished for their spon-taneous character, eventually gave way to annual assemblies with selectmen chosen to administer town government in the long inter-vals. Early religious and property restrictions on the right to vote made seventeenth-century town meetings far from pure democracies in the modern sense. Non-congregational merchants rebelled against disfranchisement and with the Glorious Revolution of 1688 William of Orange granted a new colonial charter extending the franchise to non-church members and guaranteeing the religious liberties of nearly all Protestants. Under increasingly favorable circumstances, the New England town meeting system evolved into a distinctive American institution, extending well into the twentieth century, with a tradition of free speech that became a proud heritage of democracy.

Puritanism, as noted elsewhere, tended to hold diligence and suc-cess in one's "calling" as an evidence of God's grace, thereby raising the dignity of labor, sanctioning the amassing of wealth, and glori-fying the virtue of thrift. In practice, Puritan labor ideas resembled those of Elizabethan England, which laid harsh penalties on "sturdy beggars" without relying on the Puritan idea that labor was a form of worship. England, in its efforts to force the rural unemployed to adapt themselves to new occupations and to increase the national wealth, had invented a formidable array of poor laws, which were more concerned with compulsory labor than with philanthropy.

New England borrowed heavily from English experience and from the official mercantilistic doctrines that prescribed minute government regulation of economic life as a way to achieve a strong state. Governor John Endicott was advised in 1629 by the Massachusetts Bay Company: "Noe idle drone bee permitted to live amongst us, which if you take care now at the first to establish, wil be an undoubted meanes, through God's assistance, to prevent a world of disorders and many grievous sins and sinners." Each town, being held responsible for its poor, as in England, rigidly barred newcomers likely to become public charges and "warned them out." Massachusetts ordered vagrants whipped. Connecticut bound idlers to service. Plymouth had its workhouse by 1658 for vagrants, rebellious children, and lazy servants. Rhode Island punished "sturdy beggars, masterless men, or other Notorious offenders whatsoever." On the other hand, the "impotent poor"—children, widows, the sick, and the aged—were better provided for in the Puritan towns than elsewhere.

Massachusetts, so paternalistic in regulating religion and morals, was not a whit behind in regulating wages and prices. Behind the control system were the familiar pressure groups which stood to gain by low wages and high prices or the reverse. But the members of the Massachusetts General Court, however disturbed by rising wages and labor scarcity on the frontier, were limited in their efforts to control labor by the danger that such actions might drive workmen to the west. Guild organizations, almost all of them in New England, preserved their trade monopolies, kept non-residents out, and often fixed wages by wage contracts with employers. Wages and prices in trades affected by a public interest, like those of the butchers and bakers, were thoroughly regulated. Exorbitant retail prices were condemned. When a Boston merchant was found guilty of charging very high prices, he was haled before the court. On that occasion John Cotton denounced the competitive doctrine. "That a man should sell as dear as he can and buy as cheap as he can." Instead, he insisted that one should sell at the price current at the given time and place among those familiar with the worth of the commodity. The American Puritans operated on the medieval theory of the "just price" rather than on the modern capitalist tenet of the competitive market price.

Since harsh restrictions on free labor in a sparsely inhabited country tended to defeat the purposes for which they were imposed—namely, the more even distribution of labor at reasonably low wages—another means to this end had to be found. One alternative was forced labor. Servants contracted for their services, or were contracted for by agents, under an indenture system. Not a few were taken from English jails or even kidnapped. Sometimes an opportune "juste warre" with the Indians, as in the case of the Pequot War of 1637, brought in an ample supply of slaves. Later, the thriving New England slave trade brought Africans to Boston to fill the need for domestic and other services. By the end of the century, about one thousand Negro slaves were working in the Puritan colonies on the fishing vessels, on the farms, and in the shops. Theologians discovered biblical and racial sanctions for the "peculiar institution" as did their neighbors south of Mason and Dixon's line over a century later.

The ocean attracted many a youth to an exciting seafaring career that offered an escape from labor on an unprofitable farm. New England's "Bible-quoting Yankee skippers" and her own tall ships were invading the Levant and the Far East by the 1670's. Hundreds of fishing vessels, manned by several thousand sailors, carried the prolific codfish to southern Europe to meet the religious diet of Catholics. The "triangular trade" to the West Indies after the 1640's brought New England's fish, lumber, cattle, and newly built ships for sale in exchange for wines, sugar, tobacco, fruits, and salt, some of these to be re-exported to England. Salem, which, among the colonial ports, led in the seventeenth-century slave trade, shipped rum newly made from cheap imported molasses to Madagascar or to the West Coast of Africa in exchange for slaves to be sold in the West Indies or Virginia. The Dutch and English companies monopolized the African West Coast.

The mercantilistic theories that dictated Britain's Navigation Acts of the 1640's and 1660 sought to monopolize colonial markets and to discourage local manufacturing. The Act of 1660, for example, by limiting certain "enumerated" colonial exports to the English market, often cut off more profitable foreign markets. Besides, the costly English manufactures exchanged for the bulky colonial raw products would have drained New England of specie had she not resorted to non-English markets where the trade balance was in her favor. As it was, New England had to increase her currency by adopting Indian wampum (until the ingenious Dutch broke the market by the wholesale manufacturing of wampum), by promissory notes, and by the "pine-tree" shillings coined without England's authorization. Trade with Spain's colonies brought the "dollar" or "thaler" coin from her German-speaking possessions. By the end of the century, the wealth of commerce was reflected in Boston's handsomely furnished houses, some as fine as London's best, owned by her traders and merchants.

4

The crowning glory of New England was its rich intellectual life, far exceeding that of the other colonies. While Protestant sects usually stressed the elementary ability to read the Bible, Puritans expected their congregations to understand complex theology on a much higher level of literacy. Unlike Anne Hutchinson's Antinomians and the early Quakers, who minimized higher learning in favor of personal revelation, and certain Puritan extremists who scored the universities as "stews of Anti-Christ," the Bay Colony drew many of its leaders from Cambridge University and based its theology on the rationalism of Ramean logic. A learned ministry was indispensable for them.

Hundreds of Cambridge and Oxford men brought the stimulating Renaissance spirit to higher learning. These interests were focussed upon Harvard College, the first colonial college outside of Spanish America, which was initiated in 1636 by a grant of £400 from the Massachusetts General Court and enriched by an estate of £800 and a four-hundred-volume library from John Harvard. He himself was a graduate of Emmanuel College, the intellectual model for the school bearing his name. Emmanuel pleased Puritans by its daily piety and scholarly habits and by its tutorial system of personal discussions that minimized formal lectures and made learning an intimate experience. Harvard's friends, "dreading to leave an illiterate Ministery to the Churches when our present Ministers shall lie in the Dust," intended to train ministers, it is true, but also, as Dr. Samuel E. Morison points out in *Puritan Pronaos,* they wished to advance learning in the sense of Francis Bacon. They hoped to allow ample room for literature, the arts, and science in the curriculum according to the best English standards. President Increase Mather of Harvard addressed his students, "You who are wont to philosophize in a liberal spirit are pledged to the words of no particular master, yet I would have you hold fast to that one truly golden saying of Aristotle: *Find a friend in Plato,* a friend in Socrates (and I say a friend in Aristotle), but above all find a friend in Truth."

Harvard College seemed not too impressive to a Dutch traveler of 1680 who sneered at "the only college, or would-be academy of the Protestants in all America." In an upper room of the college at Cambridge he found only eight or ten youths in residence, studying in English tutorial fashion in a smoke-filled atmosphere. The boys knew almost no Latin, according to the visitor, and the college could not afford a professor. By 1686, the college had trained 122 boys for the ministry and a lesser number for other vocations; many of these were poor boys dependent on scholarships and earning opportunities. Tuition, in that specie-scarce era, was paid in bushels of grain, in livestock, or even in shoes and boots. Lacking endowments, the college depended in part on local taxes as well as on tuition. The curriculum included the traditional liberal arts of grammar, logic, rhetoric, arithmetic, geometry, and astronomy; metaphysics, ethics, and natural science; and, in response to newer Renaissance and Puritan interests, Greek, Hebrew, and ancient history. Latin, learned in the grammar (preparatory) schools, was a prerequisite for Harvard. Morison, examining the library lists and student notebooks of that day, finds a broad Renaissance education represented in them. Student "commonplace" books showed an intimate knowledge of the amorous verse of the Elizabethans, including some definitely non-Puritan treatments of sex.

New England sought to achieve mass literacy by local taxation since she lacked endowments which, in England, made possible innumerable scholarships for worthy students. The Massachusetts Act of 1642 went no farther than to make parents or masters see to it that children be able to read and write, thus avoiding idleness and insuring their ability to read the Bible. The foundation for American tax-supported public schools actually came with the famous law of 1647 (imitated by Connecticut in 1650), which required every township of fifty householders or more to provide free elementary instruction while towns of over one hundred families were expected to offer grammar school education also. But for many years to come these laws remained aspirations rather than realities.

Small children, as in England, studied the three R's usually in a reading school conducted by a woman (later "dame schools"); needlework was often added for the girls. By seven or eight, the boys attended a writing school which prepared its pupils for the grammar school. Attendance in these schools, however, was not compulsory. The child in both England and New England learned his numbers, the alphabet, and the Lord's Prayer from the hornbook, a sheet enclosed by a transparent horn substance and fastened to a wooden frame with a handle. In Boston, his primer was likely to be John Cotton's popular catechism, *Milk for Babes, Drawn Out of the Breasts of Both Testaments,* published in 1646. The *New England Primer* appeared about 1690 and remained the principal elementary textbook for a half century. This taught the alphabet and sound theology together in couplets:

> In *Adam's* Fall
> We Sinned All

Very salutary is "F":

> The Idle *Fool*
> Is Whipt at School

"X," particularly gave the infants something to think about:
Xerxes the great did die
And so must you & I.

Grammar-school education was based on the English seven-year classical curriculum and was tailored to New England budgets, which usually meant some Latin and Greek literature for boys taught on a part-time basis by a college graduate who had other occupations to keep him busy. The oldest secondary school was Cotton Mather's alma mater, the Boston Latin School, opened in 1635, but this grammar school, like most others, offered almost nothing in the way of history, science, or modern languages.

Although the clergy scrutinized the orthodoxy of teachers and textbooks, the New England schools tended to remain under lay control. This again became distinctive of American public schools. Illiteracy was apparently far from conquered by the end of the century, for too many communities could not afford to tax themselves for an expensive school system. Some colonies, like Rhode Island, seemed indifferent. Morison finds only one boy from Rhode Island who attended college during the entire seventeenth century. New Plymouth, influenced by Brownist anti-intellectualism as well as by poverty, lagged behind. Indian wars consumed so much of the substance of New England that it is remarkable that the Puritans persisted in their efforts to establish the most complete elementary school system in the Americas.

Science was not stifled in New England despite the prevalence of folk beliefs, superstitious practices, and witchcraft phobias. The line between magic and science was not then, as sometimes since, as clear as it might have been. Increase Mather and his son Cotton who had led the credulous in the witch hunt, nevertheless co-operated with the Royal Society; for that matter, there were members of the Society who wrote intimately on witches and their habits. Yet, Cotton Mather, in the following century, was to champion vaccination for smallpox while the usually progressive Benjamin Franklin was very slow to follow. The Mathers were also the Harvard defenders of the Copernican system in astronomy which placed the sun rather than the earth in the center of the universe. Galileo had been forced by the Inquisition to repudiate this dogma in 1633, but the college adopted it by 1656.

John Cotton among the theocracy had doubted that experimental science made for true happiness, but Winthrop's own son, Governor John Winthrop, Jr., of Connecticut, proved a mighty pillar of colonial science. He was the only New Englander to win election to the Royal Society of London, founded in 1662. Educated at Trinity College, Dublin, and trained as a lawyer at the Inner Temple, he possessed over a thousand books and showed amazing versatility. He experimented with chemistry, botany, and medicine and prepared his own prescriptions, many of them, it is true, scarcely calculated to insure recovery from anything. Interested in minerals, he prospected for metals, set up the first ironworks in the colonies at Lynn in an unsuccessful effort to solve the acute iron shortage, introduced a salt manufactory to help the fishing industry, and even dabbled in alchemy.

Second only to young Winthrop was a Boston mathematician, Thomas Brattle, who had braved the witchcraft hysteria to warn his neighbors of the lasting reproach due their wanton executions. Brattle's careful calculations on the comet of 1680 were to aid Newton in formulating his theory of gravitation. Brattle made his observations with Harvard's three and one-half foot telescope, which John Winthrop, Jr., had brought over with him from England. An interesting footnote to the career of this scientist was his final bequest to the Brattle Street Church in Boston of an organ, the first in New England, to be used provided they found a "Sober person [to] play skilfully theron with a loud noise."

Literary culture was spurred on by the Cambridge Press—the first in the English colonies—which was set up in Harvard Yard in 1639 but, as in the Spanish colonies, was placed under a strict censorship. Its first product was the crudely printed *Bay Psalm Book*, edited by three university-trained ministers: Richard Mather, author of the Cambridge Platform of 1646, the constitution of Congregationalism; John Eliot, "apostle to the Indians"; and Thomas Weld, Harvard overseer and colonial agent. It was intended to be a more literal

version of the psalms than its musical predecessors and offered traditional melodies to be sung unaccompanied by instruments. Its rough
meter was scarcely esthetic but the selections were very popular,
so that the book reached a ninth edition by the end of the century
and its twenty-seventh by 1752.

Farmers enjoyed the encyclopedic almanacs, of which twenty-six
numbers were issued at Cambridge by 1670. The almanacs offered
a combination of bucolic versification, mild humor, and astronomical
data. Some interesting satire for 1670 appears in John Richardson's
Almanack:

> The Moon is habitable, some averre:
> And that some Creatures have their Dwelling there;
> Judge what you please; but yet 'tis very true,
> This year the Moon a Pair of Horns will shew.

The Cambridge Press issued in 1662 Michael Wigglesworth's extremely popular *The Day of Doom*, whose edition of 1800 copies
was exhausted the first year; many more editions were to follow in
both Old and New England. Wigglesworth, a meek person who was
a pastor at Malden, Massachusetts, and was a former Harvard tutor,
wrote verses smoking with hell-fire and brimstone theology, but
escaped the full pessimism of Calvin's predestination doctrine by
offering salvation or light punishment to those willing to do something to be saved. Generations of Puritan children memorized numerous verses of this two-hundred-stanza epic of God's wrath toward
mankind. Wigglesworth tells of infants who had died before sin was
possible, pleading their innocence of Adam's sin, but their arguments
were refuted "with ease" by a heavenly judge at the resurrection of
the dead:

> You sinners are, and such a share as sinners may expect;
> Such you shall have; for I do save none but mine own Elect.
> Yet to compare your sin with their who liv'd a longer time,
> I do confess yours is much less, though every sin's a crime.

To the Harvard-trained Cotton Mather, this was the "Book of the
Ages," the poetic counterpart of the prolific sermons and theological

works that poured from the Cambridge Press "without vain flourishes of wit." Some of these books, such as those of John Cotton and Roger Williams, have been noted already. Cotton Mather's own huge literary output straddled two centuries and reflected the eras of Puritanism and the Enlightenment. His eccentric *Wonders of the Invisible World* (1693) was fuel for the witchcraft frenzy. That year, he began his two-volume *Magnalia Christi Americana: or, the Ecclesiastical History of New England*, an interesting, if not always trustworthy, defense of the theocracy; it retailed the "exemplary lives of many magistrates, and of more ministers, who so lived as to leave unto posterity examples worthy of everlasting remembrance." Such evidence as he marshaled was intended to prove that New England's leaders were indubitably of the elect and that Massachusetts was a special concern of God's. Like many another Puritan, Mather kept a copious introspective diary that recorded his exalted moments and probed pitilessly into the weaknesses of others.

Far different was the fascinatingly honest diary of another Harvard graduate, his contemporary, the kindly Samuel Sewall, wealthy merchant and judge of the Massachusetts supreme court, who was originally trained for the ministry. His diary, covering 1673-1729, was not actually published until the nineteenth century. He embodied the Yankee virtues of thrift and prudence, which a younger contemporary, Benjamin Franklin, was to popularize. His patient courtship technique with the elusive Widow Winthrop, the welcome kisses of her maid, Sarah, and his daily observations of Massachusetts life are told delightfully. Diaries like those of Sewall, Cotton Mather, and John Hull, the wealthy mint master, represented a rising literary form peculiarly appropriate for the introspective Age of Puritanism and popular on both sides of the Atlantic.

History, teaching by moral example and revealing the Lord's will in the most trivial happenings, was a valued adjunct to Puritan literature. William Bradford's *History of Plymouth Plantation*, forgotten until its publication in 1855, was written in a plain style and skillfully told by an intelligent observer. The Massachusetts Bay counterpart of Bradford's history, though far less literary, was John Winthrop's *Journal* of which Perry Miller and Thomas Johnson have

pointed out the leading motif, "New England was the culmination of
the Reformation, the climax of world history, the ultimate revelation
through events of the objective toward which the whole of human
activity had been tending from the beginning of time." The eyes of
the world, thought Winthrop, were upon the Puritans.

Reminiscent of the golden age of Elizabethan lyrics, even through
Puritan spectacles, were the charming verses of the governor's gifted
wife, Anne Bradstreet, whose descendants included Wendell Phillips
and the Oliver Wendell Holmes family. A good wife and dutiful
mother of eight, she found time to enjoy poetry for its own sake and
to produce a large literary progeny. Her London publishers modestly
entitled her poetic volume of 1650, *The Tenth Muse Lately Sprung
Up in America*. The lyrics revealed the strong influence of the
popular Huguenot poet and soldier, William Du Bartas, whose encyclopedic epics of Creation and a universal history had been
pleasingly translated by Joshua Sylvester into the current stilted
Elizabethan euphuisms. Mrs. Bradstreet admired the poetry of
Spenser and Sir Philip Sidney and showed familiarity with contemporary and ancient historians from the Babylonian Berosus to
Plutarch and Camden. There is an echo of a recurring theme of
Shakespeare's sonnets in her poem, *Contemplations:*

> When I behold the heavens as in their prime,
> And then the earth (though old) stil clad in green,
> The stones and trees, insensible to time,
> Nor age nor wrinkle on their front are seen;
> If winter come, and greeness then do fade,
> A Spring returns, and they more youthfull made;
> But Man grows old, lies down, remains where once he's laid.

In 1820, Shelley was to write in *Ode to the West Wind:*

> If Winter comes, can Spring be far behind?

New England's reading, of course, did not stop with home pro-
ductions, comparable as these were to Puritan standards on the other
side of the Atlantic. The libraries of Brewster, Bradford, Standish,
and other Pilgrims, as already noted, showed a broad intellectual

horizon. John Winthrop, Jr.'s library of over a thousand books covered science, religion, history, travel, philosophy, and law; half of them were in Latin and the remainder in seven modern tongues. John Harvard's library gift to the college, while heavily theological, included most of the classics and the Renaissance humanists. By 1700 the college library collections exceeded those of any private library and revealed interests in contemporary literature and science.

Library lists show surprisingly few of the great Elizabethan and Stuart poets. Though Milton's prose works circulated, it is hard to find *Paradise Lost* on seventeenth-century lists and even Shakespeare's name is among the missing. The "vain romances" that Cotton Mather deplored as time-wasting for so many New Englanders seem to have escaped the legal inventories, but it is clear that popular reading tastes, as ever, were not confined to the literature of the intellectual elite. Unorthodox books from Europe or other colonies were banned by the theocracy after the fashion of the Inquisition in the New World colonies of Spain and Portugal. An important intellectual stimulus came, however, after the Restoration of 1660 as the Puritan regicides fled to New England, bringing with them fresh currents of European thought. A new press was set up in Boston in 1675, and the cause of freedom of the press improved after the Glorious Revolution of 1688, when Boston Puritanism was forced back on the defensive. When, in 1700, still another press was established in the Bay Colony's principal city, Boston became second only to London as an English publishing center.

Looking back upon seventeenth-century New England, it is clear that the Puritan world of Roger Williams was far more than a sectarian society warped by Freudian inhibitions and endless probing into the private lives of its citizens. Much of what is called "puritanical" in sex morality and social life was common to many middle-class contemporaries in Europe. The rise of middle-class culture in both Catholic and Protestant nations, rather than English Puritanism alone, produced such nineteenth-century patterns as prim Victorianism in England, crinoline ultra-respectability in America, and complacent bourgeois ideals in Louis Philippe's France and Bismarck's

Germany. The so-called Puritan "genteel tradition" of literature with its sex hypocrisy, its sentimentality, and its social evasions belongs to this nineteenth-century pattern rather than to the seventeenth-century Puritan world of the plain style and religious challenge.

The Puritans gave New England an intellectual aspiration and literary vitality which made that section pre-eminent in the world of letters for over two centuries. In religion, it is true, the New England conscience has too often meant an officious type of "brother's keeper," marked by censoriousness and book-banning; but it has also carried a quality of high moral idealism and sturdy faith in the reality of truth. This moral fervor later expressed itself in crusading for abolitionism, feminism, and peace movements. In politics, Roger Williams, the advance spirit of the Puritan Revolt, taught the Leveller's concepts of social democracy in Anglo-American terms of majority rule and minority rights. The seventeenth-century frontier, with its economic opportunities, strengthened the liberal tendencies in law and government until feudal class restrictions and narrow theocratic barriers were strongly modified and ultimately overthrown.

· 3 ·

Feudalism and the Frontier in Fitzhugh's Virginia: The Seventeenth Century

I

In 1671, young William Fitzhugh, newly arrived from Bedfordshire, England, took up lands along the Potomac River in Stafford County, Virginia, and laid the foundation of his baronial estate at Bedford on the frontier. Son of a well-to-do English woolen draper, he had come, like so many others of the first families of Virginia, with substantial capital to buy lands and servants. Two years later, he married Sarah Tucker, daughter of a wealthy planter of Westmoreland County, and his assimilation into the world of the tidewater aristocracy was complete. A shrewd land speculator and trader who aspired to the rule of a manorial estate of feudal magnificence, he acquired ninety-six thousand acres in the fertile Northern Neck of Virginia between the Rappahannock and the Potomac rivers. At his death in 1701, he transmitted almost fifty-five thousand acres in five family "seats," to as many sons, according to the Virginia custom.

Like other wealthy planters of tidewater Virginia living along the Potomac, the Rappahannock, the York, or the James rivers, Fitzhugh built a wharf for his tobacco crops nearby which was reached by deep-draft, ocean-going vessels. Pioneer Americans, north and south, who clung from necessity to water pathways, were doubly blessed in Virginia and Maryland where the numerous rivers and Chesapeake Bay afforded a ready approach from Europe on the one hand and to the scattered interior plantations on the other. Small planters could trade their crops to Fitzhugh and others like him who arranged to load them at their wharves for their agents in London and Bristol. Where the plantation fell short of self-sufficiency, planters bought directly from England, thus leaving little room for the growth of an urban financial and mercantile class of middlemen at home. Much of what became the "South" was shaped by this absence of cities and the lack of a middle class.

Fitzhugh's Virginia, wedded to tobacco as a commercial crop, was a land of small farms and a relatively small number of large plantations. The soil was exploited as elsewhere in the colonies by frontier methods of cultivation and indifference to adequate fertilizers. Tobacco tended to exhaust the soil faster than did most other crops. Besides, with an abundance of good lands and a perennial shortage of labor, there seemed to be little need to employ scientific agriculture. Planters, therefore, took up as extensive lands as they were able, cultivated a part until it was exhausted, and then opened a fresh section that could be worked with the limited labor at their disposal. This system, like that of direct marketing, discouraged the growth of towns. Even at the end of the century, Jamestown, Virginia's capital, remained a village, and its successor, Williamsburg, was scarcely more urban at that time.

Just as tobacco and rice cultivation set the pattern for the historic Southern plantation system, so it laid the basis for the future one-crop system. Tobacco was introduced to England in Elizabethan times by Sir Walter Raleigh as the gift of Virginia's Indians and it became the mainstay of the colony, especially after John Rolfe's experiments in curing the plant had made it commercially successful. The smoking and snuff habits, limited at first to Europe's upper classes, became universal. Tobacco-chewing captured the poorer classes of Europe and won an undisputed place on the American frontier.

Virginia's tobacco practically drove the Spanish product out of England; still, the English merchants, eager to insure their monopoly of this and other "enumerated" colonial exports, secured laws excluding the efficient Dutch merchants, who had managed to under-

sell England on the Continent. Between 1660 and 1682, Charles II
continued Cromwell's hostile policy toward Dutch commercial competition. Tobacco from the colonies could be shipped only to the
mother country where its re-export to the Continent entailed ware-
housing charges and other fees. But while the English merchants
waited patiently for the destruction of Holland's control of the tobacco trade in Europe, Virginia faced ruin before the falling price
of tobacco; her ample crops glutted the English market and overflowed the warehouses. Virginians, reverting to homespun and giving
up their imports of fine clothes, furniture, books, and other cherished
goods, found little comfort in the fact that English mercantilistic
policy allotted them the entire home market by preventing tobacco-
growing in the homeland, where planting conditions were less favorable anyway.

Nor did British advice to diversify their economy solve their problems, for manufacturing was badly hampered by a chronic shortage
of trained craftsmen and consequent high labor costs. Again, since
tobacco constituted much of the currency system, its drastic decline
in value meant painful inflation. Only the native abundance of food
in that fertile land prevented the economic crisis from taking the
form of starvation. Vainly, Fitzhugh and other planters sought to
raise tobacco prices by voluntary crop restriction, which proved
ineffective. In 1682, angry mobs invaded the tobacco plantations to
destroy the crops until the militia stopped the riots, arresting many
and hanging two. Finally, in that same year, recovery began to take
place in the tobacco colonies, but only after England had defeated
the Dutch in several wars and had captured the Continental market
by dumping her enormous tobacco holdings on it at bottom prices.

Great planters like Fitzhugh, John Carter, Robert Beverley, William
Byrd, and others had more than tobacco cultivation to think about.
Fitzhugh's numerous cattle, hogs, horses, and sheep, his orchard of
2500 apple trees, his grist mill for the wheat and corn he raised for
his family and servants, all brought heavy burdens of administration.
His business correspondence with agents and merchants in Europe,
his complex legal affairs, and his elaborate accounts demanded careful direction. His English servants and his fifty-one slaves—an un-

usually large group for this period—might require his medical attention and close supervision. Then there were the onerous but necessary requirements of planter hospitality, the business of government, and the duty of colonial defense.

The leading Virginia families, despite humble or mercantile origins, liked to trace their ancestry, as Fitzhugh did, to William the Conqueror; he paid a fee to the College of Heralds in London for a magnificently emblazoned coat of arms. One of Fitzhugh's descendants, George Fitzhugh of Caroline County, noted author of *Sociology for the South* (1854), added his authority to the myth of William's distinguished ancestry and the alleged Cavalier origins of the South. "The Cavaliers, Jacobites, and Huguenots who settled the South," he wrote in 1861, "naturally hate, contemn, and despise the Puritans who settled the North. The former are master races, the latter a slave race, the descendants of the Saxon serfs." Actually, as T. J. Wertenbaker has pointed out, fully 90 per cent of the Virginians were industrious small farmers rather than gay, romantic Cavaliers of King Charles, possessing limitless acres and a sword loyal to the aristocratic Stuart cause.

Nevertheless, this élite of perhaps less than one hundred wealthy planting families, as Louis B. Wright implies in *The First Gentlemen of Virginia*, took up the aristocratic tradition—although they remained busy planters, not drones—and read assiduously in Renaissance manuals on the code and manners of gentlemen. They accepted the paternalistic duties of *noblesse oblige* to one's social inferiors in return for economic services and privileges and a high status. However, instead of awaiting patiently the slow evolution of gentility through several generations, each family in this fluid social structure found money a simple touchstone for immediate acceptance. Trade carried little taint in the New World. The aspiring gentleman, explains Wright, sought a polished manner of speech, a graceful carriage, a punctilious code of honor, and a classical moderation in all things, including vice. Dueling, however, though occasionally practiced, was discouraged. This was the budding world of the Fitzhughs and their notable neighbors, the Blands, the Beverleys, the Byrds, the Carters, the Harrisons, the Randolphs, the Lees, the Lightfoots, and the Washingtons.

2

For the English tenant farmer, struggling to maintain himself on borrowed land, Virginia came as a welcome release, offering fifty acres for each member of his family who moved to the colony. For those who lacked capital, there was always the opportunity of becoming an indentured servant for three to five years in return for transportation. Youths chose indenture as an effective way of learning a trade and perhaps also of learning to read. In 1671, the year Fitzhugh arrived, there were 6000 bound servants in the colony's population of almost 50,000 and the majority of adults in Virginia and Maryland had once been under such contracts. Three-fourths of the servants were illiterate, forced to use their mark rather than a signature on the contracts.

Women, far outnumbered by men, came in ever-increasing numbers as servants. Famous in Virginia's tradition was Sir Edwin Sandys' boatload of "young, handsome and honestly educated maids," which arrived in 1621 followed by more prospective wives. Mary Johnston, romantic novelist and historian, has dwelt upon this episode in *To Have and To Hold*. The acute labor shortage in a land as rich in resources as Virginia was only partly alleviated by the indentured servant system, for the terms were too short and renewed contracts too few to solve the problem. There was little inducement to renew a contract voluntarily when farms could be had almost for the asking. Many a lesser "aristocrat" of this era failed to live up to the tradition of keeping numerous servants and retainers at work while their master lazily fanned himself, for the truer picture was one of the master sweating at his fieldwork alongside two or three servants.

Negro slavery was restricted during most of the seventeenth century. Even the notorious Dutch black cargo vessel of 1619, which is erroneously considered the cradle of Negro slavery in the English colonies, actually consisted not of chattel slaves but of twenty indentured Negroes who were later released. This system of indentures for Africans gradually merged, almost casually, into slavery. Christian scruples and colonial laws over enslaving baptized persons were overcome by the intensive drive for a more stable labor supply, especially of men inured to the beating sun and heat on the tobacco fields. After the Restoration of 1660, when the ambitious Duke of York and the Royal African Company, which included Governor William Berkeley among its directors, entered the slave trade successfully against the Dutch, slavery took on a new lease on life in the colonies. Although there were only 300 Negroes in Virginia in 1650, this had risen to 3000 by 1681; and in 1700, when the colony probably totaled 80,000 whites, some 6000 Negroes labored on its plantations and farms. Those who brought in slaves, as in the case of other immigrants, received "headrights" entitling them to extensive acreages.

This new labor competition struck a deadly blow to the indenture system, and the numbers of such servants fell rapidly thereafter. The gulf between large planter and small farmer widened as the possession of slaves by the wealthy raised the productivity of his lands and, consequently, increased his income and heightened his social status, while these factors remained static for the non-slaveholder. Finally, the rigid barriers of race, unlike the fluid relationship of master and white servant, eventually proved a sharp limiting factor to democracy in the South.

The coming of the Negro from Africa and the West Indies altered the developing pattern of a homogeneous Anglo-Saxon South. Ninety five per cent of the 100,000 white immigrants to Virginia in the seventeenth century were English, supplemented by small numbers of Scotch, French Huguenots, and a scattering of citizens of other lands. The new Negro arrivals, far from being untamed cannibalistic savages, came largely from the relatively complex cultures of West Africa where the leading slave traders had established themselves: there were Ashantis from the Gold Coast, Dahomeans from the West Coast, and Yorubas from Nigeria. Among them were ironworkers, craftsmen who had been organized into guilds, a few Negro slaveholders of kingly origin, skilled farmers, and traders. Some of the women held high social status in matri- archal fashion, regulated prices in the markets, and sometimes were independently wealthy.

These Negroes could scarcely have been "pure" racially, for recent intermixture with Portuguese, Spanish, English, and Dutch slave traders as well as medieval and ancient contacts with Caucasian peoples of the eastern Mediterranean indicated the most diverse ancestry. Mohammedan kingdoms in medieval times had penetrated deeply into northern and western Africa. Marched abjectly across the burning sands by ruthless slave drivers and packed suffocatingly into filthy ships, their voyage across the notorious "middle passage" frequently began with revolts whenever they managed to unfasten their chains. The trip proved a gruesome test of the survival of the fittest. For example, the Royal African Company, which shipped 60,783 Negroes to the New World between 1680 and 1688, lost 14,387 in the middle passage.

Once in their new home, these tribesmen might be deliberately scattered to secure docility, and the process of "breaking in" the Africans to their new plantation status began. Usually, this process was completed in the West Indies before the slaves were sold on the mainland. During the early decades of slavery in the tobacco colonies, racial prejudice seems to have been mild. The scarcity of women on the frontier sometimes gave the Negress taken by the white man more than casual status, even though out of wedlock, and even though, if she was a slave, her hybrid offspring had to remain in slavery. Still, the intermingling of the races went on. Gunnar Myrdal, the sociologist, has called attention to the fact that whole tribes of Indians were lost in the racial stream of the Negro popula- tion. A few Negro families, like the Johnsons of Virginia, rose from servitude to slaveownership. Others were freed at the death of their masters.

Distinctions between whites and Negroes, hitherto kept on a re- ligious basis of "Christians" and "heathen," were shifted in 1682 to a frank racialist plane by a law that barred Negro Christians from any claim to freedom on religious grounds. Custom had moved in this direction before law made racialism a fact. Professor Wesley F. Craven points out the attitudes of racial superiority taken by Englishmen in the colonial assemblies and courts early in the history of slave importations; he attributes their acts to a desire to maintain "racial integrity." One of his striking illustrations is taken from a Virginia court judgment of 1630: "Hugh Davis to be soundly whipped, before an assembly of Negroes and others for abusing himself to the dishonor of God and shame of Christians, by defiling his body in lying with a negro." As early as 1623 Bermuda's Assembly had forbidden Negroes to bear arms, to take part in trade, and to move without restrictions. Double penalties for whites guilty of sex relations with Negroes were imposed in a Virginia law of 1662. Two years later Maryland declared that white women marrying slaves would themselves serve as slaves during the husband's lifetime and any children of this union would remain slaves.

However, it is difficult to divorce such racial attitudes from economic factors. Lawmakers and judges (largely planters) were very receptive to the slaveowners' desire for a secure labor supply, which could be insured by a special status for the black. Before the end of the century the attempt to police the Negro population was to inspire many discriminating laws and to encourage racialism. Eventually, in the succeeding generations, an informal etiquette of race relations as well as statutory rules were to arise regulating race contacts in the interest of a dominant white society. The steady increase of mulattoes during the slavery era in American history and afterwards bore witness to a relationship of the races quite at variance with any effective goal of "racial purity" or "racial integrity."

Among the white population, the frontier did indeed act as a strong leveling force against permanent class distinctions of a feudal nature. Many an aristocratic "burgess" in the Virginia legislature had once been an indentured servant, and long-faded English gentry and parvenu tradesmen rose to the highest peaks of gentility in Virginia. Nevertheless, despite this fluid class situation, living conditions for servants and slaves, subject to the whims of masters on isolated plantations and farms, were too frequently intolerable. Some masters could plead the need for harsh discipline by pointing out that too many servants had but recently emerged from London jails or fought with rebellious Irish or Scottish armies or been recruited from depraved corners of English cities. Most servants, of course, were not of this class, but the master's practice of brutality persisted.

County courts, with justices drawn largely from among the leading planters, often showed class bias in freeing masters in cases involving rape of servant girls, torture, mutilation, severe whippings, bad food, and starvation. White servants and Negro slaves drew together in a common desire for freedom, occasionally plotted insurrections, and often escaped to the Indians or the Spaniards. A runaway servant might be punished by having the letter R branded on his cheek and be forced to serve an extended term of indentured labor. Laws were passed forbidding servants and slaves to hold meetings without their master's approval. In Maryland and the Carolinas, the story was similar, if less shocking than in Virginia.

The Old Dominion preceded New England in carrying over at least in part the prevailing English economic theories of controlling prices and wages, and of standardizing quality, especially during the early decades. Medieval restraints on competition had not yet surrendered to the individualist idea of the free market in the English colonies. Laborers were, however, too scarce in Virginia as among her neighbors to permit low fixed wages to continue for long. Skilled colonial craftsmen sometimes earned four times as much as their brethren in England. The craft guild, which clung to urban centers in New England, never took root in the agrarian South. As in the homeland, the law forced vagrants, idle persons, and orphaned or poor children to work. Poor relief was administered by the parish along lines similar to that of New England's town government. Church wardens were expected to find lodgings for the poor and orphaned at the expense of the parish.

3

Virginia's government, which ceased to be administered by the Virginia Company in 1624, began at the bottom with the English parish as a vigorous local unit concerned with church support and morals as well as with poor relief. Vestrymen, usually well-to-do freeholders chosen by a majority of the parishioners, laid local levies, appointed the Anglican clergymen, investigated moral offenses for presentment to the county court, and chose the church wardens. The latter acted as prosecutors in morals cases, audited parish accounts, and dealt with poor relief. During the early decades, this tended to be a democratic system, but by Fitzhugh's time, the vestry in too many instances had become a static unit, composed of constantly re-elected landowners, much to the resentment of the small farmers and servants.

Above the parish, though often duplicating its personnel, boundaries, and responsibilities, stood the remarkable county court, an institution borrowed from England, but with its commissioners (or justices) appointed by the governor. Unlike New England, and to a much lesser extent, the Middle Colonies as well, where the town unit dominated, Virginia and Maryland found county government best suited for their scattered rural communities. In the rural South (outside of Louisiana), the county was to have its most vigorous life for generations to come. Something of the traditional flavor of the easygoing English squire lingered in the justice of the Virginia county court.

In seventeenth-century Virginia, the county commissioners—later limited to eight in number—had a most amazing array of administrative and judicial functions. These influential men were the "squires" whose decision affected almost every phase of life—the bulk of Virginia's government in fact. Though laymen in the law, they decided or arbitrated individually the most petty neighborhood quarrel or, collectively, judged very serious cases short of life and limb. To them fell the duty of administering the numerous regulations affecting tradesmen, prices, and wages, the maintenance of roads and ferries, the recording of wills and contracts, the issuing of land titles, and the appointing or nominating of local officers. They might serve or at least control the two vital and profitable offices of tax collector and sheriff subject to the vague supervision of the governor. Usually well-to-do planters, the county commissioners too often approximated a closed self-perpetuating oligarchy with strong political strings leading to Jamestown. Even Bacon's Rebellion could not dislodge these men, and the democratization of the county court had to await another era.

At the top of the governing pyramid was the General Assembly, consisting of a House of Burgesses, elected by all freemen before 1670 and thereafter by propertied voters, and of a highly paid Council of State, chosen by the governor from the leading families. The burgesses often held at the same time posts of vestryman or justice of the peace or, possibly, colonel of the militia, making them mindful of local interests and suspicious of centralizing power in the hands of the clique at the capital. Councilors, proud of the title of Esquire signed after their names, enjoyed a chance to enrich themselves as high legal and financial officers in securing huge land grants; besides, they were immune from ordinary arrest and held partial exemption from taxes. Not far above the councilors was the governor chosen by the Crown; but a vigorous figure like Berkeley might make this office a citadel of absolutism.

William Fitzhugh shared the political duties of the ruling class as a member of the House of Burgesses for Stafford County and as judge of the county court. He even tried to make the office of "high sheriff," which was a distinguished and lucrative post in Virginia, an entailed perquisite in his family according to feudal custom, urging legal precedents for this in Scottish and English society.

Legal development, as in New England, was strongly modified by frontier conditions. Nowhere were lawyers hated more than among the debtors and the indentured classes. The popular faction among the burgesses managed at various times, especially during the Puritan Revolution when the aristocrats were on the defensive, to cut legal fees and occasionally to ban "mercenarie lawyers"—professional attorneys—altogether. Virginia, argued the popular faction, was intended as an asylum for the poor. Common-law technicalities and delays often wore out the poorer folk at law, thus defeating justice. In 1658, the Assembly reflected this popular pressure by ordering the courts to confine themselves to the "right of the cause" without regard to "imperfection, default, or want of

forme in any writt, returne plaint or process." County courts tended
to demand simple, non-technical language in pleading. Thus many
inapplicable English technicalities were eliminated.

William Fitzhugh, a county judge and practicing lawyer, and
probably the best legal scholar in Virginia, championed the common
law in all its purity as the best guide to the meaning of statutes.
As a rich planter and merchant, he had everything to lose by the
informal procedure of frontier courts and his criticism of the judges
of his day could not have been wholly disinterested. Before his
death, he had even completed a digest of Virginia's laws, though the
book was never published.

Another frontier influence on law was reflected in the resistance
of the seventeenth century to the feudal inheritance laws of primogeniture and entail, whose acceptance had to await the next century.
These laws would have perpetuated aristocratic families and estates
through exclusive inheritance by the eldest son without permitting
disposal outside of the family. In a new country such laws ran up
against the difficulty of providing younger sons with the genteel
livelihood commensurate with the family's position. As a result, the
tendency in the colonies was to favor partible inheritance, which
allowed all heirs to share in the estate. Thus Virginia set up such a
democratic procedure in 1673, and, in accordance with it, Fitzhugh
later bequeathed a magnificent estate to each of his five sons.

                                    4

The great challenge to Virginia's governing aristocracy came in
1676 in Bacon's Rebellion when the Virginia yeomanry and indentured servants made a strong bid for power. This uprising grew out
of a quarrel between the frontiersmen and Governor William Berkeley over Indian policy. In 1675, following an Indian raid on the
frontier, brutal reprisals were taken upon unsuspecting Susquehan-
nock tribesmen; news from New England regarding King Philip's
War suggested that the entire length of the frontier was aflame. The
dictatorial Berkeley and his clique, however, showed an eastern indifference to frontier problems and refused to go beyond limited

defensive measures. The frontiersmen, pressing for immediate action, found a talented leader in young Nathaniel Bacon, a Cambridge-educated planter recently arrived who had suffered heavy losses from Indian raids. Bacon at first sought to enlist the "gentlemen of Virginia" in his cause, but soon fell back upon the yeomanry and espoused their grievances not only against the Indians but eventually against the planter-oligarchy as well. Apparently he hoped to unite Virginia against Berkeley until he could win a favorable hearing from the king.

Marching upon Jamestown, after a successful sortie against the Indians, Bacon forced through laws extending the suffrage to all freemen, canceled the tax exemption privileges of the councilors, made the vestries again elective in fact, and reduced the exorbitant fees of local officials. "Bacon! Bacon! Bacon!" became the delighted slogan of his followers. While many planters deprecated Berkeley's headstrong attitude of dealing with Bacon and his men as traitors, the Fitzhughs, the Lees, the Wormeleys, and other wealthy men stood by their class against the man who had deserted his social station to join his inferiors. Bacon's men routed the governor, confiscated the properties of Robert Beverley, John Washington, and other hostile conservatives, and burned Jamestown when it could no longer be held.

At one time Bacon had almost all Virginia within his grasp. But the rebels, fighting Indians and Berkeley's men simultaneously, suffered a disastrous blow in the illness and death of their leader. Thereafter, the governor gained the upper hand. He ordered merciless executions for the rebel leaders until King Charles II, himself, angrily intervened and recalled Berkeley to England, where that ultra-Tory soon died. Although Bacon's popular laws were swept away, some concessions were later made to the small farmers. Much more fatal for Bacon's democratic cause was the sharp increase in slaves in the colony, replacing the short-tenured and less-tractable servants. Henceforth, Southern society was to be divided on racial as well as class lines, an unfavorable setting for genuine democracy.

Indian relations, which had provoked Bacon's Rebellion, had once been far more promising than they were in 1676. In Virginia's tradition there was the romantic story of the guileless Pocahontas, daughter of the mighty emperor Powhatan, who had saved Captain John Smith from death by throwing herself across his prostrate body. Surprisingly enough, the English deemed her royal blood a sufficient mark of distinction to allow her to marry a member of the English gentility, John Rolfe. In his love for the comely Indian girl, "her owne intycements stirringe me upp." Rolfe was not only willing to cherish his primitive in-laws, but took his bride, now baptized as Rebecca, to meet his family and friends in England, there to receive a cordial welcome at court. Unfortunately, the Lady Rebecca died soon after, a victim apparently of smallpox, leaving a son behind. According to John Smith, Pocahontas saved early Jamestown from starvation. Her father would have preferred to thrust the Virginians into the sea, but Pocahontas proved a sure hostage for peace.

The early settlers must have had occasion to rue their lack of more interracial unions with the Algonquian peoples. In 1622, Powhatan's successor, Opechancanough, unleashed a wholesale massacre, wiping out some four hundred whites of all ages and threatening the very existence of the colony. A second massacre in 1644 took almost as many lives, but led to the capture and death of Opechancanough. The first massacre, particularly, discouraged the Virginians in their previous high hopes of educating and converting the Indians. Dropping their plans for Indian schools and a college, they turned to a ruthless policy of extermination and victory through calculated treachery. The Indians reacted by renewing their savage attacks, notably in 1644 and 1676. A handful of converted Christian Indians remained loyal and befriended the colonists, but the bulk of the Indians, like the Pamunkey and Chickahominy tribes, retreated before the overwhelming forces of the whites, leaving behind only their tribal names for Virginia's rivers.

5

The Anglican Church, which dominated seventeenth-century Virginia, was supported by a host of severe laws punishing dissenters, but intolerance in the Old Dominion rarely attained the notoriety it achieved in New England. Puritanism made considerable headway in the southern colony, despite hostile legislation, and enjoyed the temporary triumph of turning the tables on the Anglicans during the Cromwell period. Governor John Harvey was willing to stretch a point and invite New England Puritans to the Delaware Bay area rather than see the Dutch or Swedes entrench themselves there; but Berkeley, more royalist than the king, drove the Puritans to Maryland where they soon seized control.

"Papists" were feared in early Virginia as spies of Spain and Lord Baltimore's Catholic colony in Maryland was held suspect. Catholic priests were expelled and all Catholics who persisted in living in the colony were politically disqualified. William Fitzhugh, a staunch Anglican who busied himself with the upper-class parish duty of finding an able clergyman in the faith, nevertheless dealt intimately with his Catholic law partner and neighbor, George Brent, and showed tolerance toward the increasing numbers of Catholic refugees who settled near him. Fitzhugh's tolerance, reinforced by sound elements of self-interest, included industrious French Huguenots whom he tried to attract as tenants to work his extensive lands; he even employed a Huguenot tutor for his son.

Of particular concern to the Anglicans was the rapid growth of Quakerism, then in its militant expansionist phase. Aside from their doctrinal influence, the Quaker missionaries seemed to offer a kind of unfair competition to other faiths. Their pacifist beliefs exempted them from arduous military duties on an insecure frontier. Their resistance to parish tithes for the Established Church shifted the burden to other groups. Besides, their quiet meetings seemed suspiciously secretive. "There is no toleration for wicked consciences," declared a judge bluntly to a Quaker defendant in the 1660's, shortly after an order had been issued banning the sect. Virginia's laws carried a death sentence for Quakers who returned three times after repeated expulsions, but this was unenforced. The Quaker, William Robinson, who was kept in Virginia's jails most of his time in that colony, went to New England, where his persistence won him the martyr's crown by hanging. A new day for religious toleration among Christians came with James II's "Declaration for Liberty of Conscience in Religious Matters," proclaimed in Virginia in 1687 and followed the next year throughout the colonies by the royal Act of Toleration.

If Anglicanism was somewhat behind Puritanism in revolutionary religious fervor, it continued the Reformation tradition in piety, looking upon religion as high personal adventure. Few private collections lacked *The Practice of Piety* or other popular moral and religious books. Like the Puritans, the Anglicans of Virginia had their official "days of humiliation" and thanksgiving days. The Assembly of 1619, zealous to protect orthodoxy, required all ministers to meet periodically at Jamestown "to determine whom it was fit to excommunicate."

The intention of keeping the Sabbath was as strong in early Virginia as in New England, if one judges by the numerous Sabbatarian laws and the severe judgments of the courts. To miss church on Sunday in 1618 was punishable by being tied "neck and heels" overnight and for even longer periods for repeaters. Far more practical was the punishment for fishing on Sunday, which might require that the culprit build a bridge on the road to the parish church. Laboring or traveling on the Sabbath, even carrying tools or sending a servant on an errand, was considered a violation of the holy day. In the same classification was playing cards, driving a cart, fiddling, dancing, or getting drunk on Sunday. Fines, payable in tobacco or cash, were the usual penalty. However, the parish church was far too distant for many Virginians to encourage regular attendance and the easygoing farmer often lost his way to church by dropping into a local tavern for a drink. The English Restoration of 1660, with its sharp reaction against Puritanism, discouraged the extreme Sabbatarians. Nevertheless, as late as 1690 the justices of the peace were ordered to take more strenuous steps to halt Sabbath-breaking. By this time complaints of popular indifference to the Sabbath were very common.

The Church of Virginia, separated as it was by a wide ocean from the centralized English hierarchy, developed along informal and to some extent more democratic lines than did Anglicanism across the sea. There were too few trained ministers for the scattered flock despite sporadic recruits of clerical exiles during the Puritan Revolution. The development of a strong native clergy was hampered by the personal expense of seeking episcopal ordination in England as was required. Besides, Anglican Virginia had no college for ministers as did Protestant New England nor did the Anglicans permit a simple form of ordination. Although certain ministers earned good incomes from their parishes and farms, many did not. Vestrymen were compelled to fill vacancies by choosing deacons to officiate in perhaps two-thirds of the churches. Thus laymen appeared in the pulpits, or read the burial services. In 1697, there were but twenty-two ministers in Virginia's fifty parishes. The uncertain tenure of the ministers and their dependence on the whims of the vestrymen kept —so it was reported—"all women of the better sort from matching with the Clergy."

As for the seventeenth-century Virginia church building, it tended to be far more pretentious than the early plain New England structure. Though the buildings were usually wooden frame structures, there were some examples of elaborate brick architecture like imposing St. Luke's at Smithfield, which had Gothic buttresses, pointed arches, and a stepped-up gable. Planters made gifts of costly plate and ornaments, silver communion cups, and damask carpets. As in urban New England, church members were seated in pews arranged according to social station.

6

Puritanical precepts and punishments filled the statute books of Virginia, Maryland, and the Carolinas, but there is little question that life in the South was lived more convivially than in New England. As in the land of the Winthrops and the Mathers, there was the publicity of the stocks near the church for such evildoers as sex offenders, those given to profanity, and drunken persons. A slanderous woman could be sent to the ducking stool or forced to apologize before the congregation. Ducking was a popular Virginia remedy, especially for "brabling women." Whipping, too, was a

common penalty for a multitude of offenses although gentlefolk
escaped by paying a fine. "Kissing the post," prodded by a cat-o'-
nine-tails, was one form of whipping. Bruce tells of an unmarried
mother who was compelled to appear in a white sheet before her
congregation and urged to repent—which she failed to do. In a
certain sex case, the gentleman wore the white sheet and carried a
wand before the church members while the woman, one of the
commonality, was publicly whipped. An adulteress—these laws
seemed to favor men—might be dragged in a river behind a moving
boat. Illicit sex relations among servants, who were prevented by
their contracts from marrying without their master's consent, were
common and punishable by severe whippings and public confessions. Offspring of such unions could be bound out until thirty years
of age; a child of a servant mother and a slave father could be enslaved.

Juries in the tobacco colonies seemed only mildly interested in
stamping out witchcraft, although few ventured to question the
reality of the invisible world of demons. Maryland, especially in the
Puritan era of domination, urged her justices to keep a sharp eye
upon conjurors, sorcerers, and witches; at least one such agent of
Satan did come close to being hanged in that colony. Virginia used
juries of matrons to examine accused females for the telltale marks
of the devil on their bodies, but, in general, Anglican clergymen discouraged convictions for such crimes.

Despite puritanical laws, the Virginians enjoyed a vigorous recreational life with far fewer inhibitions than their New England
neighbors. Horse-racing was a thrilling sport among all classes, for
Southerners loved to ride and to bet on horses, in fact to wager on
almost anything. On Saturday mornings, planters and farmers, including their wives, thronged the race tracks, watched their horses
and jockeys train, and speculated on their chances in the races.
However, gentlemen were bound by their aristocratic code to refuse
to run their horses against those of their social inferiors. When victory came, it called for a riotous celebration with drinking bouts
that often lasted into the Sabbath.

Even those with empty pockets could have a boisterous good time on the traditional Court Days held at the county seats where political and judicial business did not interfere with exciting wrestling matches, cudgeling, target-shooting, and half-drunken horseplay. Crowds turned to bowling or games of ninepins while others bet on their favorite cocks in the fighting pit. Finally, all rushed into the taverns where drinks in generous variety and quantity were to be had and where there was dancing to the fiddler's merry tune. There one met the shrewd Virginia horsetrader, equal of any Yankee, the none-too-coy damsels, the loquacious exhibitors of strange animals, and the wandering acrobats and jugglers. Such was Court Day not only in the seventeenth century, but in the eighteenth and nineteenth also.

For the small wealthy class of some leisure, recreation and hospitality were of course a far more elaborate and expensive business. Virginia's abundance of almost all foods was heavily requisitioned by the exacting demands of Southern hospitality, which followed the generous pattern of the English country gentleman. "If there happen to be a churl that either out of covetousness or ill-nature won't comply with this generous custom," wrote Robert Beverley, the aristocrat-historian, "he has a mark of infamy set upon him, and is abhorred by all." In the ordinary course of events, "visiting," almost on the mass scale of the English feudal nobility, proved a perennial Southern custom. Distant planting families who came a-visiting expected that their arduous journey would be fully justified by an indefinite stay and appropriate refreshments and entertainment.

It is difficult to imagine the strain that a wedding celebration or a funeral must have imposed on the host. Bruce tells of one funeral in 1691 that supplemented the imposing rites for the deceased with sixty gallons of cider, four of rum, and wagonloads of turkeys, geese, hogs, baked meats, cakes, and other tidbits to comfort the bereaved. Fitzhugh's ample mansion witnessed royal entertainment, even on minor occasions, for the guests enjoyed excellent musicians, jesters, acrobats, and the feats of tightrope dancers. Young people of this class sought the services of dancing masters and danced away the whole of Saturday night and well into Sunday morning, sometimes to the scandal of their elders, while the servants fiddled obligingly. Domestic architecture in the South, as in New England, reflected to some extent the English medieval style, stressing half-timbered frame construction, sturdy ceiling beams in Jacobean fashion, diamond-shaped casement windows, and shingled roofs. Fitzhugh's frame dwelling, surrounded by an attractive garden, had thirteen rooms, four cellars, and brick chimneys. Like those in New England, his house, too, had grown by improvised annexes as the need arose. Robert Beverley, who belonged to Fitzhugh's class, owned a pretentious residence with the distinctive Southern two-story front porch. The still-surviving Bacon's Castle, which once belonged to the famous rebel-aristocrat, shows a massive three-stack brick chimney, a porch, and a spacious interior. This large brick residence reflected the advance of the colonial brickmaking industry by the latter seventeenth century. While in New England a single chimney was built in the center of the house to conserve heat, in Virginia and other southern colonies there were often two chimneys placed at opposing ends of the roof. The familiar "Virginia house" among the lesser folk, possibly originating in Flanders, was a long narrow one-story frame house and loft with end chimneys. The village of Jamestown had rows of two-story framed timber houses with garrets, many of which did double duty as taverns. Log cabins were practically unknown at first in the familiar form, for the frontiersmen built single-room cottages of an English type, using bedcovers as walls for the convenience of visitors.

Well-to-do planters were able to emulate the English country gentlemen in furniture by importing oriental carpets, damask tablecloths and napkins, silver plate, and embroidered Russian leather couches. Despite laws restricting luxury goods, they managed to wear silk stockings, broadcloth coats with silver buttons, shirts with ruffled sleeves, and beaver hats; their ladies wore silken gowns, silver lace petticoats, and other finery. At the bottom of the social scale, the laborer was content with simple home furnishings, locally made, as on New England farms, and with buckskin or canvas suits, and wooden-heeled shoes.

7

Education in the South lagged far behind that in New England except for a very small wealthy group. Although the Anglicans agreed with the Puritans that every child must be taught at least to read the Bible, they were hampered by the plantation system where isolated farms could scarcely support a common school as did the more compact townships of New England. "Good education of children is almost impossible," complained Fitzhugh in 1687, "and better be never born than ill-bred." Two—and probably more—privately endowed free schools did flourish by the mid-century, both of them in Elizabeth City County. One was established by Benjamin Symmes, a planter; the other by Dr. Thomas Eaton; both were to survive into the nineteenth century when they merged as Hampton Academy. The Symmes and Eaton schools have usually been cited to refute Governor Berkeley who had thanked God that Virginia had no free schools. Robert Beverley later claimed that where endowed schools did not exist, "the people join and build schools for their children where they may learn on very easy terms." Possibly this refers to the Southern "field school," located on an old abandoned field and taught by a parson or a private teacher. Many of the field schools went far beyond elementary instruction into the classical subjects, particularly in the next two centuries.

Children of the upper planting class had the benefit of private tutors who often were indentured servants; these teachers might instruct children of neighbors as well and also help with the master's accounts. A few, like Fitzhugh's son, braved the hazardous ocean trip and the expense to enter the English universities.

Years of agitation were required for the chartering of William and Mary College in 1693, the second college in the English colonies. It was desired especially for the training of Anglican ministers, so scarce in the colony, as well as for the education of secular leaders. Virginians of wealth, aided by royal grants taken from quitrents and export taxes, financed the new school. In 1695 the cornerstone was laid in Williamsburg, formerly called the Middle Plantation, where the colonial government had been transferred; its presence was expected to exercise a stimulating influence upon the growth of the college. The legislature provided a classical curriculum of Latin, Greek, philosophy, mathematics, and divinity. Beginning as a classical grammar school on the English model, William and Mary was to develop as an important colonial college in the next century. Altogether, despite setbacks, the tobacco colonies showed a fair record of literacy during the era of foundations.

Popular education was also hampered by the relatively few books in the colony and by the lack of a printing press. The hard times of 1660-82, when tobacco glutted the English wharves and warehouses, brought a drastic drop in book importations. Berkeley gloated over the fact that Virginia was without a printing press and hence was free from another temptation toward error. The fact became increasingly apparent that rural conditions and a plantation economy did not favor a creative literary culture. However, the small libraries of the planters often showed highly cultivated tastes as well as strictly utilitarian ones in their well-thumbed volumes. The flavor of the Elizabethan Renaissance seemed more marked here than in the New England libraries although gentlemen of both sections bought heavily of religious tomes. The Oxford-trained Ralph Wormeley II counted among his 375 books the works of many leading Elizabethan and Stuart dramatists and poets as well as those of scientific men. In fact the presence of dramatic literature is in sharp contrast to the relative dearth of such works in Puritan towns. Fitzhugh read with extraordinary breadth in the fields of belles-lettres, theology, and science, and like many a Renaissance man ordered books on alchemy and witchcraft. Anglican ministers, far from ignoring Puritanism, often included Calvin's works in their parish libraries. The planter not only liked to purchase Jonson, Erasmus, and Bacon for his shelves, but also bought encyclopedic works on practical subjects, ranging from medicine and law to engineering and agriculture.

As to literary output, the Virginians and other Southerners trailed the New Englanders who, in letters, were so amazingly prolific for a pioneer people. It is true that Captain John Smith did write entertaining books and tracts on Virginia and the New World that were published in London, but however vivid his writing, it was not always sound history. Professor John S. Bassett, who regarded Smith as a "confirmed hack writer," nevertheless gave him credit for writing the first printed American book in *A True Relation of Such Occurrences and Accidents of Noate as Hath Hapned in Virginia Since the First Planting of that Collony* (1608).This book, written in a direct and personal style, omits the story of Pocahontas, which is supplied only in a later work, *The Generall Historie of Virginia, New England, and the Summer Isles,* thus raising the suspicion of fabrication in the minds of some critics. One of the few native Virginians to publish a book was Robert Beverley, the planter-historian, who wrote *A History of Virginia,* but this did not appear until 1705. Beverley's description of the founding of the colony does not betray the aristocratic and romantic fallacy of a Virginia peopled with Cavaliers. A Virginian almost in a nationalist sense, he urged his people to become more self-sufficient industrially and more diversified agriculturally. He was optimistic about the future of education and the possibilities of a new wine-making industry. He gave considerable attention to regional geography, the Indians, social life and government, and critically assessed the political scene, offending quite a few local politicians. Beverley's historical interests began with his early work among the public records and his book won him an interested audience in England and France as well as at home. An able historian of Virginia who has recently re-issued Beverley's work, Louis B. Wright, finds the book still very useful for social history and early geography and enjoyable for its humor and sparkle.

In retrospect, it is clear that the Englishmen who built Virginia did not transplant the life of their homeland intact. Traditional, especially feudal, ideals had to be modified to meet frontier conditions. In the rich abundant lands of the Virginia wilderness, class distinctions lost their customary rigidity; the sparse population scattered over huge parishes stripped the Anglican Church of its formality and made for more democratic religious practices; small independent farmers resisted the introduction of the common law with its expensive technicalities; and even the well-to-do elite who dreamed of becoming New World barons decided that frontier conditions in the seventeenth century did not as yet permit the adoption of such aristocratic props as primogeniture and entail. Popular education could not reach even the modest homeland standard because of rural isolation with too few people and roads to sustain adequate schools; the lack of enough books and of a printing press also hampered literary culture. Recreation, too, tended to reflect the rough conditions of life on the edge of a wilderness.

In this frontier environment, favored with unique opportunities for the hard-working farmer and the shrewd promoter, a typical democracy might have arisen in much the same form as it did later in the North and the West. However, democracy in eastern Virginia was increasingly affected by the large plantation system (though it represented the smaller part of the colony), the one-crop regime, and Negro slavery. Land speculators and well-to-do immigrants did not find it too hard to begin as large planters, once the labor problem was solved, and to capture the legislature, the courts, and local administration. Even the fluid class structure was partly concealed by the deliberate attempt to achieve a synthetic feudalism through the Renaissance manuals on the art of being a gentleman. While these factors were present in varying degree north as well as south, Virginia and its neighbors were not rescued by the diversified farming, shipping, and handicraft opportunities that enriched the more northern colonies. While New England was to find slavery unprofitable, Virginia did not and she became increasingly enmeshed in all the implications of a semi-feudal, bi-racial regime that involved inherent contradictions in a frontier society of small farmers, cheap lands, and equalitarian tendencies.

· 4 ·

Feudal Experiments among Virginia's Neighbors

I

MARYLANDERS, like seventeenth-century Virginians, filled the tide-water valleys with tobacco plantations, struggled over aristocratic designs to transplant feudalism to their soil, and fought the Indians bitterly after early failures to convert them. Their colony, named in honor of the Catholic Queen Henrietta Maria, wife of Charles I, was intended by its newly converted Catholic founder, George Calvert, Lord Baltimore, as a haven for persecuted English Catholics and as a proprietary feudal state as well. Nevertheless, the first ships, the *Arke* and the *Dove*, carried more Protestants, Puritans particularly, than Catholics among their three hundred passengers of 1634. George Calvert, raised to the Irish peerage as Lord Baltimore in 1625 despite his conversion to Catholicism, was an Oxford graduate; he displayed a love for literature as a student and eventually rose to be a secretary of state to both James I and Charles I. His death in 1632, after a colonizing failure in Newfoundland, left the actual founding of Maryland to his talented son, Cecilius Calvert, the second Lord Baltimore.

Although the Maryland charter entrusted the Calverts with the absolute political and religious power of the medieval bishops of Durham, this was considerably trimmed in practice and by later instructions. The government tended by 1650 to resemble that of Virginia, except for the position of the proprietor and his contrcl over Maryland's governor. The dream of the Baltimore family of building a feudal society under their paternal direction envisaged an aristocracy of Catholic lords, each with a thousand acres and liveried servitors, and a populace consisting of numerous small farmers with hundred-acre homesteads. This, like similar plans born in feudal mentalities, foundered on the rock of labor scarcity and cheap lands. Maryland's fertile soil, her virgin forests and well-stocked streams, and the commercially navigable Chesapeake Bay, inviting to world trade, could not easily be monopolized by a few.

In local government, Maryland borrowed Virginia's county court system, and even her assembly, which was set up to assist the proprietor, came to resemble her neighbor's independent bicameral legislature. Tobacco cultivation, indentured servants, and finally Negro slaves also united the social life of the two colonies; in both, the small farm was the dominant unit and the one-crop system soon replaced the earlier diversified crops. In paternalistic fashion, the Maryland or Virginia planter included his servants or slaves as well as his kinsfolk when he spoke of "my family." This phrase became in later years the conventional "my people" of Southern planters, even in twentieth-century times.

The religious hatreds of the Old World were difficult to extinguish in the New. The spectacle of the Jesuits, who had been driven underground in England, now actively at work converting the Indians and occasionally Protestants as well angered the enemies of the "Papists" despite the diplomatic attitude of the proprietor. Cromwell's victory over the Crown secured the ascendancy of the Puritans in Maryland as well as at home and endangered the Catholic minority. Lord Baltimore thereupon issued in 1649 the famous Maryland Act of Toleration which in effect recognized the religious rights of Anglicans, Puritans, and Catholics, but imposed the death penalty and confiscation of property for blasphemers and those who denied the three persons of the Trinity. This proved far more tolerant in practice, for Quakers, Jews, and other persecuted groups found a welcome in Maryland. But the protected status of Catholics steadily declined, especially after 1654 when the Puritans dominated the colony. Some Catholic refugees found a haven in the Northern Neck of Virginia, where George Brent, Fitzhugh's Catholic business partner, and Fitzhugh himself offered them hospitality. The century ended with Protestant domination in the colony and with the Church of England the officially established church.

A few years before the end of the century, Annapolis became the flourishing successor to the town of Anne Arundel and the colonial capital. Planters and merchants came to this urban center with its wharves and warehouses; besides, there was a small library here, which was a royal gift, and a free academy, the King William School, as well as the Assembly and court buildings. Annapolis received a city charter in 1708, but only three tiny settlements existed on the site of the future city of Baltimore.

2

Just as Maryland was carved out of Virginia's northeastern lands, so North Carolina was created from the "Albemarle Overflow" covering the southern part of the original Virginia country. While Virginia land speculators pre-empted the best lands beyond the tidewater valleys in which they lived, frontier squatters crossed into Carolina. By 1666, some eight hundred emigrants, largely New Englanders, occupied Cape Fear. If Maryland was planned with delusions of achieving manorial grandeur, Carolina, especially the southern part, appeared in the minds of English aristocrats to have even greater promise for a medieval state in the wilderness. Most of the eight original proprietors were men who had helped to restore Charles II to his throne and thus became major beneficiaries of royal favor. Among them was George Monck, newly created Duke of Albemarle, who once, as Cromwell's general, defeated Scottish, Irish, and Dutch enemies, and then, turning royalist, dissolved the Puritan Parliament and plotted with Charles II for the Restoration. Another was the time-serving Anthony Ashley Cooper, first Earl of Shaftesbury, who had switched allegiance from the royalist forces to Cromwell's standard and again back to the Crown. Edward Hyde, first Earl of Clarendon, was a consistent royalist. He was to write the pro-monarchist *History of the Rebellion* and to issue the harsh Clarendon Code which penalized religious dissenters heavily. Not least among these was Sir William Berkeley, the extremely royalist governor of Virginia, whose mind ever sought the "main chance" whether in slaves or lands, and his brother, Lord John, who participated in the extensive grant of 1663. Governor Berkeley was to administer this "province of Albemarle," the future North Carolina.

The Earl of Shaftesbury had a brilliant young protégé in the yet unknown philosopher of natural rights, John Locke, secretary to the Board of Proprietors for Carolina. Locke was asked to draw up the *Fundamental Constitutions of Carolina* in a way "most agreeable to the monarchy" and as an antidote to "a numerous democracy." He outlined a semi-feudal Carolina palatinate in which powerful hereditary lords would share power with small landowners but on terms distinctly favorable to the aristocracy. The colony was divided into counties, which set aside one "seigniory" of 12,000 acres for each of the eight "Lord proprietors." Four "baronies" of 12,000 acres each went as a unit to a "landgrave"; aristocratic "caciques" received 24,000-acre estates. Altogether about two-fifths of the land went to the proprietors and other aristocrats; even in the remaining lands, substantial grants of 3000 to 12,000 acres were subtracted for budding manorial lords. On the other hand, "headrights," or land grants to small settlers, were generous by Virginia or Maryland standards, which averaged about fifty acres received by a family head for each member or servant that he transported. Until 1670, freemen coming to Carolina were entitled to one hundred and fifty acres each with smaller grants for servants and children; thereafter the headrights fell to seventy acres and less, depending on the status of the newcomer. In a relatively aristocratic assembly, the governor had to be at least a landgrave, the elected assemblymen had to own at least five hundred acres, and the right to vote was limited to fifty-acre freeholders.

Such aristocratic ideas, though not overly conservative for contemporary Europe, had little chance of succeeding on the frontier. Many a Bacon rebel from Virginia fled to northern Carolina where he met small farmers like himself ready to contest their share of the "piney woods" against the organized land monopolists. The scheme was motivated by the desire to hasten the development of Carolina, especially the southern part, by attracting wealthy men to invest in the colony. Lands might be resold in small parcels to farmers who would pay quitrents to the proprietor. But the system never really worked to the advantage of the proprietors, for all along they had to fight to enforce their constitutional prerogatives not only against poor North Carolina frontiersmen, but also against independent traders from South Carolina who resented the efforts of the proprietors to monopolize the fur trade. In addition, the small farmers hated the cash quitrents. The settlers defended their land titles and property against the large land speculators and their agents, "the mercenarie lawyers," just as the Virginia farmers and colonists elsewhere were doing. Popular opposition to the extortionate fees charged by many lawyers led to laws forbidding payment for pleading, thus crippling the growth of a professional lawyer class and the influence of common-law technicalities which depended upon legal experts.

The proprietors themselves were too desperate for settlers and laborers and too worldly as businessmen to insist on rigid terms of settlement. Consequently, they went farther in the direction of religious tolerance than did most of their contemporaries. So long as newcomers paid their quitrents, taxes, and other duties, and were willing to behave, they were permitted the bad taste of being Quakers, Baptists, Huguenots, Puritans, or Jews instead of becoming proper Episcopalians. Any seven persons who agreed on a particular faith might form a church. Thus the solicitous proprietors hoped "that Jews, heathens and other dissenters may not be scared and kept at a distance." Within a few decades, the Quakers rose to become the dominant element in North Carolina and dissenters were moving into South Carolina as well.

Looking about for industrious immigrants, the proprietors invited the persecuted French Huguenots to come to the southern part of Carolina. These French Calvinists were in large part a highly educated, well-to-do, middle-class people. They had suffered severely during the religious wars of the late sixteenth century which had shaken their country in the tempestuous days of Catherine de Medici and her royal sons. Huguenots fled to England, to Holland, to Brazil, and to the American colonies when the Edict of Nantes, issued in 1588 by Henry IV, which had offered religious guarantees, was revoked by Louis XIV in 1685. These immigrants laid the foundation for Charles Town (formerly Oyster Point), making it the most cosmopolitan and commercial center in the Southern colonies. Quite a few of these Huguenots had lived in England and Ireland before coming to South Carolina and were, therefore, English-speaking. Not all Huguenots, of course, were wealthy or even literate but many brought with them the competitive, capitalistic psychology that had long been evident in the rising *bourgeoisie* of France and was favored by their Calvinist faith.

Another alien stock was represented by a half dozen wealthy and cultured Jewish families of Spanish and Portuguese origin who added to the commercial importance of Charleston, as it was called in the following century. To offset the political influence of the Huguenots, who outnumbered the original English pioneers, and the aggressive Puritans and Scottish Calvinists in Colleton and Craven counties, all freemen voters in other parts of Carolina were expected to come to Charles Town to vote. Economically, the port thrived upon the rich plantation hinterland and developed an important trade with the nearby West Indies; the latter had been started by pirates such as Morgan, later elevated as Sir Henry Morgan, governor of His Majesty's island of Jamaica. With tobacco a drug on the market, South Carolina planters turned to Indian corn and cattle-raising and were able to export salt pork and beef to the West Indies. Rice, the foundation of South Carolina's plantation economy, was not established until the end of the century; by then the slave population tended to equal Virginia's. North Carolina, less suitable for large plantations, was far more diversified than her neighbors, combining tobacco culture with a great number of food crops and household manufactures.

3

When William Byrd, one of Virginia's richest planters, visited New York in 1685, he was very favorably impressed with the picturesque, bustling town. He estimated that three-fourths of the inhabitants were still Dutch though England had captured this colony of 8000 in 1664. New York city, heir to New Amsterdam, stretched along parts of Manhattan Island, Long Island, and Pavonia (a former patroonship including Staten Island and later Jersey City), and consisted of seven hundred houses, reported Byrd. Brooklyn, then Breukelen, was one of a string of old-fashioned Dutch villages on Long Island, although the English were coming in there, too, in large numbers.

Even some of the new English homes must have seemed Dutch, for Holland was then in the ascendant architecturally and influenced current English styles. The word "quaint" came naturally to Byrd's lips as he walked along the curving streets and noted the stepped-up gable ends of the colored roofs, the broad arched windows, the Dutch Gothic style of churches with their conical roofs, the trim gardens of tulips, red roses, and lilies, and the picturesque windmills whose flailing arms awed Indian visitors. Flocks of geese waddled through the streets as they did in old Amsterdam.

Manhattan Island, which Governor Peter Minuit of New Netherland had originally bought from the Canarsee Indians for sixty guilders in trinkets—about $24—had every reassuring mark of a real-estate bargain. Byrd saw the comfortable brick and frame houses of the Dutch merchants, some of the buildings dating back to the prosperous fur trade era several decades before when the commercially minded Iroquois Confederacy had traded with the Dutch in the Hudson and Mohawk valleys. Along the scenic Hudson River, sturdy Dutch farmers tilled their "boueries," as their lands were called. Byrd must have been impressed by their huge barns whose broad gables, seeming to rise from the ground, were fitted with wide doors beneath stout beams, altogether resembling the German peasant homes of Lower Saxony. The Bowery of Manhattan, then a village stretching along a street which ran through Peter Stuyvesant's bouerie, was already popular among sleigh-riding parties for its houses of entertainment.

Inside the Dutch homes were the proverbially immaculate kitchen, the cloistered parlor for visitors, the great stove and clock brought over from the Netherlands, the hanging Delft plates, and,

in the homes of the well-to-do burghers, some imported silver plate
and furniture from the homeland. Family portraits and Bible pictures sometimes decorated the wall. Home life for the heavy-smoking
burgher, with his long pipe, and for his cheerful family circle was
both convivial and hospitable, despite a decided thrifty note and a
Calvinist background in many cases. Visiting ranked high among the
social arts. The land of the Van Burens and the Roosevelts, if not as
idyllic as suggested in Washington Irving's shameless caricatures of
Dietrich Knickerbocker, Rip Van Winkle, and the simple folk of
Sleepy Hollow, had its kindly traditions. The more critical, however,
might be disturbed by the burghers' smuggling activities, their collaboration with pirates, their notoriety in the slave trade, and their
reputation for sharp land speculation.

Although the coming of English rule eventually meant the establishment of the Anglican Church, the position of the Calvinist Dutch
Reformed Church remained fully protected, even though it was no
longer the favored faith originally established for the entire colony
by the Dutch West India Company. Calvinism here was far less
ascetic and more tolerant than in New England, though the statutes
forbade games or labor on the Sabbath. Governor Peter Stuyvesant,
who had surrendered the colony to the Duke of York's forces, was
indeed narrowly puritanical and intolerant, but his exceptional behavior brought a sharp rebuke from his Company. Cosmopolitan
New Netherland, where eighteen languages were spoken, had welcomed many faiths—after the initial persecution of Quakers—including Puritan sects, Catholics, Lutherans, Anabaptists, Mennonites,
and Jews. Occasionally, an extreme sectarian was banished, but the
atmosphere was most congenial for Roger Williams, who visited
New Amsterdam several times, and for the Jews fleeing from Brazil
following the Portuguese capture of Pernambuco in 1654. "They
have as many Sects of religion there as at Amsterdam, all being
tolerated," wrote Byrd, "yet the people seem not concerned what
religion their Neighbour is of, or whether hee hath any or none."

The Reverend Johannes Megapolensis, a learned but somewhat
strait-laced divine, criticized the Mennonite settlements of Long
Island during the Dutch era, "The majority of them reject the

baptism of infants, the observance of the Sabbath, the office of preacher, and any teachers of God's word. They say that thereby all sorts of contentions have come into the world. Whenever they meet, one or the other reads something to them." The conversion of the Indian proved most discouraging for the Dutch although Megapolensis worked assiduously among the Mohawks. One bright Indian who almost mastered Dutch Calvinism and the language as well, quickly fell from grace. "He took to drinking brandy, he pawned the Bible, and turned into a regular beast, doing more harm than good among the Indians." Besides, the vindictive policy of Governor William Kieft toward the Algonquins and the Dutch alliance with the Iroquois led to the savage wars and massacres of 1643-45, which exhausted the colony and relegated hopes of Indian conversion to the past. Something of Calvinist culture was recognizable in the austere interior of the Dutch churches where long benches stood against the bare walls and were set upon floors covered with beach sand.

The Dutch colony, born in 1624, had grown out of economic rather than religious motivations and their leaders were merchants and soldiers rather than clerical intellectuals as in New England. Therefore, they remained behind the Puritans in education, although those who could afford it sent their sons to Harvard or perhaps to the renowned University of Leyden. In 1650, Adrien van der Donck, a lawyer and landowner, complained, "The bowl has been going around a long time for the purpose of erecting a common school and it has been built with words, but as yet the first stone is not laid." Seven years later, this backward state was explained by basic poverty, "the people having come half naked and poor from Holland." Still, the "domines" or pastors, some of them graduates of the University of Leyden, kept the Dutch more literate than was the case in the English colonies of the South. By the end of the Dutch period, the "three R's" and catechism were taught to many in a schoolmaster's home, which usually had a large room set aside for a public school. The new regime, though respecting the Dutch language and customs, sought to encourage the English schoolmaster as an agent of assimilation.

Books were fewer in New Netherland than in New England, but those few were especially well-thumbed. Libraries were almost non-existent, for the greatest and only successful patron, Van Rensselaer, owned but thirty volumes, most of them devotional or utilitarian in nature. All reading here as elsewhere was censored, although a surprising number of critical articles appeared in the informal "newsletter," the seventeenth-century ancestor of the modern newspaper, already popularized by the Fugger bankers of Germany and their branches, including one in Amsterdam. Lacking a printing press, Dutch colonial intellectuals published abroad. Van der Donck, for example, wrote a praiseworthy *Description of New Netherland,* and the Reverend Megapolensis won note for an enlightening pamphlet on the Mohawks.

The new English ruling class, which aspired like the Dutch to create a stratified feudal social order, built on the broad basis of the princely land grants issued by the Dutch West India Company. These huge grants, like those of Maryland and the Carolinas, were intended not only to reward a small favored group but also to supply adequate labor for them through a system of permanent tenant farmers. The feudal patroonships of New Netherland, which had ultimately embraced nine ambitious landowners, were intended to stimulate colonization by offering to "patroons" who would plant colonies of fifty adults in four years, a perpetual fief of some sixteen miles along the Hudson (or eight on both sides) with interior boundaries that were gratifyingly indefinite. The patroons were promised an extensive trading monopoly and feudal control over future towns in their territory. This system had broken down under the equalitarian conditions of a new country rich in unpre-empted virgin lands. When Byrd visited Albany in 1685, he met the last of the patroon families, the Van Rensselaers, still securely anchored upon a princely estate covering practically all of Albany, Rensselaer, and Columbia counties. The widow of Kiliaen Van Rensselaer, a former Amsterdam pearl merchant noted for his paternalism, tolerance, and friendliness to learning, continued to rule Rensselaerswyck. In Dutch times, patroons had often ruled arbitrarily, even inflicting the death penalty and blocking legitimate appeals of their tenants to the governor.

The labor shortage again proved to be the reef on which the leaky craft of feudalism foundered. Prosperous Holland, unlike England, offered too few inducements for emigrants; besides, the Dutch were not a particularly emigrating people. In fact, many of the so-called Dutch of New Netherland were the French-speaking, stocky, brunette Belgian types, the Walloons, or the tall blond Flemings whose language was akin to Dutch but was still quite different. Under New World circumstances, the settlers of Rensselaerswyck, for example, were developing an independent, self-reliant spirit incompatible with antiquated feudal paternalism. Able men, emerging from the numerous servant class, profited from this fluid situation and often rose to the very top layer of the social structure. There they joined the wealthy immigrants who had come with considerable capital and experience.

The Dutch left behind them much more than quaint names and customs. Their taste of world power before the English crushed them had been made possible by their extraordinary mercantile enterprise and a rationalist outlook that was expressed in their practice of tolerance and their innovating capitalist spirit. In Holland they had been prompt to break with guild restrictions on handicraft enterprise and had adopted competitive ideas quickly. By their progressive attitude, they had freed the towns from the exclusive economic policies of medieval times. This was still the Golden Century of the Netherlands, which had begun with the displacement of the Italian bankers as capitalist leaders by resourceful Dutch businessmen who could finance the mighty Spanish and Portuguese colonial empires. Their pre-eminent career in slave trading, fur trading, and international shipping had brought them unique prosperity as well as the envy and fear of a fellow-Protestant nation, England. Dutchmen of the New World inevitably carried with them the competitive spirit of merchant capitalism, adding it to the heritage of America, which remained under a medieval handicraft tradition during the seventeenth century. Dutch families like the

Van Cortlandts, the Van Rensselaers, the Beekmans, the De Peysters, the Van Horns, and the Van Dams, while sometimes of humble indentured servant background, also reflected the rationalistic commercial spirit of old Amsterdam and provided the inspiration for the future greatness of New York city.

English feudal lords, who hoped to imitate Berkeley's aristocratic Virginia on the eve of Bacon's Rebellion, were forced to retreat by popular pressure. Thus the Duke of York gave up his personal rule over the colony in 1685, the year of Byrd's visit. Although the English upper classes went far beyond the old Dutch oligarchy of Peter Stuyvesant's time in granting a more representative assembly and various Anglo-Saxon liberties such as trial by jury, the small farmers and the town craftsmen and laborers resented the *de facto* control of the assemblies by the aristocratic clique. As in the case of the Virginia rebels who found a leader outside their class in Bacon, so the New York populace turned to a dissident German merchant, Jacob Leisler, who led a revolt in 1689 and outlawed trade monopolies. He also joined in the current anti-Catholic persecution, which followed the overthrow of Catholic James II and was, in part, a retaliation for the frontier attacks made on New York by the French Canadians, which had embittered Protestants, especially those on the border of settlement. Leisler remained in power until 1691 when he was captured together with the other leaders and hanged as a traitor. As in the case of Bacon's Rebellion, the aftermath was a bitter conservative reaction with a few adroit concessions to the commonality. Thus, after Leisler's Revolt, the New York Assembly became more popular in composition. Aristocrats drew their strength from the huge Dutch estates and the medieval practice of quitrents (common to the English colonies), a survival of the custom of commuting feudal services and dues in exchange for money payments. Though the quitrents were usually small, they were a nuisance and a challenge to democratic thinking; they were to go when the American Revolution swept away many of the cobwebs of feudalism.

Cultural assimilation moved rapidly among the easygoing Dutch, Flemings, Walloons, and their English neighbors. Just as the Dutch youth corrupted their native speech with many English terms to the despair of visitors from Holland, so the English learned to say "boss" for master, "brief" for letter, "spook" for ghost, and "crib" for cradle. On the streets, middle-class Dutch women, wearing loose gay gowns and ornamental headdress, still contrasted with fashionable Englishwomen with their close-fitting, pointed lace waists. There was little asceticism in New York attire, male or female, Dutch or English, and the ultimate blend of styles was to add to the colony's cosmopolitanism.

Among the Dutch customs adopted by the English was that of visiting and giving presents on New Year's Day, an occasion that became formalized and elaborate by President Washington's time when New York city was the nation's capital. On that day, as Alice M. Earle describes it in *Colonial Days in Old New York,* the men fired guns, went off on hunting parties, and drank whole pitchers of eggnog, bowls of milk punch, and bottles of wine. May Day was as exuberantly celebrated as New Year's Day, with the addition of the maypole—a custom abhorred by the puritanical Stuyvesant. Shrovetide was another merry Dutch holiday with men masquerading as women. Not to be outdone by the Dutch, the English introduced Guy Fawkes Day (November 5), commemorating the discovery of the "Popish" Gunpowder Plot of 1605 when Guy Fawkes had tried to blow up Parliament and the King's Council. This holiday was a real bonanza to the youngsters for it combined the fireworks of a modern Fourth of July, the pranks and masquerades of Halloween, and the old style of illuminated political processions. Boys carried effigies of the villain, Guy Fawkes, in the parade, sang anti-Pope songs, and built huge bonfires. Christmas, though far from enjoying its modern prestige and though pointedly ignored in New England, remained the holiday of the children who loved to sing to the generous giver of presents, Saint Nicholas, whose feast day was celebrated by the youngsters of the Netherlands and Belgium on December 6. Christmas Day itself was a quiet religious holiday among the Dutch until the English newcomers to New York adopted Saint Nicholas under the nickname Santa Claus and moved his feast day to December 25 to coincide with the English practice. Although the puritans in Parliament had, in 1644, banned Christmas for its wild pagan license, it was returning in a form somewhat more subdued than its saturnalian English medieval predecessor.

The Dutch Pentecostal celebration, "Pinkster Day," was adopted throughout the middle colonies and was marked by the inevitable visiting, schnapps, and festive games. Slaves, especially around New York city and Albany, developed their own variation of this holiday as they followed African-born dancers clad in native dress who beat sheepskin-covered eel-pot drums to the refrains of their tribal lands. James Fenimore Cooper describes Pinkster Day in *Satanstoe* as the saturnalia of the blacks.

Again, the Dutch, as well as the Scotch, were the great exponents of the game of golf, so popular in later years. Bowling, which Washington Irving has made part of the Kaatskill Mountain legend of Henry Hudson and his ghostly explorers in the tale of Rip Van Winkle, was widely popular. A recent historian of New Netherland, E. L. Raesly, mentions the romantic Kissing Bridge of old New York, the game of "pulling the goose" in which a horseman attempts at high speed to seize a greased fowl, and the rough pranks of farmers and workmen. Games resembling modern backgammon, pool, and croquet were popular, although the English preferred card-playing and horse-racing. As in other colonies, days of thanksgiving, proclaimed for special occasions, were festive affairs.

English rule, to some extent, meant a more sober element in this mixed society. Punishments for crime, following England's custom, were more severe for lawbreakers. Whippings, considered degrading by the Dutch, were more common. Slaves, comparatively well treated by the Dutch, showed alarming restiveness by the end of the century when dangerous slave plots were reported. On the other hand, the old Dutch oligarchy of Peter Stuyvesant, which had been so unpleasantly intrusive in personal and petty matters, disappeared in favor of wider local self-rule, at least by the tax-paying freemen. Stuyvesant, the last of the Dutch governors, had displayed the bombast and arbitrariness of the complete autocrat in his zeal for the Dutch West India Company, even violating its tradition of religious toleration.

4

When Peter Minuit, the wily purchaser of Manhattan Island, was dismissed from his post as governor of New Netherland in 1631, he quickly turned to a new career as a promoter of Sweden's colonization along the Delaware. Chancellor Axel Oxenstierna, virtual ruler of Sweden after the death of the dynamic Gustavus Adolphus, sought New World markets for his country's copper and iron. He gladly accepted Minuit's aid and chartered the New Sweden Company for the overseas venture. In March 1638, two Swedish ships under Admiral Klas Fleming, a Finnish noble, and Peter Minuit sailed up the Delaware River to the site of present-day Wilmington. Here Fort Christina, named in honor of the young queen, arose as a trading post. Thus New Sweden was born, beginning as a commercial competitor of the merchants of New Netherland who claimed the area.

At least half of the inhabitants on the Delaware were Finns—at that time, Finland had been part of Sweden for four centuries—and their simple peasant homes and pioneer background in eastern Sweden fitted them well for the task of opening a wilderness. The newcomers brought with them the technique of building the one-room log cabin with its horizontal notched logs, a type famous in the later history of the West and an American symbol of frontier equality and democracy. Their adaptation of Indian methods of girdling and burning trees and other pioneer methods of agriculture laid the technical basis for the opening of early Delaware and Pennsylvania.

As fur traders, farmers, cattle-raisers, and fishermen—noted for their eel traps and fishing spears—the Finns and Swedes thrived, becoming a permanent colony of almost a thousand by 1693 and overflowing into eastern Pennsylvania. In 1638, the year of their arrival, the Swedes built Upland (later Chester), which became the oldest settlement in Pennsylvania. Swedish architecture, notably in the famous brick Gloria Dei Church built in 1700, influenced the picturesque villages of Delaware and southeast Pennsylvania. Their customs differed considerably from those of their English neighbors, including a highly festive Christmas with special holiday bread and beer and peasant beliefs that led them to put straw crosses on their doors to drive away evil spirits. The barns of their Pennsylvania German neighbors also carried superstitious symbols. However, the imperial dream of a New Sweden vanished in 1655 with Peter Stuyvesant's war upon the colony and his capture of Fort Casimir and Fort Christina on the Delaware.

5

Like the other great English proprietors of colonial lands, William Penn combined religious and economic motives. He conceived of Pennsylvania as a "Holy Experiment" for the pure of faith organized as a Platonic commonwealth for primitive Christians, in this case a haven for persecuted Quakers; at the same time, he was actively concerned in rebuilding his declining fortunes through a proprietary land investment for the Penn family, planned along the usual semi-feudal lines of proprietors elsewhere. Born in 1644, the son of Admiral William Penn, the youth had profited by his father's services to the court in restoring the Stuarts to power in 1660. The Admiral had corrected his former error of aiding the Parliamentary cause, but his son's religious vagaries threatened to undo his sacrifices. Young Penn attended Oxford when John Locke and Christopher Wren were students, but he rebelled at the compulsory Anglican services and was promptly dropped; thereafter he had continued his education in Paris and in Italy, stressing theological subjects but finishing off with law in London at Lincoln's Inn.

Sent to Ireland in 1666 to administer his father's estate, he came in touch with the enthusiastic Quaker followers of George Fox and waived the privilege of his social station by going to jail for attending a meeting of the Society of Friends. Despite his father's angry opposition and powerful ties at court, Penn became an ardent disciple of Fox and wrote scores of erudite books, treatises, and articles on the principles of his new faith. That Penn, for all his odd Quaker mannerisms, had not exhausted his credit—and, more important, that of his father for a private debt owed by the Crown—was proved in 1681 when he received a charter, modeled after the proprietary

Maryland document, for the province named after his family. This grant was so extensive as to make him the largest landlord in the colonies. Charles II saw possibilities of imperial expansion in this venture and was not averse to a mass exodus of Quakers and other undesirables from England, where over three thousand Friends had been jailed during the first years of the Restoration.

Sailing up the Delaware River in 1682, Penn was hailed enthusiastically by the Swedes, the Finns, the Dutch, and the English who were already settled on the borders of southeastern Pennsylvania. He responded by reassuring them of the religious liberty promised all Christians by his Fundamental Constitutions of Pennsylvania. Penn had already made such a promise in 1677 in the Charter of West Jersey (the Quaker colony in New Jersey), an enterprise in which he had been a partner. "That no men, nor number of men upon earth, hath power or authority to rule over men's consciences in religious matters." He was to write emphatically, "God hates persecution." Force made for hypocrisy; only persuasion made genuine converts.

Like Roger Williams, Penn taught the principle of separation of church and state, already elaborated by George Fox, founder of the Society of Friends. The Quakers, who had been persecuted by state churches for non-conformity, rebelled against them and reduced theology to a simple perception of intuitive values revealed by the "light within" or a "manifestation" that dictated the path of right and duty. This was the Quaker's formulation of the Reformation search for a return to primitive Christianity and the most literal belief in the supremacy of the individual conscience, "Every man his own priest." The kindly Fox had taught that God incarnated redeeming love, rather than the tribal spirit of vengeance and exclusiveness, and was directly knowable by regenerate man. Even the Bible, inspired though it was, could be no substitute for the "inner light," this personal communion with God. The notion that men were equal in God's sight took on democratic significance in the political sphere, where Quakers doffed their hats to no man and used the familiar "thee" and "thou" of plain folks rather than the plural "you" of the aristocracy. No tithes to the church, no salaried minister, and no flattering salutations were encouraged in Quaker communities.

Penn's *Frame of Government* applied certain of the liberal teachings of Harrington, Algernon Sydney, and Locke. He accepted the social contract theory of government resting—in part at least—upon the consent of the governed and believed in the inalienable natural rights of men. But just as Locke had found a formula for feudal control in his constitution for the Carolinas, so Penn was very solicitous for the property rights of the proprietor. His first bicameral legislature, chosen largely by the landowners, discouraged debate, for an aristocratic Council alone proposed new laws and the popular assembly simply accepted or rejected bills. Essentially, Penn's political ideas were based on the belief that virtue and ability provided the only sound ruling class, a government of good men rather than rule by the masses. The ways of feudal paternalism and the medieval ideal of a fixed class structure shaped Penn's thinking. He could cite Machiavelli approvingly, especially during the later years when he was fighting the Pennsylvania Assembly from his English home, demanding his proprietary dues: "He who builds upon the people builds upon dirt."

Penn taught loyalty to an employer in extravagant terms, characteristic of a deep class bias, "A good servant serves God in serving his master." His laws severely punished runaway servants. He opposed the marriage of bound servants without their master's consent as detrimental from a property point of view. Laziness was a form of fraud and the idle belonged in workhouses. Like many Quakers of that century, he owned slaves, although he freed them in his will. His insistence on his quitrents, on the ousting of squatters on his lands, and on other property rights while he was an absentee owner in Pennsylvania led the popular party to attack him as an oppressor.

Alongside this indictment, however, must be noted the fact that Penn merely reflected the prevailing economic philosophy of his class. Essentially, he held to the medieval view that the wealthy were paternal stewards of God, that economic life must be subordinated to salvation, and that government must regulate wages, prices, and conditions to assure as fair a share of goods as was appropriate to each social class. A glance at the dominant economic philosophy of the other colonies shows that Penn's outlook was the orthodox one.

Despite the harsh words spoken of the Pennsylvanians during the heat of argument when Penn was in difficult personal circumstances, there is little doubt that he genuinely loved his fellow man. His oft-quoted Treaty with the Delaware Indians of 1683, which respected the rights of the red man, may be explained in terms of self-interest in view of his fur-trading plans, but certainly all too few fur traders showed so enlightened a concept of interest. Like George Fox, he preached to the Indians, whom he, like many contemporaries, regarded as the lost ten tribes of Israel, and he tried to stop abuses in the Indian trade, especially by banning the sale of liquor to them. As a result, the Pennsylvania frontier was far more stable in his day than it was to become in the next century.

His noted work, *Essay Toward the Present and Future Peace of Europe* (1693), visualized a league of nations and a world court with judgments put in effect by international force of arms. Instead of the rigid Quaker non-resistance doctrine, Penn conceded the right of force when needed to support government against overthrow and in cases where public or private rights were violated. Still, he argued successfully for exempting from military service Quakers and other conscientious objectors to war. The Quaker non-resistant tended to believe that even evil men would not injure those who really loved them. Taking up arms seemed indefensible to a sect that took very literally the commandment that "Thou shalt not kill." Besides, they had abiding faith in the power of peaceful persuasion as an effective alternative to force.

To build his Holy Experiment, especially among pietist sects throughout Europe, and to dispose of his 28,000,000 acres held by charter, Penn published a brief account of Pennsylvania, describing the virtues and defects of the new land with commendable Quaker honesty. He offered unusually generous terms for land purchase although he stressed large units of land, like other proprietors, and reserved ten acres in every 100,000 for himself. The first to respond were the English Quakers, later followed by numerous Welsh members of the sect. The latter acquired the so-called Welsh Barony of 40,000 acres on the west side of the Schuylkill, just north of Philadelphia, and built a Welsh-speaking community of Quakers numbering about 6000 by 1720.

From the Rhineland, where Penn and Fox had labored together for the faith, came the Germans and Swiss, labeled indiscriminately as "Palatinate" immigrants and later as "Pennsylvania Dutch." They fled from a land torn by the Thirty Years' War, the internal religious conflicts inspired by princes who asserted their right to impose their religion upon their subjects, and the wars of invasion by Louis XIV that made this region a battleground. Nevertheless, this group, unlike their eighteenth-century successors from Germany, were in fairly good economic circumstances; they were neither poor peasants nor servants. The German Mennonites, originally called the Swiss Brethren, were non-resistants like the Quakers and believers in simplicity of dress and habits, with a faith that harked back to primitive Christianity. They came from Krefeld, in particular, and were part of an exodus led by Penn's brilliant convert, Francis Pastorius, who with another group of German Quakers, founded Germantown six miles away from Philadelphia as a center of cultural influence for their new settlements.

Penn's Holy Experiment thus became the greatest colonial melting pot of the seventeenth century, with the possible exception of New York, and provided a successful test of tolerance among diverse nationalities. Pastorius and his Germantown settlers pioneered for the broad principle of human freedom in 1688 when, in a significant resolution, they assailed their Quaker neighbors for supporting slavery and the slave traffic. "Have these poor negers not as much right to fight for their freedom, as you have to keep them slaves?" they demanded. Pastorius, himself, worked to bring over more Germans through his pamphlet, A Particular Geographical Description of the Lately Discovered Province of Pennsylvania (1700), calling attention to the new woolen and linen manufactures and the commercial fairs.

The proprietor chose wisely in building Philadelphia, "city of brotherly love," on the site of an old Swedish settlement between the

Delaware and Schuylkill rivers. Significant for the birth of city planning in this country was his adoption of the new classical plan of London, then being rebuilt after the Great Fire of 1666. Christopher Wren, the great architect and fellow student of Penn at Oxford, had pronounced the doom of the dominating medieval half-timbered style of houses of the old London, crowded along crooked narrow streets. Boston, influenced by the older city architecture dating back to the medieval need for cramping living quarters within defensible town walls, was to rue its planlessness. The new London of Christopher Wren was laid out in checkerboard fashion with regard to the need for urban uniformity and communication. Tall brick buildings of the Renaissance type were springing up in the English metropolis. This pattern of rectangular blocks and parallel streets was adopted in Penn's Philadelphia and spread to later American cities as a regular feature of city planning. Surveyors were required to plan roads at least forty feet wide from town to town and Penn ordered that "none may build irregularly to the damage of another" in Philadelphia. Even the city's buildings began to emulate the brick, balconied homes of London during these early decades, despite the abundance of lumber.

Education in early Pennsylvania was handicapped by the intellectual implications of Quakerism. Those who subscribed to inner-light and simple pietistic doctrines did not require an educated ministry as did the Puritans who despised "enthusiasms" and stressed a high degree of intellectuality in their theology and religious philosophy. The inner exaltation of the Quaker came from the heart rather than the sophisticated mind. George Fox, who had had but little schooling himself, agreed with Robert Browne and the Separatists in regarding the universities as props of the sinful Established Church. He prescribed practical subjects for his followers. Penn, it is true, was a college man, but he tended to criticize the universities and the Inns of Court in order to enhance the glories of primitive Christianity. Like Fox, he recommended practical studies that should be taught in concrete fashion to children above twelve years of age "to the end that none may be idle" and lack sufficient literacy to read the Bible and the laws of Pennsylvania. Both Fox and Penn believed that the child should be taught to study nature directly rather than from books. Instead of overloading the minds of children with ancient tongues and formal rules of grammar and rhetoric, he wished the pupils to learn from observing everyday objects. For such reasons the *Frame of Government* authorized the legislature to establish public schools and to encourage "useful sciences" and inventions. In 1689, the noted William Penn Charter School, a public grammar school, was opened in Philadelphia, charging tuition only to those who could afford it.

In daily habits, the Quakers were no less "puritan" than the Puritans themselves. As in the case of the other colonies, such tendencies were reinforced by the prevailing laws of England, both Anglican and Puritan. Penn had affirmed this ascetic outlook in his *Conditions and Concessions to the Province of Pennsylvania,* "That the laws as to slanders, drunkenness, swearing, cursing, pride in apparel, trespasses, distresses, replevins, weights and measures, shall be the same as in England, till altered by law in this province." Therefore, the Pennsylvanians started out with the English punishments for blasphemy, profanity, lotteries, dice, and, in their own phraseology, "vain and evil sports and games."

Penn's own writings and influence helped convince the first well-to-do Quaker immigrants, who came with fashionable clothes, to give up their silks and laces and pearl satin gowns, for drab-colored dresses, while the men did without their silver buckles, long curls, and ruffled collars. Quaker homes were plain indeed, with simple furniture, but were far from being unattractive, especially for the wealthy, with whom simplicity could be a studied art. Penn condemned plays, dancing, and balls as foreign to the spirit of apostolic Christianity. Music, too, both vocal and instrumental, was attacked for its sensuality, while painting was regarded as a form of idolatry forbidden by the Bible. In the next century, one gifted Quaker child, Benjamin West, later the world-renowned artist, felt stifled by these prejudices against aesthetics, especially those against painting. Paradoxically enough, he was to be commissioned by the Penn family to paint the treaty scene of Penn and the Indians under the elms.

The humanitarian tradition of Quakerism in Pennsylvania was far more significant than their puritanism and was destined to leave a kindly impress upon future progress in social welfare. Penn's people modified the custom of public whipping and stocks, common in the English colonies, made their jails more reformative places than the usual filthy, disease-ridden cells elsewhere, and abolished the death penalty except for the crime of murder. England, it will be recalled, still kept hundreds of "crimes" as capital offenses. Penn, whose family had suffered from debtor's prison, abolished this crude institution, which aided neither creditor nor debtor. Although he operated a brewery upon his own colonial estate at Pennbury, he fought drunkenness. Dueling was strictly forbidden. None of the other colonies could claim such a degree of enlightened behavior.

Already, by 1700, when the colony had some 14,000 people, the Quakers were pressed by the coming of other sects. Two-thirds of the city of Philadelphia became non-Quaker—though the Friends retained a majority in the county. Among the newcomers were Scotch-Irish Presbyterians and German Lutherans who passed on to the yet unclaimed lands of the frontier. Still the Quakers, who had been a despised minority a half century before, had through their remarkable persistence and vitality won their way to the vanguard of the radical Reformation sects. Meetings of the Friends were held in practically all the colonies. The sect dominated not only Pennsylvania, but the Jerseys, Delaware, Rhode Island, and parts of Carolina; Quakers were also influential in New York and Maryland.

In 1676, the Quakers held New Jersey against the New England Puritans and the Dutch Calvinists. This "Province of Nova Caesaria" had been created in 1664 by the Duke of York and at first was conveyed to two Carolina proprietors, one of whom sold the southwestern portion to a Quaker society. The Duke's laws provided religious tolerance for Protestants, a system of representative government, and an attractive land policy for settlers. Despite quarrels with the proprietors over the payment of quitrents, a democratic colony of small farmers flourished. By 1702 New Jersey, which had hitherto been divided into Quaker-ruled West New Jersey and non-Quaker (for the most part) East New Jersey, was unified as a single province. Altogether the Quakers reached a high point of influence and distribution by the end of the seventeenth century. The day when the Puritans might hang a Quaker or drag one out of town at the tail of a cart was gone. The courageous disciples of Fox and Penn, who fought their battles with moral weapons alone, were nevertheless to win real victories during the next century in their humanitarian war on the cruelty of man to man.

Although feudalism among Virginia's neighbors, as well as in the Old Dominion itself, failed to overcome the frontier factors of labor scarcity and cheap land, some of its manifestations, as previously noted, took on new vitality with the introduction of slavery and the plantation system. Small farmers often gave up an unequal struggle against large landowners and their modest holdings were absorbed by the large planter, sometimes by legal chicanery or fraud. Still, the small farmer remained throughout colonial and national history the typical rural figure. In an age moving rapidly toward capitalist enterprise, led by English, Dutch, and French Huguenot merchants the persistent attempt to transplant feudal tenures may be partly explained as an effort to promote quick settlement in a wilderness through unusual incentives for wealthy investors and land speculators.

Religious tolerance, as we have seen, was not only a practical necessity in an era of militant dissenters but appealed to land promoters as the only way to attract industrious settlers in sufficient numbers to virgin lands, which, if left empty, could pay no quitrents. The political situation in England, especially after the overthrow of James II, also worked for sectarian compromise despite the widespread establishment of the Church of England in the colonies. However, the same political situation, plus the hatreds engendered by the wars against Catholic Frenchmen, left the Catholics stranded. After a glorious but brief period of complete equality in Maryland, they were denied the full privileges of citizenship and in some places driven underground as they were in England.

From the England of the Puritan Revolution and the Glorious Revolution new democratized institutions, practices, and civil guarantees, radical by early Stuart standards, were carried across the sea, strengthening the frontier factors for political and eventual social democracy. Though the large landowners and the well-to-do merchants were in the saddle, they had to contend with an independent yeomanry who might call them to account under leaders like Bacon, Leisler, or Roger Williams. The servile psychology of the Old World laboring class could not take a firm root in America. In addition, the hard practical virtues arising from subduing a wilderness were being tempered by the more idealistic dissenting sects, particularly the Quakers, who added a strong idealistic strain to the American heritage.

· 5 ·

Town and Country in the Age of Franklin

[1700-1736]

I

IN 1716, a bright ten-year-old boy of Boston, Benjamin Franklin, worked without enthusiasm in his father's new candlemaker's shop at home, cutting wicks, boiling soap, and shaping candle molds. His father, formerly an English dyer whose trade in Boston could not support a brood of seventeen children, had reluctantly taken Benjamin, his youngest, from grammar school where the boy had out-shone the rest of his classmates. Fond of swimming and canoeing in Boston harbor, the youth envied his brother Josiah who had gone to sea, a romantic career that drew so many New England boys to the strange sights of distant Atlantic and Pacific shores. Escape from the tiresome candle molds came two years later when Benjamin began a five-year term as an apprentice in a printing shop owned by his able brother James.

Boston in 1720 was a busy seaport of 12,000 souls, the largest city and the commercial metropolis of the colonies, followed by Philadelphia with a population of 10,000, New York with 7000, Charleston with 3500, and Newport with 3800. Altogether the townsfolk of English America were not more than 8 per cent of the population and even less as the decades went by and the rural West expanded. Shipping, lumbering, fishing, speculation, trade, and commercial

112

farming absorbed the energies of the rising middle class whose quality was marked by their expensive dress, fashionable powdered wigs, private carriages—still a novelty in Franklin's youth—and Georgian mansions.

Native capital had begun to exceed English investments in the fishing, lumbering, shipbuilding, and flour-milling industries in which New Englanders were pre-eminent. A few shrewd capitalists in Gloucester, Marblehead, and Salem tended to monopolize the profitable fishing industry in those key towns. Catholic Europe provided a steady market for the better grades of fish while slaves in the West Indies consumed the inferior shipments. The Peace of Utrecht (1713), closing Queen Anne's War, opened an era of marine and fishery expansion as the newly acquired colonies of Newfoundland and Nova Scotia gave Britain leadership in the codfish industry and made nearby Gloucester of imperial importance for cod exports. After 1717, colonial vessels were admitted to the French West Indies and cheap New England rum made from even cheaper French molasses displaced French brandy in the African slave trade. Whaling, which centered at Nantucket by mid-century, thrived upon the increased popularity of oil lamps in Europe. Samuel Sewall, the Puritan, who lived well into Franklin's century, was a large-scale exporter of mackerel and whale oil.

Similar concentration of capital occurred in lumbering in which large-scale operations had already denuded the coastal forests up to the Kennebec River and had moved inland to new logging camps in frontier New Hampshire and Maine. Elsewhere in the colonies, lumbering invaded the Hudson Valley, the forests of Pennsylvania, and the Carolinas. Colonial shipbuilders, drawing upon vast resources of white pine and oak, commanded a huge advantage over those of western Europe where the forests were vanishing. Their chief competitors, the versatile Dutch, were eliminated by England's mercantilistic policy of restricting imperial trade to English and colonial-built ships. Massachusetts, a leader, was building some sixty vessels—small ships to lessen the risk from storms—in young Franklin's day.

Despite brief periods of depression, many shippers prospered in both peace and war. Boston's crowded harbor, serving most colonial towns for European trade, was the home port for 489 vessels in 1749 alone. Eighty ships left Salem annually; Newport had a fleet of 120 ships, and Marblehead had 90. While England's struggle for world empire against France, Spain, and their allies tended to make mere pawns of the colonies, compelling them to fight in wars not of their making, there were rich financial benefits for shrewd colonial ship-owners who turned to privateering and captured enviable prizes among the enemy's merchant marine. Hence the successive eigh-teenth-century imperial wars, known in America as Queen Anne's War, King George's War, and the Old French and Indian War, meant a real harvest for the great colonial merchants.

Once the war ended, privateering, if persisted in by force of habit, became piracy in the eyes of the law. Such pirates, whose phe-nomenally low costs enabled them to escape being undersold in colonial trade, were popular with thrifty buyers. Besides, pirates might bring in precious metals so scarce in colonial commerce. The heyday of piracy was just passing, but the mode persisted. Boston in 1701 had the distinction of arresting the notorious ex-privateer-turned-pirate, Captain William Kidd, whose men, it was said, had mutinied on the way to the Red Sea and forced him to prey upon peaceful ships. Kidd was actually a large landowner of New York, a valiant sea captain against French foes, and a loyal defender of the Crown against Leisler's Rebellion. Still, a stern London court insisted that he hang and he left behind a tantalizing legend of buried treasure in all sorts of romantic places. A much more dyed-in-the-wool pirate, also with experience as a privateer, was the grim William Teach, the "Blackbeard" who is traditionally credited with fourteen wives. Brutal and daring in his predatory way, he ravaged the Caribbean and the North Atlantic with his forty-gun *Queen Anne's Revenge,* until a company of Virginians killed him off the coast of North Carolina in 1718.

Many a respectable New England merchant became technically a smuggler after the prohibitive Molasses Act of 1733 was passed. Powerful British West Indies planters had used their parliamentary lobby to eliminate competition with the cheap French and Spanish

West Indies products by heavily taxing such imports into the mainland. These French and Spanish islands, offering cheaper molasses
and other goods and eager for the products of the colonists, had become an indispensable source of specie, so lacking in a new country in which few mines existed and where the colonists had to
import expensive manufactures from England. John Hancock's activities as a smuggler in pre-Revolutionary days were founded upon
a generation of colonial experience and sanctioned by local opinion.

Among the princely Boston merchants was Thomas Amory, who
had left London for Boston in 1720 after business trips had convinced him that this city of the Puritans was the busiest port in the
world. At his death, he left an estate valued at $100,000, a high
figure for that day. Peter Faneuil (pronounced Funnel), who apparently held a partnership in a slaver, *The Jolly Bachelor,* in addition to more conventional forms of property, owned $75,000 in
English securities when he died in 1743; he left Faneuil Hall, "cradle
of American liberty," as a town hall whose lower floor was designed
as a public market with stalls rented out to the vendors while the
hall above was set aside for town meetings. Burnt in 1761, Faneuil
Hall was rebuilt in time for the revolutionary patriots to hold their
fateful assemblages.

Another great Boston merchant was Thomas Hancock, who left
£80,000 to his patriot-nephew, John. The elder Hancock, whose
portraitist drew him most imposingly in a handsome blue damask
gown, an embroidered waistcoat, black satin breeches, and a long
powdered wig, made his fortune in whale oil, books, rum, cloth, and
other commodities of trade. Enriched by the colonial wars and by
using smuggling tricks to evade the costly mercantilistic laws, he was
not averse to selling spoiled rations for the common soldier. His
keen speculative spirit inspired his network of ships sailing to Newfoundland, the West Indies, London, and the Mediterranean. Upon
such foundations John Hancock had no difficulty in rising to the
top of the mercantile ladder.

The establishment of fixed central markets like Faneuil Hall led
to riots by those small hucksters who had previously sold directly
at the doors of their customers or had hawked their goods on the

streets in a competitive spirit. Against the medieval idea of price controls and the survivals of the "just price," there arose increasingly the pressure for a competitive order especially among those not protected by or benefiting from local price controls. These were often set by the well-to-do classes, though nominally justified in the common interest. Harvard candidates for the master's degree were troubled by the conflict of commercial ethics. "Is it always lawful to give and take the market price?" was one controversial question of 1725 embodied in a scholarly thesis; the answer reached was definitely, "No."

The sharp Yankee trader was a popular stereotype enhanced by the old anti-Puritan libels. New Yorkers or Philadelphians might complacently repeat, "Whosoever believes a New England Saint shall be sure to be cheated: And he that knows how to deal with their Traders may deal with the Devil and fear no craft." It was easy to overlook the hard-working honest merchant against the more dramatic background of daring privateers, smugglers, and slave traders. Privateering upon enemy vessels in wartime was patriotic as well as profitable and smuggling had colonial sanction because mercantilistic restrictions were considered unjust; but slave trading was not a proud profession though slavery was generally accepted. Commercial ethics must have suffered from the necessities of evasions and concealments, especially in the slave trade. Southerners never forgot that New Englanders brought the slaves to America. In this golden age of the English slave trade, following the end of the monopoly of the Royal African Company in 1696, eighteen slavers left Rhode Island each year for West Africa, fully equipped with chains, handcuffs, vinegar, as well as rum to trap or otherwise acquire Negroes to be sold to planters of the South, the West Indies, and even Latin America. Cheap rum from Newport, sometimes watered by unscrupulous captains, was a prime commodity in the slave trade.

Those slaves who were not absorbed by the plantations were brought into New England as seamen, lumberjacks, craftsmen, farmhands, and as domestic servants. By 1763, Massachusetts alone counted 5214 Negroes in its population of 235,810 and all New

18th Century

"Benjamin Franklin," by Benjamin West. (Philadelphia Museum of Art)

Interior of Newport, Rhode Island, Synagogue, a classical structure designed by Peter Harrison during the eighteenth century. (Library of Congress)

Bedroom of Shaw house, in Hampton, New Hampshire, about 1725. The fine paneling is impressive. (Metropolitan Museum of Art)

Chamber of the House of Burgesses in the first Williamsburg capitol built 1701-1705 (reconstructed). View from the speaker's dais looking toward the clerk's table. Upon the walls are the portraits of King William and Queen Mary and the arms of colonial Virginia. (Colonial Williamsburg, Inc.)

Hall of the Van Rensselaer manor house, Albany, New York, built about 1765-69. (Metropolitan Museum of Art)

"Professor John Winthrop of Harvard" (1714-79), by John Singleton Copley. Winthrop, one of the founders of seismology, shared

"The Artist in His Museum," by Charles Willson Peale. This
self-portrait shows the details also of the popular Peale's

"The Peale Family Group," by Charles Willson Peale. (New York Historical Society)

The New York City Hall at Broad and Wall Streets, 1797. (Stokes Collection, New York Public Library)

"The Artist Showing a Picture from Hamlet to His Parents," by William Dunlap, 1788. He founded the National Academy of Design, and was influential in the growth of the American theater. (New York Historical Society)

"Tontine Coffee House," Wall and Water Streets, New York, 1797, painted by Francis Guy. This was the commercial center for eighteenth-century merchants in Alexander Hamilton's day. (New York Historical Society)

"At the Loom," an oil painting by an unknown Pennsylvania German artist about 1795. (Harpo Marx Collection, Downtown Gallery, New York)

"George Whitefield," by Joseph Badger of Boston. Though this picture misses the vibrancy and appeal of the greatest evangelist of the century, Badger shows the honesty of the "primitive" and the soberness of renascent Calvinism. Despite his humble beginnings as a glazier and sign painter, Badger may have influenced the style of Copley. (Harvard University)

England had perhaps three times as many. In those days proslavery propaganda, including a Puritan justification of slavery by the Bible, had begun to resemble the quality if not the output of certain ante-bellum Southerners. Slave revolts and arson plots frightened both Bostonians and New Yorkers—the latter especially in the hysteria of 1712 and 1741. Discipline was kept through a pass system, strict curfew laws, restrictions on the sale of liquor to Negroes, and other police measures. Still, New England slavery was rather mild. The social niceties of "white man supremacy" for a small slave population were often dispensed with; colored children went to school with whites; and race contacts on the farms tended to approach equalitarian levels. In keeping with the newer humanitarianism, Samuel Sewall, the Puritan merchant, attacked the slave trade in a tract, *The Selling of Joseph* (1701), and Cotton Mather tried to organize a society for helping the slaves.

Philadelphia merchants, catching up with the Bostonians, drew upon a vast hinterland of wheat fields, livestock, lumber, and fur supplies from Pennsylvania, New Jersey, Delaware, and Maryland. By the end of this era they had surpassed their northern rivals in both population and trade. In 1760, the town had 22,000 citizens, many of them recent immigrants from Northern Ireland and the Rhineland. The Quaker merchant aristocracy set the pace in building ocean vessels at home, shipped wheat and bar iron to New England, and traded with the West Indies and Europe. Young Franklin, leaving Boston in 1723, made a wise choice indeed in beginning his famous career as a printer and publisher in the rapidly growing city of Penn. Not very far behind were the aggressive merchant-financiers, land speculators, and fur traders of New York, the De Peysters, the Morris', and the Franks'. New York retained a strategic position in the fur trade through the Albany posts and the Mohawk Valley, being in contact with distant tribal hunters through the Iroquois Indians as middlemen. In Charles Town (later Charleston), which tapped a huge Southern fur trade with the Cherokee extending hundreds of miles in several directions, there developed a commercial-agrarian aristocracy under Huguenot and Scottish leaders. South Carolina rice planters and West Indies plantation fami--

lies came to spend a season in this pleasant city of the Barnwells, the Rhetts, the Izards, and the Pinckneys. Newport was ruled by "twenty genteel families," possessed one of the finest colonial harbors, and led in the sperm-oil, soapmaking, and rum industries.

Merchants interested in manufacturing were hampered by the lack of adequate roads, trained laborers, sufficient capital, as well as by the self-contained nature of the New England farm and the numerous mercantilistic restrictions on colonial industry. Under mercantilism, colonies were intended to be drawers of water and hewers of wood for the specialized mother country. Often traveling artisans worked on materials supplied by the farmer and rose to become store merchants. Artisan-shopkeepers dominated the small retail trade of the villages and towns and occupied themselves as wigmakers, tailors, spectacle-makers, or candle-and-soap makers like the Franklins. The European domestic or "putting-out" system, in which a merchant-entrepreneur distributed raw materials, especially textiles, among specialized workers in their homes, appeared to some extent during the century and was the predecessor of the factory system. Most businesses were still small, individual firms or partnerships; only a few fire insurance and land companies used the large-scale joint stock company form of organization. The transition from workmen to entrepreneur was still a simple one, leaving class lines extremely fluid.

The rapid rise of the American merchant class in a favorable economic environment led to a corresponding advance of *laissez-faire* individualism. Although colonial legislatures continued to use bounty systems to encourage local production and Parliament wove a complex net of mercantilistic controls over economic life, these elements of state intervention played on the whole a steadily decreasing role in colonial affairs. The mercantilistic goal of a powerful state and a self-sufficient empire in which colonists absorbed themselves in producing raw materials, especially strategic products needed for the imperial war machine, did not overly hamper the natural tendency of any young country to seek a livelihood in farming, fishing, lumbering, or any other extractive industries available. While the Molasses Act might have crippled the New England merchants by cutting off a profitable West Indies trade and by making it almost impossible to gain sufficient gold and silver coins to pay for their purchases from England, this was offset by non-enforcement— a policy of "salutary neglect" prevailing until 1763. Mercantilistic prohibitions like the Hat Act of 1732 and the Iron Act of 1750 did not prevent these two minor industries from growing. The Carolinas and New England benefited from parliamentary bounties for naval stores, ship lumber, and (for South Carolina) indigo. Even in the absence of mercantilistic interference, it is doubtful whether colonial capital and the chronic shortage of skilled labor at moderate wages would have permitted much expansion. Yet competition, far from being crippled by strict government control, was enhanced by the natural conditions of a huge country just emerging from a wilderness state, by the fluidity of classes that allowed the daring to compete for new opportunities, and by the ineffectiveness of distant traditions and dubious theories of economic enterprise. Even in Europe, middle-class champions of *laissez faire* like Mandeville, author of *Fable of the Bees*, were insisting that the self-interest of man, so long kept in chains by mercantilists and the Church, must be released in order to spur on production and wealth.

Labor, both skilled and unskilled, continued to be at a premium during this era, tending to be drawn off into agriculture. In 1751 Franklin was emphatic on this point:

> Labor will never be cheap here, where no Man continues long a Laborer for others, but gets a Plantation of his own, no Man continues long a Journeyman to a Trade, but goes among those new Settlers, and sets up for himself, etc. Hence Labor is no cheaper now in *Pennsylvania,* than it was 30 Years ago, tho' so many Thousand laboring People have been imported.

The class of apprentices to which Franklin belonged failed to meet the demand for trained workmen. Premiums paid by merchants to skilled emigrants had to compete with improved employment conditions in England wrought by the youthful Industrial Revolution. English mercantilists, intent upon hoarding skilled labor and secret mechanical processes, sought in 1699 and thereafter to prohibit the emigration of textile operatives. However, the mercan-tilists, as usual, overreached themselves; indeed, the ban of 1699 on woolen exports from Ireland and other colonies played a large part in driving thousands of skilled Scotch-Irish linen and wool makers to America. Under the putting-out system prevailing in textile spin-ning and carding, the shortage could be met by converting the household into a specialized shop where children as numerous as Franklin's brothers and sisters could be profitably employed.

On Southern plantations, where the indentured servant system was yielding to slavery, Negroes became skilled carpenters, black-smiths, weavers, and masons. While slavery proved ill-adapted to New England's small farms, small diversified industries, trading enterprises, and cold winters, Southern planters, lacking sufficient free labor, clung to slavery despite a world-wide trend toward free contract. However, toward the end of this era, Southerners, too, came to believe that it was only a matter of time before slavery be-came obsolete. In Virginia and Maryland, Negroes were only slightly fewer than whites by the 1760's and South Carolina's slaves out-numbered whites almost two to one.

Early attempts of labor to organize and to strike were held by English legal authorities in 1717 as "highly criminal at common law." Professor Richard Morris points out that "the extension of criminal conspiracy to include acts in restraint of trade actually be-gan in the Court of Star Chamber early in the seventeenth cen-tury." Thus strikes were regarded as being in criminal restraint of trade. Mercantilists, anxious to keep wages down as a means to beat foreign competitors, persuaded Parliament during the eighteenth century to outlaw labor unions. American journeymen's guilds, an-cestors of the modern trade union, tended, as in the case of the Philadelphia carpenters in 1724, to stress in their own interest price-fixing by local regulation, strict apprenticeship rules to keep com-petitors down, and the payment of various benefits to families of their members. Trades and professions "affected with a public in-terest" were licensed and their fees regulated by law—but not too effectively. Gradually, fixed wages and prices had to yield more and more to competitive rates. Freedom to choose one's occupation grew as guild restrictions against outsiders lost their effectiveness in a world that was becoming increasingly *laissez faire.*

2

City life in Franklin's day with all its drawbacks impressed travelers very favorably in contrast to conditions in London, Paris, and other aging European cities. The English visitor, Burnaby, thought Boston was a delightful English country town. Philadelphia and Charleston, laid out neatly in checkerboard fashion, seemed to have left behind the medieval heritage of cramped filthy streets (though some medieval towns had straight, trim streets) derived from the military necessity of fitting overgrown towns within narrow walls. The Quaker city won visitors' admiration for its paved streets and new lighting system, both in part the products of Franklin's initiative; shade trees and public pumps flanked the avenues. Although New York and Boston retained the narrow streets of the previous era, these were kept tolerably clean and drained by a new sewer and gutter system. New Yorkers were proud of spacious Broadway, then lined by luxuriant trees, and Boston Common was emerging from its condition of a public pasturage to a community park; ubiquitous geese often deserted the Common to waddle adventurously through the streets in search of fresh puddles. Most of the towns were surrounded by outlying country estates sometimes with classical Italian gardens in the latest mode or some other decorative setting.

Visitors, it is true, were dismayed by roaming pigs, filthy swine, or putrid animal carcasses in the streets. Reckless horsemen added that uncertainty to life and limb which only the twentieth-century pedestrian can appreciate. An even worse hazard was fire, which periodically swept away entire blocks, especially among the frame dwellings. Boston's great fire of 1760 left 220 families homeless. The first successful fire engine, invented in England, arrived in provincial America about 1731. Franklin's "bucket brigade" of voluntary firemen, known as the Union Fire Company of Philadelphia, outfitted itself so heavily with new fire engines, ladders, and fire hooks that its proud founder could claim fifty years later that "the city has never lost by fire more than one or two houses at a time, and the flames have often been extinguished before the house in which they began has been half consumed."

Travelers, riding on horseback or in carriages from town to town, were able by the end of this era to use the long highway stretching from Boston to Charleston and to stop at numerous friendly country inns for rest and entertainment. All the colonies were increasingly united by dirt roads (except in inclement weather) and above all by the intercolonial postal system, which had been taken over by Parliament in 1710 after the failure of a private patent holder. The post office had its most brilliant era under Franklin who became Postmaster-General in 1753 after serving over a decade as a comptroller for his predecessor. So successful was Franklin in improving the service that he was able to cut almost in half the six-day run between Boston and Philadelphia. By reducing rates he expanded the volume of business to such an extent that he was able to boast after British officials forced him out, "We had brought it to yield *three times* as much clear revenue to the crown as the post office of Ireland." This intercolonial post-office system helped considerably to enlarge the rural market for urban merchants and to break down provincial barriers to concerted political action and the diffusion of culture.

The plain citizen gaped at the elaborate carriages of the aristocrats who thronged the provincial capitals in the royal governor's following. Their scarlet coats, ornate knee breeches, side swords, and powdered wigs marked them off from ordinary merchants and tradesmen. With their bejeweled and gaily-appareled ladies, they attended the governor's receptions and danced the stately minuet at his balls. The wealthy merchant, visiting his favorite coffeehouse, seemed imposing in his fine frock coat trimmed with gold or silver lace and his three-cornered felt hat, and with his silver-headed walking stick in hand. In descending order, the successive lower classes wore far meaner garments appropriate to their station, down to the coarse shirts and leather breeches worn by indentured servants and laborers.

Merchants and tradesmen were fond of their town clubs, some for discussion and business, others for drinking and social life. Franklin's "Junto" of Philadelphia was the best of the discussion clubs. Prominent Virginians like Washington and New Englanders like the Adamses met in the new Masonic chapters, which carried over the ritual of the British lodges. By the end of this era, these lodges included many a revolutionist; Boston's lodge, alone, embraced such rebels as James Otis, John Hancock, Joseph Warren, as well as Sam and John Adams. Very important were the transplanted coffeehouses, noted in England for such varied activities as literature and insurance. Some of them were news centers, political clubs, playhouses, auction rooms, and financial exchanges. Some American coffeehouses furnished lodgings as well, an unusual feature by English standards.

Among the gentility, men—and often women as well—had begun to affect the elaborate ritual of taking snuff by tapping a jeweled box and offering its precious contents to visitors. This habit, originally rationalized as medicinal in value, gained prestige by the well-known lofty examples of Addison, Pope, Frederick the Great, and even Marie Antoinette. The ruling class was also marked off in the colonial college where social rank determined the cataloguing of Harvard and Yale students until the 1770's. Only reluctantly were class distinctions surrendered in the seating of church members. Despite the survival of medieval gradations of rank, society was actually fluid, as already observed, and the *nouveau riche* merchant, who began in so many cases at the bottom of the social ladder as a simple indentured servant, could quickly win honors based on wealth in this fast-changing, rootless bourgeois society.

Diet, like dress and rank, reflected the class structure, modified by the prevailing abundance of food in a prolific farm country. As in the seventeenth century, the wealthy enjoyed a large variety of meats, imported cheeses, and vegetables, topped by the new popular chocolate or, for social occasions, Madeira wine and rum punch. In New England, particularly, tea and coffee began to compete with cider and liquor. These changes were faithfully recorded and lamented in Franklin's practical-minded *Almanack:*

Many estates are spent in the getting
Since women for tea forsook spinning and knitting,
And men for punch forsook hewing and splitting.

Thus the poor were learning to ape their betters. There was something tempting in the upper-class example of the afternoon tea, served in fine chinaware amid the incessant buzz of neighborly gossip. Forks, a rarity in John Winthrop's day, came into general use among the middle and upper classes. As for the ordinary farm and city folk, outfitted at the table with the simplest of utensils, they were accustomed to the traditional English "boiled dinner" of salted meat and cabbage, or salt pork and fish, baked beans, and baked pumpkins washed down by cider.

As far as urban morals are concerned, while strait-laced statute books made no concessions to the secular atmosphere, everyday practice made savage inroads on precepts of purity. Recurrent imperial wars filled the towns and villages with idle soldiers who found immediate employment with Satan. Seaport towns, with their heavy contingents of adventurous sailors and footloose persons from England and the Continent, had substantial quotas of evildoers. Rowdies on the waterfront, mobs in the streets, and thieves, if not as vicious as London's gangs of organized crime, made urban life far from idyllic. There was, for example, Cotton Mather's graceless son, Increase, whose adventures with loose women and street gangs belied the strength of the puritanical controls. Boston's strictest laws did not halt the advance of prostitution and venereal disease even before the century of the Puritans had ended. Lawbreakers, outside of Quaker Philadelphia, continued to be exposed to the pillory or publicly whipped if their crimes did not merit execution. As these devices declined, the permanent jail became necessary, but this institution had few remedial advantages, for it was usually filthy and no more than a school for crime. Most promising were the penal efforts of the Quakers who urged a humanitarian theory of punishment in which rehabilitation and penitence—the ideal of the "penitentiary"—were the goals.

Eighteenth-century Americans shared the traditional English spirit of recreation more than did the Puritans or the first settlers elsewhere in the colonies. Town life, influenced by the governor's gay court in the capitals of the royal provinces and by the migration of easygoing upper-class Anglicans, became more secular. Strict Sabbath-day observances fell off, drunkenness and games of chance seemed more openly in evidence, and the vogue for half-pagan and lustful English ballads led Cotton Mather to lament that the good old Psalm tunes were not as popular as formerly. The aging Puritans felt degraded by the Anglican revels of the aristocrats during the Christmas holidays, recalling their black pagan origins. Around the sacred precincts of Boston and Cambridge one saw horse-racing devotees every whit as enthusiastic as Southerners; in the streets there were crowds watching fortunetellers, sleight-of-hand charlatans, and professional showmen with their tricks and exhibits.

Boston led in the violent observance of Guy Fawkes Day, or Pope's Day, which anticipated the worst pranks of modern Halloween and the Fourth of July. While small boys usually contented themselves with beating drums, blowing shrill whistles, carrying about dressed effigies of the Pope, or demanding "handouts" of neighbors, tough North End gangs battled with equally tough South Enders in a murderous combat while the constables stood by helplessly. At night, citizens' fences disappeared in a huge bonfire while festive floats exhibited the devil and the Pope. Thus to the emotions of anti-Catholicism which were kept at white heat by the incessant wars with the Catholic French and Spanish, Guy Fawkes Day added its incubus of hatred. The pranksters, of course, needed no particular justification for organized hilarity, and Boston's mobs were pliable enough to play a patriotic role during the Revolution in beating, tarring, and feathering the Loyalists. In 1708, old Samuel Sewall had a new complaint about the time-wasting Bostonians. It seemed that the ancient English festival of All Fool's Day had developed an annoying variation in which juvenile minds perpetrated "April Fool" jokes upon the unsuspecting—a practice that was to outlast Sewall and his circle by many years. Other colonial towns were not much better than Boston.

Dancing schools flourished in Boston even earlier than in other towns. The royal governor's circle and lesser aristocrats attended elegant balls and dancing assemblies where the music of the minuet, the complicated cotillions led by one couple and marked by the changing of partners, and the informal English country dances played through the night. Plain folk who enjoyed dancing above everything else kept the fiddlers sweating at public taverns and weddings. Lively dances like the Scottish highland reels were favorites among all classes; villagers, simple townspeople, and frontiersmen enjoyed lively jigs and communal dances. Boston Puritans like Sewall who had kept the organ out of the churches, though they had no objection to Thomas Brattle's organ at home, lived to see Brattle's organ become a proud instrument in the hands of the talented Anglican organist at King's Chapel. This versatile organist also taught music and dancing, repaired virginals and spinets, and even imported violins, flutes, and other instruments for the trade. By the 1760's, concerts, which had crept in under the guise of religious music, just as dramatic music had penetrated Puritan England as innocuous "opera," were a regular feature in Boston as well as in most other colonial cities.

In New York, where Dutch Calvinism, diluted by many other sects, had long compromised with things of this world, pleasure seekers flocked to the Bowery for its rows of entertainment houses and for dinner parties or picnics. The fashionable of Newport and other seaports had their convivial turtle suppers with free-flowing Madeira. Philadelphians, restrained by the Quakers, found new joys in the suburbs where Satan's reign went unchecked. Charleston, whose Calvinistic Huguenots scarcely dampened that city's love for every form of gaiety, enacted strict Sabbath laws possibly for the pleasure of breaking them, for all classes did not hesitate to combine church attendance with a later visit to the gory cockpits to bet upon their favorite battling fowls.

Maryland and Virginia planters, like Washington and his friend Lord Thomas Fairfax, enjoyed hunting as a colorful ritual in the form of the English chase, "riding to hounds" resplendent in deep blue or scarlet riding habits. This wealthy class enjoyed a perennial round of balls where they gave courtly bows to attractive belles at the fashionable Virginia capital of Williamsburg or at Annapolis.

At these towns they attended the latest plays given by English actors or by local amateurs. The plantation had its own round of amusements, including informal musicals and dances, hunting sports, and horse-racing. Mount Vernon in later years was noted for its cheerful hospitality where Washington threw off the dignified poise of a colonial leader and classical gentleman to relax completely as a sociable country squire who loved good talk as well as the pleasures of his class. Among his favorite joys were not only hunting, dancing, and plays, but also cockfights, circuses—such as they then were—and jolly dinners where comic singers would convulse him until the tears ran down his cheeks.

In this atmosphere, the victory of the theater in provincial America could not be long delayed. Occasional amateur players like those of Harvard and a brave professional or two were far from unknown in the previous century despite Puritan, Quaker, and strict Presbyterian lawmakers. In 1714, Sewall managed to halt a play that was to be acted in the Massachusetts council chamber itself. Still the American provinces could not help being dazzled by the fascinating Augustan Age of literature and drama in which the theater enjoyed a high prestige.

By mid-century, David Garrick had become the shining idol of English theatergoers, admired for his natural style of acting and speaking— that is, relatively so for his day—compared with the well-worn gestures and declamatory affectations of his older rivals. Although he remained in England, he kept in touch with the early American stage. Anglican Williamsburg had a regular theater by 1716 built by the manager of a Maryland dancing school, but this enterprise soon fell under the sheriff's hammer. Pleasure-loving Charlestonians erected their New Theatre in 1736 but high admission fees kept out all but the well-to-do. A group of English actors, Murray and Kean, came to Philadelphia and New York in 1750 and won the tolerance of the authorities as well as the acclaim of audiences. New Yorkers displayed an early fondness for the stage, though most contented themselves with purchasing books of plays.

In 1752, the American stage became a permanent institution with the arrival that year of the professional troupe of Lewis Hallam and his wife. Like other players, they found the most hospitable atmosphere in southern towns like Williamsburg where Calvinism had the least hold. However, real box-office success lay in winning over the populous cities of the North and Middle colonies, and so the Hallams proceeded to capture New York and Philadelphia. After the elder Hallam's death, his successor, David Douglass, who married the widow, took up the task of conquering New England, carefully disguising some of his plays as homilies in the advertisements. He built a chain of larger and more attractive theaters, and eventually, his efforts were rewarded with a fortune of $125,000.

Early theaters tended to be small, usually accommodating three hundred; in wintertime, most of them depended on wretched stoves in the foyers which left the auditoriums freezing so that intermissions were vital to thaw out shivering audiences. The management in some theaters "respectfully requested the audience not to spit on the stove" and also tried to discourage them from crowding the actors off the stage. In this modest setting, provincials were introduced to the comedies and tragedies of the great contemporary playwrights. After a century's neglect, Shakespeare's reputation revived and his plays attracted large audiences. Tragedies drew multitudes on both sides of the Atlantic, especially Thomas Otway's *The Orphan* and *Venice Preserved,* both of which touched off violent emotions from frenzied love to abject despair. Some critics rated Otway's tragedies second only to Shakespeare's. When *The Orphan* was enacted in a King Street coffeehouse by local amateurs, a mob of Bostonians fought to gain entrance. Comedies were always in demand, particularly those of the prolific playwright, actor, and manager of London's famed Drury Lane Theatre, Colley Cibber. Most popular were his *The Careless Husband,* warmly acclaimed by Horace Walpole among others, and *She Wou'd and She Wou'd Not.* Perennial favorites were *The Recruiting Officer* and *The Beaux' Stratagem* by George Farquhar, vigorous Anglo-Irish actor and playwright who displayed the decided taste of the day for robust humor and dubious morality.

3

Despite the attractiveness of eighteenth-century town life, it must be recalled that nineteen Americans in twenty lived in simple rural communities or were isolated upon the expanding frontier. In New England and the Middle colonies, farmers and their families toiled with primitive tools, using heavy wooden plows and hoes, and cutting grain with scythes or sickles that had evolved but slightly since the dim days of ancient Egypt. This was the era, it is true, of England's agricultural revolution, which applied in part the scientific method so sensationally effective in industry to land tillage and animal breeding. But only the large-scale farmer of some means could afford to adopt the new seed drills and straight-row planting developed by Jethro Tull or to emulate the crop rotation and fertilization methods of Viscount Charles ("Turnip") Townshend or the scientific breeding principles of Robert Bakewell.

This new learning, handicapped by the rural prejudice—too often justified—against "book farming," made American converts through the efforts of men like Jared Eliot of Connecticut, author of *Essays on Field Husbandry* (1747), which was reprinted in 1754 by the New York *Gazette* and other papers. Eliot, a friend of Franklin, rebelled against "soil butchery"—the natural temptation wherever fertile lands and too few farm workers prevailed; New England's large patches of abandoned farms already presaged a dark future. From knowledge based on his own practical experiments and inventions—including an improved seed drill—and from a careful study of the best European authorities, Eliot spread the new techniques.

Southern planters were in a far better position to experiment with the teachings of the current agricultural revolution than were small farmers with meager capital. That wealthy and intelligent country gentleman, George Washington, like many a successful planter, devoted much of his library to books on farming and never lost interest, even while President, in the possibilities of making two blades grow where one did before or in improving the weight of his cattle or the wool of his sheep. Others followed suit, for in spite of the many sports and entertainments of well-to-do planters, American conditions did not breed a genuine leisure class.

Competition with the fertile acres of the West led many planters of the Old Dominion to conclude overhastily that soil exhaustion had overtaken them and, consequently, to hurry southwestward to newer lands. Their expensive overseers, whose efficiency was measured only in immediate returns, often succumbed to the temptation of using up the soil without rotating crops or fertilizing the worn fields. With costly but inexpert slave gangs on their hands, it seemed cheaper to exploit the soil and move on to low-priced lands rather than to undertake the skilled techniques of scientific farming. So the planters of the great staples, tobacco and rice, were divided in their attitude toward the new farming methods and too often appeared indifferent to the need for diversified crops except for their own food.

The gradual advance of competitive ideals at the expense of feudal and paternalistic survivals did not leave the farmers untouched. In New England, for example, the manorial institution of the commons—lands shared communally and open to all for pasturage, fuel, and other purposes—was undermined by the tendency of aggressive older families to fence in sections of the commons as their own. Instead of keeping the older township method of conveying land and a share in the commons to new settlers, the colonial legislatures sold directly to speculators who in turn helped to create a class of powerful absentee landowners who often dominated the town meeting and overawed the small farmer.

Here was a goad for agrarian radicalism; besides, farmers tended to become chronic debtors and were tempted to escape their insistent creditors by fostering inflation either through unsecured paper money or through paper issued as legal tender against land as security. Inflationists had several motives. One was the fact that the draining of gold by expensive English imports needed by a new country led to a steady decline in the prices of crops. Inflation might reverse this tendency. Allied with the angry creditors in fighting any cheapening of the currency were Britain's mercantilists who feared the results of inflation on imperial trade. England therefore dismantled colonial mints, outlawed the inflationist land banks by the Bubble Act of 1741, and added a Currency Act in 1751 that forbade the making of bills of credit as legal tender. Those colonial assemblies which harkened to the debtor farmers were thus checked in their quest for inflationary panaceas.

At the lower rung of the rural ladder were the squatters. A Boston schoolteacher, Madam Knight, wrote disdainfully of the wretched condition of the poor squatter's house in the northern wilderness where shiftlessness was reflected in the windowless shack that rested on the bare earth and was furnished with a few improvised wooden pieces. Something of the same slothful psychology was described by the aristocratic Virginian, William Byrd II, regarding North Carolina's frontier "borderers" who had fled the planter's control to squat lazily and drunkenly on a few miserable acres. Here runaway servants and improvident debtors found a wilderness paradise in paying no tribute to God or Caesar. In these people, nevertheless, Professor Parrington notes optimistically the origin of "the coonskin democracy of Old Hickory that was to bring eventual disaster to the plans of gentlemen."

Much higher in the social scale were the fairly well-to-do farmers who could afford to own several slaves. Madam Knight, observing a family of Connecticut slaveowners, was surprised to see the easy intimacy between the races in the household, and in her journal censured this familiarity of "permitting [the slaves] to sit at Table and eat with them [as they say to save time] and into the dish goes the black hoof as freely as the white hand." Such was New England under slavery and such was the reaction of a New Englander before the peculiar institution became exclusively Southern.

The rural family, so closely knit by economic ties, was deeply affected by frontier conditions favoring equality as well as by the ideal of romance that accompanied Renaissance individualism in the western world. Strength and personal qualities counted for more here in determining the ideal suitor, even if they did not always outweigh financial assets. Courtship in a simple society where property considerations might be secondary scarcely required the tra-

ditional services of parents in haggling over dowries and selecting
a proper mate for their offspring. Substantial city people like Samuel Sewall, it is true, carried over Old World folkways in bargaining
sagely with his prospective bride and tried in the same way to
arrange his daughter's marriage—though pert Betty Sewall soon
showed she had a mind of her own. As for the maids on the farm,
the niceties of sheltered life were few and their courtships were
necessarily brief and direct. A widespread though far from universal custom reported by eighteenth-century travelers in western
Massachusetts, Connecticut, New York, and among the Pennsylvania
Germans was "bundling" or "tarrying." Engaged couples, and sometimes casual acquaintances, might spend the cold night together in
bed, but fully clad and separated by a makeshift partition. This was
not always innocent. Long betrothals, as among the Dutch who
practiced bundling, often meant prenuptial relations and led the
clergy and the authorities to condemn bundling. Jonathan Edwards,
for example, labored with his Northampton congregation to stamp
out the custom.

Marriages, which seventeenth-century Calvinists had tended to
regard as civil contracts partly because of the property aspect, were
now commonly solemnized by clergymen, although Quakers simplified the ceremony to the mere signing of a certificate in the
presence of an audience. Youthful marriages at sixteen or seventeen
and brief widowhoods were the rule. "Marriages in America are
more general, and more generally early, than in Europe," wrote
Franklin, attributing this fact to the abundance of cheap land and
to economic opportunity. Among the surviving ancient marriage
customs were those of putting the bride and bridegroom to bed and
scrambling for the bride's garter. Divorce, outside of Catholic and
the stricter Anglican circles, was usually granted for desertion,
cruelty, or adultery, and quick remarriage followed.

According to colonial books of etiquette, children were expected
to show meekness and restraint, especially at the table. "Sing not,
hum not, wriggle not," ran the rule for table manners, "Spit nowhere
in the room, but in the corner." In the periods of the great religious
revival of the 1740's, children readily imbibed the popular terrors

of damnation and a few embarked on painfully exemplary lives. Etiquette, especially for the planters studying Renaissance manuals for the perfect gentleman, was a serious discipline. Even as a youth, Washington copied these table rules for his own guidance:

> Put not your meat to your Mouth with your Knife in your hand neither Spit forth the Stones of any fruit [nor] Cast anything under the Table.
> Cleanse not your teeth with the Table Cloth, Napkin, Fork or Knife but if Others do it let it be done with a Pick Tooth.
> Rince not your Mouth in the Presence of Others.

Such sage rules were apparently necessary among all classes in that day.

Most of the recreations of townsfolk like dancing, group singing, cockfighting, and card games had their rural devotees on a large scale. More distinctive of the country were the lively southern barbecues centering about a stuffed porker basted with wine. Country dances, as already noted, were mostly Old World importations, though some of the jigs were attributed to African origin. At country fairs, sturdy farmers wrestled for prizes, competed in footraces, or chased a greased pig while others sang ballads, danced, or lost themselves in drink. Handball and a form of football were popular while hunting and fishing were universal favorites north and south. On rare occasions a wandering showman astonished villagers with a trained bear, monkey, a lion, or a buffalo from the West. Whisky and cider were the indispensable fluids for all frontier celebrations, especially among the Scotch-Irish, who usually managed, however, to consume their home-distilled drinks without undue stupefaction.

4

The colonial melting pot of nationalities digested huge non-English ingredients, though some, like the Pennsylvania Germans, stoutly resisted fusion. Besides these German newcomers, there were Swiss, Scotch-Irish, Welsh, French Huguenots, Jews of various lands, and a sprinkling of others resulting in a new composite nationality. This blend of peoples was a significant factor in the growth of an anti-English revolutionary psychology. Most of these emigrant peoples came of the poorest classes; they were packed in filthy ship quarters, fed on rotting food, exposed to thirst if the ship became becalmed, or were sometimes killed off by shipfever, smallpox, and dysentery before the vessel arrived at Philadelphia, the usual port of entry. To embark on such hell ships required the driving force of helpless poverty or frustrated religious faith. English immigrants, of course, continued to come, spurred on by the vicissitudes of politics and the resulting economic uncertainties; there was, for example, the anti-Puritan purge of the Restoration, followed, after the Battle of Culloden in 1746, by the expulsion of the defeated Scotch Cavalier followers of Bonnie Prince Charlie, the Pretender. The rising Industrial Revolution, too, for all its salutary features, compelled emigration among the rural people whose livelihood had been dislocated by the new factories.

Especially significant in shaping American frontier history were the aggressive Scotch-Irish, as the transplanted Presbyterian Scots of the Ulster counties of Northern Ireland were called. Living on the former lands of the expelled Catholic Irish, who were regarded by England's rulers as a species of untamed Indian destined for extinction, they served an apprenticeship for their future frontier life by building homes in the hostile Irish country and fighting off native attacks. However, England's shortsighted mercantilist statesmen, eager to monopolize the profitable woolen manufactures for industrialists at home passed the Woollens Act of 1699 which forbade Ireland and the overseas colonies to export this product to England and Wales. This crushed a basic industry for the Ulsterites leaving them dependent on the flax industry. Further blows came in 1717 when tenant leases began to expire, allowing absentee landlords to benefit from a rising market by doubling and trebling rents; wholesale evictions followed. Such conditions made the Scotch-Irish Presbyterians all the more resentful of the payment of tithes for the Established Church of England and by the 1720's emigration became Northern Ireland's greatest industry.

While small groups of the Scotch-Irish had come to the American colonies in the final decades of the seventeenth century, the new immigration was a deluge. James Logan, Penn's agent and himself a Scotch-Irish Quaker, lamented, "It now looks as if Ireland . . . were to be transplanted hither. They will soon make themselves Proprietors of the Province." Even their Presbyterianism, stemming directly from Calvin and John Knox, was no recommendation to Calvinist New Englanders who feared the economic pressure of these immigrants most of whom had to secure passage by hiring themselves to the captain or by contracting for indentured service with a master. Three to six thousand of them poured in annually during the 1720's, drawn to the unoccupied lands of Pennsylvania, the Shenandoah Valley of Virginia, the Carolinas, and New Jersey. Pushing beyond the Germans who had preceded them and without funds, they became "squatters" on the frontier, ignoring paper land titles and stubbornly insisting that the land belonged to him who tilled it. These frontier people bore the brunt of Indian fighting while the pacifist Quakers neglected defense and blamed them for the Indian wars. Eventually, the Scotch-Irish struck back at the Quaker rulers by capturing control of the Pennsylvania Assembly where the well-to-do easterners regulated representation and taxes in their own interest.

The Scotch-Irish adopted the log cabin and Americanized it. They took on the distinctive frontier garb of leather breeches, hunting shirt, and Indian moccasins, making them typical of the expanding West. Skilled workers in the homeland, they readily became jacks-of-all-trades until European visitors concluded that Americans tried to do everything without becoming adept at anything. They proved to be self-reliant farmers and expert riflemen in the forests and on the battlefields. To solve the problem of difficult transportation to eastern markets as well as to meet a brisk demand at home they converted their grain into liquor. Their simple but fulsome diet of fried mush with honey, hominy, pone bread, game, and fish became characteristic of western menus. Their women labored in the fields with their men, though far less frequently than did their German neighbors, and made candles and soap for market. They wore summer bonnets or winter wool hats with their short gowns or petticoats. The Scotch-Irish earned a deserved reputation for

hospitality and helpful cooperation. Professor W. F. Dunaway points
out their "grubbing, chopping, and logging bees," their cornhusk-
ings, house-raisings, and quilting parties. Outside the door hung a
latchkey in mute welcome to the stranger. Certainly, the frontier did
not breed a misanthropic kind of individualism, but a more balanced
self-reliance tempered by gregariousness. Frontier people realized
that survival and sanity itself depended upon cooperating with one's
scattered neighbors.

The story of the German and Swiss migration is a major chapter
in religious and economic history. The soldiers of Louis XIV had
devastated the left bank of the Rhine and forced the peasants of
the Palatinate to flee to America like their middle-class brethren
of a generation before. Religious persecution by the Elector of the
Palatinate and the leaders of the Lutheran state church drove other
dissidents out. After 1740, when economic pressures behind emigration became very strong, the German and German-Swiss Lutherans
themselves who had no religious motive for leaving joined with the
German Reformed sect to outnumber the rebellious Mennonites,
Amish, Dunkers, Moravians, and other "holy" sects in America.

Preceding the Scotch-Irish, for the most part, they shared the unoccupied frontier lands with the incoming Ulsterites and they tried
to select those lands rich in limestone. The Germans who moved to
the Schoharie River were so fleeced by New York speculators that
they fled into Pennsylvania. By 1727, there were 15,000 Germans in
that colony alone. Thousands more poured into the fertile fields of
the Shenandoah Valley of western Virginia or into the piedmont
lands of the Carolinas and Georgia. About 600 German-Swiss under
De Graffenried founded New Bern, North Carolina. By 1745, the
colonies had absorbed nearly 80,000 German-speaking people,
mostly Protestant; the greatest year of German immigration was
1749 when 6000 arrived. At the time the Declaration of Independence was written, one in every ten Americans was of German extraction and one of three Pennsylvanians belonged to that group.

Relatively segregated and filled with a missionary zeal concern-
ing the superiority of their culture above the Anglo-American, these
"Pennsylvania Dutch"—as they were misnamed by outsiders—clung

to their religious ideas, their notions of honest craftsmanship and labor, and their language. English ways meant cheating and slip-shod work. Foremost among craftsmen were the German gunsmiths of Lancaster and Berk counties in eastern Pennsylvania who were pioneers in the manufacture of the Kentucky rifle. These long-bar-relled guns, capable of precise marksmanship, were to be the terror of the British in the American Revolution. Another contribution to pioneering was their stout Conestoga wagons, the future "schooners of the prairies," pulled by six horses. In Georgia, the diligent Salz-burgers introduced wine-making and the silk industries. Above all, the German farmers, unlike their restless Scotch-Irish neighbors, pa-tiently replenished the soil with fertilizer and used scientific meth-ods instead of resorting to "soil-butchery," so that their descendants two centuries later could still boast of good farm lands. One of their neighbors, the Philadelphia scientist, Benjamin Rush, wrote of them in 1789:

A German farm may be distinguished from the farms of the other citizens of the state, by the superior size of their barns, the plain but compact form of their houses, the height of their inclosures, the extent of their meadows, and a general appearance of plenty and neatness in every-thing that belongs to them.

Travelers told of the German's suspicion of paper money and banks, his fear of debt, and his peasant habit of saving money in old stockings. Neighbors expressed shock at the German custom of sending wives and children into the fields for heavy labor rather than hiring hands. The pietist cults like the Mennonites continued to attract most attention, some for their simple garb, their primitive substitutes for buttons, their taboos on dancing, and their strict ideas on sex life. English-speaking Pennsylvanians remained un-certain whether they would not be Teutonized long before the Ger-mans became Anglo-American, for German schools, newspapers, and churches conceived their holy mission to be the transplanting of German ways to the New World. In this era they already dom-inated the eastern third of Pennsylvania. Though the original eighteenth-century dialect of the eastern Rhenish Palatinate eventually fused with so many English words and grammatical forms as to create the unique "Pennsylvania Dutch" speech, further assimilation was stubbornly resisted, especially by the pietist cults, as late as the twentieth century.

Even the easygoing Franklin seemed worried over the growing victory of German over English, presaging—so he feared—the destruction of Anglo-American civilization. In a letter of May 9, 1753, to a friend, he observed darkly:

Advertisements intended to be general are now printed in Dutch [German] and English. The signs in our streets have inscriptions in both languages, and in some places only German. They begin of late to make all their bonds and other legal instruments in their own language, which (though I think it ought not to be) are allowed good in our courts, where the German business so increases that there is continued need of interpreters; and I suppose within a few years they will also be necessary in the Assembly, to tell one half of our legislators what the other half say. In short, unless the stream of importation could be turned from this to other colonies, as you very judiciously propose, they will soon so outnumber us that all the advantages we have will, in my opinion, be not able to preserve our language, and even our government will become precarious.

Although Franklin's fears proved exaggerated, Pennsylvania was to see continued gains for the Teuton influence, especially in the growth of German schools and, for a time, in the bi-lingual publication of the state's laws during the mid-nineteenth century.

A far smaller, but quite influential immigrant group were the one or two thousand Jews from Spain, Portugal, the Germanic states, Poland, England—in fact from almost every corner of the world, sped by the whip of persecution. Columbus' discovery of America had coincided with the expulsion of the Jews from Spain and fresh tribulations had followed for these refugees. Beginning anew, the Jews had erected their synagogues in New York, Newport, Charleston, and elsewhere. Although Newport Jews were usually poor, a wealthy elite built a cultured and prosperous Israelite community, famed in Longfellow's poem, "The Jewish Cemetery at Newport"; its two hundred families seem to have disappeared during the Rev-

olution. Of this forgotten community of "Alvares and Rivera," Longfellow speculated in 1852,

> How came they here? What burst of Christian hate,
> What persecution, merciless and blind,
> Drove o'er the sea—that desert desolate—
> These Ishmaels and Hagars of mankind.

The wealthy Jacob Rivera of Newport had introduced the extensive
sperm-oil industry into the colonies. His co-religionist, Aaron Lopez,
shipowner and philanthropist, sent a fleet of thirty vessels to sea.
Other Newport Jews brought soapmaking as an industry to Rhode
Island, manufactured furniture, and shared in New England's "triangular trade" with Africa and the West Indies as well as in the
fortunes of privateering. Their classical synagogue was a show place
for colonial visitors.

In New York, Jewish mercantile families like the influential
Franks played a large role in eighteenth-century business and culture. The Franks, who were partners in many major trading enterprises and intermarried with the local gentry, belonged in later
years to the art patrons who sat for portraits by Thomas Sully, Gilbert Stuart, and other famous colonial painters. Many Jews were
Masons almost from the introduction of this order to the colonies.
Despite limited civic rights at first in some colonies, as in Massachusetts which lagged behind Rhode Island and Pennsylvania in
tolerance, the Jew won in dignity and kept his religious orthodoxy,
his educational organizations, and his ancient traditions.

Declining sectarian fanaticism on both sides of the Atlantic during the era of Enlightenment, together with the increasingly favorable economic environment in the uncrowded New World, softened
the virulence of group hatreds and broke down some of the barriers
between Christians and Jews. Colonial intellectuals and merchants
felt at ease in Jewish circles; Ezra Stiles, later president of Yale,
was intimate with the Jewish leaders of Newport. In Georgia, young
John Wesley, then on a religious mission with a group of Moravians,
wrote in his *Journal,* "I began learning Spanish in order to converse

with my Jewish parishioners, some of whom seem nearer the mind that was Christ than many who call him Lord."

In the wilds of Georgia, last of the colonies founded by England within the present United States, John Wesley and his brother Charles were carrying out a "second rise of Methodism" among a miscellany of nationalities—English, Scots, Salzburgers, Piedmontese, Swiss, and Jews. Anglican philanthropists founded Georgia to give jailed debtors a second chance and to save dissident Protestants of the Continent. Wesley had been sent in 1735 by the new influential Society for the Propagation of the Gospel, which was actively setting up schools and missions in the colonies; unable to make much headway among the Indians, he turned to the white settlers themselves. Despite conflicts with the founder, James Edward Oglethorpe, an unhappy love affair and difficulties arising from the High Church views he still held in the midst of a frontier society, Wesley succeeded in establishing a Sunday School—said to be the first in America—and his vigorous evangelist friend, George Whitefield, came over for a few months to establish an orphan asylum near Savannah.

Just two years before Wesley came, Oglethorpe had arrived to carry out his scheme for saving English debtors from rotting in jails. While in Parliament, he had been shocked by revelations regarding them and he had associated himself with the wealthy philanthropists who became the trustees of the new colony of Georgia, named after King George II. English statesmen saw the advantage of a buffer state south of the Carolinas that could halt Spanish expansion from Florida. During the first year, 618 came, mostly of the very poor, who were given fifty-acre farms; self-supporting immigrant families received five-hundred-acre grants. Following mercantilistic thinking, the trustees tried to direct the colonists to those crops that England had to depend on from foreign countries—silk-raising, grapes, hemp, and certain medical plants. The Indians, particularly the Creeks, were treated well and slavery and liquor were strictly forbidden under the well-intentioned paternalism of the trustees. Savannah, the capital, was laid out in the best city-planning tradition of that day with broad straight avenues and attractive park squares. Unfortunately, this regime did not work well, the malarial swamps fostered sickness, and the colonists were not adapted to the hard, persistent tasks of taming a wilderness. Only when the charter expired in 1753 and Georgia became a royal province did substantial improvement take place; experienced frontiersmen from Virginia and the Carolinas moved in and prospective planters were encouraged by the introduction of slavery. Thus South Carolina's rice and indigo fields were reproduced in Georgia and this province became culturally assimilated to the rest of the plantation South.

Franklin's America, despite its rural character, gave its chief posts of honor and economic power to the merchant capitalist of the towns and the planter entrepreneur of the South. The century began with strict mercantilistic controls and provincial regulations dominating economic life, but by 1763 all these were under attack together with the surviving guild ideals protecting the consumer against scarcity and monopolistic prices. Such inroads of the competitive spirit were encouraged by the implications of nascent liberalism. Though capital accumulations were hampered by labor shortages, the dearth of inherited wealth, and the persistence of a barter economy, this was partly remedied as in the previous century by the importation of indentured servants and slaves. Class stratification along Old World lines continued to show itself in the church pews, in the college registers, in dress, and in architecture, though this system came under increasing criticism as tradesmen and workmen proceeded, in many instances, to imitate the dress and ways of their social superiors. In the colonies, the English-born gentry styled themselves "gentlemen" or "esquire," the merchants and landowners being addressed as "Mister," while the small farmer was satisfied with being called "goodman." At the lowest stratum, workmen, servants, and slaves responded to their plain Christian names—a custom that many twentieth-century whites retain for the Negro.

Town life was unique in its wholesome outlets for group life and in the dominance of the robust English spirit of recreation. The enlightened community feeling of Franklin, the Quakers, and others created valuable civic institutions such as the hospitals, the colleges, the fire departments, the early concert halls, and the first "penitentiary" to serve as an institution of personal rehabilitation. Family life was encouraged by the favorable economic situation, which led to early marriages and numerous self-supporting children. Liberal individualism affected it in the freer divorce customs and the tendency, except where considerable property was at stake, to subordinate advantageous economic alliances to the free play of personal romantic attachments.

· 6 ·

The Enlightenment and
the Great Awakening

[1700-1763]

I

In this era of the Mathers, Franklin, and Jonathan Edwards in
America, and of Locke, Rousseau, and Count Zinzendorf in Europe,
two rival movements shaped middle-class culture and trickled
down in simplified forms to the masses. One was the classical worship of reason; the other was the romantic "religion of the heart."
Reason had been enshrined through the sensational scientific discoveries of Newton, which led optimists to believe that man could
invent social sciences as precise as Newton's principles of gravitation if he only dared to trust his understanding without leaning upon
the supernatural.

"There is nothing accidental or arbitrary in nature," wrote Leib-
nitz, the German philosopher. "Everything is ruled by universal and
necessary laws." In scientific jargon borrowed from classical writers, the "deists" reduced God from a being concerned with every
detail of the universe, even with the fall of a sparrow, to the abstract mathematical qualities of a "prime mover." This Deity had
created the immutable "natural laws" that guided man as well as
the rest of the universe. Not even God would interfere with these
laws of nature. Belief in God, according to the leading exponent of
deism, Baron Herbert of Cherbury, came through human under-

standing and God's existence was revealed in the very rational design of nature and the universal moral order. Every religion was therefore "true" insofar as it recognized only the results of natural law and of right reason. Having no monopoly of truth, all established churches that persecuted men for their faith were enemies of true religion. Here lay the seeds of Voltaire's vehement revolt against "clericalism" and the French attack on the priesthood which reached Bacchanalian extremes in the Worship of Reason during the French Revolution. Among the enthusiasts of the Enlightenment, religion was stripped of the supernatural and became a thing based on the individual conscience rather than on church authority, fostering an ever-widening split between church and state.

This intellectual revolution not only made morality independent of church sanctions but also borrowed its formal psychology from John Locke whose *Essay on Human Understanding* (1689) added the heady brew of materialism to the current secular philosophies. Rejecting Plato's mystical doctrine of "innate ideas" independent of experience, Locke asserted that "there is nothing in the mind except what was first in the senses." To him the mind of the individual at birth was but an unwritten page, a "tabula rasa." This emphasis upon experience as the sole source of knowledge, "empiricism," opened the door to the materialistic philosophy of the ancient Epicureans and Stoics, reducing the nature of the world to mere matter and motion. In some quarters, notably France and England, materialism ripened into militant atheism.

Still, the psychology of Locke gave an enormous prestige to the middle-class faith in the dominant influence of the environment. Man was no longer chained by an innately depraved human nature and his future blotted out by original sin, but had become a completely plastic being capable of perfection on this earth no less than in heaven. By changing the environment one altered man for good or evil in proportion. The implications were tremendously significant, for with the current secular shift from faith to good works, humanitarianism took on the fervor of religion. This reforming zeal also sprang from traditional sources as well as Enlightenment dogmas, but it played a mighty role in the psychology of Franklin, Jefferson, Thomas Paine, and their followers. However, while the anarchist wing of the liberals looked upon man as innately good, most liberal writers emphasized the sanctity of property and tended to exalt "self-interest" as a primary human drive; thus they brought back "innate depravity" disguised as an instinct. Middle-class American political theorists like James Madison and John Adams called for "checks and balances" in the Constitution to contain this predatory instinct and to protect the natural right of property against the communistic inclinations of propertyless majorities. The classical psychological principle of the Epicureans that self-interest leads man to seek pleasure and avoid pain became enthroned in the later individualistic (that is to say, "liberal") economics and ethics of Adam Smith and Jeremy Bentham. The phrase "pursuit of happiness" betrays its Epicurean ancestry.

From Locke, particularly in the second part of his *Two Treatises of Government* (1690), came the most influential restatement of the classical political doctrines of natural law and natural rights. He quoted the Roman jurist Ulpian for the memorable dictum that all men are by nature created free and equal. Government, he believed, rested on a "social contract" of free men who left their primitive "state of nature" to preserve their inalienable "natural rights" of life, liberty, and property in a civil state. "Men being, as has been said, by nature all free, equal, and independent, no one can be put out of this estate, and subjected to the political power of another, without his consent."

Instead of accepting the traditional Aristotelian idea of society and government as an organic growth as natural as the biological basis of the family, Locke and the liberals saw the state as a creature of individuals acting for themselves rather than as a product of an organic "society"; it existed solely because of the consent of those governed. Thinking of the Glorious Revolution of 1688 which overthrew his arch-enemy James II who had hounded him even in exile, Locke justified the right of revolution whenever arbitrary rulers violated the social contract by infringing upon the inalienable "natural rights" of the individual. This statement of the justification of revolution was to be neatly rephrased in the Declaration of Independence. John Wise was to make use of this social-contract theory, which he learned from Pufendorf, in defending the liberty of independent congregations from the arbitrary interference of centralized ministerial bodies.

The second great movement, partly described as romanticism in distinction to the classicism of the Enlightenment, was one of revolt against the aridity and coldness of a philosophy based on good works alone and confined within the narrow framework of rationalism. Among its exponents were primitivists like Rousseau, who challenged the dictatorship of reason with a philosophy of instinct and feeling, thus encouraging a popular cult of sentimentality and emotionalism. This was based on an idealization of nature and the virtues of the Noble Savage. Even the skeptical Voltaire had had his Noble Huron Indian endowed with all sorts of virtues in *Candide*. The classicists, too, could note that the prized Greek and Roman traditions were not restricted by the law of balance or the dominion of the intellect; there were the frenzies of the followers of Dionysus, the overwhelming tragic spirit of the Attic poets, and the philosophic speculations that fell outside the canons of moderation and harmony. As seen through the spectacles of the primitivists, America embodied the missionary purity of a youthful people unspoiled by the artificialities of a sophisticated civilization. The "back to nature" movement added a romantic twist to the worship of natural law by rebelling against formal memorized learning, adapting instead the subject matter to the natural bent and curiosity of the individual— the foundation of later theories of "progressive education."

In the romantic movement, America was deeply influenced by the pietists, ranging from the Quakers to the multitudes of German and Dutch sects adhering to "inner-light" doctrines or some other form of intensely personalized religion. Like the rationalists, they too rebelled against the formalistic state churches and clericalism, but unlike the mechanistic deists and their allies, they sought guidance in their own spiritual revelations based upon their interpretation of the Bible. Again, like many rationalists, pietists (like the Quakers) made humanitarianism a cardinal principle; but their philosophy was based on the Lutheran ideal of salvation by faith alone, which in effect came to be a philosophy very much concerned with good works. Idealizing the divinity latent in man, they found an overwhelming impulse to serve him by humane endeavors through a religion of the heart. Stirred by the simple pietists, many thousands of Americans were to seek the personal experience of conversion in the revival spirit of the Great Awakening. Edwards, Whitefield, and their co-workers sought to realize the Reformation ideal of the "priesthood of every believer" by inducing the mystical exaltation of the earnest penitent among their listeners.

2

Puritanism, for all its middle-class asceticism and Hebraic theocracy, had shared in the scientific and cultural ideas of the deepening Renaissance. Its university-trained leaders had eschewed unchecked religious "enthusiasms" and crude Bible literalism for a rational philosophy shaped partly by Petrus Ramus. This lessened the existing gap between science and religion. The Calvinism of the Puritans had been of the moderate English variety, for the notion of an "inscrutable and arbitrary God" had usually been lightly passed over by the clergy. As the seventeenth century ended, the spirit of religious compromise and secularism in both Europe and America, marked by toleration laws and relaxed enforcement of statutes for conformity, threatened the remnants of orthodoxy. Few eighteenth-century towns had sufficient churches to accommodate the increasing population—had everyone been inclined to attend church simultaneously. Boston's Anglicans, favored by the English government, were taking over Harvard College, the bulwark of Puritanism, from the hallowed control of Increase Mather, its ultra-orthodox president of 1685-1701; his son, Cotton, was frustrated in his ambitions to be president. A last attempt was made by these Boston theocrats to regain lost ground by making Congregationalism, under their leadership, into a rigid state church with a literal Calvinist theology. Thus in 1705, the Mathers, Samuel Sewall, and their followers issued their *Proposals* calling for a close union of

Massachusetts' Congregational churches under the control of a strong ministerial synod—an indirect scheme to imitate the centralizing system of the Presbyterian Church.

Against the clerical aristocracy, popular elements backed John Wise, an outspoken pastor of Ipswich, Massachusetts, whose father had been an indentured servant. On the eve of the Glorious Revolution of 1688, he had led his townfolk in a tax strike against the reactionary governor Sir Edmund Andros on the ground that the levy violated the colony's charter. Andros had promptly jailed him, but Ipswich paid his fine. Now he preached resistance to the theocrats, publishing two tracts, *The Churches Quarrel Espoused* (1710) and *Vindication of the Government of New England Churches* (1717). Like a true son of the Enlightenment, he based his case on the democratic social contract and the doctrine of natural rights, relying upon the theories of Baron Pufendorf. He drew an analogy between the liberty of the individual churches or congregations and the natural rights of the citizen under the social contract. Following Plutarch, he argued:

Those Persons only who live in Obedience to Reason, are worthy to be accounted free. They alone live as they Will, who have Learnt what they ought to Will." So that the true Natural Liberty of Man, such as really and truely agrees to him must be understood as he is Guided and Restrained by the Tyes of Reason and Laws of Nature; all the rest is Brutal, if not worse.

Like other liberals he fell back upon Ulpian:

As Ulpian says, "by a natural Right All Men are born free"; and Nature having set all men upon a Level and made them Equals, no Servitude or Subjection can be conceived without Inequality; and this cannot be made without Usurpation or Force in others, or Voluntary Compliance in those who Resign their freedom, and give away their degree of Natural Being.

All this was an argument for a "Noble democracy" which, for royal ears, he tactfully called a "Regular Monarchy." Church polity, it followed, must also follow democratic principles to meet the test of natural law. Cotton Mather replied with an angry denial that any attempt was being made at "Presbyterianizing" and denounced the "poison of Wise's cursed libel." Wise had indeed made his point;

and his democratic theories were to serve decades later in 1772 during the revolutionary controversy, when admirers were to reprint his two works as tracts for the times.

Meanwhile "godless Harvard," as George Whitefield libeled that institution, had proved a sad disappointment to the aging Puritans. Despite the zeal of the Overseers, there was a steady drift toward the heretical Arminian doctrines of the Anglican Church, which played havoc with Calvinist orthodoxy; it was not long before deism and eventually Unitarianism crept in. When Whitefield, the English Evangelist and co-worker of John Wesley, arrived in Boston, where crowds adored him, Harvard, unlike its more orthodox younger sister, Yale, remained cool to the rabble-rouser, much to Whitefield's chagrin. The College, again unlike Yale, resisted any attempt to impose an oath of orthodoxy upon the students. By the 1740's the philosophy students were using Locke as a textbook and others were being encouraged to study French privately, thus unlocking a Pandora's box of troublesome Enlightenment ideas. Something of the uncloistered atmosphere is suggested by such Commencement theses as one of 1733, entitled, "Is the Voice of the People the Voice of God?" which was decided affirmatively. Ten years later, Sam Adams (very appropriately for him) answered "Yes" to this thesis: "Is it Lawful to resist the Supreme Magistrate if the Commonwealth cannot otherwise be preserved?"

Aside from a minority of serious students, Harvard drew rather heavily from gentlemen idlers and merchants' sons seeking knowledge for the counting house rather than the benefits of broad college training. Sixteen-year-old Ben Franklin, who had been forced to give up hope of going to college, compensated himself by wittily repeating the local prejudices against Harvard boys. Writing as "Mrs. Silence Dogood"—the name was intended to ridicule Cotton Mather's pompous essays on doing good—Franklin ridiculed the idle fop at Harvard where dull boys "learn little more than how to carry themselves handsomely, and enter a room genteely ... and from whence they return, after abundance of trouble and charges, as great Blockheads as ever, only more proud and self-conceited." Students enjoyed amateur plays, sometimes in burlesque form, and went to Boston for the horse races or pirate hangings. (In the seventeenth century, particularly, one could listen to Boston's ministers reading admonitory lectures to the pirates just before hanging —apparently intended as a compound punishment.)

When John Leverett won the coveted presidency of Harvard, the disappointed Cotton Mather plotted to build a new citadel of Godliness out of the struggling new Collegiate School at Saybrook, New Haven, which had then about twenty-five students. Mather wrote directly in 1718 to Elihu Yale, a Boston-born London capitalist whose father had been a New Haven merchant. Yale, then living luxuriously in fashionable Queen Anne Square, was an agent for the powerful East India Company and governor of the English trading post, Fort St. George. Others, too, were at work upon Yale, particularly James Pierpont of New Haven. Elihu Yale yielded and gave £800 in goods, hoping, as Yale's historian has it, that a little more learning might bring Congregational Connecticut into the Anglican Church. New Haven won the reorganized college for itself by offering eight acres of land on the edge of town.

Gifts of books poured in: Richard Steele, the essayist, donated eleven volumes of *The Tatler* and *The Spectator;* Isaac Newton sent his famed *Principia;* and Bishop George Berkeley, the noted Irish idealist philosopher, who visited Newport in 1728-30, left a valuable collection for the Yale library. The books corrupted Yale's Congregationalism even faster than its founder had dared hope, for the Anglican theological works and Newton's science drove the brilliant tutor, Samuel Johnson, and several associates into the arms of the Church of England. Amid an embarrassing scandal, Johnson was dismissed, though he was afterwards to be compensated by becoming the first president of King's (later Columbia) College, an Episcopalian institution of New York city.

One of Johnson's successors at Yale was Jonathan Edwards, who had studied with him without losing his faith in orthodox Congregationalism. The son of an exacting Calvinist minister and schoolteacher who taught his children such axioms as "Remember you were born to die," Jonathan worked earnestly for a divinity degree. He quickly mastered the semi-medieval curriculum of Yale and apparently learned most from his own deep and independent reading. Morals at the college did not altogether please him, for he sent his father reports on the "Discovery of some monstrous impieties, and Acts of Immorality Lately Committed In the College, Particularly stealing of hens, Geese, turkies, piggs, Meat, Wood, etc—Unseasonable Nightwalking, Breaking People's windows, playing at Cards, Cursing, Swearing, and Damning, and Using all manner of Ill Language, which never were at such a pitch in the Colledge as they Now are." In short, it seemed that Yale, the hope of orthodoxy, was not much better than Harvard.

The succeeding decades were to see Yale become as secular in outlook as its Cambridge rival. At King's College, Samuel Johnson urged a non-sectarian school, but his plan met lengthy delays. His ideal of liberal studies included English composition, geography, and husbandry, as well as the traditional arts and sciences. The president, whose reputation as a philosopher and scientist was generally acknowledged, had been ordained an Episcopal minister in England and had returned to America an open enemy of Calvinist fanaticism, which was again resurgent. He placed God's concern for man's happiness above the Calvinist notion that man's chief end was to glorify God.

In 1755, the year after Johnson's King's College was founded, Franklin secured a charter for the College of Philadelphia, formerly an academy that had evolved from a charity school sponsored in 1740 by George Whitefield. If this college, which became the University of Pennsylvania by an act of 1791, did not speedily emerge as a thoroughly secular child of the Enlightenment, it was not the fault of Franklin and his friends who planned it that way. If not exactly non-sectarian, it was at least interdenominational, hence beyond Harvard, Yale, King's, and other contemporaries in escaping the control of a single church. The College of William and Mary, scarcely more than a theological seminary at the beginning of the century, developed into a more secular classical institution where Thomas Jefferson, a Latin school product, attended during 1760-62. Like other well-to-do Williamsburg boys, he enjoyed the atmosphere of parties, dancing, drinking, the theater, and the races—not to mention a short-lived love affair. Through the stimulating professor of mathematics and moral philosopher, Dr. William Small, and the brilliant and liberal lawyer, George Wythe, he came into intimate touch with the science, philosophy, law, and politics of the Enlightenment.

3

Foremost among those to strike a shattering blow against the rationalism and secularism of the Enlightenment were the German pietists, the English Methodists, the Calvinist Presbyterians, and the Baptists. This revolt became the Great Awakening, in which Yale's alumnus, Jonathan Edwards, became New England's religious leader. Germany, birthplace of Luther and the Reformation, gave pietism its chief impetus. In the sixteenth century, the ex-aristocrat and friend of Luther, Kaspar von Schwenkfeld, had broken with the Reformers by making the humanity and mystical spirit of Christ the basis of his faith. His persecuted followers, the Schwenkfelders, unable to live within the Lutheran state church, sailed to Pennsylvania in 1734, settling in Bucks, Montgomery, and Berks counties where these simple folk held prayer meetings in their homes.

Much more important in the history of pietism were the followers of Philip Jacob Spener of Frankfort-on-the-Main and Nicholas Lewis, Count Zinzendorf, leader of the Moravian communities. In 1670 Spener, a Lutheran pastor and a friend of Pastorius, had spread informal "societies of piety" whose members met at home to study the Bible, pray, and sing hymns. Zinzendorf, Spener's godson, carried on this pietist mission; he was trained at the University of Halle, which became under the theological teachings of Augustus H. Francke the beacon for pietists everywhere. Zinzendorf's estate, Herrnhut, attracted the Moravian Brethren who traced their movement back to John Hus, the martyred Bohemian reformer of the early fifteenth century. Many thousands joined this cult of primitive Christians, who practiced the "love feast" of the early apostles and cultivated church music, especially the famous part-singing. Persecuted as fanatics, the Moravians emigrated in 1735 to Savannah, Georgia, and then to Pennsylvania, founding Bethlehem and Nazareth as communistic colonies and centers of the Moravian Church in America. Considering work a holy duty, they proved very successful farmers and artisans; their emphasis upon missionary work among the Indians and frontiersmen exposed them to martyrdom as frontline soldiers of Christianity.

The pietist migrations of this period added more Mennonites to the original settlements in Lancaster County, Pennsylvania, led by Pastorius and totaling 2500 by the end of the colonial era. Visitors gaped at their ancient Biblical custom of washing each other's feet in good fellowship, their beards—mustaches were banned as too military—and the rigid rules of conduct among the Amish Mennonites who punished the refractory with total ostracism. Similar in customs and views to these pacifist groups were their neighbors, the pietist Dunkers, also known as the German Baptist Brethren, who baptized three times in a flowing stream. Mennonites and Dunkers taught plain speech and dress, and honest business dealings, and encouraged laymen to exhort the congregation. Johann Conrad Beissel, a weaver of Germantown, who had been influenced by the Dunkers, withdrew from the other pietists to build the noted Ephrata Society, a semi-monastic, self sustaining community. Saturday was their day of rest and most of their beliefs were those of the Dunkers. Beissel's talent as a composer of over a thousand hymns and his religious writings gave his Ephrata Cloister a wide reputation as a center for musical learning and religious publications. The community possessed a complete publishing business, including a paper mill and a bookbindery, as well as a printing press.

German Reformed groups sympathetic to pietism arrived in Montgomery County in 1720 to swell the ranks of primitive Christians. Even among the regular German Lutherans were the poor peasants who had come under the influence of ministers trained at Halle and were now pouring into Pennsylvania, the Carolinas, and elsewhere. Pietism was indeed a mass movement. In Germany its emphasis on the simple vernacular at the expense of Latin and its contagious appeal helped the growth of the feeling of German nationality. The American Great Awakening, too, was to prove it a cohesive national force.

While the American religious scene was seething with the ferment of a religion of the heart, England experienced a similar religious awakening. John Wesley, an Oxford-educated Anglican priest, had been influenced by the disciples of Zinzendorf, and at college his serious-minded circle had been derided as "Methodists" for their incurably pious habits. At a time when the Industrial and Agricultural Revolutions were beginning to break up traditional rural communities to create apathetic city crowds indifferent to all but heavy drinking and commercialized vice, Wesley and his friends saw an ideal opportunity to reach the masses. Breaking with the formal style of Anglican preaching, Wesley followed the example of his friend George Whitefield by braving mob attacks in 1739 to preach to 3000 Bristol workmen on a hill at the outskirts of town. Perceiving the underlying problem of poverty, Wesley was to emphasize a gospel of "good works" and social service, as well as the message to the heart. Attacking rationalist doctrines and Anglican High Church formalism, he traveled throughout Britain, sometimes preaching five times on Sundays and reaching crowds of up to 30,000 listeners—miners of Wales, workers of London, artisans elsewhere. These revivals were strengthened by tracts, hymn books, and above all by the enthusiastic congregational singing he borrowed from the Moravians. Almost a half million converts had entered the Methodist fold by the time of his death in 1791. Although Wesley spent a brief period during his youth as a missionary with a group of Moravians in Georgia, his movement did not conquer America until the Methodist revivals of the 1770's and 1780's. However, the technique of revivalism as he knew it crossed the Atlantic in the 1740's with George Whitefield, one of the original Wesley group in college.

The immediate spark for the Great Awakening came from a graduate of pietist Halle, Theodorus J. Frelinghuysen, minister to a Dutch Reformed congregation in the Raritan Valley of New Jersey. He preached a gospel of repentance and personal holiness during the early 1720's and won hundreds of converts through his emotional appeal. Soon a "New Light" faction of those who favored these induced conversions appeared in New Jersey, especially along the frontier settlements. At this point, the Scotch-Irish Presbyterians, led by William Tennent and his sons, especially Gilbert Tennent, took up the evangelizing drive. The elder Tennent set up a "log college" near Philadelphia to train his sons for missionary work. Log colleges, free from the rationalist taint of Harvard and the English universities, sprang up along the frontier, educating ministers for revival meetings west and south. Princeton College, in the heart of the New Light country, was inspired by the log college movement and chartered in 1746 at Elizabeth, New Jersey, moving to its present site in 1756. Aaron Burr, son-in-law of Jonathan Edwards and father of the turbulent future vice-president of the United States, became president of Princeton and after his death Edwards, himself, was appointed to the same post, although he died before he could assume his duties. Princeton was expected to nourish the missionary zeal of the New Lights and to train a ministry for that purpose. Yale was too far away and already suspect by the orthodox. Presbyterians not only founded Princeton, but built over one hundred log colleges, academies, and other schools in this era. The danger of an "unconverted" ministry—i.e., one that had never experienced the crisis psychology of the newly-awakened believer—had been underscored by Gilbert Tennent who argued, "Is a dead man fit to bring others to life?"

The Great Awakening gave a huge impetus to the Baptists, hitherto strong in Rhode Island, and among the Welsh and German immigrants of Pennsylvania. By the 1750's they had won hosts of converts in Virginia and a decade later they founded a revivalist center at Sandy Creek, Guilford County, North Carolina. Thereafter the Baptists as well as the Presbyterians played a major role in frontier religious history. While the Presbyterian, the Congregationalist, and the older churches stressed the need for a learned clergy, the Baptists, like most of the pietists, were suspicious of the colleges as a barrier to salvation, although their American founder, Roger Williams, had been exposed to the temptations of Cambridge. Nevertheless, their new expansion led them to recruit a clergy at their own theological college in New Jersey, which was later transferred to Rhode Island to become Brown University in 1764.

New England's experience with the Great Awakening took on

surprising violence under the subtle leadership of Jonathan Edwards. In 1726 he had accepted an invitation to the noted Northampton church of Solomon Stoddard, his grandfather. Congregationalists were then liberalizing the conversion requirements for church membership. The Half-way Covenant of 1662 had waived the requirement of an "experience" confession for children of church members, giving them all church privileges except the communion service. However, New England was yielding to "Mr. Stoddard's way," which allowed even those without an "experience" to partake in the communion with the others as long as their lives appeared unscandalous. Stoddard had also been a liberal innovator in the New Way of "praying by rule" and introducing singing classes, despite the "papist" tinge previously associated with any emphasis on rules and harmony in church-singing.

Jonathan Edwards, for all his intellectual brilliance, scientific curiosity, and personal kindliness, had no intention of perpetuating the inroads of eighteenth-century liberalism. At seventeen he had himself experienced the mystical feeling of conversion and he was convinced that God must be known directly to the heart as well as through the head. Using the methods of the German pietists, he met quietly with the youth of the town to read the Bible and for religious exhortations. His theology, an amazingly well-integrated philosophic system, revived uncompromising Calvinism, which emphasized "the sovereignty of God" whose absolute and arbitrary decrees did not require justification, and the predestination doctrines of damnation for those not of the elect. These were differences of emphasis from Stoddard's way rather than innovations in doctrine. As Edwards' able biographer, Ola Elizabeth Winslow, has wittily observed of the liberal Stoddard position, "Neither the sovereignty of God nor the depravity of man had been denied, but both had been decidedly bleached."

The truth of salvation, Edwards taught, could be intuitively learned through an inward revelation of the "divine and supernatural light." God had endowed the regenerate soul with a supernatural sense. In childhood, his father's teachings of God's sovereignty had revolted him as "horrible," but since then "a delightful conviction" and "a sweet burning in my heart" had led to his conversion. He noted in his journal, "The Reason why men No more Regard warnings of Future punishment is because it Don't seem real to them." His mission was to make hell a vivid concept and to prove that mere "good works" and respectable living did not insure salvation.

By 1734-35, his methods had raised a storm of mass emotions, beginning with "the vainest and loosest Persons" and stirring small children to hysteria. Conversions poured in steadily from the town of Northampton and throughout the Connecticut Valley. "This Town never was so full of love," wrote Edwards in a letter. In 1737, the collapse of the gallery of the decaying Northampton meeting house without injuring the crowd beneath was taken as a "sign" that Edwards was leading his flock on the right road. By the early 1740's Edwards was spreading the Great Awakening throughout the colonies in his influential work, *A Faithful Narrative of the Surprizing Work of God.*

A New England Puritan minority of Old Lights, who denounced the "enthusiasms" and terror of the revivals, made common cause with the rationalistic Charles Chauncy of the First Church of Boston. Chauncy pointed out the madness of one of the notorious revivalists, the Reverend James Davenport, who cried to his trembling audiences:

You poor unconverted creatures in the Seats, in the Pews, in the Galleries, I wonder you don't drop into Hell!—You Pharisees, Hypocrites, *now, now, now,* you are going right into the Bottom of Hell.

Upon this, according to Chauncy, "He came out of the Pulpit, and stripped off his upper Garments, and got into the Seats, and leapt up and down sometime, and clapt his Hands and *cried out*—'The Devil goes down'; and then betook himself to stamping and screaming most dreadfully." Fainting, shrieking, convulsions, and tumblings by the listeners accompanied this demonstration. To Chauncy's criticism, Edwards replied that while he rejected extremism in the form of an overheated imagination, he thought it reasonable to frighten people from hell.

In 1740, George Whitefield himself came to the northern colonies on one of his periodic tours from Georgia to New England. Gifted with a magnetic personality, a powerful voice, and a flair for telling human-interest stories, he thrilled his hearers for hours at a time, laughing, weeping, singing. Thousands in the cities as well as in the rural areas flocked to him, contributing funds for his proposed orphan home. Even the skeptical Franklin, who listened to him near Philadelphia, confessed himself deeply affected and felt compelled to empty his pockets for Whitefield's cause. Boston—save for Harvard—gave him a prolonged ovation. In Northampton, where he spent some time with Edwards, the latter wept to hear him. Wholesale conversions swept New England, emptying taverns and dancing schools, and spreading an unwonted atmosphere of holiness in his wake.

The following year, at Enfield, Connecticut, Edwards gave his most effective conversion sermon before a frightened, weeping audience, "Sinners in the Hands of an Angry God." In terrorizing words, albeit with a calm mien and level voice, he warned,

> The God that holds you over the pit of hell, much as one holds a spider, or some loathsome insect over the fire, abhors you, and is dreadfully provoked: his wrath towards you burns like fire; he looks upon you as worthy of nothing else, but to be cast into the fire . . . O sinner! . . . You hang by a slender thread, with the flames of divine wrath flashing about it.

Here was another Whitefield. Conversions continued to increase and "cryings out" became a regular feature of his meeting house.

Inevitably the reaction set in. Old Lights were encouraged to open a fresh attack on the revivalist New Lights and a pamphlet war between the two rocked New England in 1743. Edwards' tactlessness in probing the sins of his congregation after the first fears and hysteria had died down led to a reaction and finally to his dismissal in 1751. After serving a brief period as an isolated missionary to the Indians at Stockbridge, Massachusetts, where he wrote his notable philosophical essays, he accepted a call to the presidency of Princeton.

The Great Awakening was the most significant mass movement

of the eighteenth century, drawing hundreds of thousands into the churches at a time when liberalism and indifference to religion seemed dominant. Missionary activities were spurred on thereafter in all parts of the colonies. Although pietist leaders admitted the need for social service and humanitarianism, the movement in America seemed conservative, unmoved by political or economic issues. In morals and customs, the revivals produced a narrow "Puritanism," condemning as sinful "wanton tunes," dancing, horse-racing, and other popular recreations. Twentieth-century cults, following this tradition, were to label themselves proudly as Fundamentalist in opposition to their secular and modernist rivals. Still, revivalism substituted for Calvinist fatalism the optimistic belief that man could with a little effort win salvation for himself. Again, though the New Lights were too frequently dubious of the value of a liberal education, expansionist necessities led to the creation of new colleges, many with attractive futures. Finally, as Professor W. W. Sweet suggests, the Great Awakening contributed to a new national psychology just as the leveling influence of German pietism had helped knit together the scattered feudal principalities.

4

While the leaders of the Great Awakening, in the hope of securing a literate ministry, sponsored academies and colleges, primary education was still generally neglected. In this respect the Anglicans, through the Society for the Propagation of the Gospel in Foreign Parts, chartered in 1701, did notable service. Its missionaries offered children of poorer families an elementary education that combined catechism with arithmetic, reading, and writing. Avoiding Virginia and Maryland, where native Episcopal organizations dominated, the missionaries subsidized such schools from Charleston to Boston including a half dozen schools in New York City alone. This educational drive helped to revitalize Episcopalianism at a time when revivalist cults were gaining rapidly and the Church of England was leaning too heavily on the small English governing class in the colonies for support.

In Philadelphia the Quakers, spurred on by the humanitarian Anthony Benezet, sought to provide charity schools for girls as well as boys. Following the counsels of Penn, their founder, the sect brought the "three R's," rather than "ornamental" learning, to the poor. With the support of the German Lutherans and Reformed groups of Anglicans and Quakers, the Philadelphians planned charity-school projects that would help assimilate the foreign groups through the addition of English and citizenship studies. Here, according to Carl Bridenbaugh, unexpected resistance came from the German pietists led by Christian Sower's newspaper, which suspected a hidden purpose of fostering militarism and stamping out the religion, customs, and language of the German settlers. In the end, the charity-school projects limped along without much German support, for the Teutonic folk organized their own German-language schools and remained to a large extent an unassimilated group in Pennsylvania society.

"Practical studies" on the secondary level, reflecting the middle-class influence, thrived. Newspapers in colonial towns carried hundreds of schoolmasters' advertisements offering to teach "Italian bookkeeping"—the name for the double-entry system that made business planning a more analytical science—as well as surveying, mathematics, geography, astronomy, and "commercial languages" such as Spanish and Portuguese. In Philadelphia, William Penn's Charter School expanded its buildings to include the new type of "English school," which taught bookkeeping and English as well as French and German. Commercial and general night schools for working girls as well as men existed by the 1750's. Even the formal Latin grammar schools, with their classical curriculum, added a vocational course or two.

As more towns arose, especially along the frontier, middle-class families who could not afford—or did not care—to send their sons to the eastern grammar schools (primarily college preparatory in purpose) and colleges turned to the new "academies" of the mid-eighteenth century. The academy, named after Plato's famous school, taught the classics, but also gave considerable attention to English mathematics, and some practical science. The Academy of Philadelphia, sponsored by Franklin's *Pennsylvania Gazette* and various sects, opened in 1751 with a broad non-sectarian curriculum. Many of the academies, however, especially the products of the Great Awakening, remained local centers of orthodoxy. Quality varied from mere elementary rating to the superior high-school level.

The secularizing of the curriculum was marked by the introduction of formal grammar, intended to meet the middle-class demand for correct speaking and writing. Professor Stuart G. Noble has noted that, even at the time, many were skeptical of the effectiveness of learning English by "parsing" and memorizing the parts of speech. Dilworth's *A New Guide to the English Tongue*, a London textbook, was reprinted for the colonies in 1747 by Franklin. This combination of reader, speller, and grammar ran through twenty-six editions by 1792. However, the Bible was still used as an advanced reader. Rhetoric, concerned with pulpit and public eloquence, also began to be widely taught in the secondary schools. History, neglected except for providing classical background, had more champions, like Franklin, who sought its introduction to aid civic betterment. French, largely privately taught, was increasingly popular, reflecting the decisive intellectual leadership of France during the century. Italian also enjoyed cultural prestige.

Characteristic of the times was the middle-class and mechanic's movement of self-improvement in which the ubiquitous Franklin played a major role. In 1731, Franklin, who allowed himself only reading as an amusement, chartered a subscription library, the first in the colonies, supported by a society of one hundred members. "The books were imported," he later recalled, "the library was opened one day in the week for lending to the subscribers, on their promissory notes to pay double the value if not duly returned.' Donations quickly poured in and other towns hastened to imitate this example. When James Logan, agent of the Penn family and governor of Pennsylvania, died in 1751, he left his valuable collection of two thousand volumes to the Philadelphia Library. One prominent Quaker visitor, Abraham Redwood of Newport, was so impressed with the library idea that he returned home to sponsor, in 1747, the Redwood Library whose beautiful Doric structure was

designed by Peter Harrison, architect of Blenheim Castle and the
classical Newport synagogue. New York benefited in 1729 from a
gift of books for a public library donated by the Society for the
Propagation of the Gospel. Women, hampered in their education by
the man-made standards of the time, gained much in the increased
opportunities for reading.

5

Newspapers, after an uninspiring start, grew into a major form of
mass education in the eighteenth century. If the problem of public
literacy were not enough to discourage the publication of newspapers in the late seventeenth century, there was the dead hand of
clerical and royal censorship. The Glorious Revolution of 1688, followed by the comparative liberalism of William and Mary, em-
boldened Benjamin Harris to undertake in 1690 the first colonial
newspaper, *Publick Occurrences Both Foreign and Domestic,* but
this lasted exactly one issue; it was suppressed by the governor as
unlicensed, dangerously critical, and untrustworthy. The second paper, the *Boston News-Letter,* published by the postmaster and book-
seller John Campbell in 1704, was cautious enough to survive for
many decades and to profit from the privilege of being carried without charge in the mails. Better known to history is the *New England
Courant,* published by James Franklin and his apprentice and
brother Benjamin beginning in 1721. Critical of the conservatives
in church and state, James occasionally ran afoul of the governor's
party. Young Benjamin wrote anonymously the satirical *Dogood
Papers* and incurred the wrath of the clergy and the aristocrats who
were lampooned. James was also to found the *Rhode Island Gazette*
in 1732.

After moving to Philadelphia Benjamin Franklin acquired the
Pennsylvania Gazette in 1729 and transformed a dull sheet that was
then laboriously copying *Chamber's Universal Dictionary,* beginning with "A," into a witty, literary, and informative paper. Through
a partner he created the *South Carolina Gazette* in 1731, a rather
intellectual newspaper fitting for polished Charlestonians. He ex-

panded his enterprises by publishing books and pamphlets as well as newspapers and—briefly—a magazine; he also did job printing and official printing for the assembly, and sold various commodities, such as books, soap, medicines, and cheese. His connections as Philadelphia's postmaster were invaluable and by the time he was forty-two he retired, a wealthy man.

Philadelphia's leadership in journalism was strengthened by the unusual publishing activities of the German pietists. In 1738 the belligerent Christopher Sower opened a long-lived printing firm at Germantown, publishing three editions of the Lutheran Bible in the 1740's, using imported German type for the 1272-page book. His newspaper, known by various names such as the *Pennsylvania High German News-Writer* had four thousand readers in 1753, many as far away as Georgia. The Ephrata Brethren issued huge religious tomes and other publications in German. Even Franklin's *Pennsylvania Gazette* had a German edition. Scores of German newspapers were born and disappeared during the eighteenth century.

Early newspapers, faced by a dearth of news, especially in wintertime, with reports from Europe often delayed many months by Atlantic storms, resorted to wholesale plagiarism of London journals to fill the painful gaps between lucrative advertisements. A universal source for plagiarism as well as inspiration for provincial writers was Richard Steele's *Tatler* of London, which began in 1709 and was then succeeded by *The Spectator*, edited jointly by Steele and Joseph Addison. Its delightful, elegant, and brilliant essays on current events, literature, and the theater fascinated its readers and spurred on the development of journalism. Appealing to bourgeois morality in its classical aspect, Steele expressed his purpose "to pull off the disguises of cunning, vanity, and affectations, and to recommend a general simplicity in our dress, our discourse, and our behaviour." Whole issues of *The Spectator*, in that day before copyright property, were swallowed shamelessly by lethargic colonial newspapers. The Franklins' *New England Courant* was influenced by *The Spectator's* example in making the essays appear the product of a club that included the attractive character of Sir Roger de Coverley; it had its Hell-Fire Club as sponsors of

essays and satirical letters. Young Ben deliberately tried to follow
the literary model of *The Spectator* and wrote anonymous letters
to the editor quite in the Steele and Addison mode. The New England *Weekly Journal* of Harvard's gifted Mather Byles found inspiration in the Roger de Coverley papers and other moral essays of
The Spectator. Other oft-quoted English writers were Daniel Defoe,
"father of journalism" and author of *Robinson Crusoe,* and Jonathan
Swift, whose *Gulliver's Travels* furnished an arsenal of clever satire
for colonial journalists.

Memorable in the history of journalism and the freedom of the
press is the case of John Peter Zenger of New York. A struggling
printer who had come with the Palatinate emigration of 1710, he
had served as apprentice to and briefly as a partner of William
Bradford, once a radical and now publisher of the increasingly conservative New York *Weekly Gazette.* Spurred on by the popular
party, especially the merchants, which had serious grievances
against the arbitrary Governor William Cosby, Zenger began the
New York *Weekly Journal* in 1733 and printed attacks on the governor's circle. Zenger was then arrested on a charge of publishing
"a false, scandalous, and seditious libel." According to the law of
the time, as developed by the Star Chamber in the seventeenth
century, the axiom was "The greater the truth, the greater the libel"
and the jury was expected to decide merely on the question of authorship. However, the popular party whose original counsel had
been disbarred by the governor's clique quietly provided Zenger
with the best lawyer in the colonies, the former Attorney-General
of Pennsylvania, Andrew Hamilton. Before a crowded courtroom
the aged Hamilton admitted the fact of Zenger's authorship, but insisted, despite the court's protest, on the doctrine known in common law that "truth is a defense against libel." He concluded with
a challenging prediction,

The Question before the Court and you Gentlemen of the Jury, is not
of small nor private Concern, it is not the Cause of the poor Printer, nor of
New York alone which you are now trying. No! It may in its Consequence
affect every Freeman that lives under a British Government on the mainland of America. It is the best Cause. It is the Cause of Liberty; and I

make no Doubt but your upright conduct this day will not only entitle
you to the Love and esteem of your Fellow-Citizens, but every Man who
prefers Freedom to a life of slavery will bless and honor you as Men who
have baffled the Attempt of Tyranny; and by an impartial and uncorrupt
verdict, have laid a noble foundation for security to ourselves, our posterity, and our Neighbors, That to which Nature and the Laws of our
Country have given us a Right—the Liberty both of exposing and opposing
arbitrary Power (in these Parts of the World, at least) by speaking and
writing Truth.

Despite the judge's refusal to recognize that any other issue than
authorship was involved, the jury returned quickly to give a unani-
mous verdict of "Not Guilty." The crowd then gave three cheers
and Zenger was discharged the following day. Many years later, in
1805, New York State led the liberal trend elsewhere by enacting a
libel law admitting truth as a defense. England, too, moved slowly
in this direction in the Fox Libel Act of 1792 and the Libel Act of
1843. Despite this lag in statutes, the effect of the Zenger case was to
enhance the political strength of the press against arbitrary agents
of the government, giving it a major role in the revolutionary tradition of the 1770's.

6

The art of letters, much like journalism, was distinctly imitative,
except for a few notable exceptions. Still, provincial American readers and authors were closing the time-gap between the publication
of Europe's literary masterpieces and their reception in the colonies.
Alexander Pope's couplets and long English didactic poems were
freely imitated, especially in the almanacs of Nathaniel Ames of
Dedham, Massachusetts. Franklin and his publishing rivals were
busily reprinting the latest English works, not only the serious tomes
of religious, classical, and scientific learning, but the vastly popular
sentimental novels, such as Samuel Richardson's *Pamela; or Virtue
Rewarded* (1740) and his masterpiece *Clarissa Harlowe* (1744),
solidly based on the Puritan and middle-class moral tradition. Pathos, feminine innocence struggling against seduction, and high
ethical purpose dominated the Richardson tradition of the sentimental novel. This marked the birth of the modern English novel,

which aroused western Europe and America into enthusiasm for romanticism, even winning the applause of the pulpit.

Both Franklin and Andrew Bradford experimented simultaneously in 1741 with the first general literary and political magazines, but failed. One of the first American ballads published dealt with an Indian battle of 1725 in Maine and became the subject of Longfellow's first poem, *The Battle of Lovell's Pond*. Most noteworthy were the writings of Franklin, particularly his famous collection of aphorisms in *Poor Richard's Almanack*, which began to appear in 1732. So popular was the *Almanack* that it attracted 10,000 subscribers annually. His selections, borrowed from European and American folk tales, are classics of the American middle-class psychology of thrift, hard work, and self-reliance.

"Buy what thou hast no need of, and erre long thy shalt sell thy necessaries."
"God helps them that help themselves."
"The sleeping fox catches no poultry."
"Early to bed, and early to rise, makes a man healthy, wealthy, and wise."
"One to-day is worth two to-morrows."
"Not to oversee workmen is to leave them your purse open."
"A small leak will sink a great ship."
"He that goes a-borrowing goes a-sorrowing."
"Experience keeps a dear school, but fools will learn in no other."
"There are no gains without pains."
"'Tis easier to suppress the first Desire, than to satisfy all that follows it."

Franklin's notebook stressed the virtues of temperance, order, industry, frugality, sincerity, justice, cleanliness, humility, tranquility, and chastity. His formulas for success had their equivalents in the writings of Daniel Defoe. Despite his exhortations to get ahead, gain for its own sake was never a part of Franklin's outlook.

In philosophy this era was remarkable for Jonathan Edwards, Samuel Johnson of New York, Cadwallader Colden, and others. At Stockbridge Edwards wrote his defense of the Calvinistic sovereignty of God with its determinism as against the free-will doctrines of the Arminians who had won over the Anglicans and were infiltrating Congregationalism. Calvin had denied that sin is less criminal merely because it is ultimately determined by God's sovereign will. The Arminians argued that this doctrine of necessity that robbed man of his freedom to choose good or evil was opposed to morality. In his *Freedom of the Will,* Edwards argued like the materialists that nothing ever comes to pass without a cause. While man is free to make a choice, this choice is actually determined indirectly by impulses over whose control the mind is passive. The will is determined by "that motive, which, as it stands in the view of the mind, is the strongest"—the "last dictate of the understanding" (perception and apprehension). Still, for everyday purposes, there is a freedom in a limited moral sense: "if a man is not restrained from acting as his Will determines, or constrained to act otherwise; then he has liberty, according to common notions of liberty..." His metaphysical analysis drew considerably from Locke's *Essay on Human Understanding* and showed the influence of the new psychology, even if his conclusions broke with those of the Enlightenment materialists. England's Dr. Samuel Johnson reassured his friend Boswell, who felt bewildered over Edwards' reasoning, "All theory is against the freedom of the will; all experience for it."

Edwards' "religion of the heart" had been an attempt to reconcile Calvinism and pietism, to bring together the Lockean analysis of knowledge with a poetic and idealistic philosophy of Platonic love. As he put it, "There is a difference between having an opinion that God is holy and gracious, and having a sense of the loveliness and beauty of that holiness and grace... When the heart is sensible of the beauty and amiableness of a thing, it necessarily feels pleasure in the apprehension." The world was to him an ideal order of mental reality, reflecting in Platonic fashion an eternal all-comprehending mind. In this ideal world there was room for Newton's discoveries because natural science reflected the will of God.

His one-time Yale tutor, Samuel Johnson, who rejected Calvinism, became the foremost colonial disciple of the subjective idealism, or "immaterialism" of the Irish philosopher, Bishop George Berkeley, his friend and correspondent. Berkeley had sought to give the death blow to atheism by denying that matter existed independent of mind. When he criticized Newton, Johnson strongly objected, defending the scientific achievements of the Enlightenment. Berkeley's colonial influence grew when he came to Newport during 1729-31 while waiting vainly for government aid to a proposed Indian mission college in Bermuda.

One of the few outspoken critics of Johnson, Berkeley, Edwards, and the idealists was the New York scientist, politician, and philosopher, Cadwallader Colden, who accepted the materialism of the day, which made all existence depend on matter and motion. In his evaluation of Newton in *The Principles of Action in Matter* (1751), he asserted, "The intelligent agent never acts in opposition or contradiction to the material agents." His world was mechanically determined. Unfortunately for his fame, too few of his contemporaries found him intelligible.

The literature of Quaker humanitarianism forms a solid core of eighteenth-century achievement. As the century progressed, the Quakers took the lead in giving up their slaves and in urging abolition upon the world. A host in himself was the prolific pamphlet writer and ardent Quaker reformer, Anthony Benezet of Philadelphia. The French-born son of a French Huguenot, he taught in a Quaker school, founded a girls' school, taught Negroes at night in his home, and eventually sponsored a Negro school in 1758. When 450 Acadian exiles (whose plight was to be romanticized in Longfellow's *Evangeline*) arrived in the city in 1755, only to be attacked as French enemies and papists, he led a movement to provide shelter for them. His antislavery pamphlets and articles continued the pietist tradition of Pastorius at a time when slavery had many respectable friends in the North as well as in the South. He also appealed to his countrymen for just dealings with the Indians and worked for peace and reconciliation at the time of the Revolution.

No less deserving of a place in history was John Woolman, an idealistic merchant tailor and Quaker missionary to the Indians. His opposition to slavery was so effectively expressed in a tract, *Some Considerations on the Keeping of Negroes,* that one Quaker authority, Rufus M. Jones, credits him with converting the Quakers to the antislavery cause. Another essay, *A Word of Remembrance and*

Caution to the Rich, pleaded for fairness to labor and the right of every man to earn a living. The Quaker poet, John Greenleaf Whittier, performed a labor of love in editing Woolman's noted *Journal,* revealing in the latter's simple language a deep compassion for the sufferings of mankind which Woolman made his own.

In the South, genuine literature in the best tradition of the Renaissance and the Enlightenment existed not uncommonly in hidden diaries and letters, as well as in manuscript books that were occasionally printed in London. The cultured Virginia planter, Robert Beverley, as already noted, published his *History of Virginia* in London in 1705 and expressed a secular rationalist viewpoint that contrasted sharply with the contemporary histories of Cotton Mather who leaned heavily upon a supernatural interpretation of New England.

Perhaps the most enlightened literary spokesman for the South before Jefferson was Colonel William Byrd II, son of the rich Virginia planter of the same name, and educated as a lawyer in England. His unique library of thirty-six hundred books, including numerous Elizabethan and Restoration playwrights, was the largest in the South and it is clear from his writings that he could read Greek, Hebrew, Latin, and Italian and that he used his leisure as a country gentleman at Westover to acquaint himself with his books. Selected in 1728 as a commissioner to settle the North Carolina-Virginia boundary dispute, he accompanied the surveyors across the Great Dismal Swamp. Byrd left a detailed record in *History of the Dividing Line* (published for the first time in 1841), of the "other half" of Southern society, such as the shiftless squatters whose idleness was encouraged by the warm pleasant climate, fruitful soil, and woods full of game.

His unconventional humor sometimes took on a faint tinge of Boccaccio when he described the sex adventures of his men with the simple maids of the squatter families. He could speak irreverently of the founding fathers at Jamestown, "most of them Riprobates of good familys" who "like true Englishmen ... built a church that cost no more than Fifty Pounds and a Tavern that cost Five Hundred." Rather startling for his day and plantation environment was his conception of ethnic democracy, generously praising the antiracialist policies of Catholic Spain and France in their colonies. Speaking of the racialist prejudices of seventeenth-century Puritans and Virginians, he declared,

These Saints, conceiving the same Aversion to the Copper Complexion of the Natives, with that of the First Adventurers of Virginia, would on no terms, contract Alliances with them . . . Whatever disgusted them I cant say, but this false delicacy creating in the Indians a Jealousy that the English were ill affected towards them was the cause that many of them were cut off, and the rest Exposed to various Distresses.

Then, in words that went beyond the limited environmentalism of the philosophers of that day, he asserted flatly,

All Nations of men have the same Natural Dignity, and we all know that very bright Talents may be lodg'd under a very dark Skin. The principal Difference between one People and another proceeds only from the Different Opportunities of Improvement.

Though a slaveowner, Byrd believed in ethnic democracy; though a Protestant, he could appreciate the anti-racialist policies of Catholic France and Spain; and though a wealthy aristocrat, he felt a warm sympathy and understanding for the wretched poor of North Carolina's "Lubberland." Seldom does one meet such men who can emancipate themselves from their social conditioning.

7

Colonial science in this era reached a surprising stage of maturity, marking an acceptance of the scientific method and confidence in it as an instrument of progress. The *South Carolina Gazette* of March 19, 1737, partly owned by Franklin, expressed the optimistic faith of the Enlightenment in progress through experimental science. The past centuries, it contended, had been too largely "philosophy without experiments, mathematics without instruments, geometry without scale, astronomy without demonstrations, surgery without anatomy, and physicians without *materia medica.*" Proudly the *Virginia Gazette* editorialized the same year, "The world is now daily increasing in experimental knowledge, and let no man flatter the age with pretending we are arrived to a perfection of discoveries." Americans, because of a favorable physical and economic environment, were to become convinced of the inevitability of progress far more than were Europeans. Condorcet in France was to elaborate the concept of progress, showing successive stages of human advance until social inequalities ended and perfection arrived. This notion that progress was inevitable, so commonplace to the 1880's and 1890's, had been either unknown or rejected by ancient and medieval writers in favor of the idea that perfection existed only in a primitive golden age; or they held a cyclic idea of the rise and decline of civilizations.

Utility was the keynote of scientific activity in a new country, but it did not monopolize thought. Here Franklin's name clearly led all the rest, gaining undisputed world eminence. His ability to improvise experiments with limited theoretical knowledge while isolated from the main centers of European science was amazing. In 1746, just a year after Holland had developed the Leyden Jar, a simple electrical condenser, he was actively testing the new theories of electricity and introducing the concepts and symbols of positive (plus) and negative (minus) in describing electrical current. To demonstrate the identity of atmospheric electricity as seen in lightning with that of static machines like the Leyden Jar, he conducted the famous kite experiment. He did this independently, not knowing of a similarly successful experiment by a Frenchman completed in May 1752, just a month earlier. To the colonists, accustomed to explaining lightning as the blows of a wrathful God, Franklin offered a secular explanation that had important effects upon their general outlook. This point was pressed farther home when Franklin invented the lightning rod, setting one above each building to conduct the lightning strokes to earth. It immediately became very popular in Europe and abroad; King Louis XV of France even sent his personal thanks to the inventor and many other honors followed. For a brief period the adoption of lightning rods was challenged in clerical New England circles, which divided into "Electricians" and "Anti-electricians"; this quarrel ended in 1755 when Boston permitted the rod to be attached to a church.

Franklin's other inventions, betraying a remarkably versatile genius, can only be briefly summarized. In 1742 he invented the Franklin Stove or Pennsylvania Fireplace, which solved the winter nuisance of reheated stale air by introducing a circulating current; ventilation excited his interest; he even hit upon the theory that the skin breathed. He invented a smokeless chimney based on the scientific principle of draft. To keep Philadelphia bright and clean, he introduced a street lamp and established city-paving and lighting services at civic expense. He theorized regarding earthquakes, such as the frightful Lisbon holocaust of 1755, and about whirlwinds, eclipses, and storms; he even charted the Gulf Stream. In his old age he invented bifocal glasses, showed a youthful interest in balloon ascensions, and speculated upon the future conquest of disease and old age. This indeed was Franklin's era.

At Harvard, science flourished at a faster pace than at other colonial institutions. In 1722, a twenty-four foot telescope used by Halley of comet fame was secured and used in a makeshift astronomy laboratory directed by a tutor. Five years later a further step was taken by endowing the noted Hollis professorship of mathematics and natural philosophy. One of its incumbents was John Winthrop (1714-79), descended from a unique line of governors and scientists, who rose to become the foremost American scientist of his time, more profound in theoretical respects than Franklin, even in electricity. He made pioneer observations regarding the nature of sun spots and upon planetary movements. Experimentally-minded, he sponsored a New England astronomical expedition in 1761 to Nova Scotia to observe the transit of Venus across the sun. He won recognition as the founder of seismology by his study of the Lisbon earthquake and other tremors. His analyses helped demonstrate that earthquakes, like lightning, came from natural causes rather than divine displeasure. King's College under Samuel Johnson and William and Mary College under Professor William Small also showed some scientific activity.

The South, too, had its gifted scientists, though on a lesser scale. One versatile scientist was Dr. John Mitchell of Virginia, the first Southern member of Franklin's American Philosophical Society, formed in 1744. His analysis of the Lisbon earthquake led him to theorize regarding the vulnerability of various areas for such disturbances. He offered a hypothesis on a possible cause in the explosion of subterranean fire and earth. In biology his name was sometimes coupled with that of the great French scientist, Buffon, especially in regarding man as an evolutionary product. He published a treatise in 1738 on the coloration of races from this standpoint; this was republished a decade later in Nuremburg. His investigations, many appearing in the Philosophical Society's *Transactions,* included the causes of yellow fever epidemics. In the stimulating atmosphere of Charleston, noted for its medical and experimental knowledge, Dr. John Lining repeated Franklin's experiment with a kite almost at the cost of his life and corresponded regularly with him. He wrote a treatise on yellow fever, investigated metabolism, studied the influence of weather on disease, and wrote papers on meteorology.

America's unknown forests and fields offered a wealth of novel flora and fauna for examination by colonial and European botanists. In a day when the great Swedish botanist Linnaeus was founding modern systematic botany through his analytical classification method, the colonies had an outstanding disciple in John Bartram, Quaker farmer of Pennsylvania. A neighbor taught him sufficient Latin in three months to understand Linnaeus and so, as he put it, "I began to botanize all over my farm." Along the banks of the Schuylkill near Philadelphia he planted the first botanical garden in the country with native and exotic plants. Traveling all over the Alleghenies he found rare plants for Linnaeus, Queen Ulrica of Sweden, and other Europeans. By furnishing shrubs and trees to England and elsewhere he spread the current enthusiasm for gardening; in return he enriched his country with new bulbs and seeds from abroad. With his close friend, Franklin, he was among the original founders of the American Philosophical Society. His child-like curiosity regarding nature's secrets made him feel kin with the forests and its animal life, giving his science a mystical tinge. "Through the telescope," he would say, " I see God in his glory."

Cadwallader Colden added Linnaean botany and medicine to his laurels as a rationalist philosopher and historian, attracting others like himself to join a new scientific and literary society. Known for his scientific correspondence with Europe's most honored botanists, he received this flattering note from Franklin, "I congratulate you on the immortality conferred on you by the learned naturalists of Europe." Trained at Edinburgh, the best medical college of the day, Colden was prolific in his treatises on yellow fever, cancer, small-pox, and numerous other ills. He went beyond his fellow-scientists in suspecting the origin of yellow fever in the marshes and stag-nant water, though he was ignorant of the modern germ theory and the agency of the mosquito.

Far worse than the recurrent French and Indian wars, which de-moralized colonial life and carried off thousands of people, were the horrible epidemics of the time. On both sides of the Atlantic, smallpox, dysentery, measles, and kindred diseases swept away en-tire villages and denuded many towns and cities of their inhabi-tants. In 1749, for example, the village of Waterbury, Connecticut, lost 130 in a single dysentery epidemic. Measles in Charleston killed eight or nine hundred children in 1772 alone. As early as 1699, Philadelphia suffered a periodic outbreak of yellow fever costing 220 lives.

Smallpox struck terror throughout the century and filled many columns of mournful speculation in the colonial press. Fortunately, medical science proved more successful in combatting smallpox than in coping with other epidemics. From Turkey, where inocula-tion against smallpox was commonly used by laymen, England's Royal Society acquired the technique and finally overcame clerical objections to its use. In New England, interestingly enough, the Reverend Cotton Mather, leader of the saving remnant of Israel in the theocracy, took up a brave and enlightened battle for inocula-tion. The fact that early inoculation involved an occasional death (as was the case with Jonathan Edwards) made the position of its defenders a hazardous one. When Mather appealed to the Boston doctors during the smallpox epidemic of 1721, he was met by violent objections, some of them based on pious fears of invading God's province. Others threatened to prosecute any physician as a murderer whose inoculated patient died. Even the *New England Courant* of James and young Benjamin Franklin, convinced that any cause of Mather's must be wrong, joined the anti-inoculationists. A missile was thrown by an unknown hand into Mather's home with the succinct message, "Cotton Mather. You Dog. I'll inoculate you with this. With a pox to you."

However, these stubborn ranks gave way after the courageous Dr. Zabdiel Boylston accepted Mather's challenge and proceeded to inoculate at his own risk. That year he inoculated sixty; the treatment was successful in every case but one. Later efforts of the inoculationists showed gratifying results. Boylston himself became an authority on inoculation, which was then administered hazardously through portions of human smallpox pustules rather than the later cowpox vaccine that came with Jenner's discovery of 1798. Boylston's treatise on inoculation won him membership in the Royal Society.

Only after a decade of controversy following the epidemic of 1721 did enlightened Philadelphia adopt Boston's new methods. Thereafter Charleston, the capital of the Enlightenment in the South, and other towns joined the procession of inoculationists. Although Philadelphia's doctors, faced with the risks involved in the Boylston method, were caught lagging in this instance, their city speedily won leadership in medicine and public health. Their philanthropists and scientists were quick to learn from the current English hospital movement and to set up similar institutions to replace the decrepit Alms House where the physically sick and the demented were thrown together in crowded quarters. The example of London's noted Bethlehem Hospital for the insane—Bedlam in the vernacular—led to the important Pennsylvania Hospital, a project founded by Dr. Thomas Bond and heavily sponsored by the Quakers and Franklin's *Pennsylvania Gazette*. Here, in sanitary rooms, several hundred non-contagious sick and the mentally ill could go, each paying what he could afford. One of the hospital's unusual features was a medical library, a rarity in the colonies.

In this age of almanac science, astrology cures, dangerous patent medicines, barber surgeons, superstitious midwives, and outright quacks, all thriving in a credulous provincial atmosphere, the training of doctors was an important step forward. The crude system of educating doctors through apprenticeship alone was challenged by Dr. John Morgan, the first professor of medicine in the College of Philadelphia. To the medical students who eagerly studied with him, he laid down a scientific goal, "Observation and physical experiments should blend their light to dissipate obscurity from medicine." But there still remained the task of overthrowing medical folklore among the ignorant—and too often among the learned as well.

8

Art in provincial America showed the influence of secularism, the newer classical ideals, and the effects of middle-class patronage. The first colonial painters of the Puritan era were largely self-taught limners. These half-forgotten craftsmen carried over the English medieval tradition of "limning" in a flat two-dimensional plane rather than the three-dimensional perspective of the Renaissance. They escaped technical difficulties by simply filling in a clear-cut pattern, usually painting in brown and black colors; their paintings showed an ascetic quality in the plain visages and unflattering details that their subjects revealed. Gradually, the limners developed a sense of delicacy and sophistication before they gave way to the academic painters of the eighteenth century.

Merchants and planters dictated an emphasis on portraits, but rejected the plain style of the Puritan era in favor of a more urbane and flattering interpretation of the eighteenth-century subject who was anxious to impress posterity forever with his material success and classic mien. Characterizing the kind of portraiture done in this era, Oliver Larkin has written, "Sober blacks and browns have been changed for scarlet coats and for waistcoats of flowered satin brocade, as much the evidence of status as the personality in the face, or the imperious gesture." Too much of this painting was unimaginative literalism typical of a provincial society. The insistence on detailed reproduction was to characterize American taste for several generations and during this era set it apart from the satiric realism of England's ill-appreciated genius, William Hogarth, or the masters of poetic harmonies among the Flemish school like Antoine Watteau. Europe's aristocratic art patrons had achieved a high level of taste that allowed considerable artistic freedom even within the comparatively narrow range of court pictures and classical allegories.

With far more psychological insight than a colonial society might be expected to appreciate, Robert Feke of Long Island showed the originality of a "primitive" in painting and has been considered to be the best American artist before Copley. This largely self-taught painter, whose brooding eyes impressed provincials as revelatory of the true artist, found his patrons among the well-to-do families of Newport, New York, Philadelphia, and Boston, winning praise for his fidelity to the costume as well as to the person of the sitter. His best-known subjects included urbane interpretations of James Bowdoin and each member of his family and the Isaac Royall family. Intellectually, Feke belonged to a select group of deists, some of whom met with him for philosophical discussions in Newport.

When Bishop Berkeley came to Newport in 1728, he brought with him John Smibert (or Smybert) of Edinburgh, a London portrait painter who had been a fellow art student of the great Hogarth. Smibert had hoped to become a professor of fine arts in Berkeley's projected college, but when this failed to materialize he solved his problems by marrying a wealthy widow and settling in Boston. One of his pupils was a talented youth, John Singleton Copley, whose genius did so much to enhance the arts of the Revolutionary era. Smibert turned his talents to architecture as well as to painting, but succeeded best as a portraitist, pleasing his provincial countrymen by successfully meeting the demand for literalness and richness of color. Among his best portraits was a group picture of Bishop

Berkeley and his family, and the studies of Jonathan Edwards and Peter Faneuil.

In architecture, the direct influence of the Enlightenment appeared in the classical designs of the newer public and private buildings. Simple classicism, derived from the high intellectual world of the Greeks and the Romans who had inspired the Renaissance and the Enlightenment, seemed most appropriate for the Age of Reason. The harmonious and abstract English classical patterns of Inigo Jones had begun to dim the intricate baroque style and medieval forms, relics of traditionalism.

Anglican invaders of Puritan Boston built the town's most attractive structure in King's Chapel with its impressive Ionic façade. Even unpainted Puritan meetinghouses with their whitewashed interiors evolved into a charming and distinctive art style in the new mode with classical pilasters, though retaining the medieval steeple. These white rectangular churches with plain windows, though austere by the standards of the motherland, were outdone as "Puritan" (in the usual sense) by the sober Quaker meetinghouses of Pennsylvania or the primitive log cabins that served as churches for the evangelical cults of the Great Awakening, particularly along the frontier. The Jewish Synagogue at Newport, designed by the most original of the colonial architects, Peter Harrison, was an esthetic expression of restrained classicism with gleaming white interior panels. In the same spirit, Harrison was to create Newport's Redwood Library, making it a Greek temple in an English garden, resplendent with its classical porticos and harmonious wings. Boston's many-arched Faneuil Hall was designed by John Smibert, the painter-architect.

One of the best examples of the "Georgian" type of English classicism adapted to public buildings was Philadelphia's new State House, later famous as Independence Hall. This Georgian style (the term is a loose one) stressed the symmetry of fine brickwork and the balanced effect of an equal number of sash windows flanking a classically designed doorway. The Georgian building tended to omit the highly decorative baroque motifs with their intricate and sometimes extravagant ornamentation in favor of the brevity of line typical of classical simplicity. In the newer middle-class homes, roofs, once elaborately gabled after medieval English, Dutch, or German inspiration, were flattened out in the semi-Greek mode to form mild slopes or broken to form gambrels. Altogether the Georgian architecture tended to achieve such severity as to invite a reaction by mid-century when builders chose to construct rich doorways with classical pilasters and pediments, distinctive Palladian windows, and greater profusion of classical symbols and detail. Until the period of Independence, this tendency to borrow heavily from the motherland in the form of Georgian classicism rather than from the Continent—except for a minority of non-English stocks— went almost unchecked among the fashionable classes.

Architecture remained largely in the hands of amateurs, usually master carpenters who understood textbook design, or educated country gentlemen to whom the building of a mansion was almost a ritual and required years for completion. Gentlemen like Jefferson and Washington dipped into the authoritative textbooks of the Italian classicist, Palladio, and learned the art of designing magnificent estates. Washington's historic Mount Vernon began its classical evolution toward its present familiar form in 1743. It is a two-and-a-half-story wooden building with a columned porch. Southern homes, unlike northern ones, often had porches for convenience in that mild climate. Both Virginia and New England, lacking limestone, utilized their abundant supplies of good timber to build attractive Georgian frame houses, painted white.

For the humbler classes, in both urban and rural areas, some improvement in building design took place as materials became more readily available and the level of well-being advanced. Unlike the upper and middle classes, the workmen and small farmers were concerned with strictly utilitarian ideas of design rather than with meticulous classical and other borrowed patterns. Still, the traditional English yeoman cottage found wide adoption, albeit in a modified and native American style, with thatched roofs giving way to slate and tile. New England's small frame house resembled similar English-inspired cottages of the South except for the lack of a porch and briefer chimneys of a type useful in cold climates. For the simple life of the frontier, necessity promoted the widespread imitation of the Swedish and Finnish log cabins, thereafter "typically" American. One or two rooms, an earthen floor, and primitive furniture made up many a log cabin dwelling, though in the older sections, especially among the Pennsylvania Germans, the house was far more pretentious.

Well-to-do gentlefolk in city mansions and country estates looked across the sea for the new rococo and Georgian styles of furniture and consulted Thomas Chippendale's London trade catalog, *The Gentleman and Cabinetmaker's Directory,* which began to appear in 1754. Chippendale's elegant rococo chairs showed the new enthusiasm for things Chinese with their elaborately carved backs and Chinese frets and friezes. Sometimes he used the shell-like motifs of French rococo for his interlaced, rich furniture carvings and added Gothic-curved chair legs. In Philadelphia and New York, particularly, expert cabinetmakers began to reproduce Chippendale importations, though preserving certain individualistic modifications of the master's popular chairs, hanging bookcases, carved mantel pieces, and plaster relief ceiling ornaments of rosettes reminiscent of Louis XIV. Before the end of the century American cabinetmakers were to draw also from the light graceful designs, thin tapering legs, painted wreaths, and delicate inlaid tables of George Hepplewhite of England. Rich interior panels, long curving staircases, and elaborately painted wallpaper added to the transformation of the "plain style" era of the seventeenth century. Jacobean forms of medieval design, which had flaunted such interior construction details as ceiling beams and bare walls, were passing out of style.

In musical expression the most active center was Philadelphia. Despite Quaker indifference to music (as well as to painting), the German pietists, especially the Moravians who loved to sing and play instruments in honor of the Lord, furnished a creative influence. Their settlement at Bethlehem later trained leaders for a musical cult of Haydn and Bach. In 1745 their new College of Music was dedicated to teach such varied instruments as the guitar, the spinet, and the organ. As choristers they won an enviable reputation. Conrad Beissel's Ephrata Cloister developed seven-part singing and like medieval monks wrote music by hand with illuminated letters. Secular music began to creep in as outside music students flocked to the German teachers. Their concerts of violins, flutes, violas, and the French horn became famous, attracting Franklin and Washington. German and Swedish folk songs resounded to the fiddle or flute in the rural settlements. Altogether American composers drew considerably upon the musical life of Pennsylvania.

Philadelphia produced one of the first American composers in Francis Hopkinson, a lyric poet and intellectual whose home attracted devotees of all the arts. As a lawyer and patriot he proved influential, signed the Declaration of Independence, and designed the national flag. A harpsichordist, organist, and composer active in Philadelphia's musical life, he modeled his work on contemporary English sentimental music and wrote the delightfully melodious and popular "My Days Have Been So Wondrous Free" (1759), the first of his successful songs, cantatas, and oratorios. In the same talented Philadelphia circle was James Lyon, a Presbyterian clergyman and psalmodist. His *Urania* (1761), a collection of psalm tunes, anthems, and hymns, went through several editions and won him the rank of the second American composer.

Musical life flourished earliest in the middle and southern colonies. New York had in the 1750's the well-known Trinity Choir directed by the English organist and concert master William Tuckey, offering both secular and religious music. Gay Charleston, small as it was, had the most varied musical activities in the colonies suitable for the sophisticated tastes of Carolinian and West Indies planters. In 1762 it founded the famous St. Cecilia Society (destined to last until 1912), which supported a highly paid orchestra, giving performances fortnightly in the winter and spring season. Popular open-air concerts were given at its Orange Gardens after the fashion of English resorts. The town also witnessed the first opera performed in the colonies, Colley Cibber's *Flora, or Hob-in-the-Well*, a ballad opera. Other cities followed.

New England in this era freed itself of fears that "papist" musical practices would undermine the faith. Singing by note in church and even choir-singing replaced the anarchic music of Puritan congregations. Psalm-tune publications increased. A very significant product of revivalism, if not of secularism, was the acceptance of "hymns of human composure" to supplement the old psalm tunes. Boston's Anglican King's Chapel, as we have seen, adopted a long-storaged organ in 1713 following little Port Royal, Virginia, and Philadelphia's Swedish Gloria Dei Church, which had had such an instrument since 1700. The city's concerts won steady patronage by the 1760's.

While the Enlightenment added its ingredients of rationalism and individualistic liberalism to secularize the Christian heritage, especially in the minds of the educated elite, the evangelical movement of the Great Awakening gave the masses a supernaturalism of tremendous vitality. Edwards, Whitefield, and the Tennents recaptured lost ground among the indifferent sons of the Puritans as well as among the frontier settlers of the middle and southern colonies. Thereafter for several generations at least religious orthodoxy clung stoutly to the average American home, especially in the rural areas, despite defections by middle-class elements. While Whitefield had stressed a gospel of good works as well as of faith, too few of the evangelists followed suit. On the other hand, Quakers like Woolman had adopted the mystical self-communion emphasis of European Quietism rather than the aggressive conversion technique of the seventeenth century and had been able to embark upon the most fundamental program of active humanitarianism in colonial history.

The demand of the Calvinist cults for a learned ministry—in contrast to the shouting revivalist sects of the later camp-meeting era —led to the foundation of many colleges that could not escape a strong bond with the eighteenth-century world of science and philosophy. Education reflected elsewhere the domination of aristocratic and middle-class interests, hence the patronage of the academy and the college at the expense of elementary education, though the growth of commerce corresponded with an increase in "practical studies." Outside of the log colleges, the curriculum of the secondary schools and colleges grew more secular, reflecting the rationalism and urban influence of the Enlightenment.

Liberalism won a great battle for freedom of the press in 1733 and advanced in other fields as well. Economic individualism had its best exponent in Franklin, the champion of middle-class rationalism and an enlightened capitalism. The virtues of sobriety, work, thrift, and wealth-getting lent themselves to a self-sufficient individualism that looked with favor upon the liberal ideal of the weak state, though *laissez faire* was still very much restricted by British and colonial regulations. Sectarianism, strengthened by the Great Awakening, was to challenge the surviving state-established churches of the East and thus contribute to the birth of the liberal state. Even before the Great Awakening, English and German dissenters, who were rebels against the state churches in the homeland, had arrived with an inbred suspicion of centralized and oppressive government. Besides, distance from British controls at London and rural decentralization weakened the interventionist practices of a mercantilistic government. The American Revolution was to build upon such foundations of a secular liberal state, which protected religious liberty without meddling with church affairs and curbed the powers of government to allow greater freedom to private associations.

The growing secular spirit, at least among the elite, affected colonial culture as did the provincial middle-class patronage of the arts. Puritan asceticism, which had not been confined to New England during the seventeenth century, yielded to more worldly tastes. Hardheaded provincial merchants, it is true, still clung to a literalist interpretation of art, requiring portraits that were flattering or at least precise rather than imaginative in interpretation. In music, secular concerts came out from beneath the local bans and even the revivalists encouraged "hymns of human composure" to supplement the divinely writ psalms. Literature under Franklin, Beverley, and William Byrd II pictured a secular world and even the philosophy of Jonathan Edwards did not wholly break with the emergent naturalism of Locke and Newton.

· 7 ·

The Revolutionary Era of
Hancock and Jefferson

[1763-1789]

I

In August, 1764, upper-class Boston paid its final respects to the very wealthy merchant, Thomas Hancock, amid elaborate funeral ceremonies. His twenty-seven-year-old nephew and heir, John Hancock, already long apprenticed to the business, promptly assumed command of the Hancock enterprises employing many hundreds of men. In a wild scheme the young man gambled upon his proud fleet of whalers to win for him a world monopoly in oil and whalebone, but he failed disastrously as European skippers broke his "corner" with large oil deliveries. Then, to make matters worse, a general trade decline set in shortly after the Seven Years' War ended, which bankrupted several leading merchants. Hancock, continuing his uncle's profitable policy of evading the iniquitous British customs duties for his extensive importing and exporting business, was hurt even more than others of his class by England's decision to reorganize her postwar empire by tightening customs collections and by raising taxes. Inspired by the patriot leaders Sam and John Adams and fond of the plaudits of the gathering revolutionary crowds, the young millionaire of his day turned radical, being among the first to show open resistance to England. His henchmen manhandled customs officers on his ship *Lydia*, and he lost another sloop, the *Liberty*, for defying the mercantilistic laws. Soon he became too involved in town meetings and public office to heed the injunctions of his cautious business associates.

"I have a right to the liberty and privileges of the English Constitution," he declared defiantly, "and I as an Englishman will enjoy them." Like other Americans he inherited the English revolutionary outlook of the Puritans and of the Whigs of the Glorious Revolution of 1688. Middle-class liberal ideas critical of throne and altar as well as agrarian radicalism had crossed the Atlantic to ignite a receptive, individualistic people, made up in part of so many rebels against church and state. A robust democratic feeling of self-reliance and equality as well as a growing sense of American nationality had been nurtured by the common struggle against a harsh frontier, hostile Indians, and the primitive task of building a new life remote from the motherland.

Geographic isolation from the west along a compact seaboard behind the Appalachians fostered the birth of a people whose habits of thought tended to differ more and more from those of the home-bred Englishman, and who chafed at the necessity of being dependent on an authority so far away. Thomas Paine put this succinctly in his pamphlet for independence, *Common Sense*, "To be always running three or four thousand miles with a tale or a petition, waiting four or five months for an answer, which, when obtained, requires five or six more to explain it in, will in a few years be looked upon as folly and childishness. There was a time when it was proper, and there is a proper time for it to cease."

While most of the revolutionists were of English stock and demanded English political rights, some 40 per cent of white Americans were of Scotch, Welsh, Irish, German, Dutch, French, and other origins. In a population of nearly 3,000,000 on the eve of independence, some 700,000 were Negroes, nearly all of them slaves. This huge blend of non-English peoples meant a fresh cultural synthesis. An intellectual French veteran of Montcalm's armies, Crèvecœur, who became a New York farmer, later explained for the benefit of Europeans "What is an American?" in his *Letters from an American Farmer* (1782):

I could point out to you a man, whose grandfather was an Englishman, whose wife was Dutch, whose son married a French woman, and whose present four sons have now four wives of different nations. *He* is an American, who, leaving behind him all his ancient prejudices and manners, receives new ones from the new mode of life he has embraced, the new government he obeys, and the new rank he holds . . . Here individuals of all nations are melted into a new race of men, whose labours and posterity will one day cause great change in the world.

Crèvecœur, showing the current French enthusiasm of the Enlightenment for the glories of unspoiled primitivism, saw endless vistas of progress for America, rich in natural resources and opportunity. "What attachment," he asked, "can a poor European emigrant have for a country where he had nothing?" Not a few Englishmen showed misgivings about the time when their growing American offspring would take up the leadership of the entire British Empire.

Still, the revolutionary sense of nationality was very far from capturing the entire seaboard. Washington was to lament the divided loyalties of his people, the difficulties in recruiting, the tendency of many farmers to sell produce to the more solvent British rather than to the ragged Continentals, and the aggressive attitude of the American loyalists. Families were to split on the issue of loyalty to king or Congress, their members fighting on both sides. Many a merchant who began with an outspoken resentment of England's discriminatory legislation on commerce and taxes ended up with even a greater bitterness toward the restless "mob" who threatened the sanctity of property; such a man hastened to join the loyalists. Many hundreds of frontiersmen, as among North Carolina's Regulators, though angry with Britain's land policies, found their chief enemies, as in Nathaniel Bacon's day, in the eastern gentry, now of the patriot party, who had fought their efforts to get fairer representation in the assembly, even-handed tax assessments, and effective defenses against the Indians. Here were more loyalist recruits. Newly arrived immigrants from England, too, tended to cling to homeland loyalties together with the Crown officials in the provincial capitals. Wealthy colonials were torn between the unpredictable popular forces of secession among their neighbors and the stable authority of Britain, for the issue of home rule was confused by the threat to property of Revolutionary debtors who might drown the nation in a flood of paper money and repudiate contracts should independence be won.

2

Colonial merchants like the Hancocks, the Faneuils, and the Amorys of Boston, the Livingstons of New York, and the Willings and the Whartons of Philadelphia had undoubtedly been pleased with the century of commercial prosperity that ended in 1763 after the close of the Seven Years' War. The benefits of English mercantilism, which restricted the colonial shipping business to English and colonial vessels at the expense of the Dutch, enriched native shipowners; at the same time mercantilist laws granted imperial bounties to colonials on strategic naval and other materials such as lumber, naval stores, indigo, and other commodities. Merchants did resent the political might of the British West Indies planters who had persuaded Parliament to pass the Molasses Act of 1733, thus taxing a major product of their triangular trade to Africa and the Caribbean; but this law, like other customs regulations after that year, had been poorly enforced. On the whole the merchant-aristocracy before 1764 seemed content with the mercantilistic system.

Imperial ties had also protected the merchant-creditor from schemes of inflation advanced by the farmer debtor, anxious for higher prices and the means to escape fixed debts. Debtor majorities in the assemblies of Massachusetts, Rhode Island, and South Carolina fought for "land banks," which lent bills of credit to farmers on the uncertain security of land mortgages, at low interest rates, and over long periods for repayment. Rhode Island debtors not only escaped the "merciless usurers" by land-bank issues, but when these notes reached maturity, they paid them with issues drawn from a new land bank. Merchants refused to accept such land-bank issues and Parliament came to their rescue in the Bubble Act of 1741 which outlawed land banks. With colonies like Rhode

Island persisting in their sinful ways, Parliament acted again in the Currency Act of 1751, which once more banned land banks, forbade making bills of credit acceptable as legal tender, and required prompt redemption of such bills on the date of maturity. Among the land-bank subscribers ruined by this law was the Massachusetts director, Samuel Adams, Sr., father of the famous revolutionary leader. Young Sam Adams thereupon lost his proud rank among the lesser gentry at Harvard and was forced to take up menial duties to support himself. This could scarcely have endeared England to him. While the merchant-creditor class was not too happy over the painful shortage of specie and preferred limited credit concessions, they were adamant in resisting inflationary schemes. Their economic stake coincided with that of the London investors in colonial businesses which were threatened by pro-debtor legislation. Parliament was usually solicitous toward the petitions of these London businessmen.

In so favorable a setting, the new commercial laws of 1764 and thereafter came as a painful shock to the merchants. Besides, the postwar years were marked by a sharp decline of wartime prosperity and made merchants like Hancock especially sensitive to adverse economic legislation. Britain, newly expanded by empire in Asia and America, most recently by Canada and Florida, and facing the expenses of imperial reorganization, required new revenues. The costly task of stabilizing the Indian frontier was accentuated by the struggle of 1763 against Pontiac's conspiracy. One step in this direction was the Proclamation Line of 1763 along the Alleghenies, which temporarily halted the westward advance, much to the anger of land speculators as well as bona fide settlers.

More disastrous was the Sugar Act of 1764 which, though sweetened by a 50 per cent cut in duties over the old Molasses Act of 1733, dealt a paralyzing blow to the New England "smugglers" engaged in the sugar trade with the Spanish and French West Indies. The entire colonial customs system was overhauled and efficient collections stimulated. The merchants suffering from a famine of specie due to their unfavorable balance of trade with England, had hitherto relied upon the specie obtained from the foreign West Indies, and now they were indeed in a dilemma. More than ever they hated the parliamentary lobby of the aristocratic British West Indian planters who were intent upon displacing the Spanish and French West Indian planters who undersold them in the American market and paid higher prices for colonial products. Now the New Englanders were compelled to sell their lumber, fish, and livestock for ever-declining prices in the British West Indies, while they had to pay out ever-increasing sums for the product of these sugar planters. Sam Adams, quick to detect an issue, denounced these laws as a violation of the English constitutional principle of "No taxation without representation." John Hancock, frantically seeking a profitable cargo, echoed these sentiments fervently.

In the process of tightening up the customs system and the mercantilistic laws, the Crown issued Writs of Assistance, general warrants given to local officials to search the premises of suspected smugglers. Several Boston merchants engaged James Otis in 1761 to contest the constitutionality of these writs. Contending that only specific warrants describing the suspected house were legal and that general ones affecting any person were illegal, he restated certain significant principles of Anglo-American law: "A man's house is his castle; and whilst he is quiet, he is as well guarded as a prince in his castle." He then went on to higher ground, shifting from the English principle of the supremacy of Parliament to the emergent American idea that the courts could override laws contrary to the constitution, which was understood to be a fixed thing: "No acts of Parliament can establish such a writ; though it should be made in the very words of the petition, it would be void. An act against the constitution is void." He argued that "an act against natural equity is void," thus falling back upon the liberal ideal of natural rights. "The executive courts must pass such acts into disuse," he asserted, believing he had found precedent in English law for the right of higher courts to annul legislative acts opposed to the constitutional principles of England. Though Otis lost his case in Massachusetts, other colonies later ruled that the writs were unconstitutional. His theory of a fundamental or organic law superior to ordinary legislation entered the American legal system as the supremacy of the written, and relatively permanent, constitution over mere statutes. In abolitionist times, even the Constitution fell from grace among extremists like William Seward, since its protection of slavery automatically nullified that document, overridden as it was by the "higher law" of the Stoic philosophers, the law of nature itself, which stood above all human enactments.

The Stamp Act of 1765–"that D——d Act," as Hancock put it— angered the most articulate classes—lawyers, merchants, and journalists—by taxing legal documents and newspapers. Once more the merchants struck back by canceling their English orders and by organizing a boycott of English goods. James Otis attacked "taxation without representation" in a Stamp Act Congress hastily convened to crystallize resistance. Parliament, already under fire by English businessmen, capitulated, except for a face-saving Declaratory Act asserting its final authority over the colonies. Again in 1767 the merchants, of whom Hancock was one, joined in a large-scale boycott and homespun campaign to defeat the Townshend duties on glass, lead, paint, paper, and tea. Here again, repeal followed save for the tax on tea. Of constitutional importance is the protest of the conservative Philadelphia lawyer, John Dickinson, trained in London's Middle Temple. In his widely reprinted *Letters from a Farmer in Pennsylvania,* he drew a sharp distinction between taxes for the purposes of empire regulation, which he conceded as legal, and those for revenue, which he felt invaded the rights of the colonial legislatures. Differing from radicals like Sam Adams who rejected both external and internal taxation by England regardless of purposes, Dickinson made a basic distinction between taxation primarily for regulation or for revenue which entered American constitutional law. Here, as in the Otis case was another doctrine of limited government, expressing the typically American sensitivity to centralized power.

Merchant antagonism to England flared up to new heights with the famous Boston Tea Party. The East Indies Company, on the verge of bankruptcy but strong in Parliament where its annual contributions of £400,000 to England were appreciated, sought to unload its millions of pounds of surplus tea upon the colonists. By the

Tea Act of 1773 it was given the exclusive privilege of exporting directly to American consignees without the intervention of English or American middlemen. A tax of three pence on the tea was retained, but the price was still low to the consumer. At once, American merchants like John Hancock suspected a monopolistic plot to drive them out of business, beginning with tea. Thereupon patriotic "Mohawks," after meeting at Faneuil Hall, seized the tea in Boston Harbor and dumped it in the sea. No witnesses would testify against the Mohawks. Rumor had it that Hancock, a leading tea importer, was among these Mohawks, but the merchant flatly denied it. Similar "tea parties" occurred in Charleston and New York. England responded with the Coercive Acts of 1774 against Massachusetts. By this time many of the merchants were worried over the increasing violence and mob activity and the danger that their limited movement to restore the pre-1763 system might turn into social revolution.

For example, Joseph Galloway, wealthy Philadelphia merchant, land speculator, lawyer, and member of the first Continental Congress, vainly sought to halt "mob rule" by a Plan of Union which would have established home rule within a federal framework of empire. His conservatism angered the radicals who finally drove him into the loyalist camp. When Howe evacuated Boston he took with him 200 refugee merchants including some of the oldest Massachusetts commercial families. In New York, where commercial ties with Canada and England were particularly close, most of the Chamber of Commerce were Tories. On the other hand John Hancock, heir to a vast fortune, decided after a brief period of vacillation to risk everything in the cause of Samuel Adams. He urged his English agents to lobby in Parliament against the mercantilistic laws on pain of losing their American business and commercial credits. Loving popularity and adventure as well as the patriot cause, he cast his lot in with the firebrand Sons of Liberty. When General Gage marched upon Concord in 1775, one of his objects was to capture Hancock and Sam Adams whose offenses were, as he put it, "of too flagitious a nature to admit of any other consideration but that of condign punishment." Whig committees were busily at work forcing wavering or unfriendly merchants in line behind the Continental Association of 1774, which boycotted British goods and embargoed exports, expecting to lay low the entire English economy.

3

Colonial merchants drew invaluable allies among the Southern planters and land speculators. Many, like Washington and George Mason, invested in western lands whose value was injured by the Proclamation Line of 1763 blocking settlement. Tobacco prices fell sharply in 1773 and many planters shifted to grain growing. Rice planters of Georgia and South Carolina and tobacco exporters of Virginia and Maryland were under heavy debt to London mercantile houses, even mortgaging future crops to meet the burden of ancient debts transmitted from father to son. The system of marketing crops and buying goods abroad on credit proved costly and inefficient. Washington seemed convinced that he was often cheated by his English factor. So many planters joined the patriot cause that the assumption grew that this was due to a desire to repudiate debts. However, this interpretation was vehemently denied by James Madison and George Mason, though the course of planter politics after the war showed a widespread aversion to a genuine settlement of debts.

As the interior counties of the Virginia and Carolina piedmont began to be filled in by settlers, the political, social, and economic inequalities between aristocratic Easterners and democratic Westerners became acute. In 1765-66, three western counties of North Carolina organized the Regulator movement to fight the poll tax, official extortions, unfair representation in favor of the East, and laws forbidding non-Anglican ministers to perform the marriage ceremony. After a convicted official had escaped punishment for his corruption, some two thousand Regulators resorted to violence until they were defeated by the governor in 1771 at Alamance Creek. Thereafter, frontiersmen, many of North Carolina and Virginia, sought independence by moving on to form the Watauga Settlement of Tennessee; others turned loyalist. South Carolina and

Pennsylvania had equivalent struggles for social democracy against eastern oligarchies. Tidewater Virginia held fast to its privileges and overrepresentation in the legislature, although Jefferson and Madison were to win major concessions for the back country under the revolutionary pressures of the war years and afterwards. Hunters, trappers, and farmers followed Daniel Boone through the Cumberland Gap to form new homes like the colony of Transylvania (Kentucky) across the mountains, winning a territorial stake to be defended against England and the Indians as well as against eastern encroachments.

The East-West struggle about who would rule at home took on the aspect of a tenant-landlord clash in New York. There the feudal landowners depended on royal troops in 1766 to disperse the angry mobs of Levellers who marched upon Albany to compel concessions on their leases. This colony was to furnish half of the loyalists, not only from mercantile New York city but also from among numerous large landowners—though the Livingstons and Van Rensselaers remained within the patriot ranks. New Jersey debtors rioted in 1769 to destroy the property of creditors, and small farmers elsewhere showed discontent. England's tax and regulatory legislation therefore fell at an ominous period in colonial affairs and aroused deep resentments. The farmers at Lexington and Concord who "fired the shot heard around the world" were also caught between the pressure of falling crop prices and fixed debts.

Town laborers and craftsmen, too, felt the burden of hard times, unemployment, and the threat of injurious English economic regulations. British garrison troops, accustomed to supplementing their small pay by accepting private employment, competed with Boston's hard-pressed workingmen. Thus Boston laborers came to hate the redcoats for economic as well as political reasons. The Boston Massacre of 1770 was provoked by persistent goading and missiles directed against the English garrison by the laborers. Crispus Attucks, a runaway slave, led the attack, asserting, "The way to get rid of these soldiers is to attack the main guard!" He was the first to fall in the revolutionary cause. The Sons of Liberty of Samuel Adams, Hancock, and Paul Revere, which galvanized dissent into revolution and independence, drew heavily from working-class recruits. Even before the Sons of Liberty was formed, New York sailors joined in the radical Sons of Neptune to harass the British.

Aside from class conflicts which bred discontent, the revolutionary spirit was deeply affected by religious factors. New England Congregationalists, with their 660 churches, and the numerous Presbyterians, mostly Scotch Calvinists, looked upon the British cause as the bulwark of the hated Church of England. They were alarmed by persistent reports that an Anglican episcopate would soon be established; this, they believed, would endanger their religious freedom. The pulpit was therefore enlisted for independence. Most Protestant groups were also antagonized by the Quebec Act of 1774 in which the British assured themselves of French-Canadian loyalty by extending their provincial boundaries to the Ohio and giving the Catholic Church the right to collect tithes in this area. Once more the old cry of "papist" arose. While in New England's officialdom and among the people of the middle colonies the Anglicans showed a strong pro-British tendency, Virginia's Anglicans were predominantly patriots. John Wesley's new sect of Methodists, an offshoot of the Church of England, was still a small group, remaining on the whole loyal to England. Catholics divided in their allegiance with John Carroll, the first bishop, playing an active role in influencing the French-Canadians for independence, while his brother, Charles Carroll, was a signer of the Declaration of Independence. Quakers and German Pietist groups opposed the trend toward a violent solution, though some joined the Continental Army.

4

Preceding the Declaration of Independence there crystallized a liberal American idealism expressed in the phrases of the eighteenth-century Enlightenment. In 1774 Thomas Paine son of a Quaker farmer of Norfolk, England, had arrived in Philadelphia as Franklin's protégé to edit the patriot *Pennsylvania Magazine*. Two years later appeared his *Common Sense*, demanding an immediate declaration of independence, which sold 120,000 copies within three months and proved the most convincing propaganda for complete independence.

In his pungent prose, Paine based his reasoning upon the liberal theory of a free individual unhampered by a strong state: "Society in every state is a blessing, but government, even in its best state, is but a necessary evil...Government, like dress, is the badge of lost innocence; the palaces of kings are built upon the ruins of the bowers of paradise." To secure life and property, government is chosen as a lesser evil. However, monarchies and autocracies denied the equality of men and corrupted the spirit of classical Republicanism. Besides America had come of age and no longer needed England whose wars inevitably dragged the colonists into hostility against France and Spain. " 'Tis the true interest of America," he argued, "to steer clear of European contentions, which she can never do while by her dependence on Britain she is made the makeweight in the scale of British politics." Freedom from this role would permit America to trade with all nations as well as to fortify peace. "Reconciliation and ruin are nearly related," he contended, and finally demanded a declaration of independence to attract the aid of France and Spain as well as to unite sentiment at home.

Although a resolution of Richard Henry Lee of Virginia declaring independence was adopted July 2, 1776, the formal document known as the Declaration of Independence was adopted two days later. Thomas Jefferson drafted the famous paper and submitted it for amendment to his fellow committee members, John Adams and Benjamin Franklin. The Declaration began in the classical prose style of the century:

When in the course of human events, it becomes necessary for one people to dissolve the political bands which have connected them with another, and to assume among the powers of the earth, the separate and equal station to which the Laws of Nature and of Nature's God entitle them, a decent respect to the opinions of mankind requires that they should declare the causes which impel them to the separation.

Here was the invocation of the deist to "Nature's God" and the rationalist "Laws of Nature" which had derived from the Greek and

Roman philosophers. It had been distilled through the thirteenth
century thought of St. Thomas Aquinas who had recognized "natural law" as discoverable by right reason; "eternal law" as he saw
it, came from the mind of God and was partly revealed in the Bible,
church tradition, and human reason; and finally, there was "human
law," the legislation of nations. Newton, the dominant scientist of
the age, had helped give natural law a wholly secular flavor, for
God's will seemed revealed, without mystery or theology, in the
physical laws of the universe especially in the mathematical certainty of planetary gravitation. Such was the high authority of the
Laws of Nature and of Nature's God to which Americans were appealing before world opinion for the justice of independence.

We hold these truths to be self-evident, that all men are created
equal, . . .

Despite the axiomatic certainty of "self-evident" mathematical
propositions, the authors actually performed a most significant act
of faith. Christian thinking with its doctrines of the fatherhood of
God and the brotherhood of man held that all men were equal in
the sight of God. Ulpian's *Digest* in ancient Roman times had declared that all freemen at least (not slaves) were equal before the
law. This sentiment had taken on revolutionary import tinged with
economic equality when used by medieval communists and seventeenth-century English Levellers. Middle-class philosophers, like
the Englishman John Locke, had used the phrase to justify the
Glorious Revolution of 1688; James Wilson of Pennsylvania invoked
it in 1769; and George Mason, in writing the Virginia Declaration
of Rights in June, 1776, also developed this idea. By the popular
Enlightenment theory of the social contract, men were free and
equal in their original state of nature before governments were
instituted. As a liberal, Jefferson believed in removing artificial
inequalities, such as aristocracy, created by the state and class interests, and in setting up "talent and virtue," as the criteria of superiority rather than aristocratic birth and wealth. This implied a
natural and rational order in which every individual would enjoy
equality of opportunity; it did not mean pure *laissez-faire*. Shortly

before the Declaration was written, Jefferson had proposed to the Virginia legislators that fifty acres be given to the landless and that poor squatters on western land be helped to purchase the lands on which they labored.

Tories sneered at the radical affirmation of human equality, pointing out that Jefferson, Washington, and George Mason of Gunston Hall were large slaveholders and that almost 700,000 Negroes were still in bondage. However, slavery was becoming extinct in the North; even in the South, where the tobacco plantation system was in decline, the economic props of slavery seemed to be disappearing. While Jefferson and his colleagues had no idea of abolishing differences in wealth, they hoped for the early abolition of slavery and they sensed the potentialities for future social reforms implicit in this declaration of faith in fundamental individual rights. The Republican Party of 1860, dedicated to the antislavery cause, was to write Jefferson's Declaration into their platform and to assume the name of the original Republican Party begun by the Virginian.

... that they are endowed by their Creator with certain unalienable Rights, that among these are Life, Liberty and the pursuit of Happiness.

Here, again, save for the phrase, "pursuit of happiness," Jefferson was still following Locke's *Treatise on Government* and expressing the ancient classical doctrine of "natural rights" as opposed to the unreasonable restraints of the state and of tradition. As in the case of natural law, the concept of natural rights was reinforced by the popular scientific cult of Newton and hence assumed to be incontestable. Among these rights Locke had stressed that of private ownership of property. Jefferson, like James Wilson and George Mason, had preferred to broaden this right to the Epicurean "pursuit of happiness." This epicureanism was not the vulgarized notion of seeking pleasure in a selfish and sensual way, but the ethical goal of attaining the highest happiness through peace of mind. Besides, Jefferson's ethics forbade him to base the pursuit of happiness upon mere utility; going beyond the dictates of rationalism, he believed in the existence of an innate moral sense that guided man to seek the good.

That to secure these rights, Governments are instituted among Men, deriving their just powers from the consent of the governed, . . .

This was a clear statement of the social contract that made the state the servant rather than the master of the individual, being entrusted with the duty of protecting man's natural rights. Eighteenth-century liberals like Paine and Jefferson distrusted the omnipotent state of the divine-right kings and dictators and reduced its powers to the literally expressed will of the electorate. "Strict construction" of constitutional grants followed logically.

That whenever any Form of Government becomes destructive of these ends, it is the Right of the People to alter or to abolish it, and to institute new Government, laying its foundation on such principles and organizing its powers in such form, as to them shall seem most likely to effect their Safety and Happiness.

Here was the climax: the right of revolution already discovered by Locke in 1689. However, the middle-class spirit of the Declaration, again in Locke's language, closed the door to chronic violence:

Prudence, indeed, will dictate that Governments long established should not be changed for light and transient causes; and accordingly all experience hath shown, that mankind are more disposed to suffer, while evils are sufferable, than to right themselves by abolishing the forms to which they are accustomed.

The rest of the document, by far the larger part, went on to prove that the existing abuses were such that reconciliation was impossible. Dropping the conventional fiction that a good king had been misled by evil advisers, Jefferson assailed the despotic purpose of Britain's king, citing evidence in a ringing, partisan fashion that all appeals for redress had been rebuffed; he concluded with the impressive statement, "And for the support of this Declaration, with a firm reliance on the Protection of Divine Providence, we mutually pledge to each other our Lives, our Fortunes and our sacred Honor." Fifty-six distinguished signatures followed, headed by that of John Hancock, who had been chosen president of the Continental Congress the year before. His signature, written large "so that George the Third may read without his spectacles" boldly marked him off as a leading rebel to the empire for all the world to see.

The Declaration of Independence was not only to influence the course of American thought and action but to shape the ideals of the French Revolution of 1789 and the Latin American revolutions of the early nineteenth century. Scarcely less influential was its predecessor, George Mason's Virginia Declaration of Rights of June 12, 1776, derived from Puritan and other English antecedents, which also affected the ensuing liberal revolutions and the state and federal constitutions. Its resemblance to the Declaration is obvious:

That all men are by nature equally free and independent, and have certain inherent rights, of which, when they enter into a state of society, they cannot by any compact deprive or divest their posterity; namely, the enjoyment of life and liberty, with the means of acquiring and possessing property, and pursuing and obtaining happiness and safety.

Government by consent only and the right of revolution were affirmed. Then followed guarantees of suffrage, trial by jury, freedom from arbitrary arrest and judgment, freedom of the press as "one of the great bulwarks of liberty," and finally, Patrick Henry's contribution of religious tolerance based on the idea that religious duties could be performed only through reason and conviction and should not be exacted by force or violence. A similar Bill of Rights was to be drawn in 1780 for Massachusetts by John Adams, though favor was shown to Protestants by restricting public support to these sects. By the 1850's a proslavery South and its conservative Northern allies were to reject the Declaration of Independence and the Virginia Declaration of Rights, finding too many "glittering generalities"—as Rufus Choate of Massachusetts put it—in the great documents of American liberalism.

In 1776, the year of the Declaration of Independence and the Virginia Declaration of Rights, a former Glasgow professor, Adam Smith, issued an economic version of the natural-rights philosophy in his *Wealth of Nations,* which was soon republished in Philadelphia. "Every man, as long as he does not violate the laws of justice," he wrote, "is left perfectly free to pursue his own interest his own way, and to bring both his industry and capital into competition with those of any other man, or order of men." The state retained only the duty of a policeman alert against invaders, brawlers, and criminals, and of a superintendent maintaining certain essential public works that did not attract private enterprise. Smith, champion of classical free trade and competition, assailed British mercantilistic controls and the folly of using colonial monopolies as sources of profit. Here was a declaration of economic independence from the extreme system of regulation with its bounties, tariffs, state-fostered monopolies, and erratic interference with production and distribution. Nineteenth-century liberals in England and America, though with notable exceptions, were to make a cult of Adam Smith and the "natural laws" of economics in which the ideal was to let each person buy in the cheapest market and sell in the dearest. The enlightened self-interest of the individual would be substituted for the arbitrary will of the state in making economic decisions. "In political economy," wrote Jefferson in 1790, "I think Smith's *Wealth of Nations* the best book extant."

5

Was the American Revolution a social revolution in the sense of the French and Russian revolutions? Indeed, Lafayette asserted grandly, "The era of the American Revolution . . . one can regard as the beginning of a new social order for the entire world." Perhaps it was not a social revolution, but certain fundamental changes seem to have taken shape at least. So many of the loyalists were aristocrats who lost vast properties and were themselves expelled that some modification took place in the class structure, though of far less significance than the expulsion of the French aristocrats in the 1790's or of the Russian nobles or *bourgeoisie* in 1917-20. American Committees of Safety, armed with revolutionary power, probed enemy suspects, exiled many, and even condemned to death those who joined the king's army—though this extreme penalty was rare

The new state governments passed severe treason laws and confiscated loyalist estates. Pennsylvania's blacklist of active Tories was notorious. "America could carry on two years' war by the confiscation of the property of disaffected persons," advised Paine in his pamphlet, *The Crisis,* "and be made happy by their expulsion."

Tory estates, many of them princely in size, did help to finance the war; besides, confiscation seemed preferable to the aimless vandalism of colonial mobs. New York, where large aristocratic manors dotted the landscape, alone confiscated the estates of at least fifty-nine Tories worth about $3,600,000—an active precedent for the French revolutionary confiscations of clerical property that served to bolster the sagging national finances. Unfortunately, too many of the poorer tenants lost everything in this process, for the bargains in Tory estates were snapped up by speculators, merchants, and well-to-do Revolutionary leaders like the Livingstons and the Van Rensselaers. Eventually, however, most of these buyers broke up their large land parcels into small farms and lots, an important step toward an agrarian democracy. Thus the New York manors of the fabulously wealthy De Lanceys and the Roger Morris' were never reconstituted but gave way to far smaller proprietors.

Outspoken Tories of the lesser gentility were popularly treated to tar and feathers, ducking, or being drummed out of town by the "Sons of Licentiousness"—as the Tories called the businesslike Sons of Liberty. Royal sympathizers faced total ostracism. Among the most popular revolutionary literature was John Trumbull's satire on the Tories in *M' Fingal* (1775), which established the literary reputation of this "Connecticut Wit" of Hartford:

> Finding no tokens of repentance,
> This court proceeds to render sentence:
> That first the mob a slip-knot single
> Tie round the neck of said M'Fingal
> And in due form do tar him next,
> And feather, as the law directs,
> Then through the town attendant ride him
> In cart with constable beside him.

This satire, reflecting the "wit literature" of the *Spectator*, was sold through thirty pirated editions by street hawkers and peddlers, and appeared in the newspapers.

Among the Tories was the wealthy Governor Thomas Hutchinson of Massachusetts, colonial historian and descendant of the famous radical Antinomian Anne Hutchinson whom Puritan bigots had expelled from Boston. The governor's sympathies at first remained with his people, but his policy of enforcing the hateful parliamentary laws raised suspicions of his loyalty. In 1765, Boston toughs destroyed his mansion, stripping it of all valuables and throwing into the street his precious historical collections as well as the manuscript second volume of his *History of Massachusetts Bay*. His correspondence with Parliament, intercepted by the American Whigs, compromised him as a critic of the patriots. In 1774, he fled to England and there showed increasing bitterness toward the American cause. His property was confiscated by the revolutionists.

Another noted Tory was the scientist Benjamin Thompson, the later Count Rumford of Bavaria, who had been trained at Harvard. Once an apprentice to a Salem shopkeeper, he had married a wealthy widow enjoying friendly contacts with British officialdom. Though he denied disloyalty when the war broke out, he apparently furnished information to General Gage regarding the patriot forces, left his family to become a secret British agent, and finally secured a position in the British Foreign Office. Invited to serve the Bavarian Elector, he proved an able administrator and, in his official capacity, founded or improved hospitals, asylums, and living conditions. As Count Rumford of the Holy Roman Empire, he won note as a physicist. He devised improvements for home heating, cooking, and lighting, invented a photometer and calorimeter, and founded several learned societies.

Not all Tories were aristocrats—far from it. Many were plain people who failed to make the required transfer in loyalty from king to Whiggism. John Adams estimated that perhaps one-third of the colonists were either active or passive Tories. Of these, according to Dr. Claude H. Van Tyne, two-thirds were born in the British Isles. Some 60,000 left for Nova Scotia, 25,000 more went elsewhere in Canada; others emigrated to the West Indies or England. Some 2,000 loyalist planters left Savannah, for example, taking with them 5,000 slaves. For Americans, suffering through a long, painful war, harassed by Tory spies, guerrillas, and their Indian allies, as well as by loyalists within the British army, tolerance in wartime was difficult indeed.

Aristocracy not only lost many adherents as the loyalists fled, but its structure was badly shaken when Jefferson and the Virginia liberals attacked the props of feudal stability—primogeniture, entail, and quitrents. Primogeniture, which limited inheritance to the eldest son in order to perpetuate large estates, and its related law of entail, which restricted the alienation of land, were abolished in Virginia between 1776 and 1785 and were largely eliminated elsewhere in the new nation before the century ended. Entailed Tory estates, such as the vast holdings of the Penn family in Pennsylvania and of Sir William Pepperell of Maine, were broken up in favor of individualistic fee simple tenure, transferable at will. The quitrent, a feudal survival which theoretically implied personal fealty by the farm owner to an original proprietor through perpetual (though small) rents, was swept away in Virginia in 1777 and this example spread elsewhere in the southern and middle states where quitrents had existed. By 1788, Washington was to claim far too optimistically, that "the distinction of classes begins to disappear" in favor of a classical republican spirit of equality.

Liberalism, which sought the maximum of individual freedom, won another victory in the revolutionary movement for the separation of church and state. During the war years, the Virginia Assembly debated Jefferson's "Bill for Establishing Religious Freedom" until it reached the statute book in 1785-86. Here, the Anglican Church, popularly associated with the entrenched power of the tidewater planters, was disestablished through an alliance of Baptists, Presbyterians, and liberal Episcopalians. Religious liberalism swept away discriminations favoring Anglicanism in New York, Maryland, and the Carolinas, though New England continued, as in colonial days, with certain concessions, to maintain Congregationalism as the established cult. Tolerance for Catholics advanced, partly because of the necessities of the French alliance and the public appreciation of Father John Carroll's services in promoting the American cause among French-Canadians. In 1775, Washington forbade the army to celebrate "Pope Day" (Guy Fawkes Day), which must have relieved American as well as French Catholics. So far did revolutionary liberalism go in removing restrictions on Catholics that Father Carroll was able to write exultingly in 1779 to a friend, "I am glad to inform you that the fullest and largest system of toleration is adopted in almost all the American states." Thus ended the long era of discrimination against American Catholics. The Northwest Ordinance of 1787, which guaranteed religious freedom, nevertheless showed evidences of the older belief in the responsibility of the state for religion by providing that:

Religion, morality, and knowledge, being necessary to good government and the happiness of mankind, schools and the means of education shall forever be encouraged.

This ambivalent attitude regarding the separation of church and state in the Old Northwest was to be reflected in a perennial legal controversy over the teaching of the Bible in public schools. In Virginia, Patrick Henry and Richard Henry Lee fought a losing battle for state responsibility for Christianity by trying to make churches tax-supported. Some accord on the point was reached by the framers of the Constitution in the First Amendment: "Congress shall make no law respecting the establishment of religion or prohibiting the free exercise thereof."

The revolutionary doctrine of the equality of man met its severest test in the rising agitation to abolish slavery. Planters with worn-out tobacco lands and surplus slaves were ready to join the Jeffersonian movement to outlaw the slave trade. Only the resistance of South Carolina and Georgia, whose plantations still required imported Africans, prevented the framers of the Constitution from extending the state bans against the slave trade to the entire nation. Jefferson, Washington, and Richard Henry Lee, though slave-owners, wished to see slavery, itself, abolished, but they were in the minority. As a state legislator, Jefferson had proposed gradual emancipation to be followed by colonization of the blacks, perhaps to an independent Negro republic in the interior of the continent. He believed that racial prejudices and lingering Negro resentments made colonization necessary. Virginia then had 200,000 slaves, amounting to half of the entire population. In his *Notes on Virginia,* Jefferson asserted:

The whole commerce between master and slave is a perpetual exercise of the most boisterous passions, the most unremitting despotism on the one part, and degrading submissions on the other. Our children see this, and learn to imitate it... And can the liberties of a nation be thought secure when we have removed their only firm basis, a conviction in the minds of the people that these liberties are of the gift of God? ... Indeed I tremble for my country when I reflect that God is just: that His justice cannot sleep forever ...

Quaker reformers like John Woolman and Anthony Benezet persuaded Pennsylvania to undertake gradual emancipation in 1780. Benezet, whose original antislavery ideas were then being freely borrowed by John Wesley for the latter's *Thoughts on Slavery* (1774), also organized a society to help the free Negroes who had been fraudulently re-enslaved, and he convinced Quaker leaders in 1776 that they should expel all slaveowners from their sect. Vermont's Constitution of 1777 was the first to forbid slavery, and during the early postwar years, the rest of New England committed itself to some form of emancipation.

As for the Negroes themselves, John H. Franklin estimates that 5,000 served with the Revolutionary armies, though others, attracted by British offers of freedom, joined England's forces. Patriots hesitated to enlist Negroes, slave or free, because of the fears of race war, but Washington reversed this policy after the loyalists began actively recruiting slaves by promising them freedom. A French army that included 700 Haitian Negroes arrived at Savannah in 1779 as allies for the Americans. In Virginia, according to Jefferson's estimate, as many as 30,000 slaves escaped to freedom. Encouraged and often transported by the British, perhaps three-fourths of Georgia's slaves and 25,000 more in South Carolina disappeared.

Despite the liberalizing atmosphere of the Revolution, the slave-owners were to write into the Constitution a demand for the return of fugitive slaves (as well as of others "held to service or labour"), setting aside local regulations and practices interfering with the delivery of such runaways.

The liberals advanced upon still another sector, that of popular education, the prime requisite for an intelligent electorate. Young Jefferson, whose frontier upbringing and modest farm background may have predisposed him toward the interests of the small farmer and the underprivileged, despite his large plantation and a wealthy marriage, again took the leadership of the Virginia liberals in the House of Delegates in 1776 against the tidewater aristocrats. He introduced a public library bill. More important, he fought for an entire system of public education, free to those who could not afford to pay, in which the state would be divided into districts, each with an elementary school where American and English history as well as the "three R's" would be taught to both boys and girls. Promising boys of poor families would be subsidized to go on through formal grammar school and college. This proposal proved too radical for the Assembly, which refused to act until 1796 and then offered but a shadow of the original bill. The Virginian was also to help shape the federal education provision of the Land Or-dinance of 1785 for the Northwest Territory: "There shall be re-served the lot No. 16, of every township, for the maintenance of public schools within the said township."

Jefferson's bill for his Alma Mater, the College of William and Mary, is significant for its aspirations, rather than their realization. Criticizing the college as a mere adjunct of the Established Church with a narrow bias favoring an orthodox theology, he called for an institution that would provide "guardians of the rights and liber-ties of their country." He wished to abolish the school of theology, allowing a larger staff to teach "the laws of nature and of nations, fine arts, law, mathematics, civil and ecclesiastical history, medi-cine, natural philosophy and natural history, as well as ancient and modern languages." This university ideal belonged to a later gen-eration. He feared that education abroad for youth in the early

1780's meant exposure to aristocratic influences and dissipation and asserted that William and Mary offered as excellent a training in liberal arts and science as any European college. As governor of Virginia in 1779-81, he took a pioneer step in the history of American higher education by introducing professorships of law, medicine, and modern languages to his favorite college. In 1786, he wrote from Paris to his friend, George Wythe, "Preach, my dear Sir, a crusade against ignorance; establish and improve the law for educating the common people." Thus he expressed his rejection of the feudal tradition of education for the classes and manual training for the masses.

Liberals like Jefferson broke, also, with medieval traditions in promoting the secular spirit in education. Dartmouth, it is true, was created in 1769 out of Eleazar Wheelock's Indian missionary school, and Rhode Island College in 1764 from Baptist efforts. However, Howard Mumford Jones has pointed out that while of ten colleges founded by 1776 only one was non-sectarian, during the next twenty years fourteen were founded of which only four were denominational. The rationalist spirit of the Enlightenment made such inroads that orthodox Yale's students were referring to one another as Voltaire, Rousseau, D'Alembert, and other such radical idols, while the no less orthodox Princeton was said to have only two professing Christians in the student body by 1782. Deism made numerous converts among the intellectuals.

Rationalism grew during the war. An army chaplain, Timothy Dwight, later noted as a leader of the Connecticut Wits and a conservative president of Yale, recalled, "Infidelity began to obtain in this country an extensive currency and reception." In 1784 appeared *Reason, the Only Oracle of Man*, attributed to the frontier Deist and hero of Ticonderoga, Ethan Allen of Vermont, though the authorship really belongs to a British physician, Dr. Thomas Young. "Ethan Allen's Bible," as it was called, stirred up strong censure from the orthodox. At King's Chapel, the Episcopalian James Freeman, a Harvard graduate of "latitudinarian" tendencies, decided in 1785, with the consent of his congregation to omit that section of the liturgy dealing with the mystical Trinitarian doctrine, which

held that God is in three persons, the Father, the Son, and the Holy
Ghost. Like Locke and Milton, he returned to the sixteenth century
"Unitarian" rationalism of Servetus and Socinus. Thus King's
Chapel, the first Episcopal Church in New England, became the
first Unitarian Church in the western hemisphere. Within the next
decade, many liberal Congregationalists, long estranged from strict
Calvinism, were to embrace Unitarianism, as the sect came to be
called. Sabbath-day observances declined, though Boston, at least,
retained its Sunday quiet, and Samuel Adams, for all his revolutionary fervor, remained a narrow Calvinist. By 1782, New Englanders had officially dropped the use of the notorious scarlet letter
for adultery.

Still, the Great Awakening had done its work too thoroughly for
religious conservatism to lose out. Virginia Baptists staged large-
scale revivals during 1785-89, adding thousands of new members
for revealed religion. Under the leadership of the able Bishop
Francis Asbury, Methodist preachers made sensational gains in
winning converts during the great revivals of the 1780's, especially
in Georgia and North Carolina. By the 1780's the followers of Wesley had organized the well-knit Methodist Episcopal Church, which
remained independent of England. Catholicism retained its traditional theology though rationalism estranged many a Franco-American. Orthodox American Anglicanism revived in 1786, despite
revolutionary inroads, being organized in that year as the new Protestant Episcopal Church of the United States under an American
bishop who held no direct state connection with the Church of
England.

Stimulated by the liberal revolutionary spirit, popular interest
turned to criminology and prison reform on both sides of the Atlantic. English statute books, though not everyday practice, still
made 160 crimes punishable by death. Stealing a loaf of bread for
a starving family merited hanging just as did killing a human being.
The age-old emphasis on harsh punishment led to such monstrosi-
ties as Connecticut's Newgate jail, which was an abandoned copper
mine underground whose utter darkness and cold terrorized its oc-
cupants. Elsewhere, with too few exceptions, the jails were filthy,

infected with typhus, and crowded with prisoners who lived on starvation rations. Debtors and criminals, youths and hardened characters, shared a single cell. Children often accompanied imprisoned mothers. Jailers, lacking a salary, compensated themselves by graft, callously stripping prisoners of their belongings. Chain gangs working on the streets of New York and Philadelphia aroused the sympathies of bystanders instead of the condemnation intended. The situation was far worse in Europe. England retained such customs as beheading, breaking on the wheel, and whipping. Some German jails shut off practically all air and light and tortured prisoners in medieval style. Branding and mutilation were still common in western civilization.

From Italy came the epochal theories of Cesare Beccaria, a criminologist and economist of Milan, whose *Essay on Crimes and Punishments* (1767) won the praise of such rationalist reformers as Voltaire, Blackstone, Jeremy Bentham, and John Howard. Jefferson and Charles Carroll in this country were deeply impressed by Beccaria who anticipated the main lines—except for psychiatry—followed by modern criminology. Beccaria shifted the emphasis from punishment, which he regarded as only partly preventive of crime, to the idea of rehabilitating the prisoner. To deter crime, he felt that punishment must be swift and according to the nature of the damage done to society. Imprisonment must offer a scientific mode of re-educating the criminal. Capital punishment must be abolished. There was no room for barbarity in this system. One of Beccaria's disciples, John Howard, an English squire who had once been a sheriff, wrote *The State of the Prisons* (1777), which offered an analysis and program that became the bible of a generation of prison reformers.

In Virginia, Jefferson, Mason, George Wythe, and James Madison were instrumental in revising the criminal code, beginning in 1776, by abolishing most of the barbaric practices of a crude age. Capital punishment was replaced by hard labor, except for treason and murder. However, the conservatives insisted on retaining the practice of mutilating prisoners for abnormal sex crimes. Jefferson helped design the new Richmond State Prison, modeled after mod-

ern French and English examples, which separated prisoners according to both crime and sex, and he introduced the dubious improvement of solitary labor for the chain gang. Pennsylvania, which
had vacillated between the humane code of William Penn and the
harsh contemporary English and Continental practices, was influenced by the Quakers and the brilliant follower of Beccaria, Dr.
Benjamin Rush of Philadelphia, who published in 1787 *An Inquiry
into the Effects of Public Punishments Upon Criminals and Upon
Society.* He stressed the rehabilitation of the criminal as the goal of
punishment and wished to remodel the jails into communities of
homes, shops, churches, and gardens. One of America's earliest psy-
chiatrists, Rush looked upon crime as a disease of the mind. He
attacked capital punishment with an epigram, "Murder is propa-
gated by hanging for murder." In the name of "reason and humanity," he demanded the abolition of the pillory, stocks, gallows,
and whipping posts. His state, which had executed forty-nine for
burglary and four for rape during 1779-89, abolished capital punishment for all offenses except murder in 1794, and its revised criminal code forbade cruel treatment of prisoners. Philadelphia, long a
leader in humanitarian reform, reclassified her prisoners according
to crime and sex, gave her jailers fixed salaries to discourage graft,
and forbade the dispensing of liquor to prisoners. However, this
example was slow to affect other states, though prison reform was
a constant theme of discussion.

The Revolutionary era forced Americans to decide upon the future course of Anglo-American law. Hostility to things English
tempted legal minds to embark on the path of French law, which
stood high, especially in the ensuing decades. "Had there been generally available translations of French law books, the course of
American legal history might well have been different," declared
Roscoe Pound, the legal historian. The English common law with
its technicalities had helped breed a race of lawyers who were hated
by the unpropertied for their zeal in behalf of English creditors and
tidewater aristocrats. Jefferson flatly declared, "I deride the ordinary
doctrine that we brought with us from England the Common Law
rights." However, in the colonial struggle against the Crown, the

principles of the common law that Sir Edward Coke had used in fighting Stuart absolutism proved just as useful against George III. James Otis and the merchants fought English revenue inspectors in the name of the common law principle that an Englishman's home is his castle; thus the common law became the birthright of Americans in the struggle against arbitrary power. Although the common law was to hamper the growth of unions during the nineteenth century because of its doctrines of "restraint of trade" and "conspiracy," it also contained within itself an invaluable arsenal for civil liberties.

Perhaps the greatest blow for English law against its French competitor was struck by William Blackstone, judge of the Common Pleas and former professor of English Law at Oxford, who published his lectures on the eve of the Revolution as *Commentaries on the Laws of England* (1765-69). Though a Tory in outlook, Blackstone expressed the popular natural-law philosophy of Locke, Pufendorf, and Montesquieu, so attractive to the American mind. In a lucid, systematic form, he straightened the jumble of accumulated English laws into a coherent, symmetrical pattern showing their continuity and reasonableness and their relation to history and philosophy. American legal conservatives who were to dominate textbook-writing looked upon Blackstone, who spoke the language of the "scholar and gentleman," as their model until he became the ideal of the entire profession. His *Commentaries* molded generations of susceptible American law students, many of whom were thus indirectly introduced to the penology of Beccaria in whom Blackstone, as a prison reformer, was deeply interested.

6

Life in wartime was disrupted for a country upon whose soil the battles were fought despite the fact that Washington's forces, varying between 2400 and 27,000 men, took but few from a population of nearly three million people. Colonial towns like Boston, Newport, New York, and Philadelphia bore the inevitable marks of foreign occupation in destroyed buildings and goods. The enemy wasted fields, killed livestock, and abducted slaves. Atrocities were com-

SOCIETY AND THOUGHT

mitted not only by the mercenary Hessian soldier and Indians, but also by American guerrillas, vengeful frontiersmen, and free-lance lawbreakers. Britain's 30,000 "Hessian" mercenaries, actually from Brunswick as well as Hesse-Cassel, deserted in droves to the Americans—attracted by land grants. An estimated 12,500 did not return to Germany; some, of course, were killed, others went to Canada; the majority scattered among the older German-American communities where no official could sell men into foreign armies. The improvised nature of a war for independence in a divided country led to much unnecessary suffering of which the tragedy of the starving and freezing Valley Forge troops in a rich farm land is a notorious example. Soldiers were fed on unbalanced fare until John Adams could say, "Our frying-pans and gridirons slay more than the sword."

Wartime inflation, which reflected the brisk demand for native goods by Americans and British and the reliance of Congress upon such inflationary devices as unsecured Continental paper currency, forced down this paper in 1780 to a point where forty such dollars were worth but a dollar in specie. The Articles of Confederation gave Congress the power to requisition the states for funds but provided no method for enforcement. Scarcities led crowds to jostle each other to buy the available foods and goods at the local shops and stores. Infant war industries, encouraged by Congress and private societies, boomed, and so did privateering. However, the British blockade injured the tobacco planters and the withdrawal of mercantilistic bounties ruined the indigo industry. Trading with the enemy, as in the French and Indian wars, was common on both land and sea, encouraged as it was by the attractions of British gold.

The colonial press—there were thirty-seven newspapers in 1775—reflected the war spirit and colored the news according to patriot or Tory bias, using large type to achieve sensational effects. Samuel Adams depended heavily upon the influential Boston *Gazette* (though the circulation was but 2000), and rebels like Otis and Hancock wrote for it, as they also did for the *Massachusetts Spy*. The *Pennsylvania Journal* of William Bradford III published Thomas Paine's first stirring *Crisis* paper of December 23, 1776, which raised the spirits of colonial patriots during Washington's retreat through New Jersey:

These are the times that try men's souls. The summer soldier and the sunshine patriot will, in this crisis, shrink from the service of his country; but he that stands it *now*, deserves the love and thanks of man and woman. Tyranny, like hell, is not easily conquered; yet we have this consolation with us, that the harder the conflict, the more glorious the triumph.

Britons were surprised by the power of the colonial patriot press. As for the Tory newspapers in British-held areas, they were boycotted, and once the British troops withdrew, their editors were likely to be mobbed.

Science, as Carl Bridenbaugh points out, was a casualty of the war. While Paine wrote his *Crisis* paper, the eminent David Rittenhouse of Philadelphia called for breaking up the schools and concentrating upon defense. Originally a clockmaker by trade, he had through independent study risen to become a leading astronomer. He built orreries—models showing planetary motion—for Princeton and the College of Philadelphia. In 1769 he had represented Franklin's American Philosophical Society on a Harvard-sponsored project observing the transit of Venus. At that time he had built an observatory and a transit telescope, perhaps the first made in this country. Now he was buried in his work as president of the Pennsylvania Council of Safety and as a member of the state assembly. After the war he was to invent a new type of collimating telescope. Franklin himself, who began the war years by organizing a continental post-office system to replace the imperial office, became increasingly involved in diplomacy, especially the negotiations for the French alliance, and in other political problems. A notable exception to the rule of cultural sterility in wartime was William Bartram of Philadelphia, famous son of a famous father, who continued the latter's significant botanical work through his collections of plant specimens and his observations on Indian and wild life in the Carolinas, Georgia, the Floridas, and in the West. These experiences furnished the material for his book *Travels* (1791) which won acclaim here and abroad, being translated into German, French, and other languages, and even influencing in later years the romantic poetry of Chateaubriand, Coleridge, and Wordsworth. Coleridge's *Kubla Khan* carried magnificent passages based on Bartram's observations.

The battlefield did give scientific employment to a growing band of physicians, especially those of the new College of Philadelphia, the first medical school in America. One of its staff was Dr. Benjamin Rush, professor of chemistry, who had taken his M.D. at the pre-eminent University of Edinburgh. Rush relied on a balanced diet and beverages to a greater extent than he did on medicines and showed a deep interest in psychiatry long before it achieved status as a science. Despite inevitable shortcomings in the medical theory of any eighteenth-century doctor, he proved a wholesome influence in a day when charlatans were monopolizing the press with patent medicines guaranteed to cure almost every ill and half-trained physicians sent many a person to his reward long before his time.

Although the Revolutionary leaders introduced tests to determine qualified doctors, too few of those accepted were actually competent and supplies were woefully short. Thousands of soldiers were carried away by dysentery, camp fever (putrid fever), and typhoid, though doctors like Rush saved many from the recurring smallpox epidemics by insisting on wholesale inoculation. Dr. Rush, never restrained in expressing his opinions on any subject, attacked the Medical Director-General as a corrupt, inefficient politician and charged that the focal centers for infection were the hospitals. "They robbed the United States of more citizens than the sword," he contended. In 1785 he was to establish the first dispensary in the country.

War meant a total eclipse of the theater and put a damper upon public recreation. On October 20, 1774, the Continental Congress requested that Americans "discourage all horse racing and all kinds of gaming, cock fighting, exhibitions of shows, plays, and other expensive diversions and entertainments." Most players preferred to follow the example of Douglass' American Company which left for the West Indies. Possibly an exception to this rule of a vacant stage were the war plays of Mrs. Mercy Warren, sister of James Otis and wife of the Massachusetts Speaker of the House. Mrs. Warren, an outstanding intellectual of her sex who was often sought for political advice by the Adamses and Thomas Jefferson, wrote *The Adulator* and *The Group* as satires upon the Tories. Earliest of American playwrights, she was also later to write a book of poems and a three-volume history of the American Revolution.

In 1784, a reorganized American Company, now under Lewis Hallam, Jr., returned to Philadelphia and New York and once more the splendor of the theater revived. Three years later New York witnessed a performance of the first American comedy produced professionally, *The Contrast,* written by Royall Tyler. He was a Harvard-trained lawyer who had served in the Revolution and only the previous year had fought to suppress the radical farmers in Shays' Rebellion. *The Contrast* had a popular theme in contrasting the decadent fop with the plain democracy of the American patriot. The prologue began proudly in this nationalistic vein:

> Exult, each patriot heart!—This night is shewn
> A piece, which we may fairly call our own
> Where the proud titles of "My Lord! Your Grace!"
> To humble Mr. and plain Sir give place.
> Our author pictures not from foreign climes
> The fashions or the follies of the times;
> But has confin'd the subject of his work
> To the gay scenes--the circles of New York.
> On native themes his muse displays her pow'rs;
> If ours the faults, the virtues too are ours
> Why should our thoughts to distant countries roam,
> When each refinement may be found at home?

This self-congratulatory theme, elaborated in a spectacular stage setting, was developed in *The Father* by William Dunlap, a portrait painter who had studied with Benjamin West. Dunlap was a prolific playwright who wrote thirty plays--one a year in fact—and later became a theatrical manager who was to round out a long career with his *History of the American Theatre* (1832) and *A History of New Netherland* (1836-39). While the well-to-do supported the theater as a contribution to art, morals, and Americanism, and sought to establish a state-supported theater in Pennsylvania in 1785, rural leaders remained suspicious of the role of the aristocratic theater in a democratic society.

As with other wars, the Revolution had its full quota of popular songs, ballads, and hymns. From the French and Indian War had come "Yankee Doodle," which probably originated as a British thrust at the seedy-looking American militia. This burlesque of the Yankee, expressing so clearly the cheeky self-confidence of the young republic, was proudly taken up by the revolutionists in their defiance of England. Soldiers sang "The Yankee's Return from Camp" and many other political variations, including some unprintable ones, to the tune of "Yankee Doodle." The Sons of Liberty were to adopt John Dickinson's version of "The Liberty Song":

> Come join hand in hand, brave Americans all,
> And rouse your bold hearts at fair Liberty's call,
> No tyrannous acts shall suppress your just claim,
> Nor stain with dishonor America's name.

Songs dealt with the Boston Tea Party, the martyrdom of Nathan Hale, episodes of the war, and independence. Francis Hopkinson, the first poet-composer of America, lived an amazingly varied career as a Revolutionary patriot. He designed the American flag, participated in the first Continental Congress, where he signed the Declaration of Independence, and acted as treasurer for Congress. Still, he had time to write a humorous ballad, "The Battle of the Kegs" (1778), based on a wartime incident in his native Philadelphia. Hopkinson was to cap his musical career in 1788 with the publication of *Seven Songs,* considered one of the first books of music composed by an American. As a lawyer, graduating from the College of Philadelphia, he was to succeed in this field also, but his reputation lay in his musical art, his painting, and his poems and prose of social and political satire. Loyalist song writers, too, were active in the Revolution but suffered from an obvious disadvantage.

In art, the young republic remained provincial, notwithstanding several painters of unusual gifts. Patronage was limited and rustic minds classified painters with hairdressers and buffoons. Portraits were prized as a fulfillment of a filial task to preserve the memory of one's ancestors and the duty of transmitting one's likeness to an admiring posterity. Only Europe, London particularly, offered American artists the necessary patronage and appreciation. In Revolutionary days the cynosure of all eyes was upon the expatriate Benjamin West of London, "the American Raphael" who had left his native Chester County of eastern Pennsylvania with the aid of wealthy sponsors to study Renaissance works in Rome. He had been influenced by a disciple of Johann Joachim Winckelmann who was then crystallizing a bourgeois ideal in the neoclassical style, which stressed the universal, the "noble simplicity and quiet grandeur" of heroic republican Rome. This rejected the pomp and elaborate pretensions of the seventeenth-century baroque spirit. The cult of the slavish antique swept England in the age of Joshua Reynolds and Thomas Gainsborough and led art patrons to turn their backs upon the masterly sincerity and satire of Hogarth, which they considered vulgar, and to accept West's elegant, pallid classicism as expressed in his "Agrippina with the Ashes of Germanicus." West's "grand historic style" and "nature in the abstract" won him the patronage of George III, whose understanding in art as in statesmanship was sadly deficient, but who made possible the sale of his huge canvases, which were too large even for the well-to-do Englishman's home. However, West did not wholly lose the quality of realism he had acquired in his early experiments in Pennsylvania. His picture, "The Death of Wolfe," showed a sick, suffering soldier rather than a hero striking a dramatic attitude, as the classicists would have liked. The Penn family commissioned him to portray "William Penn's Treaty with the Indians," which won fame primarily for its subject matter, but was not without some realistic qualities.

Most significantly for American art, West was the painstaking teacher of an entire generation of artists from the New World, John Singleton Copley, Gilbert Stuart, Charles Willson Peale, John Trumbull, Washington Allston, William Dunlap, and a host of others. Copley, who gladly left turbulent Boston on the eve of the Revolution, as did Gilbert Stuart, had won the warm praise of West and

Reynolds for the realistic "Boy with Squirrel" painting he had sent
to London and had been encouraged by them to desert his provincial aristocratic clients for study in Rome. Thereafter, in London,
his work tended to be derivative after West's style, though financially successful. However, "The Death of Chatham" showed genuine technical brilliance and outshone West's historical canvases. The
Marylander, Charles Willson Peale, displayed the neoclassicism of
his teacher in "Pitt as a Roman Senator," which pictured the statesman in a toga. After returning to America in 1769, he won many
clients for his elegant portraits picturing Washington in the convincing pose of a country gentleman rather than as an elusive
abstraction; in later years, he executed an honest craftsmanlike
likeness of "Franklin at 81." At Valley Forge he completed forty
excellent miniatures of American officers and, with Copley, he was
to occupy a pre-eminent rank in the early American tradition. The
story of West's other remarkable students belongs to a later era.

7

The "realism" of the Constitution of 1787 has often been unfavor-
ably contrasted with the "idealism" of the Declaration of Independence and the liberal revolutionary spirit. Yet, by the world standards
of 1787 at least, the Constitution represented a major step toward
democratic equality as well as a series of compromises between
economic groups in which the propertied creditor class held the
chief advantages. The so-called Critical Era of 1783-87 was scarcely
a "Thermidorian reaction" in the French revolutionary sense, when
in 1794 the conservative counterrevolutionists were to snatch the
ship of state from the Robespierre terrorists. It is true that once the
question of independence was decided, Hancock, Patrick Henry,
Hamilton, and John Jay reverted to the older colonial question of
who shall rule at home, creditors or debtors, merchants or farmers,
East or West. Still, the clock could not be wholly turned back to
the days when the colonial gentry ruled the country. The Enlightenment and the social effects of the Revolution had caused the unfolding of liberal ideas, institutions, and economic changes that

could only culminate eventually in an enhanced role for the masses.

Charles Beard, in his challenging book *An Economic Interpretation of the Constitution of the United States* (1913), rejected the older view of John Fiske that this document grew out of the virtual collapse of the Articles of Confederation during the Critical Era and that it was a product of popular forces. Instead, he stressed the role of four pressure groups among the fifty-five men who completed the Constitution: public security-holders, manufacturers, shipping interests, and financial speculators. "As a group of doctrinaires, like the Frankfort assembly of 1848, they would have failed miserably," he wrote, "but as practical men they were able to build the new government upon the only foundations which could be stable: fundamental economic interests." Thus, security-holders counted upon the effect of a strong government in raising the value of depreciated securities; manufacturers expected uniform tariffs against foreign competition, which the Articles could not offer; shipping interests likewise sought effective commercial legislation; and creditors wished to keep debtors from dangerous schemes of repudiation and reckless inflation. In a day when property qualifications for voting eliminated the poorer classes, it was possible for the Constitution to be ratified by a vote of about one-sixth of the adult males. Thus, as Beard put it, the Constitution "was the work of a consolidated group whose interests knew no state boundaries and were truly national in their scope."

The economic background of the Constitution is therefore significant. While the war ended the bounties and guaranteed markets of British mercantilism and the French hesitated to grant commercial equality to the new republic, American shippers managed to win new markets in the Baltic and the Mediterranean. Smugglers broke through British restrictions in the West Indies. More serious was the postwar decline in prices and the end of war scarcities, which meant that the farmer was weighed down once more by fixed debts and declining money income in a land perennially short of specie. Again they sought a panacea in inflationary paper money to save their farms from foreclosure. Most states, especially Rhode Island, resorted to the printing press. Disgruntled farmers as well as new immigrants moved to the West and settled along the Mississippi; there Spain played the role of siren to Westerners who were driven by need as well as by geographic distance to calculate the advantages of union over separatism. Secession, not an unfamiliar idea for American revolutionists, might give them the commercial navigation of the Spanish-controlled Mississippi River.

In Massachusetts, Governor John Hancock and his conservative coalition of merchants and lawyers entrenched themselves behind a constitution of their own liking. The distressed farmers, hurt by the commercial depression of 1785-86, violently protested the heavy poll taxes, exorbitant legal costs, high official salaries, uncompromising foreclosures, and debt imprisonment. Hancock himself managed to keep his popularity by withdrawing temporarily from politics on the eve of the debtor's revolt, returning thereafter triumphantly to be re-elected governor year after year until his death. His aristocratic carriage drawn by six horses and accompanied by four servants and his equally aristocratic case of gout did not hamper his vote-getting talents.

Captain Daniel Shays, who had fought in the ranks at Bunker Hill and Saratoga, led an armed revolt of farmers from the Connecticut Valley and the Berkshire Hills in 1786. The rebels surrounded the local courts including the state supreme court until routed by Governor James Bowdoin of Massachusetts and General Lincoln's militia. Congress, anxiously watching this incipient social revolution, was prepared to recruit and to throw in federal troops if necessary.

Here was an overwhelming argument, especially for creditor groups, for a government stronger than that possible under the Articles of Confederation. The new federal Constitution was to protect economic minorities by a system of indirect elections, by the separation of powers, and a check and balance system. State legislatures, such as those of Rhode Island and her imitators, were to be forbidden the power to limit bills of credit, to "make anything but gold and silver coin a tender in payment of debts," or to pass laws "impairing the obligation of contracts." This, it was hoped, would end the paper money menace and debt repudiation. The Lockian idea that the purpose of government is to protect property was clearly expressed in the arguments for ratifying the Constitution, especially in the *Federalist Papers* issued in 1787 by John Jay, Alexander Hamilton, and James Madison. All stressed the idea of checks and balances against undesirable majority action, authority for which was founded in Montesquieu and Polybius and implied in the classical Newtonian world of neatly poised planets suspended in space by the gravitational forces of attraction and repulsion. The theory that democratic government had its principal task in reconciling, through a system of checks and balances, the claims of conflicting interest groups into which all societies are divided is best expressed in the famous Tenth Number of *The Federalist*, written by James Madison. It dealt, significantly, with the idea of the *inequality* of men:

The diversity in the faculties of men, from which the rights of property originate, is not less an insuperable obstacle to a uniformity of interests. The protection of these faculties is the first object of government. From the protection of different and unequal faculties of acquiring property, the possession of different degrees and kinds of property immediately results; and from the influence of these on the sentiments and views of the respective proprietors ensues a division of the society into different interests and parties . . .

But the most common and durable sources of factions have been the various and unequal distribution of property. Those who hold and those who are without property have ever formed distinct interests in society. Those who are creditors and those who are debtors fall under a like discrimination. A landed interest, a manufacturing interest, a mercantile interest, a moneyed interest, with many lesser interests, grow up of necessity in civilized nations, and divide them into different classes, actuated by different sentiments and views. The regulation of these various and interfering interests forms the principal task of modern legislation, and involves the spirit of party and faction in the necessary and ordinary operations of the government.

For this new task of realistic government with its factions and party spirit, Americans had had a long apprenticeship. Allan Nevins has effectively expressed this in a pungent sentence: "Throughout British America the governments were governments by parties, and the Legislatures came to be run with nearly as much wire-pulling, log-rolling, party bossism, and political bargaining as would exist in American communities of the same size today." The state legislatures under the Articles of Confederation had inherited this experience and had transmitted it to the structure and working of the federal Constitution. But there was far more concern for property rights in the new instrument. Its Bill of Rights, previously adopted by the states, reflected the freedoms won through the common law, the Puritan Revolution, the Zenger Case for freedom of the press, and the experience of religious tolerance derived from the necessity of diverse cults to live side by side as well as from Enlightenment influences. The middle class had invoked these individual rights in its struggle for ascendancy, but their liberal logic could not long stop short at narrow class lines but eventually strove for a formula that would cover all groups and all classes.

· 8 ·

The Old South and the
New West in Jefferson's Day

[1789-1830]

I

THOMAS JEFFERSON, born on the Virginia frontier in 1743 when the English colonies were but seacoast settlements with a "West" that began east of the Alleghenies, lived until 1826—long enough to witness the amazing expansion of his country toward the Rockies and the Pacific Northwest. By then his Virginia and her southern neighbors had become the Old South paying deference to the upstart New West. In 1790, more than half of all Americans lived south of Mason and Dixon's line, scattered among farms and plantations except for a single sizable city, Charleston, which was soon to be outstripped by Baltimore. But from the time that his fellow-Virginian, George Washington, assumed the presidency until another Virginian, James Monroe, left it in 1825, the Old Dominion steadily lost its primacy among the states as its sons moved to Kentucky, Tennessee, and beyond, or to the deep South along the Gulf; by 1820 it had fallen behind New York in population and by 1830 was also behind Pennsylvania. The nearly 4,000,000 Americans at Washington's first accession to office, with no more than 5 per cent west of the Alleghenies, had more than doubled by 1820 and were not far from 13,000,000 in 1830, a figure augmented not only by natural increase and foreign immigration, but by the purchase of Louisiana

223

in 1803, which doubled our territory, and by the addition of the Floridas.

Virginia's pessimism dated back to the decline of the tobacco industry in pre-Revolutionary times and a sense of doom filled many who were now convinced that soil exhaustion had sterilized the lands of their state. Only the grain trade, stimulated by Europe's war necessities, offered relief. The private wharves of the Fitzhughs and their neighbors along the Rappahannock, the James, and the Potomac rivers were permitted to wear away against the pressure of the current while the large tobacco warehouses stood partly empty.

Those who could afford to use the latest scientific techniques of England like the Jeffersonian, John Taylor of Caroline County, a disciple of Arthur Young (England's champion of crop diversification and soil science), and George Washington, leader in scientific husbandry, especially in merino sheep breeding, did impress visitors with their model plantations. Taylor became a militant defender of an agrarian philosophy and a bitter foe of Hamilton's business theories. Jefferson, like Taylor and Washington, was an innovator in farming, although he had to neglect his plantation for politics. He introduced the nectarine and the pomegranate to his state, cultivated grapes for wine, experimented with orange trees and Egyptian rice, and set up plantation industries like nailmaking. Most small farmers, however, continued to be suspicious of "book farming," as they called scientific agriculture. Forecasting the later agricultural revival was the work of a young planter, Edmund Ruffin, who began in 1818 to introduce marl, a clay marine deposit mixed with calcium carbonate, as fertilizer to restore Virginia's soil by correcting the acidity of the worn lands.

Among the aristocratic planter allies of the Old South were the rice and sea-island cotton growers of South Carolina and Georgia. Spurred on by the insatiable demand for cotton by England's textile factories during this early phase of the Industrial Revolution, planters of the sea-island areas raised a black seed, long-staple, silky cotton to make fine textiles, defraying the high cost of ginning and cultivation by charging fancy prices. But sea-island cotton produc-

tion could scarcely begin to meet the demand and, in the drier upland regions where the coarse green seed, short-staple cotton grew,
the costs of hand-ginning to separate the seeds from the cotton boll
were far too prohibitive, considering the modest prices for the short-
staple crop.

Nevertheless, upland planters found the demand for cotton
tempting enough in a day when the new textile machines of Hargreaves, Arkwright, and Crompton threatened to leave spinners and
weavers idle for want of raw cotton supplies. Ingenious souls tink-
ered with various cotton gins, some fairly workable. The real triumph was reserved for the Connecticut Yankee, Eli Whitney, a
friend of the widow of General Nathanael Greene and a former
Yale student and mechanic. His cylinder-type wire gin, which
easily separated the seed from the lint, captured the immediate attention of the planters, including Jefferson himself, but patent litigation and his attempts to monopolize the business led to personal
financial disaster. This was later retrieved through his invention of
the interchangeable-parts rifle (the noteworthy ancestor of American mass production technique). Thereafter, as historians have so
often related, upland cotton spread swiftly, easily adapting itself
to the Southern soil, which had proved fickle to many other crops.
Even Virginians turned cotton planter until the frosts of 1825 and
the drop in prices discouraged these marginal producers. In a few
decades Southerners would insist "Cotton is King" and fasten the
one-crop system on the South. Cotton replaced grain as the chief
export of the United States, while Charleston, and later New Orleans became the region's chief cotton mart, dealing with New York
and Liverpool importers. By the 1820's the exports of Georgia and
South Carolina, largely cotton, more than matched in value those
of the rest of the nation together.

From the 1790's on, but especially after 1800, planters and small
farmers from the upper South began to pour into the deep South,
into frontier Alabama and Mississippi, often bringing a cavalcade
of slaves with them, some on horseback, others afoot, some heavily
guarded, and others moving freely in high hopes of "Beulah land."
Most of these white migrants were actually nonslaveholders and

some of them were content to come as squatters. Tennesseans of Virginia or North Carolina origin led this migration in the pre-1830 era; Indian barriers held back the South Carolina and Georgia emigrants. Alabama lands, whose limestone basin assured fertility, became part of the "black belt" as the planters discovered this soil, which was free from the thinness, sandiness, or barrenness of the coastal plains along the southeastern seaboard. Too often the planter's wasteful methods of tillage left excellent topsoil to be carried away by heavy rains, leaving eroded pits and gullies. The primitive hardwood forests were disappearing because of Indian wastefulness as well as squatter "soil butchery" and soft pines had taken the place of the huge trees. In the moister pockets and coastal areas of the otherwise sun-baked South, grew magnificent magnolias, cypresses, and bays, hung with ancient veils of Spanish moss. Early plantation houses in northern Alabama and Mississippi were double log-cabin "mansions" built by slaves. The lands were cultivated in piecemeal fashion with additional acres planted each year, at first with considerable crop diversification.

In the story of the Virginia and North Carolina migrations westward, history has few stranger tales than the sagas of the Lincolns and the Scotch-Irish and Welsh Jefferson Davises who moved into the backwoods of Kentucky. The Lincolns had come to Massachusetts in 1638 from England, later moving, as did many Puritan neighbors, to Virginia. In 1780, Grandfather Abe Lincoln crossed the mountains into Kentucky as part of the Virginia migration. He lost a son during an Indian attack while building his frontier cabin. Another son, Thomas, father of the future president, proved to have too few of the pioneer virtues of success and left Kentucky to settle in southern Indiana, where Southerners were already in the majority, and then went to Illinois. His son, Abe, was born in Hardin (now Larue) County, Kentucky, only a few months before his infant neighbor, Jefferson Davis, and about ninety miles away; in Illinois, young Lincoln adapted himself to life as a small farmer, clerk, and rural lawyer, and eventually rose to the presidency. Davis, also intellectual and idealistic, whose family settled in the rich Mississippi black belt and became wealthy planters, advanced to the presidency of the Confederate States, leading the Gray against the Blue of the Illinois rail splitter. On Davis' side was at least one branch of the Lincolns, a family who did not cross the Ohio.

Just as the Virginia Lincolns had followed parallel westward lines into Kentucky—the usual tendency—so another frontiersman moved from North Carolina to Tennessee. This was Andrew Jackson, who was to become a backwoods lawyer, trader, and successful land speculator—substantial vocations supplementing his prowess as an unrivaled Indian fighter and the national hero of the Battle of New Orleans—and of course, president of the United States. Despite several economic setbacks, Jackson owned a 640-acre cotton plantation, worked by slaves, and an elegant mansion, The Hermitage. Of the younger generation of North Carolina migrants to Tennessee was the far better educated lawyer, James K. Polk, another of the Western leaders to replace the Virginia dynasty and the Massachusetts Adamses in the White House.

The annexation of Louisiana brought another major cohort to the planter ruling class, the sugar-growing French and American planters. Louisianans, enriched by French technological progress abroad in utilizing power-driven sugar mills, possessed by the end of this era over three hundred sugar-producing units with an output of 90,000 hogsheads and a working force of 21,000 slaves. Tall cane fields lined the Mississippi River, where the rich soil, though requiring strong plowmen, was free from stones.

In this era of frontier beginnings for the plantation system in the deep South, John Bernard, the English actor and traveler, noted striking variations of the planter type from Virginia to Georgia. There was the aristocratic elite of the pre-Revolutionary generation, educated in England or France and graduating to the status of gentlemen after making the traditional grand tour of the Continent. "Their favourite topics were European," he wrote of Virginians in 1798, "and I found men leading secluded lives in the woods of Virginia, perfectly *au fait* as to the literary, dramatic and personal gossip of London and Paris." Their personal warmth beneath a veneer of classical dignity impressed him. As he entered the newer plantation country, as in Georgia, he met the semi-literate type who made a cult of indolence, rising late, reclining at length after breakfast while a Negress or two fanned the flies away, drinking heavily and plotting craftily to entice his neighbors for an outing of fishing, hunting, horseracing, and more drinking. After making the necessary visit to the overseer for information about his affairs, he could retire to the village to talk prices or horses, or to gossip and play cards. Hunting might even be pursued after dinner by torchlight, but the abundance of game discouraged the elaborate English ritual of hunting in groups, for each hunter was quickly absorbed in his own target. Horseracing grew in popularity, partly at the expense of the colonial sport of cockfighting. Womenfolk had the solace—and problems—of the continuous rounds of protracted visits by kinsfolk and friends. Bernard did not find worthy of note the prosaic but more typical picture of thousands of pioneer Georgia planters sweating in the fields with their slaves.

That there was a genuine leisure class in America, however, was emphatically denied by Jefferson who pointed out the tireless, unremitting duties of the average planter. "In our private pursuits," wrote Jefferson, just as if he had read and rejected Thorstein Veblen's *Theory of the Leisure Class* of almost a century later, "it is a great advantage that every honest employment is deemed honorable." Besides, inherited fortunes were too few for men to endanger their accumulations by frivolous indifference to serious planning and labor.

2

The rapid increase of free Negroes in Virginia and Maryland not only reflected a humanitarian desire to end slavery, but also the decreasing local value of slaves during the era before 1830. It seemed but a matter of time to these planters of the upper South before the peculiar institution, so loathed by the best Virginia spokesmen, would disappear. In retirement, Washington expressed emphatic antislavery sentiments to John Bernard, "Not only do I pray for it [abolition] on the score of human dignity, but I can clearly foresee that nothing but the rooting out of slavery can perpetuate the existence of our union, by consolidating it in a common bond of principle." First of all before freedom, he cautioned, must come the education of the slave.

In 1800, while campaigning for president, Jefferson received from Governor James Monroe the startling news of the Gabriel insurrection, involving a plot of some 1100 slaves led by a young slave of a notorious master near Richmond. Monroe wrote: "It is unquestionably the most serious and formidable conspiracy we have ever known of the kind. While it was possible to keep it a secret, which it was till we saw the extent of it, we did so." Gabriel had been influenced by the example of Santo Domingo, where Toussaint L'Ouverture had borrowed French equalitarian ideas to overthrow the masters in a bloody revolution and to launch a virtual race war to establish an independent Negro state. This event had been impressed upon the slaveowners, especially at Norfolk, by the thousands of French refugees escaping the island, and convinced many like Jefferson that manumission without removal of the Negroes would be dangerous. Gabriel's plan was to seize the arsenal and other strategic buildings of Richmond as a prelude to a general war in which at least 50,000 Negroes would join. This was exposed by a faithful slave and averted by an unusual cloudburst that demoralized Gabriel's army. Mass arrests, slave trials, hysteria, and hasty executions followed with more plots discovered elsewhere. Slave patrol laws, as always after an insurrection panic, became more stringent and an impetus was given to the formation of the American Colonization Society which took active form by 1816. More plots disturbed the sleep of Virginians particularly in 1802, 1808, 1809, and constantly during the War of 1812; at least one involved the leadership of a white military officer. Practically every slave state in this era heard repeated rumors of actual uprisings and of slave plots to escape or to burn towns. Slave crimes against masters added to this ugly situation. Upon such a keg of powder, Southern liberalism could not thrive and proved to be an exotic plant that scarcely survived Jefferson.

Insurrections usually occurred among field hands, while the informants tended to be the domestic servants in the Big House who enjoyed special privileges and were intimate with the master's

family. Some slaves enjoyed the privilege of hiring themselves out
and of holding property. The relatively mild French black code,
which continued to prevail after the purchase of Louisiana, forbade
the selling of young slave children apart from the mother and guaranteed the property of slaves. By 1830, among 2,000,000 whites of
the South Atlantic states there were almost as many slaves, together
with 300,000 free Negroes—the latter a hunted group, suspect in the
eyes of the law as an incendiary influence or as a mischief-maker.
Northern states, especially Illinois and Indiana, showed little sympathy for free Negroes, even enslaving many under the guise of
long-term apprentice laws.

To the planter, the slave was an indispensable source of labor,
suited for the enervating "90 degrees in the shade" of the Southland
and for simple repetitive tasks. He was also an investment whose
speculative worth might rise much faster in good times than did
ordinary bank investments. There was, therefore, the temptation to
sink one's ready cash in more and more slaves ahead of production
needs. As a result of increased slaveholding during the era after
Eli Whitney's gin, the gap between farmer and planter widened
more than ever. Still, in this frontier stage of plantation life, the
small slaveowner could work alongside the slave without losing
caste though hired men might refuse to accept this degree of intimacy. How profitable the system was, appeared disputed at this
date as in later times. Jefferson's learned friend, Thomas Cooper,
noted as an economist as well as a scientist, wrote from South Carolina, "The usual work of a field hand is barely two thirds what a
white day labourer at usual wages would perform." Slave labor has
ever been given unwillingly and generally inefficiently whether in
ancient or in modern times.

The small farmer, who filled most of the occupied South, whether
in the Blue Ridge valleys of Virginia and Tennessee or the broad
piedmont from the Carolinas to Georgia, usually raised a variety of
crops for his own use. Piedmont farmers might raise an acre or two
of low-grade tobacco and several more of grain; other upland
farmers raised a few acres of cotton, which the family helped separate from the seeds as well as food crops. Indian corn was a staple,

roasted or fried; corn pone, hoecake, muffins, or spoonbread was varied in the daily menu with candied or roasted sweet potatoes, bacon, and "cowpeas." The piedmont back country of Virginia and the Carolinas raised hogs, cattle, and horses for the early "long drive" of Jefferson's day to the seaboard town markets. By the 1820's droves of perhaps 5000 hogs were eating their way through the woods and interrupting travelers on the few good roads available.

Many of these farmers were eventually to accumulate enough to buy a few slaves, though the rising prices of these slaves, as already noted, made it increasingly difficult to bridge the gap between them and the cotton, rice, and sugar aristocracy. The Southern yeomanry, who constituted most of the Southern people, varied from the well-to-do farmers who could afford a few luxuries to the poorer sort who depended wholly on barter. Most of them were uneducated, but honest and independent in outlook. There were several gradations of poverty and simple living. Frontiersmen on both sides of the Ohio, like the Lincolns in Indiana and Illinois and their neighbors in Kentucky and Tennessee, tended to be restless and lived in temporary shelters. "They only make such improvements as they can leave without reluctance and without loss," wrote Timothy Flint of them. The split rail fence and log cabins were standard fixtures in the wooded areas. John Bernard, visiting the Carolinas, sniffed disdainfully at the primitive one-and-a-half-story log cabin lined with bunks for beds and containing two chairs and a table "in the last stage of palsy." The table scene is unforgettable:

No sooner were you seated than the house-dog (of the large wolf-breed) would arrange himself beside you, and lift his lank, hungry jaws expressively to your face. The young children, never less than a dozen (the women seeming to bear them in a litter in those regions), at the sight and smell of these victuals would set up a yell enough to frighten the wolves.

Elbowed aside by the aggressive planter and the yeoman farmer were the scattered pockets of "poor whites," failures in the race for worldly goods, who dwelt in rural slums in ramshackle huts lacking floors, dishware, and furniture. Isolated upon the thin soils and irregular terrain of the Cumberland plateau, or eking out a miserable living in the sandy barrens of the coastal plains and deep South, these listless, slothful people were spoken of contemptuously by slaves as well as white farmers as "crackers," "sandhillers," or worse. Hookworm and other diseases, as a later generation discovered, accounted for much of their abject condition rather than genetic taint, as some believed. The poor white has often been confused with the Southern highlander, isolated in the inaccessible parts of the southern Appalachians and similarly illiterate, but far more alert in spirit and independent economically.

3

Cheap lands, of course, exerted the mighty suction for the westward movement that was upsetting the balance of the Union against the original thirteen states and threatening to dwarf federalist New England. Six frontier states entered the Union during the years from 1816 to 1821 alone, all but Maine being states with public lands. Already in 1792 Kentucky had assumed statehood, followed four years later by Tennessee, in 1803 by Ohio, and in 1812 by Louisiana. Kentucky's lands, selling in 400-acre tracts at twenty-five cents per acre, had been swiftly taken. Georgia was even more generous in disposing of her lands. As for the federal "public domain" lands north of the Ohio, these became more attractive after Congress responded to frontier pressure by reducing the minimum price and the size of the unit by successive laws until by the Act of 1820 the minimum price was $1.25 an acre, the minimum unit cut to eighty acres. Speculators, and many bona fide settlers as well, were checked by cash requirements. Thus the Great Migration, following the War of 1812, was channeled increasingly into the excellent lands still available at low prices north of the Ohio or in the deep South and the trans-Mississippi country.

Politically, this growth of the West was reflected in the fight of New England Federalists to keep their favored position within the Union. During the War of 1812, Federalists at the Hartford Convention demanded constitutional amendments that would require a two-thirds vote in Congress before admitting new states or declaring war. As late as 1830, Connecticut's Senator Samuel Foote proposed a resolution to suspend the sale of public lands. On this occasion, the Webster-Hayne debate revealed the need of both the North and the South, facing a deadly sectional feud, to make an ally of the New West.

The young republic saw the rapid settlement of Kentucky and Tennessee; Lexington, Louisville, Nashville, and Knoxville grew from defense or trading posts into bustling market towns. Daniel Boone's historic Wilderness Road, which opened the way to Kentucky's blue-grass limestone region, became a substantial wagon road during the 1790's, in time for the new waves of migration. As the frontier process of development matured into a settled community stage, a new Southwestern ruling class emerged of land speculators, lawyers, planters, and middle-class groups. Even before the purchase of Spanish and French Louisiana, the restless frontiersmen had begun to cross over to foreign soil, many accepting nominal Spanish citizenship. Dissatisfied Kentuckians like the Lincolns crossed the Ohio to mix with New York State men and Pennsylvanians in the southern parts of the Old Northwest. At the fringes of settlement were the squatters, farmers, and hunters who moved on impatiently into Indian lands, indifferent to land titles.

New Englanders disliked the murderous habits of frontier fighting, especially among the river men or the gamblers. Once the participants agreed to rough and tumble rules of "bite, kick, and gouge"—sometimes these tactics began spontaneously—one was likely to see ears bitten off, noses deformed, eyes gouged out, hair pulled, and flesh rent until honor was satisfied. Pistol duels among "gentlemen," despite legal penalties and public criticism, allowed bullies to remove outspoken critics. Lincoln narrowly escaped a duel in frontier Illinois. In a frontier community, unchecked by traditions of stability, and often exposed to Indian and wild animal dangers as well as to new diseases, life was lived dangerously and boisterously.

Frontier recreation reflected a strong social spirit that belied the notion of "individualism" in the narrow uncooperative sense. Newcomers shared the benefits of logrolling both as a contribution to cooperative house-raising and to jollity. English, Irish, and colonial sports persisted as the migrants introduced their familiar songs and games. Dancing on the green with bran or sawdust scattered on the ground—the "brandance"—became the "barn dance" to a later generation. Among the fiddler's favorites were such homely titles as "Old Dan Tucker," "Zip Coon," "Sailor's Hornpipe," and "Leather Britches." Bottles of whisky frequently passed along from lip to lip among both sexes and were indispensable for dances and every festive occasion.

Wooing, as Everett Dick, the frontier historian, declares, was brief and to the point. Suitors in Kentucky might even practice lassoing the maid, not too difficult a feat with the proper cooperation on both sides. Bundling as a form of courting persisted from the mid-eighteenth century to the opening of the new century. Kissing games took a variety of ingenious forms such as "hanging onto the doorknob"—a kind of chain reaction among partners of both sexes. Marriages, as in colonial times, were somewhat earlier than in eastern cities and Europe, widowhood lasted briefly, and children became a prime economic asset almost at infancy.

From the fabulous salt licks of Kentucky, a state since 1792, vast herds of deer, elk, and buffalo were disappearing, with the buffalo becoming a mere legend to the new generation despite the efforts of Boone to prevent their extinction. Among the young men of Tennessee, Davy Crockett, hunter, humorist, and later politician, trained his giant dogs to slaughter bears, killing 105 during the winter of 1825. Visitors to the West were startled by the number of dogs everywhere, even in the churches. Kentucky's horses of the blue-grass lands were prized as far away as South Carolina, where they readily sold during the opening years of the century. Well-fed cattle, sheep, and hogs were driven to distant markets in the deep South or the East. Small farms, many with rich wheat fields, alternated with farms and plantations of hemp and tobacco, the large units cultivated by gangs of Negroes. With more than an ordinary share of western boastfulness as to the virtues of their own state, Kentuckians could agree with a certain Methodist preacher in their midst, "In short, my brethren, to say all in one word, heaven is a Kentuck of a place." Kentucky and Tennessee farmers, eager for profitable markets down the Mississippi, had once fostered separatist intrigues with Spain; in 1803, they inspired the Jefferson administration to buy all of Louisiana. Improved transportation led hemp growers and other producers to reach out for distant markets beyond New Orleans, there to be met by foreign competition. As a result, Kentuckians listened sympathetically to their Virginia-bred son, Henry Clay, whose American system included a protective tariff, internal improvements at government expense, and a central financing institution, the United States Bank.

At crossroads and boat landings, frontier stores sprang up, some of them merely the front part of the log cabin or house. Bartering, accompanied by sharp bargaining, was the rule, whether in Bibles, playing cards, fish, or hardware. Shortage of change on the frontier led to the "chopping" of available silver dollars into "bits" or eighths with "two bits," for example, becoming the current term for twenty-five cents.

Competing with the stores were the sharp Yankee peddlers selling "notions" ranging from pins, needles, and scissors, to books and clocks. The Connecticut Yankee inventor Eli Terry, in 1807, reduced the size of the cumbersome grandfather clocks to shelf size and soon Terry's Waterbury factory produced clocks in quantity for the nation and furnished a major staple for the peddlers. Some peddlers traded clocks for southern mules and drove the latter to a profitable northern market. The Southerner's stereotype of the Yankee was the bony, hawk-beaked peddler, possessed of vulgarity, slyness, a scriptural name, and a nasal twang. This unfriendly impression was strengthened along the Ohio when the Kentuckian contrasted his own easygoing land surveys with the rigid geometric lines of the Yankee's townships and the lots surrounded by carefully guarded fences.

4

With the acquisition of Louisiana territory the "homogeneous" Southerners added more diverse cultures to their own. Tens of thousands of French and Spanish Creoles of New Orleans, St. Louis, and the back country, predominantly Catholic, suddenly found themselves transferred to an alien power. They were overwhelmed by the dynamic Anglo-Saxon Protestant who despised their paternalism and had little understanding of their Continental legal tradition. Many wept, anticipating the worst, as the American flag went up in the transfer ceremony. In upper Louisiana, the original 7000 population on the eve of the transfer became almost 21,000 in 1810, and 66,500 a decade later as a result of the American influx. Louisiana Territory altogether had in 1806 26,000 whites, of which 13,000 were mostly Creoles—French or Spanish native whites and 3500 Americans. In this era there were already 40,000 French settled on American territory such as the Old Northwest Territory and Vermont. Kaskaskia, Detroit, Vincennes, Cahokia, and other French settlements had played a large role in the American Revolutionary era when George Rogers Clark had made his northwestern thrust against Britain's frontier outposts. Americans like Moses Austin of Connecticut exploited the lead mines of Missouri, John Jacob Astor and his rivals sought a fortune in furs, and thousands of farmers loaded their produce on river barges and keelboats destined for the high prices offered in the New Orleans market. One distinguished visitor, Washington Irving, later described in *Astoria* the workings of the St. Louis melting pot of 1810, already a central supply point for the river trade and the military posts of the upper Mississippi:

Here is to be seen, about the river banks, the hectoring, extravagant, bragging boatmen of the Mississippi; with the gay, grimacing, singing, good-humored Canadian *Voyageurs*. Vagrant Indians of various tribes loitered about the streets. Now and then a stark Kentucky hunter, in leathern hunting-dress, with a rifle on shoulder and knife in belt, strode along. Here and there were new brick houses and shops, just set up by bustling, driving, and eager men of traffic from the Atlantic States; while, on the other hand, the old French mansions, with open casements, still retained the easy, indolent air of the original colonists; and now and then the scraping of a fiddle, a strain of an ancient French song or the sound of billiard balls, showed that the happy Gallic turn for gayety and amusement still lingered about the place.

The subdued skyline of St. Louis was broken by the high, massive stone walls of the pretentious estate of the fur trader, Auguste Chouteau, the elder. This property covered an entire square and included an attractive artificial lake that also served as a reservoir for a private grist mill. Here the well-to-do Creole ruling class gathered to discuss business or public problems. Newcomers were impressed by the gleaming whiteness of an old white Spanish fort and the lime-covered mud walls of other homes in St. Louis, Ste. Genevieve, and elsewhere. In the streets, French-speaking slaves, better treated than under American customs, often engaged in petty disturbances. Humble log cabins of the French type were made with timbers upright rather than in the American horizontal style.

American Protestants wondered at the gaily-dressed French crowds which listened politely to Sabbath-day sermons and then went to the billiard table or played cards. In turn, the French had their own opinions of the Calvinists, believing, as a sympathetic observer put it, "that a sullen countenance, an attention to gloomy subjects, a set form of speech, and a stiff behavior, are much more indicative of hypocrisy than of religion; and they have often remarked that those who practice these singularities on Sundays will most assuredly cheat and defraud their neighbors during the rest of the week." Again, French and American attitudes toward the Indian contrasted, for not only did Frenchmen often live in conventional family manner with Indian wives, but occasionally a Frenchwoman turned up as an Indian squaw. Children of such racial crossings, as well as those of illicit unions with Negro women, were commonly noted. At public affairs the French grouped together as families, from the oldest to the smallest child; Americans kept the sexes apart, presumably to protect the women from exposure to bawdy jokes.

An American official complained of the Creoles: "The summary decree of a military officer, however tyrannical or absurd, is much better suited to their ideas of the fitness of things, than the dilatory trial by jury and glorious uncertainty of the common law." But the new Anglo-Saxon rulers did not interfere with the French and Spanish legal traditions of the Roman law, leaving Louisiana outside of the Anglo-American common law system prevailing else-where. In 1825, Louisiana adopted the Civil Code, which was bor-rowed almost verbatim from the Code Napoleon, and retained the parish system of local government. Religious liberties were scrupu-lously protected by the new government.

By the 1820's French speech had lost out to English in the streets of St. Louis and New Orleans, though resisting successfully in the villages of Ste. Genevieve, Carondelet, and other back-country Mis-souri towns as well as in the parishes above New Orleans. French dress, *capots*, moccasins, and headkerchiefs had almost disappeared. Benjamin Latrobe, the architect, predicted in his New Orleans jour-nal of 1818, "In a few years this will be an American town." Holy Week declined in pageantry; the long religious processions on the streets and public square disappeared behind the cathedral walls as Protestantism advanced. In upper Louisiana, French names in the mouths of Americans were transformed; thus Vide Poche was Wheat Bush, Ste. Genevieve was Send Jimaway, and Bois Brûle came out Bob Rowley. Government surveyors, poetically individ-ualistic in their spelling, helped along this linguistic fusion. St. Louis itself, on the eve of the German invasion of the 1830's, was a typically American western city—even a metropolis. As the city accumulated the exports of the river towns and the trade des-tined for the Gulf and Atlantic coasts, it grew to nearly 50,000 by 1830.

While the fur and mercantile aristocrats of St. Louis, like the Chouteaus, looked impressive in their mansions furnished with fine libraries and furniture, the French sugar and cotton aristocrats of New Orleans and the beautiful plantations along the intricate bay-ous of lower Louisiana were even more magnificent and cosmopoli-tan. Here were French revolutionary refugees and Napoleonic exiles, and planters who had fled from the race war of Santo Do-mingo. By 1809, over 6000 French-speaking people had come—whites, free Negroes, and slaves. Stories were still fresh and were to be charmingly retold in 1847 in Longfellow's *Evangeline* of the sad eighteenth-century Acadians of whom so many came to Lower Loui-siana; the tale of Evangeline was to be enshrined in the Evangeline

Oak near St. Martinsville, where the heroine supposedly met her beloved Gabriel.

The Louisiana planter lived in a fine house; he played on his piano, read novels and more serious tomes, and was proud of his imported furniture; he sent his daughter to the fashionable New Orleans convent school of the Ursuline nuns, frequented the large French theater, bet avidly on the horses, and hunted with carefully bred hounds. Even the lesser planters shared these privileges and tastes on a proportionate scale. "The pernicious habit of novel-reading," complained Timothy Flint, "which is an appetite at the North, has here an insatiable craving." Anglo-Americans, shocked at the French play or concert bills posted on the Sabbath morning announcing an evening performance, retaliated by adding a note to the poster, "Remember the Sabbath day to keep it holy." More difficult to understand was the French custom of frankly recognizing the existence of brothels and roulette gambling houses. "Much is said in defence of this practice," wrote Flint, "that since vice will exist, they had better have a few houses filled than all spoiled." The presence of the beautiful octoroon or mulatto, the mistress of the Creole planter or his son, had already become romanticized in the style that George Washington Cable was later to adopt in his sympathetic stories of the exclusive New Orleans Creole. Octoroon balls, noted for their lovely ladies and exotic atmosphere, attracted visitors from afar.

Slavery, with certain French variations, was everywhere in evidence in the city as well as in the rest of the territory. Many of the slaves actually supported down-at-the-heel masters by their earnings through self-hire. Despite the relatively mild nature of French slavery, reports of slave insurrection plots busied the American territorial governor and in 1811 there broke out the worst insurrection in slavery times. This one was aimed at New Orleans itself, the objective of a force of slaves estimated variously from 180 to 500 persons. Troops fought a pitched battle to crush the rebellion that had originated in a plantation just thirty-six miles above the city. To intimidate others, the troops decapitated many of the rebels and stuck their heads on poles along the Mississippi.

Whatever its tragedies, New Orleans was a gay city, "little Paris" to the American river men who came in their thousands for at least one long look at the effete Creole city of sin, especially during the winter. River gangs, devilishly skilled with bowie knives and guns, and ready to escape to the swamps, terrorized the city. With 1200 to 1500 boats and perhaps 50 steamers coming to the city annually, adventure-seeking crews filled the streets, elbowing aside Frenchmen, Spaniards, Portuguese, Indians, and Negroes, as well as Americans. By the 1820's an American residential and commercial quarter, largely brick, had grown along the Faubourg St. Mary while the old stucco cathedral with its thick walls remained the imposing center of the ancient French quarter. Repeated fires during the 1780's and 1790's wiped out most of the old French buildings and left the newer Spanish-American architecture as the typical style. Thus Spanish arcades, inner courts, balconies, and one-story stucco homes stood out among the numerous humble adobe houses and the few surviving French-style buildings. French coffee houses with their lively billiard and card games upstairs awaited the visitor. At the doors of the residences Negresses with baskets of goods on their heads called their wares. Chronic outbreaks of yellow fever epidemics inspired some efforts to safeguard the water supply and keep the refuse-filled streets clean. The connection between yellow fever and the mosquito pest in those half-drowned lands surrounding the city was unsuspected.

Above all, New Orleans was the gateway to distant continents, with vessels filled with cotton, sugar, molasses, and other plantation products destined for the West Indies, the Atlantic coast, and even beyond. Just south of the city was the Baratarian coast where Jean Lafitte ruled over a fortress settlement of pirates and privateers. Lafitte's low prices, due undoubtedly to his low basic costs, attracted thrifty merchants to his city warehouse and store. Never at a loss for idolators who romanticized him, Lafitte won fresh laurels during the War of 1812 when his men joined Andrew Jackson behind the cotton bales of the city in battling the British invaders. Though he was pardoned by President Madison, Lafitte's enterprising days here were numbered, for his newer colony at Galveston was dispersed by naval forces.

5

Westward immigrants, following parallel lines in the main, gave New Englanders and those of the middle states an increasing share with the predominant Southerners in the Old Northwest. In these early decades pioneers here, as elsewhere, clung to the Southern timbered lands until the 1840's when they mastered the art of cultivating the hard, level, and treeless prairies. "I'm going to strike out for the tall timber," announced the early pioneer; he was thinking of his needs in fuel, building, fencing, and other materials and felt convinced of the superior fertility of these heavily wooded regions along the rivers. His successors found the vast rich prairies far above the banks of the Ohio to be anything but a farmer's bogey, The hopeful songs of the pioneer told his optimistic story in marching rhythm, as one of their descendants, Hamlin Garland, recalled:

> Cheer up, brothers, as we go,
> O'er the mountains, westward ho,
> Where herds of deer and buffalo
> Furnish the fare.

> Chorus: Then o'er the hills in legions, boys,
> Fair freedom's star
> Points to the sunset regions, boys,
> Ha, ha, ha-ha!

> When we've wood and prairie land,
> Won by our toil,
> We'll reign like kings in fairy land,
> Lords of the soil!

The Ohio River and its tributaries and the Great Lakes provided the most convenient approaches to the West, and hence the earliest towns and villages were settled along these ways. Travelers from the east relied on several wide wagon roads and Indian trails in the days before the Cumberland Road section, between Cumberland and Wheeling, of the New National Pike was completed in 1818; this road followed, at the outset, Braddock's route in his ill-fated expedition of 1755. After 1825 the road was continued to Columbus, Ohio. Sturdy Conestoga wagons, pulled by six-horse teams and carrying settlers or laden with heavy freight for the frontier stores, were the railroads of the West. Their drivers are said to have introduced the American custom of driving to the right—for Englishmen kept to the left.

Along Lake Erie's southern shores, Moses Cleaveland, the Yale-trained lawyer, soldier, and land speculator, came in 1796 with fifty settlers and surveyors from Connecticut; at an Indian site along the Cuyahoga River they found the town named after him which, in simplified frontier spelling, became "Cleveland." This was in Connecticut's Western Reserve left from her old sea-to-sea colonial charter, a three million acre tract retained by that state to satisfy the Revolutionary war claims of her citizens. It was made part of the Northwest Territory in 1800. Here was born a new Connecticut with familiar New England institutions, architecture, and attitudes —the village commons, the tall spires of the white meeting houses, and the Calvinism of Congregationalists and Presbyterians. The Puritan's faith in schools and colleges, his crusading reform spirit as well as his houses of prayer took root in the Old Northwest. From two townships set aside by the Ohio Company for a college was born Ohio University at Athens, founded by the New Englanders, the Reverend Menasseh Cutler and General Rufus Putnam, and opened in 1809 as the first college of the Old Northwest.

Contrasting with the Western Reserve type of culture was that of the transplanted South whose emigrants settled on the north side of the Ohio River. Here were the Southern-style houses, the courthouse buildings that served to some extent the official uses of the New England meetinghouses, and the relative indifference to popular education as distinct from college training for the professions. Southerners were entrenched in the Virginia Military Lands, a four-million-acre triangular tract with a broad base on the Ohio River intended for Virginia's Revolutionary veterans.

The group of New England veterans and speculators who fo...
the Ohio Company purchased 1,500,000 acres in the lower Muskin-
gum Valley, which included the new capital of the Northwest Territory, Marietta, named in 1788 for the ill-fated Marie Antoinette.
A more direct French influence appeared in the second oldest
settlement, Gallipolis, whose promoters beguiled 800 simple Frenchmen to take up lands without giving them a proper title. Most of
these stranded immigrants escaped by 1807 to their compatriots in
upper Louisiana and Canada. With the victory of "Mad Anthony"
Wayne in 1795 in the Battle of Fallen Timbers at the forks of the
Miami River, the way was clear for the inevitable series of Indian
cessions further opening the southeastern part of the Northwest
Territory—the prelude to far more extensive cessions in another decade or so.

The boom town of Cincinnati situated at the high bank of the
Ohio grew from about 8000 after the War of 1812 to almost 25,000
by the end of this era. Its corn hinterland gave it crop exports, cat-
tle-feeding, and slaughtering activities, which made it "Porkopolis
of the West." With the steamboat era, it became a major port for
Ohio commerce and a chief shipbuilder as well, compelling Pittsburgh to turn to manufactures. Looking at the daily life of transplanted New Englanders, Pennsylvanians, Kentuckians, and Tennesseans, Flint felt critical of the bluster and cheap glitter of the
frontier which disregarded the poor outcasts stranded in the westward movement. "The elegance of the houses, the parade of servants,
the display of furniture, and more than all, the luxury of their over-
loaded tables, would compare with the better houses in the Atlantic cities," he observed.

In the Ohio tradition of this period was the story of Johnny Ap-
pleseed, a backwoods version of the kindly St. Francis. He was actually John Chapman, a Massachusetts nurseryman who had moved
to Ohio in 1805 and prospered by realizing the future importance
of planting and selling young fruit trees in the wilderness where
a monotonous corn diet made apples welcome. In the astonishing
legend that developed he was an eccentric mystic who was loved
equally by Indians and whites, who gave what he had to the poor,

who understood wild life intuitively, and who fascinated children
with his Indian tales. Above all, he collected seeds from the refuse
of cider presses in little bags to scatter them benevolently through
Ohio, Indiana, and Illinois. Stories of his heroism and goodness
multiplied after his death to ripen into a major American tradition.

In Indiana and Illinois, where population clung to the rich lands
of the Mississippi, Ohio, and Wabash river bottoms, Southerners
outnumbered those from the free states in this era. A Kentucky
family like the Lincolns lived in typical frontier Indiana style, first
building a "half-faced camp" which was a three-sided pole cabin,
then putting up a one-room log cabin, and finally a larger, more
substantial house. The influx of Southern frontiersmen gave Indiana
its "hoosier" character, with a distinctive pronunciation dating back
to the eighteenth-century speech of the plain people in rural England. Like these forebears, Hoosiers made "join" rhyme with "line"
and dropped the final "g" in such participles as "singing," "walking,"
and "going." When newcomers knocked at their cabins, they called
out, "Who's here?", rendering it "Who's yeer?"—hence, so it is believed, came the name "Hoosier." Opportunities for education were
so few despite the log-cabin schools here and there that illiteracy put
Indiana behind all other free states. Lincoln's schooling during his
Indiana childhood did not aggregate one year and he carried away
a lifelong supply of frontier superstitions.

The French *habitants* were probably less literate though they
brightened the drab scene observed by visitors by their colorful
Mardi Gras spectacles, New Year calls, and folk songs derived from
the troubadours and jongleurs of medieval Provence. They sang
about wicked knights seducing fair maidens, of a noble king hopelessly smitten by a beautiful lady, and boating songs about royal
hunters. The Americans could match these by old sentimental English ballads and ditties and lively dances they had known in Kentucky and Virginia. In Vincennes, the early political and cultural
center where the Creoles dominated politics throughout this era,
Americans could boast of introducing by 1808 amateur dramatics,
several newspapers, a literary club, a library of three or four thou-

1800-1846

"President Thomas Jefferson," by Rembrandt Peale, 1805.
(New York Historical Society)

Fairview Inn, built in 1801, as it appeared in 1827. This inn stood on the National Turnpike, now Frederick Road, three miles from Baltimore, Maryland. (Maryland Historical Society)

"Boston Harbor," by Robert W. Salmon. (Metropolitan Museum of Art)

Above, left: "War News from Mexico," by Richard C. Woodville, one of the outstanding genre painters influenced by the Dusseldorf school. (National Academy of Design)

Above, right: "Post Office," by David G. Blythe, genre painter, whose skill at caricature suggests the style of his French contemporary, Daumier. (Carnegie Institute)

Opposite, top: "Stump Speaking," by George C. Bingham. A painter's view of frontier politics in Missouri. (Boatmen's Bank, St. Louis, Missouri)

Opposite, bottom: "Yankee Peddler," by John W. Ehninger. (Newark Museum, Newark, New Jersey)

Below: "The Jolly Flatboatmen," by George C. Bingham. A native artist's view of life on the Mississippi. (City Art Museum, St. Louis, Missouri)

The Iron Horse wins, 1830. Although Peter Cooper's Tom Thumb locomotive actually lost the race because of a breakdown, the victory of steam locomotion was clear enough. (Bureau of Public Roads, Department of Commerce)

The Shaker ritual dance, the "Square Order Shuffle." This lithograph shows the pantomime of hands shaking off sin. (Western Reserve Historical Society)

The National Pike. Its first section, the famous Cumberland Road, ran from Cumberland, Maryland, to Wheeling, Virginia; later it was extended to St. Louis. (Bureau of Public Roads, Department of Commerce)

"Tammany Society Celebrating the Fourth of July, 1812," by William Chappel. (New York Historical Society)

Hiram Powers' "Greek Slave," 1843, at the Dusseldorf Gallery, New York, from an engraving by R. Thew. The nude figure aroused hostility until clergymen de-

"The Park Theatre," New York, November, 1822, painted by John Searle, showing a scene from *Monsieur Tonson* by the popular English playwright and pro-

sand books contributed by citizens, and even a Vincennes Historical and Antiquarian Society. By 1810, Indiana had 24,500 people
and one of her frontier heroes, a transplanted Virginian, William
Harrison, was destined for the White House.

Her neighbor, Illinois, which reached statehood in 1818 with
35,000 people, was a similar frontier community. Pioneers believed
that dirty, disorderly Shawneetown, for all its lack of schools,
churches, jails, and courthouse, would nevertheless become the
metropolis of the future—the gateway to the rich Wabash country.
Chicago was but a village, remembered for its frightful Fort Dear-
born massacre during the War of 1812, a war that finally ended the
worst of the Indian peril. An interesting immigration experiment
by an English tenant farmer, Morris Birkbeck, and his friends
brought some 400 Englishmen to English Prairie in Edwards
County. The founders hoped that they might establish a duplicate
of the English manorial estates here, but this dream was quickly
dissipated by the alacrity with which the colonists hastened to become independent farmers on easily available lands of their own.
Roads were poor here as in Indiana, but gradually the stagecoach
and better roads helped unify the southern half of the state. In the
treeless prairies those who could afford to buy their own timber
transported it to their farms. Timothy Flint was moved by the
beauty of the prairie horizons mingling the blue of the skies with
the brilliant hues of the wild flowers.

Prosperous Cincinnati and Louisville and other river towns grew
partly at the expense of Pittsburgh, the "jumping off" place for
pioneers entering the Ohio valley, whose boat-building and supply
business they invaded. When Flint visited Pittsburgh in the 1820's,
it was a substantial town of numerous brick homes situated on a
romantic river setting, but coal dust was already tinting the skies.
Too many rogues waxed rich on poor immigrants and gambling and
prostitution flourished. "The traveller was too apt to think of her
as immersed in 'sin and sea coal,'" observed Flint, "for the constant
use of fossil coal, both for culinary and manufacturing purposes, has
given a sooty and funereal aspect even to the buildings." Improved

connections with the East, especially the National Road, were breaking down the key position of Pittsburgh as the gateway to the Ohio.

This was the heyday of the keelboat era on the Ohio and Mississippi rivers with two or three thousand crewsmen engaged in this traffic by 1815. These light shallow boats, sometimes a heavy barge type on the deeper rivers, measured forty to eighty feet long and seven to ten feet across, and were often fitted with passenger cabins. They could navigate upstream where flatboats were helpless, propelled by poles and oars and perhaps carrying square sails. While an upstream trip from New Orleans to Louisville required three or four months, the return trip could be made in four weeks. This meant a powerful economic and cultural link between the South and the Old Northwest. The French boatman preferred his canoe above all, but the Kentuckian liked the wild boastful life of the keelboatman, dancing, fiddling, and flirting to the delight of girl spectators, fighting in pitched battles against townsmen, river pirates, and Indians, and proudly demonstrating his prowess at wrestling or telling tall stories. Mike Fink who had been born in Pittsburgh when it was a mere frontier post typified these hardy virtues and vices as the prince of keelboatmen and bullies on these rivers until the day he was shot, leaving an amazing trail of extravagant legends behind him. By the 1830's the keelboat was in decline, conquered by the steamboat. Hunters still used it for traveling up the Missouri, Arkansas, and Red rivers or along minor streams where the ponderous steam vessels would not deign to follow.

The steamboat arrived on western waters in 1811 when the *New Orleans* left Pittsburgh for the Gulf. Its builder, the Ohio Steamboat Navigation Company, was associated with Robert Fulton, the inventor, and Robert R. Livingston, the promoter, who, when serving as minister to France, had met Fulton, an American art student in Paris, and decided to back him. Fulton's successful steamboat, the *Clermont*, had already won world attention—though Europeans had also launched successful models—for its trip of 1807 from New York to Albany, covering a hundred and fifty miles in thirty-two hours. By the 1820's at least a hundred steamboats were puffing their way along the western rivers, many already being transformed esthetically by the distinctive architecture of the steamboat era.

6

French and English rationalism, culminating in the eighteenth-century Age of Reason, reached its apogee and decline during the years 1789-1830. It was checked in this country by the Second Great Awakening, which drew its vitality from the unlettered southern and western frontiersmen. At first the West shared in the wave of rationalism spread by the French Revolution and by the French Alliance of 1778, which introduced many French ideas to this country. Isolation did not prevent a sympathetic reading among Vermont settlers of Thomas Paine's *Age of Reason,* issued between 1794 and 1796, which questioned the authenticity of the Bible while affirming a belief in God and in a hereafter and pleaded for a universal religion of humanity outside of sectarian limits and church control. Against the atheism of certain of the French revolutionaries, however, Paine offered his philosophy of deism. Vermonters had only recently read the deistic book of their late neighbor, Ethan Allen, who had published *Reason, the Only Oracle of Man* in 1784. Masonic literature, the Jacobin clubs of the eastern states, and the rationalistic society of the Bavarian Illuminati, which had influenced Paine, also affected liberal religion in this country. The orthodox could only hope that the Reign of Infidelity of the 1790's, so evident in the colleges, might presage the Second Coming of Christ. Preachers at that time were never certain of a dignified reception along the frontier, where agnostics and atheists sometimes styled themselves "nullifidians." Baptist and Methodist membership along the eastern seaboard fell off. In Virginia, Chief Justice John Marshall thought that the Episcopal Church was "too far gone to be revived."

In Louisiana the French leaders responded to the influence of Paris, buying books by Voltaire, Diderot, Rousseau, Buffon, and Montesquieu. One Protestant minister, visiting St. Louis in 1818, asserted flatly that "every Frenchman with whom I formed an acquaintance, of any intelligence and influence, was of the school of French Liberalism—an infidel to all Bible Christianity." Even among the humble *habitants* there were obvious signs of religious indifference. One visiting priest reported a comment of a St. Louis citizen during the Catholic revival in Missouri, "If Bishop Du Bourg had not come in time to our relief, the last spark of faith would have been extinguished in our country." By 1830, the reaction against eighteenth-century rationalism and deism had set in on both sides of the Atlantic.

The Second Awakening obviously drew much of its inspiration and techniques from the first Awakening when Jonathan Edwards, George Whitefield, and the Tennant family popularized the idea of the induced conversion, which, in effect, made salvation available to all men of good will. Liberal Arminian ideas emphasized free will instead of Calvinist predestination and encouraged religious democracy in the form of Freewill Baptists, Methodists, and Universalists —the latter designated the "poor man's Unitarianism" because of its promise of salvation to all men and its popularity among unlettered folk. Once the prestige of the French Revolution and rationalism was shattered by the romantic reaction following the Reign of Terror, all that was lacking was a spark to revive crusading evangelism, which taught the idea of an intimate Saviour and the certainty of salvation through repentance and faith. To the isolated families along the frontier the birth of the camp meeting through the Second Awakening meant a much-needed social outlet and a new contagious form of excitement as well as a purely religious experience.

The cradle of the camp meeting was shaped during the late 1790's in Logan County, Kentucky, by a Scotch-Irish Presbyterian preacher, James McGready, who left North Carolina, already a raucous, shouting preacher, indifferent to the restraints of his church, which still taught that predestination alone opened the way to salvation. Fascinated crowds, unable to return to the routine of the farm, came back with their wagons filled with bedding and cooked victuals, prepared to stay for days. Logan County, notorious for its Rogues Harbor of escaped cutthroats and thieves, was palpably shaken as the converted swore off crime, blasphemy, Sabbath-breaking, and crude methods of fighting, such as gouging out each other's eyes. The camp meeting idea developed rapidly, spreading at first along the banks of the Cumberland in Kentucky and Tennessee, and shouting preachers became the vogue after the exciting summer revivals of 1800. However, the Calvinistic Presbyterians shook their heads at McGready's meddling with predestination and allowed the primitive Methodist and Baptist exhorters to gather a rich harvest of souls.

In the famous Cain Ridge meeting of 1801 in Bourbon County, Kentucky, ten to twenty-five thousand people came equipped to stay a week. At night, while torches and campfires cast a mystical spell over the multitude, a powerful chorus sang the stirring hymns of Watt and Hart. Three preachers of the Baptist, Methodist, and Presbyterian sects took turns in denouncing sin, provoking sobs and shrieks. Hysterical, spasmodic laughs—euphemistically called the "religious laugh"—broke out; spasms, jerking and rolling of the body, fainting, dancing, and even barking by the possessed who "treed the devil" distinguished the Cain Ridge and other of the more successful meetings. Even the well-dressed, including some who had merely come for the excitement, "took the jerks." Awed crowds watched impulsive women with their long hair flying in the wind dance wildly, shrieking above the cries of the men, seemingly oblivious of their surroundings. Those affected might lie motionless for hours, breathing with difficulty, staring at mystical visions, and then, awaking, might turn from moods of black despair to exaltation—and then back again.

The Cumberland revival captured the frontier. Even the Connecticut Congregationalists who had moved to Vermont were affected despite their Calvinism; one Vermont county experienced twelve definite revival periods during the first decade of the century. Universalism, tainted with rationalist ideas, "was almost driven from the land," wrote Peter Cartwright, the Methodist exhorter. Here was the beginning of the "old-time religion" that persisted, especially in southern rural areas, well into the twentieth century, acting as a conservative check upon the social gospel of the more rationalistic cults. From the Vermont frontier across northern

New York blazed the "burnt district" of revivalists and wild cultists who inspired new churches and "isms" of astonishing varieties.

Methodist, Baptist, and later Presbyterian churches also were overwhelmed by hundreds of thousands of converts during the next decades. Bishop Francis Asbury, much of whose life was spent in the saddle, rode over 300,000 miles, organizing the Methodist faithful in the West and the South through a circuit system of traveling preachers devised by John Wesley himself. Laymen with an "exhorter's license" rode through vast circuits, sometimes hampered by the attacks of rowdies or unappreciative Yankees who disliked shouting, illiterate preachers. Baptists, too, used the lay preacher who was appointed to "exercise his gifts" and was poorly paid for them.

None wrestled for souls more strenuously than the tempestuous Methodist circuit rider, Peter Cartwright. Converted to a burning evangelism in the Cumberland revival, he shouted down miserable sinners for hours at a time in the backwoods of Kentucky and Tennessee; in 1824, he transferred his gifts to Illinois, finally entering the rough and tumble of frontier politics, even running for Congress in 1846 against the successful Lincoln. His frank *Autobiography* boasts of his bare educational attainments, his freedom from "the high toned doctrines of Calvinism," and his heaven-sent skill in inducing the jerks. "I always looked upon the jerks as a judgment from God," he insisted, though he observed one drunken sinner snap his neck fatally in a violent display of the jerks. He saved hundreds from the "blasphemous Shakers" and the "diabolical Mormons" and outdid the stiff-necked Calvinists. "The Predestinarians of almost all sorts put forth a mighty effort to stop the work of God," he recalled complacently.

In a Kentucky Presbyterian schism certain of the seceders joined the rapidly growing Shaker sects of Ohio. This celibate sect had originated in eighteenth-century England under the sponsorship of Quakers and the leadership of "Mother" Ann Lee as "The United Society of Believers in Christ's Second Appearing"; its members were called the Shaking Quakers because of certain peculiar rhythms characteristic of their ritual dances. Mother Ann Lee, daughter of a poor English blacksmith, stressed the sinfulness of sex; this conviction was intensified in her by an unhappy, forced marriage and by the death of her infants. Influenced by her own torturous dreams, she became attracted to a French pietist group in England of "shaking Quakers," called Prophets, who preached the Second Coming of Christ and urged a return to primitive Christianity. She took up these doctrines, elaborated them to include celibacy, the equality of the sexes, the principle that she was the feminine incarnation of Christ, the public confession of sins, the virtues of humility and charity, and the Bible as the source of faith. Persecuted in England, where she was arrested for violent preaching on the Sabbath, she emigrated with eight followers to New York in 1774 and settled near Albany where she drew many followers in the "burnt district," especially among the revivalist Baptists. She died a decade later, her church securely established.

By 1800, there were twelve Shaker communities, most of which quickly spread into the West, into Ohio, Indiana, and Kentucky. The Shakers, like other millennial sects, taught the Universalist ideal of salvation for all and a mission to gather the elect and to save all sinners. To offset the practice of celibacy they increased their numbers through converts and the adoption of orphans. In the spirit of primitive Christian communism, so they believed, they set up villages in which they collectivized property and achieved an admirable and prosperous regime based on careful farming and craftsmanship in cabinetmaking, weaving, and farm industries under a self-perpetuating theocracy. The religious advantage of maintaining these isolated communities was to preserve their orthodoxy against the secularism and temptations of the outside world. Curious visitors, freely permitted at one time, thronged to gape at the Shaker ritualist dances, accompanied by rhythmic handclapping and the singing of revival songs. So rapidly did the sect grow that by the end of this era there were five thousand members scattered over twenty communities in seven states, including the original New England and New York centers.

Another of these Utopian community faiths was that of the pietistic Rappites. In 1805, George Rapp, a Württemberg pietist who had rebelled against the rationalist tenets of German Lutheranism, came to Pennsylvania to build a millennial Christian communistic society for his 600 followers, mostly laborers. Annoyed by unsympathetic neighbors, Rapp moved on in 1814 to Indiana to set up Harmony for his German followers under his ministry and autocratic rule. The beautiful setting on the banks of the Wabash was enhanced by Rapp's botanical pleasure garden, arranged according to the scientific Linnaean system, his huge flock of scientifically bred sheep, and the neat orchards of grafted fruit trees. Girls sang while they worked at their spinning jennies and a band played religious tunes. High German ideals of craftsmanship animated the farmers, the smiths, the weavers, the tailors, the shoemakers, and others who lived in this paradise. But in 1825, for various reasons, they decided to sell their holdings to another Utopian—this time a secular Socialist, Robert Owen, the English manufacturer who built New Harmony. As for the Rappites, they began anew at Economy, near Pittsburgh, until schisms and the death of Rapp split their ranks and left only fragmentary societies, which, however, outlived the century.

Another German pietist group founded by William Otterbein, a German reformed minister, and Martin Boehm, a Mennonite preacher, was organized in Maryland and Pennsylvania in the fateful revivalist year 1800 as the United Brethren in Christ. "We are brethren," was the greeting of these evangelical folk who believed in the "inner experience" and the attainability of salvation through personal goodness. In the West they found a ready response to their doctrines, which quickly spread through Ohio, Indiana, and Illinois among the German-speaking settlers.

American Catholics, under the statesmanlike leadership of John Carroll, recovered from the losses due to French rationalism and the conflicting claims of English, French, and Irish Catholics to exclusive hegemony over the Church. They gained numerous communicants in the West, especially among French refugees and Louisianans. The Jesuits, dissolved in 1767, were revived and rose in prestige in the battle against secularism. Father Carroll founded Georgetown University, the first Catholic college and a pillar of the faith in 1789. The following year, in deference to the Maryland clergy and the flourishing state of the Church, the Pope permitted the Americans to choose Father Carroll as their first bishop, administering from Baltimore a diocese consisting of the entire United States. By 1808, the scattered Catholics in Kentucky, Tennessee, the Old Northwest, and the north trans-Mississippi area, were organized within a new diocese centering at Bardstown, Kentucky. That year Bishop Carroll was elevated to archbishop. A decade later, in response to further Catholic growth derived from annexation, Louisiana and the Floridas were detached to form a separate diocese and other areas in the Northwest were reorganized into new dioceses. Between 1789 and 1815 the Catholic population of 30,000 tripled, but the most sensational growth was yet to come with the influx of Irish and Bavarians in the 1840's and 1850's.

7

As with the Great Awakening of the 1740's, the task before the revivalists of 1800 was to recruit a learned clergy in the West—and even the extreme "holy sects" made some concessions to this aim, however grudgingly—and this, naturally, stimulated the growth of colleges and other schools. Presbyterians and Congregationalists, particularly, who clung most tenaciously to the Calvinist ideal of an educated ministry, took the leadership over the Methodists and Baptists. The first college founded west of the Alleghenies was the Presbyterian-sponsored Transylvania College, which opened its doors in 1780 with a law school, a medical school—itself a unique achievement—and a general arts college. Jefferson Davis studied in this orthodox school with its intensive nine-hour day of study and daily prayers, acquiring a classical as well as religious education. Liberals seceded to form Centre College in 1823 at Danville, Kentucky. North of the Ohio, where the Presbyterian revival had taken on momentum, simple theological schools—"log colleges"—were built after the eighteenth-century New Jersey model of the Tennants. Congregationalists founded Marietta College in 1790 and gradually Baptists and Methodists sponsored small theological seminaries.

Below the college level, frontier education showed extreme diversity, most of it poor and largely supported by private sources. Southerners carried over the neighborhood "field school" of colonial days where a schoolhouse cabin on an abandoned piece of land was managed usually by a semi-literate schoolmaster meagerly paid by the pupils' parents. "There were some schools, so called," wrote Lincoln of his Indiana days, "but no qualification was ever required of a teacher beyond 'readin', writin', and cipherin' to the rule of three.'... There was absolutely nothing to excite ambition for education." Professor Everett Dick tells of the not-so-apocryphal schoolmaster candidate in Missouri who was asked by the board of trustees whether he taught the earth was round or flat. The candidate indicated that he had not considered this fine point, but offered to teach it either way. Upon this, the trustees were impressed and hired him, deciding, after consultation, that he teach that the world is flat.

Occasionally, an educational endowment on the English model might enable a fortunate town like Alton, Illinois, to provide a free-public school system. Girls' schools taught needlework and other domestic arts believed fitting for the circumscribed intellectual horizon of women. The wealthy, of course, had the choice of tutors and eastern schools for their boys. Squatters, on the other hand, forced to keep beyond the settled areas, left their children bereft of schooling and religious training; these happy-go-lucky illiterates developed, instead, a rich lore of superstition and sometimes a deadly facility with bowie knives. An influential religious and educational institution, the Sunday school, won ready acceptance throughout the nation and lessened the prevailing ignorance on the frontier, culminating in 1824 in the American Sunday School Union, which was formed to coordinate such education and to publish children's spelling and hymn books.

For those who could afford it there were hosts of pedagogical itinerants, prepared to teach almost anything from dancing to commercial and classical subjects. In a day before adequate dental and medical schools in the West there was every inducement to acquire professional status by apprenticing oneself to an itinerant dentist

or doctor. Likewise, law schools were too few for the demands of
the frontier and thousands of men like Lincoln rose in the profession after a brief office apprenticeship of "reading law."

8

With the opening of the trans-Mississippi West, American science,
particularly geography, geology, botany, and ornithology, made its
own distinctive contributions. President Jefferson, an ardent sponsor of science, sent off his private secretary, Merriwether Lewis,
with William Clark to explore the Louisiana Territory and the Columbia River Valley to the Pacific. During their journey of 1803-6
from St. Louis they sailed up the Missouri River to the Mandan
Indian villages near present-day Bismarck, North Dakota, a strategic trading point in the Great Plains. After wintering there, the expedition continued toward the Rocky Mountains and then down
the Columbia River to the ocean; thereafter, splitting into parties,
the two leaders explored the Yellowstone and then were reunited in
St. Louis. Their reports threw new light upon the Plains Indians,
particularly, and the geography, resources, and characteristics of
the upper Missouri Valley. Upon the treeless, open plains, they had
been appalled by the force of the wintry winds suggestive of the
blasts of the open sea. How could the frontiersman ever conquer the
Great Plains?

   In this historic phase of marking trails across the Far West, another of Jefferson's official explorers, Zebulon M. Pike, also left St.
Louis in 1806 for the Great Plains, ascending to the source of the
Arkansas River and then south into the Spanish-occupied valley of
the Rio Grande. Although arrested as an interloper by the Spanish
and escorted back to Louisiana by way of northern Mexico, he had
much to report upon the discouraging semi-arid deserts. This er-
roneous notion of a Great American Desert held by Pike and the
Spaniards, who had preferred to remain on the periphery of the
Great Plains, was given further official sanction by the Stephen H.
Long Expedition of 1819-20. Long had followed the Platte River to
the present site of Denver and then had moved south to the Arkan-

sas and Canadian rivers. Like the others, he saw thousands of buffalo, the hostile nomadic Indians, elusive on their swift horses, the
sandstorms, and the treacherous quicksands. Above all, the scarcity
of water—averaging less than twenty inches annually—depressed
him. "In regard to this extensive section of country," he wrote, "I do
not hesitate in giving the opinion that it is almost wholly unfit for
cultivation, and of course uninhabitable by a people depending
upon agriculture for their subsistence." He conceded the value of
the Great Plains as a barrier against the dispersal of population
westward to the detriment of the East. At Washington, President
Monroe apparently agreed, writing off the Great American Desert
as a national asset save for its use as a giant Indian reservation.

Jefferson, himself, keenly interested in fossils and other prehistoric evidences, stuffed a room of the White House with ancient
bones discovered at Big Bone Lick, Kentucky. He sent zoological
specimens gathered by the Lewis and Clark Expedition to the versatile artist and showman, Charles Willson Peale, who had opened
his popular Philadelphia museum with awesome relics of prehistoric
monsters. Scientific speculation grew with the discoveries of ancient
mastodons and other huge survivals of a forgotten past. In a limestone cavern of Tennessee curious visitors gazed at two pygmy-size
Indian bodies in an excellent state of preservation. Frequent discoveries were made, upon the Cahokia prairie of Illinois and elsewhere in the Northwest, of the silver and copper ornaments and
elaborate funerary pottery once belonging to the ancient mound
dwellers of this region.

The "father of American ornithology" was a Scottish poet, Alex-
ander Wilson. He had been influenced by his friendship with the
botanist William Bartram of Philadelphia, whose extensive Bartram
Gardens in Pennsylvania attracted foreign botanists and travelers.
Bartram's description of nature awakened the enthusiasm of the
European romanticists, influencing Coleridge's *Ancient Mariner*,
Wordsworth's poems of nature, and Chateaubriand's *Les Natchez*.
Wilson was encouraged by Jefferson whose scientific adventures
were necessarily vicarious. He explored the great West as he moved
down the Ohio and the Mississippi to New Orleans, traversed the

unbroken forests, and as he went along, crammed his pockets with
the skins of birds. His restlessness led him in 1804 to walk for two
months through the wilderness snows to Niagara, and on another
occasion to ride on horseback from New Orleans to Florida, playing
his flute for diversion. In 1813, the year of his death, Wilson published the seventh volume of his epochal *American Ornithology*.
Although his anatomy and taxonomy tended to be somewhat more
poetic than precise, his descriptions were superior to those of his
contemporaries on either side of the Atlantic. He expanded William
Bartram's list of 215 native birds to 278.

While the achievements of Wilson have been almost forgotten,
Americans have immortalized his disciple, John James Audubon.
John James was born in Haiti in 1785 of a wealthy French planter
and merchant who had fought at Yorktown against Cornwallis, but
who lost his Haitian properties in the Toussaint L'Ouverture revolution which took the life of John's mother. Young Audubon was
trained in drawing, geography, mathematics, and the violin, but preferred to remain outdoors as an amateur naturalist. After a visit to
France and a brief career as a dandy, he settled for a short time
on his father's Pennsylvania estate and then, bereft of his fortune,
he moved westward along the Ohio, hunting and fishing with his
elderly friend Daniel Boone, and peddling. In French-speaking
Ste. Genevieve he turned store merchant, but his idling in drawing
pictures of birds disquieted his practical Creole neighbors and lost
him his business. He read Buffon, the leading French naturalist,
learned to classify birds, and, influenced by Wilson in 1810, decided to prepare his drawings for publication. Meanwhile, he
earned a livelihood in the then popular art of crayon portraits, as
well as in oil paintings; he taught dancing, stuffed birds for a museum, and gave children lessons in drawing in Cincinnati and New
Orleans. He returned to Philadelphia and studied painting with
Thomas Sully and Rembrandt Peale. Naturalists scoffed at the
handsome youth, insisting that he might be an artist but certainly
no naturalist.

On a trip to London and Edinburgh, he found a venturesome
publisher for his gigantic folio, *Birds of America*, which combined

art and extensive knowledge of frontier American backgrounds. He recorded 509 species of which 473 are now recognized, going beyond Wilson's achievement in this respect. The descriptions he offered were in the form of episodes but were original and fascinating; his drawings of birds usually showed painstaking care though marred by "poetic license" in technical aspects. *Birds of America* appeared in parts between 1827 and 1838 and has been praised as "the greatest tribute ever paid by art to science." Whatever Audubon's technical shortcomings were he made ornithology a tremendously popular and inspiring subject for generations of Americans and induced many to become ornithologists. By the end of the century disciples of Audubon were to organize Audubon societies to study "bird lore" and to protect wild life from extermination.

Magic and superstition made up much of the everyday science of frontier America. Miracle healers and local wizards, often inferior in technique to the better sort of Indian medicine men, followed the prescriptions of folklore to cure sick men and ailing animals in Lincoln's Indiana. To stop the hateful spells of witches, there was the trusty remedy of shooting the image of a witch with a silver ball. Omens of all kinds, such as the movements of the moon, freak animals, night shadows, and curious coincidences provided reliable guides to farming, soapmaking, and important daily decisions among rural folk. Lincoln, according to his law partner, Herndon, never wholly escaped the influence of his childhood folklore, remaining a fatalist at certain crises of his life. He visited a Voodoo fortuneteller in New Orleans in 1831, once tried to cure his son Robert of a rabies infection by turning to the virtues of a "mad-stone," and often pondered over the supernatural symbolism of his dreams. A rich cosmology, built of Christian and pagan elements, made formal religious practices seem too thin for the psychological needs of the unlettered frontiersman.

· 9 ·

The Northeast: Business and Society under the Astors and the Lowells

[1789-1830]

I

From the outbreak of the French Revolution in 1789 until the final crash of Waterloo the fate of America was partly determined by revolutionary France or embattled Britain. The French *bourgeoisie*, echoing the revolutionary slogans only recently invoked by their American brethren like the Adamses, Hancock, Franklin, and Jefferson, added fresh fuel to the fire of middle-class liberalism. Thousands of French refugees—by no means all aristocrats—expelled by successive factions who captured power at home, clustered largely in the eastern cities and influenced the culture and political activity of their adopted land. Jacobin clubs flourished in Philadelphia as well as in Paris, resembling the revolutionary committees of Sam Adams' day. American enthusiasts sang and danced the audacious sans culotte tunes such as "*Ça ira.*" In this local version of the war of all peoples against all kings, American champions of the French Revolution directed their attack against the allegedly monarchist followers of Alexander Hamilton, John Adams, and the pro-British federalist aristocrats. Orthodox religion and traditional political ideas in the colleges as well as in political parties were challenged by the implications of liberty, equality, and fraternity.

From the battles of 1792 until the defeat of Napoleon in 1815 with only brief periods of truce, France and England and their respective allies engaged in a world combat that inadvertently made the United States an ally of one side and then the other; first in the undeclared naval war with France in 1798-99, and second during the War of 1812 with Britain. Economically, we were no less directly affected. During the fat years of American neutrality, while Europe's farmers and laborers left their lands and trades for the battlefield, our exporting farmers prospered as never before and the eastern shipbuilders and men of commerce grew in wealth, for Europe's war needs gave the infant republic a solid form of nurture.

Not only did the shipowners, merchants, and their associates enrich themselves during the Napoleonic wars by supplying embattled Europe, but the fisheries, the whaling industry, and the Oriental trade opened up a new page in the prosperity of the maritime states. Boston, Salem, New York, and Philadelphia fought for a share of the rich and exotic Pacific trade.

In 1790 Captain Robert Gray and his vessel *Columbia* of Boston had opened the fur trade with the Northwest, thereby furnishing a profitable link with the trade of the Orient opened six years before by New York's *Empress of China*. Americans competed with Spaniards, Englishmen, Russians, and others to carry the sea otter's fur to Canton, port of entry for Chinese trade. Upper-class Chinese— and many Europeans too—reveled in the craze for the sea otter's glossy black skin which could shine with a rich silvery cast. Mandarins wore otter-skin robes while aristocratic ladies used this fur in capes, sashes, and trimmings for silk gowns. The Winships of Boston even arranged a deal with the powerful Russian American Fur Company, in return for half the profits, to use their supplies and to hire Aleutian Indian hunters provided by the Russians to catch the sea otter.

Boston registry dominated Pacific shipping but little Salem became famous for its intrepid captains, such as those employed by the very wealthy Elias Hasket Derby, who had inherited great means from the colonial West Indies and West African "triangular trade" and had amassed a second fortune by outfitting privateers during the Revolution. "King" Derby's *Grand Turk* had in 1786 opened the trade with the South Seas, especially with the island of Mauritius in the Indian Ocean. His ships established a trade route to Canton, Java, and other Far Eastern points with an outbound cargo of iron, salt fish, ale, soap, whale oil, and furniture. Profiting from a flourishing trade in pepper from Sumatra, the town of Salem became a world center for the distribution of this highly popular commodity, and when the bottom of the pepper market collapsed it drew upon Arabian coffee from Mocha to fill the gap. American sailors, at home upon the fast vessels developed by privateer needs during the Revolution (built without the cumbersome high quarterdecks), found adventure in distant islands like Hawaii and those of the South Seas by fighting unfriendly Polynesians. Far better off than their English compeers in this inhuman era of Captain Bligh and the *Bounty*, they enjoyed relatively high pay and tolerable conditions.

But Jefferson's Embargo of 1807 and the War of 1812 dealt a disastrous blow at least to our European commerce, curbing the American merchant marine and throwing thousands of sailors out of work. Then American capital and labor shifted to the nascent industries, potential heirs to an ever-growing domestic market. New England, which owned half of the nation's ships, escaped disaster by switching to industry. Many a flourishing seaport, like Salem, after the Lowells took hold in New England, settled down into a prosy cotton mill town. By 1831, New England's cotton mill products were valued at over $15,500,000 and her woolen goods rose to more than $11,000,000, impressive figures by early standards.

Before the industrialist captured power in New England, the glorious world of the merchant had seemed forever fixed. But Daniel Webster's political metamorphosis in Massachusetts from a belligerent States' rights man and an ardent free trader to an equally bellicose nationalist and tariff protectionist is revealing. This somersault merely reflected the basic shift of his state's economy from a trader's society, which loathed the burden of tariffs, to an industrial one, which thrived upon them.

No businessman eclipsed the hard-bitten John Jacob Astor in the swiftness and extent of his rise. This gifted German youth, who had arrived in New York City in 1784, was to amass a fortune in the continental fur trade and in real estate estimated at his death in 1848 at $20,000,000—perhaps the largest fortune in the world at that time. From peddling furs and musical instruments, he developed eventually an international fur business, extending at one time from New York across to the Pacific Northwest and China. According to his critical biographer, Parton, he held "the simple object of giving the least and getting the most," allowing his fur agents to intoxicate the Indians in order to dispossess them more easily. By 1800, he had already amassed a quarter of a million dollars as a merchant and fur trader; eight years later, he founded the American Fur Company, which not only wrested leadership from the powerful British Northwest Company, but after 1817 dominated most of the fur trade in the Great Lakes region and the Missouri Valley.

Astoria, a trading post at the mouth of the Columbia River, was intended as a keystone in Astor's world system of fur trading, but he had to sell it at a loss during the War of 1812. Then, however, he turned to even more profitable investments in real estate, especially in Manhattan, the Middle West, and Canada. During the war with England he joined with Stephen Girard in financing the nigh-desperate federal government—saving it at a fancy price and thereafter improving his influence at Washington. Thus, his fur representatives were able to defy federal agents, even to threaten with dismissal those who enforced inconvenient government regulations in the western trade. In 1816, for example, he was able to eliminate Canadian competitors by persuading Congress to exclude aliens from the fur trade, except as employees. As "the landlord of New York," as he (and particularly his son) was known, Astor proved to be an unyielding creditor. He was energetic and shrewd, aware of the opportunities that came with the British evacuation of the western fur-trading posts, and soon lifted himself from his lowly status in a squalid house to become a parvenu aristocrat in a Manhattan mansion, the friend of Washington Irving and the theater. Practically all of his vast wealth, except for the $400,000 Astor Library left to the city, was hoarded for his children.

Second only to Astor in renown, and far more philanthropic in outlook, was the former French sea captain, Stephen Girard, who had come to Philadelphia in 1776. Thoroughly familiar with the maritime markets, he first accumulated a fortune in shipping and trade; thereafter, attracted to banking, he moved into the building occupied by the defunct first Bank of the United States and became, like Astor, intimately involved in government financing during the second war with England. Girard's contribution to banking was an efficient and elaborate international credit system based on cooperative agreements with a host of small banks, the dominant English House of Baring, and the federal government.

With the end of the war, which demonstrated the need for a national bank, the Jeffersonians regretted their junking of the useful Bank of the United States, even though it had been created by their aristocratic enemy, Alexander Hamilton. The Administration allowed Girard to subscribe $3,000,000 to a second such bank, appointing him as a government director. Astor, who had been a leading lobbyist in Congress for the bank charter, became associated with Girard as a member of the board and as president of the New York branch. Before his death in 1831, Girard climaxed a lifetime of philanthropy as well as money-making by endowing an orphan school with $6,000,000, the nucleus of Girard College. Philadelphians also honored him for his heroic leadership in the terrible yellow fever epidemic of 1793, when he acted as hospital superintendent, bravely nursing the victims whose illness was killing off thousands.

2

These were also the early decades of the Industrial Revolution when textile machinery inventions, thriving on the infinite mass demand for cheap cotton cloth, altered the map of the world even more decisively than had the legions of Napoleon, Wellington, and Blücher. Southern cotton planters and their slaves, aided by Eli

Whitney's gin, fed the voracious English machines until New England textile competitors began to absorb a substantial part of the raw cotton output. By following the mercantilistic policy of jealously hoarding new machinery and skilled workmen, England tried to prevent industrial rivals from springing up elsewhere.

Hopeful American manufacturers were hampered not only by England's restrictions but also by the ban on European emigration arising from the desire to keep men of military age at home. Only five or six thousand immigrants came annually, rash souls who braved the typhus and "ship-fever" in the crowded, filthy steerage holds across the Atlantic. Most avoided the slave-dominated South, while the French refugees preferred Gallicized Philadelphia. In reply to the pleas, advertisements, and bounties offered by American state legislatures for experienced textile workmen and machinists, a significant, if small, vanguard appeared. Young Samuel Slater, destined to establish the American cotton industry along the new lines, brought his precious information regarding the textile machines of Arkwright, Hargreaves, and Crompton to the United States as he escaped to New York in 1789 in disguise. The following year he began his fruitful partnership with a leading Providence manufacturer, Moses Brown, who had thus far failed to set up a satisfactory spinning frame, because he lacked both skilled workmen and tools. In 1793, both men built the first American textile factory in Pawtucket, Rhode Island, to make sewing thread of fine cotton yarn. Five years later the firm of Samuel Slater and Company erected the first cotton mill near Pawtucket and was soon producing yarn-spinning machinery for other manufacturers as well. By 1827, as a rich textile manufacturer worth almost $700,000, Slater built the first steam mill at Providence.

Among the first mills to combine all textile operations were the Waltham plants of Francis C. Lowell, a Harvard-trained importer who had spied out the latest textile techniques of Lancashire. Aided by a talented mechanic and by the support of New England's rising merchant, Nathan Appleton, he introduced the power loom to America in his Waltham mills, in the year 1814. To protect his infant industry from foreign competition, he turned lobbyist, skillfully sponsoring the Tariff of 1816, then advocated by John C. Calhoun and William Lowndes of South Carolina. These Southerners, expressing the eager hope of Charleston to become a diversified industrial and commercial city, were, at that time, nationalists rather than States' rights men and therefore ready to raise duties on manufactured cotton in the Hamiltonian protectionist spirit.

Whether the tariff helped the new textile industry is dubious; certainly it did not prevent the textile depression of 1819. Nevertheless, along the fall line of the New England rivers which furnished power grew the bustling towns of Lowell, Fall River, and Waltham. Americans repaid their British benefactors by inventing labor-saving machinery of their own. Thus it happened that, in New England, whose rustic homespun had lent much reality to the ludicrous caricature of the Yankee with his awkward-shaped clothes, the technical perfection of standardized textiles took firm root. Capital poured in eventually from small shops, as well as from the wholesale transfer of wealth from commerce to manufacturing that accompanied and followed the Embargo and the War of 1812.

New industries, like woolen and iron manufactures, which followed the better entrenched cotton manufactures, suffered from the inevitable instability resulting from limited capital and labor, inexperience, uncertain markets, and violent business fluctuations. Victor Clark, historian of manufactures for this era, has concluded, "Unoccupied land drank up liquid capital as thirstily as a desert, and its call for labor was the primal command to human effort." Barter deals dominated in this era with the Lowell factories among the first to pay regularly in money rather than in kind; private fortunes were still too few for large-scale expansion; local depressions, often confined to a single industry, were caused by risky speculation, inefficiency, or shortages. Such were the early growing pains of American industry.

The tariff, according to the noted economist Taussig, contributed little to the solution of these problems; on the contrary, tariffs in the iron industry even encouraged producers to lag behind the efficient English processes by using obsolete machinery and antiquated methods rather than raise their costs by the purchase of new

machinery. Virtually unlimited resources, an expanding domestic
market, and intelligent leaders and workmen were far more significant in building industry than the tariffs that stirred up so much
commotion in the political world.

The spinning wheel and the hand loom stubbornly held out
against the advance of the machine in the self-sufficient homespun
world of early nineteenth-century America, especially in the West
and in rural New England; but the mill towns along the fall line
steadily altered the social structure. The four textile spinning factories of 1803 grew to sixty-two in 1809; three years later there were
fifty plants within thirty miles of Providence alone. Wealthy pater-
nalists, like Slater and Lowell, ruled with a mixture of benevolence
and severity over a newly recruited labor force. Slater borrowed
from England the family system of labor in which father, sons, and
daughters bound themselves as a unit to work at the mills for wages
varying in 1815 from $5 weekly for able-bodied men to 75¢ for
eight-year-old girls. In this way many poor families were able to
earn several times as much as they would have done in scratching
the soil of a small worn-out farm from dawn to dusk—though the
social environment of a mill town was scarcely an improvement
over the freer out-of-doors. A similar system obtained in Connecticut and western Massachusetts as well as in Slater's Rhode Island.
To Slater goes the credit for introducing the first Sunday school,
which was also borrowed from England, as well as for founding a
day school for his employees.

Lowell usually recruited his mill hands from the unmarried
farmers' daughters of New England. A girl of this class was often
eager to work for a wage in order to accumulate a dowry, to pay off
a burdensome mortgage, to support a needy family, or to "make
a gentleman" of a brother by earning enough for a college education. Occasionally, as Arthur W. Calhoun observes, "a woman with
a past" drifted into the idyllic community of sheltered females living
in company-owned and supervised boarding houses, and attending
company-built churches, libraries, and stores. However, Lowell's
girls worked only a few years before returning to the farm or marrying; by the end of the 1820's child labor was increasingly relied

on in New England and elsewhere to operate the prevailing twelve-
or thirteen-hour shift at the mills. While the long hours were a
familiar routine from farm days, there were the additional disturbing factors of confining factory discipline, unregulated working conditions, often dangerous to safety and health, and other problems.
A kindly employer like Lowell might mitigate these abuses by
paternalism but others would not. Fortunately, the American labor
situation was too favorable to bear a strong resemblance to the
startling industrial abuses revealed by parliamentary investigations
in the British Isles. American spokesmen of the new industrialism,
like Alexander Hamilton, defended child labor on moral grounds,
dwelling paternalistically upon the spiritual value of training "the
little innocents" to early and honest habits of industry.

Highly skilled artisans whose tasks were being absorbed by
machines competed at a decided disadvantage with the low-paid
women, children, and unskilled men in the factories. Although anti-
machine riots did not prevail, the mechanics organized trade unions, ignoring legal restrictions. It was apparent that the wage rate
for the unskilled was rising while pay for trained craftsmen was
not. In self-defense the relatively well-paid printers, shoemakers,
and carpenters united into local craft unions to exclude their unskilled competitors from certain tasks and to control prices wherever possible. Agitation centered around wages, working conditions,
and control over the number of apprentices. Sporadic strikes broke
out. Philadelphia cordwainers, as early at 1794, invoked the "closed
shop" by compelling employers to hire none but union members.
Organized printers in New York city even showed something of
"labor consciousness," for, as a militant spokesman insisted in 1817,
"The interests of the journeymen are separate and in some respects
opposite to those of the employers." Actually, the employer "class"
was not as yet separated by any wide economic gulf from their
workmen, for many an artisan worked for himself as well as for
others within the same week or even hired others to work for him.

Historically, such labor organizations seem to be a direct outgrowth of the medieval journeymen's guilds or societies. These
sprang up when the craft guild became a class-dominated society

under the thumbs of wealthy masters instead of remaining a relatively democratic institution where every apprentice might reasonably hope to become a master. The journeymen's societies and their successors retained the guild ideal of stabilizing wages and prices through collective action. They differed fundamentally, it is true, from the traditional guild, which accepted the organic religious principle that the local community as a whole, rather than any class alone, must regulate wages, prices, and other economic conditions There had been, then, a fear of individual or class monopoly that might create an artificial scarcity of goods or alter income distribution beyond that justified by each "according to his station."

Employers of the early industrial era, far from embracing the Adam Smith ideal of free competition, also organized into associations to control prices, to outlaw competitive advertising, and to check troublesome union men through the black list, which barred known organizers from local employment. The masters, championed by the conservative Federalists, invoked the old English common law, which treated combinations of men intent upon raising wages as criminal conspiracies in restraint of trade. Jeffersonian Democrats, on the other hand, refused to abide by this aspect of the common law, just as they had rejected certain other phases of the English legal tradition that seemed aristocratic. In the famous Philadelphia union case of 1806, involving the application of the common law to unions, the Jeffersonian defense counsel asked challengingly, "Shall all others, except the industrious mechanics, be allowed to meet and plot, merchants to determine their prices current, or settle the markets... and yet these poor men be indicted for combining against starvation?" In spite of this challenge, however, the defense lost the case; the federalist judge condemned both unions and strikes as illegal by the common law doctrines of "conspiracy" and "restraint of trade." In a Pittsburgh labor case of 1815 the closed shop, too, was specifically condemned. Successive conspiracy trials—six between 1806 and 1815—turned mostly against the unionists. Not until 1842, in the influential Massachusetts case of *Commonwealth v. Hunt,* did labor win legal recognition for the right to organize. Still left unsettled were the issues of the strike and the legality of the boycott weapon against employers' goods. Thereafter, the common law champions fell back on an attack upon certain methods of unionization as illegal by expanding the definition of coercion or intimidation.

3

The pace of immigration declined until the very end of this era when Irishmen and Germans fled the economic and political unrest in their native lands to build homes in America. Rural folk, like those from the stone-fenced New England farms where sheep-raising was displacing thousands of farm hands, moved to the towns looking for factory and commercial jobs. In 1800, only five towns had more than 10,000 people: Philadelphia led with 70,000, New York followed with 60,000, Boston trailed with 25,000, Charleston with 18,000, and Baltimore with 13,000. By 1830, New York alone was to exceed 200,000 inhabitants, becoming the chief city of the nation.

The Erie Canal, in 1825, had united the wheat, corn, lumber, fur, and mineral hinterland of the Great Lakes with the Hudson River towns and assured the primacy of New York city, although that metropolis had already shown the commercial advantages of a great natural harbor that would have led it to displace Philadelphia in any event. The canal came in time to divert the lumber and flour of western New York, then being rapidly settled, away from the St. Lawrence valley and toward the Hudson and New York city. One canal after another swiftly opened the interiors of Ohio, Indiana, and Illinois, joining them to the Great Lakes and adding to the resources of Manhattan. Thus the city's population soared to 123,000 in 1820 and 202,000 in 1830; by the latter year, its real estate was valued at $125,000,000 and its imports at $36,000,000.

The visitor of 1815 still felt the flavor of New Amsterdam as he walked along the streets and gazed at the high gable-end roofs and whitewashed houses and the Dutch farm village called Brooklyn. Streets tended to be narrow and crooked, as in Boston, though Broadway and some of the newer streets were straight, with broad walks and graceful trees. Wall Street was a center of both fashion and finance, where merchants gathered at the Tontine Coffee House, an American version of Lloyd's of London, to read shipping news and to drink coffee or liquor. Business houses were springing up along the East River of lower Manhattan. Since the turn of the century the city had been provided with drinking water by the Manhattan Company and sanitation was making some advances.

Ominously, however, the beginnings of New York's lower East Side slums had taken root in a half-dozen streets around Chatham Square, where poor German and Irish immigrants lived in cellars and crowded into single rooms in filthy ramshackle houses along unpaved walks. In these streets lay dead dogs, cats, and mice, while numerous swine, the chief scavengers as late as 1867, grunted noisily as they buried their snouts in the piles of refuse. Immigrant ships discharged their passengers at wharves within a stone's throw of the slums where pestilence wiped out hundreds of lives annually. Along these East Side streets white and Negro prostitutes were already plying their profession, at least by the 1790's. With the industrial era and with the increased immigration after 1815, the rudiments of the fetid tenement emerged, often a remodelled old Dutch rear house behind a former garden of tulips and cabbages, with wooden stories piled unsteadily upward to accommodate more newcomers. The traditional shell-paved walk between the main building and the rear house evolved into a noisome alley. Human mortality mounted swiftly; yellow fever epidemics in 1798 and 1803 carried away hundreds of victims and stirred a panic among the citizenry. In 1800, the city was protected by a night police force of seventy-two men, two captains, and two deputies, but there were no day police to restrain thieves and assassins.

Still, the city of John Jacob Astor, which was to inherit his $400,-000 library as a sizable part of the city library, had its attractive mansions, churches, and public buildings. Columbia College was emerging as an important institution. Fires spurred on this "Liverpool of America" to construct brick sidewalks with curbstones. The excellent harbor was developed through the work of almost the entire population, each able-bodied man being required to give a day's labor to this construction. During the French revolutionary years, when numerous refugees like Talleyrand lived in New York, the streets witnessed stirring processions of French Jacobins singing the "Marseillaise." Van Wyck Brooks, noting the Gallic influences upon New York in 1800, especially in the French boarding houses and cafés, the French hats, gowns, and scarves, adds this observation, "Meanwhile, the bogus count and baron were already a part of the picture, drawn by the gaiety and grace of the New York girls and the dollars that rose in fountains from their gullible fathers." On Sundays, thousands of New Yorkers descended like locusts upon Long Island to strip the eastern section of all fruit, the resentful cries of the farmers notwithstanding.

The Tammany Society, formed in 1786 from patriotic and revolutionary antecedents, was then in its relatively idealistic phase, although it went through a certain "realistic" education in the days of Aaron Burr; it tended to champion the popular cause by fighting for manhood suffrage and for the abolition of imprisonment for debt. Its namesake, Tammany, supposedly the Indian chief who signed the half-legendary Treaty under the Elms with William Penn, was generally admired as the patron saint of the nation, and a Tammany museum in his honor was set up at the City Hall.

Philadelphia, though bested by its Knickerbocker rival and no longer the nation's capital, was still regarded, in the late colonial period, as "the London of America." Still, it had other competitors: in the South, Baltimore benefiting by the National Road, absorbed a good part of the eastern and central Pennsylvania trade; in the West, young Pittsburgh had usurped the gateway to the Ohio Valley, and its forges attracted the iron ores and bituminous coals of western Pennsylvania. State legislators tried to help Philadelphia in 1800 with an extensive network of turnpikes and after the Erie Canal was built introduced an elaborate system of canals connecting the city with Pittsburgh and the northern interior. It never lost first place as the chief outlet of the eastern Pennsylvania farmers and a major Atlantic port.

Philadelphia merchants could boast that London's famed financiers, the Barings, had married daughters of their city and hence strengthened the economic ties between the two metropolises. As in the Franklin era, the city led in civic spirit and cooperative welfare projects, notably in health, sanitation, fire prevention, science, and in patronage of the arts. Besides the colleges and hospitals of Franklin's day, there was now the fascinating Peale Museum, which Charles Willson Peale, the versatile artist and taxidermist—America's first—had organized. Here one might see the latest geological, anthropological, and other discoveries of the Lewis and Clark expedition—a gift from Jefferson—rare animal species in realistic poses against a skillfully painted background, the mounted bones of fearful prehistoric monsters that had once inhabited the New World, and even Franklin's prized Angora cat from France.

With most of the French refugees preferring Philadelphia to other towns, the Quaker City, which was never actually very prim, became even more luxury-loving and gay. French styles and manners dominated the wardrobes and behavior of the well-to-do who promenaded along the fashionable tree-lined avenues. Nobles of Versailles taught fencing and dancing; expensive hairdressers of Paris prepared fancy wigs for the rich federalist politicians; and gay Frenchmen thrilled Quaker girls with their outdoor serenades. A Massachusetts girl, writing home about her stay in Philadelphia, wailed, "I have not one minute to spare from French music, balls, and plays. O dear, this dissipation will kill me." French pastry, cosmetics, shoes, and cabarets were among the current importations. The disease of "Gallomania" infected thousands. Louis Philippe, destined to rule France, held a miniature court of his devoted followers. Bankrupt French planters from revolutionary Haiti arrived to add to the Gallic invasion, supported by congressional funds and private charity.

Fleeing from English reaction during the French revolutionary era was the noted chemist and philosopher, Dr. Joseph Priestley, the discoverer of oxygen, who had been mobbed by Tories for his revolutionary sympathies. Arriving in 1794, he attempted an idyllic life in the nearly primitive wilderness along the Susquehanna and refused to give this up for a professorship of chemistry at the College of Philadelphia. Intellectuals, especially the newly arrived romantics, flocked to Bartram's Garden where the botanist William

Bartram, already famous on both sides of the ocean, entertained such distinguished visitors as the novelist Charles Brockden Brown and his circle.

Boston, reviving under its shipping, fishing, and industrial activities, evolved only slowly from its resemblance to an old-fashioned English country town. Rounded cobblestones paved its streets and sidewalks. Civic affairs were in the hands of parsimonious selectmen and in 1800 organized police were still lacking, only a few oil lamps guarding the foolhardy stranger traveling at night. The Lees, the Cabots, and the Lowells were moving in from the country, some of them advancing through annexed Tory property. State Street, then in the middle of Boston, was the mercantile center and commercial "exchange." A surprisingly elegant theater accommodating twelve hundred persons was erected in 1793 at a cost of $6000 despite hostile state laws. One might hear the "*Ça ira*" played by the orchestra, which occasionally bowed to the gallery by rendering "Yankee Doodle." The finest building was still King's Chapel, now belonging to the Unitarians, and nearby was the pleasant green park ascending from the sea, Boston Common. Among the attractive residences was the elaborate crescent-shaped Tontine with fourteen to sixteen mansions grouped together. To a British visitor there seemed to be a marked democratic spirit in popular manners and activities, especially at the taverns. "A man with the title of Major sometimes holds your horse," he noted, "and Captains are digging by the roadside; it is a vestige of the Revolution." Animated conversations and quick acquaintances were part of the American way, even in federalist Boston.

Born of a political deal to capture Southern votes for Hamilton's speculative bill transferring state debts to the federal government, the town of Washington along the Potomac had little to commend it when President Jefferson arrived—the first Chief Executive to move into the chosen capital city. In that miry "city of magnificent distances" and poor transportation, a mushroom growth of buildings, fed upon speculative hopes, came to an abrupt end during the second administration, leaving half-finished, crumbling houses for the unemployed workmen to take over. During the War of 1812 the British retaliated for the American burning of Canadian parliament buildings by burning the Capitol and the White House.

In the capital city the French Revolution and simple Jeffersonianism altered the aristocratic ways of the federalist rulers in New York and Philadelphia. From the revolutionary sans-culotte of Paris came the workmen's style of pantaloons to replace knee breeches among the well-to-do. James Monroe was the last of the presidents to cling to the genteel knee breeches, silk stockings, silver buckles, and queue. At the White House, Jefferson dropped the frequent and formal federalist balls and their stiff etiquette for occasional and less restricted dinners and receptions, while the pleasure-loving Dolly Madison pleased western Democrats with the spontaneous spirit of her dances and musicals.

Most promising in the history of city planning was the revival of the tradition of Sir Christopher Wren, builder of London, through George Washington's protégé, a French army engineer and architect serving in the American Revolutionary army, Major Pierre Charles L'Enfant. His plan for a city of streets radiating from the capital center may have been influenced by one of Wren's rejected models for the rebuilt city of London; in buildings, L'Enfant sought to follow the advice of Jefferson and to substitute an American version of the classic for the English influences, now under a cloud among patriots. Others were to carry out L'Enfant's plan. The originator was to die in poverty. When Benjamin H. Latrobe, the architect, visited Washington in 1806, he commented bitterly at the ruin left by speculators, "Daily through the city stalks the picture of famine, L'Enfant and his dog."

Especially hopeful of the future was nearby Baltimore, the outlet for the products of south central New York, western Pennsylvania, and Virginia, as well as of the immediate Chesapeake vicinity. Its natural harbor on the bay was admired by George Washington who confidently predicted that it would be "the risingest town in America, except the federal city." He also believed that Philadelphia would decline because of its navigation handicaps while New York, because of its extremely fine harbor, would always be commercially important. In American Revolutionary days Baltimore's fleet of daring privateers had won distinction in their forays on English shipping and now its gleaming clipper ships revived its nautical reputation.

Like Philadelphia, the city was proud of its spacious, well-planned rectangular streets lighted by traditional English lanterns. In 1816, at a time when American streets were generally unsafe at night, Baltimore took the lead in introducing gas lighting despite a good deal of popular distrust regarding its safety. That year Baltimore's citizens had been dazzled by the spectacular gas lights of Rembrandt Peale's museum; and the city council had then decided to follow the vogue of Europe where the discovery of gas made from coal had begun to revolutionize urban lighting. This example was promptly followed by other American cities for both streets and public buildings, though fears of explosions delayed the general adoption of gas lighting for homes until after the Civil War.

4

Recreation in America reflected the growing sophistication of town life, the increasing wealth of the country, and the gay French influence. More pretentious theaters and appreciative audiences in the West as well as in the East attracted such talented English players as Joseph Jefferson the comedian and Junius Brutus Booth the tragedian.

Jefferson, who was strikingly similar in appearance as well as republican sympathies to his famous American namesake, came to Boston's new Federal Theatre in 1795. Finding the Boston theater unprosperous, he moved on first to New York and then to Philadelphia. He originated an effective role as a humorous and kindly interpreter of old men and became the pillar of the Quaker city's Chestnut Street Theatre, newly resplendent with gas lighting in 1816. A member of a family of actors, he trained seven of his eight sons for the stage, and a grandson named after him even eclipsed his reputation as an actor.

Related to the radical—and erratic—Wilkes family was the temperamental and handsome Englishman, Junius Brutus Booth, who had once tried to run way to join the American Revolutionists and had actually gone as far as Paris. So great were his talents as a realistic tragedian—he even played Shylock with a convincing Jewish accent—that he was hailed while in England as the peer of the great Edmund Kean. In 1821, he toured the leading theatrical cities both North and South, impressing audiences with his gamut of emotional expression especially in Shakespearian roles. Never repressing his feelings, he could, and did on occasion, step out of his role to utter his contempt for stolid American audiences. Ten years after his arrival he became manager of Baltimore's Adelphi Theatre, where he introduced many talented English actors to the American stage.

Surviving heir of the eighteenth-century classical school of passionless declamation was the aging Lewis Hallam, who tried pathetically to retain his favorite role against the rivalry of the popular and younger romantic actors. His oft-repeated "last and only performance" at Philadelphia in 1806-8 barred him from the dignity of a graceful exit. His versatile partner, William Dunlap, continued to manage the Old American Company, translated some thirty French and German successes for the American stage, and even wrote about the same number of original plays himself. Author of an interesting *History of the American Theatre,* he earned from a later generation the title of "father of the American drama." His versatility included a moderate talent as a portraitist and miniaturist, as a magazine editor, and as a writer of the early Gothic plays of terror. He wrote a novel, a biography of Charles Brockden Brown, history textbooks, and temperance tracts. Dunlap's enthusiasm and competence almost made up for certain failings in creative genius. Crowds in New York and elsewhere in the latter 1820's were fascinated by Dunlap's "Eidophusicon" or moving diorama, a sort of travelogue that used 250,000 square feet of canvas to picture the Hudson Valley in a rapid succession of scenes.

Emerging from the Southern plantation, where the slaves blended Africanisms with native music, came the minstrel tradition to the eastern cities. Negro singers accompanied by banjo strumming were familiar sights in post-Revolutionary streets; in Boston, for example,

Negroes sometimes appeared on the stage. An occasional white comedian, aware of the ludicrous in the stereotypes of the shiftless black, fond of chicken, watermelon, and long words, introduced the blackface part. But the great age of the minstrel belongs to the succeeding decades, though the whites were already familiar with the shuffling steps, jig dances, and river songs that became basic ingredients of the minstrel show of the 1840's.

For both town and country, itinerant entertainers formed the chief staple of commercial recreation. Salem citizens, for example, had the opportunity at various times to witness the feats of magicians, ventriloquists, operators of Punch and Judy shows, fencing masters, and exhibitors of panoramas, kaleidoscopes, and grim waxwork figures. Townsmen might even go up in M. Blanchard's captive balloon, the new sensational French invention. An enterprising New York sea captain put an elephant on exhibition in various cities and villages; others displayed trained monkeys, acting dogs, or wrestling bears. Even in rural Pennsylvania, countryfolk could gape at life-size automatons representing a French aristocrat and a sans-culotte, cleverly contrived through inner springs to dance and to battle each other.

5

Until the turnpike era was well established, cities were tied together only loosely through such roads and paths as there were. In 1800, it required three days to go from Boston to New York by stage coach. Philadelphians needed sixteen days to reach Lexington, Kentucky, and twenty-two for Nashville, Tennessee. Beyond the Potomac, roads were far worse or simply nonexistent. To make matters worse many eastern rivers could not be crossed by bridge. Dignified judges of the Supreme Court, traveling within their local circuits to dispense justice in traditional style, were severely jolted on rough, unpredictable roads, or even thrown bodily into the mud or snow. Little wonder that they rebelled against a post that exposed them to such dangers and indignities.

City merchants found a partial solution for bad roads, especially in sparsely populated regions where local funds were lacking. This was in the turnpike movement, beginning slowly after the Revolution when private corporations financed the building of better roads through fees collected at toll gates. By 1825, the eastern cities were closely bound by a network of turnpike roads, including major links with the West, such as the well-known Albany-Buffalo road. Droves of horses, cattle, hogs, and sheep sometimes shared the turnpike with crowded stagecoaches, carrying from eight to fourteen passengers and an indefinite amount of baggage. By 1830 the influence of the Scottish engineer, John McAdam, affected a large part of American transportation; "macadamized" roads firmly built of small stones and a solid roadbed assured stable and properly-drained surfaces for the swelling traffic of vehicles.

Even on the best routes, such as the main road between Philadelphia and Baltimore, the traveler had to put up with packed, uncomfortable, and filthy inns. One visitor, inquiring innocently of an innkeeper whether lodgings were available, heard these reassuring words, "Don't trouble yourself about that. I have no less than eleven beds in one room alone." This appeared no exceptional experience. A fastidious New York State innkeeper put up this sign, "No more than five to sleep in one bed. No boots to be worn in bed." The dawn of a better day came after 1790 when the French introduced the more commodious "hotel" idea, which spread throughout the more populated centers. For the well-to-do in New York city there was the fashionable City Hotel, built in 1793, which replaced the historic Fraunces Tavern (formerly the De Lancey Mansion) patronized by Washington.

6

Religious life in the East, especially in the 1790's, continued to feel the strong classical influence of eighteenth-century French rationalism until overwhelmed by the romantic reaction that followed the French Revolution. More than in the West, rationalism in the East swept the colleges. Masonic literature, which broke with religious traditionalism, infiltrated the cities and towns, even the frontier settlements, and Thomas Paine's *Age of Reason*, far more than his *Rights of Man,* aroused a sensation. Sabbath-day observances declined. In 1805, over the bitter opposition of the Yale-bred minister and geographer, Jedidiah Morse, and the Congregationalists, the rationalistic Unitarians managed to make one of their members, Henry Ware, the occupant of the pivotal Hollis professorship of divinity at Harvard. This controversy hastened the secession of liberal Congregationalists into an independent Unitarian church.

Outstanding among the Congregationalist ministers of Boston who were turning away from orthodox Calvinistic dogmas was "the apostle of Unitarianism," the gentle William Ellery Channing, an active humanitarian as well as religious leader. A Platonic idealist of the newer romantic current rather than a strict rationalist or Lockean empiricist of the classical eighteenth century, he stressed pietist ideas and the general benevolence and idealism of Christianity. "I always write the words Right, Love, Idea, etc., with a capital letter," he asserted in affirming his indebtedness to Plato. Reared for a time in the liberal atmosphere of Jefferson's Virginia in its Jacobin days, he had reacted against traditionalist doctrines based on man's depravity. He was influenced by both the moral liberalism of the Edinburgh Enlightenment and the new German idealism that he discovered through the writings of Madame de Stael. With the other romantics of the pietist tradition, Channing spoke and wrote exalting the religion of the heart above the limited empire of the intellect, and taught a benevolent doctrine of man's natural potentialities for goodness and perhaps perfection. Aided by Channing's exposition of Unitarianism, which rejected Trinitarianism for the doctrine of God in a single person and taught universal salvation and a tolerance of dogmatic differences, the new American Unitarian Association drew up its platform in 1825.

Allied in faith and activities with the Unitarians were the Universalists, the common man's simplified version of Channing's teachings. The first Universalist church in this country was founded in Gloucester, Massachusetts, in 1780 by the Reverend John Murray of London. He managed to convince suspicious patriot neighbors that he was not an English spy and taught that God's divine grace would save every person from sin. His associate and successor,

Hosea Ballou, preached in 1791 that Jesus was a man and that a good God would not consign frail mankind to damnation. Ballou gave the Universalists their basic organization, wrote prolifically on religion, and founded the *Universalist Magazine* in 1819.

Against the current of rationalism and the newer heretical doctrines came the Second Awakening at the opening of the century, reinforced later by the post-Napoleonic conservative and romantic reaction on both sides of the Atlantic. At Yale, which led all other colleges in enrollment, the grandson of Jonathan Edwards, President Timothy Dwight, led an effective war during his twenty-one year rule against deism, materialism, Jeffersonian and foreign radicalism, and the French ideas of his scholarly but tainted predecessor, Ezra Stiles. For a time dancing, plays, and other college frivolities gave way to Calvinist austerity. Foreign professors were suspect to Dwight; when he found no trained American available for a professorship of chemistry, he decided to train a promising Yale law student for the position, Benjamin Silliman, who turned out to be a surprisingly good choice. Religious conservatism spread from Yale to Dartmouth, Williams, and Amherst, and was reinforced by the new theological colleges founded after the Second Great Awakening. The evangelical fervor of the Methodist revival stirred up the New England advocates of the old-time religion and halted the inroads of rationalism, while a home missions program helped the orthodox to recover lost ground.

Another prop for orthodoxy was the tractarian movement, originating with the gifted Hannah More of London in 1795. By 1807, it had been firmly established in Dwight's Connecticut and had spread into the South and West, where its orthodox doctrine and strict morality were planted in fertile soil. From England, too, as already noted, Samuel Slater the industrialist borrowed the educational example of the pin factories where the Sunday school flourished and transplanted this instrument of orthodoxy among New England's mill families. Shortly afterwards, under Lyman Beecher, father of the famous Harriet, the Sunday school became a vital adjunct to the church.

By the 1820's the orthodox movement, which drew the mighty support of economic conservatives in politics, was spearheaded by a concentrated demand for laws to enforce the Sabbath. New England states forbade the transaction of business, unnecessary travel, or public entertainment on the Sabbath; so did many a state in the South and West. Numerous petitions descended upon Congress, demanding that federal laws halt the mails on Sunday. Railroad companies yielded to a large extent in the succeeding decades by stopping their cars on the Sabbath. Conservatives hoped that this new orthodoxy might stem the radical economic panaceas and "isms" that came in the era of Jacksonian democracy.

Under Bishop Asbury's guidance free Negroes of the North took a major step in 1799 toward a separate church in which their own evangelical variations of the services could develop unhampered. This was the foundation by an ex-slave of the Bethel African Methodist Episcopal Church in Philadelphia. Branches elsewhere in the Cotton Kingdom grew so rapidly that an interchurch union became necessary. Likewise within the Baptist church Negroes withdrew to organize the Abyssinian Baptist Church.

Evangelical religion in at least one major respect democratized America. By multiplying the number and size of sects, it inspired a powerful coalition of dissenting groups, which challenged the power of the established Congregational Church of Massachusetts, Connecticut, and New Hampshire. Behind the official church to which all taxpayers owed support were the federalist conservatives and many from the well-to-do classes. Liberal republicans, tainted with French rationalism, would have been unable to separate church and state without the aid of the Baptists and the Methodists, as well as the Episcopalians. Thus it happened that New Hampshire disestablished the Congregational Church, routing the Federalists shortly after the War of 1812. Connecticut followed a few years later, though in Massachusetts, where the conservatives fought a clever delaying action, separation of church and state had to wait until 1833. Elsewhere, in frontier Maine and Vermont, dissenting sects and small-farm democracy were too strong for aristocratic

Calvinism or any other officially established faith to take hold. What was best in Puritanism, the crusading spirit in education and in social reconstruction, remained as a heritage to New England and to the West, which drew so many of its citizens from the land of John Cotton and Roger Williams.

· 10 ·

Culture in the East: From French Classicism to German Romanticism

[1789-1830]

I

EVERY historical period has its dominant pattern of ideas as well as a group of secondary or "recessive" patterns. The eighteenth-century world of Benjamin West, Madison, and Hamilton had been dominated by classical ideas derived from Greece and Rome, stressing perfection of form, universality, and pure reason. Man, being primarily a creature of reason and calculating selfishness, had to be controlled in the general interest by checks and balances, as Madison had argued, in order to achieve an equilibrium between interest groups or classes. Whatever Jefferson and other levelers had in mind, the oft-repeated classical dictum that men are created equal had been taken by practical men to mean little more than equality before the law—not intellectual, biological, economic, or social equality. Like the strict Calvinists whom they had supposedly pushed aside to set up a secular world, eighteenth-century American classicists looked upon man primarily as a lowly son of Adam because of the innate selfishness of human nature far more than as an exalted son of God. But classicism had been so long wedded to leisure class patronage that classical education had come to be widely regarded as the precious heritage of the elite, as learning for the few rather than for the many. This meant more academies, colleges, and universities for landlord and merchant families.

Infiltrating the dominant classicism of the American eighteenth century until it gained a complete victory in its own right in the era of Horace Mann was its "recessive" rival, romanticism. Professing to rediscover the emotions neglected by the Age of Reason, and thus bowing to the dominion of the heart rather than the head, the romantics looked upon man as endowed with a divine spark and infinitely plastic, regardless of social background, capable of perfection if given a favorable environment. It was the common man, of the frontier, the new factories and the small shops rather than the intellectual elite, who inspired them. Beginning with Horace Mann at the end of this era, the victorious romantics were to crusade for elementary and normal schools to serve the education of the masses rather than of the classes. The ideal of a missionary democracy spreading enlightenment among all mankind had been implicit in both the American and French revolutions and carried the obvious corollary of mass education. This era of 1789-1830 that saw the transition of American cultural life from the dominance of French classicism to the rule of German romanticism revealed in education as well as in other fields the conflict between a conservative type of classicism and a radical romanticism.

Next to environmentalism in reforming the schools was the influence of liberal nationalism. Not only was a new nation born whose leaders anxiously sought to stress its distinctiveness from England, but a revolutionary notion arose that Americans had a democratic mission to put down tyrants and decadent aristocrats everywhere. So thought Thomas Paine and Jefferson, thereby exalting the dignity of the state above the isolated individualism suggested in Locke's social compact. No one was to express these forces more clearly than Noah Webster, "schoolmaster to America" and a major architect of American nationalism.

Fittingly enough, Webster was a descendant of William Bradford of Plymouth, spent his youth in a rural Puritan household in West Hartford, Connecticut, volunteered to fight in the Revolution, was graduated from traditionalist Yale, and emerged as a schoolteacher, lawyer, and journalist. For a time he fell beneath the liberal influence of the French Revolution, but after the Terror he became critical of democracy and proclaimed ardent federalist ideas, especially after 1800. Still, he remained an environmentalist, believing that the school could indoctrinate the young American in principles of virtue and loyalty. Like Jefferson and other Americans he believed that youth could escape foreign vices and tastes by a good native training in improved schools. To him, American teachers, American textbooks, American publishers, and American travel were prime necessities. His nationalism assumed an isolationist and anti-foreign hue. Distrustful of classical education as a leisure-class product, he urged English translations instead of "dead languages" and called for more attention to vocational needs.

Out of Webster's early work of 1783-85, *The Grammatical Institute of the English Language,* evolved a series of influential spellers, readers, grammars, and finally after 1806 the famous dictionary that made "Webster" a part of the American vocabulary. His speller, like that of his popular English predecessor, Dilworth, whom he replaced, encouraged the teaching of the "a, b, c," method of learning to read instead of the word method. He introduced phonetic devices, campaigned against the colloquial use of "kiver," "chimbley," "bust," and "sparrowgrass," and popularized American history, Connecticut geography, and American folklore. His grammars tended to enslave future schoolchildren to a heavily formal study of language rather than to follow current usage. The moralistic Webster readers, forerunners of McGuffey's equally moralistic texts, were grist to the mill of amateur elocutionists in that age of patriotic and didactic oratory. The combined speller-readers proudly "taught millions to read and not one to sin" and made the "spelling bee" enormously popular as a social and educational pastime in elementary schoolhouses, as Eggleston's *The Hoosier Schoolmaster* of a later generation attests. Some 200,000 copies of the *Blue Black Spelling Book* were selling annually by 1807 and thirty years later Webster claimed to have disposed of 15,000,000 copies—an amazing total for a heavily rural nation whose population was less than

4,000,000 in 1790 and 12,866,020 in 1830. For countless Americans, Webster's speller was the first and final contact with "culture."

The successive dictionaries of 1806 to 1828 had the virtues of excellent definitions, marred, however, by inaccurate etymologies, and useful pronouncing features that helped standardize American speech. In the 1850's Southern nationalists like J. D. B. De Bow and George Fitzhugh were to war upon Webster's dictionary because its pronunciations were "Northern cockney," at variance with the correct speech spoken by Southerners. The dictionary furthered Webster's mission of fostering an American language as a distinctive organic growth. A champion of simplified English, he taught Americans—on somewhat arbitrary principles—to drop the "u" in honour, candour, errour, etc., while retaining it in serious, famous, and furious. He reversed the "re" in theatre, centre, lustre, and similar words, dropped the "k" in words like cubick, musick, and publick, and substituted s for c in offence, defence, and expence.

Webster became a staunch champion of nineteenth-century middle-class respectability, already evident in the euphemisms of the current sentimental novel. Girls were "betrayed," not seduced, breasts became "bosoms," legs, "limbs"; he buried many a harsh Anglo-Saxon word that was a staple in Shakespeare's vocabulary, including stink, womb, and spew.

Elementary-school education had to await Horace Mann and his generation for significant advances. As late as the 1830's the few public schools that existed were poorly supported and the burden rested individually upon parents, leaving the stigma of "charity pupils" on those who came from families who could not pay taxes or tuition. Massachusetts and Connecticut sought with only fair success to realize their ambitious colonial laws for compulsory tax-supported schools. New York, under the energetic Jeffersonian leadership of Governor De Witt Clinton, champion of popular education as well as builder of the Erie Canal, extended regular state subsidies for elementary school, but the conservative legislature blocked his demands for a state-wide normal school, a free high school, and an elementary system. As yet, the classical influence meant an emphasis on class, rather than mass, education.

While still mayor of New York city, Clinton had given his enthusiastic support to Joseph Lancaster's experiments in mass education which could meet the demand for inexpensive schooling in a
day when compulsory taxation for schools was stubbornly resisted
by the propertied classes. Lancaster's monitorial system, according
to its English founder, could educate poor children at a cost of a
dollar a year by employing a staff of the older and brighter pupils
to assist a head teacher in instructing as many as a thousand
children in a single classroom. Britain's Bible and missionary societies, handicapped by shortages of funds, were sponsoring these
experiments at home and abroad. In 1805, Clinton organized the
Free School Society to introduce the Lancastrian system in classrooms capable of seating five hundred pupils. Encouraged by such
influential sponsorship the movement spread and Lancaster, himself, came to Baltimore in 1818 to further his ideas. However, the
shortcomings of this semi-militarized system with its mechanical
disregard for the child's personality became patent by the end of
this era when the new Swiss ideas of informal individualized training espoused by Pestalozzi and Fellenberg liberalized popular
education.

Some indication of the growing challenge to the classical spirit
came in the 1820's with the birth of the free public high school as
a rival to the Greek-inspired academy. Although this classical institution had already yielded to the utilitarian spirit of the times
by adding practical subjects leading to technical and liberal professions, it remained too expensive and exclusive for any broad
program designed to help the common man. In 1821, Massachusetts,
already possessing twenty-six incorporated academies, took the lead
in introducing the first high school in Boston with a curriculum
that included "practical subjects." Within a few years, a girls' high
school, quickly filled by eager applicants, was added. Before the
decade ended, Massachusetts led in requiring every town of over
five hundred families to maintain a high school teaching American
history, bookkeeping, surveying, algebra, and geometry. Popular
pressure eventually determined that the American high school curriculum be a simplified and imitative version of college studies to

serve those who could not afford to go beyond the preparatory-school level, thus involving a type of duplication open in later years to serious criticism. More decades were to pass before the new system relegated the academy to the background. In New York, for example, aristocratic defenders of the academy prevented Governor Clinton from achieving the free high school ideal that he advocated as early as 1817.

One of the products of the Enlightenment and the French Revolution had been an incipient feminism based on the ideal of equality for women and championed most effectively by Mary Wollstonecraft, who was the talented and unconventional wife of the English philosophical anarchist, William Godwin, and the author of the influential *Vindication of the Rights of Women* (1792) and *Thoughts on the Education of Daughters* (1787). In Connecticut, Emma H. Willard, a self-educated schoolteacher and a daring feminist, fought the prejudices of her day against the teaching of "men's subjects" like mathematics, science, and philosophy to young women, whose minds, many of that generation believed, were too delicate to endure such disciplines. Mrs. Willard, encouraged by the sympathy of Governor Clinton and the aid of other well-wishers in New York, founded the first women's high school in 1821 as the Troy Female Seminary. She offered all those harsh subjects of men's preparatory schools, which, it had been feared, would rob the girls of charm, refinement, and health. Indefatigably she wrote suitable history and geography textbooks, introduced modern teaching methods, trained herself to teach as many sciences as possible, and made Troy a model for European as well as American experiments in higher female education. A sentimental age was to recall Emma Willard best as the poet who wrote, "Rocked in the Cradle of the Deep," but a large corps of women schoolteachers, scattered strategically over the nation, remembered her as a pioneer leader in education.

Higher education came in for the lion's share of attention in this era, reflecting the needs arising from the Second Great Awakening for more theological colleges, the patriotic desire for a national university, and the persistence of European classical ideals. Washington and Jefferson, among others, advocated a national university, but this hope faded except for the fulfillment of Washington's plan for the United States Military Academy at West Point in 1802. Jefferson eventually turned his attention to a state project for the University of Virginia. West Point on the picturesque Hudson River, once Washington's military headquarters and the strategic site that General Benedict Arnold had tried to betray to the British, evolved from a postwar supply depot to a training school for cadets. After 1817, with the arrival of the imaginative Major Sylvanus Thayer, "father of the military academy," a chaotic stage in West Point's history ended. Trained as an engineer in the famous École Polytechnique, Thayer brought back outstanding French engineers, translated French technical textbooks, and raised the scientific work to national eminence. Army engineers, like Major George W. Whistler, father of the great painter, helped to industrialize the country through vast roads and railways and Whistler, himself, even directed the industrial birth of faraway Russia. Disciplined cadet companies under their own officers, though under regular army surveillance, marched proudly in the new West Point tradition and among them were Lee, Grant, Sheridan, and Stonewall Jackson.

Jefferson believed in a modern, democratic university. His plan for the new University of Virginia avoided an aristocratic class basis by making the state university part of an integrated system, which included, also, elementary and preparatory schools, and by making it free at the lower levels. Without neglecting classical learning, he found ample room for modern languages, the sciences, modern history and government, and the fine arts. One could specialize vocationally by choosing the right "electives." He refused to set up a professorship of divinity, then the core of every college staff, arguing that the university's mission was first to develop a secular democratic philosophy free of church dogmas. He even invited as the first professor of chemistry, Thomas Cooper, the radical English Unitarian refugee, though a local outcry forced the cancellation of this appointment. Though the University of Virginia did not realize the sweeping plans of its founder for an integrated elementary and collegiate system, its early solid academic achievements were not inconsiderable.

This age of brilliant but conservative lawyers included John Marshall, Daniel Webster, James Kent, and Joseph Story and had its counterpart in the advance of legal education. James Kent, a Federalist who ardently believed that manhood suffrage would lead to some form of communism, was on the other hand, a craftsman of the law who served as a law professor at Columbia and influenced the course of American law while chancellor of New York by introducing the practice of handing down written decisions in major cases and building up from English practices an influential body of equity decisions. Most eminent of American jurists and federalist lawyers, John Marshall did much to fasten the influence of Blackstone and the common law—then heavily conservative in its practical bearings on unions and property—upon the United States at the expense of French and continental influences. When Harvard established the Dane professorship of law, the donor insisted that Judge Joseph Story, creator of American patent law and many international law precedents, be chosen. Thereafter, as an influential teacher and textbook writer, Story strengthened the English legal tradition in this country. Most influential—though the only one of its kind for years—was the Litchfield School in Connecticut of the federalist lawyer, Tapping Reeve, who trained such men as Calhoun, Augustus Longstreet, and Horace Mann, and many future governors, senators, and supreme court justices. Altogether, the amount and quality of legal education was impressive for a youthful nation though stunted in an extreme individualist direction at the expense of the intellectual influences of the French revolutionary and Napoleonic eras.

Heralding the future dominance of German ideas in American education were the stream of German university-trained American scholars and men of letters. Germany, Prussia particularly, had escaped the intellectual as well as military bondage of France through the War of Liberation against Napoleon and sought fresh creative energies in her folk traditions and native scholarship. German romanticism expressed itself in the folk tales and linguistic studies of the Grimm brothers who were rediscovering the ancient German past; in the Aryan myth of Teutonic uniqueness; in Hegel's philosophic glorification of the state and the evolution of Germany to world pre-eminence, and in Friedrich Jahn's patriotic *Turnverein* which combined gymnastic exercises with the propagation of nationalistic ideas. As yet the common goal of German unification was largely encased in a liberal ideology and gave romanticism a constructive force. Father Jahn's gymnastics had a wholesome effect on the American school curriculum and on the country by spreading interest in physical fitness, just as the Grimm tales amused American children; and German idealism was channeled here into reformist activities.

To be sure, as Heine later observed, while England ruled the waves Germany ruled only the clouds—the mists of heavily theoretical studies. George Ticknor, future literary historian and one of a group of young Bostonians to study at Göttingen University, described to Channing in 1816 the ivory tower spirit of German scholasticism, which was eventually to be imported into American universities:

A man of science here lives entirely isolated from the world, and the very republic of letters, which is a more real body in Germany than it ever was in any country, has no connection with the many little governments through which it is scattered without being broken or divided.

Göttingen, whose 300,000 volumes exceeded Harvard's proud collection eight times, made the library the center of the university and shamed American colleges which tended to skimp on books. From scholarly Göttingen, too, came Edward Everett, Harvard's professor of Greek literature and editor of the pontifical *North American Review*.

Another Göttingen Doctor of Philosophy, George Bancroft, the historian and statesman, brought back the German-Swiss version of early "progressive education" derived largely from Rousseau and Pestalozzi. Bancroft's college preparatory school, Round Hill, of Northampton, Massachusetts, was opened in 1823 (jointly supervised with another Göttingen student) and based its program largely on Pestalozzi's ideal of social reform through education rather than political revolution. Pestalozzi, who was to influence the best in the American educational tradition, had rebelled against the passive learning implied in formal lessons and memorized assignments and preached education for the masses; followers of this pioneer had invented important practical teaching devices for Pestalozzian education. Thus the Round Hill School used foreign-language tables where all had to converse in the language studied and, under an ardent German disciple of Jahn, it opened the first American gymnasium, adding supervised outdoor activities and sports to its well-rounded modern course of studies. Unfortunately the school, like many later progressive experiments, proved too expensive and finally closed its doors.

Harvard itself, after an era of torpor, revived its leadership by training selected scholars in the best German universities, its administrators initiating the century-long trek of American scholars to receive a higher education in Germany. Largely as a result of this policy its linguistic studies rose in distinction, and the curriculum grew by advanced courses in modern languages, history, government, economics, and medicine. Rivaling Jefferson's University of Virginia in its new interest in German studies, Harvard invited the scholar and stormy petrel, Karl Follen, as its first professor of German literature. Follen, like *Turnvater* Jahn, had studied literature at Jena, had fought in the War of Liberation, and had been exiled for republican conspiracies against the Prussian monarchy. After teaching several years at the University of Basle, he was dismissed through German police pressure. At Harvard he was encouraged to take on the additional duties of sponsoring the first college gymnasium, which he opened in 1826. This innovation was taken up shortly by Yale, Williams, Amherst, and Brown, though as a movement it declined temporarily between 1830 and 1860.

One of Follen's close friends was Francis Lieber, another disciple of Jahn who had taken a Ph.D. at Jena and had spent much of his youth dodging political police. Lieber arrived in Boston in 1827 and with the help of Follen opened a gymnasium and swimming school. Eager Bostonians had even tried to get Jahn himself to take over the supervision of their gymnasium. At first Lieber enjoyed considerable popularity in his teaching of calisthenics and swimming exercises among both young and old, but American youths and their parents, raised in the English tradition of sport and competitive play, grew bored with regimented exercises and withdrew. Though he failed and physical education declined as a movement for thirty years, eventually German calisthenics was to be blended with the Anglo-Saxon sport tradition and with Swedish medical gymnastics to become the American system of physical training. Boston was to see this victory in 1861 when the Normal Institute for Physical Education was incorporated to train teachers in this field by offering anatomy, physiology, hygiene, as well as gymnastics and other subjects. Lieber himself during 1829-33 turned toward the editing of a thirteen-volume *Encyclopedia Americana*, the original for the well-known later editions, modeling this work upon the high German standards of Brockhaus' *Konversations-Lexikon*, from which the *Americana* was partly derived through translation. Among a generation whose education owed something to Lieber's work—scores of able collaborators took part—were the young lawyer Abraham Lincoln, President Andrew Jackson, and a number of notable Harvard professors.

2

Science and scientific education continued the unfolding of the modern experimental spirit. Harvard's first professor of medical theory and practice, Dr. Benjamin Waterhouse, introduced Edward Jenner's discovery of vaccination. This replaced the hazardous method of coping with smallpox through direct inoculation of the smallpox virus by the safer process of using cowpox virus, which produced a vaccine that was relatively harmless. In 1809, Massachusetts tried to make vaccination compulsory. Medical education made important strides, going beyond the colonial custom of mere apprenticeship to a doctor to require at least the degree of Bachelor of Medicine, taken after finishing two school terms—a demand still less than Edinburgh's requirement of four years' training. In a day when the equivalent of high school was a sufficient prerequisite for entering a medical school, Harvard's medical school, which was founded in 1782, attracted a majority of students with general college degrees. Medical journals began to flourish. But nearly all American medical schools had scanty equipment and no hospital affiliation. Those who could afford to do so, like Harvard's illustrious graduate Oliver Wendell Holmes, left to study at Paris, the Mecca for ambitious American medical students in the years between 1825 and 1860.

The shortcomings of medical science were but too patent during such catastrophes as the yellow fever epidemic of 1793 in Philadelphia, the worst up to that date. Even Benjamin Rush, who was entrusted by the College of Physicians to draw up a plan of attack, continued to insist stubbornly on purges and bleeding. Privately, he wrote that he knew of only one preventive and that was to flee from the city—as many Philadelphians had already discovered. The layman's remedies were wine, bark, and hot vinegar baths to supplement the doctor's bleeding and purges. Patients began with alternating seizures of chills and high fevers, developed a yellow skin and bloodshot eyes in three or four days and usually died after the fifth day. Thousands perished in Philadelphia and other cities, their corpses abandoned by panicky relatives and friends. While some attributed the plague to the putrid exhalations of decayed coffee, a few guessed that there was some connection between the mosquitoes bred in the swamps and the transmission of yellow fever. After these epidemics Philadelphia's city fathers urged cleaner streets, meat and water inspection, and other sanitary practices.

Yale College was fortunate in its choice of Benjamin Silliman as its first professor of chemistry and natural history. Silliman, trained under Sir Humphry Davy, inventor of the miner's safety lamp, and other scientists of western Europe and Philadelphia, became an effective teacher though only a fair research man; still his publications were respected in the Old World and the New. In 1818 he founded the *American Journal of Science and Arts*. Jefferson's friend, Thomas Cooper, who had once collaborated with the famous refugee chemist, Joseph Priestley, became a professor of geology at Dickinson College while Jefferson himself continued to observe science at home and abroad and to encourage scientific work in a host of varied fields. Philadelphia and Charleston, with their museums and numerous scientists, kept in the foreground of the scientific advance.

3

In social and economic philosophy, the battle flared between the liberals who looked to Thomas Paine's France for inspiration and the traditionalists who found their guidance in Edmund Burke's England. Under Presidents Washington and John Adams the Federalists were in the saddle. Economic thinking centered about the problems of protecting property rights against the onslaught of majorities and of preserving the existing class structure threatened by the Jacobins at home and abroad. Alexander Hamilton, a self-made man who married into the wealthy Schuyler family, had worked during the Constitutional Convention for a powerful centralized state to head off agrarian radicalism and the confiscatory tendency of Daniel Shays and his imitators. Like other Federalists, Hamilton had no high opinion of human nature and still less of the people en masse. Like John Adams, another self-made man who had risen with a successful law practice, he believed that the fundamental task of government is to protect property through a system of checks and balances. Their enemies insisted that both were simply monarchists aping the aristocratic society of England.

Counting heavily on the personal motive of self-interest as the mainspring of history, Alexander Hamilton had tried to cement the new republic to the bedrock of the capitalistic schemes of the speculators, the manufacturers, the men of commerce, and the holders of stocks and bonds. Firstly, to these men of substance he offered a United States bank, largely privately owned and controlled though federally chartered, to protect the creditor classes against the debtor-controlled local banks; secondly, he secured a mildly protective tariff to encourage manufacturers and to diversify economic life; thirdly, he obtained a profitable deal for speculators and reassured creditor groups at home and abroad by funding the federal debt, then sadly depreciated, at par and assuming the state Revolutionary debts; and finally, he added the excise tax to strengthen the central government against the disaffected farmers. He did win for the young nation an enviable record for credit and solvency.

As a professed realist, Hamilton built up an argument for his tariff and its moderate economic nationalism on the fact that the young republic faced a mercantilistic world in which bounties, premiums, tariffs, and other devices of discrimination aided foreign competitors. He did not reject Adam Smith's theoretical discussion for free trade and economic liberalism, but insisted, "If the system of perfect liberty to industry and commerce were the prevailing system of nations, the arguments which dissuade a country, in the predicament of the United States, from the zealous pursuit of manufactures would doubtless have force." His arguments for the diversification and the preservation of infant industries, as history revealed, did not allow for the very human unwillingness of these industrial infants to shed the protective covering of the tariff after the period of incubation ended.

Strengthening the solicitude for property rights of Hamilton and the Federalists were the anti-majority beliefs of John Adams, once a radical of the natural-rights school of liberals. In all societies, Adams believed, there are the few, the "natural aristocracy," who win wealth through their abilities and virtues and create a stable social structure. These men of property must be saved from the passions and ignorance of the many through such political checks upon the majority as might be provided by an independent Senate. Still, Adams retained his suspicions of Hamilton's speculative capitalism, fearing that the rich, like the poor, could oppress and destroy society.

In New York another believer in strong checks on the majority, Chancellor James Kent, eulogized the prevailing system of allowing the well-to-do to select governors and state senators and attacked radical proposals for more elective offices and manhood suffrage. "The tendency of universal suffrage," he asserted, "is to jeopardize the rights of property and the principles of liberty." But he and his friends were fighting a losing cause against the upsurge of the common man.

The great constitutional architect of Federalism, bent on arraying the courts and the law against embattled radical majorities, was John Marshall. As Chief Justice of the Supreme Court from 1801 to 1835, Marshall was able to engrave federalist regard for economic minorities into the fundamental law of the land, writing his famous decisions in a convincing literary style. The Supreme Court rose in prestige and power by asserting effectively its right to declare acts of Congress (*Marbury* v. *Madison*) unconstitutional and acts of state legislatures (*Fletcher* v. *Peck*) invalid, thus strengthening the centralizing tendency exemplified by Hamilton's federalist program. He gave a hostage to future corporate business by declaring a corporate charter to have the force of contract and hence immunity from hostile state legislation (*Dartmouth College* v. *Woodward*); and upheld the constitutionality of the second Bank of the United States on the authority of the implied powers belonging to Congress (*McCulloch* v. *Maryland*). Thus the protection of economic minorities—which proved of limited serviceability at a much later day in defending cultural and racial minorities—advanced at the expense of the States' rights cherished by agrarian interests. To a later generation was left the onerous task of building up the "police power," i.e., the rights of a sovereign community to legislate broadly for the welfare of its citizens, which the individualist interpretation of Marshall had hampered.

Against the commercial-industrial philosophy of Hamilton and Marshall was squarely posed the agrarianism of Jefferson and John Taylor of Caroline, Virginia. Jefferson's economic views have been noted in part. Like the French physiocrats with whom he corresponded he believed that the farmer was the human cornerstone of a democratic state; he distrusted cities and favored—most of the time, at least—liberal economic principles of *laissez-faire*. Opposed to Hamilton's ideas of a strong government with a permanent national debt to attract speculators, he favored a "rigorously frugal and simple" government whose duty it was to discharge the debt, to keep military costs down, to provide "little or no diplomatic establishment," and to maintain free commerce with all nations though no political connection with any. A friend of liberal France,

he was shocked by the excesses of the French Revolution, but re-
solved to prevent war with her or any other country. As president,
he proved to be no doctrinaire free trader nor passive *laissez-faire*
advocate, even calling for a mild tariff for manufactures, against the
opposition of the shipowners, in order to maintain "a due balance
between agriculture, manufactures and commerce." The War of
1812 led him to introduce thirty-five spindles and numerous looms
to his own plantations and convinced him that more farm labor
could be diverted toward manufacturing.

From Virginia, the scientific planter and Jeffersonian statesman,
John Taylor, took up the cudgels for agrarianism against Hamilton,
Adams, and Marshall. Though he, too, was suspicious of unrestrained majorities—"geographic majorities" aimed at Southern
planters—he offered, instead of federalist checks and balances, the
sword of States' rights which Calhoun and the South soon accepted.
Taking issue with Adams' idea of a "natural aristocracy" of talent
and virtue, he pointed out that this often led to an artificial aristocracy based on speculative wealth. "As the aristocracies of priest-
craft and conquest decayed," he wrote, "that of patronage and paper
stock grew." The masses, hitherto exploited by ruling classes under
such psychological devices as "loyalty to the throne and altar,"
were now dominated by the capitalistic stock-and-bond speculators
nurtured on government favors who appealed virtuously to "publick faith, national integrity, and sacred credit." Hamilton's system
of tariffs, the bank, and inflated stocks had created this parasitic
class, which drew sustenance from the toil of the farmer, and thus
had led to the origin of the Federalist and anti-Federalist parties.
The only remedy, Taylor felt, was confiscation of special privilege
without compensation. Before his death in 1824, he was to see his
party compromise its agrarian philosophy with the Federalists, and
John Marshall rivet his federalist interpretation upon the Constitution, while even the trusty Jefferson retreated in his old age from
pure agrarianism to an avowed willingness to tolerate government
aid to merchants, shipbuilders, and factory owners.

4

Literature in this age of Walter Scott in England and Cooper, Irving, and Charles Brockden Brown in America left its classical moorings for the uncharted voyage of romanticism. Professor G. A. Borgese, in an illuminating article on romanticism, points out the following elements: Even in ancient Greece, as one cultural vogue after another was exploited, there appeared alongside classicism romantic Dionysian or Platonic traits of fantasy, exaltation, "unrepressed passion," and deep melancholy. Within the Reformation tradition there was also the romantic doctrine of "justification by faith alone" in which mystical inspiration and the revolt against authority were essentials. The growth of a large female reading public, thanks to the educational developments of the eighteenth and early nineteenth centuries, encouraged the vogue of the sentimental novel with its romantic love theme.

Music dropped many classical conventions for Bach's appeal to esthetic fervor and allied itself with the imaginative realm of folklore. Philosophy moved toward the super-rational, the transcendental, often with mystical overtones from the Orient. Germany, the matrix of the new romanticism that infiltrated America, found this movement an escape from French classicism just as she was freeing herself from French military domination. Romantics, fleeing from utilitarianism and the culture of nascent industrialism, often found shelter in medievalism, chivalry, Gothic tales, and the idealization of primitive peoples like the Indians. Politically, the romantics, especially in America, inclined toward a kind of primitivism that expressed itself in a cult of the common man, manhood suffrage, abolitionism, feminism, pacifism, mass education, and utopia-building. No phase of culture wholly escaped the enthusiasm of the romantics. The pendulum had begun to swing from the overintellectualized side to the emotionalized side.

Americans, north as well as south, were entranced by the Waverly novels of the German-influenced Sir Walter Scott who transmuted the barbaric crudities of the Middle Ages into chivalric romance. Scott even drew the character of Rebecca in *Ivanhoe*

from the model of the beautiful Rebecca Gratz, daughter of a
Jewish merchant in Philadelphia. Between 1814 and 1823 about a
half million copies of Scott were printed by the American press
alone. Imitators of Scott in America, turning toward Indian themes,
were legion. Drawing from the same Gothic inspiration were the
popular English novelists of mystery, terror, and the supernatural,
the late eighteenth-century Horace Walpole, author of *The Castle
of Otranto,* and Mrs. Ann Radcliffe, who wrote *The Mysteries of the
Forest.* Ruined castles, secret panels, and the sinister filled their
pages. Here were the intellectual ancestors of the modern authors
of detective stories, a field in which Edgar Allan Poe was to dis-
tinguish himself.

Most important of American novelists before Cooper was the
Philadelphian, Charles Brockden Brown, author of the popular
mystery novel, *Wieland,* the product of a single month's toil. In this
story the chief character is driven by a supernatural voice to murder
his wife and children; ventriloquism and somnambulism are sus-
pense-building devices. Melodrama, romantic melancholy, and
pathological analysis characterize the novel. In other books Brown
showed the utopian influence of Godwin's philosophical anarchism
and Mary Wollstonecraft's feminism. Man's innate goodness, his
right instincts, are exalted over the evil wrought by unnatural social
institutions.

Romanticizing the American Indian (at least some of them), the
frontier, and the sea, James Fenimore Cooper used materials he
knew as a child on his father's semi-feudal lands, "Cooperstown,"
in upper New York, or later as a sailor. He enjoyed amazing success
with his *Leatherstocking Tales,* particularly the suspense-filled
novel, *The Pioneers,* and the highly adventurous story, *The Pilot,*
which was intended to excel Scott's *Pirate* in the accuracy of its
sea descriptions. Especially lasting in popularity was *The Last of
the Mohicans,* published in 1826, which idealized the Indian Uncas,
last of the Mohican tribe, and created another of nature's noblemen
in Natty Bumppo, the frontiersman. However, unrealistic the *Leatherstocking Tales* might be—and Westerners failed to recognize noble
savages in the degraded, sullen redskins of their day—the novels

were enjoyed for their sustained adventure and unsophisticated beauty.

Encouraged by Walter Scott himself, Washington Irving, a business representative of a bankrupt New York firm, turned to literature as a career. In 1809, he published the folkloristic and humorous *A History of New York* under the pseudonym Diedrich Knickerbocker. This good-natured caricature of the colonial Dutch as solid over-robust burghers and simple folk tended to obscure the historical Dutchmen who settled New Netherland. Even more enthusiastically received were Irving's sketches of 1820, such as *Rip Van Winkle*, and *The Legend of Sleepy Hollow*, which exploited still further local legends, notably the Henry Hudson tales of the river bearing his name, such as the headless horseman, and folk stories carried over from the Old World. By the late 1820's and early 1830's Irving was turning to the rich Spanish and Moorish history and the folklore of *The Conquest of Granada* and *The Alhambra*. Thereafter he turned to frontier novels and biographies.

Written more in the realistic spirit of Cervantes than of Walter Scott was the four-volume novel *Modern Chivalry* by Hugh H. Brackenridge. Son of a poor Scottish immigrant, he had nevertheless acquired a Princeton education, become a frontier judge in early Pittsburgh, and founded the town's first newspaper, the *Gazette*. Though a Jeffersonian, he wrote a satiric, entertaining novel of intriguing western politicians, the crudities of the frontier, and the incompetence of many would-be saviors of the people. He portrayed pot-bellied politicians who waddled among their constituents, winning their electorate through kegs of whisky and piles of cigars. Brackenridge retained the classical distrust of the demagogue and was not yet swept off his feet by the ensuing era of rough Jacksonian democracy and the romantic deification of the common man.

Popular reading tastes, especially among middle-class women, clung to the sentimental novel, so successfully typified in Richardson's *Pamela*. Out of a mountain of eighteenth-century manuals on etiquette and model letter books on morals and the proprieties, the letter-construction formula of *Pamela* had opened wide the door of respectability to the novel. Pamela became the idealized type of

sheltered, middle-class womanhood, one who wept in embarrass-
ment when receiving a gift of silk stockings from her master. Foremost among American best sellers was *Charlotte, a Tale of Truth*
(or *Charlotte Temple*) written in 1791 by Mrs. Susanna Rowson,
a daughter of an English revenue officer stationed before the Revolution in Massachusetts. Mrs. Rowson, married to a musician and
herself a stage singer who made an American tour, wrote a highly
sentimental tale of seduction in the best moralistic manner of
Richardson, and won the ready tears of multitudes. Outdoing all
competitors, *Charlotte Temple* had sold 50,000 copies by 1812 and
during the nineteenth century reappeared successively in two hundred American printings.

Another best seller in the idealized manner was the extraordinary *Life of George Washington* by Mason Locke Weems, "Parson Weems," a former minister turned book peddler who had sold
many a copy of *Charlotte Temple* among Southern readers. Recognizing the huge market that existed for idealized biography, particularly one of Washington whose parish rector he claimed once
to have been, he mixed fact and myth to construct an informal life
of the first president that would patriotically inspire American
youth. Weems insisted that Washington never told a lie and embellished the famous cherry tree story. When the enraged father
asked who cut down his favorite tree, George responded bravely,
"I can't tell a lie, Pa; you know I can't tell a lie. I did cut it with
my hatchet." This very popular book ran through twenty editions
and the cherry tree episode was immortalized for children through
McGuffey's Third Reader.

English writers accounted for much of American reading. After
a century of neglect Shakespeare returned to public favor on both
sides of the ocean, aided in this country by American editions
of his complete works in 1795-96. Even the frontier audiences
found Shakespeare on the stage exciting as well as "improving."
Milton's *Paradise Lost* had more friends than ever. The melancholy
of the "graveyard poets" like Thomas Gray and Isaac Watts found
an appreciative response. The English and French historians, from

William Robertson and David Hume to Voltaire, went through successive American editions.

Children read books intended originally for adults, such as Defoe's *Robinson Crusoe*, based on the experiences of a shipwrecked Scottish sailor, Swift's subtle *Gulliver's Travels*, watered down in successive editions for simple tastes, and *Aesop's Fables*. Mother Goose, probably dating back to Charles Perrault's French *Tales of My Mother the Goose, or of Mother Goose*, published about 1697, was made available to American children through eighteenth-century Boston and London collections of nursery rhymes. One of the first American printings of Shakespeare appeared about 1786 in a volume of Mother Goose rhymes, which contained some of the charming songs of the bard of Avon.

The sensational growth of newspapers from two hundred in 1800 to over five times that number by the end of this era, together with a circulation exceeding that of any other country, showed how far we had progressed toward becoming a nation of newspaper readers. Partisan conflicts and government printing contracts stimulated the growth and activities of the newspapers. Alexander Hamilton himself established a federalist organ during 1801 in the New York *Evening Post* while the Jeffersonians had such editorial champions as Thomas Ritchie's outspoken Richmond *Enquirer*. Conservatives could boast of an effective journalist in Hezekiah Niles, editor until 1811 of the Baltimore *Evening Post* and thereafter of the very influential *Niles Weekly Register*.

So hot did partisan war become that libel suits multiplied and challenges to duels between editors were not infrequent. Successive crises broke out over French issues in Adams' era when the federalist majority in Congress, angered by the savage pro-French position of their opponents, passed the Alien and Sedition Acts. The latter particularly defined sedition as "false, scandalous, and malicious" statements against the government. Fortunately, the Zenger precedent, which made truth a defense against libel, remained. It proved impossible to muzzle the American newspapers effectively, trained as they were in the hard colonial school.

5

The story of architecture reflected the social forces that were re-
molding the United States, though in this field classicism took on
increasing vitality after French models. A deliberate attempt by
Jefferson and his associates to achieve an American classicism free
from English Georgian influences left its impression particularly
upon public architecture. The desire for a "pure Renaissance" style
going back to Republican Rome grew out of the middle-class concept of republican "virtue" popularized during the French Revolution and already expressed in such Roman ideas as the Senate, the
aristocratic veterans' Order of the Cincinnati, Polybius' ancient
theory of the separation of powers, and a tendency to portray Washington wearing a toga. Even the Roman eagle became naturalized
as American.

Jefferson, a student of Palladio's Renaissance textbooks but now
rebelling against their heavy theoretical nature, visited France during the latter 1780's and gazed "whole hours at the Maison Quarrée
(in Nîmes), like a lover at his mistress." The resultant "pure classicism" was partly exemplified in the Doric order of his Monticello
home with its four-column high porch and impressive pediment.
Antedating the European classical revival by years, the American
classic was adopted at Jefferson's instigation for the Virginia state
capitol. His University of Virginia used all the classical orders in
its rotunda which was connected by pavilions and colonnades intended to be useful as models for architectural students. He followed
French practices in solving the problems of modern doors and
windows for the monuments of antiquity. The plan of the original
capitol was designed by Jefferson's protégé, Dr. William Thornton
of Philadelphia; its low central dome was modeled after the Roman
Pantheon. The ideals of the exact classic were strength and grace
and thus the classic temple became the enthusiasm of Jefferson's
generation. After 1820, the Gallic Roman classic was to be followed
by an enthusiasm for the Greek classic, nurtured by the exhilarating
spectacle of ancient Greece coming to life again, aided by Byron
himself, through its fight for independence from the Turks.

English classicism retained its hold in the North where the influence of the distinctive Scottish architects Robert and James Adam, inspired by certain Roman imperial models, molded classic columns to achieve lightness of proportion and the utmost delicacy —"prettifying" and effeminate details, according to Talbot Hamlin, the historian of American architecture. Most significant of the disciples in America of the brothers Adam was Charles Bulfinch, who set the dominant tone of delicate English classicism for culturally conservative Boston. Praised as the "first American architect" —others had been amateurs or carpenter craftsmen primarily rather than professionals—he designed New England's first theater, the Federal Street Theatre, the Boston State House with its gilded dome which influenced most future state capitols, and numerous courthouses and residences. The Adam influence bore most heavily upon Salem, where Samuel McIntire, woodcarver-architect, and his sons designed scores of fine residences, such as the Elias Derby House, noted for exquisite interiors, low projecting carved cornices, and ornamental mantels. Graceful spiral staircases frequently marked the Adam style. Variations of this "late colonial" style also dominated the Hudson Valley, Long Island, and elsewhere. Some variety was lent by imported Italian marble mantels, Chinese porcelain and lacquers, and French brocades. In the cities French refugee architects offered competition to the Adams' baroque by French classicist designs.

Painting wavered between the classical canons of Benjamin West's pupils and the realistic impulses of less academic souls. One of West's greatest students, Gilbert Stuart, dominated the American scene of Jefferson's day. In the bosom of the wealthy Federalists of Boston, Stuart, whose family claimed a political tradition going back to aristocratic Stuart pretenders, found a generous patronage for his portraits. Noted for magnificent transparent colors and perceptive interpretation of character, he could easily outstrip his famous teacher in the field of portraiture, though he seldom ventured upon other forms of expression as did Benjamin West.

Leaving Europe in 1792 when his extravagance had dissipated the substantial earnings of his brush, he decided to recoup his fortunes by portraying Washington. Ever resourceful, he overcame the president's boredom as a sitter by discussing farming and horse-racing with him. He gave to posterity a realistic and luminous like-ness in the Vaughan portrait, a three-quarters profile of a kindly country gentleman of the South with twinkling eyes. More in keep-ing with the classical ideal, he also drew the so-called Athenaeum portrait, known to Americans today largely because its stoic fea-tures still grace a penny postage stamp. This latter portrait en-riched Stuart who copied scores of the original—some with curious unintended variations—for an eager middle-class clientele. Among his other striking portraits were those of General Horatio Gates and the beautiful "American Sappho," Mrs. Perez Morton.

Lagging far behind in the arts was sculpture. John Trumbull, one of West's ablest pupils who continued the "grand historical style" of the master, discouraged a hopeful stone-cutter in 1820 with the pessimistic observation, "Nothing in sculpture would be wanted in this country for yet a hundred years." Such work as appeared could scarcely escape a derivative style and a lifeless classicism.

Among the arts, music reflected most clearly the advance of American nationalism, even if the tunes were usually English, for this era marked the appearance of such patriotic songs as "Hail, Columbia," "The Star-Spangled Banner," and "America." The first song originated in 1798 when an undeclared naval war with France seemed to presage a major conflict in which the pro-English Fed-eralists pressed for retaliation against French attacks upon American ships and rode roughly over the civil liberties of the pro-French Jeffersonians in the Alien and Sedition Acts. In Philadelphia, a young singer-actor decided that he could play to a full house if his federalist classmate, Joseph Hopkinson, the eminent lawyer and son of Francis Hopkinson, would write a patriotic song to the stir-ring popular tune of Philip Phile's "The President's March," written during Washington's administration. Intended to appease both po-litical factions as well as to gain an audience, "Hail, Columbia" did both magnificently. Singer, chorus, and full band joined in the grand refrain:

Firm united let us be
Rallying around our Liberty
As a band of brothers join'd
Peace and Safety we shall find!

"The Star-Spangled Banner" grew out of the War of 1812—America's second war for independence, though the music was from the very popular English classical song, "To Anacreon in Heaven," which had already served for the verses of "Adams and Liberty" and "Jefferson and Liberty." As has been so often told, a young Washington lawyer, Francis Scott Key, wrote the words of the future national anthem while detained by the British on a frigate during the night bombardment of Fort McHenry, Baltimore's chief defense. Inspired by the dogged resistance of the American garrison and the sight of the flag still flying at dawn, he jotted down the famous words on an envelope and had the words printed in Baltimore a week later. Though "The Star-Spangled Banner" did not become an official anthem until the Spanish-American War, it shared national honors with "Hail, Columbia" very quickly.

To the music of "God Save the King" and its many continental predecessors, a theological student of Andover, Massachusetts, Samuel Francis Smith, casually dashed off "America" in 1831. So amazing was its success that Smith himself was startled, admitting later that he had found the tune in a German music book, unaware of the British use of the music. "It was struck out at a sitting, without the slightest idea that it would attain the popularity it has since enjoyed." The generation after Independence was indeed ripe for the birth of a national anthem.

From the British Isles, as Sigmund Spaeth relates in his history of popular music, came scores of catchy songs and ballads. "Auld Lang Syne" quickly captivated the public as a nostalgic New Year's song and "Believe Me If All Those Endearing Young Charms," which began its American career in President Jefferson's day, was eventually naturalized by Jackson's time as "Fair Harvard." Another English favorite, "The Last Rose of Summer," was widely known here long before Flotow borrowed it for his opera *Martha*. A dulcet English tune won world fame through the sentimental words of a homesick American playwright in Europe, John Howard Payne, author of "Home Sweet Home." Payne later recalled pathetically, "How often have I been in the heart of Paris, Berlin, London or some other city and have heard persons singing or hand organs playing 'Home Sweet Home,' without having a shilling to buy the next meal, or a place to lay my head." In 1818 an Austrian organist, Franz Gruber, gave Americans as well as Europeans one of the most enduring Christmas hymns, "Silent Night." Elsewhere on the American continent ballroom couples waltzed to the new compositions of Weber and Schubert, and concertgoers listened to the symphonic "modern" music of Handel, Haydn, Mozart, and Beethoven. Succeeding decades were to herald the arrival in America of the famous melodies of the nineteenth-century German romantics.

The birth of American nationality was the keynote of this era, but it remained to be seen upon whose terms the synthesis would take place, whether of conservative Federalists or of liberal Jeffersonians, whether of commerce or of agriculture. Federalist merchants, looking upon England as the bulwark of order against French anarchy, preferred to temper nationalism with the traditional philosophy of Burke's England rather than with the liberalism of Jefferson's Francophiles. Their ideal of American nationality embraced Hamilton's economic nationalism and the Marshall constitutional façade of nationalism. In the cultural sphere, Noah Webster, convert to Federalism, did more than any other individual to create an American language and a nativist outlook. Despite the break with England, Federalists preserved a major cultural tie by sponsoring Blackstone and the common law against the French law.

Hoping to keep their favored position in the Union, the commercial classes fought to keep back the tide of universal suffrage and to stave off an incipient revolution for mass education that had been brewing in Switzerland and Germany. Within the upper-class framework of the colleges, they did contribute generously to experimental science and medical schools; many in fact dabbled as respectable amateurs in home laboratories. Not all men of substance thought alike, for self-interest did not always run in the same channels. John Taylor and other Southern planters expressed agrarian ideals at variance with Hamilton's stockjobbing. Even John Adams was far too eighteenth century in his thinking to acquiesce completely in speculative finance.

Jefferson, friend of the small farmer and mechanic, did win a unique victory for things French by replacing the English Georgian style in architecture with French classicism. Northern merchants, on the other hand, clung stubbornly to the graceful English classicism. In painting they gave their patronage to Gilbert Stuart, preferring his stoical Washington to the realistic picture of the first president as a very human country gentleman. Nationalism for all classes was sealed in song, but cultural ties were far too strong for Americans to forget the English tradition in music whatever the new words might be in the national anthems. Literature, too, was largely English in derivation, though the republic could boast of Cooper and Irving as indigenous writers. Next to English influences, as we have seen, were marked French and German tendencies.

Washington's Farewell Address expressed a nationalism that was meant to reconcile all classes. He disliked parties because he felt that they put geographic and economic interests above the national good. In foreign affairs, he advised his countrymen to make no favorites of any European nation or bloc, implying that such action in a day when English and French warships preyed upon American shipping might destroy the young republic. Like Jefferson, he was too much a part of the classical cosmopolitan world of the eighteenth century to counsel rigid isolation for all time—though politicians have sometimes assumed that such was his intention. Both presidents condemned permanent alliances that might be "entangling" for a newly-born nation whose weakness would make it a pawn of some European giant just as in colonial times. The "hands-off" hemisphere idea of the Monroe Doctrine was based upon similar considerations.

Despite Washington's nationalism, class interests continued to plague the course of unification. Western farmers, desperately anxious to win an outlet for their produce at Spanish New Orleans or to secure new lands, conspired with Spain or talked secession until the Louisiana Purchase of 1803 solved the problems of navigation and expansion. Thereafter, New England Federalists, jealous of the ascendancy of the West, doubted the benefits of the Union. When the lust of western War Hawks for Canada precipitated the War of 1812 and thus cut off the commerce of New England, federalist extremists challenged the fiction that this was primarily a war for the freedom of the seas and demanded hostages of the Union as the price of their continued membership. In those days, the gifted spokesman of federalist commerce, Daniel Webster, seemed indeed to be calculating the value of the Union, as Southerners later charged. Only after the North had been cemented by industrialization and other economic ties did Webster find the Union glorious, "one and inseparable." American nationality had yet to face its severest test in 1861 when sectional interests as well as ideals arrayed Yankees and Confederates upon the battlefield.

· 11 ·

The Melting Pot of
Carl Schurz' Day

[1830-1861]

I

Not since the time of the Goths did Western Europeans (and Orientals, too) forsake their ancestral homes in such multitudes as they did during the mid-nineteenth century. In 1854 alone, the year immigration reached its zenith, some 400,000 wanderers entered the United States, most of them through the human funnels of crowded New York city, Boston, and San Francisco. By 1860 there were 4,136,000 foreign-born residents in a population of only 31,443,000—almost one person in eight. Huge segregated colonies of Irish, Germans, Scandinavians, and Chinese, isolated by language or religion or other cultural traits, made assimilation to the eighteenth-century English standard improbable.

The mounting babel of nationalities was permeated with the current nationalistic idea of preserving the purity of each immigrant stock through separate schools, churches, newspapers, and lodges. This forecast a long wait for an ultimate American type of society which could blend the contributions of many lands and diverse peoples. With the arrival of the human tidal wave of the 1840's and 1850's the United States faced its greatest test of group accommodation and tolerance, a test far exceeding the eighteenth-century absorption of Palatinate Germans and Scotch-Irish whose

311

coming had dismayed Franklin's generation. Here were discouraging hurdles of language, clashing religious attitudes, illiteracy, extreme poverty, temperament, and often undemocratic traditions as well that must be overcome before a cultural synthesis could arise from what a later generation called the "melting pot." Would this experiment of large-scale assimilation to free institutions succeed?

Whatever religious and political grievances had spurred on their thousands to uproot themselves from European soil, these were relatively minor to the lash of economic need, famine, and suffering that drove away their hundreds of thousands—millions in fact—to escape grinding poverty or starvation. The deepening agricultural revolution in the British Isles and Germany eliminated countless farmers and created a burden of local relief that worried aristocratic landlords. In many cases, the landlords decided that it was cheaper to pay passage for local emigrants than to continue costly relief rates. In Ireland and much of Germany a chronic potato blight, beginning in the 1820's and attaining famine proportions in 1845-46, goaded millions to flee across the ocean. The humble and extremely prolific potato, originally the gift of the New World, had long been respected as the savior of the small Western European farmers, whose multiplying numbers pressed perilously close to the subsistence level. According to the immigration historian William F. Adams nine-tenths of the Irish emigrants came from classes dependent upon the potato for survival. As the potato shriveled, even in storage, these farmers and tenants, especially in Ireland, were doomed.

Illiteracy and rural isolation did not prevent prospective emigrants from learning about the unique expansion of the United States during the early nineteenth century. Not only had the purchase of Louisiana in 1803 doubled its territory, but the annexation of the Floridas, Texas, and, after the Mexican War, a new empire in the Far West, especially across the Great Plains and the Rockies to the Pacific, opened up lands almost without end. Then came the Gold Rush to California, which attracted emigrants from every part of the globe. Indian titles melted away before the white man's advance, particularly after the Black Hawk War, which opened up

Wisconsin and Iowa to Germans, Scandinavians, Irish, and other nationalities as well as to native whites. Among the special attractions were cheap fertile lands, colonization experiments, generous land laws like the Preemption Act, which offered low prices to existing settlers, and early admission to all the privileges of citizenship. At the same time American factory owners, checkmated by a shortage of cheap labor due partly to the westward movement which drained the population of the seaboard, eagerly courted millions of workers from the Old World, who were glad to accept any wages above subsistence levels. Prospective immigrants were tempted by glowing prospectuses of steamship companies, railroads, state agents, and industrial firms.

Ireland's woes, particularly in the Catholic South, were indeed greatest, partly as the badge of a conquered people. Here an exploited Irish tenantry worked on five-acre to fifteen-acre patches of estates belonging to English absentee landlords. These owners were too often indifferent to the welfare of the illiterate Catholic peasant and were themselves pressed by declining prices after the long Napoleonic wars that ended in 1815. Catholics paid tithes to the established Church of England besides supporting their own clergy. With no incentive to improve their farms, since improvements reverted to the landlord, and almost no opportunity to add to their incomes by other work, many of the Irish turned to idleness and whisky, anxious not to miss any fairs, wakes, dances, or convivial visiting. In his turf hut, which lacked furniture, windows, and, consequently, ventilation, the simple Irishman lived with his large brood and shared his quarters with the family pigs. Cholera, typhus, and famine gave Ireland the heaviest mortality in Christendom by the 1840's with less than one-fifth of the population living beyond the age of forty. Periodic civil wars, as in the past, added violence to this picture, with gangs of "Ribbonmen," and "Peep-o-Day" boys, and individual clashes to disturb the peace. The revolutionary cause of Young Ireland, led by liberal Protestant intellectuals who made common cause with Catholics against the English, reflected the rising nationalist ferment of the thirties and forties. In view of all these factors it is not surprising to note that even before the potato blight of 1845 about one million Irishmen had arrived in the United States.

The breaking point of human endurance, even for peasants inured to suffering, came with the potato rot. To make matters even worse, the government's decision in 1846 to reduce the price of food for labor by repealing the Corn Laws, which had restricted wheat imports, removed the remaining protection for the English landowners against foreign competition. This inspired the landlords to undertake large-scale evictions of their Irish tenants, involving over a million persons in a few years and furnishing unforgettable scenes in Irish history. Rebellion flared in Limerick; thousands stole to maintain themselves; and one local priest even threatened openly that if the government failed to offer relief, he himself "would show them where food could be had." An English Quaker visiting Mayo and Galway, wrote this description of a village in 1847: "Out of a population of 240 I found thirteen already dead from want. The survivors were like walking skeletons—the men gaunt and haggard, stamped with the livid mark of hunger—the children crying with pain—the women in some of the cabins too weak to stand." Animals disappeared as food. Altogether Ireland lost one-fourth of her people through famine and emigration—one of the few Western European countries that failed to gain population during the expansive era of the Industrial Revolution.

Out of this tragic, famine-ridden island, by 1860 came 1,611,000 Irish-born Americans, almost 40 per cent of all foreign-born residents. Usually they came penniless, fortunate in once having accumulated the passage money, or having it remitted by a relative (or granted by the Irish landowner). They felt deeply embittered against England, and were adrift as a suspect religious minority in a Protestant land. Elbowing the Negroes aside as their chief competitors, the unskilled and unlettered Irishmen went to work on construction gangs, building canals like the Erie, which employed 3000 Irish in 1818, and laying railroad tracks. They filled the labor gap left by the westward movement, for only 10 per cent became farmers, while the rest, generally too poor to buy land, and too intensely gregarious to endure the isolation of pioneer life, preferred to live in the city. In rural Ireland with its small farms close to each other, one seldom lacked neighbors. Besides, farming in Ireland had not been a pleasant experience and American city wages seemed very high. More of the Irish, being penniless, remained in New York city, chief port of entry, than in other cities. Next to New York's 203,000 Irish of 1860 came Philadelphia's 95,000, then Boston's 46,000. Substantial Irish colonies also existed in St. Louis, Milwaukee, and Chicago.

Boston, a major port for British ships on their way to Canada, attracted, by 1860, more than 46,000 Irish, almost half as many as there were natives, and 3200 Germans. Such immigrations threatened to overwhelm this erstwhile Puritan capital. An analytical historian, Oscar Handlin, has told how the Irish immigrant, with his readiness to work for low wages, stimulated New England industrialism by his cheap labor in the factories, thus reviving stagnant industries suffering from high costs and giving life to mass-production industries like ready-made clothing, which now pushed aside the competition of custom tailors. Irishmen sweated in the expanding copper and brass foundries, locomotive works, and forges of New England, filling most of the manual jobs. Comparatively few became merchants and professional people. While Paddy helped prosper the rising class of New England industrialists, his daughter Bridget added the touch of aristocracy to these families by serving as a maid at low wages, thus solving the perennial shortage in domestic help.

Eastern employers, satisfied on the whole with their huge immigrant labor reservoir, dropped their hostility to the westward movement and to western issues like pre-emption (giving squatters the right to buy their lands without competing bids), which had previously seemed to threaten their existing labor supply. Professor Fred Shannon has argued that the West was never a "safety valve" for eastern labor discontent; certainly the large-scale flow of Irish immigration to the cities offset any corresponding movement of urban natives to the frontier. With an ample supply of unskilled labor, factory employers looked with increasing favor upon a *laissez-faire* philosophy of industry.

However much the untutored Irishman might like "to take justice in his hands" in a fight against crooked subcontractors who cheated him, or to beat his foes insensible with the trusty cudgel of the homeland, the shillelagh, he kept his conservatism in politics, religion, and economics. While he joined the Democratic party as a "poor man's party" that had few of the nativist prejudices of the Whigs and captured control of Tammany Hall as early as 1820, he did not fully share the Jacksonian reform spirit of his day except on the issue of manhood suffrage. Politically, he disliked the pro-British views of the Federalist-Whig tradition and, like the Irish senator Edward Hannegan, was incensed by the boundary compromise with England, when Polk yielded "Fifty Four, Forty or Fight" in the Oregon dispute. The Irish vote, like the German vote and that of other immigrant groups, was never deliverable as a package by priest or politician, though substantial blocs did freeze into cohesion upon the threat, real or fancied, of danger to them in local or national elections. Aided by the Irish-controlled Tammany Hall, the privilege of voting was easily won by newcomers despite the law.

Like other nationalities of a similar economic and cultural status, Irish immigrants afforded numerous recruits to corrupt politics, notably the Tammany leaders. But while Whig politicians virtuously denounced the wholesale corruption of voters by Democratic bribes of food, clothing, and shelter at the taxpayer's expense, they did nothing to lessen the wretchedness and squalor among the festering slums of the cities. Tammany, of course, sold its favors in the most profitable market, but its lieutenants were warm, seldom condescending, in their manner—unlike the bloodless philanthropists of the charity societies that reflected middle-class fears of overpopulation by the poor and improvident.

As a bitter competitor of the Negro for a livelihood, the Irishman developed race prejudices comparable to those of the submerged "poor whites" of the South, and he hated abolitionism as a threat to his livelihood. In the factories he depressed wages, even driving the newly organized Lowell girls out of the mills, thus enabling employers to resist unionization. From Ireland, he imported the weapons he had forged in the desperate struggle for survival. There he had terrorized competing workmen who sought his job; his unions had fixed minimum wages, and even enforced the closed shop. Along the Chesapeake and Ohio Canal, County Cork laborers organized a secret society to keep out County Longford intruders as well as German and Yankee competitors. During the thirties, Irish belligerency blew up into a murderous civil war among canal construction gangs, which brought local militia and even inspired the first use of federal troops—Jackson's—in any labor dispute.

While Irish Protestants made up much of the immigration from Erin before 1845, the Catholic proportion grew ever more dominant. Nativists, sneering at the "priest-ridden Irish," were ignorant of the intimate role that the Irish priesthood had played in Ireland's history, giving the Emerald Isle primacy in the origins of Western Christianity and offering leadership in the struggle against the foreign oppressor. The Irish Catholic press, led by the clergy, fought the rationalist and irreligious trend of the Jacksonian era, condemned the revolutions of 1848—except for a brief enthusiasm for the Young Ireland uprising—and attacked the liberal "isms" of the romantic era. Irish families, traditionally proud to give a son or daughter to the Church, stimulated Catholicism in the United States far more than did Catholics of other nationalities and thus shaped the course of American Catholicism. This meant Irish leadership among the 4,500,000 Catholics of 1860, resulting in stricter doctrinal practices, a greater emphasis on parochial schools as against public schools, and a determined battle against the use of the Protestant King James version of the Bible in the schools. Despite their poverty the Irish undertook the building of Sunday schools and parochial schools, and founded Catholic colleges like Holy Cross (1843), Boston College (1863), and St. John's College (1841), later Fordham University, to preserve the purity of the faith. Their protracted resistance to the use of the Protestant King James Bible in the public schools, where many Catholic children remained, ended in the withdrawal of the Bible altogether.

Irish churchmen campaigned successfully against alcoholism for a brief period in the late 1840's, assisting the noted Irish visitor, Father Theobald Mathew, "Apostle of Temperance," who had crusaded for prohibition among the poor in the cities of the British

Isles. In 1849-51, he launched a spectacular campaign in the United States, persuading thousands to take the pledge for total abstinence. However, the Irishman, whose distillery industry at home had survived British mercantilistic restrictions, soon repented his hasty pledge, abetted by tempters in the form of gang bosses and calculating subcontractors on public works.

Even before the flood of Celtic and German immigrants after 1845, Irishmen bore the brunt of the worst anti-Catholic excesses in American history. The Puritan inheritance of anti-Catholicism had been materially strengthened by the numerous Protestant dissenting sects to whom anti-Popery was a cardinal tenet of the Reformation spirit. With the evangelical revivals, headed by Charles G. Finney in western New York during the latter twenties, Protestantism renewed its militancy, as Ray Billington shows in *The Protestant Crusade*. It was strengthened by the rise of proselyting Bible and tract societies on a national scale, new missionary organizations, a Sunday school movement, and a Protestant press. England's Catholic Emancipation Bill of 1829, a belated effort to restore Catholics to the full civil rights of Englishmen, aroused controversy in America as well as in Britain. Then there was also the disturbing Oxford Movement, which stressed "Anglo-Catholicism" within the Anglican fold, but led nevertheless to the conversion of its leader, John Henry Newman, to Roman Catholicism in 1845. As a priest, Newman was to take an active role thereafter in fighting the "No Popery" agitation in England. European liberals, too, including the tremendously popular Louis Kossuth of Hungary, identified the Catholic Church with the reactionary Hapsburgs, arousing liberals to join the workmen in the Protestant Crusade. Altogether, the atmosphere was favorable for a campaign portraying an aggressive temporal Pope who was armed with faggot and torture instruments to impose Catholicism upon the New World.

From "Brimstone Corner" in Boston, Lyman Beecher, father of the immortal Harriet, cast his pulpit lightnings upon Popery as part of a world conspiracy to break down free institutions. Others eagerly followed his lead, repeating salacious rumors that the convents were centers of Dionysian orgies. Beecher's incendiary sermon of 1834 provoked a mob of about fifty workmen to burn the Ursuline Convent in nearby Charlestown where many upper-class Unitarians had sent their daughters for an education. Irish homes and Irishmen walking the streets were also attacked. The community was disturbed, but not sufficiently so to pay for the damage done.

The burning of the Ursuline Convent had been preceded by such placard incitements as this one: "To Arms!! To Arms!! . . . Leave not one stone upon another of that curst Nunnery that prostitutes female virtue and liberty under the garb of holy Religion. When Bonaparte opened the Nunnerys in Europe he found Cords of Infant skulls!!!!!" This theme of Catholic immorality soon proved to have lasting financial value to newspaper and book publishers who could offer pornographic stories in the gentle guise of uplift literature. The best of the various "escaped nun" stories from this viewpoint was Maria Monk's *Awful Disclosures of the Hotel Dieu Nunnery of Montreal*. Maria charged, with suitable details, that she saw convent sisters killed for refusing to surrender to the lusts of priests and that she herself was now with child. Her story of secret crevices in the convent where the bodies of infants were hidden made such fascinating reading that at least 300,000 copies were sold before the Civil War, and it continued to attract thousands of readers even during the 1928 presidential campaign of the Catholic Alfred E. Smith! As it turned out, investigators not only found the tale a complete fabrication but the innocent Maria proved to be a prostitute of long standing, easily induced to serve as a tool of unscrupulous publicists. This episode added materially to the anti-Catholic incitement. In 1844, Philadelphia mobs burned two Catholic churches and thirty Irish homes and clashed with Irish bands, leaving about thirteen dead and many more wounded.

In New York, Irishmen stood staunchly behind their new militant archbishop, John Hughes, a formidable orator and mass leader. He had risen from poverty in County Tyrone, Ireland, to prepare himself for college and the priesthood by beginning as a day laborer in 1817 upon his arrival in America. Contemptuous of the docile reaction of Philadelphia Catholics to persecution, he let the mayor know that since New York city would not protect his churches or pay compensation, he was stationing 2000 armed Irish guards around Catholic buildings. This apparently cooled off the rioters and the crisis passed. Actively absorbed in founding Catholic schools and colleges (one became Fordham University later), he fought aggressively for Governor William Seward's controversial proposal to use public funds for Catholic as well as Protestant schools. This would have solved the problem for Catholic parents who were unable to prevent their children from using the King James version of the Bible under Protestant teachers and listening to anti-Catholic books. Archbishop Hughes' newspaper even applauded the act of an irate priest in burning the Protestant Bibles sent to his communicants. As Professor Billington points out, the archbishop did a good deal of harm in a delicate situation by tactless public lectures on "The Decline of Protestantism and Its Causes" and by predicting enthusiastically the victory of Catholicism over the heresies of the West. The final result of the public-school controversy was the elimination of all Bible reading from tax-supported schools and a sharper separation of church and state.

Nativists, their numbers swelled by new recruits from the middle classes, organized nationwide secret societies to combat the power of the immigrants and the advance of "Popery." The Order of the United Americans was formed in 1844 and the Order of the Star-Spangled Banner came five years later. Grips, pass words, distress signals, and other lodge mummery that "a nation of joiners" liked to keep, as well as benevolent old-age pensions and services, became part of the "Know-Nothing" movement bent on anti-immigrant legislation. During 1854-55, the American Party, which garnered these groups, captured many of the local political organizations of the older parties but failed to overcome widespread constitutional scruples about passing exclusionist laws. Besides, public opinion had been largely outraged by the reckless advance of mobbings, election violence, conspiratorial movements, and the intolerance of the entire nativist movement.

Sharing with the Negroes the invidious distinction of being the "mudsills" of society by accepting jobs no longer attractive to older immigrant groups who had risen in the social scale, the Irish showed all the secondary features of poverty and the backwardness derived from the rural slums of Ireland. In Boston, for example, they created a new slum in overrunning the neighborhood near the wharves and around the commercial and industrial centers where they found employment. Formerly aristocratic mansions evolved into filthy tenements, subdivided by shrewd entrepreneurs who, knowing the shanty background of the very poor, dispensed with windows, inside privies, and other such luxuries. These landlords filled in the spacious gardens with one shack after another and the immigrant practice of taking in lodgers even worsened the crowding. The ubiquitous saloon, dance hall, and political club added their faint cheer to the slum. Delinquency, adult crime, prostitution, disease, and improvidence flourished insidiously in this environment. The mortality among the Irish was startlingly worse than for other foreign and native groups, especially from bronchitis, tuberculosis, and Bright's Disease. Boston, which had begun to forget large-scale outbreaks of cholera and smallpox, woke up to find these diseases virulent in the Irish slums.

New York city, the home of Archbishop Hughes, and the residence of over 203,000 Irish in 1860—four times as many as in Boston—had much the same story on an aggravated scale. Slums at Five Points and Greenwich Village were firmly entrenched. Leaders of this city, half of which consisted of foreigners, complained of the heavy charity tax burdens. "Our city," reported an official, "operating like a sieve, lets through the enterprising and industrious while it retains the indolent, the aged and infirm, who can earn their subsistence nowhere, to become a burden and often because of their vices, a nuisance to the community." The Irish poor, followed by the Germans, represented the heaviest load upon the taxpayer.

A closer view of the Irish-American of the mid-century reveals a far more diverse group than mere generalizations would indicate. The more sensitive Irish, proving unsuccessful in the rough-and tumble of politics, withdrew from the field, leaving the spoils to the post-Civil War generation of the Kelleys, Crokers, and Murphys of Tammany Hall. New York state government was enriched by the election in 1812 of the intellectual attorney-general, Thomas A.

Emmet, brother and fellow-conspirator of the romantic Irish patriot
Robert, who had been executed after heading the Society of United
Irishmen in a desperate revolt against English power in Dublin.
Irishmen wept with their poet Thomas Moore over the Emmets in
the sentimental verses of "Breathe Not His Name." Thomas, exiled
by England, became an Irish-American leader, and his sons and
grandsons won distinction in the New World as educators and scientists. Philadelphia had a most enterprising publisher in another
Irish political refugee, Mathew Carey, associated with his able son
Henry. The Careys founded the *Encyclopedia Americana* under
the editorship of the scholarly German refugee, Francis Lieber,
selling a hundred thousand of these sets. Their large corps of book
peddlers on the road once included Parson Weems, builder of the
cherry tree legend. Both Careys were ardent protectionists, helping
to formulate Henry Clay's American System of internal improvements at federal expense, protectionism, and a national bank. But
the Anglophobia of the Careys led them to label free-trade ideas as
an English scheme to close the furnaces and factories of America
and continental Europe.

Thrifty Irish girls sent millions of their savings home to their
kinsfolk as did many Irishmen in the smaller towns, where the
saloon did not take such a toll. At least $5,000,000 a year was being
remitted to Ireland by the 1860's. Whatever their immediate burden
to the taxpayer and their temporary influence in reducing wages
for the unskilled, this was offset in the long run by the industrial
renaissance in the factories of New England and the mines of the
Middle Atlantic states that accompanied the Irish immigration. In
the cities, Irishmen took over the hazardous occupations of police-
men and firemen. As the Irish filled the pick-and-shovel jobs, or became miners, longshoremen, and mill hands, natives moved up in
the economic scale to become heads, foremen, and skilled workmen.
Edward Everett Hale, Boston Unitarian clergyman who defended
the Irish in his *Letters on Irish Emigration* (1852), concluded,
". . . the consequence is that we are, all of us, the higher lifted because they are here."

The Irish, however strict their doctrinal orthodoxy, added a strain of sprightliness, audacity, and humor to the American character. Like the German forty-eighter, the Irishman celebrated the Sabbath as a cheerful day of robust recreation as well as abstinence from labor. Again like the German, he liked to sing the tearful sentimental tunes of the homeland. His dances, like the jig and the Irish reel, were marvels of dexterity, and frequently of grace as well. Irish plays quickly became popular upon the American stage, especially during the 1840's. With the Celtic love of pageantry, he clad himself in outlandish uniforms—as did other immigrant groups—and marched in lengthy parades on St. Patrick's Day and the Fourth of July, stopping traffic for the day. Free of the inhibitions of Anglo-American traditions, the irrepressible Irishman, who had learned to laugh and joke and poeticize amid the most painful circumstances of centuries, helped to shape the unconventional and idealistic American psychology of the modern city. He was indeed a far more complex character than the simple figure suggested by the stage Irishman of the red flannels and suspenders, and the thick brogue.

2

Not far behind the troubled sons of Erin were the German immigrants, of whom 1,301,136 had landed by the outbreak of the Civil War, representing almost one-third of the foreign-born. The western and southern German states had experienced some of the economic evils besetting Southern Ireland, such as the potato blight, which began with the bad harvest of 1829 and reached its worst extent in 1845. They suffered from landlordism and the pressure of population upon limited resources, although there were non-economic reasons, too, for leaving the homeland. Entire German villages left en masse for the promised land so attractively pictured in numerous books, pamphlets, advertisements, and letters. In the agricultural revolution of Western Europe, which marked the shift from a nearly static system of serfdom and traditional farm practices to a scientific and capitalistic mode of agriculture, the newly-freed peasant often found the subdivided farms too small for a growing family; besides, the pasturage and common lands used in manorial days were now appropriated by the nobility. Many of the forests had been stripped by the Napoleonic Wars, leaving a chronic shortage of fuel and building materials.

Farmers, borrowing heavily to equip themselves for a role in the new commercial farming, were too often left stranded with unpaid mortgages during the many bad harvest years after 1829; credit became tighter as capital was increasingly attracted to the booming urban industries born during the Industrial Revolution. Like the Irish, the German peasants had to pay burdensome tithes to a state church not always of their own choice, and the payments to the landlord, more recently required in money rather than in kind, were more difficult to meet than ever. Little wonder that the roads to Le Havre, Bremen, and Hamburg, the ports of embarkation, were crowded with long lines of carts drawn by drooping beasts and loaded with women, children, and the sick, together with their household goods. Protestants from the north and Catholics from the south joined in this exodus to seek the cheap fertile lands unpre-empted by a landlord caste on the other side of the ocean.

Accompanying the farmers and tenants displaced by the agricul-tural revolution were the urban craftsmen unable to find places in the factory system bred by the Industrial Revolution. Remorselessly, the machine took away the livelihood of the old-fashioned craftsmen. In *The Weavers*, Gerhart Hauptmann, whose grandfather had starved as a textile worker in Silesia during this era, dramatized the futile weavers' revolt of 1844 against unbearable conditions. For those craftsmen who could escape to America and find a niche within its prosperous economy the struggle for existence in the homeland usually ended with a happy sequel.

Among the German emigrants were thousands who wished to es-cape the harsh conscription laws of the Continent and others, com-paratively well-to-do, who saw far greater opportunities for social advancement in the New World. Some of the emigrating German nobles—and there were a few—and the radical nationalists were motivated by the dream of a new Germany in sparsely settled west-ern America. A small but influential middle-class minority, the famous forty-eighters, left their country after total reaction had overthrown the short-lived liberal revolutions of 1848. Some German radicals like Karl Marx were fed on French socialistic doctrines as well as German communistic theories; Marx and Friedrich Engels had issued the startling *Communist Manifesto* that year; this presaged a far more sweeping revolution than the bourgeois uprisings of that day against surviving feudal aristocrats and the Metternich system of censorship and political repression. However, most radicals of 1848 preferred to remain home, even in jail, rather than to embark upon an overseas exile, despite the offer of Baden and other states to pay the passage of political prisoners. Thus emigration became a mighty industry for Bremen especially. The tobacco merchants of that port had already garnered the American distributing trade and now they saw their gains rising as the tobacco vessels returned to America with profitable passenger cargoes. During the thirties, 9000 to 13,000 embarked annually from Bremen, and the number continued upward in the forties and early fifties. The peak of the German migration came in 1853-54 when bad crops and foreclosures broke the will of hundreds of thousands of home-loving peasants and laborers to remain in their ancestral land. Going to America dwarfed all other industries. Few returned home; for every one who came back to Germany in 1854, thirty-two remained in their adopted home.

In 1830, when a new wave of German immigration began, the older Teutonic settlements of Pennsylvania and Ohio remained unassimilated, a cultural isle in an American ocean. Besides German Lutherans and Reformed Church members, there were those who practiced pietist doctrines and primitive Christian economic theories, spoke a German dialect at which educated forty-eighters sniffed, and maintained an unworldly ideal that contrasted sharply with the rationalism and modern economic radicalism of so many of the nineteenth-century immigrant leaders. The bulk of the new immigrants, it is true, were not rationalists or radicals, but simple peasants. Like their distant Pennsylvania kinsfolk, they built permanent homes in the wilderness rather than hasty structures thrown together for speculative profits; in traditional style, they conserved their soil and clustered together in German-type villages instead of dwelling in isolation upon the frontier like the Scotch-Irish and the Yankees.

Just south of the New Englanders of the Western Reserve in northern Ohio stretched a fifty-mile belt of Pennsylvania German villages. Here, near Mansfield, arrived in 1848, along with other new immigrants, the Altgelds, a poor peasant family whose baby, John Peter, was destined to be governor of Illinois and a famous progressive leader. Ohio, like other states with large German populations, was studded with village names like Berlin, Hanover, Strassbourg, Dresden, Spires, and Frankfort. Neighboring Pennsylvania sects of German Moravians, Dunkers, Amish, and Mennonites built the scriptural outposts of Bethlehem, Nazareth, Salem, and Canaan.

German nationalism, nurtured upon the War of Liberation against Napoleon and the romantic rediscovery of the German past, inspired several major ventures. Aristocrats and large private settlement societies of the homeland planned to build a New Germany in America, which would resist assimilation with the superficial, uncultured, puritanical Yankees. This was the story of the Giessener Society, the nationalistic Burschenschaften, and other German settlement societies which hoped to transform Missouri, romantically described by Gottfried Duden's writings in 1824 as a wilderness paradise, into a Germania. From Giessen poured out pamphlets regarding a free German state, a "rejuvenated Germany" in North America. Missouri, a state in 1821, and but recently emerged from the era of dominant French culture in the St. Louis area, became the center for the Germanic experiment. Moving westward along the Missouri River, just beyond the old French towns, were the new Holsteins, Hamburgs, and Westphalias. In the German village of Hermann, Gasconade County, dwelt the hopes of many nationalists who expected to perpetuate the memory of ancient Arminius, teutonized as Hermann, the German conqueror over three Roman legions in the Teutoburger Forest. Though it became a center for freethinkers and rationalists, Hermann village never advanced beyond a cozy little German community of neat farms and German schools. Gallic St. Louis proved a far greater magnet to the German newcomers. They also overflowed across the Mississippi into southwestern Illinois, especially St. Clair County where Belleville became a Teutonic center. Slaveholding Missouri was considerably leavened by the Germans who preferred to reproduce their own type of compact farm villages in which free labor could be recruited from their own large families. Southern families who had hitherto competed successfully for farms in the border states and in the southern counties of the Old Northwest against the Yankees were increasingly outnumbered by the Germans as well as by native farmers who found slavery out of place in the wheat and corn lands above the Ohio.

Apart from Missouri's "New Germany" advocates were a number of religious rebels. In American religious history the Missouri colonies are noteworthy for the work of Pastor Karl F. W. Walther, "the Lutheran Pope," who came with a group of 700 Saxon Lutherans in 1841, rebelling against the rationalism and radicalism infecting religion, and rejecting the formalism of the state church. German rationalism, especially the "higher criticism" movement emerging from Tübingen University, had assailed the supernatural basis of the Bible and questioned its complete historicity. Most shocking to the traditionalists was the currently popular book of a young lecturer of theology at Tübingen, David F. Strauss' *Das Leben Jesu* (1835-36), which treated the life of Christ and the miracles in this critical rationalist fashion, suggesting the skeptical spirit of Voltaire, though the methods were hailed by scholars as scientific. In Missouri, Walther gave aggressive form and content to the traditionalist Lutheran position, organizing the Missouri Synod in 1846 and a year later uniting with conservative congregations elsewhere as the Evangelical Lutheran Synod of Missouri, Ohio, and other States. Walther not only served as a Missouri pastor but acted as an editor of several influential German Lutheran journals and founded the Lutheran Theological Seminary, which became the Concordia Theological Seminary in 1850 when he transferred it to St. Louis. Walther's theology assumed a straitlaced puritanical quality that his critics termed Calvinism despite his emphasis on universal salvation rather than predestination. His attack on rationalism and secularism led his followers to embrace a kind of religious fundamentalism at variance with the radical implications of experimental science. Despite constant church secessions and doctrinal quarrels with other Lutheran factions of various nationalities, Walther's militant theology, asceticism, and economic conservatism deeply influenced the Lutheran Church in America. Before the century ended a powerful international Lutheran youth movement, the Walther League, was to come into being, devoted to an active missionary program and to the founder's principles.

Another projected New Germany, hardly more successful than the Missouri idea, seemed destined for Texas during the era of the Lone Star Republic after 1835. A group of nobles under Prince Solms of Braunfels, the *Adelsverein,* planned in the middle 1840's to eliminate German pauperism and to offset emigration losses for the fatherland by planting a permanent German colony in one of the least populated areas of the Mississippi Valley. Despite the Indians, the war with Mexico, and inexperience that led to much unnecessary suffering, the emigrants founded New Braunfels as a flourishing German community and others moved near Austin and San Antonio, totalling about 35,000 German colonists in 1861. Here, as in Missouri and elsewhere, the Germans remained non-slaveholders and despite their Democratic party affiliation and general indifference to political power were suspected by the natives to be abolitionists. The highly educated "Latin farmers" and the aristocrats among them seemed exotics to their American neighbors upon the Texas plains. Frederick Law Olmsted observed, "The German Romanticist is grieved because the speculating Yankee lacks all appreciation of the magic and fairy world of medieval poetry, and the German titled landowner in New Braunfels, Texas, is vexed because no one but he himself uses his title of 'herr von—.'" Not quite lost among a multitude of plodding German peasants were the "Latin farmers," intellectuals from the German universities who were determined to realize the romanticist's wilderness utopia discovered by Chateaubriand and his literary generation. Olmsted saw some of these in a German Texan community of 1857, "You are welcomed by a figure in blue flannel shirt and pendant beard, quoting Tacitus, having in one hand a long pipe, in the other a butcher's knife; Madonnas upon log walls; coffee in tin cups on Dresden saucers; barrels for seats; to hear a Beethoven's symphony on the grand piano."

The third great project for a New Germany, similarly unsuccessful, was for a German Wisconsin. Climate and soil seemed reminiscent of Germany; and the early immigrating Teutons quickly filled in the three southeastern counties about Milwaukee. Catholics from Bavaria, Austria, and the Rhenish provinces were attracted in large numbers to Milwaukee, partly because of the efforts of the first bishop in the new Catholic diocese of that area; these leaned toward orthodox religious universalism rather than rationalist and radical nationalism. After 1848 Milwaukee became a German Mecca. But growing German reaction after 1848 dampened the enthusiasm of liberals and leftists for a New Germany. Although Wisconsin remained a Yankee commonwealth, by 1860 its population of 775,000 included 124,000 German-born residents (about 16 per cent), a high proportion that declined thereafter. As in Missouri, the German Lutheran influence was a major one. In this migration were the Old Lutherans, dissidents against the official Lutheran state church in the homeland and founders of the Lutheran church in Wisconsin. Nowhere did the Germans capture a state though the Teutonic elements were greatest in Wisconsin, followed by Minnesota (10.6 per cent), Illinois (7.65 per cent), Missouri (7.5 per cent).

Among the Germans attracted to California, even before the gold rush, was the educated Baden-born John A. Sutter, who had been active in the caravan trade of the Santa Fe trail. Near Sacramento he had founded New Helvetia and for a time prospered as a large wheat and cattle baron. His own sawmill overseer, J. W. Marshall, made the fateful revelation on January 24, 1848, that gold had been discovered upon Sutter's lands. In the gold rush, miners trampled down Sutter's property, squatters seized his lands, and rustlers stole his sheep and cattle, leaving him a tragic bankrupt by 1852.

Other German emigrants went to San Francisco and the mine fields; many prospered as leaders of the wine industry in California and as fruit growers.

Germans, like other immigrants, tended to avoid the South, except for the experiments in Texas and Missouri. This was not due exclusively to slavery or to the plantation economy, for most Southerners did not own slaves and the South remained predominantly a region of small farms. Rather, transportation lines were poor, the climate seemed unbearable part of the year, and the race issue lent a decided element of insecurity. Still, the Shenandoah Valley in Virginia and western North Carolina had its large pockets of German-speaking farmers from colonial days; and sizable groups of Germans lived in New Orleans, Louisville, and Charleston. Governor John A. Quitman of Mississippi, noted leader of the "fire-eating" Secessionists, was partly of German parentage. In South Carolina, the brilliant historian Francis Lieber was professor of history and political economy at South Carolina College, having succeeded Jefferson's protégé, Thomas Cooper; he found the atmosphere sufficiently congenial to remain twenty years, leaving for the North only in 1855 after he failed to secure the coveted college presidency. A slaveowner himself, he was not without philosophical anti-slavery leanings, a duality reflected in the political opinions of his sons, one of whom gave his life for the Confederate cause while another lost his arm for the Union. In general, southern Germans were far more concerned with the nativistic prejudices of their neighbors than with abolitionism, for they remained Democrats. Only during Reconstruction did German Texans emerge as Republicans. Of the one-half million foreign-born in the slave states on the eve of the Civil War, one-third were in Missouri and were overwhelmingly German.

In common with the Irish, though on a far lesser scale, a substantial number of the German immigrants, especially after 1848, lived in the cities. By 1860, the young town of Milwaukee where Carl Schurz lived for a time had 15,981 Germans as against 22,292 native-born citizens and its Germania reflected the language and customs of the homeland. Europeanized New York, first in its share of immigration, had a German-born population of 120,000, almost one-third the size of all native groups. Gallic St. Louis of the Chouteaus and the French fur traders became Germanized with 50,500 Teutons almost matching the 61,400 natives. Philadelphia, as in colonial times, had its large German-speaking neighborhoods, although its 95,500 Irish outnumbered the 44,000 Germans. In Cincinnati, whose German population rose from 5 per cent in 1830 to 30 per cent in 1860, the Germans built the first iron foundry and first sugar refinery in the West as well as textile factories and mills. This major role of German and Irish immigration in the cities (although the native-born were far from extinct) was indeed significant in shaping American urban culture. As the nation became urbanized, city life did much to set the standard and tone for the rest despite the conservatism of large isolated rural areas, and German and Irish influences became too great to be extinguished by programs of assimilation.

The most politically-conscious Germans came in 1848 and after· wards, the "Greens," as their press referred to them, to succeed the "Grays" of the pre-1848 immigration. While the two groups had their own internal differences, they were compelled to unite against the growing forces of nativism.

Much of the story of these highly cultured forty-eighters can be told through the career of Carl Schurz. Born near Cologne of poor parents who sacrificed much in their hope of making him a professor of history, young Carl had gone as far as his candidacy for the degree of doctor of philosophy at the University of Bonn in 1847 when the first rumblings of the revolutions of 1848 against the reactionary Metternich system began to sweep the western European cities. As a dashing leader of the student liberal movement and a devoted follower of Professor Gottfried Kinkel of the university, he joined the rebel forces at once, rising to become a staff officer in Baden and the Palatinate. Finally, when the monarchists were able to regain control in 1849, Schurz fled to France and thence to the German refugee colony in Switzerland. In an exciting episode that became a saga of the 1848 movement, Schurz secretly re-entered Germany to rescue Professor Kinkel, then jailed for life near Berlin. On the night of November 6, 1850, Schurz conspired to spirit Kinkel out of prison and to convey him to England. Hounded by the Prussian police, even in Paris and elsewhere, Schurz mixed with revolutionists like Louis Kossuth of Hungary and Joseph Mazzini of Italy until he decided to leave in 1852 for the United States. He bought a small farm in Watertown, Wisconsin, where a relative lived, ready to become a "Latin farmer" like many other cultured forty-eighters.

Soon he turned restlessly to politics, campaigning in German and in English, which he quickly mastered, in behalf of Frémont in the election of 1856. Frémont, the first Republican candidate for president, was idolized by the liberal anti-slavery Germans who deserted the Democratic party despite the stigma of nativism associated with the new party as a heritage from the Whigs. This was the significant election when the nativistic foes of the Germans, Irish, Italians, and other immigrants ran former President Millard Fillmore as head of the American Party ticket, the "Know-Nothings." Schurz and the Germans battled the Know-Nothings—so called because of their secret fraternity formula of responding "I don't know" to the inquisitive. German rationalists and other groups resented the attempt to make the Bible compulsory in the schools; they fought the demand that the probation period for naturalization be lengthened and that the power of aliens in American politics be reduced. "America for the Americans!" ran the Know-Nothing slogan. "We have had enough of 'Young Irelands,' 'Young Germanys,' and 'Young Italys.' We have had enough of insolent alien threats to suppress our 'Puritan Sabbath' and amend our Constitution." Mob attacks on Germans in Cincinnati, Columbus, and other cities led the German press to call for a larger German militia—which appeared promptly with uniforms and standard arms. During the elections of 1855, when nativism rose to high tide, Germans demanded pledges of their candidates against Know-Nothing laws, and in some towns, as in Texas, where nativists threatened lynching, they marched in a body to the polls, carrying German flags and singing songs of the fatherland. German Democrats demanded that their candidates support the equality of German with English as the language of instruction in heavily German districts and, in states like Pennsylvania, obtained legislative sanction that the laws be published in both languages. After 1856, the nativist strength in politics, though capturing most of New England, New York State, Maryland, and much of the South, began to decline, submerged by the slavery and sectional issues as well as by the organized strength of the American and Irish voters.

Schurz had cooled toward the Democrats, especially since Stephen A. Douglas had secured the passage of the Kansas-Nebraska Act of 1854, which repealed the Missouri Compromise limiting slavery north of 36° 30'. From Congress, Salmon P. Chase had launched a major appeal of the "Independent Democrats" to the Germans and other newcomers, warning that the new law would bar them from the western territories since these lands were now open to slavery. In 1858, Schurz campaigned for Lincoln against Douglas in that senatorial campaign. The following year he had the difficult task of stamping out nativism in his own party when the Republicans of Massachusetts tried to postpone the privileges of the ballot and of officeholding for foreign-born voters until two years after federal naturalization. In this matter, anxiously watched by both Germans and Irish, Schurz aided Senator Henry Wilson of that state in blocking the law.

Again, in the crucial election of 1860, Schurz, though he had been a Seward man in the Chicago Convention, helped—according to William E. Dodd, though disputed by others—to convert enough German votes for Lincoln to turn the tide in the pivotal northwestern states. Thereafter, Schurz' career became increasingly active as minister to Spain, Civil War general, United States senator, civil service reformer, and finally, as a very able Secretary of the Interior under Hayes. Like other forty-eighters, he combined a talent for music with politics and played the piano skillfully. More tactful than most of the refugees, he displayed a sense of humor and personal charm. But unlike those refugees who brought Marxism and other radical panaceas, he clung to the conservative economic philosophy of the Republican party. His talented Jewish wife, who had studied with Friedrich Froebel in Hamburg, was to adapt the progressive methods of her teacher to this country's needs by introducing the first kindergarten in the United States to Watertown, Wisconsin, in 1856; in this sphere, she influenced others to follow her example.

Much farther to the left were the German socialists and communists who added their collectivistic schemes to the milder reforms demanded by Schurz and his middle-class forty-eighters. Like other German protesters, they denounced slavery, Sabbatarianism, compulsory thanksgiving days, and formal oaths on the Bible. Their press condemned land speculation, proposed state arbitration of labor disputes, equal rights for women, and a free school system with at least one German teacher in partly German-speaking districts. Certain extremists like the "philosophical tailor," Wilhelm Weitling, experimented in Iowa with a German communist colony and organized Workingmen's Leagues (labor congresses); German communists were heavily represented in the Icarian Colony at Corning, Iowa, founded by Étienne Cabet and a band of Frenchmen who had seceded from their original colony in Nauvoo, Illinois. These communists were mostly of the utopian and anarchist variety rather than of the Marxian discipline, except for a handful of emissaries of Marx and Engels who, sponsored by the Communist League of London, were spreading the *Communist Manifesto* of 1848.

Communist opinions accounted for little of German editorial opinion, which ranged from as far right as the conservative Lutheran position of Walther, through such influential middle-class papers as the *New Yorker Staats-Zeitung*, founded in 1834 by a political refugee, and the nationalist Illinois *Staats Zeitung* of Chicago, all the way to the left-wing press. There were 133 German publications in the nation by 1850 and over 200 a decade later; these included some twenty-seven dailies, especially numerous in New York, Cincinnati, Chicago, St. Louis, Buffalo, and San Francisco. Despite the predominantly bourgeois character of these newspapers and their contributions to democratic habits, the nativists of the American Party frequently lumped the Germans together as communists or atheists.

German Christian Communism, which owed nothing to Marx and

little more to the forty-eighters, had its expression in the Rappite colony of Pennsylvania and among the German pietists along the Iowa River known as the Community of the True Inspiration. The Iowa colony, Amana, founded in the 1850's, consisted of German peasants led by semi-literate prophets, who practiced communism in order to bind the group closely together and to solve the immediate economic problem. Many had left Germany to escape military service, which spared neither mystic nor intellectual. They had moved in 1842 to western New York before settling in Iowa. Best-known among the Inspirationists of Iowa was Barbara Heinemann, revered for a generation as a gifted prophetess.

Iowa also attracted Hungarian revolutionists at the time that Louis Kossuth, the liberator, visited the United States, but these were largely intellectuals rather than farmers, dreaming of building a New Buda among the Iowa cornfields in the medieval image of Budapest. Though they were unsuccessful in this project, other Hungarians did build settlements in Iowa. Another foreign blend came in 1847 with hundreds of Dutch Calvinist rebels against the State Church of the Netherlands. Many of these were rebellious artists and poets as well as farmers, and they built "Pella"—meaning place of refuge.

William Dean Howells, the future father of the realistic novel, knew the German farmer well during his Ohio youth. He admired his lust for life—tempered though it was among the isolated ascetic cults and the very strict Lutherans. The new German-American combined Old World habits of patient frugality and stubborn perseverance with an unquenchable love for social life, in contrast to so many of his New England neighbors. To the German, who could not build enough beer gardens for dancing and drinking, or music halls, theaters, athletic clubs, lodges, and singing societies, the Yankee's recreations seemed unimaginative, mere frontier crudeness, or anaemically puritanical in the narrowest sense. On Sundays the German took his family and friends along with bulging picnic baskets to the meadows, singing the sentimental *lieder* of the homeland, competing in sharpshooting contests, playing German games, and drinking large steins of the lager beer that was already tempting American de-

votees. Instead of Yankee pork and beans and pie, the *hausfrau* la-
dled out sauerkraut and wienerwurst, and served torten (fancy
pastry) for dessert. Howells admired the German fondness for the
plays of Schiller, which they enacted on the stage, and their friendliness, but was struck by the cultural gulf that separated the Germans
from the natives. Few Germans were invited to native homes and
intermarriage with non-Germans was rare at this time, despite the
fact that, in the new country, nationalities, classes, and church
groups seemed far less rigid than in the Old World. Small native
children shrank back in terror, Howells recalled, at the sight of the
German peasant immigrant with his heavy beard, long drab coat,
odd visored cap, and long crooked pipe.

A soured visitor of the 1850's, Karl Griesinger, once a liberal
editor, saw little that he liked in American cities. His travel books
satirized the narrow bourgeois spirit of his Americanized countrymen and the holier-than-thou puritanism of the natives. To him, it
seemed that all Germans had turned grocer, selling everything
under the sun except church steeples, and profiting heavily on the
sale of liquor in the general stores that occupied almost every city
intersection, sometimes three or four on a corner. Thrifty grocers
saved on wages, he wrote, by bringing over relatives to work at
low pay—actually a familiar practice among all nationalities. The
Pharasaical Sunday closing laws were evaded by the German
"sacred concerts," which sounded suspiciously like Strauss waltzes,
and by saloons kept closed only in front. Green immigrants were
swindled by land companies or by calculating damsels with "breach
of promise" suits, which presented the unhappy man with an alternative of marriage or prison.

However, Americans were captivated by the colorful German
Christmas with its beautiful Christmas tree dating back to ancient
pagan times. Although Santa Claus had arrived as Saint Nicholas
back in Dutch colonial days in New York, German children enjoyed
an especial familiarity with the delightful ways of the jolly saint
derived from centuries of folklore. After the Civil War, Thomas
Nast, talented German cartoonist whose satiric drawings blasted
the corrupt Tweed Ring of New York out of existence, also devoted

his holiday efforts in *Harper's Weekly* to portraying the German Santa Claus, correctly attired, busily filling stockings with toys, and riding in a sleigh drawn by reindeer. German toymakers found a permanent niche for themselves in juvenile hearts. For German-speaking people everywhere this was the *biedermeierzeit*—the naive, sentimental years of the age of romanticism. One popular gift for bourgeois America was a cheaper and better cigar made possible by the thousands of German cigar-makers whose coming revolutionized the industry. Their cigar stores seemed to arrive at the same time as the wooden Indian who stood as a sentinel on the sidewalk during the 1850's and afterwards.

Very significant in preserving the *Deutschtum* (Germanism) of the newcomers was the nationalistic *Turnverein*. In the Prussian schools, Friedrich L. Jahn, widely known as "Turnvater Jahn," the state teacher of gymnastics, mixed his studies in history, literature, and German folklore with a dream of making his people as physically impressive as the ancient Teutons appeared to Tacitus. An agitator for German nationalism, then in its liberal phase, he helped organize the influential *Burschenschaften,* the student patriotic fraternities centering at the University of Jena, where he pursued the Ph.D. degree for literary studies. His popularity led his conservative enemies in the German states to move cautiously, much as they preferred solid feudal and dynastic principles to the subversive teachings of romantic nationalism. Jahn taught the Prussians to break away from their cultural servility to France and cosmopolitan ideas, to take up proudly the tales and songs of medieval Germany, and to learn gymnastics and military exercises—*turnen* as they were called. Thus arose the popular German social and athletic society, the *Turnverein,* whose nationalistic features swept continental Europe and whose emphasis on formal drill in calisthentics competed in the United States with the English recreational ideal of athletic games and informal sport.

For American Germans the *Turnverein,* together with kindred societies such as the Sons of Hermann, the Veterans' Leagues, the sharpshooter clubs, and the fire-engine companies, proved a powerful institution for resisting assimilation. When the Turners united at Cincinnati in 1850 as a union of gymnastic societies, they had significant political potentialities. By 1859, according to Faust, there were at least 156 such societies with a total of 9300 active members. Nativists scored the socialists, freethinkers, and other radicals in the *Turnverein*. To Americans, the Turner movement, aside from nativistic annoyances, meant a major impetus to the cause of gymnastics, especially in the colleges.

Other nationalities too, had their full quota of lodges and societies, ranging from the Sons of Erin and the Ancient Order of Hibernians of the Irish to the B'nai Brith of the German Jews. Nativists struck back at these foreign organizations by forming hostile secret societies, such as the Order of the Star-Spangled Banner and the Order of United Americans. Apart from the political nativists and the immigrant societies, gregarious Yankees, too, were joining in their hundreds of thousands the newly imported English secret orders, especially the popular Odd Fellows and the Order of Druids; despite the anti-Masonic movement of this era, Masonry also had revived in strength by the time of the Civil War. "The American has dwindled into an Odd Fellow," lamented Thoreau, "one who may be known by the development of his organ of gregariousness."

After 1848, with the new wave of cultured German immigrants, the German-American theater ceased to be a crude affair that attracted patrons by free beer and folk dances. It became a relatively high type of playhouse in which the romantic German literary themes of the *Sturm und Drang* movement, inaugurated by Goethe himself at the end of the eighteenth century, led to the popularity of Shakespeare on the German stage as well as of Goethe's own works of genius and of the plays of his gifted friend Schiller.

Germans clung to the hasty notion that the Yankee "Puritans" hated music, but left no doubts of their own intense devotion to almost every kind of musical expression. The youthful Theodore Thomas who left Germany as a child in 1845 was to insist stubbornly that he would teach Americans to appreciate good music, willy-nilly—and *did* in the course of a brilliant career as a symphony conductor in Chicago and the East. The gregarious Germans loved choral singing in *Gesangvereine, liederkranz, männerchor, musik-vereine,* especially in the clubs of Milwaukee, "the German Athens"; they preferred huge national singing festivals to the more individualized musical expression of the Anglo-Americans. In 1846, one unusually successful musical festival in Cincinnati of choral societies drawn from the various Germanias attracted fifteen to twenty thousand spectators. The forty-eighters and their successors introduced the fanciful musical world of Felix Mendelssohn, particularly his music to Shakespeare's *A Midsummer Night's Dream.* After 1848, the Germania Society of New York offered the music of Richard Wagner who had begun to intoxicate the German nationalist, as well as to charm the world, with his stirring operas, *Rienzi, Tannhäuser,* and *Lohengrin,* so many of whose themes were drawn from the warrior's world of medieval and ancient folklore.

In 1795, young Gottlieb Graupner of Hanover arrived in Charleston where he became acquainted with the banjo and Negro singers. Four years later he introduced himself in blackface as "The Gay Negro Boy" in a between-act characterization at the Federal Street Theatre of Boston. He seems to have been the first of the Negro minstrels and the originator of the popular stage tradition of minstrelsy. More in keeping with his German background was his organization in 1810 of the Boston Philharmonic Society, a group largely of amateurs who practiced Haydn's symphonies and other classics, introducing a vogue of popular symphonic concerts. This came in part as a reaction against the crude "fuguing" of William Billings and his eighteenth-century Boston school which suggested to some extent the rhythm of modern syncopation. In 1815, Graupner initiated the long-lived Handel and Haydn Society and introduced the great oratorios to this country, some of them heard at the Christmas festivals. He died in 1836, hailed by music historians as "the father of American orchestral music," though forgotten for his pioneer role in the minstrel tradition.

Faust, the historian of German-America, has called attention to the part German makers of musical instruments have played in the culture of America. While New Hampshire could boast of Jonas

Chickering, the piano maker who helped devise the iron plate frame of that instrument, the Germans could mention a long list of noted German-American names in the history of contemporary piano-making: Steinway, Lindemann, Weber, Steck, Knabe, and others. Henry Steinway, for example, who left his German instrument factory in 1851, dissatisfied with the guild restrictions on large-scale production, came to New York with his four sons to apply mass production methods to piano manufacture. He did much to eliminate the prevailing metallic, nasalized tone of the instrument. By 1859, Steinway and Sons had constructed a huge factory with eight hundred workmen turning out sixty pianos a week.

In the development of painting the German influence led to a vogue of literalism of a middle-class, sentimental type, derived originally from seventeenth-century Holland. Americans who believed that painters should be primarily concerned with telling a story with technical skill found their journey's end in the artists of the Düsseldorf school who in turn affected the Hudson River school of scenery and landscape painters. One of these landscape painters, Albert Bierstadt, was born near Düsseldorf and, though leaving for Massachusetts in his infancy, returned to this town in 1853 to study the techniques of Karl F. Lessing and his pupils. In 1859, he accompanied an expedition to the Rockies and observed its rugged scenery for months, emerging within a few years with paintings that won him fame for their interpretation of nature's sublimity—"Laramie Peak" and "View of the Rocky Mountains—Lander's Peak." One of his Düsseldorf teachers had been Emanuel Leutze, also an American of German birth who had left his country as a child, later to return to study with Lessing. From his master Leutze learned the popular historical style with all its vices—conventionality and stiltedness. Among his extremely popular paintings were "Columbus before the Council of Salamanca" and the often reproduced "Washington Crossing the Delaware." Critics of a later realistic age, looking at the picture of Washington, chuckled at his theatrical pose and questioned his wisdom in standing up in a small craft while it was trying to navigate through dangerous ice floes. Leutze, who had portrayed the Delaware from a Düsseldorf studio, using the Rhine as a convenient substitute, allowed Washington to use a flag that belonged to a later era. Still, Leutze was one of the few painters to emulate John Trumbull in selecting patriotic American subjects, ranging from Indians to Revolutionary leaders.

3

Within the German migration and yet somewhat apart from the main stream were the Jews, particularly those from reactionary Bavaria. In some of the German states Jews long buried behind medieval ghetto walls had begun to inhale the air of emancipation under the influence of the Enlightenment and of Napoleon's leveling of the ghetto walls. With the Metternichian reaction they were again plunged into compulsory segregation, even being expelled from several states, denied entrance into many vocations, and restricted in everyday movements. By 1839, ten thousand Jews had left for America from Bavaria, whose restrictions on Jewish marriages and extortions of ghetto taxes exceeded those of other countries. Among these refugees whom the Bavarian government seemed so desirous to lose were the Straus family, who were to enrich their adopted country by founding modern department stores such as Abraham and Straus in Brooklyn and the present-day form of Macy's in Manhattan. Oscar Straus became Theodore Roosevelt's progressive Secretary of Commerce and Labor and the first American ambassador to Turkey; Nathan, merchant and philanthropist, lived to be voted, in 1923, the citizen who had done most for public welfare in the first quarter century of Greater New York's history, and his son became an ardent public-housing enthusiast and was chosen administrator of the United States Housing Authority under the New Deal in Franklin D. Roosevelt's administration.

Nearly all of the incoming German Jews, like the Strauses, came with few worldly goods, though many never rose, as the Strauses did, beyond the peddler's stage of commercial enterprise, and many stopped at the next level, the second-hand clothing store. Succeeding the Yankee peddler, who had risen in the economic scale, the Jewish peddler became an unfavorable stereotype in the American mind as had his native predecessor. Those who earned enough were able to drift back as merchants to the larger cities, where Jews might find social acceptance among their coreligionists, as well as opportunities to engage in commerce. Never hampered psychologically by restrictive medieval guild ideas that were intended to bind Christians by restricting output, prices, and styles at the same time, the Jew thrived in the relatively free American atmosphere of economic experimentation and competitive spirit. The ready-made clothing business unlocked rich opportunities for the shrewd entrepreneur and made cheaper goods accessible to the masses.

The German Jew was attracted to such German-speaking cities as Cincinnati. This city became the center of the Reformed sect of Judaism, largely sponsored by German Jews. The Reformed groups, in contrast with the older Orthodox synagogues, reflected the Enlightenment ideal of Moses Mendelssohn. He had rejected the oriental customs of the synagogue and had stressed the use of German and western traditions rather than the exclusive use of Old Testament Hebrew in the prayer service and in religious education. In the American environment, this meant using English in the services as soon as it could be mastered and even included the use of the organ. German Jews, like their Spanish and Portuguese predecessors, looked upon philanthropy and mutual assistance as of central importance in Judaism, and founded numerous societies, lodges, and orphanages. Rebecca Gratz of Philadelphia earned a wide reputation as a leader in social work; her unusual personal history and charm gave Walter Scott, who learned about her through Washington Irving, the character of Rebecca in *Ivanhoe*. In 1843, a New York group of working-class German Jews founded the influential Independent Order of B'nai B'rith (Sons of the Covenant) to combine religious interests with lodge insurance and literary meetings. As yet, these newcomers were looked upon as a crude and illiterate lot by the older Jewish groups, but they were soon to make their mark in education as well. Middle-class German

Jews usually felt at home in the Teutonic cultural milieu, held offices in German organizations, and shared in their nationalist or reformist programs.

Whatever Southern opinion might be regarding slaves and Negroes, the ante-bellum South displayed marked hospitality toward Jews. According to the *Charleston Mercury*, the Jews were "amongst the most faithful and patriotic of the people of South Carolina." The only Jewish members of the United States Senate came from the South—Judah P. Benjamin of Louisiana and his friend David Levy Yulee of Florida—and these men were twice elected. Both were born in the West Indies of Portuguese-Spanish Jewish extraction, married Christian maids, and won acceptance in the most conservative circles—Yulee becoming a Presbyterian, while Benjamin never renounced his faith; and both rose to great success as railroad builders and brilliant statesmen. Enthusiastic Southerners, they adapted themselves readily to the ardent proslavery and secessionist beliefs of the deep South. Benjamin, a successful lawyer and an expert in international law, served the Confederacy as its Attorney-General, then its Secretary of War, and finally, as Secretary of State. Even in the final hours of the war, when critics maligned Benjamin and his proposal to arm the slaves for the South while offering them their freedom, he kept the long-established confidence of President Davis. The South also welcomed the Philadelphia-born Jewish sailor, Uriah P. Levy, who became a commodore and, like Herman Melville, agitated for a law abolishing stripes in the Navy. Captivated by the idealistic philosophy of Jefferson, Levy bought Monticello, later converting it to a public memorial.

4

Lutherans of the Middle West received substantial allies in the new Scandinavian wave after 1839, which brought, by 1860, about 44,000 Norwegians, 18,600 Swedes, and over 2000 Danes. Like most other immigrants, they were spurred on by economic pressure, though religious factors did affect various special groups. Scandinavia once again, as frequently in the past, faced the problem of adjusting a growing population under outmoded agricultural methods to the small precious patches of arable soil. Beautiful Norway with its wild mountains, fjords, and forests profoundly impressed the visitor but to the practical peasant and fisherman it was a hard land of which three-fourths was uncultivable and most of the remainder was forest and meadowland. With heroic efforts the frugal peasant managed to raise a few acres of oats, barley, and a little wheat. The Swedes (including the Finns as well) were only slightly better off, having almost the same problem on their mountainous lands of thin soil, marshes, and crops that could not always thrive in the short growing season. As for the Danes, eking a livelihood from the sandy coast of Jutland, many needed only a little guidance to rush across to the American Utopia. On the religious side, the Scandinavian Lutherans, like the Germans, had their numerous pietist rebels who fought the tide of nationalism that was breeding intolerant state churches; many sought escape in America where compulsory military service did not exist as it did on the Continent.

Norwegian farmers shared in the potato rot that infested Ireland and Germany, and they suffered periodic famines such as the one of 1839. Uncertain crops, small lands inherited through a painful subdividing process, foreclosures, political grievances against the official class and the clergy, made these people ripe for the propaganda of the "America books," written by enthusiasts like the idealistic Ole Rynning. This early immigrant of the thirties published his *Account of America* to praise the good lands, free institutions—excepting plantation slavery—and brilliant future of the United States. Though his premature death discouraged some, thousands came to northern Illinois along the Lake Michigan shore and to southern Wisconsin; by 1850, they were entering Minnesota whose history was to be intimately allied with Scandinavia. High wages and low food prices encouraged young men to begin as farm workers or laborers, accumulating enough to buy their own precious land. Even the difficult journey, the sickness, and the fraud practiced upon them by speculators did not dim their purposeful enthusiasm. Many came as seamen, feeling rich on the eighteen to twenty-five dollars earned monthly by the ordinary sailor. Norwegians joined the gold rush, writing home to boast to their Bergen friends who earned ten cents a day that Sacramento City laborers earned fifteen dollars a day.

In keeping with the nineteenth-century spirit of liberal nationalism some Norwegians dreamed of a New Norway in America, as had the German proponents of a New Germany. Ole Bull, Norwegian violinist and composer, whose soaring American popularity had won him a small fortune in a few years, planned a huge colony of "Oleana" in northern Pennsylvania. "We are to found a New Norway," he declared, "consecrated to liberty, baptized with independence, and protected by the Union's mighty flag." All Norway watched, many to scoff, at the rise of New Bergen and Walhalla in Bull's utopia. Finally, the enterprise collapsed after it was discovered that the unbusinesslike violinist had been swindled by land speculators who did not hold title to the land they sold. But Bull continued to help his settlers who finally moved to the upper Mississippi Valley.

Although this era had not yet witnessed the great Swedish migration, the pattern of the future movement of the Swedes, like that of the other Scandinavians, was already clear. By the 1840's, the Swedes had moved into the northern Illinois area in Chicago, Galesburg, Rock Island, Rockford, Moline, and Bishop Hill—the latter a communistic theocracy under the pietist Eric Janson. With pietism in full swing in Sweden the newcomers tended to religious conservatism similar to that of the Missouri movement led by the German Lutheran correspondent, Karl Walther. They adopted the Methodist techniques of the circuit rider, the missionary conference, and the Yankee meetinghouse and Sunday school. These pietistic Lutherans kept their clergy under lay control, taught a strict moral code, and preached temperance to curb the heavy drinking of the time. Swedish pietists, aided by gifts from one of their own fervent faith, Jenny Lind, "the Swedish nightingale," founded the Augustana Synod to spread and to defend their doctrines. By 1860, they had established Augustana Seminary at

Chicago (transferred in 1875 to Rock Island) as a focus of Swedish-American culture. Despite their emergent puritanism the Swedes retained their festive holidays and an enthusiasm for their medical gymnastics system. Although American physical education built heavily on German foundations, this was not altogether so, for the "curative gymnastics," a form of therapy taught by the Swedish poet and university fencing instructor, Per Henrick Ling, also became part of the American system. Ling's work was contemporary with and to some slight extent he anticipated that of "Turnvater" Jahn. Both Swedish-Americans and Norwegian-Americans—the honor is shared—popularized the infinite variety of Scandinavian dishes comprising the smörgåsbord; and the Swedish Christmas remained a pageant in itself, sharing with the German tradition the introduction of the Christmas tree.

The future development of Minnesota as a second Scandinavia, whose best features it resembled, was suggested in the 1850's by Fredrika Bremer, the prolific Finnish-born poetess and novelist, in *Homes in the New World* (1853-57). One of the most popular novelists in Sweden, especially admired for her sentimental themes, her writings were extravagantly praised by Walt Whitman, Longfellow, and James Russell Lowell. Visiting early St. Paul, she rhapsodized:

What a glorious new Scandinavia might not Minnesota become. Here would the Swede find his clear romantic lakes, the plains of Skåne, rich in corn, and the valleys of Norrland—the climate, the situation, the character of the scenery agrees with our people better than any other of the American states, and none of them appear to me to have a greater or more beautiful future than Minnesota.

In 1851, the Sioux relinquished extensive lands to the new territory of Minnesota organized in 1848; a few years later the Ojibway tribes, too, consented to sign a similar treaty. Thus the gates were opened to pioneer immigration, and in 1857 Minnesota entered the Union. Mud-plastered, one-room log cabins, furnished with little more than rude tables, chairs, and beds, sprang up across the horizon.

5

France seemed to have reached a fairly stable economic balance by mid-century except for the industrial unrest in the cities, but her recurrent political revolts, such as those of 1830 and 1848, and her changes of regime in 1815, 1830, 1848, and 1851, created a good number of political refugees. With Napoleon's overthrow thousands of adherents of the First Empire joined the ex-king, Joseph Bonaparte, in American exile. The French liberal's admiration for American institutions had no greater exponent than Alexis de Tocqueville, whose *Democracy in America* (1835), expressing faith in the final victory of popular government, became a classic. In 1851, some 20,000 French immigrants arrived, many of them former revolutionists fleeing the dictatorship of Louis Napoleon. By 1860, the census reported almost 110,000 French-born residents in the country with a small but growing number of French-Canadians.

After the Mormons fled Nauvoo, Illinois, a group of several hundred Frenchmen under Étienne Cabet, exiled lawyer, editor, and French deputy, who had fought the regime of Louis Philippe, arrived in 1849 to establish a communist utopia. Cabet, who had written *Voyage au Icarie* in 1840 under the influence of the socialistic ideas of Robert Owen, proposed a communistic society along rationalist lines. This Garden of Eden was soon disrupted by dissension, leading Cabet with some 200 followers to abandon Nauvoo for another "Icarian" community at Cheltenham, Iowa, but factionalism and secession pursued him there also. Small Icarian communities appeared in St. Louis and elsewhere before they finally disappeared.

6

Offsetting to some extent the Germans, Irish, Scandinavians, French, and a sprinkling of other nationalities who modified the Anglo-American tradition was the continued movement of Englishmen and Canadians into the United States. In 1860, there were 431,690 Americans who had been born in England; thousands more came from Canada, including many French-Canadians. Parliament, worried over this loss to the Empire, learned that three times as many Englishmen went to the United States as to the British colonies. Landlords, like those of Kent, shipped their paupers to New York, hoping to escape the parish cost of twenty pounds annually for each couple. One unsentimental landlord of East Sussex wrote in 1826, "Unless we can be relieved of the surplus labourers, the consequences in a short time must be dreadful, nearly every parish in this part of the country has a large surplus of labourers, with an immense increase following very close. The great cause of this has been by the overindulgence of the magistrates towards the poor." Most hand weavers, competing in a hopeless struggle with the power loom workers, worked fourteen hours a day —if they were employed—at less than five shillings a week.

Once the mercantilistic restrictions upon the emigration of skilled workmen abated, thousands of English artisans, such as the unemployed weavers, came to New England and the Middle States to handle the complicated machinery of the factories. In this movement they met comparatively little competition, and their presence, except for the caustic remarks of Anglophobes, excited little comment. One unfriendly critic insisted that few bothered to become naturalized or, if they voted, sided with the aristocratic Whigs and therefore on the opposite side from the Irish. "They are patriotic John Bulls," wrote one journalist. "They take British papers, frequent British beer-houses, drink British ale, and are proud and happy to call themselves 'British residents.'" On the other hand British visitors were appalled by the ease with which their conationals forgot their former loyalties and identified themselves with their adopted country. Once the first nostalgia wore off—and their letters revealed a painful homesickness especially on the isolated prairies—they came to appreciate the unique opportunities for buying good land at $1.25 per acre and improved land at not much more.

7

Nowhere else did segregation and persecution discredit the melting pot ideal of cultural fusion as it did in frontier California among the 50,000 Chinese residents by the time of the Civil War. California miners and laborers, resentful of their hard-working Chinese competitors with their exasperating thrift and willingness to toil for low wages, struck back at them as the sinister "tools of the capitalists." They were ready to believe that the industrious and neat Chinese were the scum of the oriental river towns. The Chinese were branded as loathsome lepers, coolies imported as virtual slaves under contract to rob the white laborer of his bread, hardened criminals engaged collectively to import thousands of Chinese women as prostitutes, and cunning merchants whose suave manner and etiquette cloaked their devious plots. "California for the Americans!" ran the nativistic slogan here, echoing an indictment that was generally and cruelly false.

Thousands of Chinese farmers and laborers, fleeing to Hong Kong and Canton from the famine and disorders of the sporadic Taiping rebellion of the fifties, felt compelled to disregard the injunctions of Confucius against leaving the village of their clans and the graves of their ancestors. Many embarked as laborers under contract to Latin America or filled in the gap left by the abolition of slavery in the British colonies; others tried their luck in the exciting gold rush of California, and later, the gold era of Australia as well. Unsentimental brokers financed the immigrant whose property did not suffice for passage money, insuring the investment by onerous interest charges. Like other emigrating groups the Chinese newcomers were young, half of them being unmarried, and at first transients, hoping to return soon with enough to take care of their families. Moving into the mining counties they tended to choose the older abandoned claims rather than to stake out new ones, their patience being often rewarded by profitable returns. Others found highly attractive wages as domestic servants and laborers, filling an emergency need when the mines were drawing off most able-bodied men. In laundering, for example, neglected by the Californians who preferred to pay fabulous prices for such menial tasks, many Chinese discovered a genuine bonanza and were able to cut prices drastically.

In San Francisco a Chinese quarter grew rapidly around Sacramento Street and what later became Grant Street, forecasting the "Chinatown" of the post-Civil War era. Before the great fires of 1849-51 demolished them, many of the Chinese dwellings and business houses were constructed, partly at least, from quaint sections imported from the homeland. Californians gaped at the Chinese with "their long plaited queues or tails, very wide pantaloons bagging behind, and curiously formed head coverings, some resembling inverted soup plates." As a substitute for their traditional village and patriarchal self-government they founded the "Four Societies," which later became the unfairly abused and hence notorious "Six Societies." These were intended to be purely voluntary and benevolent associations, offering lodgings and cheap kitchens to Chinese immigrants, settling disputes, helping the sick and the poor, offering burial insurance, and acting as an organ of the Chinese-American community. As the lot of the Chinese worsened, the Societies became the channel of public expression for the resentments of their race, replying to the accusations of the state legislature and the press.

Before 1852 the Anglo-Saxon Californian was too obsessed with his feud of Mexican War days against the spirited Mexican and Chilean competitors to give more than an amused tolerance to the useful and aggressive "Celestial," as the Chinese was then called. One governor even suggested that Chinese immigration be stimulated by offers of land grants. The *Daily Alta California* predicted on May 12, 1852, "The China Boys will yet vote at the same polls, study at the same schools, and bow at the same altar as our own countrymen." That same year the atmosphere suddenly changed with the expulsion of the Latin American from the mines through license taxes and crude force, leaving the Chinese the chief target for the nativists. Tough Missourians and other Southerners, some arriving with their slaves, allied temporarily with Irish and German immigrants to force the state legislature to pass anti-Chinese laws until the status of the "Celestial" was reduced to that of the

Negro and the despised "Digger" Indian. Chinese were increasingly laden with heavy special taxes, forbidden the right to vote or to testify in court against whites, and adjudged aliens ineligible to citizenship. Only the courts prevented the politicians in the legislature from excluding Chinese altogether. Lacking legal protection against whites, many Chinese miners were driven out of their holdings and scores were brutally murdered or dispossessed each year, sometimes killed by avaricious tax collectors whose fees depended upon their success at extortion. Chinese submissiveness, born of a long anti-military tradition, did not turn away the wrath of the Californians; the whites themselves were suffering from declining wages and a fall in the yield of placer mining after 1853, thus sharpening the economic competition between the races.

So far did the prejudice against Chinese mount that a nativistic school superintendent defiantly asserted in 1859 of the Chinese, Negro, and American Indian peoples, "The great mass of our citizens will not associate on terms of equality with these inferior races, nor will they consent that their children should do so." Steadily a hateful stereotype of the segregated Chinese developed and early assimilation ceased to be a possibility. Although some temporary improvement in race relations took place under the Republican administration of Governor Leland Stanford during the Civil War, this proved to be but the calm before the storm of post-war years. The stereotype of the cunning oriental, popularized later in Bret Harte's humorous poem, *The Heathen Chinee,* remained to plague race relations.

The Great Migration of the forties and the fifties put the tradition of American tolerance to its most severe test. While thousands of Englishmen could easily be absorbed in an Anglo-American society, there were cultural barriers to segregate the Chinese and also the Mexican-American, who was involuntarily added to the Union by the war with Mexico. As for Indians and Negroes, they had long been placed outside the pale of assimilation. Cultural prejudices took an overt form usually when economic or other types of personal insecurity inspired it. Irishmen learned to hate Negroes or

Chinese or Germans in the brisk competition for the better-paid jobs as semi-skilled laborers. Plain German immigrants in the Middle Western Yankee communities might escape economic conflicts but they found it impossible to surmount the social distance between New Englanders and Teutons. Until the old communities could accustom themselves at least to the grown-up children of immigrants, if not to the immigrants themselves, the newcomers fell back upon the inner warmth that segregation provided for Scandinavians, Germans, Irishmen, and others, allowing them to follow the familiar ways of the homeland undisturbed.

Protestant America, rebelling against the Catholic influx of Irishmen, Bavarians, and French-Canadians, became ever more mindful of the separation of church and state as a fundamental principle. Though the King James Bible had long been used in the schools, the necessity of meeting Catholic criticism of the Protestant Bible led to a secular compromise of excluding the Bible altogether from the public schools, with the separation of church and state as an afterthought. Protestant attempts to curb Catholics as well as other newcomers through Know-Nothing and Whig politics failed against the united opposition of immigrants and American anti-nativists. Within the urbanized Democratic party, anti-nativist resistance could easily be channeled, and the ballot proved a mighty prop for religious and cultural minorities. Extremists might burn churches and attack Catholics on the streets, but this kind of reaction merely aroused decent public opinion. Hatreds continued to smoulder, but everyday contacts between Protestants and Catholics within the framework of a free church in a free state reduced frictions considerably.

Economically, it is clear that the immigrant's willingness to accept the least attractive tasks raised the status of the native; and the vast reservoir of immigrant labor encouraged industrial expansion and the spirit of *laissez-faire*. "It is seldom indeed," wrote the English traveler, Alexander Mackay, "that you find a native American, or the descendant of an emigrant, occupying a lower position than that of an artisan." European doctrines of radicalism, notably those of Owen, Fourier, Cabet, and even Karl Marx, affected this generation largely in the form of innumerable short-lived utopias—some, like the Mormon community, quite indigenous in origin—or in militant trade unionism. Idealistic forty-eighters fought for social justice to the slave and the laborer—although many of this group were economic conservatives. Such contributions could be appreciated as American industrialization called for more and more cheap labor and agriculture, too, continued to expand westward to meet the demands of the urban centers here and abroad that had been created by the Industrial Revolution.

· 12 ·

The West of Jackson and Francis Parkman

[1830-1861]

I

ROMANTICS in America and Europe dominated literature during this era and often turned folklorist to rediscover the misty past of their nation and the Golden Age of unspoiled virtue. While President Jackson and the frontier states, believing that the only good Indian was a dead one, evicted the redskins without undue sentimentality, seaboard writers, from Longfellow and Cooper in the North to William Gilmore Simms in the South, dealt sympathetically with the aborigines—at least with the *dead* good Indians. Francis Parkman, the Harvard-bred historian, and Washington Irving, friend of Astor, the fur trader, hesitated before subscribing to the noble Indian theme and wrote more realistically on the natives than did most contemporaries. Longfellow, captivated by the newly discovered German and Scandinavian folklore, adapted the spirit and trochaic meter of the Finnish epic *Kalevala* to the story of an Indian St. Francis—Hiawatha. This hero was actually an Iroquois wizard, orator, and statesman of the sixteenth century who helped to organize the Iroquois Confederacy, but the Harvard professor confused him with an Algonquian demi-god resurrected from the dead. Western readers preferred the frontier-minded novelist of Philadelphia, Robert Montgomery Bird, whose *Nick of the Woods* sought in realistic fashion to show that Indians were nothing but brutal "varmints."

Novelists turned almost instinctively to the fascinating legends and customs of the numerous Algonquian stocks whose dialects and folkways could be recognized from Labrador to the Ohio River Valley and far across the Mississippi to the Northern Great Plains along the Rockies. In colonial times their feud with the Iroquois of the St. Lawrence Valley had been stirred up and kept aflame by the rival French, English, and Dutch traders and officials in their struggle for empire. Famous Algonquians such as Pocohontas, King Philip, Pontiac, Tecumseh, and Black Hawk became part of the larger American story. Daniel Boone had known their Shawnee and Delaware kinsmen in the Ohio Valley and young Abe Lincoln was to be mustered in the service of Illinois against Black Hawk's Sauks and Foxes. In the Great Plains other Algonquian groups, such as the nomadic hunters of buffalo, the Cheyennes, the Arapahoes, and the Blackfeet blocked the path of pioneer intruders into the Far West.

Algonquian peoples taught whites the art of canoeing, coasting on a toboggan, and the ball-and-racket game of lacrosse. Northern settlers learned from them the methods of making maple sugar and syrup. Contact between the races added scores of Algonquian words to American-English as it evolved independently of Elizabethan English, such as caucus, mugwump, sachem, tomahawk, Tammany, totem, hominy, persimmon, squash, moccasin, raccoon, caribou, and squaw.

As Algonquians, the Foxes and Sauks believed in Manitou, an Algonquian word for the Great Spirit, and had a vague but persistent faith in a hereafter. Food was left at the graves to accompany spirits in the long journey from the earth. According to Black Hawk, the Sauk chief, the souls of scalped enemies could not leave their dead bodies and hence would not plague the living. Medicine men, combining magic and the healing art, had a most tenuous position among certain tribes; in the Northwest, for example, relatives of a dead patient might kill the unsuccessful healer. As a custodian of tradition the medicine man often helped to arrange the rites of puberty for Indian youths. In the corn country of the Foxes and Sauks and among numerous other tribes as well, folklore centered about the supernatural origin of corn, beans, and tobacco, which was attributed to the generosity of a divine culture bearer. This suggests a cultural borrowing through successive tribes linked to the ancient Toltec and Aztec people who worshipped Quetzalcoatl, a deified hero who once taught men the arts of civilization. He was known to the Mexicans as "the fair god" because of his light-colored hair; and his story captivated the contemporary Indiana novelist, Lew Wallace, whose popular romance of the conquest of Mexico, *The Fair God,* was to appear in 1873. In the ceremonial music of the Iowa Indians, drums and crude wind instruments as well as tribal choruses played a large part. The tribesmen made their drums of hollowed logs covered with rawhide, partly filled with water to achieve a liquid tone.

Living in palisaded villages and cultivating maize, the Iroquois linguistic group, historic enemies of the Algonquians, had earned a reputation for militarism and barbaric methods of torture. In colonial times the Iroquois had armed themselves with the guns of the Dutch and the English to battle the Algonquians and their French allies and to carve out an imperial federation along the Great Lakes and the St. Lawrence Valley; their famed League of the Iroquois dated back to the seventeenth century. Under the leadership of Hiawatha, an Onondaga described variously as a statesman of peace and as a wizard, the original League of the Iroquois had embraced Mohawks, Senecas, Oneidas, Onondagas, and Cayugas. After the Revolution, when the Iroquois had made the mistake of backing the British, the tribes were scattered, some to Ontario, others to western New York and Wisconsin.

Best known to the whites, next to Hiawatha, were Joseph Brant, the fierce Mohawk chief who championed Christian assimilation for his people against the stubborn traditionalist Red Jacket of the Senecas, and Sequoia (or Sequoyah), an inventive Cherokee assimilationist. Names of the Iroquois peoples marked the new maps of the United States and Canada, including places like New York's Genesee Valley, Niagara, Oneida, Seneca, Chautauqua, and Lakes

Ontario, Erie, and Huron. Noted everywhere for the high position held by women in tribal councils, the Iroquois also reckoned descent and inheritance through the mother's side (matrilineal) and were divided into totemic clans. The Algonquians, on the other hand, adhered to an organization based on succession through the father. Certain of the Iroquois, at least, seem to deserve the rather exaggerated present-day praises of their democratic organization and love of peace. Among the notable southern branches of the Iroquois were the progressive Cherokee of the Southeast who became a national issue in President Jackson's day. These people were associated with another gifted though non-Iroquois stock, the neighboring Muskhogeans, numbering about 50,000 and including the Choctaw, the Chickasaw, the Creek, and the Seminole, who with the Cherokee later won distinction as the Five Civilized Tribes (or Nations) of Indian Territory (Oklahoma). Sequoia, crippled son of a white man and a Cherokee mother, showed marked ingenuity as a silversmith, artist, and writer, and compiled in 1821 an alphabet for his people with the aid of an English speller. Assisted by devoted New England missionaries, he and his tribal fellows made this alphabet the basis of a newspaper, *The Cherokee Phoenix*.

The Cherokee evictions, though not altogether dissimilar from the hopeless retreat of the red man on other fronts, show most clearly the futility of assimilation to the white man's ways as an escape for the Indian. Since 1700, when they had occupied extensive lands south of the Ohio, they had been reduced to fragments of northwestern Georgia, the Carolinas, Tennessee, and Alabama. Encouraged by the missionaries and Sequoia, the Cherokee of northwestern Georgia had deliberately embarked upon the path of Christian assimilation, hoping to keep their lands and to escape the fate of the neighboring Creeks, evicted by Georgia during 1827-29. Their advancing literacy, modern printing press, prosperous farms, neat houses, schools, mills, and spinning wheels— all were external evidences of their intentions. They had even turned slaveholder, owning over 1300 slaves in approved civilized style. Intermarriage or concubinage with whites and Negroes had altered the racial composition of the Cherokee.

In 1827, the Cherokee Indians, invoking a constitution of their own, declared themselves an independent nation, and, when Georgia promptly annulled their laws, they appealed to the Supreme Court. In the case of *Cherokee Nation* v. *Georgia,* Chief Justice John Marshall frankly expressed his genuine sympathies for the Indians "once numerous, powerful, and truly independent, found by our ancestors in the quiet and uncontrolled possession of an ample domain, gradually sinking beneath our superior policy, our arts and our arms..." But he denied that the Supreme Court had original jurisdiction in their case since they were not actually sovereign nations but "domestic dependent nations."

Meanwhile, a slave had discovered a gold nugget on the Cherokee lands, squatters rushed in, and Georgia began to insist emphatically upon the written promises made her by the federal government to evict the Indians. Race hatred flared as Georgia put the Cherokee under martial law, ordering the missionaries out and jailing Samuel Worcester and ten missionaries for abetting the Indians. In the case of *Worcester* v. *Georgia* (1832), Marshall declared the Indian nations to be "distinct political communities, having territorial boundaries, within which their authority is "exclusive"; therefore, the laws of Georgia, infringing on Indian autonomy, were null and void. However, President Jackson, who was so ready to hang a South Carolinian or two for defying federal authority in the fight over nullification, proved a friend of States' rights in this instance by refusing to enforce the Supreme Court's decision and by assisting Georgia to expel the Cherokee. "John Marshall has made his opinion," he was reported to have remarked, "now let him enforce it." On the Indian issue Jackson remained true to his frontier past and the Indian prejudices of the West.

A few Cherokee were persuaded by federal agents to sign away the tribal lands at a modest sum and over 15,000 of the Indians were rounded up for the tragic "trail of tears" of 1838-39 to the Cherokee reservation in Indian Territory (including later Oklahoma). Prodded by General Winfield Scott's regulars at the beginning of the journey along a curious roundabout way through Kentucky, Missouri, and Arkansas, they were hurried ahead by unfriendly townsfolk, and utterly demoralized, many bartering away their goods for liquor. An estimated 4000 are believed to have died along the way. For many trans-Mississippi tribes, the fate of the Cherokee was an object lesson in the futility of adopting the white man's culture as the price of survival. The aged Sequoia himself was to move on restlessly, dying three years later in northern Mexico, his memory kept green by the majestic, giant redwoods of the Pacific Coast that bear his name. The policy of Indian removals among the southwest Choctaw, Chickasaw, and others continued, though not among tribes like the Florida Seminole, of whom many fled for refuge into the vast swamps of the impenetrable Florida Everglades. There for years the Seminole resisted transfer to Indian Territory, defeating federal troops and thwarting the bloodhounds put upon their trail. With the Indians now largely across the Mississippi, federal officials felt confident that the problem was practically solved, since the land beyond the river seemed desolately arid, according to Zebulon Pike, Stephen H. Long, and other outstanding explorers. Atlases and history books were labeling most of the trans-Mississippi West as the Great American Desert.

Explorers, traders, and settlers who entered the broad Missouri River Valley which extended far into Montana, met the warlike Siouan peoples—Dakotas as they called themselves—including Dakotas, Crows, Mandans, Assiniboins, Winnebagos, Osages, Arkansas, Kansas, Iowas, Missouri, Hidatsas, Omahas and others, whose names reveal the process of place-naming upon the Great Plains and in the Mississippi Valley. Next to the Algonquians, the Siouan Indians were the most numerous. Once dwellers as far away as the South Atlantic coast, they had long since migrated and altered their woodland and prairie culture by life upon the Great Plains, adopting the horse from the Spaniard, becoming more nomadic than ever, and much more formidable.

Siouans developed a "buffalo complex" in their way of living and in their religious symbolism. In the Dakotas and adjacent Montana with their grassy prairies interspersed with huge forests, rolling hills, and large stretches of jutting Bad Lands of amazing buttes and bluffs, the Sioux lived, following the retreating herds of buffalo and other game, and occasionally turning farmer or stock raiser. With buffalo skins they made their shields, robes, boots, and clothes or fashioned their distinctive *tipis*, often painting them a gleaming white. Buffalo meat was a daily staple and Buffalo dances, despite their recent adoption, dominated their ancestral ceremonies. The white man's swift extermination of the buffalo shattered the culture of the Sioux. "When the buffalo are extinct," predicted Francis Parkman as he visited these tribes, "they too must dwindle away."

Thanks to Buffalo Bill and his Wild West shows, Americans have usually pictured the Plains Indians—all Indians, in fact, from Pocahontas down—as Dakotas, the most impressive, artistic, and numerous branch of the Sioux. Clark Wissler, the historian, has pointed this out, adding that these tribes were publicized through the exploits of Sitting Bull and Crazy Horse, the Custer Massacre, in which the Teton Dakotas triumphed, and Longfellow's Minnehaha, a Dakota heroine. Their expansive eagle feather headdresses, sharp aquiline nose, painted buffalo robes, and white *tipis* were generously attributed to most Indians by illustrators and painters, even by the engraver of the familiar Indian profile on the five-cent piece.

The Ogalala Dakotas even developed the famous sun dance out of many ancient as well as environmental elements, including buffalo details. This was a combination of rituals and supplicatory dances initiated by an individual to fulfill a vow made at a time of crisis and directed by the priests. The sun dance began with the bringing in of the sacred tree, which only a virgin might cut down, and all the tribesmen joined in making offerings to the sun, upon which they steadfastly gazed while dancing. Observers were appalled by the self-torture practiced by a group of young men among the dancers. When Parkman visited the West, missionaries were beginning to make some progress in converting the Dakotas to a literate culture by devising an English alphabet for the Dakota language.

Other Siouans were far less in evidence than the Dakotas. The Mandans, for example, whom Lewis and Clark had known so well, and the Assiniboins had been almost wiped out in the smallpox epidemics of 1837 and afterwards.

Siouan peoples had their full share of folklore derived from the vanished Aztecs and Toltecs, especially within their cosmology. Giant Thunderbirds, suggestive of Quetzalcoatl and the Feathered Serpent stories, had created lakes by digging up vast holes and had shaped the mountains and rivers. Even now in their retirement to the clouds, they could be heard in the lightning and thunder that they evoked. The Mandans had their own ancient flood story including a Noah's Ark breasting the waves.

Romance and suicides for love were not unknown and wives who were abused could divorce their husbands. However, polygamy was common and among certain tribes like the Mandans and Arikaras sexual hospitality toward favored strangers prevailed, being reflected on the frontier by the large number of "half-breeds." As among most Indian peoples, there was a strict sexual division of labor in which women labored at home and in the fields while men hunted or made heavy household utensils.

Again, in common with practically all other Indian tribes, they had no equivalent to the white man's notion of absolute private ownership or to a competitive, individualistic economy. The Indian had no desire to imitate the successful white man who multiplied his daily wants in the churning beehive of a modern city or town and sweated to accumulate dollars in a bank; however, the Pacific Northwest tribes who practiced the potlatch, as we shall see, could readily understand the high prestige gained for an aspiring individual by the amassing of wealth. Instead of the "cash nexus" between man and man, the Indian was part of an intricate communal system of relationships that stressed mutual assistance and an equitable distribution of food and land suitable for each family's need. Whites, ignorant of the Indian's ways, denounced his faithlessness in observing land cession treaties—never doubting that it was instinctive with man to surrender land through paper transactions. The Westerner overlooked the fact that so many of the Indian land cession treaties were secured through individual Indian signatures that had no traditional binding value over an entire tribe. Petty thieving, sometimes no more than the usual Indian custom of taking gifts or other things that captured his fancy, irritated nearby settlers. Horse-stealing, which lent prestige to the successful Indian raiders, as among the Sioux and the Apache, goaded the whites into taking savage reprisal. "Mine" and "thine" was a far less rigid distinction among Indians than among white men.

For the Dakotas, driven from Minnesota (a Sioux phrase for "sky-colored waters") a century before by the guns of the Chippewa, war became a major activity. On horseback in the Great Plains, they were swift riders and formidable warriors. Parkman, who had left his scholarly books in New England to study the Indians of the Far West along the Oregon Trail, came to this unsympathetic conclusion regarding the Dakotas, "War is the breath of their nostrils. Against most of the neighboring tribes they cherish a rancorous hatred, transmitted from father to son, and inflamed by constant aggression and retaliation." As allies of the Americans during the Black Hawk War, the Dakotas hunted down relentlessly the fleeing Fox and Sauk warriors.

Nomadic life on the Great Plains gave the Indian sign language renewed vitality. Scattered tribesmen accumulated a substantial vocabulary of pantomime and gestures for distant communication. Their famous smoke signals, reinforced by maneuvers with blankets and mirrors flashed from horseback, represented a technological advance over the white man in the years before the telegraph. Army officials were deeply impressed by the military importance of such communication and adopted the Indian's idea as part of the signaling system that came into general use during the Civil War and thereafter.

Westward beyond the land of the Dakotas and beyond the Rockies lay the numerous Pacific Northwest tribes of the Oregon country, stretching from Alaska to the boundary of California. Here amid scores of mutually unintelligible languages and dialects, a trade language developed among some hundred thousand Indians, a sort of Esperanto known as the Chinook jargon. Most arresting among these tribes was the common practice of deforming the head at birth by pressing it with a board, the "flathead" style of the Salish stock of western Montana. Other tribes preferred the "aymara," a conical shaped type of head deformation. When Americans asked several

Chinooks from the Columbia River Valley why they deformed their heads, one retorted aptly, "Why do your women make themselves so small about the waist?"

Another widespread custom, especially around Puget Sound, was the potlatch, a feast given by an aspiring chief or a clan at which valuable gifts were given away. Recipients were not necessarily overjoyed, for they were expected in many instances to reciprocate in a competitive way, sometimes by a feast grander than the first, with even more valuable gifts. At the potlatch not only tangible goods were given away but non-material things as well, such as ceremonial songs and memberships in a religious society. The custom could be used maliciously to impoverish any person by bidding up the exchanges of gifts. Wealthy chiefs sometimes enhanced the potlatch by wastefully burning scores of blankets or breaking valuable copper plates, thus raising their prestige. Here was a literal use of Thorstein Veblen's theories of "conspicuous consumption" or conspicuous waste as practiced by an Indian leisure class to prove their high status or rank! As in white society, only a few had unlimited quantities of blankets or money to burn; to be able to do so was therefore infallible evidence to the masses that one belonged to the leisure class.

Among many coastal tribes little or no clothing was worn by men and only a trifle more by women; interior tribes eastward behind the Cascades had a fuller wardrobe, similar to that of the Plains Indians. Tsimshians, Haidas, Kwakiutls, and Tlingits of the Northwest coast lived on salmon, codfish, and halibut, spearing the fish from a canoe or along the banks and sometimes catching them with nets or traps; berries and game supplemented their diet. Slavery and a good deal of polygamy existed together with an animistic religion, which, for the Kwakiutls at least, contained elements of cannibalism. Tattooing, as among the Haidas, and considerable totemic art characterized the Pacific Northwest. The seafaring Tlingits, extending from southern Alaska to the United States border, practiced the potlatch, slavery, and elaborate shamanistic rites. They excelled in making superb totem poles. These masterly wood carvings, usually of fine cedar, stood in front of the houses to let everyone know the distinguished origins of each clan, exhibiting animal and mythological symbols and representations of ancestral heroes and noted events. As in the case of the potlatch, the totem poles revealed the competitive psychology of their makers.

A far cry from the highly complex cultures of the Pacific Northwest was the simple society of the California tribes, whose members have been estimated as high as 150,000 for all Spanish California, and their kinsfolk of Utah, Nevada, and Arizona. These were all lumped together as Digger Indians by the early American settlers. In contrast to the clean-cut Siouans, racing across the Great Plains on fast horses, these Diggers—so derided because they grubbed for roots and stored acorns for food—seemed filthy in their primitive brush shelters. Yet they were good basketmakers and, until the whites destroyed the game, good hunters as well. Their degradation by liquor and poverty was widely commented upon by newcomers. Those who had lived in the Spanish missions had had at least some measure of security, even if accompanied by close surveillance; but Mexico's secularization of the missions in 1833 scattered this flock to the winds and left them to die of the white man's diseases and exploitation.

Farther south, east of the Sierras, lived the Navaho and the fierce Apache warriors of the New Mexico and Arizona territories who became the rebellious wards of the United States after the Mexican War transferred them to new masters. The Navaho, then a warlike people, lived in low cone-shaped huts of grass, earth, and sticks, which they deserted at the death of an occupant. Stimulated by Aztec traditions and Spanish contacts, they evolved into an ever more artistic and industrious people, noted as blanket weavers, jewelers, and poets of nature. The nomadic Apache, invincible on horseback, preyed upon their neighbors and proved doughty opponents for the American soldiery. In their crude way they borrowed much of their culture, like the Navaho, from the Pueblo Indians whose villages were scattered along the Colorado and Rio Grande rivers from Mexico to Utah and Colorado.

The name Pueblo suggested the sedentary community life of these tribes who lived in adobe houses on semi-arid lands Like their ancestors, the cliff dwellers of the canyons and mesas of the Southwest, they had been strongly influenced by the Mayan, Aztec, and Toltec civilizations. They were outstanding in painted pottery work, cotton and wool weaving, basketmaking, masonry architecture, and jewelry craftsmanship. Eclipsing their northern Indian neighbors in agriculture, they grew maize, squash, beans, and cotton, and kept turkeys and some cattle. Much of their material advance was stimulated by the Spanish who introduced oxen and sheep as well as horses from the Iberian peninsula and taught the arts of their homeland as well as the skills of the Aztecs. In their ceremonies the Pueblo Indians were noted for their rainmaking rituals and, especially among the Hopi and Zuni tribes, for their snake dances, which contained such Mayan devices as the great plumed serpent and the Aztec-Toltec symbols of Quetzalcoatl's story. Monogamy prevailed and the status of women was high.

2

Contact with the white not only disrupted the unity of Indian cultures but proved a costly experience in other ways as well. Most catastrophic were the epidemics of smallpox against which the Indians had little immunity. In the epidemic of 1837, initiated through the ignorance of an amateur inoculator of the American Fur Company, who injected the smallpox virus among the Siouan tribes, 17,000 were wiped out. Only the nomadic Sioux, then away on a hunting trip, escaped the contagion. The tribes of the Great Plains were so depleted as to shatter an already declining fur trade struck by the current depression and the vogue for silk hats that replaced beaver hats for the eastern gentry. Venereal diseases and cholera outbreaks also took their toll.

Whisky, sedulously distributed by cunning traders—the original "bootleggers"—despite federal and local laws, completely demoralized the Indians who quickly acquired a taste for the firewater. Once under the influence, the Indians embarked on a spree that began with a free-for-all fight, the men battling each other and the women scratching until all achieved the Nirvana of the final stupor. So desperately did the Indians crave drink, despite a long past as teetotalers, that some were ready to sell their daughters to the trader; and no price in furs and government supplies seemed too high for the magic fluid. The Plains Indians often courted starvation and exposure in winter by selling anything at hand for a few more gallons—even for the heavily watered variety of liquor that they accepted unsuspectingly. Here and there in the Far West, beggary and theft spread among the tribesmen.

To protect the Indian, Congress established in 1824 a Bureau of Indian Affairs and created a commissioner with sweeping powers in 1832. The Bureau, at first under the unfriendly control of the Department of War, was transferred to a more independent position within the new Department of the Interior in 1849. Indian agents tried to stamp out the liquor traffic and to track down corn distilleries and bootlegging on the frontier. Empowered to protect Indians from white encroachment, they supervised the movement of outsiders upon Indian lands, calling troops when necessary. Tribal lawbreakers as well as illegal traders came under the scrutiny of these agents who exercised dictatorial powers over Indian life. Among their chief duties were the encouragement of Indian schools and the payment of federal annuities to the Indians, usually large cash sums as well as expensive supplies due under existing treaties. Indian agents—except for some notoriously corrupt ones—battled the traders who would have siphoned off all the federal cash and goods.

Another spokesman for the Indians was the missionary. Some were as steadfast as Samuel Worcester, the Yankee missionary among the Cherokees, who preferred martyrdom to the betrayal of Indian rights and who became the center of a famous Supreme Court case. Many struggled to master the complex Indian tongues and to teach their charges to read and write as well as to pray, much to the trader's disgust. Missionaries were handicapped by the lack of adequate terms in the Indian vocabularies for the abstract concepts of Christianity. Unlike the white, who analyzed his experiences in the form of abstract ideas of science and religion, the Indian combined or synthesized the world of nature and the magic of animate and inanimate objects into a simple, unified whole, with a vocabulary enriched by nature imagery. Catholic missionaries in the North-west tried to bridge this gap through visual methods, using the "Catholic Ladder," a six-foot-long chart illustrating their religious ideas and the rudiments of church history.

In the Pacific Northwest, Methodist, Presbyterian, and Catholic missionaries combined Christianizing with colonizing efforts. Catholic missionaries, as far back as early French and Spanish times, had set up scores of missions, particularly along the Pacific Coast, only to suffer a major disaster after 1833 in California and the Southwest when Mexico decreed that the missions be secularized. Especially successful was the sturdy Belgian-born Jesuit, Father Pierre Jean De Smet, whose conversions ran into thousands and whose missions dotted the Great Plains country. With numerous duties that included a trip to Rome and missionary work from Iowa to Oregon, he traveled some fifty thousand miles from 1840 to 1847—an especially arduous task in those days. His fame rested chiefly on his ability as a peacemaker among the tribes as well as between the races. However, the missionaries were discredited in the minds of perhaps most Indians by the advancing westward movement that encroached upon their treaty lands. The noted Presbyterian missionary of the Oregon country, Marcus Whitman, was murdered by neighboring tribes, an event marking the opening of the Cayuse War. Taming the Indian who was fighting for his rights was no easy task.

The relations between the Indian and the white man at his door were not always unfriendly. Fur traders had their Indian "princesses" with whom they often lived in conventional marital fashion, thus cementing racial friendship as well as helping business along. While other traders and garrison soldiers might take their matrimonial ties or sex adventures lightly, there were instances of genuine romance and devotion. Children of mixed marriages often bound both groups together. Friendly tribes saved the lives of many an exhausted pioneer, while trappers succored starving Indians during bad winters. However, when whites and Indians fought, both turned savage, scalping and mutilating without compunction. American officers denounced the sadistic cruelty of the Plains Indians, their prolonged torture of enemies, sometimes burning, beating to death, flaying, or dissecting their foes. Yet the white man often paid the Indian the compliment of imitating his wardrobe, as is evident in his adoption of the buckskin hunting suit and coonskin cap. He even imitated the Indian's savage treatment of his enemies, and his wolfish eating habits.

3

As Charles Dickens and his wife traveled along the Ohio Valley in 1842, noting the crudities of their American cousins, they saw the trans-Allegheny West well past its early frontier beginnings. Towns and villages clustered about the northern Ohio banks from Pittsburgh to Cairo, while the numerous canals of the 1830's and early 1840's in Ohio, Indiana, and Illinois were diverting settlements into the interior, reinforcing the tributaries of the Ohio River and the Great Lakes. Although Dickens had been shocked by New York's filth and the pigs that acted as chief scavengers through the streets, he felt that Cincinnati, then the queen city of the West, had much in its favor. Situated in the great corn belt of Ohio, Cincinnati had risen as a market and packing center for corn-fed cattle and hogs, proudly titling itself Porkopolis. Kentuckians, it is true, still found it most profitable to drive huge herds of cattle a thousand miles to populous New York city, but this "long drive" was to end with the coming of the railroads in the late 1840's. While the Erie Canal had tapped the commerce of the Old Northwest and tied East and West economically, the Ohio Valley still looked upon Pittsburgh, Cincinnati, St. Louis, and New Orleans as focal centers of trade. Within a decade or two the railroad was to rivet East and West again, this time making Chicago the chief entrepôt, but when Dickens visited Cincinnati, Chicago had scarcely begun to display its importance.

Cincinnati, then a city of over 115,000, one-fourth of which was German, became ever more Teutonic in appearance. German wine-makers, merchants, and industrialists helped diversify the industries of Porkopolis. In 1840, it had been the center of the sensational Log Cabin campaign of the presidential candidate, William Henry Harrison, who capitalized on the rising national enthusiasm for the simple ideals of the frontier. At the city's Lane (Theological) Seminary, founded by a New England philanthropist, Arthur Tappan, who had amassed a fortune from New York dry goods, President Lyman Beecher of Connecticut was carrying out the mission of making Cincinnati safe for pure Calvinist Presbyterianism. Southern and New England students rocked the institution in their quarrel over slavery. Beecher's thirteen children, including the famous Henry Ward, Harriet (Stowe), and Catherine, grew up amid the ferment of reformist, religious, and literary controversies of young Cincinnati. In 1849-50, Cincinnati was to suffer the worst scourge of cholera in western history, which carried off nearly 8 per cent of its population.

Dickens did not care to see much of the West beyond St. Louis, and this town seemed less attractive than Cincinnati, though the French quarter was interesting in a quaint way and the new St. Louis theater, costing $60,000, was quite impressive. The predominance of the northern fur trade in its economy had recently begun to decline, though some 67,000 buffalo skins alone arrived in 1840. This city had prospered through the fur activities of the cultured Chouteaus, the resourceful Manuel Lisa, and John Jacob Astor's American Fur Company. Between Dickens' visit and the Civil War the city grew sensationally from 17,000 to 160,773 people, became heavily German, and manufactured brewery products, consumer goods of all kinds, and steamboats for the river trade, with New Orleans and the colonizers of the Far West as leading customers. Its chief rival for the trade of the Upper Mississippi Valley had become Chicago, strategically located at a conjunction of the Great Lakes and the advancing eastern railroads. Like other cities of wood, St. Louis suffered most devastatingly from fire, notably in 1849; before the survivors could congratulate themselves on their escape, they were overtaken by a cholera epidemic that wiped out four thousand lives.

Of the French quarter, relic of another regime, Dickens had this to say:

In the old French portion of the town, the thoroughfares are narrow and crooked, and some of the houses are very quaint and picturesque: being built of wood, with tumble-down galleries before the windows, approachable by stairs or rather ladders from the street. There are queer little barbers' shops and drinking houses, too, in this quarter: and abundance of crazy old tenements with blinking casements; such as may be seen in Flanders. Some of these ancient habitations, with high garret gable-windows peeking into the roofs, have a kind of French shrug about them: and being lop-sided with age, appear to hold their heads askew, besides, as if they were grimacing in astonishment at the American Improvements.

In contrast to the backward French quarter appeared the new wide streets and the marble-fronted shops of the American sections.

Missouri was not only the jumping-off place for traders to the Sante Fe and Oregon trails, but also a fast-growing land of farmers and slaveholders, increasing fivefold in population between 1830 and 1850. It was heavily Southern in origin, although it included 72,000 foreigners, largely Germans around St. Louis, by the latter date. Its lead mines, like those of Iowa, had attracted many settlers into the interior. Since 1830, Galena, Illinois, had become a new focus for mining towns. The year of Dickens' visit Galena was preparing to ship a million dollars worth of lead; and Milwaukee, benefiting from the Wisconsin lead production, eclipsed St. Louis a decade later as a port for the lead trade. Mining towns of the lead era suggested the picturesque adventure and lawlessness of a later period. Another English visitor, describing the lawlessness of the lead country with its easy homicide by pistol or bowie knife, its heavy drinking and gambling, concluded, "Its miners, like those of Galena, are worse than savages."

Wagon routes to the East from the lead country of the Upper Mississippi led to Milwaukee, which had less than 10,000 settlers in 1845 when it was incorporated as a city. A newspaper of that town reported in 1847:

The lead schooners are constantly arriving from the mineral region. These singular teams drawn by six, eight, or more yoke of oxen, excite some curiosity in those who are not used to such sights at the East. They sleep under the canopy of heaven, with the camp fires and the primitive meals of a military encampment, pitching tents with the first dusk of evening and rising with the early dawn.

From Milwaukee such shipments were sent over the lakes to Buffalo. However, by the end of the forties the old lead diggings became too expensive to continue and miners joined the 1849 gold rush to California or went on to the new iron and copper mines of Michigan. By the 1850's the mineral wealth and timber of Michigan had laid the pioneer foundations of a new state as steamers carried its products eastward to the Erie Canal.

In 1842, American pioneers were invading the large prairies of the Upper Mississippi Valley, overcoming their earlier reluctance to leave the timbered regions of the Ohio Valley. Farmers with sufficient capital could buy additional lumber for homes and fences and prairie-breaking implements. Freed from the Indian danger by the removals following the Black Hawk War, they built clusters of homesteads and were delighted with the bountiful wheat of the rich soil. England's decision in 1846 to repeal the corn laws that had previously discouraged wheat imports added a huge foreign market for American farmers in addition to the ever-expanding domestic demand for foodstuffs. In 1847, Cyrus McCormick, Virginia-born inventor of the reaper, left Cincinnati for Chicago, already a major outlet for the prairie crops. There he built a factory and sold his machines on the installment plan among the prosperous wheat farmers of the Upper Mississippi Valley. By 1855, almost 10,000 reapers were in use and the American types of mowers and reapers, being much faster than their French and English rivals, won first prize in the French Exposition of that year. This first stage of prairie settlement, like the opening of the mining frontier, had its share of western anarchy. "In the early forties," writes Frederick Jackson Turner, "the Illinois prairies were in parts a lawless frontier, sometimes infested by desperadoes who burnt courthouses, defied the constituted authorities, and in places even elected the constables and justices, as in the later frontier of Montana."

Chicago's sensational growth from an insignificant village came in the 1850's after railroad and steamship navigation had opened up new eastern markets and had provided cheap transportation for New Englanders and other newcomers from the North and Europe.

Between 1850 and 1860 the city of the prairies expanded from less than 29,000 persons to 109,000, one-half of these foreign born—Irish, German, Welsh, and English. Harriet Martineau, a visiting English economist, had expressed in the 1830's her unflattering opinion of the mud streets and improvised frame houses, "Chicago looks raw and bare, standing on the high prairie above the lake-shore." When Dickens visited Chicago's rival, St. Louis, the Illinois city boasted wide, symmetrical streets, one of the best hotels in the West, and a polished elite of city leaders. Still, even in the 1850's, signs of frontier improvisation remained, though broad Michigan Avenue along the lake front gloried in a block of fine stone-built stores and beautiful homes. Shabby frame houses, awkward plank walks, sewers emptying their slime into the street, and cholera epidemics that killed off 150 daily during the summer of 1854 disgusted many. Fredrika Bremer, who had admired Minnesota's beautiful prairie lands as a future Scandinavia, rebelled at the crude commercialism she saw in the 1850's: "Chicago is one of the most miserable and ugly cities which I have yet seen in America, and is very little deserving of its name, 'Queen of the Lake,' for, sitting there on the shore of the lake in wretched dishabille, she resembles rather a huckstress than a queen."

But even its crude speculative spirit and its new eminence after 1850 as the hog-butcher of the West—almost a million dollars were invested in the meat-packing business—did not wholly obscure the city's amazing energies and progress. "No man has seen the West who has not seen Chicago," wrote Henry Ward Beecher in 1856. The Republicans who nominated Lincoln for president at Chicago in 1860 could already see the beginnings of famous cultural institutions—the early Chicago University, academies of science, libraries, musical societies like the Philharmonic, Garrett Biblical Institute, Rush Medical College, spacious theaters like McVickers, and scores of newspapers and magazine publishing offices.

Lumbermen, following closely upon the fur traders and missionaries, opened the Upper Mississippi Valley, especially in the vast pine forests around Lake Superior, upper Lake Michigan, and Lake Huron. From the old timber lands of the East came the "State of

1847-1865

Washington Irving photographed in his study at "Sunnyside."
(New York Historical Society)

Libby Prison, Richmond, Virginia. Formerly a tobacco warehouse, this prison acquired considerable notoriety in the Northern press during the Civil War. (Brady Collection, Western Reserve Historical Society)

"Contrabands." This picture shows a group of newly freed slaves at Cumberland Landing, Pamunkey River, Virginia, 1862. (Brady Collection)

Confederate Charleston at the end of the Civil War. (Brady Collection)

Atlanta after Sherman marched through Georgia. (Brady Collection)

"A Cotton Plantation of the Mississippi." This print was a Currier and Ives favorite. (Western Reserve Historical Society)

Ward in Armory Square Hospital, Washington, D. C. In hospitals such as this, Walt Whitman, Dorothea Dix, and Louisa May Alcott ministered to the Civil War wounded. (Brady Collection)

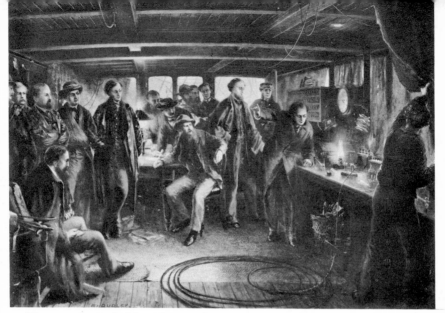

"Awaiting the Reply," by Robert Dudley, 1866. Cyrus W. Field (tall bearded figure seen against window) watching in test room of S.S. "Great Eastern" as first message was sent over Atlantic Cable. (Metropolitan Museum of Art)

New York Draft Riots of 1863. Woodcuts from the *New York Illustrated News*, August 8, 1863. (Museum of the City of New York)

—RESUMPTION OF THE ICE TRAFFIC.   CRUELTY PERPETRATED BY THE RIOTERS ON A NEGRO BOY NEAR THE ORPHAN ASYLUM ON FIFTH AVENUE.   SCARCITY OF MILK—ONE OF THE EFFECTS OF THE RIOT

THE RIOTERS ON BROADWAY, ABOVE THE LAFARGE HOUSE, CHARGED ON BY THE POLICE UNDER INSPECTOR CARPENTER. See page 226.

The Union Stock Yards of Chicago, 1865, a lithograph. (Chicago Historical Society)

Chicago in 1858: State Street, looking south from Lake Street. (Chicago Historical Society)

San Francisco in 1856: a view over the Plaza. (New York Historical Society)

"In Auburn Ravine," 1852, daguerrotype of the
California Gold Rush. (California State Library)

"The Albany-Schoharie Stage Coach Line," 1855, a water color by F. Stucker.
(Halladay-Thomas Collection, Sheffield, Massachusetts)

"The Champions of the Mississippi," a Currier and Ives lithograph of a famous race.
(Western Reserve Historical Society)

Maine" logging system and type of logger camp, which was a low, log-built house where innumerable lumbermen were wedged together at night to rest in canned sardine fashion. Singing French-Canadians, red-shirted Irishmen, and burly Scandinavians in the 1850's dragged the massive tree trunks to the river banks where they cut them into logs which they floated in huge rafts down the Great Lakes or the Mississippi. Notorious for their robust horseplay, they worried the settlements along the way by their pranks and fights. As yet the business could be handled with small capital, using the ax until the double-cut saw replaced it to bring down the trees, but this phase did not last long. In 1848, when Wisconsin entered the Union, there were 24 sawmills in operation; ten years later this had grown to 107 and over 3000 men were employed in the state's lumber industry. Michigan's growth, and later, Minnesota's as well, owed much to this forest activity; unfortunately squatters slashed down the trees, regardless of legal restraints, upon the assumption that the public domain was open to all and that the riches of the forest would last forever. Outlets for the lumber, minerals, furs, and wheat of these new states and territories grew at Milwaukee as well as Chicago, especially after railroad connections were made in the 1850's, and across the Mississippi at Fort Snelling, St. Paul emerged as a major river port.

Out of the lumber camps, perhaps originating with the French-Canadian, came the astonishing saga of Paul Bunyan, a mythical bearded and muscular giant whose adventures multiplied in the retelling in the trans-Mississippi West as well as in the Old Northwest. In the western tradition of the tall tale Bunyan kept company with his elephantine Blue Ox, Babe, who measured only "forty-two ax handles and a plug of tobacco between the eyes," and after some earth-shaking adventures gluttonously swallowed a red-hot stove and died. Bunyan, who bewailed Babe's death with tears that became the Missouri River, built a fitting memorial of rocks known to posterity as the Black Hills. In the South, Bunyan-like tales were attributed to John Henry, and these stories too, entered the stream of native American folklore. Among American Scandinavian lumbermen Bunyan bore a suspicious likeness to Thor.

While Southern planters, farmers, and hunters had moved along contiguous areas westward and, to a lesser extent, northward across the Ohio River, a swelling stream of New England and Middle Atlantic pioneers moved across the continent, largely along parallel lines. Rural New Englanders, bereft of jobs because sheep farming required few hands, crossed into "Greater New England," especially New York, and the northern parts of the Old Northwest. Vermonters, who did not share in the industrialization of Massachusetts and Connecticut, advanced into the Western Reserve of Ohio. Indiana, cut off at the north from easy access to Lake Michigan by monopolistic speculators, by the sand dunes, and by the bad roads of the northern swamps, was slow to absorb the Northerners, giving the Hoosier state a heavily Southern complexion. The 1850's, coinciding with the completion of railroad and steam navigation across the Great Lakes region, marked the heaviest flow of Northeastern and European migration. This east-west movement was celebrated in 1854 with the completion of the Chicago and Rock Island Railroad (at Rock Island, Illinois), which united the Atlantic and the Mississippi.

Southerners, moving up the Mississippi River into the Des Moines, shared with equal numbers of Northerners the task of planting the Iowa prairies. From Missouri and Tennessee came many a future Arkansan. This brawling frontier territory, once part of Missouri, was admitted as a slave state in 1836 and had a bit more than its share of desperadoes, lynchers, and wielders of the lethal "Arkansas toothpicks," as the bowie knives were called.

In Texas, which enjoyed the dignity of being an independent republic in the years between 1836 and 1845, Tennesseans, Kentuckians, and others of the South outnumbered the settlers from the North and Germany. Cotton, sugar, and slavery drove a wedge for the South into the Lone Star Republic and state until, in 1850, the settlements crossed the ninety-eighth meridian into the semi-arid Great Plains. By that time there were almost eight thousand slaveholding families, nearly one-third of the population, with a planter elite of 6 per cent who held more than twenty slaves each. In the fertile southeastern part of Texas, pioneer farmers and lumbermen drew heavily upon the thick forests of pine, oak, and cedar. Just below San Antonio, in the Nueces Valley, lay the cradle of the Texas cattle industry. On the eve of the Civil War the state possessed almost 5,000,000 head of cattle, as yet tough, lean types that offered little milk and rapidly declined in value. Occasional attempts to drive thousands to markets in Chicago, New Orleans, and California failed to take hold, and it seemed as if the wild cattle would multiply as serious pests comparable to the jack rabbits and prairie dogs of the Plains.

Stephen Austin, father of Texan colonization, had created a defense force on the edge of the Plains against the warlike Comanche in the mounted Texas Rangers of 1826, but this organization took active form during the Texan Revolution. Battling Indians and Mexicans, the Rangers learned to ride hard and fast and to avoid the swift arrows of the Indians. By the 1840's the Rangers adapted the newly invented "six-shooter" of Samuel Colt of Connecticut to their defensive needs with devastating effect upon the nomadic Indians. No longer were the Texans compelled to rely upon the single-shot "horse-pistol" or the slow cap and ball rifle whose delay in reloading exposed them to deadly spears and arrows; survival had then required almost superhuman marksmanship with a solitary shot.

4

Pioneer individualism and self-reliance were, as already noted, seldom anarchic, for most settlers cooperated not only in fighting Indians and combatting catastrophe, but also in "house-raisings" for newcomers and in innumerable social activities such as the corn-husking parties and quilting bees. Hospitality was signified by the pioneer phrase, "the latch string hangs outside," indicating an open door to both neighbor and stranger. Still, the test of survival made life far from merely "colorful." Large broods of children earned their keep by doing an endless series of chores that left few months for schooling, except for what a literate mother might teach in the evenings with the aid of Webster's speller or reader. Little girls, entrusted with the care of babies, did not need store-bought dolls.

Gambling at cards, stimulated by the new engrossing game of poker, was universal, except where evangelical faiths gained a strong foothold; the roar of the bettors at cockfights lent excitement to the community. State fairs, frontier "lyceums" for local discussions, newspapers, and the peddler's stock of sentimental novels, biographies, and homilies kept rural life from stagnating mentally. Dancing on the rough cabin floors proved better suited to shuffling and galloping steps than to the smooth rhythms of the East. Dancing schools took quick root in the West. Wrestling contests in which Abe Lincoln was notably adept, and rowdyish weddings stirred up villagers. Diet on the frontier, more copious than selective, centered about pork as the chief staple with parched rye substituting for coffee. English visitors, almost unfailingly, singled out for record gluttonous American breakfasts and equally gluttonous table manners. Tobacco chewing and a cultivated art of spitting led Dickens and other foreign critics to forget the magnificence of western forests and prairie horizons.

Very significant in American culture is the impact of the frontier jury upon American law. In this debtor's paradise "twelve good men and true" could scarcely be anything but sworn enemies of all creditors. The tobacco-chewing judge, whittling away, with his feet upon his desk and spitting skillfully in the direction of a cuspidor, abdicated his traditional English power in the courtroom to the jury, an institution that was invoked wherever possible. Frontier lawyers like Lincoln mastered the art of melting rural juries to tears. In those days before the double-feature motion picture bill, the jury trial was expected to be an entertaining spectacle that no judge could be permitted to dampen. Judges chosen for short terms were shorn of their common law powers and juries often decided the law of the case as well as the facts, even fixing the punishment. While England was restricting the use of the jury in civil cases, frontier America gave it a fresh lease on life and encouraged perennial appeals and inefficient justice. Depending upon the prejudices of the community, light sentences for assault and murder and a sympathetic view of "self-defense" pleas were demanded of jurymen. This laxity and the easy victories of legal shysters sometimes led to the organization of vigilance committees or law-and-order men who corrected what they conceived to be the shortcomings of the courtroom.

As far as basic constitutional forms are concerned, the frontier states were usually imitative, each new commonwealth borrowing its constitution, bill of rights, and local government structure from eastern models. The single executive, the bicameral legislature, and the graded court system appeared unfailingly together with the hallowed if cumbersome principle of separation of powers. New England's historic township system in a modified county-township form remained the model not only for the entire Old Northwest but also far beyond to the Pacific, except for the importance attached to county government in areas like southern Illinois where Southerners abounded. Likewise, new towns and cities followed eastern patterns of municipal organization.

But within this traditional framework the radical frontier spirit still had ample room for political experiments and innovation. There was no cultural lag in the speed with which western states cast off property and religious qualifications for voting and for officeholding. Popular election for most officials made far more rapid headway in Mississippi, Illinois, and Wisconsin during this era than in the East. While eastern spoilsmen for office could applaud western attacks on the merit system idea, it was a western president, Andrew Jackson, who best expressed his section's confidence in the ability of the common man to fulfill the duties of almost any office: "The duties of all public offices," he asserted in his message of 1829, "are, or at least admit of being made, so plain and simple that men of intelligence may readily qualify themselves for their performance." Here was a dynamic western impulse of majority rule, even with its obvious abuses, which converged upon the country at a time when the English Chartist movement and the continental revolutions were infusing liberal sentiments from the East.

5

The magnet of the frontier advance, except for the gold and silver rushes, was the cheap land that a sympathetic government made ever more accessible. When Westerners complained of the law of 1820, which required the purchase of no less than eighty acres under the auction system at a minimum of $1.25 per acre, altogether an investment of at least $100 cash, it was liberalized in 1832 by reducing the purchase unit to forty acres. Squatters who occupied land solely by virtue of possession had protected themselves through claims associations, which prevented competitors from bidding against them at auction, by boycotting, tarring-and-feathering, or even hanging such outside bidders or claim-jumpers. In 1841, despite grumbling from conservative congressmen, the squatters won the Pre-emption Act, which allowed them the privilege of buying the land they occupied at the minimum price.

Quite commonly the farmer was a speculator as well, buying additional land for the sake of a quick profitable turnover. Congressmen with easy consciences sometimes withheld from sale for speculation large tracts of public lands. Speculators grabbed the veteran's land scrip for little or almost nothing. Land sales up to the panic of 1837 set an amazing tempo with almost 13,000,000 acres sold in 1836 alone—exceeding all previous sales by far. Walking along the streets of Chicago just before the crash of 1837, Harriet Martineau watched the lines of storekeepers loudly soliciting her party to buy lands before the prices rose any higher. A Chicago settler who paid $150 for his land in the morning sold it that afternoon for $5000. The wolves, lurking on the edges of this yet unborn metropolis, did not discourage the extravagant dreams of promoters that land values would soar indefinitely based on immediate expansion. Thus large islands of undeveloped lands held for a speculative rise separated the frontier settlements.

Unaware of impending doom from the iron rails of the East, the majestic Mississippi River distributed the commerce of its rich valley among the river towns and gloried in the golden era of the steamboat, which had driven the keelboat into the smaller streams. Samuel L. Clemens as a small boy in Hannibal, Missouri, shared the ambitions of his friends to be a steamboatman on the great river. As "Mark Twain," a pseudonym derived from steamboat lingo, he was to immortalize in *Life on the Mississippi* his experiences as a pilot when he had memorized every curve and jutting of the river. His *Huckleberry Finn* and *Tom Sawyer,* romanticized the Mississippi as distilled through the eager adventurous eyes of youth in the decades before the Civil War. He belonged to the highly paid association of steamship pilots—"the tightest monopoly in the world," as he put it—which protected its favored position by severely restricting the number of apprentices and by charging exorbitant initiation fees.

Mark Twain saw the steamboat era in its most hectic phase, when reckless crews pushed full steam ahead to race each other madly along the river, paralyzing all other river craft. Suave gamblers and footloose women added color to the background of gilded steamship architecture and over-decorated cabins. Twain felt outraged when he read that Dickens denied that the steamboats were magnificent floating palaces; at least they seemed all this and more to the plain people along the banks. Especially vociferous among the tough river characters who fascinated Twain was the braggart whose mouth-filling boasts showed a certain order of creative ability. Thus, in *Huckleberry Finn,* there is this amazing self-introduction by the river bore about to begin a fight who "jumped up in the air three times and cracked his heels together every time":

"Whoo-oop! I'm the old original iron-jawed, brass-mounted, copper-bellied corpse-maker from the wilds of Arkansaw! Look at me! I'm the man they call Sudden Death and General Desolation! Sired by a hurricane, dam'd by an earthquake, half-brother to the cholera, nearly related to the smallpox on the mother's side! Look at me! I take nineteen alligators and a bar'l of whisky for breakfast when I'm in robust health, and a bushel of rattlesnakes and a dead body when I'm ailing . . . Cast your eye on me, gentlemen! and lay low and hold your breath, for I'm 'bout to turn myself loose."

However, Sudden Death and General Desolation proved to be a disappointment in his fracas, emerging quite a meek soul.

Steamboating on the Upper Mississippi to present-day St. Paul and the Falls of St. Anthony attained heavy excursion dimensions by the late 1830's and thereafter. This trip along the river through the towering bluffs near Prairie du Chien and its environs became popular as "the fashionable tour." Visitors could watch the Chippewa and Sioux dance and sing, ride by carriage to Minnehaha Falls, see the American Fur Company's large post at Fort Snelling, or observe life in the old lead mines. Mark Twain was to take this tour again in the postwar years, butchering the sentimental Indian legends of the upper river with his inimitable humor.

6

In the spring of 1846 a young but ailing Harvard graduate, a descendant of John Cotton, left with his cousin for St. Louis, bound for the great adventure he had long planned, to know the Indian at first hand in the Far West. Francis Parkman, later renowned for his literary and scientific histories of the colonial struggle between France and England for possession of North America, was to spend five months in the West and to publish his first book in 1849, *The Oregon Trail.* Broken in health and with failing eyesight, he was to face utter exhaustion under a burning desert sun and to be prostrated by dysentery and fever. Yet he fulfilled his mission of learning the world of the Missouri Valley, its Indians and trappers, and its settlers headed for Oregon or California.

The Oregon Trail, stretching for two thousand miles from Independence, Missouri, to the Williamette Valley had already been worn smooth by covered wagons when Parkman saw it in 1846. Only a few years later Father De Smet noted the reaction of the Indians,

Our Indian companions who had never seen but the narrow hunting paths by which they transport themselves and their lodges, were filled with admiration on seeing this noble highway which is as smooth as a barn floor swept by the winds, and not a blade of grass can shoot up on it on account of the continual passing.

Following the Platte River across some five or six hundred miles of the Great Plains, the trail became rugged after leaving Fort Laramie, then, cutting through the mountains at South Pass, it paralleled the Snake River to Fort Boisé (now Boise, Idaho) and beyond as far as the Columbia River. Along the route appeared the mute testimony of castoff possessions and graves with crudely carved inscriptions. By this time the old blue and red painted Conestoga wagon with its broad wheels and canvas top, drawn by four to six horses, had evolved into the mammoth "prairie schooner" capable of carrying heavy freight as well as entire families. Its six or seven arching wooden bows, covered by canvas, gave it the appearance on the prairie of a ship at sea. It had been first used in the Santa Fe trade, but quickly became the chief vehicle for emigrants to Oregon, California gold seekers, and Mormon travelers.

A long line of explorers, traders, and trappers from the Lewis and Clark expedition and afterwards had opened the Oregon Trail and other routes to the West. Primitive Indian trails, too, originated many of the white man's pathways. Adequate water and abundant grass for livestock were the determining factors that made the Trail generally acceptable. In the prairie schooners were families who had read glowing books about how the Oregon country stretched from the southern border of Alaska to northern California and from the Pacific to the Continental Divide. In 1830, Hall J. Kelley, a Bostonian pioneer, wrote an enthusiastic description of the climate and soil of Oregon. A few years later, Washington Irving publicized the western prairies and the Pacific Northwest in his exciting "westerns" on *Astoria, A Tour of the Prairie,* and the *Adventures of Captain Bonneville.* A close associate and publicist for the fur magnate, John Jacob Astor, he felt that the fur trade of the Far West was the most romantic of themes.

Missionaries like the Methodist, Jason Lee, and the Presbyterian, Marcus Whitman, made the colonization of the Oregon country one of their chief objectives. Whitman's ride to Washington during the winter of 1842-43 has been romantically construed as a dramatic effort to keep Oregon from absorption by England. Actually, he had made a trip to his missionary superiors, the American Board at Boston, in a successful effort to keep open two small Oregon mis sions; then he had gone on to Washington to ask the Secretary of War to assure a safe route for the great covered wagon migrations expected the following year. Already in the year of Parkman's journey a large cluster of immigrants had settled on the choice lands of the Willamette Valley. Such settlements had stiffened the determination of Congress and the administration to end the joint occupation of the territory with England, although they yielded on the belligerent slogan of "Fifty Four, Forty or Fight" in favor of forty-nine degrees. Even the California gold rush of 1849 slowed down the Oregon movement only temporarily.

In Oregon the pioneer culture of the Mississippi Valley was imitated, with the New England element demanding public schools and popular education. Generous land laws, such as the Donation Land Act of 1850, gave Oregonians over eighteen grants of 320 acres each—double to married couples—and thus diverted capital to agriculture rather than industry. The small farmers made Oregon a free state in 1859 but Southerners were sufficiently numerous in the election of 1860 to give the Secessionist candidate, Breckenridge, over 5000 votes, only a few hundred less than Lincoln won and substantially more than Stephen A. Douglas. By 1853, Washington Territory, where several additional centers of settlement existed, was detached from Oregon; its promising village, Seattle, was named after a friendly Indian chief.

Parkman came during the decline of the once-glorious fur trade, after an era had passed of the adventurous French-Canadian *voyageurs*, who were superlatively proud of their skill with the canoe. He could still hear exciting stories of the French era and take part in the prairie hunt himself. Indian tales, taken from the historic and contemporary life of the tribesmen, fascinated him, though the dirt and noise of the Indian villages offended his sensibilities. In 1822, the large-scale fur trade had shifted from the Upper Mississippi Valley to the Upper Missouri where over one thousand men were engaged in a business worth one million dollars annually. Astor's aggressive American Fur Company, which absorbed several powerful rivals, had a string of trading posts and forts along the Missouri and the Platte rivers and an army of trappers, boatmen, and traders. Also operating from St. Louis was the competing Rocky Mountain Fur Company of Colonel William H. Ashley, whose staff included the best known explorers of the Far West such as Jedediah

Smith as well as Ashley himself. Ashley replaced the fort system when the fur trade shifted again to the Rockies, and introduced an annual rendezvous of "mountain men" and proprietors at several selected points on the eastern edge of the mountains. Parkman met some of these mountain men along the Platte River near the American Fur Company's Fort Laramie and later described their half-savage cabin:

The walls and floors were of black mud, and the roof of rough timber; there was a huge fireplace made of four flat rocks, picked up on the prairie. An Indian bow and otter-skin quiver, several gaudy articles of Rocky Mountain finery, an Indian medicine bag, and a pipe and tobacco-pouch, garnished the walls, and rifles rested in a corner. There was no furniture except a sort of rough settle, covered with buffalo-robes, upon which lolled a tall half breed with his hair glued in masses upon each temple, and saturated with vermillion. Two or three more "mountain men" sat cross-legged on the floor.

Though traders were forbidden to enter Indian camps after 1844 they managed to bribe the natives to come to the fort, where they had the privilege of buying coffee, sugar, and soap at exorbitant prices. Pleasing the parents by kissing Indian babies helped business, and alliances with Indian maidens were even better. Life for the trader at the post was enlivened by celebrations, buffalo chases, gambling, heavy drinking, and squaws.

That same spring of 1846 saw the United States and Mexico at war while the Far West became the scene of intense activity. Trade, however, was cut off along the Santa Fe trail of the Southwest, which since 1821 had seen annual caravans, sometimes of a hundred prairie schooners and numerous mules, laden with finished goods, leave Independence for New Mexico—a few even to go on to Chihuahua, Mexico. In Santa Fe and the surrounding country, where isolation from central Mexico had made manufactured goods scarce indeed, the traders reaped wealth in silver bullion, hides, and mules. During the Mexican era they had evaded the burdensome tariffs on expensive objects by concealment such as false wagon tops and cleverly-devised bottoms, which became standard in the trade. Along the route, when not fighting thirst in the Cimarron Desert or battling

Comanches or Kiowas, they camped at night in an improvised fort of wagons with locked wheels arranged in a square.

The Mexican War caught the Mormons in the midst of a series of westward migrations. Driven out of Nauvoo, Illinois, and mobbed in Missouri, the Latter-day Saints under Brigham Young's leadership sought to isolate themselves in a Far Western utopia. Mormon missionaries abroad added thousands of English recruits to this trek of the forties and fifties. On February 6, 1846, the first exiles crossed on the ice of the Mississippi. Then, braving the snow and cold despite scanty clothing and a shortage of wagons, which forced many to sleep on the ground, they crossed the Missouri near Council Bluffs, Iowa. Just outside of later Omaha they set up the so-called winter quarters, "misery bottoms" as their experience led them to call it, and prepared a base for successive westward expeditions. A federal recruiting officer carried off over five hundred men, the Mormon Battalion, but although these suffered thirst, hunger, sickness, and frequent mortalities in being marched across deserts to Santa Fe and then to San Diego, they did not actually see combat service. After Brigham Young and his advisers had decided that the land of Canaan lay off the Great Salt Lake, the Mormons moved parallel to the Oregon Trail on the north bank of the Platte until a cutoff was made to the lake. Their wagons and curious handcarts devised by Young to save expenses, brought them to the promised land in the unsettled Great Basin beyond the Rockies.

"Great Salt Lake City"—as it was first called—sprang from a plan devised in 1833 by Joseph Smith while the Saints lived in Kirtland, Ohio, This provided for unusually wide streets throughout a checkerboard design of blocks ten acres each. Devoted to large-scale community planning as yet foreign to American taste, the industrious Mormons constructed irrigation canals and made the semi-arid land bloom. The gold rush, while attracting some Mormons to California, actually benefited the land of "Deseret" because of the profitable trade in supplies with miners headed for the gold hills. In 1850, when Congress created the territory of Utah, Salt Lake City had 6000 inhabitants. Mormonism was one of the very few socialist cults of the mid-nineteenth century to survive into the next century.

7

While Parkman rode along the Oregon Trail, Polk launched the war, begun, so he said, "by act of Mexico." Like his predecessors, the President had his eye on the annexation of Spanish California. Our trade along the Pacific, the penetration of Oregon, and increasing interest in the fertile "land of the dons" brought the thinly populated province within the orbit of Manifest Destiny. Even the California climate had already won its eastern enthusiasts. A St. Louis fur trapper, Robidoux, visiting southern California in 1840, came back with enthusiastic talk about the oranges and the extraordinarily healthful climate. When a Missourian asked whether there was any fever or ague there, Robidoux replied reassuringly in western "tall-story" style, "There was one man in California that ever had a chill there, and it was a matter of so much wonderment to the people of Monterey that they went eighteen miles into the country to see him shake." But only a handful of Americans lived in California before the war and Mexican governors kept an unfriendly eye upon intruders who might wish to make another Texas of the province.

This "land of the dons" had recently become more than ever before a province of large ranchos whose boundaries were so extensive that a man could ride all day on horseback across his own lands. In 1833, Mexico's government had decided to abolish the historic mission system that had attempted to Christianize and to educate the Indians under a paternalistic segregated system that some critics condemned. But the mission system was never intended to be more than transitional, suitable for the first stage of conversion among the primitives. It is true, however, that the wealth of the missions seemed tantalizing. There were at that time twenty-one prosperous missions with thirty thousand Indian neophytes tending many hundreds of thousands of horned cattle, horses, goats, sheep, and swine; they raised seventy thousand bushels of wheat annually, and manufactured a large variety of home products. The Mission San Fernando covered three hundred and fifty square miles and San Juan Capistrano held even more. Mexico hoped to create a free self-reliant Indian population organized into pueblos and aided by a secular, rather than a regular, clergy. This legislation, while ending ancient abuses, created far worse new ones. The Indian sank into a degraded peon, living precariously in a filthy rural slum of mud-plastered or brush huts without windows, his torpor shaken periodically by drunkenness, and his body often racked by venereal diseases, smallpox, or tuberculosis. This class of landless and dependent natives grew as Mexico gave away the huge mission lands in indigestibly large grants of no less than forty-five hundred acres; thus there flourished a small class of semi-feudal landowners and wealthy merchants. Schools and publications were neglected, some of the landowners being illiterate themselves. Roads were almost nonexistent while heavy wagons with wheels cut from cross sections of trees plodded along at a snail's pace. The ranchero practiced few of the best Spanish farm techniques, neglecting milk and dairy products to concentrate on the hides his cattle provided; the market for meat, especially his tough beef, was limited. Scientific breeding had to await the American occupation. Barter, with hides as the chief unit of currency, prevailed in these early days.

Upper-class Californios, despite a good deal of Indian blood, prided themselves on their Castilian ancestry and looked down on the American as an uncouth "gringo" who believed time was money. They lived in attractive Spanish haciendas with inner courts and gardens that gave this pre-American era an idyllic, festive flavor. Ladies wore silk shawls over full-skirted Spanish dresses, drew their hair back smoothly in braids fastened by silk ribbons and often wore colorful head coverings. The men liked to wear decorative jackets, vests, short breeches, and broad-brimmed wool hats held on by chin straps. Less pretentious farmers lived in bare adobe houses with thick walls, tiny windows, and earthen floors; after the secularization of the missions had enriched many of these farmers, their humble houses were replaced by elaborate haciendas befitting their new positions. The more reliable Indians became *vaqueros*, or cowboys on the ranches; they were unbelievably dexterous with the lasso, an art which the American cowboys learned from them.

During the decade before 1846, Californians absorbed themselves in factional wars unrestrained by the distant authorities at Mexico City; and the landowners began to speculate ever more tolerantly upon the stabilizing benefits of American rule. By 1846, the trickle of immigrants from the United States had increased from Pacific vessels and from the Western trails, despite barriers of burning deserts and formidable mountain chains. Many were befriended by the hospitable German, John A. Sutter, who had once lived in St. Louis and now ruled as a frontier governor over his settlement of New Helvetia, the foundation of Sacramento. Despite his American sympathies the Mexicans helped him to prosper as an official and a large landowner with thousands of head of cattle.

Among those he aided was the tragic Donner party, who had left Independence, Missouri, in May, 1846, apparently well-equipped and provisioned for the trek to California. After vexatious delays and accidents they arrived at the foot of the towering Sierra Nevadas late in fall and with their food almost gone. Through his servants, Sutter sent supplies to the rescue, but they proved insufficient. A violent winter snow storm caught the Donners as they reached the crest of the mountains; had they known it were possible, they might have broken through the remaining fifty miles of snow. As it turned out, they froze amid the high Sierras in canvas shelters and make-shift cabins. Starving, they fell ravenously upon the twigs and mice about them and finally resorted to cannibalism, even eating Sutter's servants. Only forty-five out of seventy-nine persons survived. Despite this ghastly event overland immigration continued, encouraged by the letters of the optimistic American consul at Monterey and by the leadership of John C. Frémont, "the pathfinder," and other pioneers.

The oft-told event of the gold rush of 1849 began in Sutter's colony, leaving him completely impoverished in the end. There James W. Marshall, a recent immigrant who was building a saw-mill for Sutter, discovered gold just forty miles from Sacramento on January 24, 1848. So fast did the Sacramento Valley grow that the town itself, which was laid out the same year, quickly became a thriving miners' supply center; it was incorporated in 1850 with nearly 7000 people, and within a few years became the capital of the new state of California. Thousands in prairie schooners followed the Oregon Trail to Fort Hall, where they turned off to the California Trail. Soldiers deserted the garrisons, crews left their ships, and tradesmen and workers dropped their prosaic tasks for hopes of romantic California gold. Discouraged, the Commander of the Pacific Squadron reported to the Secretary of War, "No hope of reward or fear of punishment is sufficient to make binding any contract between man and man on the soil of California."

French lotteries gave steamship tickets to California as a prize. Englishmen, Norwegians, Germans, Chileans, and Australians filled the steamers. Many preferred the slow water route around Cape Horn or the brief mosquito-infested jungle trip across the Isthmus of Panama to the difficulties of the overland passage. Impatient miners, loaded with equipment and supplies, took their chances, once off the boat at the Isthmus, upon the burning Panama trail with its exhausting horseback journey, jungle insects, and cholera while vultures circled contemplatively overhead. Confusion marked these early years of the gold rush. Least desirable were the ex-convicts from the penal colonies of New South Wales including dissipated criminals known in California as "Sydney Ducks."

The shabby adobe buildings of San Francisco housed no more than 800 people in 1848. Two years later some 30,000 to 40,000 persons jammed the numerous ramshackle houses, canvas tents, and treacherous muddy streets. Free-spending miners threw away fortunes in the saloons and gaming houses of the city, which were decorated in the tinselled finery of large imported glass mirrors, prism chandeliers, and ponderous furniture. Six times during 1850-51 fires swept the city over entire blocks, destroying at least twelve millions in property. Fantastically high prices for everything and the speculative mania wiped out the modest gains of many. A small store might rent for $3000 a month and lots worth a few hundred dollars rose to as many thousands within several months. Boots sold for $100 and the smallest usable change was a quarter. Instead of becoming a magnate, many a fortune hunter turned bankrupt, tramped aimlessly about, died of cholera or pneumonia, or committed suicide.

Lawlessness, comparable to that in frontier Illinois, Missouri, and perhaps to "bleeding Kansas" as well, dominated San Francisco as well as the "diggings." Between 1849 and 1856 at least 1000 citizens were murdered. Murderers, thieves, and toughs, benefitting by the protection of corrupt politicians and lawyers, plied their trade with little worry over retribution. One notorious San Francisco gang, the "Hounds," paraded occasionally, robbed foreigners, left town to raid ranches in open daylight, and murdered many in the Chilean quarter. To combat these vicious elements citizens organized private police and courts in 1849 to protect the city, which they did for a time, driving the Hounds out of San Francisco. When wide-scale lawlessness revived, a Vigilance Committee was formed in 1851, promptly arresting over ninety, hanging four, and expelling twenty-eight, besides frightening other criminals away. More elaborate and famous was the second Vigilance Committee of 1856, which almost invoked civil war as it disregarded formal courts and even state officials to smash gangs and to punish protected murderers and corrupt officials. Vigilante justice in San Francisco, though carefully restricted by responsible leaders, set an unfortunate model for other Western and Southern communities. Still, by the time of the Civil War, crime and rowdyism had declined to normal urban proportions.

In the diggings, where unskilled men worked in unscientific fashion at placer mining, washing up gold dust among the boulders and gravel of the streams, life was reduced to elementals and the survival of the fittest. At first a cooperative spirit and a reasonable degree of honesty prevailed; soon a horde of gold seekers descended, ready to try any methods to outwit or to bully more fortunate rivals. As previously noted, Mexicans, Chileans, and above all Chinese were victims of these mining toughs who robbed them of their claims. Sunday was the grand day of recreation, which varied from horseplay, gambling, and visiting brothels, to minstrel shows, phrenology exhibitions, wrestling, dancing, and sports. At camp dances the men tried to make up for the scarcity of women partners by dancing with each other. Inevitably, illness carried off many who were unaccustomed to camp life or were weakened by exposure and disease. More money was apt to be made by the shrewd Yankee storekeeper with an eye on the main chance than by the average miner. Finally, even the gold rush era had its collapse, for in 1853 the diggings fell in output, imported goods broke local high prices, the bottom dropped out of the real estate market, and men turned to any job for a livelihood.

The cattle frontier south of Monterey expanded and prospered as the thousands of mining immigrants sharply raised the demand for meat and hides. Steers once worth $4 a head sold in 1849 for $75, and even for $100 in the cities. As the herds of sheep and cattle grew, the rancheros took to wearing gold spurs and silver-trimmed saddles, or entertained on a princely scale, and gambled recklessly. Others expanded their ranchos speculatively. This proved too good to last, for when the competition of incoming livestock from New Mexico and Texas poured in and the mining boom lost its first impetus, ruin faced thousands who lost their property.

The American regime in California, though prospering the former Mexican province on the whole, did not benefit all While the Treaty of Guadalupe Hidalgo ending the Mexican War sought to safeguard the property and personal rights of the natives, Californios were angered by the American inquisition into land titles. Lands had been surveyed carelessly and recorded inefficiently in the old days; now, the strict Anglo-Saxon demanded evidences and expensive title procedures that could not always be met. Too many were deprived of their lands on technical grounds. Still, under American rule the aristocratic latifundia system declined in favor of moderate-sized farms, although many of the vast estates survived. As for the Indians, the new rulers tended to place them on the same socially and politically disfranchised level as Negroes and the trend to alcoholism, vagrancy, and lawlessness continued. They relapsed into a peonage of which Los Angeles offered a peculiar variety. Indians would be given whisky, then jailed as drunken vagrants, and finally auctioned off to prospective employers for a week or so; thereafter the process could be repeated as often as desired. They died off rapidly in many villages.

Los Angeles itself, which had been the largest town in the territory in 1846 when its population of 1600 had dwarfed that of San Francisco, did not catch up with its rival again until the twentieth century, though as a cattle town it prospered sensationally though indirectly from the gold rush. A small elite developed of well-to-do natives and Americans who supported the Los Angeles *Star*, outstanding in caliber by western journalistic standards and bilingual in makeup. Illiteracy, inherited from the Mexican regime, was difficult to stamp out, but the Americanized town council (*Ayuntamiento*) did much to improve sanitation and public health, handicapped though it was by the fact that the city's drinking water flowed in open ditches. In frontier lawlessness, at least, Los Angeles caught up with San Francisco, for by 1854 scarcely a day passed without a murder. Here, too, vigilance committees were organized, the worst offenders were hanged, and many more were driven out. Elsewhere in the cattle country of Southern California, Indian outlaws penetrated through the Sierras to raid the ranches and to carry off thousands of cattle. Cutthroats on horseback, sometimes immortalized in the Robin Hood type of legends, roamed at will.

In towns or "pueblos" like Los Angeles, San Diego, and San Antonio, the Spanish or Mexicans had systematically laid out large oblong squares or plazas as the town's nucleus with the four principal streets running at right angles from the corners, usually broad stone-paved thoroughfares. The typical Spanish-American plaza included a busy center of merchants' arcades, a market place, fountains for household uses, and a recreational park. Some of the towns grew out of missions or military presidios. In California, most of these old towns expanded and became Anglo-Saxon, though San Diego, near the Mexican border and somewhat off the main routes, remained heavily Mexican and grew only at a slow rate. San Bernardino was one of the new towns and was founded by Mormons between 1851 and 1858 as a new Salt Lake City, a Pacific outpost for the Latter-Day Saints. However, their ambitiously planned industries and irrigation works were forfeited to others, for in 1858 Brigham Young, then at odds with President Buchanan's troops, recalled his settlers. Little Anaheim, southeast of Los Angeles, took its name from its German settlers of 1857 and began as a communal settlement, later developing as a citrus fruit center. In 1845, California had no more than 5000 white persons, most Spanish Californians; five years later it entered the Union as a free and largely Yankee state of 92,600 people. When the Civil War broke out, California's sensational growth gave it a total of 380,000 and the twenty-sixth rank among forty-one states and territories.

8

Western Americans, too busy in their race for land and riches to cultivate esthetics, sometimes gaped at the architectural inheritance from Catholic Spain and the pagan Indians. The old mission buildings, the Mexican presidios, the haciendas of the native Californians, and similar constructions scattered elsewhere from Florida to California shone in the beautiful natural setting of clear desert horizons, reddish, twisted canyons, rolling foothills, or valleys where fanciful rivers had chronically shifted their course. In Texas, the Alamo, which was nothing but a fort and a death trap at that to Travis' bold men who had fought to the last against Santa Anna, had been founded in 1718 as a peaceful Franciscan mission. Its lovely baroque ornamentation recalled the sixteenth-century plateresque style, the first architectural expression of the Spanish Renaissance. In its shell-like extravagance of design and rich interiors, the Alamo reflected the distant influence of José Churriguera of Madrid whose "churrigueresque" style set the vogue for church architecture in seventeenth-century Spain. Mexican architects liked to blend the profuse ornamentation of the churrigueresque with native Aztec patterns.

Talbot Hamlin, historian of architecture, praises the Mission San José de Aguayo of San Antonio, which was built in 1731, as being "as rich, as perfect, and as sophisticated a piece of Spanish Baroque design as one would find in the Spain of half a century earlier."

Cultural lag in Spanish America accounted for the delay in borrowing the newer distinctive Spanish styles. At Tucson, Arizona, the San Xavier del Bac Mission remains today a gleaming white tribute in the desert to the best of Mexican church baroque with a dome suggestive of the Moorish past as well as the fanciful pilasters, spirals, and rich surfaces of the Spanish Renaissance.

Within New Mexico early Spanish missionaries of the sixteenth and seventeenth centuries had encouraged the native craftsmanship of Indian workmen in their adoption of a mission plan with plain, ponderous masonry and flat roofs familiar to the more advanced southwestern tribes who were linked in the past with Aztec culture. Even in the more sophisticated Arizona missions or in those of California from Friar Junipero Serra's San Diego to the twenty other clerical citadels northward, Indians left their influence. Sometimes, it was expressed negatively in the errors of architectural proportions, but at other times it was much more significantly shown in the Indian types of terraced buildings, the interior paintings in brown and red or black and white, and the use of familiar Indian patterns. Though the mission showed an ingenious variety of Spanish and sometimes native motifs, depending on the date of founding and the skill of the architects and workmen, the persistent aspects were the impressive bell towers, the ornamented chapels, the flowered patios, the multiplicity of arched doorways, the thick protective walls, and sometimes, as at Santa Barbara, the arcaded cloisters with their beautiful proportions. Built at different times over several centuries, the missions within the United States told the story of Spanish, Mexican, and Indian architectural history, ranging from Indian austerity or classic simplicity to the most intricate Spanish rococo.

With California's accession, the United States had filled out its modern continental boundaries except for the Gadsden Purchase and Alaska. By 1860, more people were living west of the Mississippi than had inhabited the entire nation when President Washington took office. The Far West had 4,500,000 inhabitants of whom 653,000 were of foreign birth, and many of these lived in Spanish-speaking communities. The motley frontier procession had been long: explorers of many nations, tough mountain men, resourceful missionaries, adventurous forty-niners, rowdy keelboat and steamship crews, huge prairie schooners with eager immigrant families, persecuted Mormons, and solitary restless wanderers. Literary men like Mark Twain had begun to discover the rich folklore and epic elements in this tremendous westward movement. After 1860, the frontier movement became one of filling in by internal migration the "wide open spaces" in the Great Plains. But this had to await the solution of the problems of water, shelter, defense, livelihood, and personal adjustment that had discouraged the Spaniards in conquering the semi-arid lands still suspect as the Great American Desert.

· 13 ·

Cult of the Common Man:
Horace Greeley's Era

[1830-1861]

I

DEFENDERS of tradition on both sides of the Atlantic dolefully watched the march of manhood suffrage, mass education, unionism, feminism, and radical schemes of social reconstruction. They longed for the good old days before the French Revolution when the masses knew their place and the weight of authority kept rebels from disturbing church and state, family and property. The conservatives had won a breathing spell in Europe and to a lesser extent here after the defeat of Napoleon in 1815 and again after the triumph of reaction with the defeat of the 1830 and 1848 revolutions—but only for a moment. While paternalistic landowners in the American South and in parts of continental Europe romanticized the dear dead past of a stratified courtly society, victory came to the invincible forces of the Industrial Revolution and the ideology of liberalism. Organized labor in the factories and the mines, acting far more militant in settled Europe than in frontier America, forged ahead to a place in the sun. Middle-class liberals, after winning the right to vote, yielded to the logic of their own principles as well as to the strength of urban labor by eventually conceding the suffrage even to the propertyless. Women, whose natural role as man's inferior in the Oriental world of Saint Paul and the biblical

395

prophets seemed forever fixed, chafed at their bonds of subjection as the Industrial Revolution brought to many of them considerable economic independence.

Those traditionalists who felt that society was falling apart into warring segments cited the contemporary abuse of the Reformation principle of "every man his own priest" in the multiplication of cults—Shakers, Mormons, Millerites, Universalists, Perfectionists, and scores of other new faiths. As old certainties were discarded for new, extravagant "isms" thrived in an atmosphere of romantic optimism offering such panaceas as agrarian communism, spiritualism, mesmerism, Bloomerism, millennialism, Grahamism, and starry-eyed anarchism. Hasty utopias tried to rediscover the innate goodness of man beneath his encrusted greed and evil by experiments with communal living in isolated model settlements. What seemed to be "freedom's ferment" to liberals was denounced as the suicide of civilization by conservatives.

"Free society is a failure," asserted the Southern proslavery propagandist, George Fitzhugh of Virginia. As proof he cited the utopian activities of Horace Greeley, influential editor of the New York *Tribune*, the "political Bible" of the Common Man. Had Greeley not condemned *laissez-faire* as a failure? Was he not an ardent exponent of socialism, feminism, Fourier communities, spiritualism, agrarian anti-rent causes, trade unions, prohibition, and "land to the landless"? Greeley's undeniable influence on the Republican platform of 1860, which embodied the Declaration of Independence, the Homestead Act, and an antislavery plank, suggested to others as well as to Fitzhugh that he symbolized the triumph of the masses against the shackles of feudalism.

This era of utopia-building, like other current forms of romanticism, harked back not only to Thomas More's *Utopia* and the revolutionary sects of Luther's Reformation but also to the medieval outbreaks of revolutionary peasants and heretical sects. These medieval rebels, usually drawn from the poorest classes, preached Christian communist utopias, the imminent fulfillment of biblical prophecies of an earthly reign of social justice under Christ, the achievement of universal peace, and the doctrine that all men

would know the truth from the Holy Spirit without the mediation
of priests or rulers. Protestantism became the heir to this spirit of
individualistic revolt against authority; and American Utopianism,
with few exceptions, was Protestant in motivation.

2

Although antebellum Americans were largely small farmers, laborers, shopkeepers, and artisans, the growth of sizable labor and
factory-owning classes came quickly as the Industrial Revolution
captured New England and the Middle States. City growth reflected
this rapid pace of industrialization. In 1790, when the population
fell short of 4,000,000 persons, there had been only six cities with
more than 8000 residents and all city dwellers totalled 131,000 or 3.3
per cent of the nation's inhabitants. By the time Lincoln was elected
there were 141 such cities (largely north of Mason and Dixon's
line) and these aggregated 5,000,000 citizens, thus representing
16.1 per cent of the 31,443,321 Americans estimated by the Bureau
of the Census. With an increase in private fortunes and inherited
wealth, industrial capital piled up from shipbuilding, whaling, small
shops, and existing textile mills. In 1820, the factories had absorbed
$50,000,000 in capital; by 1840, they were worth $250,000,000, and
on the eve of the Civil War, over $1,000,000,000. From New Eng-
land's barren fields and declining sheep-raising industry, both hurt
by western competition and deprived of traditional home industries
by the factory, came a stream of unskilled labor of all ages. Thousands of impoverished Irish immigrants rushed to the factories,
lowering wages temporarily, it is true, but also stimulating new
enterprises through the reduced costs they afforded.

In the late 1840's the chief cotton mill owners of Lowell and
Lawrence and two hundred smaller investors pooled their impressive corporate capital of $2,450,000 to build the company-owned
mill town of Holyoke, Massachusetts, at the Connecticut River falls.
Impatient with the older paternalism of Samuel Slater and Francis
Lowell, these absentee owners pushed their opportunities for quick
speculative profits in badly ventilated cotton mills and disease-

breeding company tenements, herding the Irish into slums. Working hours, as yet unrestricted by law, began at five o'clock in the morning and ended at six-thirty in the evening. Here was an early type of *laissez-faire* industrialism that led the proslavery propagandists in the South to assume virtuous airs and that presaged a deeper class cleavage than had hitherto existed in a land of small entrepreneurs.

Vast native resources of metals, coal, and timber, strategically located near rivers, canals, and, later, railroads, insured a solid foundation for efficient production and low costs. In western Pennsylvania, the Ohio River and the state's extensive coal fields, together with the new anthracite smelting processes for iron ore, gave Pittsburgh its lasting advantage over eastern cities. By the 1850's the ores of the Lake Superior region were beginning to reach this city, confirming its leadership as a national iron and industrial center. Michigan's rich copper output alone on the eve of the Civil War was almost one-half that of Great Britain's, and her vast virgin forests supplied many of the industrial regions with fuel and building materials.

The Pittsburgh-born shopkeeper, William D. Kelly, even anticipated the revolutionary Bessemer method of decarbonizing iron, thus making flexible steel possible in quantity by the end of this era. Kelly, whose tireless ardor for the protective tariff earned him the title "Pig Iron Kelly," showed that Yankee ingenuity which characterized the Industrial Revolution in America, but the greater glory and rewards were destined for his English rival, Sir Henry Bessemer.

Significant in the American mass production tradition were the sewing-machine inventions of two mechanics, Elias Howe, a former textile machinist of Lowell, and Isaac Singer, a workman of New York. Howe invented a practical eye-pointed, needle-type of machine in 1846 and after prolonged litigation set up the Howe Machine Company in 1865. His ingenuity gained him a fortune. Singer, who invented the foot-treadle type of machine, opened a factory and central office at New York in 1853, taking the leadership in the large-scale manufacture of machines and also becoming wealthy in the process. The Civil War, with its scarcity of labor and its need for vast quantities of uniforms and other clothing, enriched the sewing-machine manufacturers and helped give this country permanent leadership in the manufacture of sewing machines for all parts of the globe.

Another inventor-manufacturer who strengthened the tradition of large-scale machine techniques was Cyrus Hall McCormick of Virginia, who invented the reaper in 1831 and wisely kept up with the latest mechanical improvements thereafter. In 1847, he opened a large Chicago factory, sending out salesmen to convert the farmer to machine cultivation. A few years later he extended his sales to England and then to the Continent. Finally, the creation of an expanding market and enlarged business operations owed much to the invention in 1832 of the first practical electromagnetic telegraph by Samuel F. B. Morse. By 1843, he had persuaded Congress to subsidize his experiments and to build a telegraph line between Baltimore and Washington the following year. By 1860, the telegraph had displaced the short-lived Pony Express to the Pacific and had spread throughout Europe. Prophetic of the future American rubber industry was the invention of vulcanized rubber by Charles Goodyear in 1840-44, though he was compelled by financial reasons at first to develop his rubber business in Europe.

As the American economy became more closely integrated with that of western Europe, it shared in the recurrent commercial crises of international trade that replaced the formerly local breakdowns of small-scale industry and finance. England and the United States in the terrible panic of 1837, for example, experienced a concurrent era of speculative fever followed by a crash. In this country, President Jackson's Specie Circular of 1836 had pricked the monstrous land bubble by demanding payment in specie rather than paper money for public lands of which 20,000,000 acres had been sold that year. The paper pyramids of inflated land values hitherto sustained by the dubious credit of western speculators and innumerable wildcat banks utterly collapsed. With this general debacle went the canal-building craze, in which entire communities and states had heavily mortgaged themselves. Many of these failed to recover in time to meet the competition of the railroad boom. Ohio, for example, which spent $8,000,000 for a canal network in 1836-37, was saddled with an enormous debt for so youthful a state. In the lesser panic of 1857, the railroads, too, were to feel the sharp pains of hasty, speculative growth.

By September, 1837, nine-tenths of the eastern factories had closed. At least 33,000 commercial and industrial failures were reported through the nation involving losses of $440,000,000. Beggary multiplied, unchecked in that *laissez-faire* era save for a few philanthropic agencies that were quickly overwhelmed. In New York city where some 20,000 were unemployed, angry crowds demanded lower prices for food, rent, and fuel; mobs broke into large flour houses and warehouses, trampling down everything until they were subdued by troops. Businessmen demanded governmental subsidies; others urged the restoration of the second United States Bank, so recently destroyed by Jackson as a "Monster" dominating the economy in the interests of foreigners and eastern speculators. These demands for government intervention were flatly rejected by President Martin Van Buren, whose message in the so-called Panic Session exemplified the strain of Jeffersonian *laissez-faire* dominant in American thought until the Great Crash of 1929.

After the panic of 1837, canal construction, which had united the Great Lakes with the Ohio and Mississippi valleys as well as with the East in a vast domestic market, declined, but new cities marked its influence. Cleveland, for example, after being connected in 1832 by the Ohio Canal with Akron and the interior, prospered with the ensuing economic importance of northern Ohio, becoming a major outlet for mining, farming, and industrial products of the state and growing from a drowsy hamlet on the lake of scarcely 1000 inhabitants in 1830 to a modern city of 43,400 by 1860. When Lake Superior's newly discovered iron ore region opened its traffic with Pittsburgh, Cleveland's strategic location gave it primacy in shipping and manufacturing; here the coal of Ohio and Pennsylvania met the iron ore of the Lake Superior mines.

During the 1840's and 1850's railroads fulfilled cheaply and efficiently the uncompleted mission of the canals, uniting the Atlantic

Coast with the Mississippi Valley. More than the canals and other internal improvements, the railways inspired the age of iron and steel by their own voracious wants. As this era began, steam locomotives and iron rails, following British leadership, displaced the horse-drawn carriages, sometimes outfitted with sails, which had precariously ridden the wooden or stone tracks overlaid with strap iron—a contraption that frequently fell apart or curled up, derailing or overturning the cars. In that day before Pullman cars travel was an ordeal and passengers had the unpleasant choice of opening windows and being singed alive by flying locomotive sparks, or keeping them closed and being smothered. Jerky cars, suffocating smoke, and puddles of tobacco juice gave many a European visitor his most lasting impression of American life. But these little inconveniences did not prevent the railroads from expanding their mileage from less than 3000 miles in 1840 to over ten times as much on the eve of the Rebellion.

As in the canal era, states and localities weighted themselves down with huge bond issues and heavy taxes to help finance the railroad construction companies. From Maryland, the Baltimore and Ohio Railroad reached out to Cincinnati and finally, by 1857, to the Queen City of the Mississippi, St. Louis. By 1860, east-west traffic had been assured by a succession of short-track lines that were gradually consolidated. Thus Bostonians achieved uninterrupted connections with Albany and then with the New York Central and by the consolidation of eleven local lines in the Mohawk Valley and along the Great Lakes they could finally reach Chicago. The Erie Railroad, directed by the unscrupulous cattle-driver, Daniel Drew, served southern New York, neglected hitherto by both the Erie Canal and the railroad; and the Pennsylvania, which inherited the old state system of internal improvements between Philadelphia and Pittsburgh, extended its tracks toward Chicago and St. Louis to head off the B. and O. invasion of Pittsburgh.

The South, lacking the freight and passenger advantages of the urbanized North, had fewer lines, but Charleston had direct connections with Memphis, Richmond with Chattanooga, and a beginning was made on a Vicksburg-Savannah line before the war broke out. Of the few important North-South links, necessitated by the traffic in farm products, mules, cotton, and cattle, the most impressive was the Illinois Central sponsored by the railroad-minded Stephen A. Douglas of Chicago, and completed in 1856 with the aid of federal land grants. This railroad strengthened Chicago's position as the natural railroad center of the Mississippi Valley and the nation, connecting it with the profitable traffic of Cairo and "Little Egypt," with Mobile, and finally with populous New Orleans. The next step, all agreed, was some sort of transcontinental railroad, but sectionalists battled in Congress and in the newspapers about whether the enormous line across the Great Plains and the Rockies should be Northern or Southern.

With a rich and expanding domestic market for the products of industry and the farm, foreign trade played a humble role in the nation's economy except for the South whose cotton, rice, tobacco, and sugar accounted for over three-fourths of our exports in 1860. The historic Canton trade declined, for the sea otter, so valuable to the Chinese buyer, had disappeared while Americans developed an enthusiasm for European porcelain in preference to Chinese pottery, and drank Brazilian coffee instead of oriental tea. Promising for the future seemed the visit to Japan in 1854 of Commodore Matthew C. Perry, brother of the famous naval hero of 1812. This opened the isolated island empire to westernization and trade under the sponsorship of the United States. In the West Indies, a mainstay of American trade since colonial days, American commerce fell off.

Although this era was to see the American merchant marine decline from a position of parity with England to a permanent level of inferiority, American shipbuilders and captains proudly launched ever swifter and larger clipper ships that seemed to leave the British far behind. These vessels, like sculptured works of art, were designed to cut across the waves, propelled by tall masts sustaining broad canvases, and could cross the Atlantic in less than fifteen days. Clippers developed in time to serve the gold argonauts to California in 1849, to transport wheat to Europe during the starving forties, and to evade patrols along the West African coast while carrying off thousands of Negroes into slavery. Portending the

doom of the clipper was the new transatlantic steamer which won
supremacy during the years that the clipper was deeply engaged
in the California trade. While Britain subsidized the steamships of
the Nova Scotia merchant, Samuel Cunard, Congress backed the
E. K. Collins lines; but Americans proved indifferent to the policy
of continued large-scale subsidy to the merchant marine and the
Collins lines lost considerable prestige because of a series of wrecks.
British technical superiority and cheaper labor costs conspired to
eliminate Collins by 1858. Thus the American steamship lines fell
well behind Britain's.

3

The rise of the common man in America during the heyday of
romanticism seemed to be—far more than in the case of the parallel
advance of European workingmen—an individualistic, antimonopo-
list, and antiaristocratic movement rather than a class-conscious,
anticapitalist crusade. Skilled workmen who were themselves self-
employed part of the time, did not join unions or "workingmen's
parties" to launch a class war. Recent studies suggest that the
so-called "Workies" and the mechanics' press of Jackson's day were
heavily middle class in composition and ideals, though radical
formulas of socialist reconstruction and communist utopias had
their exponents.

In 1828, both Jackson and John Quincy Adams wooed the labor
vote as expressed in the ten-hour movement and its slogan "From
Six to Six." According to Arthur J. Schlesinger, Jr.'s noteworthy
study, *The Age of Jackson,* the Tennessean drew considerable support from Eastern mechanics and tradesmen as well as Westerners,
but this view has been contested. Certainly, Jackson became the
leader of the war of 1832 on the second Bank of the United States,
alleging that it favored parasitic speculation and foreign interests—
though many western Jacksonians thought that this bank was far
too active in restraining speculation. In Jackson's day, labor and
other popular forces were strengthened by several decades of
franchise reform, for one state after another stripped away prop-

erty qualifications for voting. Southern states, too, joined the procession toward white manhood suffrage.

While the age of Jackson coincided with the greatest agitation for mass reforms in American history up to that time, Jackson himself was scarcely better than neutral toward the labor movement. Professor Richard B. Morris has proved that it was Jackson and not Rutherford B. Hayes who was first to use federal troops in a labor conflict. In January, 1834, Irish strikers raised havoc on the Baltimore and Ohio Canal, then directed by Jackson's former Secretary of War and confidant, John H. Eaton. The President quickly responded to Maryland's call for troops by ordering two companies of regulars to the scene. At the desire of Eaton, he kept the soldiers policing the canal for the remaining winter months, thus overawing the strikers. In so doing, says Morris, he gave unprecedented aid to "a company which did not scruple to employ the blacklist, private police, and labor spies to maintain discipline among its workers."

Labor sentiment, concerned with improved status rather than with political power, resented the stigma of pauperism upon those who attended schools without paying tuition and the patronizing attitude of the rising business and professional classes. Conservatives cited the popular Malthusian theory that population tended to outstrip the food supply; they condemned taxes for the support of the poor, since by "encouraging the poor to depend on them, they foster their idleness and improvidence and thus produce, or at least increase, the poverty and distress they are intended to relieve." Next to nothing was done about the slums of New York, Boston, and Philadelphia where thousands were huddled together in filthy tenements lacking even privies and windows. The panics of 1837 and 1857, as already noted, awakened no tendency toward state intervention.

In a landmark case in labor history, the right to organize was upheld by a Massachusetts supreme court in *Commonwealth v. Hunt* (1842). The Boston Journeymen Bootmakers Society had agreed not to work for employers who hired non-union members; they were indicted for violating the common-law doctrine of conspiracy. Chief Justice Shaw defined that doctrine:

The general rule of the common law is, that it is a criminal and indictable offense for two or more to confederate and combine together by concerted means to do that which is unlawful or criminal to the injury of the public or portions or classes of the community or even to the rights of an individual.

Refusing to consider the diminishing of the employer's gains as proof of a criminal conspiracy, he concluded:

... we cannot perceive that it is criminal for men to agree together to exercise their own acknowledged rights in such a manner as best to subserve their own interest... The legality of such an association will therefore depend upon the means to be used for its accomplishment.

Although the language of common law was vague enough to allow conservative judges in later cases to assume that unions had an intent to oppress individuals, Shaw's decision meant a major step toward recognizing the legality of labor unions.

The trade union movement witnessed some substantial advances, encouraged by the legalization of unions. Philadelphia inaugurated the modern trade union movement in 1827 by forming the Mechanics Union of Trade Associations, which united all the unorganized trades of the city. Stressing equality of citizenship to be achieved through public education and leisure, this organization never called a strike but leaned upon political action on the principle (later espoused by Samuel Gompers and the American Federation of Labor) of rewarding one's friends and punishing one's enemies. Although the Mechanics Union died in 1830, it was succeeded by the short-lived Workingmen's party, which tended to favor the Jackson program. The unprecedented panic of 1837, like other economic crises of the nineteenth century, reduced the unions to impotence as workers cut under each other's bids for wages and failed to pay union dues. Industrial expansion over an ever-widening market all over the country led the unions to begin during the 1850's to form national organizations within a single craft such as the typographers, the iron molders, the locomotive engineers, and the bricklayers.

Next to the demand for free schools the most persistent among the demands of the "Workies" was the ten-hour day. This, like the contemporary British movement, was largely motivated by job scarcity and the desire to share the work, though there was also the hope that more leisure would enhance the culture and hence the status of the workingman. Strikes for the ten-hour day were frequent and often successful. In England, Robert Owen, the humanitarian factory owner who built New Harmony in Indiana as a collectivist experiment, tried vainly to convince industrialists that shorter hours need not reduce output because the additional rest would raise the productivity of every worker. Part of the shorter hours movement was devoted to attacks on child labor, which led Massachusetts to curb this evil in 1836, followed several decades later by other industrial states.

Another demand of the workingmen's parties and press was for the abolition of imprisonment for debt. In 1830, five of every six persons in the jails of New England and the Middle States were debtors, most of them humble citizens whose debt amounted to less than twenty dollars each. That generation of Charles Dickens, who had sentimentalized the plight of the debtor in *Little Dorrit* and other novels, was torn between the sacredness of contracts and the humanitarian impulse. Other workingmen's programs called for land reform, equality of taxation, the abolition of all licensed monopolies, especially banks, an effective mechanic's lien law, the revision or abolition of the militia system, and the repeal of all conspiracy and combination laws hampering the growth of unions. Altogether, spokesmen for labor—and many were small businessmen and middle-class idealists—had no revolutionary aims. As one put it, "Our object is not to excite jealousy in one class of society towards another."

Labor's keen interest in land reform set in motion the free homestead movement of the forties, which culminated in the Act of 1862 granting 160-acre tracts of land to prospective farmers. Labor newspapers, despite their high mortality, campaigned effectively for free public lands to all, directed by an English immigrant printer, George Henry Evans, whose *Workingman's Advocate* and other publications proposed a New Agrarianism after the ideals of Paine and Jefferson. Evans organized the National Reform Association with branches in many states to make the western public lands a genuine "safety valve" for eastern labor unrest. Homestead laws and cheap lands would draw off excess workmen and keep wages high and shop conditions attractive, he believed. Evans also agitated for laws restricting land ownership to small farmers.

Among his most enthusiastic converts was the professional reformer, Horace Greeley and his New York *Tribune*. Greeley had read copiously in the writings of the utopian socialists and had emerged a determined enemy of corporate monopolies, swollen fortunes, landlord domination, and *laissez-faire* industrialism. During the panic of 1837 he counselled the unemployed, "Fly, scatter through the country, go to the Great West, anything rather than remain here." Like Andrew Johnson, congressman of backwoods Tennessee, he had also introduced a homestead bill while in Congress and did much to cement the land reform alliance between eastern labor and the western farmer. The icy opposition of the slaveholders toward a West of small farmers disappeared after the outbreak of the Civil War when the alliance of Northeast and West prevailed to pass the Homestead Law.

Related to the labor agitation for free homesteads was the Anti-Rent movement of the thirties and forties in New York State. The ghost of Patroon Van Rensselaer plagued tenants along the Hudson with the survival of feudal rents required in perpetuity by the Dutchman's heirs. When the landowners refused to sell their lands in fee simple, which would have terminated all claims, and insisted upon the payment of $400,000 worth of unpaid quitrents on pain of eviction, tenants rebelled and fought off the sheriffs until troops arrived to restore order. Finally in 1846, the new state constitution wiped out such vestiges of feudalism by forbidding landlords to reserve perpetual dues or services when selling or leasing lands.

4

One of the most striking characteristics of this era in the history of labor was the tendency to construct utopian communities on a collectivist basis, either communist or socialist, as an answer to the evils of the Industrial Revolution. Owen's New Harmony, situated on the banks of the Wabash, succeeded another communistic experiment, that of the Rappites, by purchasing their properties in 1825. Owen and his son, Robert Dale, who believed that man was completely plastic and capable of total regeneration in a favorable environment, frightened middle-class sympathizers by attacking the churches, the strict marriage laws, and private property. Investigating English factory abuses with his small son, Owen had denounced the exploitation of little children and women as worse than American slavery and had influenced the Parliamentary passage of far-reaching factory legislation. His own textile plants at New Lanark were models of profit-sharing and attracted international attention.

About 1000 settlers arrived in 1825 from Europe and the East to participate in the lectures, concerts, dances, and community life of New Harmony. The founder plunged his group into pure communism, destroying individual incentive by distributing goods according to need solely, regardless of the labor contributed. Too many had their own radical brands of salvation, too few were pioneers, secessions were frequent, and dissensions broke up the colony within a few years. Owen and his heirs were unable to retrieve the fortune he had sunk in this enterprise. Although his utopianism failed in the individualistic American environment, his ideas of economic cooperation were to influence England's powerful cooperative movement. Nine smaller Owenite communities sprang up in Indiana, New York, Ohio, and elsewhere, but these too, gave up the ghost by 1828. Owen persisted in building new collectivist communities in England and Wales on a larger scale, but these eventually failed.

Associated with Owen's son, Robert Dale, in many quixotic reform enterprises was the beautiful but erratic Scottish immigrant, Frances Wright. Her miniature utopian community of Nashoba, near Memphis, consisted of a few ex-slaves and whites. At first she planned to train former slaves there for settlement in Africa by enlisting the aid of the federal government and philanthropists, but soon changed her mind to make her project an experiment in race relations with the object of breaking down prejudices against color. Nashoba was assailed for its practices of race mixture out of wedlock, and, finding little outside support, it became bankrupt.

Especially influential upon utopianism in this country were the theories of François M. C. Fourier as expounded and practiced by Albert Brisbane. Fourier, though a son of a wealthy Lyons merchant impoverished by the French Revolution, turned to anarchist ideas with which to combat the wastes and injustices of unbridled competition. He believed that "pure reason" rather than traditions should determine social institutions, and that man's instincts or "passions" should be allowed free expression within a cooperative society. To achieve these goals he drew up a utopian scheme of "phalansteries" (or phalanxes). Each ideal phalanx would have 1620 persons cultivating 5000 acres of land or working on crafts in "joyous labor," permitting each person to try a variety of congenial tasks. Unlike Owen, Fourier was an "anarchist-communist" who rejected a society based on the machine for an agrarian and handicraft system; he made innate individual differences the basis for the phalanx plan, while Owen's environmentalism would try to change human motivations by altering the social structure. Investors in the phalanx included non-participating capitalists who were promised dividends and interest.

In the United States, Albert Brisbane, a youthful but wealthy social theorist who shared Fourier's antipathy to both competition and the class struggle idea, propagandized for the Frenchman's system in his *Social Destiny of Man* (1840) and in several Fourierist newspapers, which he edited with Horace Greeley, an ardent sympathizer. Brisbane organized several "Furyite" phalansteries during the 1840's, of which the North American Phalanx near Red Bank, New Jersey, about fifty miles from New York city, came closest to his specifications. Here the experiment in "associative living" was carried on by over 100 people in a huge three-story phalanstery on 673 acres of good farm land; excess production was shipped to nearby Manhattan. Men and women received the same wages for equal work, labor was restricted to thirty hours a week, and intellectual life, like that of New Harmony, was intense and varied, including frequent literary discussions, plays, and concerts. As in the case of other utopias, the members did not find it easy to drop their competitive psychology, and after a destructive fire in 1854, the community disbanded.

Much more famous, though less consequential in size and economic significance, was Brook Farm, near Boston, where the dis-- tinguished transcendentalists came at various times—Emerson, Hawthorne, William H. Channing, Bronson Alcott, Margaret Fuller, Orestes Brownson, and many others. Under Brisbane's guidance, this cooperative community was reorganized in 1844 as the "Brook Farm Phalanx of Agriculture, Domestic Industry, and the Mechanic Arts." This experiment in "simple living and high thinking" never paid for itself and dissolved after a major fire in 1846. The "Furyite" forties saw at least thirty-three phalanxes established throughout the Middle Atlantic and Middle West areas based on the ideas of "joint-stockism," a single building, "joyous labor," and rewards according to classifications of "necessary," "useful," and "agreeable."

Going beyond other utopians in his consistent adherence to philosophical anarchism was the Boston businessman, musician, and inventor, Josiah Warren. He had lived at New Harmony but had rejected its collectivism after two years in favor of his ideal of "the sovereignty of the individual." He set up anarchist villages with such names as Equity and Utopia in Ohio and one, Modern Times, in Long Island. Condemning competitive as well as monopolistic prices as unjust, he set up "equity stores" with a price system based on cost; this was intended to include a fair reward for the producer and the seller. Widely hailed by American philosophical anarchists such as Stephen P. Andrews, his followers too often tended to be eccentrics of various schools.

The utopian record for longevity belongs to the communistic experiments of Étienne Cabet and his "Icarians" whose settlements were scattered in Texas, in California, and throughout the Middle West, in Nauvoo, Illinois (where they succeeded the departing Mormons), in Cheltenham, Missouri, and in Corning, Iowa. The Icarians were French and German settlers directed from Paris; they emphasized traditional family life, but, like the New Harmony colony, they practiced the communistic principle of "From each according to his ability, to each according to his need." Despite periodical secessions and quarrels over Cabet's dictatorial policies, some of the western communities lasted at least a decade or two before succumbing like the others to the contagion of the flourishing system of free competitive enterprise prevailing by mid-century.

Christian socialism and Platonic communism offered ready-made formulas for collective living for those whom the Industrial Revolution and secularism had uprooted. "Mother Ann," English founder of the Shakers, was the daughter of a blacksmith and herself a factory hand who gathered her flock from among the poorest classes. Joseph Smith and Brigham Young, founders of Mormonism, attracted thousands of recruits from the factories and mines of England and America. Often, it is true, the communistic form of the religious experiment was used for the sake of isolating converts from the influence of "Gentiles" or in order to pool effectively the limited resources of the faithful. This romantic age of utopia-building inspired such a host of religious communistic experiments as to outstrip the cults of previous centuries. A persistent ingredient in these newer utopias was millennialism—the fervent belief in the imminent Second Coming of Christ to reign on earth. To the strict millennialist, therefore, the process of heaping up treasures upon this earth could only corrupt the seeker for salvation and made no sense to those who believed that the millennium might come at any day soon.

The Shakers, already considered in a previous chapter, reached their maximum numbers—about 6000, living in over a score of communities—by mid-century when periodic revivals in Kentucky and elsewhere prepared many a soul for millennialist life. New societies with "families" of thirty to ninety individuals each were formed in Kentucky, Ohio, and Indiana, as well as in several eastern states. As in the days of Mother Ann, who had died in 1784, they made pure communism work by their self-effacing psychology, their notable skill in weaving, cabinet work, and other crafts, as well as in farming, and by their self-perpetuating theocracy. Following

Mother Ann's teachings, they regarded sex as a barrier to purity and offset the losses due to celibacy by adopting orphans into the community. Men and women were treated equally and wore simple clothes; they followed the monastic virtues of humility, charity, cleanliness, and chastity. After 1860, the Shaker communities declined rapidly, though a few survived well into the twentieth century.

From western Vermont across the Mohawk Valley between Albany and Buffalo lay the "Burnt District" where the constant fires of evangelism had made that part of Greater New England hospitable to the bewildering pageant of strange faiths and religious nostrums that were witnessed by New York and Yankee farmers. Many who found salvation here were ready to join the Shakers, the Mormons, the Millerites, the Inspirationalists, and other sects. The family of Joseph Smith, founder of Mormonism, had seen the rise and fall of locally born cults and were ready to believe their sons' revelations, couched in biblical terms, and expressing in modified form the familiar ideas of an Old Testament theocracy and the promises of the Christian dispensation. To the authority of the Bible, Smith added the divinely inspired Book of Mormon, which he translated and published in 1830, the year that his new church of the Latter-day Saints was founded. Possibly influenced by Owen's teachings, Smith founded a communistic colony at Kirtland, Ohio, based on a "United Order," which required all church members to consecrate their property to the community in return for individual "stewardships" or limited control over these goods. Profits went back into the common fund, which was managed by Smith or his successors in the general interest.

Harassed by the Gentiles and internal dissensions, which were aggravated by Smith's revelation sanctioning polygamy, the Mormons looked for a "land of Zion" at Independence in Jackson County, Missouri, where all Israel would be gathered together. But the Missourians feared the political dominance of this strange cult with its plurality of wives and its large abolitionist wing; therefore, in 1833, mobs drove the Saints out of Independence. A new attempt at a Mormon Commonwealth was made at Nauvoo, Illinois, on the

Mississippi where 15,000 settled within a few years. Here again local prejudices and unwise Mormon politics led to fresh mob attacks, resulting in the murder of Joseph Smith and his brother. In 1847, the new leader, Brigham Young, led the Mormons westward until they decided that isolated, bleak Utah would offer permanent shelter for the Saints. Collectivist ownership of the farms, irrigation canals, and waters became the foundation of the new Zion. Tens of thousands of Mormons from Europe and the East came to the self-proclaimed Provisional State of Deseret to which Congress denied statehood, although afterwards organizing it as the territory of Utah. Young's Mormon theocracy, fearful of being overwhelmed by the Gentiles who would profit from the painful sacrifices made in the desert, clashed with President Buchanan over territorial rights and narrowly escaped war in 1857. Fortunately, the Mormons were left alone to continue their amazing pioneer work of building a prosperous community amid rugged, barren mountains and parched soils.

Driven from Vermont was another utopia and its radical religious leader, John Humphrey Noyes, a Dartmouth-trained minister who had been expelled for his heterodoxy. Noyes, who had been influenced by the revivalists of the Burnt District, thought that conversion meant freedom from sin and that communion with God required the rejection of personal property and individual marriage. In New York, his Oneida community shocked outsiders by their "complex marriage" system, a latter-day version of Plato's community of wives in which every woman was the wife of every man. Though these "perfectionists" pointed out that "complex marriage" obtained only in the eugenic sense, their group practice of deciding upon the sex partners aroused outside antagonism to this "free love." Life at Oneida was intended to be both simple and scientific with vegetarianism and spiritualism thrown in. Women were equal with men, bobbed their hair almost in masculine style, and wore "bloomers," then taken to be evidence of complete emancipation; their children were cared for scientifically in community nurseries. The Oneida experiment lasted from 1848 to 1881, being toned down to meet sharp outside criticism; individual marriage finally returned and communism gave way to a socialistic scheme of joint-stock ownership. Oneida became famous—and highly solvent—through the production of steel traps and the beautiful workmanship of its community plate silver.

Other communistic and socialistic experiments of the day absorbed the interests and hopes of thousands, including many peasants from Germany, Sweden, and, later, Russia. Especially long-lived was the German Separatist group of Christian communists at Zoar, Ohio, which practiced pacifism, brotherliness, and—for a brief time—celibacy. Aided by English Quakers, Zoar endured from 1817 to 1898 when it was dissolved. One group of Christian socialists under the Reverend Adin Ballou organized the Hopedale Community in Massachusetts, based on pacifism, temperance, and a humanitarian "practical Christianity," which allowed wide doctrinal freedom to members. Ballou's ideas, especially his desire to inaugurate Christ's kingdom on earth, was to interest Tolstoy intensely; the famous Russian novelist and idealist even considered Ballou as the greatest American thinker.

Millennialism and revivalism bore astonishing fruit in the Millerite movement of the 1840's. William Miller, a Yankee who had lived in his youth in the Burnt District, used the exciting technique of the revivalist in preaching the imminent Second Coming of Christ. A Bible literalist, he claimed (in the thirties) to have discovered scriptural proof that the present world would end in 1843. Revivalist tents were crowded and millennialist newspapers sprang up with the ubiquitous challenge, "Are you ready to meet your Saviour?" Alice F. Tyler, in *Freedom's Ferment*, notes that in such circles, children's stories were apt to conclude, "And that's the way the world is coming to an end." Miller himself estimated that he had between 50,000 to 100,000 followers; the less restrained claimed for him a million converts. When 1843 came and passed uneventfully, the malicious reported that the faithful had climbed hills, trees, and roofs in ascension robes to await the heavenly hosts. Disillusionment crippled but did not kill the movement. In 1861, the followers of Miller organized the Seventh-day Adventists who were destined to achieve a world membership of over one-half million by the mid-twentieth century. They took over the belief in the visible return of Christ and observed Saturday as the Sabbath.

Another effervescent ingredient in so many of the utopias of the day was spiritualism, with its search for direct heavenly revelations as in the days of Abraham and Moses. While the phenomena of spiritualism dated back to ancient history, the times seemed most suited for an outburst of revivalistic trances, mystical jerks, the revelations of child mediums, and spirit-rappings. Shakers, "Fury-ites," Millerites, and Ballou's Hopedale Community shared in this ferment; even rationalists like Robert Owen and his son Robert Dale Owen, who had long ago given up belief in formal religion, became staunch champions of the scientific basis of spiritualism. At Emerson's Brook Farm the assembled intellectuals drank deeply of Swedenborgianism, as revealed by the Swedish theologian, who combined a mystical contact with the spiritual world with doctrines of millennialism and human perfectionism. Nothing made spiritual-ism respectable more than the publication in 1860 of Robert Dale Owen's *Footfalls on the Boundary of Another World,* which dealt sympathetically with the phenomena of presentiments, second sight, haunted houses, ghosts, somnambulism, and dreams. Freethinkers were stunned by this defection from their ranks, and spiritualists, of course, were correspondingly elated and lauded Owen. Intellectuals like Horace Greeley, Harriet Beecher Stowe, William Cullen Bryant, and Theodore Parker seemed convinced of the truth behind spiritual phenomena. Orestes Brownson, the Transcendentalist author who had sampled in succession Presbyterianism, Unitarianism, and Catholi-cism, rejected spiritualism, not because it was false but because it meant traffic with evil demons. The "best people" as well as the masses patronized the rising cult of mediums, the vogue for phre-nology, and the revival of "animal magnetism" associated with the hypnotic spells of the late Dr. Mesmer.

An intense popular outburst of spiritualism broke out in the Burnt District during the 1830's. In 1848, the modern American vogue for spiritualism began—also in the same region—with the sensational news of the Fox sisters who lived near Rochester, New York. These girls demonstrated to the satisfaction of visitors that sounds of

mysterious spirit-rappings filled their room. The Fox sisters established the profession of mediums, and newly-discovered mediums
quickly came into existence to reach the spirit world through
(paid) drawing-room exhibitions of clairvoyant perceptions into the
unseen, table-rappings, spirit writing, and ghostly visitations. Although the sisters, later stricken with remorse, admitted a hoax
explaining that they cracked their toe joints to make the rapping
sound, the spiritualists doubted this recantation. On the eve of the
Civil War they could claim thirty magazines and newspapers at
home and abroad serving over 1,500,000 converts. Pioneer American
spiritualists like Andrew Jackson Davis believed that this science
would open the door to genuine truth and to the brotherhood of man.

5

The exaltation of the common man and his "rights" could scarcely
leave the status of women untouched. With factories and shops
opening up new careers to women, numerous utopias welcoming
them to equality with men, and liberals preaching feminism in England, France, Germany, and the Scandinavian countries, the future
of woman's rights seemed optimistic. Yet the work confronting reformers was staggering. The common law, as well as biblical tradition, bound women to an oriental status of inferiority. Blackstone,
the revered legal authority, had disposed of the independent rights
of women by the simple common law rule, "The husband and wife
are one and that one is the husband." In this state of wardship the
wife had no control over her property and her person was exposed
to beatings short only of murder; as a ward she could not sue alone
in the courts. If she ran away, her husband could forcibly reclaim
her, as if she were a slave. If she resorted to divorce, where religious
factors or complicated legal procedures permitted it on certain
grounds such as male infidelity, she might lose her home, her children,
and her property. Drunken husbands sold their wives' clothing or
forced her employer—if she had employment—to turn over her earnings to him. It was simple to stop the complaints of a wife overly
conscious of human rights by committing her to an insane asylum.

This was actually done in the case of the wife of a Massachusetts state senator who replied to his spouse's proofs that he had been unfaithful by throwing her downstairs and then confining her to an institution for the insane. Nor was society as a whole willing to hear the woes of womankind, for the lecture platform and the pulpit were traditionally denied to her. Yet American women, due to frontier conditions, which modified the common law, and their increasing economic independence, were far better off than their European sisters. The rebel leaders came from the middle class and were aided by sympathetic male reformers.

Harriet Martineau, Alexis de Tocqueville, and other European visitors condemned the life of upper-middle-class American wives as intellectually dull, restricted to formal duties at home, and pampered after the fashion of pet animals. Their daughters, it is true, enjoyed far more freedom from chaperonage than did European girls. The current vogue for romanticism and sentimentality added a kind of exaggerated chivalry and stupid etiquette that was as confining to intellectually vigorous or sensitive women as the whalebone corsets and steel hoops that encased them in this ultra-respectable Age of Crinoline. Victorian propriety formed a stereotype of female delicacy: the fragile "lady," subject to fashionable faints, indifferent to exercise after marriage, languidly playing with her ringlets or idly moving her delicate fingers over the piano keys, and faithful to the minute ritual of the etiquette books. Women were educated for marriage in a patriarchal society that revolved about their fathers and brothers and stressed property relationships rather than marital companionship. Despite women's biological functions, they were expected to know as little as possible about sex and to accept uncomplainingly the double standard of morality for men and women.

Still, busy American merchants and industrialists, who had already cultivated the art of bolting their dinners—to the distress of sensitive foreign visitors—and immersing themselves in money-making to the neglect of the refinements of life, left a large sphere of art patronage to their wives. There were strong incentives for ambitious matrons in this fluid American social structure to overcome their humble beginnings by asserting their family status in an exclusive "society" that patronized "culture." Thus the lack of an hereditary aristocracy was a standing temptation to create a social plutocracy. The acute New York editor and poet, N. P. Willis, wrote emphatically in 1855 of the collective power of wealthy women in American life:

> It is the women who regulate the style of living, dispense hospitalities, exclusively manage society, control clergymen and churches, regulate the schemes of benevolence, patronize and influence the Arts, and pronounce upon Operas and foreign novelties, and it is the women . . . who exercise the ultimate control over the Press.

However, this was obviously not the lot of the average American woman. She lacked such pleasant compensations for her restricted opportunities in a man-made world.

In this country, the woman's rights movement owed much to the liberal ideas of Godwin's gifted wife, Mary Wollstonecraft, who had argued passionately for justice to women in the name of human dignity. Her influential work, A Vindication of the Rights of Women (1792), urged that trades and professions be opened to women according to their ability, that women be educated in coeducational schools, and that society abolish the existing double standard of morality. Certain of her ideas were popularized by the novelist Charles Brockden Brown and the scholarly transcendentalist, Margaret Fuller, whose Women in the Nineteenth Century (1845), a plea for the economic and intellectual emancipation of women, became the bible of feminists. Most belligerent and resourceful in a long career beginning at seventeen devoted to woman's rights was Susan Brownell Anthony, a keen- witted oratorical schoolteacher and the daughter of a Quaker abolitionist. She spent her energies in planning the strategy of her cause, allying it with temperance, abolition, and education crusades. Disregarding critics, she became a public lecturer and, when the male temperance organization refused equality to women in their movement, she organized the Daughters of Temperance. Her lifelong friends, Mrs. Elizabeth Cady Stanton, a graduate of Emma Willard's Academy, and the

Quaker abolitionist, Mrs. Lucretia Mott, launched the first woman's rights convention in the United States at Seneca Falls in 1848. Their "Declaration of Sentiments and Resolutions," couched in the fighting style and historic form of the Declaration of Independence, relegated man to the oppressive position erstwhile held by King George III. The impressive list of grievances denounced the denial of suffrage to women, the status of civil death and wardship for wives, the unjust divorce laws, the limited educational and economic opportunities for women, the double standard of morals, and the exclusion of their sex from public participation in church affairs. In the succeeding resolutions the convention pledged themselves to organize against these evils.

During the 1850's Miss Anthony and Mrs. Elizabeth Stanton induced the New York legislature to give women an independent legal status, allowing them the right to sue as individuals, strengthening their rights over their children, and safeguarding their property and earnings. Indiana, under the prodding of Robert Dale Owen, made similar concessions. So began the long crusade that was to culminate in 1920 with the passage of the Nineteenth Amendment— the Susan B. Anthony Amendment. By that time another federal amendment that she had sponsored, the Eighteenth, covering prohibition, had been passed to begin its brief controversial life.

Education for women, being a prerequisite for freedom and economic opportunity, was pressed by the feminists. When liberal Oberlin College opened its doors to women in 1833 it led the way to coeducation, an innovation that endeared itself further by its economy. Among Oberlin's earliest women graduates was Lucy Stone, the uncompromising suffragette whose eloquence in behalf of antislavery and women's causes converted many hostile audiences. When she married in 1855 the public was aghast to learn that by mutual consent she would retain her maiden name instead of taking her husband's. Mary Lyon, a lifelong enthusiast for the higher education of women, founded Mount Holyoke Female Seminary in 1836. A few women managed to win acceptance to the medical schools despite stiff opposition; the New England Female Medical College was begun in 1842 and a similar institution was later created for New York. The normal school movement added to the facilities for women's higher education.

Feminists like Elizabeth Stanton pressed for a reform of educational methods for girls so that they might learn self-reliance like the boys through athletics, freedom of movement, and practical dress. Reform in dress received its sensational impetus through the advertisements of Amelia Jenks Bloomer, reformist editor of *The Lily*, published regularly at Seneca Falls after the meeting of the Woman's Rights Convention. This "Bloomer" costume, a combination of long Turkish trousers and knee-length coats, had its advantages for mothers who had been compelled to lift their wide floor-length skirts in one hand while carrying a baby and a lamp with the other up a long flight of stairs. To the feminist, it meant physical freedom of motion as well as a symbol of emancipation. However, the public outcry and hoots at the Bloomer girls and the malicious distortion of their motives, compelled even the hardiest of the reformers to retreat. In the field of sport some of the milder changes made by the dress reformers managed to hold on.

Sara Josepha Hale, the editor of the popular woman's fashion magazine, *Godey's Lady's Book,* usually devoted to style pictures and sentimental tales, campaigned for middle-class women to learn to play without inhibitions, to discard their tight corsets, to swim, to ride horseback, to sponsor and patronize public playgrounds, to watch their diet, and to enjoy the "picnic"—a term and practice she popularized. This Victorian journal, which she edited for fifty years, had a circulation of 150,000 and undoubtedly influenced the generation before and after the Civil War in the direction of greater social and educational opportunities for women.

6

Dwarfing all other battles for liberal ideas and a higher status for the common man were abolitionism and its milder antislavery aspects. Colonial Quakers like John Woolman and Anthony Benezet had been the vanguard of the humanitarians in the cause, but this crusading generation paralyzed affairs of state and finally precipitated one of the major wars of history to stamp out human bondage. By the middle 1850's the slavery discussion was monopolizing the pages of the *Congressional Globe* while 200,000 men and women were active in some 2000 antislavery societies and propagandized for the slave's freedom through their newspapers and books. Feminists deplored the fact that so many of their leaders like Lucretia Mott were too deeply absorbed in the abolitionist cause; on the other hand, the antislavery men showed less tolerance even to aggressive abolitionists like William Lloyd Garrison, editor of the *Liberator*, for devoting the time he did to woman's rights and pacifism.

In 1833, English abolitionists won their hard fight to free the slaves of the British West Indies, offering financial compensation to slaveowners. They went on to press their cause against American slavery, Russian serfdom, and bondage everywhere. While economic factors, more than humanitarian ones, had extinguished slavery north of the Mason and Dixon line and Americans had abolished the slave trade, almost 4,000,000 Negroes remained chattel property in the South. In the competitive world of the Industrial Revolution free wage contract had replaced fixed servile status and therefore slavery had become an anachronism—though in the South, where Eli Whitney's cotton gin and the expanding mass demand for cheap cotton had revived the profitableness of slavery, the peculiar institution had taken a new lease on life.

Although American antislavery sentiment crystallized about "free soil" doctrines that barred slavery from expansion into the West, the spearhead of aggressive abolitionism was a remarkable group of rebels and martyrs who favored immediate emancipation. The unsparing Puritan mentality, naturalized in the Greater New England of northern New York and Ohio (especially the Western Reserve), as well as Quaker humanitarianism galvanized the conscience of a people. William Lloyd Garrison, son of a turbulent Massachusetts sea captain who had deserted him and his mother, had become a fiery journalist full of the divine wrath of an Old Testament prophet. He fought for the great causes of this era—immediate abolition of slavery, international peace, woman's rights, and the abolition of capital punishment and imprisonment for debt. A strict Christian non-resistant, he used only the moral weapons of his vitriolic pen to prod the churches and public opinion everywhere against slavery. A former associate of the Quaker antislavery publisher, Benjamin Lundy, he renounced publicly the latter's idea of gradual emancipation in 1829, adopted the British abolitionist slogan of "immediate emancipation," and founded in 1831 the militant *Liberator* whose motto showed his common ground with European reformers: "Our country is the world—our countrymen are mankind." There was no hint of passive non-resistance in his language:

> Let Southern oppressors tremble—let their secret abettors tremble—let their Northern apologists tremble—let all enemies of the persecuted blacks tremble. . . . I am in earnest—I will not equivocate—I will not excuse—I will not retreat a single inch—AND I WILL BE HEARD. The apathy of the people is enough to make every statue leap from its pedestal, and to hasten the resurrection of the dead.

He narrowly escaped lynching in 1835 at the hands of Boston "ruffians in broadcloth" who marched him through the streets with a rope about his body. Undeterred, he was later to burn the Constitution for sanctioning slavery, condemning that document as "a covenant with death and an agreement with Hell."

Out of the "New Calvinist" Presbyterian revivals of Charles G. Finney during the 1820's and thereafter, especially in New England and the Burnt District, came an evangelical impetus for abolitionism. Finney could not only evoke the singing ecstasy and convulsions of the converted, but his well-trained mind enabled him to win over men of discernment for reformist causes. A theological professor and president of Oberlin throughout this era, he made his college a pioneer in coeducation and a hotbed of abolitionism, furnishing several recruits to John Brown's raid on Harpers Ferry.

One of Finney's evangelists, Theodore D. Weld, played a far more effective role in furthering abolitionism than did Garrison. While Garrison angered the South more than any other man, he confused the cause by harnessing it to a purely pacifist and anarchist position that rejected political action. Weld, on the other hand, in cooperation with British and American reformers, patiently organized local societies within the new American Anti-Slavery Society of 1833, which he helped convert to the goal of immediate emancipation. He trained "the Seventy," a group of abolitionist agents, to use the revivalist technique throughout the land, to distribute tracts written by him, and to lobby among the politicians at Washington. Modestly, he concealed his achievements from the glare of publicity.

The movement had its martyrs too; a few of the abolitionists were lynched both in the North and South. Elijah P. Lovejoy, editor of a Presbyterian sheet at St. Louis that advocated gradual emancipation, was murdered by a mob in 1837 at Alton, Illinois, where he had attempted to set up a new press. Most electric in its effect was the execution of John Brown in 1859 for seizing a federal arsenal and attempting to ignite a slave insurrection through the South. Though right-wing antislavery forces as well as conservatives condemned Brown as insane, Cleveland and the Western Reserve went into general mourning upon his death. Brown was one of a host of rebels who operated the "Underground Railroad," especially active in Ohio, to aid slaves escaping to freedom in Canada despite several federal laws aimed at such fugitives. This "system" of underground stations was manned by sympathizers with "depots" as far east as Philadelphia and as far west as Missouri. Beginning in the 1820's, it achieved a record volume of escapes under the leadership of Levi Coffin of Indiana after the passage of the Fugitive Slave Act of 1850.

Southern abolitionists were not wanting among the martyrs. Coffin himself was a North Carolinian by birth; James G. Birney, an Alabama slaveholder, freed his slaves, organized the Kentucky Anti-Slavery Society, frequently fought off hostile mobs, and in 1840 and 1844 ran for president on the newly formed Liberty Party ticket; and Angelina Grimké (later the wife of Theodore Weld) and her sisters, daughters of a wealthy South Carolina slaveholder, went North as lecturers and pamphleteers for abolition and woman's rights. In Stafford County, Virginia, Moncure D. Conway turned renegade to his angry neighbors by forswearing his aristocratic slave-owning heritage to join the literary antislavery cause of New England and to become a distinguished author. The Jeffersonian influence had not wholly disappeared south of the Mason and Dixon line, but its adherents tended to flee north or to remain silent except in the Allegheny areas.

The roll of antislavery leaders is long and the nature of their varying programs complex. Out of the struggle over the annexation of Texas and the War with Mexico emerged many militants. As a Whig congressman from Illinois, Abraham Lincoln was moderately antislavery and antiwar, but rejected total abolitionism until the Civil War made it imperative. Wendell Phillips, the cultivated but impassioned follower of Garrison, was, like him, ready to accept secession rather than a union with slaveholders and savagely denounced the national churches for their neutrality upon the slavery issue. The Quaker poet, John Greenleaf Whittier, a lifelong friend of Garrison's, joined the cause early in his life but, unlike the editor of the *Liberator,* took an active role in political activities in behalf of the slave. His *Ichabod,* a poem excoriating Daniel Webster's conciliatory sentiments in the famed Seventh of March speech as a traitorous act against freedom, is the best known of his antislavery poems. On the whole, however, abolitionism and race equality remained radical ideas to the average Northerner. When the gifted woman writer, Lydia M. Child, wrote her noteworthy plea for racial understanding as well as tolerance, *An Appeal in Behalf of that Class of Americans Called Africans* (1833), she lost for years her popularity as an author of historical novels. Like other reformers of her sex she was also active in a number of other causes—temperance, the peace movement, and the status of the Indian.

Very important in this movement were Negro abolitionists, ex-slaves and freedmen, of whom the best-known was the talented mulatto, Frederick Douglass, who escaped slavery in Maryland to take work as a day laborer in Massachusetts, educating himself sufficiently to become a popular lecturer and an abolitionist newspaper editor. Even more remarkable than Douglass in some ways was the quick-witted colored woman, Sojourner Truth, a freed slave and religious cultist. She showed exceptional tact and colloquial skill as a public speaker and reformer, moving audiences of both races in behalf of Negro rights and feminism.

Garrison, Phillips, Sumner, Chase, and other antislavery leaders also tried to eliminate racial prejudices and to extend full citizenship rights to the Negro in their midst. Despite the small Negro population in the North, practically every state admitted some type of compulsory segregation or discrimination against Negroes, usually expressed in "black laws." Ohio, Indiana, and Illinois, where Southern influence was strong, passed sweeping laws barring the entry of Negroes into the state (or requiring heavy bonds to insure against their becoming public charges), forbade them to vote, refused to permit them to serve on juries, and denied their children access to white public schools. Before 1849, Ohio did not permit Negroes to testify against whites. Both Northern and Southern states used a racial classification system, defining the limited amount of Negro blood that a white might possess before losing status as a Caucasian, and penalized intermarriage between the races. Even in humanitarian Massachusetts, Negroes were at times barred from service on trains and otherwise segregated. Churches, reflecting public opinion, often excluded Negroes or relegated them to the crude "Negro pew."

Free Negroes themselves did most to achieve the privileges of citizenship. They were greatly encouraged in 1848 by the news that the French revolutionary government had abolished slavery in the colonies and by other democratic reforms in England and elsewhere. In Massachusetts, according to a recent article by the sociologist, Louis Ruchames, major gains were won through a talented Negro historian, William C. Nell, who labored patiently for twenty-six years to abolish segregation in the public schools of the state. After repeated reverses, he still managed to carry one town after another for non-segregated schools and in 1855 succeeded in getting passed a state law forbidding school segregation. Among the antislavery reformers who aided Nell was Senator Charles Sumner who appeared before the state supreme court in 1848 in a test case, *Roberts* v. *The City of Boston,* which involved a petition by a Negro father to be permitted to send his daughter to a white public school in her neighborhood. Sumner lost the case because the court (including Chief Justice Shaw who had previously justified the legality of trade unions in *Commonwealth* v. *Hunt*) decided that segregation involved a reasonable use of the power of classification by the school authorities. This idea was later to be canonized as the familiar "separate and equal" accommodations doctrine justifying segregation that followed the defeat of the civil rights laws in the eighties. In his argument, Sumner was to popularize the fighting slogan of the next decade, "Equality before the Law." He likened American segregation to the institution of the medieval ghetto and to the Hindu caste system. Even before the Massachusetts law of 1855, other New England states, New York, and Ohio had already taken substantial steps toward granting the Negro citizenship.

Ohio's progress toward civic equality for the races was largely due to a coalition of Negro clubs and antislavery sympathizers, particularly those from the Western Reserve area where New Englanders were in key posts. The Oberlin Collegiate Institute, the first college to admit Negroes without restriction, angered the state legislators who retaliated with an inquisitorial official investigation into the affairs of that institution. In 1848, when the European revolutions stimulated reformers everywhere, the Cleveland *Plain Dealer* campaigned for the abolition of Ohio's notorious Black Code, "dictated by Kentucky slaveholders," according to the editor. A transplanted New Englander, Salmon P. Chase, pushed through the law of 1849, which removed the ban on Negro immigration and permitted Negroes to testify in court. However, nothing was done to extend to them the privileges of jury service, suffrage, or nonsegregated schools. Matters were far worse in Indiana and Illinois where the voters renewed their ban on Negro immigration and continued the older patterns of discrimination. As for the proslavery South, the racial situation seemed too explosive for concessions to the free Negro who was widely regarded as a menace to the security of slavery; new vagrancy laws were added to other policing measures. Altogether, the antebellum gains of the Negro, while substantial, still fell far short of any notion of full citizenship.

7

✓ One of the opiates for poverty in the new urban slums was heavy drinking, though this habit also had its votaries among the upper classes as well, even reaching into the dignified legislative halls at Washington. From the Old World, German beer-drinkers and Irish whisky-drinkers arrived to contest the field with the gathering forces of temperance advocates. To the Germans, beer gardens and taverns seemed part of the order of nature and, together with the Irish, they believed in a festive and not-too-dry Sabbath. Both tendencies were anathema to many New Englanders, though the Puritans had been anything but prohibitionists, decrying only drunkenness as worthy of the colonial penal letter, "D." Middle-class industrial leaders in England and America condemned alcoholism as inimical to factory efficiency and to the strict discipline of the machine. Their favorite argument against factory reforms was the charge that drink rather than low wages or unemployment caused improvidence and poverty. In 1818, for example, the New York Society for the Prevention of Pauperism campaigned against liquor as the root of poverty.

In industrial countries, too, where feminism had evolved from the liberal creed of the middle class, much of the energies of woman's rights movements was diverted to temperance in an effort to strengthen the home. Among the sects, Quakers and Methodists attacked what Bishop Asbury called the "demon rum." In the camp meeting revivals after 1800, Methodists, Congregationalists, and Presbyterians developed an evangelical technique to combat drunkenness. Catholic churchmen, led by Father Mathew who was credited with millions of pledge-takers in Ireland, claimed great success among the Irish.

Revivalistic movements for "signing the pledge" against drink swept the country, the most significant being the Washington Temperance Society organized by a half dozen ex-alcoholics; they claimed one half million pledge signers by 1843 through their evangelical appeals. Ex-drunkards stood up before awed multitudes to offer lachrymose testimonials. The Cold Water Army of the

Washingtonians drummed up much of the original enthusiasm of
the Children's Crusade. Choice grain for the prohibition mill were
the unabashed, tearful songs of which the best-known was written
by Henry Clay Work in 1864, "Come Home, Father." The first verse
began:

> Father, dear father, come home with me now!
> The clock in the steeple strikes one,—
> You said you were coming right home from the shop,
> As soon as your day's work was done.

In 1854, Timothy Shay Arthur wrote his long-lived temperance play,
"Ten Nights in a Bar Room And What I Saw There"; eventually, the
song "Come Home, Father" found a place in this drama.

Antislavery leaders, including Gerrit Smith, Garrison, Frederick
Douglass, and Lucretia Mott, helped make the temperance movement international. In Maine, Neal Dow, later mayor of Portland
and a national prohibition leader, culminated his fiery orations on
the liquor traffic by securing statewide prohibition through the
Maine law of 1846, which became the model for prohibitionists
throughout the Union. Difficulty in enforcement led to repeal or
modification of the strict Dow-inspired laws that forbade the sale
or manufacture of intoxicating drinks. In some states prohibition was
left to local option as a compromise.

The German press attacked total abstinence as the product of a
pharasaical Puritanism and as a deprivation of human liberty comparable to slavery. Together with the alleged Puritan threat to their
"Sabbath freedom," prohibition seemed to them a plot of the intolerant nativists. In Wisconsin, the Germans were strong enough
to block statewide prohibition in 1853 after being defeated previously on this issue. German brewers, already prominent in the distillery business, were especially vocal in this battle against "Yankee
fanaticism" and they joined forces with Irish saloon-keepers and
distillers as well as with native anti-temperance men. By the mid-
fifties the high tide of prohibition successes had begun to recede
and the slavery crisis temporarily eclipsed the movement by 1861.
Still, thirteen states had already abolished the sale of liquor and,

despite later relapses, Maine, New Hampshire, and Vermont continued throughout the century to keep their temperance laws.

8

The generation that fought the Civil War, ironically enough, was reared in the era of a great peace crusade in which many thousands of organized advocates of peace had condemned war as contrary to Christianity and progress and had labored on a national and international scale to develop peace machinery. Upon the humanitarian foundations left by the colonial pietists, non-resistants, like Garrison, Adin Ballou of the Hopedale Community, Whittier, and Thoreau, refused to fight under any circumstances—though Garrison and others weakened in this resolve during the Civil War. Middle-class free traders, pointing out the causes of war in hostile tariff systems, were active in the organized peace movement on both sides of the Atlantic. Indeed, American and English reformers helped greatly to cement Anglo-American friendship after the War of 1812 through their intimate cooperation in the causes of peace, temperance, abolition, feminism, factory legislation, and cheaper international postal rates.

The Russian Czar, Alexander I, had in 1815 offered to the world the mystical, ineffective Holy Alliance as a Christian weapon against war. Despite Russia's obvious cynicism in taking this step, the project stimulated the growth of American peace societies such as those led by the Reverend Noah Worcester of New England. He wrote the Czar that in the very week that the Holy Alliance was announced, the Massachusetts Peace Society was organized in Boston to spread "the very principles avowed in the wonderful alliance." Secretary of State John Quincy Adams, well-informed on Russia's aggressive intentions, was irritated by this public pressure to force the country into the Holy Alliance. Branches of Worcester's peace movement scattered periodicals and tracts throughout the Union in the conviction that the United States had a mission to establish universal peace.

The task of uniting the various peace societies existing before

1830 fell to William Ladd, a retired New England shipowner and merchant who infused a crusading fervor into the movement and organized the powerful American Peace Society in 1828. By 1837, spurred on by the uncompromising stand of Garrison's wing of non-resisters, the Society condemned all wars, defensive as well as offensive; but, going beyond the usual statement of the Christian principles of peace, it actively sponsored Ladd's specific program for a congress of nations and a world court of arbitration and per-suaded the Massachusetts legislature to petition the President that he negotiate abroad toward this end. The Society also urged the principle of arbitration—a movement that was to win wide adoption beginning with the Alabama Claims dispute of 1871—and with other peace advocates and pacifists fought against the War with Mexico. James Russell Lowell expressed the current Christian pacifism in his *Biglow Papers:*

> Ez fer war, I call it murder—
> There you hev it plain an' flat;
> I don't want to go no furder
> Than my Testyment fer that.

The credit for advancing the American peace movement to a world stage belongs to the Connecticut Yankee, Elihu Burritt, known as the "learned blacksmith," who had educated himself while a workman at the forge to read foreign languages and to understand world geography. Devoted to Ladd's program and sympathetic to other reforms of the day, he initiated the first world peace congress at Brussels in 1848 and organized the League of Universal Brother-hood as an international society whose members pledged themselves "never to enlist or enter into any army or navy, or to yield any vol-untary support or sanction to the preparation for or prosecution of any war. . . ." He urged workmen in 1850 "to unite and refuse to fight" and helped to avert war with England over the Oregon dis-pute in 1846 by newspaper and pamphlet appeals—the so-called "friendly address" movement—in the press of both countries.

Many well-wishers abstained from the peace movement because it had been too thoroughly infiltrated with anarchistic non-resistant ideas that seemed a standing invitation to would-be aggressor nations. Differences over strategy both here and abroad split the movement, especially during the Crimean War. In the decade before the Civil War, when many felt that the "irrepressible conflict" could only mean a war basically over slavery, the American Peace Society decided that loyalty to the Union came first. So ended a major phase of the peace movement, but before it closed, it had fashioned the chief institutional forms of the twentieth-century organizers of peace.

9

In this utopian generation the fervent belief of the liberal that man is by nature innately good, plastic, and rational, except when corrupted by evil institutions, produced major reforms in the treatment of prisoners, dependent children, and mental cases. With capital punishment declining, prisons ceased to be places of brief detention, except for debtors, and became large institutions of lengthy incarceration requiring new penal theories. Philadelphia Quakers, leaders in American penal theory and practice, rebelled against the notion that prisons were chiefly places of punishment and tried to prevent their jails from becoming schools of crime. Pennsylvania, under their instigation, had abolished capital punishment except for first-degree murder. In the old Walnut Street prison and in their new Eastern State Penitentiary, completed in 1829, the Quakers introduced the "penitentiary" theory of isolated cells to induce a truly penitent spirit and to prevent the more incorrigible prisoners from corrupting others.

Alexis de Tocqueville and Gustave de Beaumont, French investigators of the American prisons, recommended the Eastern State Penitentiary to their government, though they observed, "Gigantic walls, crenellated towers, a vast gate of iron give to this prison the aspect of a vast chateaufort of medieval times." The food and care seemed good to Tocqueville, but he was privately disturbed by the fact that inmates never left their cells, which faced an inner corridor opening upon separate tiny walled gardens. Prisoners felt cowed by the solitude, even welcoming the face of the warden. "Ah, Sir," sighed one inmate, "it's the most frightful torture one can imagine." To alleviate this situation the discipline was later relaxed to admit frequent visitors, more books, and varied occupations for each cell.

From the Eastern State Penitentiary the Auburn prison system borrowed the idea of isolated cells, but drastically altered it by allowing the men to leave them during the day in order to labor in general workshops or outside on contract to private firms. But the prisoners were harshly punished if they spoke to each other and the whip appeared to be the foundation of the system. Taxpayers, pleased by the fact that such institutions could pay for themselves through the contract labor system, were convinced that the tiny cages—about three and one-half feet wide—in which the inmates slept and the outside activity were far more humane than the Eastern State Penitentiary's solitary system. As a result, the Auburn model was copied throughout the country. Despite shortcomings in penal theory, the nation went far toward replacing the crowded, filthy prisons and crude underground pits of the day by modern prisons, equipped to segregate different types of offenders.

Americans were ahead of Europeans in separating youthful delinquents from hardened law breakers and in introducing "houses of refuge" and reformatories to rehabilitate these youngsters. De Tocqueville—and Francis Lieber, too—praised the House of Reformation in South Boston, which was managed by an Episcopal minister. Here whipping was abolished in favor of "moral discipline" in which each child was ruled by a majority of the boys, judged by a jury of his peers, and sentenced, according to gravity, to loss of privileges, ostracism, or, in extreme cases, solitary cells. Spying and tattling were discouraged. The system provided considerable schooling, wholesome recreation, and an indeterminate sentence that was shortened according to the progress of each inmate.

The liberal belief that to change the environment was to change man had its most severe test in the reforms for the insane. Over-optimism in Europe and America governed the early experiments in restraining the feeble-minded and salvaging the insane. Nevertheless, considerable progress, spurred on by the Quakers particularly, was made in building new state institutions for the care of the insane, and glowing reports appeared regarding the cures effected by sympathetic care in institutions. However, thousands of mental cases remained unprovided for and thousands more were locked in cages, cellars, and closets or were chained to tables, and were beaten into submission. No one aroused the conscience of the nation more forcefully than did a semi-invalid, Dorothea Lynde Dix of Massachusetts, who headed a school for girls, wrote children's books, and gave instruction on Sundays to the women of the East Cambridge House of Correction. There she noticed in addition to the usual prisoners several insane persons left neglected in a separate unheated room and she determined to investigate the plight of such people.

Dorothea Dix's search for aid took her to Dr. Samuel Gridley Howe, head of the Perkins institution for the blind at Boston, who was then winning national attention for achieving the first successful training of a blind deaf-mute, Laura Bridgman. This girl not only learned to read and write but became a teacher of sewing. A confirmed environmentalist, Dr. Howe encouraged Miss Dix to undertake her three-year investigation of the insane, an amazing physical feat for a fragile woman, which took her 10,000 miles about the country during 1842-45 to visit 300 jails and houses of correction, 500 almshouses, 18 state prisons, and other institutions. Investigating Massachusetts, she found patients chained, locked in closets and cellars, clad in filthy rags and sometimes left completely naked, and neglected by indifferent or ignorant keepers amid overpowering stench. In her *Memorial to the Legislature of Massachusetts* (1843), she wrote frankly of what she had seen, unable to conceal the loathing she felt for the wretched asylums of her state:

I come as the advocate of helpless, forgotten, insane and idiotic men and women; of beings sunk to a condition from which the most unconcerned would start with real horror; of beings wretched in our prisons, and more wretched in our almshouses.

Supported by leading reformers and philanthropists of her state, she obtained a large appropriation for the insane and continued her journey to stir others to act. Twenty states and Canada adopted her recommendations. Thereafter, for another decade, she traveled abroad, moving England to reform its asylums and Japan to introduce its first modern institutions for the insane. At home, she persuaded Congress to provide generous land grant assistance for the care of the insane, the blind, and the deaf and dumb, only to see the action vetoed by President Pierce, but she succeeded in getting some limited legislation for certain classes of insane. During the Civil War she was to place her countrymen under further obligation by acting as the superintendent of women nurses. Overcoming the prevailing criticism of women in public life, she set into motion a powerful movement for the reform of state institutions that continued for decades. Though this generation was too credulous of an early cure for insanity, its unbounded faith in human potentialities showed how thoroughly this was the age of the common man.

The keynote of this era of democratic reform, as has been amply illustrated, was an enthusiastic faith in environmentalism with its assumption that man is innately good and infinitely plastic. This encouraged the numerous utopian experiments, already grounded in the individualistic Reformation tradition of dissent. Hence, the kind of "collectivism" sought in this period was strongly individualistic, being opposed not only to state churches but also to coercion in government. The weak state of Jefferson and the liberals was still the ideal, and the "collectivists" were primarily concerned with freer status for the individual.

Labor followed middle-class aims in their opposition to monopoly, aristocracy, and landlordism. They favored mass education as the grand gateway to freedom of opportunity. Unions did not mean the advancement of the class struggle in the Marxian sense but another free association in a land ruled by many such voluntary groups in preference to the dictates of a coercive state. The search for improved status was to emancipate women and slaves as well as laborers. One of the dynamic factors that made environmentalism into a crusade was evangelicalism, despite the social conservatism that characterized so many of its adherents. Such fiery gospels as those of the Burnt District and millennialism, while diverting many to an exclusive concern with salvation, also left their influence upon the technique of abolitionists, temperance exhorters, peace crusaders, and other reformers, and upon the forms taken by utopianism. Finally, environmentalism, coupled with an optimistic belief in progress, inspired pioneer efforts to rehabilitate prisoners and the mentally ill as well as to create a just social order.

· 14 ·

The American Renaissance of Mann and Emerson: High Tide of Romanticism

[1830-1861]

I

THE GENERATION of Horace Mann and Ralph Waldo Emerson saw a rebirth of seventeenth-century Puritan intellectualism that steeply raised the national level in education, literature, and science. To the Puritan mind, learning and godliness were inseparable. Harvard College, symbol of that fusion, was no mere theological seminary, regardless of the preponderance of ministers among its early graduates. The invigorating breath of Elizabethan and Stuart literature as well as of classical learning had been transferred from Cambridge University to Harvard College; the new experimental science of Francis Bacon and Galileo had been accepted at the college long before it had been at many a respectable European university. Puritanism, for all its vagaries from a modern point of view, had been a rational cult with an integrated philosophy refined by the Huguenot, Peter Ramus, and by the Cambridge university reformers.

Even more significant than Harvard College as an evidence of the Puritans' thirst for learning was their concern with mass education. The unique Massachusetts law of 1647 laid the foundation for the American system of tax-supported public schools, being distinctly

436

different from the English idea of privately endowed schools. That law, copied by Connecticut in 1650, required every township with fifty or more householders to offer free elementary instruction; and towns with more than one hundred families were ordered to set up "grammar" or college preparatory schools. This goal, far too ambitious for a simple wilderness community, receded in the distance with the decline of Puritanism and the advent of strict eighteenth-century Calvinism with its emphasis on theology at the expense of liberal learning. Evangelical groups of the Great Awakening and afterwards did, it is true, set up colleges to train ministers for their increasing flocks and to preserve sectarian differences, but they lacked the humanism of Harvard. Indifferent to philosophy, the evangelical churches permitted emotional interpretations of dogma —"enthusiasms," the Puritans called them—to affect their intellectual life. Hostile to the Enlightenment of the eighteenth century, the new Calvinism and the evangelical churches tried to stem the advance of secularism in the state and in the schools.

Several forces made for the separation of church and state in American schools. The Puritan theocracy, of course, contributed little in this direction, though it left its heritage of moral idealism through the American emphasis on ethical training in the schools. The Enlightenment and its American disciples, Franklin and Jefferson, made steady encroachments on narrow sectarian education. The University of Pennsylvania, opened in 1751, and the University of Virginia, founded in 1819, began with relatively modern and secular courses of study. More important, non-sectarianism came about as a result of the conflict of rival Protestant and Catholic groups for free expression and the consequent need for compromise. A union of dissenters with doctrinal liberals, as noted elsewhere, overthrew the Calvinist state-church in Massachusetts in 1833 and accounted for the separation of church and state in other states.

A landmark in the history of secular education is the Massachusetts School Law of 1827. This act, passed with a good deal of unanimity in the General Court, revived a law of 1789 forbidding the use of sectarian schoolbooks and in effect outlawed oral instruction favoring any particular creed. Moral instruction remained as long as it was not permitted to cloak sectarian proselyting. That this law did not become a dead letter, following the fate of similar older legislation, was largely due, as we shall see, to Horace Mann.

Since the days of the Puritans, the ideal of free public schools had declined in New England and elsewhere, leaving only expensive private schools or impoverished district schools. In the public schools, memorized assignments, corporal discipline, and untrained teachers were the rule, and no profession ranked lower than teaching. Schoolmasters in Massachusetts earned $185 annually in 1838 and women were paid one-third of this sum. In many villages, teachers took their pay partly in being "boarded around" for brief stays with the families of their pupils. In numerous districts, the school year scarcely lasted three months. As Francis Bowen of Harvard put it in 1835, New England's school system "had degenerated into routine, it was starved by parsimony. Any hovel would answer for a school house, any primer would do for a text-book, any farmer's apprentice was competent to 'keep school.'" The system of decentralized schools meant in effect unsupervised school districts. Even worse, children of poor parents had to accept the stigma of pauperism in order to attend school since support came from tuition.

During the quarter century following 1825, the struggle went on for tax-supported non-sectarian schools, publicly controlled and directed; this struggle was accompanied by great agitation and bitter quarrels until victory was achieved. Labor unions resented the stigma of "pauper schools" and fought for free schools as a guarantee both of equality of opportunity and of the leveling of class barriers. Enlightened industrialists supported mass education in the belief that the efficiency of labor would thus be greatly increased. Thus the original Puritan tradition in education was to be transmuted into the very optimistic American faith in education as the touchstone of all public and private good.

In this era of romanticism, with its faith in the potentialities of the individual, the common school revival began. As already noted, George Bancroft had introduced at his Round Hill School the "progressive" educational theories of Rousseau's Swiss disciples, Fellenberg and Pestalozzi; and Robert Dale Owen, who had studied in Pestalozzi's schools, propagandized for a national system of education on the Swiss model. In Prussia, Herbart and Froebel were elaborating the Swiss educational theories, while their nation adopted the methods of Pestalozzi in its elementary schools; this was done despite the fact that the Swiss ideal of the free natural development of the child's personality seemed incongruous in a paternalistic, semi-feudal state where repression rather than expression seemed the rule. Yet Prussia made education from top to bottom a genuine responsibility of the government and raised the literacy level. In France, Victor Cousin gave his official endorsement to the Prussian school system as worthy of emulation, regardless of reactionary German politics. His report, translated into English in 1835, aroused the enthusiasm of Calvin E. Stowe, Horace Mann, and other American educators.

The Swiss educators and their German disciples stressed the instinctive activity of the child and made the school an instrument for self-realization in which harmonious living and social duty took precedence over mere fact-gathering. Froebel, creator of the kindergarten, gave the child an introduction to the world of utility, beauty, and creative imagination through ingenious play devices. Herbart, like Froebel, a disciple of Pestalozzi, helped make the art of pedagogy into the science of education, stressing scientific method, clarity of classroom concepts, and variety of school interests.

Chief among those to admire the Prussian schools with their kindly relations between teacher and pupil, their natural teaching methods, and their teacher-training system was Horace Mann of Massachusetts. The son of a farmer, he rose to success as a lawyer and a socially minded state legislator. Keenly interested in mass education, he gave up a profitable law practice and political career to become in 1837 the poorly paid Secretary of the State Board of Education, a new agency he had sponsored while in the State Senate. In 1843 he spent six months in Europe studying educational conditions. He returned an ardent admirer of the Swiss-Prussian system and urged that these new methods be adapted to American conditions in his famous Seventh Annual Report of 1843. He called the attention of school committees to the school law of 1827, forbidding catechisms in the schools and opposing the efforts of zealots to make the public schools the agencies of their particular sects. However, he made it clear that he favored non-sectarian moral instruction, including the use of the Bible within the limits of the law. He was attacked by the churches for his "godless schools" and by the Boston schoolmasters who disliked his fondness for Prussian methods. During Mann's twelve years as Secretary, the Board succeeded in more than doubling the salaries of teachers, established a minimum school year of six months, vastly improved the schoolhouses, and sponsored the opening of fifty new high schools. Since mass education required teachers trained in the best methods of elementary instruction, the Board set up in 1839 at Lexington the first state normal school in the United States.

The example of Massachusetts was followed in several other states, and even in faraway South America the idealistic Sarmiento, who had come under the influence of Mann, fought successfully the conservative classicists of Chile and Argentina in the name of normal schools (Cousin's "école normale") and mass education. In 1848, Mann was elected to Congress and for five years was prominent in the House as an antislavery advocate. In 1853, he became first president of Antioch College, already dedicated as a "progressive" school of a non-sectarian, coeducational type. Here he hoped to repeat his successes by revolutionizing higher education, but lack of funds and sectarian suspicions plagued him until his death in 1859. Both his wife, Mary Tyler Peabody, and her sister Elizabeth were among the outstanding women of their day. Mary wrote children's books and urged various reforms; Elizabeth, also a reformer, brought to Boston in 1860 the first English kindergarten in the United States, following the example of her friend, Margaret Meyer Schurz, who had established at Watertown, Wisconsin, in 1856 a German kindergarten on the model of Froebel.

Typical of the best reformers of his day, Horace Mann was an ardent believer in environmentalism, that faith which held that to improve the environment was to improve man. He agitated effectively for state hospitals for the insane, supported temperance laws, and backed the rights of the Negro. One critic asked him, "Would you advocate the slaves to an equal social and political condition with the white race?" To this he replied confidently, "I would give to *every human being* the best opportunities to develop and cultivate the faculties which God has bestowed upon him.... Having done this, I would leave him, as I would leave every other man, to find his level—to occupy the position to which he should be entitled by his intelligence and virtue." Here was the clear-cut position of a nineteenth-century liberal who believed that once the artificial restraints imposed on man by the state were removed self-reliance would do the rest. He fought for public schools as the best method of opening the door of opportunity to the individual. Pauper schools and charities were poor substitutes, he felt, for personal initiative.

In 1848, the very year that Karl Marx was circulating his *Communist Manifesto,* which declared all history to be merely the story of an exploitative class struggle, Mann expressed his belief in the power of education to bring about class reconciliation. This was in the *Twelfth Annual Report* during his period as Secretary, which stated in part:

According to the European theory, men are divided into classes,—some to toil and earn, others to seize and enjoy. According to the Massachusetts theory, all are to have an equal chance for earning, and equal security in the enjoyment of what they earn....

Now surely nothing but universal education can counterwork this tendency to the domination of capital and the servility of labor.... But, if education be equally diffused, it will draw property after it by the strongest of all attractions; for such a thing never did happen, and never can happen, as that an intelligent and practical body of men should be permanently poor. Property and labor in different classes are essentially antagonistic; but property and labor in the same class are essentially fraternal....

Education then, beyond all other devices of human origin, is a great equalizer of the condition of men—the balance wheel of the social machinery.... It does better than to disarm the poor of their hostility toward the rich; it prevents being poor.

Such was the optimism of Mann and his age.

Connecticut, also, had an educational crusader of national importance in Henry Barnard, who shared Mann's enthusiasm for

Prussian schools and was particularly attracted to the German emphasis on educational theory as a science. In 1838, he became Secretary of the Connecticut Board of School Commissioners and after the Board was abolished he was appointed, in 1843, State Superintendent of Schools of Rhode Island, giving that state, according to Mann, one of the best systems of public instruction in the world; thereafter, for a few years, he returned to Connecticut, where, as Superintendent of Common Schools and principal of the state normal school at New Britain, he carried out the progressive ideas that were then transforming the Massachusetts school system. During 1859-60, he was chancellor of the University of Wisconsin and later was president of St. John's College in Annapolis.

Barnard won lasting distinction and influence through his editing of *The American Journal of Education* in the years between 1856 and 1881. This pioneer journal showed the new Swiss and Prussian influence, especially in the numerous translations of German books and articles on educational methods and philosophy. Barnard also published similar discussions by American educators and brief biographies of the leading educators of the world, altogether furnishing a basic encyclopedia of valuable information and ideas for American teachers and administrators. As the first United States Commissioner of Education (1867-70), Barnard invited German educators to occupy key posts in American schools. Following the leadership of Mann and Barnard, other states began to publish vast quantities of school reports, set up free public schools, trained teachers in normal schools and teachers' institutes, reformed textbooks, and introduced school libraries.

In Ohio, Professor Calvin E. Stowe of Lane Seminary, whose scholarly achievements were to be obscured by the later fame of his wife, Harriet, was among the first to recognize the significance of Victor Cousin's germinal report on Prussian education and to propagandize for the acceptance of its message. In 1837, following his own visits to the European schools, he reported upon his findings to the Ohio legislature and recommended an Americanized version of the Prussian system. He was largely responsible for the passage of legislation devoting revenues from the canals and state banks to a free common school system. In Virginia, Stowe's report converted many legislators to the theory of general taxation to support normal and elementary schools and encouraged a broadening of the three R's in the grade school curriculum to include science, art, music, and citizenship. Stowe was critical of the Prussian system of libraries, which were intended to serve the teaching staff alone; he recommended that common school libraries be set up for the use of children as well.

New York continued its generation-old battle to provide a system of free tax-supported schools for the entire state. The gains made by Governor De Witt Clinton were broadened to cover far more school districts, although complete victory had to wait until the decade after the Civil War. In Pennsylvania, a major public school law was passed in 1835 after a campaign had been launched in the legislature by Thaddeus Stevens who made the issue one of "Free Schools versus Charity or Pauper Schools." In New Jersey, the story and result were much the same and fully as enheartening. In the West, where the settlers held an extravagant faith in the virtues of tax-supported schools as the gateway to opportunity, the territorial legislatures were usually generous in appropriations for state-supported school systems. The opposition, which varied from state to state, was often formidable. Not only did well-to-do taxpayers put up a last-ditch stand, but religious groups, both Catholic and Protestant, resented the secular trend that allowed the state to intervene between parent and child in behalf of compulsory education. Both fought to retain their parochial schools or to gain a share of the public funds for the partial support of such religious institutions. Many of these conflicts, especially those involving church and state, were to break out chronically, but by the time of the Civil War the battle for free public schools had been largely won.

The "Prussian idea" of a supervised state school system ranging from the elementary grades to the university attracted many American reformers who were dissatisfied with sectarian control over higher education. This influence was especially pronounced in the organization of the Michigan school system in 1835, which combined a hierarchy of schools culminating in the new University

of Michigan with its program for school supervisors. In turn, the
Michigan system became the model for the educational plans of
the western states.

At the same time, the Prussian invasion carried with it the spread
of German language teaching as the key to the intellectual riches
of German romanticism. Jefferson made German part of the University of Virginia curriculum in 1825; Harvard followed closely that
same year by appointing Carl Follen as German instructor; the
University of Pennsylvania and Columbia, too, revived their long
dormant German studies. The New England transcendentalists, encouraged by Carlyle and Coleridge, struggled to master the intricacies of the German language and idealistic philosophies. American
scholars hastened to Germany in ever-increasing numbers; by the
Civil War at least three hundred Americans had graduated from
German universities—forerunners of an elite of perhaps ten thousand who were to take degrees in that country during the nineteenth
century.

Little wonder, therefore, that the conservative proslavery apolo-
gist, George Fitzhugh, could condemn in 1860 the mounting influence of German romanticism upon Northern liberalism:

German learning and research, and German speculation have unsettled
or subverted everything: established nothing. In history, it has not established a fact, but undermined and shaken all faith in half what was
hitherto believed as facts. In religion, it tried, and at one time had well-
nigh succeeded in overthrowing all that is historical or miraculous in the
Bible, and in leaving to its votaries nothing but a set of moral maxims
and fine sentiments. In politics, its transcendental speculations have
destroyed all time-honored loyalty, all faith in past experience, and be-
gotten a presumptuous revolutionary Utopian spirit, restless under restraint, and ever anxious for change, that has made society in Europe
a heaving volcano.

2

Simultaneous with the common school revival was the crusade for
adult education, another victory for the common man. Lyceums,
mechanics' institutes, debating societies, library associations, and

all kinds of lecture courses drew hundreds of thousands of eager adults whose education had been neglected or seemed too meager for the times. Such education varied from the "genteel" and "improving" type to the strictly utilitarian sciences and trades. Borrowing a leaf from Aristotle's famous lyceum of learning, Josiah Holbrook, a Yale graduate who had experimented with teaching manual arts combined with book learning, opened adult courses at Millbury, Connecticut, in 1826 and thus established the "lyceum" movement. So swiftly did the lyceums spread that eight years later, there were three thousand town lyceums, scores of county lyceums, and eight state lyceums, culminating for a time in a national lyceum in New York city. Massachusetts alone had 137 in 1839 with an average annual attendance of 33,000. Lyceums existed in practically every state in the Union, in frontier towns and Southern cities, as well as in New England's cultural centers. Lectures and discussions dealt with such diverse topics as corporal punishment, manual training, educational reform, and applied science.

The lyceums gave mass impetus to sentiment for the common school revival. Holbrook himself was among the first to demand normal schools and state departments of education and to promote popular science education. He gave lyceum instruction in mathematics and the sciences with actual apparatus, magic lanterns, and other devices of visual education. He fostered textbook reform to improve instruction. Distinguished and well-paid lecturers like Emerson, Oliver Wendell Holmes, and Wendell Phillips attracted crowds. This is particularly remarkable in the case of Emerson whose transcendental mysticism filled so many of the famous lectures he wrote for lyceum audiences. Like the intellectual Puritan ministers of old who spared not their congregations in elaborating upon difficult points of theology, Emerson serenely held forth on the mysteries of the Oversoul, Transcendentalism, Swedenborg, and kindred subjects. Boston, of course, shone in the lyceum movement, its extensive lecture programs enhanced by a gift of $250,000 left in 1839 by the industrial Lowell family for the still-extant Lowell Institute lectures. Though the lyceum movement had run its course by the Civil War and had become corrupted by concessions to cheap entertainment, it left or inspired numerous institutions for adult education such as the Chautauqua movement after 1874.

The lyceum and the political stump gave the arts of oratory and elocution their golden age. In the democratic society of Jackson and Lincoln, the spoken word swayed public opinion mightily whether on the frontier or in the Senate. A two-hour oration, replete with humor as well as encyclopedic information, was a standard form of entertainment and mass education. The Boston federalist historian and novelist, Richard Hildreth, prefaced his six-volume *History of the United States* (1849-52) with the understatement, "Of centennial sermons and Fourth-of-July orations, whether professedly such or in the guise of history, there is more than enough." Political barbecues north and south gave ample opportunities for bombastic spread-eagle oratory; and the dramatic rhetoric of Daniel Webster, Henry Clay, and Edward Everett, whose polished speech at Gettysburg was overshadowed only by Lincoln's far greater and briefer address on that day, inspired a generation of schoolboys. Webster's *Reply to Hayne* gave many a budding orator the most memorable phrases upon which to try his wings as a public speaker. College literary societies everywhere simulated the rounded periods, the persuasive logical devices, and the sonorousness of the great orators.

In the common schools, elocution owed a great deal to the stories and sentimental poems in the six McGuffey Eclectic Readers of 1836-57 written by William Holmes McGuffey, who had done much to organize Ohio's public school system. In his long career, which began with teaching elementary subjects in a rural schoolhouse near East Liverpool, Ohio, he was professor of languages at Miami University, president of Cincinnati College, president of Ohio University at Athens, and finally, from 1847 to 1873, professor of moral philosophy at the University of Virginia. His fascinating readers dispensed morality and a great mass of information; they reflected the newer textbook reforms then being championed in New England. So influential were his schoolbooks upon two generations of children—Henry Ford regarded the McGuffey Readers as one of the most valuable experiences of his childhood—that by 1925 some 122,000,000 copies had been sold. Who could not recite:

> Woodman, spare that tree
> Touch not a single bough,
> In youth it sheltered me
> And I'll protect it now.

or quote from his selection from Mrs. Felicia Hemans' *Casabianca:*

> The boy stood on the burning deck . . .

3

No device of mass education quite excelled the penny press—the outstanding journalistic event of this era. European visitors swore that Americans read nothing but newspapers. The New York-Brooklyn area for example, with a population of 300,000, reported a daily circulation for its penny press of 70,000—about one newspaper for every family. In England, where printing technology had also developed the penny press—actually, papers sold there for two cents as compared to one cent in the United States—the habit of newspaper reading was confined largely to adult males. The speedy double-cylinder presses, run by steam power, were capable of 4000 impressions an hour, and the rotary press of 1847 could double this record. While the rural press made haste slowly with a slightly improved hand press, which remained a common fixture of pioneer communities, the urban presses rushed thousands of newspapers to the waiting hands of newsboys. With a white population that was 89 per cent literate in 1840 and 91 per cent in 1860, the nation possessed an enormous market for cheap newspapers. In an era of democratic agitation the primacy of the newspaper was almost unchallenged. Political parties, antislavery organizations, temperance movements, and others had their own newspapers, either at the penny press level or slightly above. Nevertheless, the very technological improvements that made cheap newspapers, magazines, and books possible, had their anti-democratic implications, too. In the day of the hand press or the simple machine presses a small printer could easily acquire the capital necessary to enter the publishing business. But with such expensive machines as the "lightning" rotary press introduced in 1847 by the *Philadelphia Public Ledger,* which cost at least $20,000 each, publishing became a big business and journalistic opinion showed an increasingly conservative bias.

The first successful penny daily was the *New York Sun,* which appeared on September 3, 1833, as an experiment of Benjamin H. Day of Massachusetts. From the London newspapers Day borrowed the sensational police court daily column with the story told in the sentimental and humorous style of Dickens' day. After featuring a scientific hoax regarding the discovery of batlike people on the moon, the *Sun* passed the 19,000 mark in daily circulation, even eclipsing by 2000 the record of the London *Times.* To maintain its circulation in this Age of Barnum, the *Sun* could scarcely rely on the "merely important"—to use a later phrase of William Randolph Hearst; it fed its readers exciting stories of sex scandals, horse races, prize fights, and other such fare at the expense of political editorials and genuine news.

This formula laid the foundation in 1835 of the *New York Herald,* published by the resourceful Scottish immigrant, James Gordon Bennett, who is often considered the father of yellow journalism. Determined to reach the businessman as well as the literate worker, Bennett combined a most thorough financial service in which he covered Wall Street personally with grossly sensational news camouflaged under a moral exterior. Dropping Victorian euphemisms, he told with zest his salacious "human interest" stories of sex, murder, and disaster, adding a little detective work of his own on choice cases, and carrying profitable advertisements of quacks and vice merchants. Upper-middle-class readers enjoyed reading about themselves in the "Society Page" which he invented, while working-class readers, fascinated by the daily array of sensationalism, forgave Bennett his conservative economics and easy tolerance toward slavery. From a technical standpoint, at least, Bennett could boast of his leadership in news-gathering, his large-scale use of pictorial news, his facility in adopting the latest devices of telegraph and printing machinery, and his alertness in reporting "scoops." It was James Gordon Bennett who later made journalistic history by "scooping" the newspapers of the entire world in the 1870's by sending the plucky explorer, Henry M. Stanley, to find the missing missionary, David Livingstone, lost somewhere in central Africa.

Reaction against Bennett's callous indifference to morals and ethics helped Horace Greeley to succeed beyond his fondest hopes with his influential *New York Tribune*, founded in 1841. Greeley, a Vermont printer, had campaigned with unusual effectiveness for "Tippecanoe and Tyler Too" in 1840 with his paper, *The Log Cabin*. He was an independent in politics with liberal Whig tendencies. Few of the "isms" escaped his sympathetic attention and his concern for labor insured to unionism a fair hearing in the *Tribune*. While waging his war against the salaciousness of the *Sun* and the *Herald* and attacking the immorality of the theater, he also championed abolitionism, feminism, temperance, Fourierism, free homesteads, and a protective tariff in behalf of high wages. A later generation recalled his enthusiasm for the West and the future of the farmer. "Vote yourself a farm" was his slogan for the new Republican Party and he advised a friend, "Go West, young man, go West!" Without resorting to the scandals, police reports, and "degrading" advertisements of his competitors he captured his readers by his wholesome, if sentimental, human-interest stories of the Dickens variety and his feature columns on books, poetry, crusading reforms, and agricultural interests. His reporters were resourceful and his columnists included some of the most gifted of Emerson's circle—Margaret Fuller, George Ripley, and Charles A. Dana. Most significant was his popular *Weekly Tribune*, also begun in 1841, which attracted over 100,000 readers especially in rural districts. "The *Tribune* came next to the Bible in the West," observed the popular lecturer and poet, Bayard Taylor.

Former *Tribune* associates, impatient with Greeley's reformist policy, banded together in 1851 to start the *New York Times* on its enduring career of accurate, dispassionate journalism. From the beginning it established its policy of remaining independent in politics and of giving special attention to foreign affairs.

In New England, which lagged behind New York in journalistic enterprise, the family of Samuel Bowles managed the thoughtfully edited *Springfield Republican* whose editorials were widely reprinted and pondered on by national leaders. In the West, Joseph Medill who had once edited the *Cleveland Leader* became, in 1855, a partner in the *Chicago Tribune;* it was he who built it into a powerful Republican paper, one of the earliest to press for the nomination of Lincoln in 1860. Although a radical on several issues, Medill's extreme economic conservatism was to shape the future policy of his influential paper. Elsewhere, from coast to coast, newspapers flourished as never before. Professor Frank L. Mott notes that their number rose from 1200 in 1833 to 3000 by 1860, altogether several times as many as in England or France.

The sensational growth in magazines of almost every type aroused the comment of that generation. In a day before international copyright law adequately covered literary property, pirating was in full flower in Europe and the United States. Unfortunately, America was too heavily a debtor to Europe in the literary field for her piracy to be taken as a matter of course. Dickens never forgave the American publishers for stealing his work with little or no payment rendered. Aided by this habit of pirating as well as by technological advances, American publishers reprinted the five leading British journals and sold them at one-third of the price paid by English readers.

The most enviable record of magazine sales was made by *Harper's Monthly Magazine,* published in 1850 in New York, and regaling the family with a variety of pirated stories from Dickens, Bulwer-Lytton, and other popular romantic novelists. Anxious to overtake that fortunate journal, the English immigrant printer and engraver, Henry Carter, issued *Frank Leslie's Illustrated Newspaper* in 1855. Imitating the literary and pictorial features of *Harper's,* he added sensational news accounts, sports stories, popular science, and successful health crusades. By the end of the sixties he had over 200,000 subscribers.

Another journal that was widely read was *Graham's Magazine* of Philadelphia. This combined literature and travel and was noted

for its able articles written by such men as Lowell, Cooper, Longfellow, and Bryant. Poe's great stories, "The Murders in the Rue
Morgue" and "The Masque of the Red Death," first appeared in
Graham's Magazine. Some of these writers, together with Whittier,
Hawthorne, and Whitman, also wrote for the *United States Democratic Review* (1837-59). Ladies of fashion preferred the sentimental tales and advice on clothes in *Godey's Lady's Book,* edited
by Sara Josepha Hale; the magazine's circulation almost reached
100,000 by 1861.

In New England, there was the *North American Review,* which
adopted the formal, chaste style of the leading British reviews and
enjoyed prestige, though not mass circulation. At first, under the
editorship of men like Edward Everett, who had drunk deeply of
the German springs of literary inspiration, it was heavily European
in emphasis. Later under the historian, Jared Sparks, and others it
gave considerable attention to American themes, biography, economics, science, and other neglected subjects. Bryant made his
debut in the *North American Review* with "Thanatopsis" and "To
a Waterfowl." While this magazine had a few thousand subscribers,
the intellectual organ of the transcendentalists, *The Dial* of Boston
(1840-44), never went beyond three hundred. Edited by Margaret
Fuller, Emerson, and others, this magazine accepted the work of
such contributors as Bronson Alcott, Theodore Parker, and Orestes
Brownson. *The Dial,* like the *North American Review,* did much to
acquaint Americans with German literature, especially with the
writings of the post-Kantians and Goethe.

4

Popular reading tastes in this era would hardly conform to the
recommendations of modern college reading lists for the age of
Emerson and Hawthorne. Walt Whitman's *Leaves of Grass* (1855)
won the admiration of Emerson who wrote, "I greet you at the
beginning of a great career"; but his sales were modest enough—
less than five thousand copies disposed of by the Civil War. Herman
Melville often puzzled the critics and his *Moby Dick* bored too

many readers. The heavy sales of Emerson's *Essays* and Thoreau's *Walden* were made to the grandchildren of the antebellum generation rather than to contemporaries. Longfellow's idealistic poetry was sufficiently close to the popular middle-class spirit to win him tens of thousands of readers for his *Hiawatha* (1855) and other works. Nathaniel Hawthorne, after many false starts, managed to make a financial success of *The Scarlet Letter* (1850), possibly because its subject matter seemed promising to those scenting scandal, but, as the author lamented, his fellow townswoman of Salem, Maria S. Cummins, wrote a sentimental novel, *The Lamplighter,* which sold 40,000 copies in its first eight weeks, far outselling his own book. "America is now given over to a d——d mob of scribbling women...," he complained bitterly to his publisher.

Foremost in this "mob of scribbling women" who dominated the "feminine fifties" was of course Harriet Beecher Stowe, whose *Uncle Tom's Cabin* appeared in 1852. This intellectual daughter of Lyman Beecher had been raised in the antislavery atmosphere of New England and Cincinnati and had married the able public school reformer Calvin E. Stowe. She knew little of the South at first hand, except for an occasional trip across the Ohio into Kentucky, but she had a vivid picture of certain slave types through contacts with fugitives. The slavery issue had long been discussed in the Beecher household. Stealing a few hours each day from the task of rearing six children, Mrs. Stowe finished *Uncle Tom's Cabin* and sent in chapters serially to Gamaliel Bailey's abolitionist newspaper, *The National Era.* So overwhelming was the response of the readers that the story was lengthened interminably. She adopted the idealized and sentimental style of the day and created sharply contrasting stereotypes such as the saintly Uncle Tom and the fiendish ex-Yankee overseer, Simon Legree. When a hesitant publisher finally issued the story in novel form, the results were truly amazing. Edition after edition was exhausted by an engrossed public, touched by the book's pathos and scriptural righteousness; one half million copies were sold by 1857. In Britain, *Uncle Tom's Cabin* did even better, selling, according to F. L. Mott's *Golden Multitudes,* about 1,500,000 copies in the very first year of English publication. Ambitious proslavery novelists replied with an "anti-Tom" literature, showing that life in the South was not as bad as Mrs. Stowe thought it to be.

Another "scribbling woman" in this age of George Sand, George Eliot, Frederika Bremer, Mrs. Mulock, and the gifted Brontë sisters was the American author of perennial best sellers, Mrs. E.D.E.N. Southworth. She wrote over fifty novels for a highly appreciative, and largely female, audience. A self-reliant schoolteacher who had been deserted by her husband and was supporting two children, she followed the success pattern of her friend, Harriet Stowe, and capitalized upon an excellent story-telling ability. Mrs. Southworth adapted the formulas of Scott, Dickens, and Stowe to her tales and conjured up innumerable melodramatic situations, thrilling crises, and villains as unspeakable as Legree. Her best-known novels were *Ishmael, The Deserted Wife,* and *The Curse of Clifton;* these and scores of others reappeared in successive paper-backed editions well into the twentieth century.

By 1840, prices for novels fell from two or three dollars to as little as fifty cents or even a quarter. This was due to technical advances in printing and paper manufacture, bitter price wars, and the use of paper-bound books. The ensuing flood of literature raised the question in many minds of whether the net result was necessarily good. Still, there were multitudes of discriminating readers for literature at the level of Dickens, Thackeray, Hugo, Scott, and of the best American and English historians, notably Prescott whose *Conquest of Mexico* sold about 25,000 by 1861; Macaulay, too, had his devotees here. The prolific English novelist, Bulwer-Lytton, author of *The Last Days of Pompeii* and *Rienzi,* reached the masses through his exciting historical romances. "I think no one is so much read as Mr. Bulwer," declared Harriet Martineau in 1837. "I question whether it is possible to pass half a day in general society without hearing him mentioned." Walter Scott's fascinating Waverley novels, with their medieval flights of fancy, pageantry, idealized morality, and sentimentality, were scarcely behind Bulwer-Lytton's books in popularity; both, however, faced the increasing competition of Dickens. In poetry, this era began with an enthusiasm for Greece and her champion Byron whose personal affectations as well as poetry enchanted thousands. By the Civil War, Tennyson had won an even firmer place in America in the hearts of lovers of poetry than in England.

Children shared in this avalanche of cheaply printed books, reading avidly the newly-published folk tales of Hans Christian Andersen and the Grimm brothers. Many thousands were decoyed into reading the "improving" juvenile books of Peter Parley or the Rollo books of the Boston schoolmaster, Jacob Abbott, who dispensed encyclopedic information in the sugar-coated guise of children's talk at picnics and during rambles in the woods. Juvenile magazines, weighted down with moral homilies in a style now considered unbearably stilted, kept their popularity by virtue of good storytelling and left a cheerful recollection in the minds of the children in after years.

The tremendous popularity of American novels and poems of this era in England stood in sharp contrast with their limited acceptance a generation earlier. "Who reads an American book or goes to an American play, or looks at an American picture or statue?" sniffed Sidney Smith in the *Edinburgh Review* of January, 1820. Untrue as this was even in 1820, no one could any longer make this remark sound faintly plausible a few decades later. Britons were too curious about the American scene and too appreciative of the rising talent on the American side to ignore the writings of Harriet Beecher Stowe, Emerson, Hawthorne, and even far lesser figures.

5

In the intellectual ferment that affected so much of antebellum America, the New England renaissance left the most enduring literary and philosophic monuments. "From 1790 to 1820," wrote Emerson sweepingly regarding Massachusetts, "there was not a book, a speech, a conversation, or a thought in the State. About 1820, the Channing, Webster, and Everett era began, and we have been bookish and poetical and cogitative since." Out of the ashes of an old order rose a latter-day Puritan intellectualism, fervent in the cause of schools and self-culture. From a Puritan viewpoint, however, Emerson's circle was tainted with a heresy suspiciously like Anne Hutchinson's Antinomianism, a kind of "inner-light" intuitive doctrine that Bostonians called transcendentalism. Yankee individualism, fed by a class of generous patrons enriched by the Industrial Revolution, blended its Puritan heritage with a tincture of the mysticism of Plato, the German idealists, Emanuel Swedenborg, and the Orient. The transcendentalism of Emerson and his followers took its name from Immanuel Kant and in effect proclaimed that intuition was superior as a source of knowledge to mere sense experience. This was but another manifestation of the romantic spirit that idealized man and nature and exalted the imaginative, the intuitive, and the emotional over the pure intellectualism and cold artistic symmetry attributed to classicism. Idealism, whether in the form of transcendentalism or otherwise, was a fitting philosophy for the romantic, impatient with things as they were and often anxious to build vast utopias solidly in the clouds. For the democratic era of Mann and Emerson, Jackson and Lincoln, idealism was a heavy stimulant, inspiring liberal experiments and reforms in society based on the assumption of man's perfectibility and his power to master his environment. This provided a philosophical justification of American individualism and produced the cult of the common man. In a real sense transcendentalism was the direct offspring of the Protestant Reformation, for its doctrine of divinity latent in every man implied the "priesthood of all believers" and the exaltation of the personal conscience above man-made traditions and laws.

Transcendentalism was fostered in the 1830's by Harvard Unitarians who had sipped the mysteries of German romantic philosophy. Its capital during the 1840's was Brook Farm and its organ, *The Dial*. The Transcendental Club included at various times Bronson Alcott, Margaret Fuller, Elizabeth Peabody, Thoreau, Theodore Parker, Orestes Brownson, Emerson, and other distinguished authors. Though Ralph Waldo Emerson was not its founder, he was the high priest of transcendentalism. Like so many other Bostonian intellectuals he was a "Brahmin," a Unitarian minister—

in fact, his ancestry went back in a direct line of seven ministers well into the seventeenth century. But he found that Unitarianism did not go far enough in stripping away the formal institutions that separated man's direct communion with God and he left the pulpit in 1832 after failing to convince his Boston congregation that they ought to give up the communion service. Thereafter, he devoted himself to lecturing and to writing.

Emerson's lecture on "The Over-Soul," a kind of pantheism in which the souls of all men commune within a universal soul imbued with God's own spirit, showed his exaltation of the nature of man. "I am part or parcel of God," he exclaimed in describing an ecstatic experience. A descendant of Calvinists who had lamented the depravity of man's nature, he could nevertheless confidently preach the divinity latent in him. His apotheosis of the individual was most emphatically expressed in "Self-Reliance," perhaps the most optimistic statement in literature of man's self-sufficiency.

There is a time in every man's education when he arrives at the conviction that envy is ignorance; that imitation is suicide; that he must take himself for better for worse as his portion. . . The power which resides in him is new in nature, and none but he knows what that is which he can do, nor does he know until he has tried. . . We but half express ourselves, and are ashamed of that divine idea which each of us represents. . . Society is a joint-stock company, in which the members agree, for the better securing of his bread to each shareholder, to surrender the liberty and culture of the eater. . . .

Whoso would be a man, must be a nonconformist. . . . Nothing is at last sacred but the integrity of your own mind. . . . It is easy in the world to live after the world's opinion; it is easy in solitude to live after our own; but the great man is he who in the midst of a crowd keeps with perfect sweetness the independence of solitude. . . . A foolish consistency is the hobgoblin of little minds, adored by little statesmen and philosophers and divines. . . . Speak what you think in hard words and to-morrow speak what to-morrow thinks in hard words again, though it contradict everything you said today. . . . To be great is to be misunderstood.

Such was the extreme individualism and idealism that Emerson taught in "Self-Reliance" (1841), based on his belief in the guidance of a divinely sent intuition that one must labor to discover. From such premises it was simple indeed to call for a declaration of cultural independence of Europe. He decried our imitation of foreign architecture, foreign tastes, foreign opinions, and our inclination to "follow the Past and the Distant." Foreign travel added nothing to our true inner experiences and self-revelation. "It is for want of self-culture that the superstition of Travelling, whose idols are Italy, England, Egypt, retains its fascination for all educated Americans. The soul is no traveller... Travelling is a fool's paradise. Our first journeys discover to us the indifference of places." This call for cultural independence was made before an enthusiastic audience at Harvard in Emerson's Phi Beta Kappa Society address of 1837 upon "The American Scholar." Oliver Wendell Holmes called this "Our intellectual declaration of independence." Proclaiming his doctrine of self-trust, Emerson expressed his hope that "the sluggard intellect of this continent will look from under its iron lids and fill the postponed expectation of the world with something better than the exertions of mechanical skill. Our day of dependence, our long apprenticeship to the learning of other lands, draws to a close." He called for courage and originality from the American scholar, free of mere bookishness. "Man Thinking must not be subdued by his instruments." Without self-trust men become of no account and lose their identity in "the mass" or "the herd"; they live vicariously through the hero or the genius. Believing that the individual had a mission to realize his divine capacities, Emerson shared with his good friend Carlyle a deep faith in the historic role of the hero and the genius and conceived of history as the lengthened shadow of the great man. In his essay on "History," he argued, "...there is properly no history, only biography." To him, history was the record of that universal mind in which the perceiving individual could recognize himself and identify his own experience.

Emerson's philosophy was compounded of German idealism, oriental mysticism, and Yankee individualism. His essays and mystical poems were basically Christian and democratic in their exaltation of the individual, but too introspective—at least until the militant 1850's—to unite with social action. Though he decried the new commercialism and materialistic ethics, he showed marked impatience with the reformer who sought practical means to set things right. During the decade preceding the Civil War, he descended from his ivory tower and threw himself actively into the antislavery crusade. He felt that John Brown had lost his head at Harper's Ferry, but nevertheless, he praised him in his Boston lecture, "Courage," in these moving words: "The Saint, whose fate yet hangs in suspense, but whose martyrdom, if it shall be perfected, will make the gallows as glorious as the Cross."

At least one genius in America was ready to follow Emerson's doctrines of self-trust and self-sufficiency to the letter: his protégé, Henry Thoreau of Concord, a penniless Harvard student who practiced the philosophic anarchism that his patron merely preached. Thoreau was filled with Rousseau's love of nature, the Greek ideal of living a full life, and the spirit of individual craftsmanship. He retired to the shores of Walden Pond to live an independent existence, free of all superfluities. "I went to the woods," he wrote in his journal, *Walden,* "because I wished to live deliberately, to front only the essential facts of life, and to see if I could learn what it had to teach, and not, when I came to die, discover that I had not lived." At idyllic Walden Pond, where he wrote his forthright contemplative accounts of outdoor life, he lived the Emersonian role of the self-sufficient individual, becoming a St. Francis of the woods to the birds who perched trustfully upon his shoulder and to the strange animals whom he befriended.

As an isolated individualist he learned to his dismay that the state had certain claims upon him. Holding all government to be tinged with evil, especially in a nation that demanded taxes to pay for the iniquitous Mexican War and tolerated the slavery of one-sixth of the population, he refused to pay taxes and was jailed for one night. Disappointed that some meddler had paid his poll tax, he nevertheless elaborated upon his ideas of passive resistance against evil in a notable essay, *Civil Disobedience,* destined to influence Gandhi and the passive resistance of India's patriots in the twentieth century. His technique was simple. "If the alternative is to keep all just men in prison, or give up war and slavery, the State will not hesitate which to choose." He went beyond the Jeffersonian liberals who advocated limited government and the slogan, "That government is best which governs least." Thoreau would rephrase it, "That government is best which governs not at all." He wished no part of the collective guilt for invading Mexico, hanging John Brown, or reducing man to a machine. Clinging to the Puritan and Stoical ideal of the conscience as a "higher law" standing above the Constitution and man-made fugitive slave laws, he shared an attitude familiar among such antislavery men as Theodore Parker, Wendell Phillips, William Lloyd Garrison, and William Seward.

While Emerson and Thoreau sought self-realization in extreme individualist ideas, their associates of the Transcendental Club which met in Ripley's home, leaned toward collectivism. A former Unitarian minister of Boston, George Ripley was to become the influential literary editor of Greeley's *New York Tribune*, and to found Brook Farm in 1841, which by 1844 became a Fourier phalanx, attracting over 140 members within a few years. Here came Margaret Fuller, versatile and erudite feminist, "progressive" educator, and admirer of Goethe and the German romantics. Another frequent arrival, Orestes Brownson, a former minister who had shifted from Presbyterianism to Unitarianism and was to end as an aggressive champion of American Catholicism, was then editing the *Boston Quarterly Review* and belligerently espousing various labor and socialistic causes as well as the idealistic doctrines of transcendentalism. Several of the Brook Farmers were to follow Brownson when he startled the literati in 1844 by his conversion to Catholicism. To Brook Farm, also, came Bronson Alcott, erratic and original, who had experimented with the new German ideas of pedagogy, even introducing sex education until indignant parents withdrew their children. His short-lived experiment with a cooperative community, "Fruitlands," had been a trial for his family, including his gifted daughter, Louisa May Alcott. Emerson and Thoreau came and looked on in their detached manner upon the enthusiasms of Brook Farm, unwilling to submerge their individualistic ideals in a semi-socialist experiment.

Among the best-known residents of Brook Farm was Nathaniel Hawthorne, whose most successful novels and short stories were yet unwritten. From his native Salem he had imbibed the grim tales of colonial witches and fanatical Puritans as well as the bustling atmosphere of a historic seaport for the oriental trade. Melancholy by temperament and obsessed by the Puritan sense of sin, he did much to popularize a distorted version of Puritan intolerance that came to be accepted as authentic history. Struck by Emerson's doctrines of non-conformism he showed the harsh fate of the social rebel in his treatment of Puritan adultery in *The Scarlet Letter,* in which the beautiful heroine Hester Prynne suffers from social ostracism by her people. Again Hawthorne showed his pessimism in *The House of the Seven Gables,* which dealt with the theme of retribution falling as a curse on a succeeding generation of usurpers, in which the innocent are broken in spirit by an undeserved imprisonment. There is much of the romantic Gothic literary influence of England and Germany in Hawthorne's novels and short stories, revealed in characters who move in a murky, nightmarish atmosphere to symbolize the triumph of the pure conscience over evil. His originality was expressed in his imaginative total canvas and in the art of the short story, which he helped to raise as a major literary vehicle in this country.

Outside of Hawthorne and possibly Emerson, scarcely any of the transcendental circle wrote a "best seller" or even a work of moderate popularity. Strangely enough, from Harvard College and its Cambridge and Boston environs came voices that reached masses of readers both here and abroad. Foremost was Henry Wadsworth Longfellow, professor of modern languages at Harvard, who had disposed of 300,000 copies of his books by 1857. An erudite scholar who fell in love with the sentimentalism of the German romantics after the tragic death of his young wife and who investigated the folklore of Europe in long trips abroad, he showed little interest in the Jacksonian battles for the common man. Yet he captivated generations of school children and adults by the sweet melancholy or the idealistic exhortations of "A Psalm of Life," "The Village Blacksmith," "The Day Is Done," "The Children's Hour," and "Paul Revere's Ride." Just as the European scholars were unearthing folk tales to serve the rising sense of nationalism, so Longfellow used the meter of the Finnish epic "Kalevala" for an incursion into American folklore in the idealized Indian tale, *The Song of Hiawatha* (1855). Unlike Hawthorne, he found only beauty in the colonial traditions, expressing them in *Evangeline* (1847) and *The Courtship of Miles Standish* (1858). His learned predecessor at Harvard, George Ticknor, who had been among the first to study at Göttingen and to bring back the learning of Germany, had lost his heart to the literary past of Spain and Portugal, writing a major work, *The History of Spanish Literature,* that circulated well despite a certain aridity of treatment.

Harvard's distinguished historian was the industrious Unitarian minister Jared Sparks, who collected mountains of letters belonging to Washington, Franklin, and other Revolutionary figures. His lives of these men tended to be idealistic; he even resorted to the practice of correcting the grammar and removing the colloquialisms of these heroes. Far more inspired historians than Sparks were three Harvard graduates, Francis Parkman, whose work on the Oregon Trail has already been described, William Hickling Prescott, and John Lothrop Motley. Prescott, influenced by Ticknor, chose the glamour and excitement of fifteenth-century Spain for his popular work, *The Reign of Ferdinand and Isabella* (1837), completing it brilliantly despite a partial blindness that forced him to rest sometimes for hours after reading for ten minutes. Following an understanding with Washington Irving, who had written on the glories of Moorish Spain and was now considering a book on the conquest of the New World, Prescott pre-empted the latter subject and produced in succession *A History of the Conquest of Mexico* (1843) and *The Conquest of Peru* (1847). Despite Prescott's erratic treatment of the Aztec and Inca civilizations in a day before modern archaeological research, his relative accuracy and critical sense later won him praise as the first American scientific historian, and his literary gift of narrative, if not sufficiently analytical, entranced thousands. Over 160,000 copies of his first book were sold by the Civil War and many more editions were exhausted thereafter; the volume on Peru did even better in both America and England.

Motley, who had studied at Göttingen and Berlin as well as at

Harvard, was a moderately successful historical novelist before he embarked upon history. His absorbing narratives of real incidents drawn from numerous European archives raised him to the popularity and substance of Prescott and Parkman. Such was his *The Rise of the Dutch Republic* (1856), which suggested to him the parallel story of the rise of the United States. Alone of the Harvard-Göttingen scholars, George Bancroft, politician, educator, and historian, infused a dominant democratic content into his work, particularly his *History of the United States*, which was quarried —not always carefully—from enormous original sources. Like Hegel, he thought of history as revealing the unfolding of a divine plan, but unlike the German philosopher, he thought the final goal was Jacksonian democracy rather than Prussian monarchism. Motley, Prescott, Parkman, Sparks, Ticknor, Everett, and others of the Boston-Cambridge "Brahmins" were content to leave fundamental social implications and democratic ideologies to others.

Oliver Wendell Holmes, Harvard's outstanding medical professor, was a celebrated amateur in literature, lavishing his wit and keen insight in *The Autocrat of the Breakfast Table* on the mild problems besetting the well-to-do Brahmins of Boston. As an eighteenth-century rationalist with classical tendencies he ridiculed Calvinism and challenged its doctrines of predestination and sin as unscientific. His deep personal tolerance was influenced by his scientific belief that environmental and prenatal factors often robbed man of complete responsibility for his actions—though he professed to believe that man was a free moral agent.

Among the New England literati who agreed with Bancroft and certain of the transcendentalists in uniting literature and democratic social action were James Russell Lowell and John Greenleaf Whittier, both effective antislavery poets and essayists. Lowell had imbibed many conservative tenets at Harvard, but his marriage to an abolitionist poet, Maria White, may have redirected his sympathies toward a militant rejection of slavery. His *Biglow Papers,* excoriating the Mexican War, furnished a rallying point for Whigs who believed the war was a slaveholder's plot for expansion. At the same time his masterly Yankee dialect in these verses was adopted

by numerous "local-color" storytellers thereafter, making realistic
dialect a permanent part of national literature and serving as an
ideal vehicle for American folklore and regional expression. But
Lowell was to revert to his Brahmin heritage of economic conservatism after the Civil War at a time when his prestige made him
a literary arbiter. The self-educated Quaker, John Greenleaf Whittier, wrote verses of moral fervor praising toil in *Songs of Labor*
and condemning slavery. When the idol of Massachusetts, Daniel
Webster, delivered the Seventh of March Speech upholding the
compromise measures of 1850 even though they included a fugitive
slave law, Whittier expressed his protest against the fallen angel in
"Ichabod." After the war he too, like Lowell, was to forsake "the
opinion mill" and fall back on neutral New England themes of
nature, which he developed most successfully in *Snowbound.*

The New England renaissance was the most arresting phase of
what Professor Mathiessen has appropriately called the "American
Renaissance." Washington Irving of New York, then held to be the
finest prose writer in America though his quality was fast declining,
was publishing his books on the Far West and his biographies of
Goldsmith and Washington. A transplanted New Englander, William Cullen Bryant, was vigorously editing the antislavery and Jacksonian New York *Evening Post,* and justifying his youthful poetic
promise with such well-remembered poems as "The Fringed Gen-
tian" and "The Battlefield." Most significant, though there were
too few to appreciate it, was the ascending star of Walt Whitman,
a former carpenter, country schoolteacher, and editor of Brooklyn
who published his *Leaves of Grass* in 1855. Sharing much of Emerson's doctrine of self-reliance and buoyant individualism, Whitman
broke with traditional meter to express in free verse the infinite
moral capacity of man and the masses:

> One's-self I sing, a simple separate person,
> Yet utter the word Democratic, the word En-Masse.

His robust song to the pioneers, to the limitless future of America,
to the frank Greek joy of living uninhibitedly the life of the flesh as
well as of the spirit, all struck new notes at variance with the

bowdlerized manners of crinoline America and our Victorian culture. His rich original sense imagery discovered a pulsating world that had been mutilated by far-fetched metaphors, similes, and worn adjectives borrowed slavishly from Greek and Roman mythology. He heard and beheld God in every object, but felt untroubled that he did not understand the deity in the least; he remained confident that nothing is greater as an object of wonder than man is to himself. Unfortunately, Whitman discovered America long before his country truly discovered him. Only shortly before his death in 1892 was his pre-eminence as an American poet widely acknowledged.

Just as Whitman made sense only to some, Herman Melville of New York, a whaler who had been to the South Seas, had to await the twentieth century for a full sympathetic hearing. His novels seemed too pessimistic for the optimistic 1850's and he lacked the easy storytelling virtues that made Hawthorne's melancholy forgivable. For that romantic age *Moby Dick* (1851) was too realistic and even slow-moving with its symbolism, its exoticism, and its allegory of the world struggle between good and evil as expressed in the story of Captain Ahab revengefully pursuing the white whale that had bitten off his leg. Some of his autobiographical books on the South Seas, like *Typee* (1846) and *Omoo* (1847), attracted readers because of the exotic pictures of Polynesian life and adventure among his cannibal captors. But he could not remain long in the conformist literary pattern and launched out as a social rebel, a severe critic of western exploitation of the natives and of flogging in the Navy.

6

In the utilitarian atmosphere of a fast-growing nation, newly industrialized, science had numerous devotees among the masses, including inventive Connecticut Yankees as well as college scientists. Holbrook and his associates did much for science education in the schools and lyceums. Taxpayers, as Professor Dirk Struik points out, responded by supporting large appropriations for state geological surveys and national exploratory expeditions. In 1830, the Massachusetts legislature sponsored state geological exploration which revealed significant fossil findings in the Connecticut Valley; in the subsequent years, some eighteen states imitated this example of becoming patrons of science. As for the federal government, it did not hesitate to sponsor "pure science"—on a modest scale of course—as well as strictly utilitarian aims. Industrialists and merchants, like the Appletons and Lowells, also came forward as patrons of research. The American faith in progress was hitched to a belief in the benevolence of science in shaping the destiny of the country. As religious dogmas weakened, the worship of science grew.

This era of 1830-60 is noteworthy in the history of the conflict between science and religion, for it began with the quarrel with geology over the antiquity of the earth and it ended with a much deeper quarrel over Darwin's *Origin of Species* (1859). The English geologist, Charles Lyell, who lectured on and studied geological formations in the United States, published, between 1830 and 1833, his *Principles of Geology*, which awakened religious controversy. He disagreed with the "catastrophists" who kept the antiquity of Creation down to 4004 B.C. by explaining complex geological changes in terms of catastrophes like the Flood. Instead, Lyell supported "uniformitarianism" which estimated the age of ancient geological formations on the same basis as similar processes of modern times, thus upsetting the literal interpretation of the Creation completed in six days. Many articulate Americans and Englishmen tended to follow the English theologian, William Paley, author of *Evidences of Christianity* (1794) who believed that science could be relied upon to reveal God's design in nature. Lyell and other scientists met theological critics by embracing Paley's theory of God's design and enclosing their scientific findings within the framework of a broader interpretation of the Bible.

The reception of Charles Darwin's *Origin of Species* and its theories of natural selection and sexual selection as explanations of organic evolution was another matter. For one thing, Darwin's book appeared in 1859 and was reviewed here in 1860 on the eve of the Civil War when the attention of the press was entirely absorbed in domestic affairs. Secondly, the great Swiss-American naturalist, Louis Agassiz of Harvard, who had contributed the comparative method to biology, rejected Darwin's idea that new species come about through the selective agency of the environment. Prevailing opinion held that all species were immutable since Creation. Long an investigator of fossil fishes and morphological structure, he had marveled at the striking similarity of animal skeletons in spite of widely different appearances and habits, but he refused to believe that this proved an evolutionary idea. Instead he insisted that such similarities merely illustrated the many-sidedness of God's creation. As long as Agassiz lived—he died in 1873—New England scientists preferred to avoid the controversy over evolution and its implications that were so unfavorable to the literal interpretation of the Bible regarding Creation.

Of the few who dared challenge Agassiz in America, Asa Gray, his resourceful Harvard colleague in botany, was the most outspoken. Gray had won an international reputation for his widely used textbook *Manual of Botany,* and had modified the older Linnaean system of classification by a more effective method. Under his leadership Cambridge had become a center for botanical instruction and Darwin had privately confided to him his startling secrets of the evolutionary process years before the publication of *Origin of Species.* Defending Darwinism against both professional and clerical critics, Gray argued that this theory did not conflict with religion but illustrated more grandly and more truthfully the divine plan of human creation.

American medical science, far more beholden to Paris and Edinburgh than to Germany, enjoyed a major triumph in the significant paper of the French-trained Oliver Wendell Holmes on "The Contagiousness of Puerperal Fever" published in 1843 in the *New England Quarterly Journal of Medicine.* Although not an original discovery, Holmes' arguments on child-bed fever pointed out that the ignorance of doctors and midwives regarding contagiousness made many a maternity hospital a death house. As a hard-headed practitioner as well as theorist, Holmes showed a wholesome skepticism of medical cure-alls and relied heavily upon wholesome diet and pleasant surroundings for natural cures. He saw no conflict between science and religion. "Science represents the thought of

God discovered by man," he wrote, and adopted Darwinism shortly after its appearance.

Surgery and dentistry entered a new stage with the successful application of ether to deaden pain—anesthesia, as Oliver Wendell Holmes christened it. In 1846, a dentist, William T. G. Morton, used sulphuric ether for a patient who was having a neck tumor removed. In the presence of a skeptical crowd, he demonstrated that the sick man scarcely felt the pain of what would otherwise have been an excruciating experience. Morton had scarcely secured his laurels before a disturbing article appeared in the *Southern Medical and Surgical Journal,* written by a Georgia surgeon, Dr. Crawford W. Long, who claimed to have anticipated Morton as early as 1842. Long recorded eight operations in which he had used anesthesia. There ensued a bitter conflict between these men—and still other claimants. In any event, anesthesia came in time to mitigate the pain of thousands of wounded soldiers in the war with Mexico and promised even better things for the future.

In the study of physics, the logical successor to Franklin was Joseph Henry, head of the Smithsonian Institution. His basic experiments with magneto-electricity showed Samuel F. B. Morse the possibility of the electric telegraph in long-distance communication. Henry may even have preceded Morse in demonstrating the electromagnetic telegraph sometime in 1830-31. His invention of the first electro-magnetic motor opened the way for the use of electricity as industrial power in later times. He published studies of solar radiation and the heat of sunspots and observed the temperature of steam under varying conditions. As head of the Smithsonian Institution, recently bequeathed to the United States by a wealthy English chemist, James Smithson, for the "increase and diffusion of knowledge," Henry issued weather maps, published original scientific works, and performed many other services later taken over by the Library of Congress.

Samuel F. B. Morse, painter and inventor, was the son of the New England geographer, Jedidiah Morse. He was studying art in France when he came into contact with the semaphore signal system of Claude Chappe. From Joseph Henry and Dr. Charles T. Jackson (who also claimed priority in the invention of anesthesia), he learned the principle of electromagnetism. He invented the telegraph at least by 1836 and revealed it to the world in 1844 with the completion of the Baltimore to Washington line. The telegraph was to reduce the hazards of a divided nation severed by the diverging development of East and West. Morse was a technical adviser to a New England businessman, Cyrus W. Field, who was interested in the new ideas of telegraph transmission via a submarine cable. In 1858, Field succeeded in laying the trans-Atlantic cable and, when it broke down thereafter, his company painstakingly rebuilt it in 1866.

Among the alleged sciences, phrenology converted thousands of laymen and not a few specialists of England and America into enthusiastic supporters. This art of reading the character and mental powers of man through a study of the outer surface of the head had been systematized by Dr. Franz J. Gall of Vienna about 1800 and had been popularized by his pupil, Dr. J. K. Spurzheim, who lectured on it in Boston in 1832. Rejecting the tendency to follow Aristotle in stressing the unity of the mind (or soul), Spurzheim outlined within the brain separate mental organs such as "amativeness," "combativeness," "philoprogenitiveness," "concentrativeness," and other basic "propensities" and "sentiments." The truth of phrenology, observes Professor Edwin G. Boring, was still scientifically possible in a day before the physiology of the brain was known. Phrenologists eventually courted disaster at the hands of modern psychology by insisting that external head protrusions or recessions reflected corresponding faculties of the brain; but they contributed the sound idea that the brain was the "organ of mind." Even their errors regarding the significance of external "head bumps" anticipated the modern idea that mental functions are localized in various parts of the brain. As Boring concludes, "For this reason it is almost correct to say that scientific psychology was born of phrenology, out of wedlock with science."

Environmentalists like Horace Mann, who was influenced by the prolific Scottish phrenologist, George Combe, believed that education could strengthen the desirable faculties and weaken the undesirable ones. In Boston, the Fowler brothers founded *The American Phrenological Journal* in 1838, encouraging the craze for phrenology in parlor séances and educational gatherings. The *American Journal of Science,* edited by the cautious Sillimans, father and son, of Yale, gave phrenology respectful attention. Edgar Allan Poe praised that study in his *Southern Literary Messenger* of 1836, "It has assumed the majesty of a science; and as a science ranks among the most important which can engage the attention of thinking beings." He heightened the novelty of his supernatural tales by borrowing a concept or two from Spurzheim, as in the story "Ligeia." The craze for phrenology was to outlast the century and find enduring hospitality in this country even after Englishmen lost their enthusiasm for it. The *Journal of Phrenology,* organ of the movement, originated in Edinburgh in 1823, but it was to die in Philadelphia in 1911 after a protracted life here.

From Vienna, too, came Dr. Friedrich A. Mesmer's eighteenth-century studies of animal magnetism and "mesmerism," the foundation of modern hypnotism. In certain respects, Mesmer anticipated Freud's use of hypnosis in curing mental diseases, but as yet mesmerism remained a fad, fashionable in European and American séances. By mid-century, as the word "hypnotism" replaced "mesmerism," which was associated with fantastic cure-all ideas, more and more professional scientists found considerable validity in the use of Mesmer's method as a tool of diagnosis. By this time, however, mesmerism and spiritualism had become closely allied as the stock in trade of clever mediums.

Another Austrian scientific importation of tremendous popularity in a credulous age was the system of hydropathy that attempted to cure disease through internal and external uses of hot or cold water. American health journals and hydropathic institutes acclaimed the virtues of this latest revelation together with diet panaceas such as vegetarianism. One noted vegetarian of the day, Sylvester Graham, advocated fruits and vegetables as a cure for practically any disease, and popularized a kind of unrefined wheat flour, Graham flour, which became a national fad. "Grahamism" was not the least of the "isms" of Lincoln's day.

7

In the arts, mid-century Americans of the middle class craved
the current romantic styles imported from Europe despite the
Emersons and Whitmans who called for original self-expression.
The rise of mass education following the Jacksonian era and the
prosperity of the factories and trade brought into existence a
larger, more democratic, but unsophisticated, patronage that fos
tered work of a utilitarian, spectacular, or uncritical "prettifying"
nature. Besides, the ascetic inhibitions of the numerous pietist
and evangelical cults, both native and immigrant, and the practical
pioneer tradition discouraged estheticism. A technical feat like
Clark Mills' rearing steed of the Andrew Jackson statue led an
enthusiastic Congress into voting more than twice the original
contract price of $15,000. In music, a shrewd French concert man-
ager attracted thousands by advertising that forty pianists would
play simultaneously with five orchestras and 1800 singers, or that
a thousand candles would be illuminated. Musical critics rated
a performance by every criteria but art, while art critics stressed
the storytelling factor and literary reviewers scrutinized the morals
of a novel or poem. In 1838, bored Americans in the gallery at a
Haydn concert interrupted with yells, "Stop that noise! Give us
'Bonaparte Crossing the Rhine,' 'Washington's March,' or 'Yankee
Doodle'!"

In architecture, the romantic motifs in Europe inspired an era
of American Gothic that gradually replaced the Roman and Greek
phase of the neoclassic revival typified by the Capitol building at
Washington and the "Republican style," which Latin Americans
were also imitating. Classical architecture retained its firm grip
in the plantation style of the Southern slaveholder. Indicative of
the romantic neo-medievalism that the revived English Gothic
brought in was Washington Irving's home "Sunnyside." More and
more homes, especially in the North, were built with pointed
arches, pinnacles, and decorative Gothic motifs. These were the
architectural equivalents of the Gothic tales of mystery in literature
so effectively told by Edgar Allan Poe.

Romanticism in painting won its chief distinctiveness in sentimentalized landscape art, particularly of the Hudson River School,
whose "Dusseldorf" elements have already been noted in the works
of Leutze and Bierstadt. Aside from the direct German influence,
there was the impact of Dutch seventeenth-century art and the
frontier, notably in the work of the English-born self-taught painter,
Thomas Cole, who expressed the grandeur of the Catskills and the
White Mountains. Another self-taught portraitist and engraver,
Asher B. Durand, who shared with Cole the honor of founding
the Hudson River School, brought a sincere, if somewhat literal
and detailed technique, to this group. Cole, Durand, and their
associates, as Robb and Garrison among other art historians point
out, limited themselves to natural scenery, forgetting the human-
ized landscapes of farms and roads. The American patron's insistence on storytelling in art caused painters to concentrate on
numerous precise details. This is best illustrated in the unusual
vogue for the "genre" painting—the good-natured depiction of
the foibles and the pleasanter aspects of everyday life. Especially
in demand were the canvases of the Dusseldorf-trained Eastman
Johnson, whose rich, vibrant colors and native realism gave tremendous appeal to his sentimental themes. His "The Old Kentucky Home," a picture of an idyllic slave quarter and plantation
house, was known to tens of thousands through cheap lithographs.

More of the actual America of Stephen Foster and the young
Mark Twain appears in the keenly observant and frequently
humorous genre paintings of George Caleb Bingham, William
Sidney Mount, and Richard C. Woodville—to mention the more
successful artists in this category. All three combined optimistic
subjects with craftsmanship in the handling of warm colors and
meticulous detail. Bingham had been reared in Missouri and
trained at one time in Dusseldorf. He combined these influences in
his river and western pictures: "The Jolly Flatboatmen," "Raftsmen Playing Cards," "Stump Speaking," and the idealized "Daniel
Boone Escorting a Band of Pioneers into the Western Country."
He sketched the raftsmen, gamblers, and drunkards from real life
and he knew the rural politician because he himself had been a

Missouri Whig official. His interpretation of the Jacksonian common man shows the tongue-in-cheek attitude of a conservative
Whig.

More in the conventional groove of subject matter was Samuel
F. B. Morse, who enjoyed a national reputation in painting before
he invented the telegraph. He was one of Benjamin West's distinguished pupils and had also studied with the Southern-born
painter, Washington Allston. Like the genre painters, he was a
master of precise effects and color and displayed these qualities
best in "Congress Hall," which plainly depicted at least eighty
people and even expressed in mathematical proportions the details
of the dome. However, "Congress Hall" did not prove sufficiently
interesting or moralistic for the visitors who saw his exhibit, and
he returned to the safer avenue of middle-class portraits. In 1825,
he gave an impetus to native artists by founding the National
Academy of Design, making it an artist-controlled institution to
compete with old John Trumbull's American Academy of Art,
which was dominated by wealthy lay patrons and tended to ignore
the exhibits of living American painters.

For the lower middle classes and the farmers who could not
afford the originals of the genre painters and the idealized pictures that seemed so admirably suited for the walls of a home
alongside of a few well-chosen mottoes, there was an easy path to
inexpensive art patronage in the colorful prints of Currier and
Ives of New York. More zealously than their competitors, this firm
could satisfy the homely taste by reproducing the genre paintings,
copying some raging contemporary fire or idyllic forest subject,
or delighting thousands with a cheerful New England winter scene
of snow and sleigh bells. For two generations their simple narrative
pictures of American life and history decorated the walls of homes
all the way to California and familiarized countless persons with
the work of the genre painters.

Even more important than the Currier and Ives vogue as art for
the common man was the sensational popularity of the daguerreotype in the 1840's and 1850's. A French painter and physicist,
Louis Daguerre, had invented this early form of photography, and

American firms quickly led the world in producing the technical apparatus for these pictures. Almost anyone could afford this kind of portrait and would cheerfully suffer the discomfort of having his head fixed in place by an iron clamp while waiting several minutes for the sunlight exposure to take effect. Inevitably, most of the early daguerreotypes betray the unnatural poses and strained expressions that result under such conditions, though one Boston firm at least, Southworth and Hawes, showed the esthetic possibilities of informal, unposed pictures. Oliver Wendell Holmes was among the first Americans to appreciate the esthetic possibilities, aside from mere literalness, inherent in photography. Best-known of the early photographers was the New York Irishman, Mathew B. Brady, who transmitted to posterity realistic pictures of Lincoln, Whitman, and Barnum. During the Civil War his resourceful camera captured thousands of battlefield scenes in spite of unappreciative soldiers. These pictures provided an indispensable record of the human side of warfare.

Sculpture was far more retarded in an artistic sense than painting, though enthusiasm bubbled over for Hiram Powers, a former Cincinnati creator of wax works for the city's dime museum, who had been raised on a farm in Vermont. Going to Italy in 1837 when neoclassicism was at its height, he absorbed the classical techniques of idealizing figures and applying abstract symbols. Therefore it happened that the popular Powers fastened an outmoded style upon America and retarded the growth of realism in national sculpture. His controversial statue, "The Greek Slave," displayed in 1843, was daring in a moral rather than in an artistic sense, for it displayed a naked woman, albeit a somewhat sexless figure; this stirred up speculations regarding the possible use of a live model, a practice strictly condemned in Victorian America. However, a thorough inspection of the lady by the Cincinnati clergy gave the imprimatur of the church to the statue as tending to stress refined and exalted sentiments. Its simple allegory of Greece in chains to the Turks recalled the surviving cult of Byron who had symbolized martyrdom for Greek independence.

Also in this neoclassical style was the overrated work of Horatio

Greenough whose statue of Washington competed for attention with the "Greek Slave." Originally intended for the Capitol, this twenty-ton Jove-like figure proved a white elephant, being moved from place to place before being finally lodged with the Smithsonian Institution. The meticulously tailored father of his country appeared half naked, save only for loose classical robes, which unfortunately revealed Greenough's ignorance of anatomy, and pointed his right finger upward in an apostrophe to his countrymen. While lucky artists like Greenough found generous patronage from the taxpayer, others managed to locate their neoclassical busts and patriotic figures in private homes and museums.

American music among the elite, as already suggested, continued to owe much to high German musical standards and the public school teaching of music fostered in Boston and elsewhere by Lowell Mason. Boston, a major center for musical expression, delighted not only in Mason's compositions and leadership but was quick to appreciate the German symphonic programs of Beethoven and Mozart, and the novel music of Wagner. Italian opera, the newest expression of European romanticism, carried its sentimental plots and melodic arias to New Orleans, New York, Baltimore, and other cities. One of the first native American musicians to enjoy an international reputation was Louis Moreau Gottschalk of New Orleans, once a child prodigy of the organ and piano whom Chopin had praised as the future king of all pianists. Women particularly thronged to New York's Niblo's Garden and other concert chambers to hear this sentimentalist play in a vigorous sparkling fashion his own emotional compositions as well as the music of Chopin and others.

For the masses, the music of nostalgia, sweet melancholy, and folk songs had an irresistible appeal. This was the era of Stephen Collins Foster, the gifted son of a cultured middle-class family of Laurenceville, Pennsylvania. With little formal musical training he adapted the folksong technique to most of his nearly two hundred songs. His nostalgic notes were a fitting expression of his own tragic, seemingly futile life of marital unhappiness, excessive drinking, poverty, and early death from an accident in a Bowery lodging house. Habitually indifferent to money matters, he earned little from his masterpieces and quickly dissipated these sums. Influenced by the demands of the newly popular minstrel shows, which featured the happy-go-lucky, nostalgic Negro stereotype, and borrowing certain ideas from Negro camp meetings, he wrote, as John T. Howard points out, "Old Folks at Home" without the trouble of crossing the Ohio. California forty-niners took comfort in singing "O! Susanna" as they trudged across the Great Plains and the western deserts. Foster was inspired by his wife to write "Jeanie with the Light Brown Hair," whose real popularity was not attained until the mid-twentieth century. His own age also enjoyed "My Old Kentucky Home," "Old Black Joe," "Come Where My Love Lies Dreaming," "Nelly Was a Lady," and finally, at his death, "Beautiful Dreamer." His biographer, H. V. Milligan, writes that "the Negro ceases to be a caricature and becomes a human being. . . . This is not the Negro of 'Jump Jim Crow' and 'Zip Coon' but of *Uncle Tom's Cabin.*" Though Foster's tunes were not true folk songs, their tremendous appeal to Americans—and Europeans too—raised them to a secure status as American music.

The picturesque minstrel tradition in America, attributed to the early efforts of a German immigrant, Gottlieb Graupner, who was reported to have used blackface, took on its definite form after 1830 under a remarkable group of showmen. During the early 1830's Thomas ("Daddy") Rice, a white comedian, borrowed the "Jim Crow" song and clothes from a Negro for his appearance in Pittsburgh. Soon a routine of blackface, with Negro songs, dances, and costumes spread throughout the theaters, earning handsome salaries for the "minstrels." The first troupe of blackface song and dance men was the Virginia Minstrels of Dan Emmett, later composer of "Dixie" and "Old Dan Tucker." Emmett wrote "Dixie" in New York in 1859 as a "walk around" tune for Bryant's Minstrels. When war came the Confederates appropriated the song before the Union forces could think up suitable words. One of the original Virginia Minstrels, Edwin P. Christy, earned a well-deserved reputation for the choruses of his own Christy's Minstrels, especially for their introduction of Foster's tunes. Christy, with the consent of Foster, who feared to jeopardize his future by being associated with "Ethiopian music," even assumed credit for a time as the composer of several Foster pieces.

With a finger in almost every pie of public amusement Phineas T. Barnum, a Connecticut showman who had learned a few tricks while serving patrons in a country store, tried his hand at music as well as other kinds of entertainment. In 1842, he merged two of New York's museums to form the American Museum, which combined freak shows, educational exhibits, and stage performances in a medley scarcely known in Europe, and until then only to a limited extent in this country. No other man had taken the public pulse so accurately as Barnum in devising and publicizing the kind of sensationalism of a morally "wholesome" kind to appeal to millions. The incessant blaring of Barnum's brass band outside the Museum drew crowds to see the Wild West Show, the baby beauty contests, the moral lectures, the astonishing exhibits of all kinds, and other attractions. Before he acquired the Museum, he had awakened a sensation with Joice Heth, who claimed to be no less than 161 years old and recalled her slave days when she nursed "dear little George Washington." In 1842, he exhibited the embalmed Fiji Mermaid to credulous thousands, who felt not too badly cheated when they afterwards learned that this prodigy was a cleverly-sewn contraption of the upper half of a female monkey and the lower half of a large fish. That year he introduced to the world General Tom Thumb, a five-year-old dwarf whose age was suitably raised to eleven and who measured two feet, one inch in height. The general toured Europe with Barnum, being fondled by the delighted Queen Victoria herself, petted by the crowned heads of the Continent, and adored by huge throngs of the plain people.

Barnum tried to offset his national reputation as "the great humbug"—said partly in affection—by risking his fortune to guarantee a concert singing tour for Jenny Lind, "the Swedish nightingale." Appalled to learn how few Americans knew that Jenny was a singer and not a dancer, he developed the art of publicity to a degree known only to modern Hollywood and created a lovable "personality" of the strait-laced and rather plain Swedish girl. Newspapers gladly publicized her every move and her astutely advertised charities. Firemen paraded for Jenny Lind, portraits of her appeared everywhere, and even "Jenny Lind sausages" joined the manifestations in her honor. The response was truly unique in American entertainment history. Not only were Barnum and Jenny Lind enriched, but American musical tastes were stimulated and many more European and native artists felt encouraged to hazard an American tour. Jenny Lind gave ninety-three concerts throughout the East and usually chose a simple repertoire that enchanted multitudes who adored the chaste voice and white-clad figure of the singer. In 1871, Barnum was to found his circus and ten years later he joined T. A. Bailey in establishing the long-lived tradition of what they modestly called "the Greatest Show on Earth."

Barnum's success does not prove that Americans were more naïve or gullible than their contemporaries in England, France, Spain, or elsewhere. The great showman, himself, disproved this recurrent charge during his European tour. Englishmen, for example, to whom dwarfs were not unknown, shared the excitement of Americans for Tom Thumb once the Court had shown Barnum its favor. M. R. Werner, biographer of Barnum, tells of the English painter, Benjamin Haydon, who was driven to suicide by the final evidence of the futility of his life when his painting exhibit was ignored by English crowds at Egyptian Hall in favor of his competitor, Tom Thumb. He noted despairingly in his diary:

> They rush by thousands to see Tom Thumb. They push, they fight, they scream, they faint, they cry help and murder! and oh! and ah!.... It is an insanity, a rabies, a madness, a furor, a dream. I would not have believed it of the English people.

This was the last straw for Haydon, whose disappointed career had long weighed upon his mind. So he ended his life, convinced that Barnum had captured the universe.

The optimistic belief in environmentalism that encouraged reformers to emancipate labor, women, and slaves had its direct cultural expression in the new agencies for mass education. The status of the common man was enhanced by the public school movement, the lyceums, the mechanics' institutes, the penny press, and the cheaply produced novels, magazines, and biographies. In art, the patronage of the masses, in which the middle class actually played a leading role, meant a bonanza for those who offered literalness or romantic idealization, such as the manufacturers of the daguerreotype cameras, the printmakers, notably Currier and Ives, the Hudson River School, and some of the successful "genre" painters who dealt with contemporary scenes. In music, these patrons preferred minstrel and sentimental tunes and especially Stephen Foster whose memorable melodies did not require a cultivated ear for appreciation. Science, too, benefitting from the widespread belief in the beneficence of applied science and technology as well as faith in the inevitability of progress aroused enthusiasm at all levels, ranging from those content with spiritualism and phrenology to the most exacting devotees of physics and chemistry. Finally, the man who best took the measure of this credulous age on both sides of the Atlantic, Phineas T. Barnum, reaped fittingly the financial rewards that his insight gave him.

The culture of the elite also reflected the contemporary emphasis on environmentalism and the goodness of man. From abroad German romanticism—if one may use this much-abused term to describe what was happening—carried with it the Teutonic enthusiasm for a national literature, a native folklore, and a national educational system. The Swiss-Prussian ideal of education, deriving from the teachings of Rousseau, gave an enhanced status to the child, whose natural bent was to be cultivated and not repressed. In literature, Emerson, Whitman, Melville, Thoreau, Hawthorne, and others of the American renaissance added an esthetic form to the belief that man was not an earth-bound son of Adam but the exalted son of God, whose divine inheritance included latent genius and mystical insight. Such assumptions, however extravagant, added immeasurably to the American dogmas of self-reliance and individual freedom.

The Antebellum South:
From Jefferson to Jefferson Davis

[1830-1861]

I

WHEN the aged Jefferson died in 1826, the spokesmen for the South were the belligerent cotton planters of South Carolina. They were suffering more than planters elsewhere from an agrarian depression and exhausted soils at a time when the competition of the rich Black Belt of the Gulf states was being felt. To the South Carolinian there seemed no question that Northern industrialists were exploiting the South by a tariff that benefited almost no one in an exporting section while taxing the cheap cotton clothes for slaves and burdening other Southern imports. They spurred on Vice-President John C. Calhoun to find a formula in "nullification" as a weapon against the latest atrocity, the "Tariff of Abominations."

But genuine Southern power, reflecting the westward expansion of the Cotton Kingdom, was already shifting to the land of Jefferson Davis, the fertile Gulf states from Georgia to eastern Texas. By 1861, the Southwest accounted for over three-fourths of the four million bales of cotton exported from the Cotton Kingdom and most of the slaves. New Orleans, the largest city of the South, replaced Charleston as the chief port of the South as cotton, sugar, and rice from the newer lands led the procession of plantation exports. Georgia, aided by railroads in opening up untouched lands in her interior, had a planter elite class of 902 with estates exceeding a thousand acres each. Alabama had nearly seven hundred in this class of cotton nabobs and Mississippi and Louisiana each had hundreds of such great planters. So large were the sugar plantations of Louisiana, due to the expensive machinery and heavy capitalization required for investors, that 160 planters accounted for half the crop. While small farmers of the non-slaveholding class were in the overwhelming majority in every Southern state, these large planters heavily influenced politics, social life, and culture.

Despite an alleged democratic revolution in the South beginning about 1830 and supposedly serving the common man, the planter did not abdicate his rule before 1861—and certainly not then. It is true that under the leadership of the frontier counties of the lower South, state after state did break with the oligarchic Virginia model of county government that had been entrenched in the South since the seventeenth century. The aristocratic justices of the peace, usually chosen for life and in effect self-perpetuating, had long wielded regal power in local affairs—legislative, executive, and judicial—whether in taxation, the selection of local officers, or the hundred and one details of community life. Within the all-powerful county court, the justice of the peace exercised his sweeping powers on the most intimate concerns of the citizen. While the "revolution" gave the right to vote to nearly all white men and made local offices elective, thus stripping the county court oligarchs of their acknowledged supremacy, the basic economic and social structure remained untouched. The right to vote among the illiterate, anti-Negro, and superstitious poorer classes —and the planter did very little for mass education—meant too often a travesty of democratic processes in which crude rural politicians replaced the better-educated statesmen in state and congressional halls. Four million Negroes were excluded from the ballot and their fate was entrusted to the other classes who were united by the ideal of white supremacy; this slogan, however, had to await its most effective use during the generation after 1890, when the resurgent small farmer of the South led by Ben Tillman

and other demagogues captured power. Professor Charles S. Sydnor has pointed out how belligerently the new men in office served
the planter. Governor Henry S. Foote of Mississippi observed that
the slaveholders of his state were "more discreet and moderate in
spirit than the noisy and in general unscrupulous *non-slaveholding*
champions who assumed to represent them." Non-slaveholders
initiated the movement for reviving the African slave trade and
fought most militantly for Southern rights against the North.

Planters, concerned with the sanctity of property, tended to join
the conservative Whig party rather than the more popular Democratic party, although both parties appealed so successfully to all
white classes as to divide the vote of innumerable Southern counties almost evenly. The well-to-do feared the provocative fire-
eaters who might plunge the Southland recklessly into war and
the wealthier planters voted in 1860 to a large extent for John
Bell and the National Constitutional Union party in order to prevent secession and war. The small farmers of the deep South,
hoping to become planters in their own right and frequently
united by kinship ties as well as by consciousness of racial soli-
darity against the Negroes, were more bellicose for the rights of
the South than the planters. After the national Whig Party broke
down in 1852 with the dismal defeat of Winfield Scott by Franklin
Pierce, planters and farmers moved steadily toward a one-party
system, hallowed by slavery, white-man supremacy, and Southern
nationalism; thus the Solid South was crystallizing even before
Reconstruction.

The lower South, where Jefferson Davis was developing his
Mississippi plantation after giving up his frontier army service,
had gone through a wild expansive period during the 1830's and
1840's, marked by all the western incidents of unscrupulous speculators and debtors, homicidal gamblers, and outlaws. A newly-rich
class of "cotton snobs" ruled the plantations. Impecunious Virginia lawyers rushed in to profit from the perpetual litigation of
fast-growing frontier communities. By 1861, the region had sobered
considerably, though the frontier flavor lingered and the class
structure, except for Negroes and poor whites, remained fairly

flexible. Mississippi prospered, boasting of a superior type of cotton boll imported from Mexico, which could be easily picked and thus insured increased productivity. Alabama, whose fertile limestone basin was free of the thinness or sandiness of the eastern coastal plains, shared with Mississippi the rich Black Belt. Georgia's primacy in cotton obscured her vast diversified crops of corn, wheat, oats, and rice. More fortunate than her sister states in possessing a good railroad system as well as rich crops, Georgia was indeed to be a tempting morsel to General Sherman when he devastated her countryside as a major part of a plan to cripple the Confederacy.

Still, there were in 1860 only 384,000 slaveholding families owning the nearly four billion dollars worth of slaves; this meant that only 1,500,000 persons had a direct connection with slavery among a white population of over 8,000,000. While all but 250,000 of the 4,000,000 Negroes were enslaved, these were usually owned in small groups; for example, only 300 planters in the entire South could boast of owning more than 200 slaves apiece, 2300 held over 100 each, and fewer than 200,000 owned as many as ten or more slaves. Sensational exceptions existed of course. In South Carolina, Wade Hampton, reputed to be the largest slaveholder in the South, owned about 3000 Negroes working on his widely scattered plantations. The magnificent Samuel Hairstons of Virginia possessed at least 1700 slaves; Nathaniel Hayward of Charleston accumulated fourteen rice plantations and over 2000 slaves; and Joseph Davis, brother of Jefferson, belonged to this feudal aristocracy of lands and slaves.

Planters, too, liked to carry on the tradition of the gentleman that ambitious colonial Virginians had studied from Renaissance handbooks. At their best this class suggested Washington, Madison, and Jefferson. Alexander Stephens, for example, who had risen from poverty, practised a kindly paternalism that endeared him to his slaves; he struggled to get public schools for the masses of Georgia and fought the secessionist fire-eaters almost until the actual war began when he decided to yield as did so many former Unionists to the dictates of Southern nationalism. Many a planter romanticized the feudal ideal as a pattern for upper-class society, so fascinatingly described in the pages of Sir Walter Scott, and encouraged the code duello, the horse-racing tournaments, and the chivalrous cult of chaste Southern womanhood.

At the same time this cult of Southern womanhood did not always prevent the male pursuit of a double moral standard as far as slave girls were concerned; the existence of 518,000 mulattoes and other mixed bloods in 1860 attests to this fact. While miscegenation was far commoner among lower-class whites than among planters, it occurred among both. Southern wives sometimes complained bitterly that they were but members of their husband's harem. Mulattoes whose faces revealed too embarrassingly the image of their masters might be disposed of to a distant plantation; others were well treated by their white fathers and even endowed with a comfortable inheritance. "I knew the dissolute half of Legree," said one Southern lady in an intimate parlor discussion of *Uncle Tom's Cabin*, forgetting that Legree was an overseer, not a planter. "He was high and mighty, but the kindest creature to his slaves, and the unfortunate results of his bad ways were not sold. They had not to jump over ice blocks. They were kept in full view, and were provided for handsomely in his will. His wife and daughters, in their purity and innocence, are supposed never to dream of what is as plain before their eyes as the sunlight."

Only the fortunate few in Southern communities could emulate the fine style of a latter-day Scott noble. More often, large rickety frame houses with utilitarian porches or even double cabins were the residences of the planters. The classical elegance of Andrew Jackson's "Hermitage," which stood on the latter's 640-acre plantation, showed the invasion of "Plantation Greek" to which wealthy planters had readily succumbed. But many a planter's home, like Jackson's, was Greek only as an afterthought with a two-story portico attached to a plain house. As elegance increased among the rich planters in the 1850's, sugar, cotton, and rice palaces sprang up along the Mississippi and French classical architectural influences from Louisiana did much to give the characteristic style to these mansions. Wooden columns were replaced by impressive white stuccoed brick pillars in Corinthian style supporting elegant cornices. French balconies and wrought ironwork covered three sides of the plantation house; inside, French wallpaper and crystal and bronze chandeliers and huge gilded mirrors, newly imported from Louis Napoleon's Empire, showed the Gallic impress on the plantation Greek of the Gulf states. Large rooms, high arched ceilings, and long winding staircases provided an expansiveness that was not only esthetic but useful for ventilation in a hot climate. Referring to the shining new plantation homes along the Mississippi, Professor Oliver Larkin, art historian, concludes, "Their very names suggest Creole sensibility and Yankee push: Asphodel, Belle Grove, and Rosedown; Rattle and Snap, and Uncle Sam."

Recreation for the planter varied, of course, according to his means and cultural level. The plantation house could offer the pleasures of dancing, jolly parties, and festive occasions. There seemed no shortage of fried chicken, roasted sweet potatoes, and mint julep; remote plantations were relatively self-sufficient in food and entertainment. Hunting offered every inducement of success in the well-stocked Southern forests. Fox hunting flourished especially among the planters of Virginia and Maryland, though the fox did not always get the sporting consideration he did in England. Carolina rice planters could escape the malaria of the warm months in their swampy lands by going to Charleston, enjoying its good talk, colorful society, music, balls, and races and residing in the English-style mansions with their gardens of azaleas, oleanders, and camellias. For others, there were the watering places, where the family could meet people of their class while young ladies could pursue courtships in the proper milieu.

Yet the planter was a businessman, too, anxiously concerned over the downward trend of crop prices and the upward movement of slave prices. In the Gulf states where frontier conditions pushed "culture" into the background, the planter was kept busy between hunting and planting. "Dogs and horses, 'coons and 'possums, crops and prices did prevail in conversation," writes Professor Ulrich B. Phillips, "while Caesar and Cicero were more often

the names of Negroes in the yard than of authors on the shelves."
In the Southeast—and increasingly in the Southwest, too—where
the toll of soil-butchery and slavery had produced exhausted hills,
ghost towns, and vast eroded gullies, the more intelligent planters
followed Edmund Ruffin of Virginia and turned to scientific agriculture to undo the damage. Planters sponsored numerous agricultural societies, trained slaves on many plantations to use new
plowing methods to check erosion, encouraged valuable soil experiments, and introduced technological improvements. The importation of guano from Chile and Peru during these decades was
almost revolutionary in effect. However, overseers had no genuine
incentive to conserve the soil and the destruction of the land went
on faster than did the reclamation measures that a *laissez-faire*
Southern community could or would take to restore fertility; this
system left only barren hills for the poor whites to squat upon and
grub for a living. The planter sold in an uncertain world market
with prices declining during the 1830's and 1840's and with his
profits often siphoned off by marketing fees and interest charges
to New York banks, warehouses, and other transportation agencies,
as well as by Northern-inspired tariffs. He often denounced the
Yankee as parasitic and hypocritical, fattening upon his enterprise while pharasaically abusing the slave system that created
the wealth of the Cotton Kingdom.

Historians disagree on whether slavery actually paid in an economic sense. Capital funds, it has been frequently observed, were
poured into more slaves to raise more cotton to buy more slaves.
Too little capital was diverted into permanent local and community improvements. Had the planter put his money out at interest in a Northern bank at 6 or 7 per cent he might in many
instances, at least, have been far ahead by the end of the year. To
provide for a slave force of which a large number were too young
or too old to do effective work involved serious losses and risks.
The death of several able-bodied hands might be a crushing blow
—financially at least—to the smaller planter. Pregnancy among the
slave women meant a loss of labor for some time. Supervision by
an overseer and his assistants was costly because slaves, as in all

times, gave their labor unwillingly. Overseers usually expected
a free hand from the planter to carry out the difficult task of squeez-
ing profits out of the plantation. Not infrequently planters expressed the opinion that free labor was cheaper than slave.

Aside from slavery the plantation system was handicapped by
a defective marketing and financing system that did not improve
with the advent of emancipation. "My husband supported his
plantation by his law practice," complained the wife of Senator
James Chesnut of South Carolina. "Our people have never earned
their own bread." For the wealthy Chesnut family the plantation
system was a way of life rather than a mode of enrichment. Mary
Chesnut could not understand her husband's criticism that the
lavish dinners she gave in traditional Southern style were examples
of "hospitality run riot."

By the Civil War tobacco plantations dotted the border states
from Virginia, Maryland, and North Carolina to Kentucky, Tennessee, and Missouri, with a piedmont marketing capital in Richmond. This crop, unlike cotton, required painstaking care and
hence was not suited to the labor of large gangs of unskilled slaves.
Small farmers could raise tobacco profitably on five or six acres
and send their crops to compete with those of the planters under
the warehouse auction system. Nine-tenths of the plug and twist
tobacco—which made this a nation of tobacco chewers and spitters
—were manufactured in the slave states, particularly in the border
areas. The aristocratic eighteenth-century snuff habit had become
quite plebeian and had joined pipe-smoking and tobacco-chewing
as evidences of the common man's day. Jackson's wife, Rachel,
and Mrs. Zachary Taylor aroused derisive comment in sophisticated circles by their Southern frontier habit of smoking pipes.
As for the tobacco chewing habit, Charles Mackay, the fastidious
English poet, suggested that the American eagle emblem be replaced by a cuspidor. While the manufacture of the bourgeois
cigar largely belonged to the Northeast and to foreign lands,
Southern planters and small farmers resented the anti-smoking
campaign of certain Northern reformers who were spreading another
one of the subversive "isms" against the existence of the South.

The planter elite had a very articulate ally in the lawyer class, which the South produced in overabundance considering the limited legal opportunities in a rural society. This restless, dissatisfied intelligentsia usually served the slaveholder's interests enthusiastically in the courts and legislatures, even writing the novels, poems, newspapers, and proslavery books that made up Southern literature in the Cotton Kingdom. George Fitzhugh, a Virginia lawyer unhampered by much law business, devoted almost all his waking hours to writing books, pamphlets, and articles for slavery. So prolific was he in publishing anonymous articles for Southern newspapers and magazines that his extreme proslavery sentiments came to be looked on by Lincoln and Congress as typical of the South. Leonidas W. Spratt, a Charleston lawyer, politician, and journalist, even inaugurated a widespread movement to revive the African slave trade for the South.

The planter's record on mass education was less than mediocre. At least 90 per cent of 4,000,000 Negroes were kept illiterate as a necessary police measure. About 1,000,000 poor whites, living largely in the rural slums created by the wasteful plantation system, were not much better off. Planters preferred the aristocratic English custom of supporting education for the gentry through tutors and private schools. The Yankee endorsement of the tax-supported elementary and high schools was no argument in its favor. Besides, the small farmers—who made up 5,000,000 out of the 8,000,000 whites in the South—seemed unenthusiastic about laws to tax themselves and they were wedded to the traditional ideal of manual labor for the poor. As a result, children whose parents could not afford to pay tuition might get schooling if they qualified under a means test; but funds for such "paupers" were exceedingly limited in most states. There was also the persistent rural problem of providing inexpensive schools in an area of dispersed population. Alexander Stephens of Georgia, recalling the limited educational opportunities of his youth, campaigned for a modern tax-supported school system to remove the pauper stigma on free schools. Though he succeeded in putting through the desired legislation, public apathy led to the repeal of these laws. Large planters joined the

small farmers in preserving a state tax system that scarcely made
any demands on anyone.

Aided by congressional land grants in some cases, federal gifts
of President Jackson's surplus revenue in 1838 and a variety of
local expedients, most Southern states and cities made some advances before the Civil War toward the educational ideal of Calvin
Stowe and Horace Mann. New Orleans, with a thriving commerce
and a rich cultural background, led Southern cities in organizing a
centrally supervised free school system. In 1847, Louisiana offered
at least three years of free schooling to her youth. Mobile, far ahead
of rural Alabama, also set up a tax-supported school system. Beginning in 1845 Alabama began to develop a state-wide system of
free schools along the lines of Massachusetts, but even in 1859 the
superintendent of education reported that almost half of the children were attending no school at all. In nearby Mississippi planters
and farmers blocked such educational bills throughout this era
and the state depleted its existing funds by bad investments.
Florida, delayed economically and culturally by the long war
against the Seminole, took few steps toward free schools before
1850. Tennessee, where Andrew Johnson escaped illiteracy only in
adulthood, and where too many of his neighbors in the eastern
section never left that condition, was indefinitely delayed by the
school superintendent's embezzlement of school funds, though it
did set up legislation for a free school system in 1845. Virginia never
succeeded in carrying out Jefferson's ideal of free public schools.
Leaving school financing to the counties, the Old Dominion
achieved very little for mass education except of the pauper
school variety. South Carolina and Georgia kept the decentralized
school idea, leaving the notion of free tax-supported systems for
some hazy future. Exceptional progress, however, was made in
North Carolina, where the small farmer was strongly entrenched;
here, in 1839, a system of free schools was created for the state
after Horace Mann's model. By the end of the fifties there were
3000 schools in North Carolina operating under an annual revenue
of $279,000—a princely sum by the standards of that day.

For the planters collegiate education was a far different question from mass schooling and their new state universities and private colleges compared well with the best in the North in quality, attendance, and number, even including female seminaries. The University of Virginia, which Poe attended, had a splendid staff and a rounded curriculum. The legislature, it was reported, had even invited the distinguished French historian and statesman, Guizot, to the faculty, though the offer was not accepted. Francis Lieber, the erudite German-American political theorist, taught for years at the College of South Carolina. The brilliant Le Conte brothers won their reputation in geology at the University of Georgia (Franklin College) and at the College of South Carolina. Good state colleges existed in Mississippi, Alabama, Louisiana, Tennessee, and Missouri. These were supported by various means: tuition, endowment, public land sales, and often by public lotteries.

This emphasis on well-financed, excellently staffed colleges and academies contrasts sharply with the shoddy elementary schools and reflects the racial and class atmosphere of the antebellum South. The pall of illiteracy among the Negroes and poor whites affected the intellectual climate. The federal census of 1850, tabulating the illiteracy rate among the native white population over twenty years of age, showed the South with an illiteracy rate of 20.3 per cent, the Middle States with 3 per cent, and New England, despite immigration, had only 0.42 per cent. The rise of the common man in the South too often meant the bigoted influence of illiterate voters, fed on anti-Negro, anti-Yankee, and anti-foreign prejudices. Under such circumstances, the true self-interest of the majority was completely confused by irrelevant issues.

2

The yeoman farmer, who made up the bulk of the Southern people, worked his small farm of diversified crops and considerable cattle; most of this class was content with self-sufficiency but many added cash crops of tobacco, hemp, cotton, and meat for the market. The South was a "one-crop" section only in a very general sense, for it produced bumper crops for export from large fruit orchards, from thousands of corn and wheat fields, as well as from the plantations of sugar, rice, and cotton. Working in the fields with his sons, perhaps assisted by a slave or two, the small farmer was very far from being the poor white with whom the North often confused him. Many small farmers aspired, with a reasonable chance of realization, to become substantial slaveholders.

In the deep South, particularly, the farmer could see eye to eye with the planter on major issues relating to slavery. The presence of 4,000,000 Negroes among 8,000,000 whites created a problem of security that often drew whites of various classes together. By 1861, Negroes outnumbered whites in South Carolina and Mississippi; in Georgia, Alabama, and Louisiana, the whites held only a narrow margin; and many counties in other plantation states had Negro majorities. Thus the Southerner was reared in a psychological environment that gave the doctrines of majority rule and equalitarian democracy a definite Caucasian flavor if it did not destroy them altogether. The contradiction between the facts of Southern life and Jeffersonian liberalism was painfully apparent during the antebellum decades.

Nevertheless, class cleavage existed. Andrew Johnson and the farmers of eastern Tennessee hated the planter aristocrat and loyally defended the Union in 1861 as did the farmers in western Virginia. In North Carolina an erratic spokesman for the small farmer and poor white, Hinton Rowan Helper, who hated Negroes and planters alike, blamed the relative backwardness of the South, both material and cultural, on slavery. His influential book, *Impending Crisis of the South* (1857), bitterly assailed the planter in language that shocked the South and conversely impressed anti-slavery forces elsewhere.

As slave prices soared until two-thousand dollar slaves made their purchase impossible for most small farmers, the flexible white class structure seemed in danger of crashing. Lawyers, planters, and journalists, including Alexander H. Stephens of Georgia, William Yancey of Alabama, L. W. Spratt of South Carolina, J. D. B. De Bow of Louisiana, fought to increase the stake in slavery of the non-slaveholding classes by illegally reviving the slave trade.

"Our true purpose," declared Governor James H. Adams of South Carolina, "is to diffuse the slave population as much as possible and thus secure in the whole community the motives of self-interest for its support." Besides, it was believed that reviving the slave trade would enable the South to win the western territories for the planters. However, Virginia, with its large slave-exporting trade, denounced new foreign importations and the Whig party, reflecting the conservative planter's attitude, rejected the plan as disguised secessionist propaganda, too radical for Southern property interests. Therefore, the South itself killed this dangerous issue before the North could take action. Nevertheless, substantial "bootlegging" of Africans into the lower South did occur, with an estimated 15,000 entering in 1859 alone, according to Stephen A. Douglas who claimed to have seen 300 Africans in a slavepen in Memphis. Frank advertisements of Africans for sale appeared in the Southern press and Southern juries seemed loath to inflict the piracy penalty on patriotic slavers.

Even without a direct material stake in slavery, the yeoman farmer who did not have to compete with slave labor could accept the institution as an indispensable policing device. Slave insurrections and plots chronic since the days of the slave ship mutinies were facts not easily minimized, though the blame could be placed on free Negroes or, by those of short memory, on William Lloyd Garrison's militant abolitionist paper, *The Liberator*. Southern writers pointed out that within eight months of the founding of Garrison's paper in 1831 the Nat Turner insurrection broke out. A young lay preacher or "leader," Nat Turner of Southampton, Virginia, led slaves to kill fifty-five whites before his band was put down.

Most revealing is the slave insurrection panic of 1856, which gripped the South during the exciting Frémont-Buchanan election, in which the "Black Republicans" had nominated their first presidential candidate, while Dixie extremists threatened secession if Frémont won. Gossip and evidence forcibly taken from slaves suggested that in one slaveholding community after another, from Texas to Florida, the Negroes were plotting a general slave in-

surrection in the event that Frémont was defeated. Local mobs
lynched suspected plotters when the courts were too slow in hanging the Negro leaders. Little wonder, therefore, that John Brown's
seizure of the arsenal at Harpers Ferry, Virginia, intended as a
prelude to a general slave uprising, angered the South as a deliberate plot of the North to incite the long-dreaded race war.
Planters and yeoman farmers could easily unite on this issue.

This charged atmosphere, intensified by frontier influences, made
violence all too prevalent even in settled communities. Gentlemen, of course, like the rival editors of two Richmond newspapers,
the *Enquirer* and the *Whig*, could shoot it out on the dueling field.
This reflected the bitter personal note in Southern journalism.
Henry Clay and W. L. Yancey were among the better-known duel-
ists of the South. In Georgia the frail Alexander H. Stephens was
stabbed eighteen times by a local lawyer and saved his life only
by grasping the knife blade aimed at his throat. A German musician, visiting Mobile in 1846, wrote of a petty dispute between
two Creoles that almost became murder: "The adversaries, without any regard for the crowd in which they found themselves,
and at the risk of wounding innocents, reached into their pockets
and each drew out a revolver. They exchanged a dozen shots in
the open street and the fight did not end until one of them fell
with a shattered shoulder... No one was astonished at this im-
promptu duel..." For the North, such violence was taken as
typical, particularly after the brutal and nearly fatal caning of
Charles Sumner in the Senate chamber by young Preston Brooks
of South Carolina—a deed for which his state honored him in a
celebration although certain Northern bystanders, too, had stood
by in the Senate without interfering.

The camp meeting revivalist tradition of Kentucky and Tennessee, although affecting both North and South, took on added
fervor amid the frontier and rural conditions of the Southwest
particularly, giving impetus in numbers and orthodoxy to Methodists, Baptists, and Presbyterians. Churches took over many
schools and colleges in the South such as Emory College (1836),
molding them after the pattern of the "old-time religion." The

non-revivalist Southern churches such as the Episcopalian, Lutheran, Quaker, and Catholic trailed behind the communicants of the camp meeting cults.

But while the radical religious and secular panaceas thrived even in the rural North—Mormons, Shakers, Perfectionists, Fourierists, and other such groups—the erstwhile radical South of Jefferson's day turned conservative. There were few Unitarian or Universalist churches in the South. Of 257 Unitarian churches in the nation, only three were in the South and of 634 Universalist churches, only about twenty existed below Mason and Dixon's line. The radical "isms" no longer thrived there; the few Southern abolitionists like the Quaker Grimke sisters, James Birney, a former slaveholder of Alabama, and Moncure D. Conway of Virginia hastened North, away from the narrowing horizon of Jefferson Davis' land. A North Carolina Quaker, Levi Coffin, moved to Indiana and organized the vast radical network of the famous Underground Railroad, establishing friendly "stations," including sewing circles, to take care of the destitute slaves. However, the Southern churches did encourage the temperance movement and Southern humanitarians responded to the pleas of Dorothea Dix before their state legislatures by building asylums for the insane and modern schools for the deaf.

In this sectional, evangelical, proslavery atmosphere, the Southern white grew increasingly intolerant of abolitionist and religious heresies. Logically enough, considering this emphasis, the churches led the procession to disunion, although the challenge came from the Northern churches. In 1845, Baptists split along the Mason and Dixon line in a controversy regarding the refusal of the antislavery faction to allow a slaveholder to act as a missionary. Out of this cleavage was born the Southern Baptist Convention. A year later, after antislavery Methodists had forbidden a slaveowning Georgia bishop to exercise his office, Southern delegates organized the Methodist Episcopal Church, South—a schism destined to endure almost a century. By the late 1850's Southern Presbyterians, too, broke with their Northern brethren on the slavery issue and organized the United Synod of the Presbyterian Church.

Catholics and smaller denominations managed to remain intact, but they, too, had to make concessions to the etiquette of white supremacy and the exigencies of the slavery cause.

3

By 1850, the Southern highlanders had become a substantial white minority group and their isolation in the southern Appalachians was now undisturbed by any major population movements through the mountains. While the successful farmers had taken up the valleys and lowlands, the highlanders were forced back upon the isolated mountainsides and peaks where they earned a scanty living from the poor soil and by hunting and fishing. As each generation subdivided its lands to provide for married descendants, the standard of living went down. Descendants of the pioneer English, Scotch-Irish, and German settlers who overflowed Pennsylvania, Virginia, and the Carolinas, these highlanders had scarcely emerged from the eighteenth century and their culture was largely a blend of old British folk traits and the religious evangelism of the Baptists and the Methodists. Their children might be named after Reformation heroes or classical poets like Homer, Vergil, and Pliny, and some even possessed copies of the classics proudly inscribed by their colonial ancestors, but many could not read and their culture revolved about an oral tradition in true folk style.

However simple his house and however backward his education, the highlander, like the Scottish clansman, had a fierce sense of independence. In isolation he preserved feudal attitudes toward family honor and obeyed the traditional code that required him to seek out the enemy who insulted any member of his family and exterminate him and his adult male relatives and descendants until a truce was arranged. Shooting in the back, treachery, and ambush were sanctioned in such clan feuds. In the Baker-White blood feud of 1844 in Clay County, Kentucky, which originated over an adultery case, the aggrieved husband provoked a war that flared up in successive generations with pitched battles fought even as late as 1901 and 1932.

Outsiders who later discovered the highlander were fascinated by his store of long-forgotten English and Scottish ballads, his distinctive folk dances, his handicrafts, and his folkways. All Southerners, it must be pointed out, liked to sing and antebellum songs included hundreds of improvisations based on the old ballads. There was "Lord Randall" in which a girl kills her sweetheart with "a cold cup of pizen"; and in "Edward," the distraught boy confesses that the telltale blood on his coat belonged to his brother. Whites and Negroes sang improvisations on the English themes of frustrated love, matchless bravery, and cruel blood feuds. Southerners even exchanged ballads and folk tales with New Englanders, as scholars later discovered. While whites in the minstrel shows affected Negro song, dialect, and humor, the Southern Negro sang the secular songs of the white community with original rhythmic versions of work songs and religious melodies. The rediscovery of the Southern highlander in the twentieth century offered an insight into the musical and folk expression of the entire Old South.

Ranking below the highlander and even ridiculed by the slaves as "po' white trash" and "buckra" were about 1,000,000 poor whites of the decaying rural slums of the South. Isolated among the abandoned or undesirable lands of the plantation states were the "sand-hillers" and "pineywood tackies" of the Georgia and South Carolina pine barrens and woods; the "red necks" and "crackers" of Georgia and the Gulf region; the "wool hats" of the South Carolina back country and the "clay-eaters" of other scattered areas; even in French Louisiana there was the large shiftless element among the "Cajuns," descendants of Longfellow's Acadians in the day of Evangeline and Gabriel.

The poor white dwelt in a primitive single-room and windowless log cabin furnished with a filthy bed or two and equipped with the indispensable frying pan or skillet. He eked out a living by hunting with his mangy cur, by fishing, or by planting a few patches of corn, potatoes, and tobacco and raising a few chickens.

The razorback hogs that ran wild in the woods supplied lean pork for his daily diet. Though both man and beast appeared emaciated, it was difficult to starve in the well-provisioned Southern country. The year-round mild climate made the struggle for existence far easier than in the inclement North and did not tax one's ingenuity for planning ahead. But "90 degrees in the shade" combined with disease and lack of opportunity reduced the poor white's physical movements to absolute essentials, giving the impression of ingrained laziness and mental torpor, and cut down his speech to a painfully slow drawl.

Hookworm, growing out of the larvae of worms living in infected feces in the soil, played havoc among the barefoot poor whites, penetrating even the unbroken skin and seriously enervating the victim until anaemia and malnutrition set in. The disease gave him a craving for dirt or clay—hence the term "clay-eater"—and a bony, awkward, pot-bellied appearance. While relatively few were as degenerate as Erskine Caldwell's Jeeter Lester in *Tobacco Road*, they seemed hopelessly backward, and they nourished their pride on the supposed inferiority of the Negro. They, thank God, did not "work like a nigger" and could relax among their homemade potations of whisky and pass around the "red eye" untroubled by masters or discipline. As early as 1736, William Byrd II had written of this peculiar psychology: "They [the Negroes] blow up the pride and ruin the industry of our white people, who, seeing a rank of poor creatures below them, detest work for fear it should make them look like slaves." Because of slave competition, wages for white farm hands in the South were extremely low.

But the tragedy of it all was that the poor white *could* work and do it well under less discouraging conditions. Already in several cotton factories of the South, such as that of Daniel Pratt, a Northerner operating a plant near Montgomery, and in William Gregg's textile factory in South Carolina, the poor whites were found to be definitely salvageable. Many of them worked hard in the turpentine industry among the pine forests of central Alabama. The potentialities of this class were to be further revealed in the

New South when the expanding cotton mills absorbed thousands of them.

Meanwhile, the poor white basked himself in the sun of racial superiority and sometimes identified himself with the upper white classes. When the Civil War came he was flattered to be solicited for army service and to wear a shiny new uniform, and he gave a good account of himself on the battlefield with his rifle. But military discipline irked him and he led the vanguard of deserters, bored with the prolonged war. Southern politicians, by flattering this class, built themselves a bulwark of personal power founded on the poor whites and their pineywoods constituency. One oft-repeated story still worth retelling is of the eastern Mississippi congressional campaign of Franklin E. Plummer. When one candidate ingratiated himself with parents by industriously kissing babies, the other walked over to pick up a babe and proceeded to "lay it across his lap, turn over its little petticoat, and go to hunting red bugs." This enchanted the proud parents! There was now no question of whom the father would vote for. The native humor of the poor whites, enriched by a crude frontier flavor, gave Southern literature, as Shields McIlwaine points out, its most original and indigenous flavor of the entire antebellum era. Their gander-pullings, orgiastic camp meetings, rough jokes, and localisms gave invaluable literary material to the scholarly Georgia humorist, Augustus B. Longstreet, for his boisterous dialect sketches in *Georgia Scenes* (1835).

4

The "mud-sill" of Southern society was, of course, the nearly 4,000,000 slaves working on the plantations and farms, or hired out as laborers in tobacco factories, mines, mills, and wharves. Living in slave cabins along the "street" away from the master's house and given an annual maintenance worth about $40, they were rewarded with minor incentives in clothes, trinkets, payments, extra time for their own little garden patch, and hunting and other privileges. Some learned skilled trades on the self-sufficient plantation and enjoyed a higher status than their fellows. But they were

largely subject to the whims of their master, unlike the feudal serf
to whom well-established custom usually gave certain securities
against the lord. For example, while the lenient French black code
forbade masters to sell young children of slaves apart from their
mothers and allowed slaves to hold their own property, these concessions outside of Louisiana depended too often on the kindness
of the master. Custom had protected feudal serfs in these matters.
"We are yours, but the land is ours," ran the medieval argument of
the serf who felt the security of established tenure. While visitors
to the South usually found no first-hand evidence of brutality—and
Horace Greeley's reporters as well as antislavery visitors were avidly
searching for this—the court and newspaper records do reveal many
such cases.

It would seem that men in their right minds would not impair
the value of slaves worth possibly as much as $2000, and indeed,
the planters often treated their slaves well for that very reason.
Frederick Law Olmstead, a careful observer visiting the South in
the 1850's, watched Irishmen on a ship at Mobile being given the
most dangerous tasks in loading 400-pound cotton bales while slaves
were assigned to safer jobs. A ship's officer explained, "The niggers
are worth too much to be risked here; if the Paddies are knocked
overboard, or get their backs broke, nobody loses anything!" James
D. B. De Bow, editor of *De Bow's Review* and for a time a federal
superintendent of the census, cited figures to prove that Negro
mortality was higher in Philadelphia than in Charleston. He published model plantation rules governing the treatment of slaves. One
Mississippi planter, for example, forbade his overseer to work Negroes in the rain or to keep them out after nightfall except when
necessary for weighing or putting away cotton. Labor was forbidden
on the Sabbath, and punishments for crime were often tempered
by the fact that it seemed to make no sense to execute a valuable
slave or to put him away for life.

Some planters had almost saintly records in dealing with their
slaves and perhaps thousands, like Alexander Stephens, could even
claim the love of their household retinue. Former Governor Aiken
of South Carolina, who owned a magnificent 1500-acre rice planta-

tion worth $380,000 at least, lived himself in a plain cottage surrounded by shrubbery, while treating his 700 Negroes as well as slavery could possibly permit. They occupied clean double frame houses with two or three rooms for each family and had available two general hospitals and a lying-in hospital. In Mississippi, Jefferson Davis took pride in his kindly and successful supervision of slaves, allowing them unusual autonomy. Slave juries tried petty offenders among their race on the Davis plantation Southern defenders never wearied of pointing out that slaves were cared for in sickness and in health, in old age and in infancy, and that the master watched over his flock like a father. On a Sunday afternoon or at a Negro funeral the stranger might be startled by observing long processions of well-dressed colored men and women promenading. Some of the clothes were, of course, cast-offs from the Big House, others came from second-hand shops, still others were new garments bought in nearby towns with earnings gained in spare time.

Once the slave accepted his status and obeyed his master uncritically—striking back at a white man even in self-defense was a crime—interracial contacts might progress far beyond the most tolerant customs of the North. Olmsted watched black and white children playing together and Negro women carrying both black and white babies together in their arms. The Mammy acting as wet nurse for white children was a familiar plantation figure. The races need not separate in public conveyances provided the Negro was a servant of the traveling master or mistress. On this point Olmsted concluded, "Where the negro is definitely a slave, it would seem that the alleged natural antipathy of the white race to associate with him is lost." This situation recalls the story of the quick-witted Southern Negro woman in more recent times who managed to retain her seat in the white section of a "Jim Crow" railroad car by hastily donning a servant's apron.

The practice of hiring out slaves gave Negroes some measure of independence, often allowing them the privilege of selecting their own employers and bargaining for their services. In the Virginia tobacco factories, where intelligence and skill were expected, qualified slaves could count on far better treatment and pay than as field

hands. Charles Dickens was impressed by the excellent morale of
the slaves in the Richmond factories and warehouses and enjoyed
their spirituals and their lively tunes.

But slavery, for all its mitigating factors, left a heavy blight of
social disorganization upon the Negro family. While the amount of
slave breeding was undoubtedly exaggerated by abolitionists, there
were some instances of it; this practice suggests, at least, the
peculiarly influential role of the master in the most intimate aspects
of Negro life. The rape of a female slave was not a crime but a
violation of chattel laws if the assailant was an outside white; besides, Negroes could not give testimony against whites. With the
burden of family responsibility removed from the male Negro, the
matriarchal tendencies in Negro family life were enhanced. Polygamy, promiscuity, and miscegenation involving slave girls and the
master's sons were often ignored as long as the plantation regime
moved smoothly. While public opinion frowned on the practice of
breaking up slave families, a bankrupt master usually found it expedient to sell as few or as many Negroes as the purchaser required.
The economic stability of the Negro family was injured by the time
freedom came by the careless habits learned in plantation slavery,
which offered too few incentives for steady work habits. To labor
overzealously in the fields merely encouraged the overseer to raise
the standard of output expected.

Although Southern public opinion and the planter's self-interest
reacted against brutality toward the slaves, it is plain that a regime
in which Negroes could not testify in court or bring charges against
masters could scarcely escape cruel deeds by irresponsibles. Besides, there is ample evidence of such devices of repression as white
patrols, curfews, exemplary hangings or beatings, the requirement
that slave gatherings be supervised by a white, and the psychological ritual of white-man supremacy. These police measures were
strengthened after insurrections or rumors of one, or after slave
crimes against masters (and there were many of these). Runaway
Negroes were hounded and advertised for like any escaped felon,
if not exactly in the melodramatic style described in *Uncle Tom's
Cabin*. Not infrequently free Negroes were enslaved, for the burden

of proof of free status rested upon the black. Negro illiteracy, as we have seen, was more the product of white fears of black conspirators who could read and write than of local poverty. As for life in the slave quarters, all too few planters were as progressive as kindly Governor Aiken. The *Southern Cultivator* described the slave huts in these blunt words, "Small, low, tight and filthy, their houses can be but laboratories of disease; whilst on every side grow weeds..." Altogether, slavery in the South would have required a community of saints to make the peculiar institution as humane as the proslavery propagandists claimed it to be.

The lot of the free Negro was not a happy one in Illinois, Indiana, or California, where attempts were made to exclude him; but in the South, where he was regarded as an incendiary influence upon slaves, it was often impossible. Virginia's leadership in the colonization movement fostered a fond hope in the border states that all Negroes could eventually be shipped back to Africa. That state and others in the South by the 1850's encouraged a form of peonage for free Negroes under local authorities, offered assisted emigration, and opened the way for his re-enslavement by a system of petition. Because most states had begun to forbid manumission without exile, several hundred free Negroes turned slaveholder and bought their own relatives and friends as slaves. There was, however, a small, relatively prosperous class of craftsmen, among them barbers, mechanics, carpenters, masons, blacksmiths, as well as farmers and fishermen.

That the life of the Negro remained effervescent is a tribute to his elasticity of spirit rather than to the humaneness of slavery. His festivities were colorful in their originality and flavor in French New Orleans, where the processions and dances of the carnival season, blending French, Catholic, and African elements, became a civic tradition. On Sundays at Congo Square whites stared at the spectacle of hundreds of Negroes of all ages leaping, swinging, and gliding to African rhythms, modified by French steps and tunes set to the measured beat of the drum. Upon their newly acquired Catholic faith were engrafted African magic, sorcery, and primitive religion. Most astonishing and awesome to the whites were the

Negro Voodoo cults of Louisiana. From West Africa and Haiti came
their serpent worship, the Voodoo doctor, and the powerful "queen
of the Voodoos," interesting in the world of spirits. Superstitious
slaves—and impressionable whites as well—bought the Voodoo
charms, amulets, love philters, and even poisons of the Voodoo
doctors and queens. Their meetings, festivals, orgiastic rites and
incantations were well known to the New Orleans press.

In the Cotton Kingdom, where Negro gatherings were suspect,
slave leaders developed their own African modifications of the
white man's religion within the existing Southern churches. That
the Negroes were not only apt pupils of the revivalists but improved
upon their techniques was emphatically attested by the bluestock-
ing wife of a South Carolina senator, Mary Chesnut, who confessed
in her diary how the words of a plantation Negro preacher carried
her away:

He became wildly excited, on his knees, facing us with his eyes shut.
He clapped his hands at the end of every sentence, and his voice rose
to the pitch of a shrill shriek, yet was strangely clear and musical, occasionally in a plaintive minor key that went to your heart. Sometimes
it rang out like a trumpet. I wept bitterly ... The Negroes sobbed and
shouted and swayed backward and forward, some with aprons to their
eyes, most of them clapping their hands and responding in shrill tones:
"Yes, God!" "Jesus!" "Savior!" ... I would very much have liked to shout
too ... Suddenly, as I sat wondering what next, they broke out into one
of those soul-stirring Negro camp-meeting hymns.

Blending the white spirituals of the camp meetings with the
African solo and chorus renditions, the plantation singers rang out
with their melancholy psalms and hymns and their improvised
folk-tale versions of the Bible stories as well as their rhythmic variations of more secular music. How much of the revivalist technique
was borrowed from Africa may only be conjectured. Rhythmic
hand-clapping and shouts were part of the white spiritual tradition.
However, West Africa had its cults of religious dancing under priests
governed by a hypnotic rhythm, marked by hand-clapping, shouts,
drum-beating, and the hysterical acts of the possessed. In their
singing was the beginning of the beautiful Negro spiritual that

matured in the late nineteenth century and became a distinctive part of American music. Professor Bell Wiley has identified some of the songs of freedom that Southern Negroes sang openly during the Civil War. One may perhaps infer such motives when Negroes rendered this famous spiritual:

Go down, Moses,
Way down in Egypt land,
Tell old Pharoah
Let my people go.

Slaveholders, who felt that slave religion and the emphasis on sin and future rewards helped stabilize the plantation system, would have been seriously disturbed had they suspected a subversive note in the moving songs.

5

Overshadowed by the sensational material progress of the North, the Southern states could still show substantial advances. Baltimore was a pioneer in both the canal and railroad era and the Charleston-Hamburg (S.C.) railroad line of 136 miles was in 1833 the longest railroad in the world. Senator Robert Y. Hayne of South Carolina was not only the Southern orator who debated with Webster in 1830 but also an economic planner who promoted transportation ties between his state and the Ohio Valley while his fellow-politician Calhoun directed part of his energies to a railroad link for Charleston across the Lower South. However, Southern state treasuries and their banks collapsed during the panic of 1837, carrying many promising projects down with them. Tennessee and Texas had practically no railroads before 1850 and Mississippi and Alabama had only a few. Rapid improvement in railroad building did take place during the 1850's although it was insufficient for the demands of war in 1861.

Before the California gold rush, North Carolina led the nation as a gold-producing state with a mint at Charlotte coining as much as $478,000 in a prosperous year. Increasingly appreciative of the industrial possibilities of the local water power and exceptionally cheap white labor, the state embarked on textile manufacture. *Niles National Register* reported in 1843, "A complete revolution in the trade in cotton yarns has been effected in North Carolina within a few years by the establishment of a number of factories in that state." By 1850, according to a rather optimistic estimate in *De Bow's Review,* there were 250 cotton mills south of Mason and Dixon Line consuming about 150,000 bales annually out of the half-million used in American home manufacturing. Tennessee led the South by 1840 in the making of pig iron, followed by Kentucky and Virginia. Alabama's industrial progress was impressive. Daniel Pratt, the wealthy industrialist of that state, owned an iron foundry besides a factory producing $160,000 worth of cotton gins a year, and a cotton factory employing 150 hands. By 1860, that state had fourteen cotton mills capitalized at $1,316,000 and a working force of 1312. Georgia, benefiting from rich diversified resources, the best railroad system in the South, and excellent leaders, including not a few Yankee mechanics, factory owners, and teachers, led the South in cotton manufacturing with $18,483,000 worth produced in 1860. Altogether, Southern industry, if not able to catch up with Northern factories and shops, seemed capable enough in 1861-65 of waging a major war against a superior foe for so many years. Something of the promise of the industrial New South was forecast in the antebellum years.

Beginning in 1830, industrialization as well as scientific farming were encouraged (as in the North) by the new agricultural societies, local, county, and statewide. These introduced the significant annual state fairs that not only offered prizes for cattle and improved farm methods, but also rewarded successful manufacturers and propagandized for economic diversification. *De Bow's Review* and the *Southern Cultivator,* both of the lower South, led in this agrarian-industrial renaissance; De Bow particularly was the most militant champion of an industrial South in his entire section, making his program part of a larger scheme for Southern nationalism. During this era, also, began the state agricultural and geological surveys, an important cooperative step toward scientific agriculture and the development of natural resources.

Yankees like Sergeant Prentiss of Maine, who became a pro-slavery Whig orator of Mississippi after marrying a planter's daughter, migrated in droves to the South to mend their fortunes long before "Carpetbagger" became an epithet for such outsiders. John A. Quitman, an Ohio lawyer, moved to Natchez at twenty-two and after building a plantation assumed the attitudes of a Southern imperialist and filibusterer, hungry for empire in the Caribbean. As one of the new aristocracy, he rose to become governor of Mississippi and a leader in sectional politics. While most foreigners preferred the free North to Dixie, many did come to the Southern cities, later furnishing Irish and German regiments to the Confederacy and quickening economic life. French Louisiana, especially New Orleans, scarcely belonged to the Anglo-Saxon South. One out of every three or four citizens was foreign-born in Natchez, Richmond, Memphis, Baltimore, Charleston, and Mobile. Europeans made up a good part of the mechanic's class in the South. Unions were few, because wages were often forced above the average in the North simply by the scarcity of skilled workmen. However, the unskilled Irishman, being thrown into competition with slave labor, seems to have been worse off than similar classes in the North.

The few cities of the South were mild exceptions to the rural nature of that section. Only New Orleans and Charleston, both outlets for the plantations of the lower South, compared in size with the great cities of New England and the Middle Atlantic States. St. Louis, Baltimore, and Washington were more Northern than Southern. New Orleans, an exotic Latin plant in the Anglo-Saxon South, could boast of its expansive trade, a bilingual press and literature, numerous libraries, an excellent school system, scientific societies, and a medical school. Here a former Charlestonian, James D. B. De Bow, who became a professor of political economy at the new University of Louisiana, managed after a struggle to keep his literary and commercial *De Bow's Review* alive. Such a project would have been quickly buried in Charleston, that graveyard of magazines. In the Delta were submerged, mosquito-breeding lands where cemeteries had to be built with tombs several stories above the ground; yellow fever was a perennial visitor. Still, New Orleans'

Charity Hospital, which admitted over 2800 yellow-fever patients in 1847 together with 1500 typhus and typhoid cases, claimed to be the largest fever hospital in the world.

Charleston, with its 43,000 citizens in 1850 could vie with New Orleans in traditions, society, cultural institutions, and beautiful subtropical flower gardens. In music there was the old trained St. Cecilia Society, in education, the College of Charleston, which was perhaps the first municipal college in the country, championing classical learning more than De Bow in New Orleans thought was desirable, and craftsmen attended the Apprentice's Library while others went to the century-old city library or the Museum. Unfortunately, Charleston emulated New Orleans' drawbacks too, especially in ghastly yellow-fever epidemics. Even worse were the defective water cisterns that left the city prey to the worst fires on the continent. In 1835, a fire destroyed about 60 houses; three years later one-third of the city was wiped out with insurance losses of $4,000,000. Only New York's great fire of 1845 could exceed this figure for losses.

Fanny Kemble, the English actress married to the planter Pierce Butler, felt more at home in Charleston than in any other Eastern city because of its surviving colonial architecture and old-fashioned atmosphere, though she was shocked by the large tumble-down slum districts. Eighteenth-century English Tudor mansions with wrought-iron gates and quaint English garden estates like "Runnymede" and "The Oaks," blossoming with magnolias, live oaks, and palmettos, added their charm to the Charleston of William Gilmore Simms and his literary circle. But in this pleasant town Fanny was startled to hear an ominous beating of drums and tolling of bells: the slave patrol was gathering to cope with a reported slave insurrection.

Richmond, future capital of the Confederacy and eastern commercial port and center for the tobacco business, had about 30,000 residents when Olmsted visited it in the 1850's. He sniffed at the little town with its unpaved though newly gaslit streets, its few sidewalks, and the cheap stucco imitation of granite in the Virginia State Capital designed by Jefferson. Olmsted failed to see newer cultural landmarks like the *Southern Literary Messenger* building, where Edgar Allan Poe had so recently held forth, the Virginia Mechanics Institute, the University of Richmond, and the picturesque details that had entranced Thackeray and even Dickens. Thackeray had lectured there in 1853 on eighteenth-century English literature, had spent considerable time at the *Messenger*, and had quite won the hearts of Richmond folk. He concluded that this town was the most picturesque in America. Dickens, wearing his brown suit and red cravat and accompanied by his shy wife, had visited in 1842 and, despite his obvious hostility to slavery, had thrilled the town with his presence. At the Swan Tavern lived the greatest actor of the day, Joseph Jefferson, manager of a stock company that performed at the Marshall Theatre. This young Philadelphia-born comedian, the third actor of that name in his famous theatrical family, was to find a permanent role for himself in 1859 when his version of the ne'er do well, Rip Van Winkle, captivated audience after audience in Washington and elsewhere. There were also the grim slave auctions and the slave-operated tobacco warehouse and ship chandlery, notorious during the Civil War as the Libby Prison.

Memphis, on the broad, rolling Mississippi, was rising in national importance in 1857 with its new railway connection to Charleston and the experimental navy yard constructed by Congress. As a center of the newly opened eastern Tennessee plantation lands, it grew very fast in the fifties, reaching a population total of 22,600 by the Civil War, but the town seemed too crudely western with its flashy gamblers, bawdy houses, homicidal boat crews, and bad hotels, to attract fastidious visitors. Mobile, whose cathedral recalled the fact that it had once been the capital of French Louisiana, had become largely Americanized as the commercial seaport center of Alabama and Mississippi, exporting a million bales of cotton in 1861. Local railroads met the advancing Illinois Central Railroad from Chicago. A Mardi Gras carnival second only to that of New Orleans and various other amusements drew planters of the Gulf states to that pleasant town of about 15,000 whites and 5000 slaves. Vigorous civic leaders were making real headway against the periodic epidemics of scarlet fever and dysentery by draining the local swamps, and De Bow claimed that Mobile had a far lower mortality rate than New York or Philadelphia.

The South, as we have seen, suffered from basic agrarian and class problems, some traceable to the inefficient and monopolistic one-crop system and slavery, and others due to the costliness of the marketing system. The tariff controversy of Jackson's day had been partly solved by the lower import duties of the forties and fifties, but Southern suspicions of sectional exploitation lingered on. Charleston, the pride of the old aristocracy, had failed to fulfill its early promise of becoming an industrial center and even New Orleans was far behind its extravagant forecasts. Northern industry and urban growth continued to outstrip the South at an accelerating rate. Imperceptibly, the conviction grew in Southern minds that the South was but a colonial province of Yankeedom, paying forced tribute to the banks, railroads, and middlemen of the North. Southern commercial conventions of the 1850's agitated for "direct trade" with Europe through enlarged Southern ports and ships, hoping to bypass New York, to reduce freight costs, and to escape high interest charges. Comparing their plight with that of the American colonies suffering under British mercantilism after 1763, the planter felt something of the revolutionary impulse of 1776—but it was the reactionary Calhoun rather than the liberal Jefferson and George Mason who inspired the new rebellion. And over 4,000,000 Negroes, 1,000,000 poor whites, and many small farmers had no genuine stake in the world that Jefferson Davis tried so vainly to preserve.

· 16 ·

Intellectual Trends
in Southern Nationalism

[1830-1861]

I

In the minds of hundreds of thousands of non-slaveholding Southerners who marched shoulder to shoulder with the planters for the
Lost Cause, the slavery causes of war were closely bound up with
a complex of related motives centering upon Southern nationalism.
State and local loyalties were particularly strong amongst rural
Southerners, and even transcended national ties, as in the case of
Robert E. Lee, who disliked both secession and slavery. Proslavery
arguments and abolitionist attacks had popularized the hateful
stereotype of the puritanical Yankee who had plotted to stir up race
wars in the South and was now invading the chivalric Southland. The
antagonisms of a conservative agrarian people against a liberal,
urban, industrial society had been spurred on by a belief that tariff
beneficiaries and Northern banks had artfully exploited the wealth
of the South. The Unionist traditions of Washington, Jackson, and
Jefferson were not dead, but quiescent; the secessionists were to
seize power in the state conventions of 1861 under the guise of
outraged Southern nationalism.

In 1829, at Virginia's constitutional convention the parting of the
ways was symbolized as three distinguished but aged members took
their seats among younger statesmen who had lost their enthusiasm

for Jefferson's philosophy. James Madison, James Monroe, and John Marshall, surviving Jefferson, awakened momentary cheers; but in the convention and outside were those like President Thomas R. Dew of the College of William and Mary who questioned the liberal tradition and called for a realistic acceptance of slavery as a perpetual institution. John Marshall, Chief Justice of the Supreme Court since 1801, looked back with satisfaction upon a generation of judicial statesmanship in which he had immeasurably strengthened the sovereignty of the nation over the states and the power of commerce and industry over agriculture. In economic philosophy, he was a Hamiltonian and an old-line Federalist, suspicious of majorities and mindful of property rights; he had added to the sacredness of contracts in such cases as *Dartmouth College* v. *Woodward* and *Fletcher* v. *Peck*. Like Adam Smith and Madison he believed emphatically that self-interest was the pivot of human motives. He had built a protecting rampart around the rights of property that at times encroached upon the rights of the community. Conditioning his background was the fact that he was a conservative businessman, a bank director, and a leading legal adviser in property cases. In the Virginia Convention, he saved the eastern conservatives from utter rout by offering timely, but inconsequential, suffrage concessions to the landless faction.

Yet Marshall was a major architect of American nationalism, as most of his precedent-making cases prove. Ironically, his broad interpretation of commerce in *Gibbons* v. *Ogden* as something far greater than mere buying and selling was later to serve the champions of a "welfare state" as a precedent for passing far-reaching social legislation. As a nationalist, he stood courageously for the rights of the Cherokee as wards of the nation against Jackson and the Georgia frontier. Despite his high respect for property, he disliked slavery as a divisive force in the American Union and worked actively for a plan to colonize the Negroes in Liberia. In his old age, he was still engaged in putting down sectionalism and in reconciling extremists to a peaceful continuation of the Union.

When he died in 1835, another Southerner, Roger B. Taney of Maryland, a vigorous Jacksonian, succeeded him. In his own state, young Taney had attracted attention in the Jacob Gruber case for his willingness to defend a man believed to be guilty of inciting a slave revolt. As Jackson's secretary of the treasury he had angered conservatives by carrying out the President's directive of removing government deposits from the United States bank. For this, apparently, he was rewarded by Jackson with the highest judicial office in the nation. On the bench he pleased Jacksonians by his modification of Marshall's strict contract doctrines, strengthening the state's "police powers" over individual rights. In the noted case, *Charles River Bridge* v. *Warren Bridge* (1837), involving the question of whether a state grant (or contract) to build a bridge had been impaired by a later legislative grant for a competing bridge, Taney modified the strict contract doctrine of Marshall's Dartmouth case. He rejected the assumed monopolistic rights of the original grantee on the ground that no state could be presumed to surrender indefinitely its right to advance the public interest; thus he established the principle that legislative grants are to be construed narrowly in favor of the state. "While the rights of private property are sacredly guarded," he said, "we must not forget that the community also have rights."

The famous—or notorious—Dred Scott decision demolished Taney's reputation among liberals in the North. In this case he had to decide whether the slave Dred Scott of Missouri was freed after he had been taken to Illinois, a free state under the Northwest Ordinance, and then to Wisconsin Territory, free under the Missouri Compromise of 1820. Taney, in a lengthy historical review, tried to prove that Negroes were never considered to be citizens of either the state or the nation and hence could not sue in the courts. Professing to describe the state of public opinion in 1776 regarding "that unfortunate race," he used words that were needlessly offensive, "They had for more than a century before been regarded as beings of an inferior order; and altogether unfit to associate with the white race, either in social or political relations; and so far inferior that they had no rights which the white man was bound to respect; and that the negro might justly and lawfully be reduced to slavery for his benefit." Here Taney overlooked the humanitarian tide in the Negro's favor that had already begun under the colonial Quakers, spreading to the Virginia slaveholders themselves. Even worse was Taney's conclusion, which thoroughly upheld the contentions of Calhoun and Jefferson Davis that slavery as a form of private property was protected by the Fifth Amendment against unfriendly national legislation. This dismayed the Republicans whose new party was founded on the assumption that Congress could prevent the extension of slavery. The Marylander, who could find evidence for the constitutionality of Jackson's antibank acts and could justify the rights of the community against the sacred contract clause, failed to show any judicial ingenuity in favor of human freedom—though two colleagues could.

Symptomatic of the conservative revolution in the South was the conversion of the gaunt, humorless, Scotch-Irish statesman and planter, John C. Calhoun of South Carolina, from his early nationalism to rigid States' rights and nullification. By the thirties, Charleston had given up its hopes of considerable industrial eminence, and the drop in cotton prices had precipitated a crisis in which Southerners could no longer tolerate a high protective tariff at the expense largely of Southern imports. As vice-president under Jackson, Calhoun could not follow the nationalism of his leader and prepared his belligerent "South Carolina Exposition" on nullification, denouncing the tariff law as unconstitutional and offering a mode of redress. Calhoun now argued that the Union was a product of individual sovereign states which had delegated certain powers to their agent, the federal government, and that, therefore, even a single state could rightfully nullify a usurping action by the general government. Daniel Webster, on the other hand, made it clear in his debates with Hayne that the Union was a product of the *whole people,* not of the states as such. Following Calhoun, South Carolina passed an ordinance of secession and was halted in its course of resistance only by the determination of Jackson, the hesitation of other Southern states, and the prompt action of peacemakers.

To suit his times Calhoun constructed a political theory that warred upon Jeffersonian liberalism, root and branch, and developed many of the most militant proslavery arguments. With him slavery ceased to be a necessary evil but became a positive good, far superior to Northern wage slavery. "Many in the South once believed it [slavery] was a moral and political evil," he declared in 1838. "That folly and delusion are gone." Liberty can only be enjoyed by the truly equal—certainly not by the poor laboring class.

Like many eighteenth-century philosophers Calhoun believed that extreme selfishness was rooted in man's nature and therefore government must be strong enough to control him. He denounced the compact theories of Locke and Jefferson, which presupposed that men were created equal in a state of nature and manufactured governments only for the convenience of better preserving the "unalienable rights" of life, liberty, and property. Governments were to him as organic as plants and therefore the social compact theory was a myth. His doctrine of the "concurrent, or constitutional majority" meant to replace the "numerical majority" with one in which an economic minority could veto the acts of the majority—"considering the community as made up of different and conflicting interests as far as the action of the government is concerned; and takes the sense of each, through its majority or appropriate organ, and the united sense of all, as the sense of the entire community." A later generation would call this "functional representation" but as Calhoun presented it, the minority rights of the propertied—particularly those of the slaveholding planter—were safe against any winds of public opinion or community needs by the veto of a single interest. Such a theory offered no protection for the legal rights of racial or cultural minorities or for any liberal program of civil liberties. Men are born unequal and from this inequality stem differences of wealth and a potential class struggle that government must prevent by protecting the propertied from the envious assaults of the majority. Calhoun in his "concurrent majority" had deserted the Declaration of Independence for the feudal class doctrines of the Polish magnates whom he had apparently studied; they had allowed the veto ("liberum veto") of a single magnate to halt legislation that endangered his property interests and privileges.

By the time of his death in 1850, the year of his speech on the admission of California, Calhoun was ready to challenge the North on slavery, secession, and civil war. "At all events," he asserted, "the responsibility of saving the Union rests on the North, and not on the South. If you are unwilling we should part in peace, tell us so, and we shall know what to do, when you reduce the question to submission or resistance." Calhoun had guided the South down the path of secession and war; younger men were to take up his cause.

2

The intellectual tragedy of the South was the waste of mental energies in the intense effort to justify slavery and to exalt Southern nationalism. A morbid emphasis on proslavery themes diverted native talent to a blind alley of achievement; besides, the rural South lacked publishers and its heavy illiteracy handicapped creative literature.

Southern writers wasted their talents in defending an anachronism. Not only had slavery long ago disappeared in the North, but the British Empire had freed its slaves in the nearby Caribbean in 1833 and her example was soon followed by France. During the latter 1850's, even Russia began with a series of edicts that finally abolished serfdom by 1861. Mexico had abolished slavery in 1829 and other Latin American states adopted various measures of emancipation, leaving Cuba and Brazil to save the South from complete isolation by antislavery countries. Meanwhile, chronic revolutions in Haiti and the memory of the race war nightmare that had inaugurated that republic discouraged or frightened slaveholders. The "back to Africa" movement, sponsored by the colonization societies, seemed so futile a solution that another door to escape was closed for the South. By 1850, the articulate South was militantly aroused in defense of its institutions, a "conscious minority," as one writer puts it, isolated in the liberal Western world, which had shifted from fixed status for labor to freedom of contract.

Most uncompromising among the proslavery writers was the group associated with James D. B. De Bow. Like Calhoun and numerous other militants, De Bow idealized the "Greek democracy" among the whites of the South. "No white man at the South," he argued in

The Interest in Slavery of the Southern Non-Slaveholder, "serves another as a body servant, to clean his boots, wait on his table, and perform the menial services of his household." Proudly he boasted of the homogeneous Anglo-Saxon stock of the white Southerner and his freedom from "all the absurd and degrading isms which have sprung up in the rank soil of infidelity." De Bow, as already noted, worked actively for the revival of the African slave trade to diffuse slaves among the underprivileged whites. His writings as well as *De Bow's Review* championed Southern nationalism in almost every aspect, calling for an industrialized, more self-sufficient South, Southern textbooks, a Southern literature, and finally secession.

His most prolific and militant contributor was the Virginia lawyer, George Fitzhugh, author of *Sociology for the South* and *Cannibals All!* and contributing editor for the *Richmond Examiner* and the *Richmond Enquirer.* Personally kindly and affable, somewhat introspective in manner, he nevertheless ground out the most aggressive propaganda against "the failure of free society." Like Calhoun, he rejected the entire liberal philosophy of Jefferson, including the Virginia Bill of Rights and the Declaration of Independence. More logically consistent than most proslavery writers, he identified liberalism with *laissez-faire* in economics and denounced free competition as a jungle idea of the devil-take-the-hindmost variety that sanctioned a perpetual class war. He argued that the Negro was racially inferior to the white and would be destroyed if he tried to compete with the Caucasian under a *laissez-faire* system. Only some kind of patriarchal system based on a permanently servile rank for the Negro would protect him from the consequences of a class war.

Fitzhugh stressed the phrase, "slavery principle," using it in a sense similar to Marx's idea of the class struggle as the dominant theme of history. He tried to show that some form of slavery or serfdom, of master and servant relationship, had been universal in society until modern *laissez-faire* times. "Liberty and Equality are new things under the sun," he wrote. "The free states of antiquity abounded with slaves. The feudal system that supplanted Roman institutions changed the form of slavery, but brought with it neither liberty nor equality." This was his central argument in his pamphlet, *Slavery Justified*, which urged the re-enslavement of the free Negroes in the South. Like Carlyle, whose sneers at British abolitionism and liberalism convinced Southerners that he was one of them at heart, Fitzhugh dwelt upon the growing slums, the starvation, and the human degradation among the factory workers of England under an unregulated competitive system. *Laissez-faire* left Ireland to starve and France and Germany to flounder about in recurrent revolutions; hence socialism was making advances everywhere amid the collapse of free society. Believing that only cheap western lands acted as a safety valve for Northern unrest, he felt that eventually the evil consequences of *laissez-faire* must descend upon the Yankees. In an editorial for the *Richmond Enquirer* of May 6, 1856, he presented the conflict of *laissez-faire* liberalism against slavery in language that may have influenced a certain interested reader, Abraham Lincoln, whose later House-Divided speech echoes this thought from an anti-slavery viewpoint:

Social forms so widely differing as those of domestic slavery, and (attempted) universal liberty, cannot long co-exist in the Great Republic of Christendom. They cannot be equally adapted to the wants and interests of society. The one form or the other must be very wrong. . . . The war between the two systems rages everywhere, and will continue to rage till the one conquers and the other is exterminated. . . . We do not hope, nor wish to see slavery like ours introduced at the North. There is no room for the black slaves, and we never wish to see white men made slaves. But we do hope, and expect, and believe that conservative men everywhere are about to adopt the principle that men should be governed, not "Let Alone," and that each one should be governed according to his wants, and moral and intellectual capacity.

After the Civil War, Fitzhugh was to carry his war upon the competitive system to the extreme of sanctioning monopolistic business.

Fitzhugh had a greater influence than even he imagined. Lincoln, Charles Sumner, and William Lloyd Garrison took his extreme statements to be typical of the South's advanced position and quoted him at length. Frémont-for-President clubs distributed leaflets in 1856 with Fitzhugh's favorite assertion, "Slavery is the natural and normal condition of the laboring man, whether white or black." A careful examination of the slavery debates in Congress during the 1850's shows that Fitzhugh's writings were more often referred to by the antislavery members than those of any other proslavery propagandist except Calhoun, though the speakers were not always aware of his authorship. A Republican leader, Senator James R. Doolittle of Wisconsin, expressed a common antislavery view that Fitzhugh's doctrines were typical of the South, "You [the South] have not until within the last few years assumed the doctrine that the natural and normal condition of the laboring man is that of a slave." So, also, said Senator Sumner and his colleague Henry Wilson of Massachusetts. In the House this belief was echoed by the Republicans Sidney Edgerton of Ohio and Henry Waldron of Michigan. When war came, Union pamphlets quoted Fitzhugh's ideas frequently as illustrative of the war aims of the South—white laborers as well as Negroes were to be enslaved.

Among the rank weeds of slavery was the stimulus given to racialist thinking in the South. Since legal competency depended on one's complexion, it was necessary to define a Negro. One South Carolina lawyer, reviewing the diverse laws determining Negro racial purity, advised, "When the blood is one-quarter or more African, the jury must find the party a mulatto." But he recommended that juries ought to consider individuals with less than one-eighth Negro blood as white. Proslavery writers usually assumed that intelligent Negroes were probably part-white in ancestry and that Africa's backwardness through the centuries proved the incapacity of blacks to create a high culture.

One of De Bow's most famous colleagues at the University of Louisiana was Dr. Josiah C. Nott, professor of anatomy. He was co-author with George R. Gliddon of *Types of Mankind* (1854), a racialist work that maintained that all races of men sprang from different permanent types and that the Negro belonged to an inferior type. In 1856, Nott helped to edit an American translation of *The Moral and Intellectual Diversity of Races* written by the French racialist, Count Joseph Arthur de Gobineau, whose book was to become a major authority in Hitler's Germany for the Nazi doctrines of "Aryan" superiority—the latter term borrowed from Gobineau and his school. Proslavery anthropological science, as represented by Dr. Samuel A. Cartwright of Louisiana, tried to demonstrate that the Negro's inferiority stemmed from the "fact" that he consumed less oxygen than whites.

Southern laymen echoed these opinions in the magazines. Fitzhugh and others were converted to the truths of racialism by the book, *Negroes and Negro Slavery* by Dr. John H. Van Evrie of New York. Van Evrie's "science" had still more of the Nott-Gliddon type of proslavery illustration and, though attracting Northern sympathizers, too, had its real ovation in the South, notably from Nott, Cartwright, Fitzhugh, Jefferson Davis, and Alexander Stephens. While popular prejudices, North and South, had long assumed the inherent inferiority of Negroes, the new racial science, at a time of growing humanitarianism, lent its prestige to the lore of the illiterate. Fitzhugh, who reviewed enthusiastically the books of both Gobineau and Van Evrie, added his own myth of the superior blood of the Cavaliers from whom Southerners were descended, as against the fanatical Puritans who begat the tribe of Yankees. "The gentlemen of the South," he wrote proudly, ". . . have the lofty sentiments and high morals of a master race." When Stephens became Vice-President of the Confederacy, he was to echo Fitzhugh:

Our new government is founded upon . . . the great truth that the negro is not equal to the white man; that slavery—subordination to the superior race—is his natural and normal condition.

Long after slavery died the everyday etiquette of white-man supremacy was based heavily on the assumptions of racialist thinking. Those who subscribed to the myth of a Cavalier South and the cult of chivalry were in many instances not averse to the notion that they belonged to a superior race.

Proslavery thought definitely turned Southern speculation toward the creation of a possible science of society, ostensibly based on the inductive principles of Francis Bacon, but, in reality, a pseudo social science that could rationalize slavery as an eternal principle. Already during the years between 1830 and 1842, Auguste Comte, French "father of sociology," had published his epochal six-volume *Cours de Philosophie Positive* but the most extensive analysis in the United States of this philosophy of positivism was made by a Southern scholar, George Frederick Holmes of Virginia. The son of an English slaveholder in British Guiana, something of a youthful prodigy in his brief college career at the University of Durham, he had left his home after a family quarrel and had wandered for several years through Canada and the United States, training himself for law. Failing to find a legal practice, he had turned his unusually erudite mind to history, political economy, and literature, teaching at various Southern colleges and, during the years 1857-97, serving on the staff of the University of Virginia. Holmes had long speculated in numerous articles upon the possibility of creating an inductive science of society that would integrate every phase of man's history and thought. Since liberal doctrines, in such forms as abolitionism, secularism, and *laissez-faire,* he thought, were disintegrating traditional society, the time seemed ripe for a sociology allied to a sound Aristotelian philosophy that could prescribe the cure for current social evils. However sympathetic he felt toward Comte—and Comte himself entered into an enthusiastic correspondence with him—he objected to positivism as too secular. Yet he went so far as to write Comte:

Throw out altogether the consideration of matters supernatural, segregate from the range of contemplation, as well as discussion, the whole circle of religious topics, not as untrue, but as being beyond the prescribed horizon, and I am even now a sincere positivist, in spirit, aim, and even mode of procedure, and have long been so.

Especially significant is the fact that Holmes' "sociology," unlike that of his proslavery contemporaries, outlasted the Civil War, though it bore the impress of the antebellum ideological struggle. In 1882, he was to publish one of the earliest college textbooks in sociology, *The Science of Society,* which had a remarkably sound framework in many respects; it even escaped the extreme individualism of Herbert Spencer and the fallacies of the social evolutionists which then dominated the thinking of William Graham Sumner of Yale and his numerous followers.

Holmes preceded Fitzhugh in developing the notion that Aristotle sanctioned slavery as part of an organic social order in which governments grew as a natural offshoot of society, not by an artificial social compact as described by Jefferson and the liberals. Fitzhugh's *Sociology for the South* (1854) revealed the influence of Holmes. This book and another proslavery work, *A Treatise on Sociology* (1854), written by Henry Hughes of Mississippi and appearing simultaneously, were probably the first titles in English to bear the word "sociology." Thus slavery apologetics had some incidental relationship to the emergence of sociology in this country. However, the North had its "sociologists" too, notably the eccentric and amazingly erudite Stephen Pearl Andrews of New York, a philosophical anarchist who published *The Science of Society* in 1851; this was a brief outline of a sociological system based on unrestricted individualism allowing only for voluntary forms of cooperation. Strangely enough, Andrews even corresponded with Holmes and Fitzhugh, meeting the latter in New York in a futile effort to collaborate with him on a basic work on sociology. But Andrews the anarchist was too hopelessly subversive for the Virginia traditionalists.

Nearly all the proslavery writers drew upon the Bible to prove the divinity of human bondage. In slavery days, colonial New Englanders had also found arguments in the Bible for slavery, though Northern theologians had since discovered that the Scriptures sanctioned the use of "servants," not slaves. In the evangelical atmosphere of increasing religious orthodoxy, Southern writers gave considerable weight to the scriptural proofs for the justice of slavery; they could readily quote the apostle Paul on the duty of slaves to obey their masters.

Proslavery writers drafted Aristotle into the service of the South. His heavily qualified and contradictory observations on the justice of slavery were taken as a flat endorsement. In the current ideal of a Greek democracy of free white men resting on a "mud-sill" of slaves, Aristotle's place seemed assured. Calhoun and Professor

Albert T. Bledsoe of the University of Virginia had tried to build
their political science on Aristotle's organic theory of government,
and Holmes suggested the outlines of a proslavery sociology in a
remarkable essay, "Observations on a Passage in the Politics of
Aristotle Relative to Slavery," published in the *Southern Literary
Messenger*. Since Aristotle stressed the natural role of slavery, government, the family, and a traditional social system, he made a good
Southerner, unlike the subversive Plato of the scandalous *Republic*
whom Northern liberals were exalting. "Plato is philosophy, and
philosophy Plato," Emerson was telling his Northern audiences.
Thus the antithesis of a good realistic Aristotle and a bad utopian
Plato was developed by Holmes, Fitzhugh, and others. The Puritan
tradition in New England, which associated Aristotle with "papist"
scholasticism, tended to be suspicious of the Stagirite.

3

Proslavery propaganda could not wholly kill native literary ability,
but it could direct literature into a cultural blind alley with hundreds of orators, lawyers, and sentimental poets sounding the
beauties of slavery and the Cavalier South. Encouraged by *De Bow's
Review*, literary nationalism grew and added its influence to the
emergence of a Solid South long before Reconstruction. During
the three years following the publication of *Uncle Tom's Cabin*,
at least fourteen proslavery novels appeared, all of them ephemeral.
"Thank God," wrote Hinton R. Helper in the *Impending Crisis of the
South*, "a 'Southern literature' in the sense intended by the champions of slavery, is a simple impossibility, rendered such by that
exility of mind which they demand in its producers as a prerequisite
to admission into the guild of Southern authorship."

Literate Southerners were not as parochial as the propagandists
would have liked. They preferred Northern or English novels, even
reading *Uncle Tom's Cabin* avidly and subscribing to *Harper's
Weekly*, *Godey's Magazine*, *Graham's*, and *Blackwood's* while neglecting their own journals. Even in newspaper preferences the
Yankees had the advantage. "Where is the newspaper South," asked

a discouraged South Carolinian, "whose circulation in a week will begin to compare with that of the political weather-cock of the *New York Herald* in a day?" Still worse was the textbook situation, for Southern teachers (many of them Yankees) chose Northern books like Peter Parley's histories, which were eventually re-edited for proslavery tastes. Noah Webster's readers earned large royalties in the South despite their antislavery leanings while trusted books like William Gilmore Simms' *Geography* and M. M. Mason's *The Southern First Class Book* made little money for their authors.

It is likely that the Southern tradition of chivalry owes a great deal to the British consul at Richmond, G. P. R. James, author of a hundred novels and stories modeled after Scott, and especially liked for the widely published *History of Chivalry* (1831). Bulwer-Lytton, as in the North, had a tremendous vogue. As for the immortal Sir Walter Scott, whose romantic medieval plots could be read in numerous cheap editions, he was so popular among Southerners that upon his death in 1832 the *Richmond Enquirer* carried heavy black edges along its columns "as in honor of a departed figure of national importance," according to Grace W. Landrum. Mark Twain, with his customary license, blamed the entire Civil War on Sir Walter.

The *New York Tribune* and other Northern papers refused to consider the Boston-born Edgar Allan Poe as a Southern writer despite his education and literary work in Virginia. Greeley considered Simms to be the only novelist of the South, Richard Henry Wilde the sole poet, and Hugh Swinton Legaré the only successful essayist. This cruel estimate, reflecting sectional hatreds, had considerable plausibility in it. Even Simms diverted some of his energies to proslavery propaganda when he collaborated with Dew, Governor Hammond of South Carolina, and Chancellor Harper on the huge tome, *Pro-Slavery Argument* (1852). His contribution to literary nationalism was a glorification of the chivalric traditions of South Carolina and a more attractive restatement than his contemporaries offered of the idea that the South was a Greek democracy with equal opportunity for freemen and security for slaves, both of which Northern wage workers lacked.

Simms, although born and reared in Charleston and selecting a Southern locale for most of his novels, biographies, and histories, was actually no parochial novelist. His literary friendships and contacts spread as far afield as New England and New York. His early poems showed a Byronic influence and he shared both the chivalric cult of Sir Walter Scott and the frontier literary tradition of James Fenimore Cooper, whom he excelled in portraying flesh-and-blood human beings. As a Charleston newspaper editor in his earlier years he had shown Jacksonian leanings, escaping the fascination that Calhoun exercised upon other Carolinians, and even endangering his life in 1832 when a mob surrounded his office after he had defied the nullificationists. But Simms tried to make his peace with aristocratic Charleston despite his plebeian origin, married the daughter of a planter and manufacturer, and became a planter in his own right. Soon he was safely in the orbit of the proslavery, secessionist circle.

From his prolific pen poured forth over twenty novels and about fifty-eight stories, novelettes, histories, and biographies. In *Guy Rivers* he told an adventurous tale of Georgia's gold mining frontier filled with Creek and Cherokee, poor whites, Yankee peddlers, gamblers, and circuit riders. Another popular border romance, reprinted in recent years, was *The Yemassee*, a story recalling the Indian clashes of colonial South Carolina and realistically portraying good as well as bad Indians. Readers, North and South, liked these Southern variants of Cooper's Leatherstocking formula, a frontier tradition in which the best of Southern writers, from Mark Twain down, have distinguished themselves.

Far less fortunate were Simms's efforts to drum up a "Southern" literature through the various Charleston magazines that he edited from *The Magnolia* to the *Southern Quarterly Review* and *Russell's Magazine*. Despite a talented local circle, patronage was lacking and the proslavery contributors, with Simms's encouragement, were permitted to dominate the subject matter at the cost of literary achievement. In this group was the aging poet, William Grayson, who decided to answer *Uncle Tom's Cabin* with his interminably dull poem, "The Hireling and the Slave," an act of proslavery loyalty

that was rewarded by frequent republication in Southern maga·
zines elsewhere. A more promising member of Simms's Charleston
circle, which met at "Lord" John Russell's bookstore, was Henry
Timrod, grandson of a German immigrant, destined to win recognition as the poet of the Confederacy, particularly for the lyric
"The Cotton Boll." The lawyer, young Paul Hayne, later "laureate
of the South," published his first book of poems in 1855 and helped
to edit *Russell's Magazine*. George Frederick Holmes wrote scores
of literary articles for Simms's *Southern Quarterly Review*, receiving
the editor's highest praise, "Your contributions to the *Review* have
been the very best which have appeared in its pages."

One of the most erudite classicists and legal philosophers of the
South was Simms's one-time associate, Hugh Swinton Legaré, who
came of a plantation family. Acquainted with many literatures, he
idealized the trained classicist who could express thoughts in correct, elegant Latin and Greek and he read these languages easily. As
a conservative Whig politician he advanced from local politics to
Congress. He opposed Jackson's fight on the bank and rose to become
Attorney-General under Tyler, even serving as Secretary of State
for a few weeks before his death in 1843. Always a Unionist, he led
the opposition to Calhoun's nullification scheme. A friend of higher
learning though hostile to the new science, he was a leader in the
cultural renaissance in Charleston of the twenties and thirties; his
passing opened the way for the antebellum fire-eaters.

Related after a fashion to the Charleston circle was the German
immigrant Francis Lieber, professor of history and political economy
in South Carolina College until 1856, when he left for Columbia.
Author of *Political Ethics* and *Civil Liberty and Self-Government*,
he developed a "pluralist" political theory that stressed the role of
social institutions rather than political structures as the true foundation of government. However, while Lieber corresponded with the
Charlestonians and apparently knew some of them well, and his
repudiation of natural-rights ideas should have pleased them, he felt
himself an alien in the South and returned to the North. During the
Civil War he became Lincoln's expert on international law and

issued "General Orders No. 100," the basis for later efforts to codify the international rules of war.

Charleston, as Professor Trent insists, was a graveyard of magazines, thirty-four of them, despite the militancy of Simms's circle and the valiant efforts of the fiery Charleston *Mercury* and its editor R. B. Rhett, "father of secession." To feud with Northern journals and call vociferously for Southern books did not make up the deficit left by laggard subscribers. De Bow probably saved his *Review* from an early death by opening it in bustling New Orleans rather than near his decaying Charleston birthplace. In that delta city the French elite had already built up a respectable literary tradition and the public school system was one of the best. There the literary leader was the meticulous historian and statesman, Charles Gayarré, whose sound four-volume *History of Louisiana* had begun to appear in 1851. Nevertheless, even in New Orleans De Bow did not have an easy time, being compelled to slave in his little office day and night to keep expenses within his meager income. He combined, as we have seen, a host of projects for a diversified South and promotion of a substantial Southern industry with his ardent proslavery propaganda.

In Richmond and its environs, where Poe's star was in the ascendant, creative literary life did not escape the dead hand of proslavery agitators, though the situation was far better there than in Charleston. At the College of William and Mary were the proslavery defenders, Professors Thomas R. Dew and Nathaniel Beverley Tucker. Though the son of a liberal Jeffersonian, Tucker fell in love with "the gallant cavaliers from whom we spring" and in his novel *The Partisan Leader,* he forecast the secession of Virginia led by a Calhoun-like politician. Hating industrialism, abolitionism, and Jacksonian democracy, he wrote privately to Simms, "And what are our democracies but mobs?" The "slough of democracy," he believed, had no sense of honor. From nearby Port Royal came the stream of Fitzhugh's books and articles during the fifties to champion Southern nationalism. His friend, George Frederick Holmes, moved to Virginia and became a leading contributor to the *Southern Literary Messenger,* being chosen in 1852 by its editor, John R. Thompson, to write a parting review of *Uncle Tom's Cabin* for the dying magazine, "as hot as hell-fire, blasting and searing the reputation of the vile wretch in petticoats who could write such a volume." Holmes enthusiastically complied, adding, as Thompson had desired, a bitter criticism of the failure of Southerners to patronize their own literature:

What Southern author has not occasion for bitter complaints of the neglect, injustice and illiberality of the Southern communities for which he has lived and written? . . . What Southern periodical, established for the development of Southern intellect, for the defence of Southern institutions, for the creation of a Southern literature, has not languished for the want of adequate encouragement?

Novelists and poets of the thirties and forties escaped much of the miasma of the proslavery atmosphere. During the thirties, Dr. William Alexander Caruthers, a Virginia liberal, became a literary exponent of Jeffersonian humanitarianism as well as of Scott's romanticism. His historical romance, *The Cavaliers of Virginia,* was better than its title, for it not only gave a sympathetic picture of the fox-hunting, dueling gentry, but also showed sympathy for the democratic cause in Bacon's Rebellion. Another of his books, *The Kentuckian in New York,* devoted considerable attention to the small farmer and the poor white and attributed the debasement of labor to slavery. Even more popular among those who liked prose romances were the novelists, Philip Pendleton Cooke and his brother, John Esten Cooke. The latter used the frontier tradition of Cooper and the regional technique of Irving, notably in his novel, *The Virginia Comedians.* His thirty novels, biographies, and histories pleased readers so much that he became one of the best-paid literary men in the South.

More talented than these novelists and no less steeped in the Virginia plantation tradition despite his staunch Unionist sympathies was John Pendleton Kennedy. Circumstances made him a conservative, for he was the son of a Baltimore merchant, the son-in-law of a wealthy Baltimore textile manufacturer, and the head of the Baltimore and Ohio Railway. In politics and in his law connections, he was a nationalist Whig; still his literary gifts as well as his money made him an intelligent patron of the arts. He "discovered" Poe by voting him a literary prize for "Ms found in a Bottle" and got him the editorial post—though it paid but $15 a week—with the *Southern Literary Messenger*. His own literary art, still appreciated after a century, shows the influence of Irving and Scott as in *Swallow Barn;* his *Rob of the Bowl* was a cavalier-style novel of the Protestant-Catholic clash in colonial Maryland; in *Horse Shoe Robinson* he dealt with the western Carolinas during the Revolutionary era; and in *Quodlibet,* he drew a mild satire of Jacksonian democracy. In his plantation novels appear the color of county court days, fox and 'possum hunts, and the hospitality of the planter rather than life among the slaves.

Edgar Allan Poe, an indubitable genius, can scarcely be explained in terms of Southern literary traditions, though he attended the University of Virginia for a year, edited the *Southern Literary Messenger* most effectively for two years, and subscribed on occasion to the proslavery and anti-Jeffersonian views of his neighbors. Left an orphan in Boston by a penniless stage couple, he had been adopted by John Allan, a Richmond merchant (to whom he showed little gratitude), and educated in English and Scottish schools. After his brief experience at the University of Virginia he attended West Point until expelled, then moved to New York for a time. Except for his work with the *Messenger* at Richmond, his literary career usually took him and his family outside the South to New York and Philadelphia. He gave an impression of shyness, and lost himself in alcoholism, neurotic ideas, and melancholia.

The Gothic romance style of Mrs. Radcliffe, which he cultivated with such art, may have furnished a necessary outlet for the mysticism, fantasies, presentiments of evil or terror that he may himself have felt. From a craftsman's point of view he has come to rank as the peer of the American short story and mystery tale. His "Fall of the House of Usher" illustrates his famous literary formula of writing nothing but what is necessary to create the total effect that the story was intended to have. He gathered the most successful of these Gothic and Saracenic stories in his book, *Tales of the Grotesque and Arabesque* (1840). His "Murders in the Rue Morgue" and "The Gold Bug" are the brilliant forerunners of the best modern detective stories in their clever deductive skill. However much he satisfied sentimental tastes with his poetical themes as in "Annabel Lee," he enriched them with his characteristic originality and feeling for realistic imagery as well as his traits of otherworldliness, particularly in "The Raven" which suggested Coleridge's influence.

As an editor of the *Southern Literary Messenger* he showed unusual awareness of esthetic criteria in judging contributions. The *Messenger* remained well above the literary level of any Southern journal and was comparable to the best in the North, though the steady invasion of proslavery contributions, especially under Thompson, must have cost it many antislavery readers. Poe so thoroughly emancipated himself from the current American vogue of evaluating literature according to didactic or moral qualities that his estheticism went to the other extreme of "art for art's sake" which made pure subjectivism and even unintelligibility acceptable as art. This tendency was carried over to France in the 1850's by a poet-devotee, Charles Baudelaire, and Poe's principles were taken up by the French "Symbolists" of the 1880's who rebelled against the artificiality of poetical meters and naturalism in favor of deeper subtleties of personal experience. Poe's pessimism, graveyard images, and indifference to rationality were to attract the French "decadents" who found release in pure subjectivism of the irrational "Dada" variety and in a craving for novelty in any form. Whatever values lay in Poe's esthetic theories, he was one of the earliest Americans, next to Franklin, to be hailed as a master by any significant circle of European intellectuals.

In the Gulf states there were original minds who saw literary possibilities outside the plantation tradition, especially in the humor and folkways of the small farmer, the highlander, and the poor white. A former Virginian, Joseph G. Baldwin, who practiced law and politics in the Gulf states during the 1830's and 1840's, caught this indigenous spirit of the deep South. His autobiographical book *The Flush Times of Alabama and Mississippi* (1854) portrayed the varied types of the frontier: the speculators who used "credit without capital and enterprise without honesty," the newly-rich class of "cotton snobs," and the lawless men who kidnapped slaves, preyed upon planters, and gambled with the less sophisticated card players until driven out by vigilantes. Like other Virginians from that soil-exhausted state, Baldwin was definitely out to make a career in the Gulf territories:

> To the Southwest he started because magnificent accounts came from that sunny land of most cheering and exhilarating prospects of fussing, quarreling, murdering, violation of contracts . . . in fine, of a flush tide of litigation in all of its departments, civil and criminal. It was extolled as a legal Utopia, peopled by a race of eager litigants. . . .

Georgia's frontier past received a good deal of humorous attention in the unconventional *Georgia Scenes* (1835) by Judge Augustus B. Longstreet, a Methodist Episcopal clergyman and the president, at various times, of the University of Mississippi and the University of South Carolina. Though he laughed unsympathetically at the poor white, he could picture the fighting, drinking, blasphemous, and gambling frontier types of the lower South at a time when Southerners thought them unworthy of literary notice. In his snobbish way Longstreet enhanced the realism of his portrayal by the use of dialect, then a unique form of literary expression. In New England, James Russell Lowell was to "originate" the American literary use of dialect—so the critics were to say—over a decade later in *The Biglow Papers*. Georgia had a rather promising poet in Dr. Thomas Holley Chivers, a friend of Poe. Chivers was the son of a rich Georgia planter, but he married a Massachusetts girl. His poem "Isadore," appearing after Poe's death, in *Eonchs of Ruby,* was so similar to "The Raven" that Simms charged Chivers with plagiarism; but the Georgian, whose own work was of a high order, insisted that Poe was the plagiarist and that "Isadore" antedated "The Raven." Here, as Professor Spiller and his associates point out, the controversy rests to this day. Another Georgian poet,

Richard Henry Wilde, won a national reputation for his sentimental lyric, "My Life Is Like a Summer Rose," which was later set to music by Sidney Lanier.

<h1 style="text-align:center">4</h1>

Both social science and natural science had to run the gantlet of proslavery and religious fundamentalism; fortunately this experience was not necessarily fatal and scientific thought remained far from dead in the antebellum South. Sociology, as we have seen, emerged as a proslavery discipline, stressing the organic social structure of the stratified plantation system. Anthropology took on a marked racialist bias, restrained only by the Southern clergy who protested the notion of Nott and Gliddon that there had been more divine creations than that of the original pair in the Garden of Eden. Thomas Cooper, the South Carolina scientist and religious rationalist, shared the difficulties of Northern geologists in combatting the objections of the clergy to Lyell's principles of geology, which made the earth quite an aged planet at the alleged time of creation in 4004 B.C.

Still, as Professor Thomas C. Johnson points out, amateur and professional scientists were legion in the South. Edmund Ruffin, whose discoveries in soil chemistry helped to revive Virginia's spent lands, was of national stature, however extreme his secessionist leanings happened to be. The agricultural revival in antebellum times owed much to Ruffin's conclusion that organic acids hampered fertility and that lime-bearing marls could remedy the difficulty. In the Shenandoah Valley, Cyrus McCormick had invented the reaper, destined to begin the mechanization of American agriculture. Another Virginian, the lame Matthew Fontaine Maury, wrote the first classic of modern oceanography, *The Physical Geography of the Sea,* and put mariners further in his debt by his famous wind and current charts of the Atlantic and his sponsorship of the United States Weather Bureau. His researches into the Atlantic Plateau led him to suggest the feasibility of the oceanic cable to Cyrus Field. Teaching at various Southern colleges, including the University of Georgia and South Carolina College, was an out-

standing disciple of Louis Agassiz, Joseph Le Conte, whose geological studies showed originality and depth.

While the rural South was dwarfed intellectually by the urban,
industrial North with its more stimulating atmosphere, certain
educational tendencies are noteworthy. The New England lyceum
movement affected a number of states below the Potomac, especially North Carolina, which, according to one historian's count,
had some such adult education society in every town and village.
The ideal of classical education, highly revered in plantation circles,
was hard-pressed by a vigorous demand for laboratory sciences by
the students in the colleges, as in the University of Virginia. As
for the sweet Southern belle, says Professor Johnson, she was far
from the vacuous, simpering girl that the novels portray. His
analysis of the *Richmond Enquirer* for 1835-37 shows advertisements of over one hundred girls' schools that taught natural science
as well as the "useful" arts and skills. The leadership of the South
in "female seminaries" for the middle and planter classes and in
colleges for which Southerners spent over twice as much as Yankees
shows the high role allotted to the education of the ruling classes.
The upper-class woman's desire to converse intelligently and to
help direct the elaborate plantation gatherings, rather than any
marked concession to feminism, was one of the motives of female
education; co-education, however, was another matter. The well-
to-do plantation lady, Mary Chesnut of South Carolina, belonged
to a feminine circle that read with some critical acumen the European and American novelists and poets, translated the best in contemporary German literature, and wrote letters and diaries with
genuine literary facility.

In a remarkable study, *Freedom of Thought in the Old South,*
Professor Clement Eaton of the University of Kentucky has shown
the baneful effect of the slavery controversy upon free speech and
a free press in the South until the liberal Jeffersonian heritage had
been irreparably damaged. The North barely escaped a similar
situation. During the thirties, an Illinois mob murdered the abolitionist editor, Elijah Lovejoy, in Alton; hoodlums at Cincinnati
destroyed the press of James Birney, a former slaveholder who

had turned abolitionist; and "ruffians in broadcloth" almost lynched William Lloyd Garrison. With the rising victory of abolition and the "isms," the lot of the Northern reformer ceased to be an unhappy one.

On the other hand, the South, where emancipationists, colonizationists, Jefferson liberals, and Quaker humanitarians had long badgered the conscience of the slaveholder, reversed its attitude after 1830. In 1829, David Walker, a Boston free Negro, wrote a fiery pamphlet calling upon all slaves to overthrow their masters. One Southern state after another took extraordinary action to stop the circulation of such incendiary appeals; some, like Georgia, imposed the death penalty, and nearly all restricted in some way any expression that might stimulate slave discontent. Insurrections like Nat Turner's outbreak in Virginia and the circulation of Garrison's *Liberator* led to tighter regulations. Though easygoing Southern habits usually meant non-enforcement of such laws for long periods, numerous cases involving free speech were heard. At Washington, President Jackson instructed Postmaster-General Kendall to handle the delivery of abolitionist papers in such a way as to publicize the identity of Southern abolitionists. Calhoun's leadership also led to the famous "gag rule" in the House against receiving antislavery petitions—a palpable violation of the freedom of petition. Unorthodox editors like John Pleasants of the *Richmond Whig* could be silenced by a fire-eating rival who accused him (wrongly) of being an abolitionist and a coward—the prelude to Pleasants' death on the dueling field.

The colleges, pride of the planters, dropped antislavery professors while students at the University of North Carolina burnt an antislavery professor in effigy, demanding his dismissal. Discouraged Quaker radicals deserted Virginia and North Carolina for Indiana and Ohio; Southern Catholics were instructed in caution by their Charleston bishop, being told that slavery was not a sin, though the abuses against the Negro were of religious concern; Germans, except for antislavery militants, developed an attitude of neutrality. Unitarian and other varieties of religious rationalism declined; three major churches, as we have seen, split

on antislavery matters, and evolved along ever more conservative
evangelical lines. By the time of secession the Unionist elements
of the South, possibly a majority, had been largely overawed by
the aggressive proslavery forces. The spirit of John Calhoun had
triumphed in a conservative intellectual revolution that was to
outlast the Civil War.

It is easy to exaggerate the responsibility of the Southern cult
of chivalry for the Civil War. Mark Twain, writing in *Life on the
Mississippi*, originated a savage indictment of Sir Walter Scott
and the chivalric ideal in the South:

There the genuine and wholesome civilization of the nineteenth century
is curiously confused and commingled with the Walter Scott Middle-
Age sham civilization, and so you have practical common sense, progressive ideas, and progressive works, mixed up with the dull, the inflated
speech, and the jejune romanticism of an absurd past that is dead, and
out of charity ought to be buried . . . It was Sir Walter that made every
gentleman in the South a major or a colonel, or a general or a judge,
before the war . . . Sir Walter had so large a hand in making Southern
character, as it existed before the war, that he is in great measure responsible for the war.

Twain was ready to admit that the North as well as the South
shared in the romanticism and sentimentality of Scott, but the impact was fatal for semi-feudal Dixie—so he thought.

Twain was never disturbed by facts and refutation would have
left him unmoved. The class origins of Southern society of course
antedated Scott and were due to economic rather than literary
facts. If there was a cult of manners it can easily be traced to the
Renaissance manuals for gentlemen that tidewater planters had
studied assiduously during the seventeenth and eighteenth centuries. The "sheltered female," a pet rather than a companion for
her husband, was a contemporary feature of prosperous bourgeois
life in that Victorian age and originated far earlier. In the patriarchal plantation families, resisting the advance of feminism and
other expressions of liberalism, women of the well-to-do classes
were given by those who sought to rationalize the situation the

dubious consolation of membership in the cult of pure Southern womanhood. This meant a form of social futility that many of their Northern and European sisters would have understood and commiserated with them upon. Lynchers were later to rationalize their anti-Negro brutalities by asserting their concern for the chastity of Southern women. Even among the impoverished Southern highlanders, who hardly knew Sir Walter and worked their women into an early grave, the dominant "code of the hills" protected women from clan feuds and made the honor of that sex sufficient grounds for a perpetual feud until extermination overtook the less fortunate clan. Here was an example of feudal borrowing that mountain isolation preserved.

Elsewhere in the less isolated rural South, feudal attitudes and beliefs inherited from seventeenth-century England and Scotland had long taken on a new lease on life with the adoption of slavery and the expansion of the aristocratic plantation system. The "code duello," not unknown above the Mason and Dixon line, continued to exist here despite Southern laws, not because of Scott but because it fitted into the medieval social inheritance which plantation life had preserved. The same explanation partly applies to the knightly tournaments, jousts, and horse-racing, though these sports were often clad in the romantic form prescribed by the Waverley Novels. Besides, Southerners of various classes, it will be recalled, carried over the love of horses characteristic of English country gentlemen.

The proslavery novelists and pamphleteers, pressed by the barbs of American and British abolitionists in a world rapidly shifting to free wage labor, naturally turned in self-defense to the feudal inheritance of the South. George Fitzhugh frankly explained his attack on "free society" as not due to any desire to change Northern institutions—as would be implied in any fervent devotion to Walter Scott—but merely to defend the South. There was some psychological compensation for hard-pressed Southern planters during an era of falling cotton prices in regarding Northern finance and industry as ruthlessly exploitative while unsophisticated Dixie harked back to the glorious feudal world of brave honest knights, devoted

squires, and fair, helpless damsels. To defend an anachronistic social order, proslavery novelists, poets, and journalists of the plantation school resorted to the obvious strategem of charging that the
rest of the world was out of step—not they. Under such circumstances
far too many Southerners swallowed Sir Walter Scott as a popular
antidote to Harriet Beecher Stowe; others were even ready to embrace antimajoritarian and racialist theories to purge themselves
of the guilt that abolitionism fastened upon the South.

In that age of romanticism, marked by the enthusiastic Greek cult
of Byron, the Southern proslavery writers were alternately attracted
to the Calhoun idea of a Greek democracy and the feudal ideal of a
stratified social order, regardless of their mutually contradictory
nature. In either case slavery and white-man supremacy were
secure and the South set the norm of a well-ordered society. Sir
Walter can therefore be at most a very minor war criminal in provoking the attack upon Fort Sumter, even if his tales did lend a
certain amount of color and content to Southern nationalism. Besides, his influence among Southerners was shared by the prolific
G. P. R. James and Bulwer-Lytton, both deep-dyed romantics. The
causes lay far deeper than these literary fantasies, being imbedded
in economic, political, and social conditions, of which the chief
factor was the South's rejection of human freedom in an age of
triumphant liberalism.

· 17 ·

Civil War: Triumph of American Nationality

I

THE CLASH at Fort Sumter of secessionists and champions of American nationality initiated the war that was to cost almost 600,000 lives and countless treasure. To unite his divided following, Lincoln had reduced his war aims to a simple denominator, "My paramount object in this struggle is to save the Union and is not either to save or to destroy slavery." After the Emancipation Proclamation was issued on January 1, 1863, freeing all slaves within rebellious areas in the hope of breaking Southern resistance, Lincoln could then drastically alter his statement of war aims. At Gettysburg he reminded his countrymen that this nation had been "conceived in Liberty, and dedicated to the proposition that all men are created equal." In words that clearly rejected Chief Justice Taney's notion that the Declaration of Independence had nothing to do with Negroes, Lincoln called for "a new birth of freedom—and that government of the people, by the people, for the people, shall not perish from the earth." This immortal phrase, borrowed from the felicitous phraseology of Theodore Parker, the antislavery leader, raised the level of war aims to its highest democratic expression.

Hatreds, North and South, had been fanned too long by proslavery orators or abolitionists to require any philosophical statement of war aims in 1861. Volunteers, carried away by patriotic bands, speeches, posters, the kisses or threats of young ladies, and other community pressure, overwhelmed the recruiting stations. Sons of wealthy planters organized cavalry companies under their command and in many instances arrived with a personal slave to lessen the inconveniences of war. Confederate flags flew on Southern college campuses even before hostilities began, and classrooms emptied quickly, forcing some institutions to close. In the North, college youth came in substantial but far smaller numbers though an abolitionist institution like Oberlin must have been almost deserted, for it later claimed almost one hundred dead. Princeton, with a heavy Southern enrollment, lost one-third of her students to the Confederate cause; hundreds of other Southerners left their Northern colleges and academies for Dixie. All expected that the war would be short and glorious, but they were to be terribly disillusioned by the reality of the bloodiest war in American history.

Eleven seceded states, with 5,500,000 whites and about 3,500,000 slaves, constituted the Confederate States of America. Against them were twenty-three Northern states with 22,000,000 people and a superb industrial machine, which the rural South could not hope to match even under the best of circumstances. The Confederacy managed to put about 600,000 men in the field during the war, but these were compelled to accept long enlistment terms to fight the 2,500,000 Union soldiers who served at various times under federal generals. On the side of the South were the advantages of a defensive war with good interior lines against a more dispersed enemy; but the deteriorating Southern railroads, never too good even in peacetime, collapsed under the burden of over four years of fighting. Most crucial was the problem of ordnance in an agrarian country. Southerners depended desperately upon the Tredegar Iron Works of Richmond, noted for its high quality tensile iron, which provided nearly eleven hundred cannon for Lee's armies. Southern ingenuity and personal sacrifice tried vainly to catch up with superior Northern production or to offset it by slipping vessels through the tightening Yankee naval blockade. Inflation and taxes were especially painful in the South. So serious were their shortages that women stripped their homes of carpets to provide coverlets for the soldiers. The paper shortage was so grave that many newspapers simply disappeared; at least twelve resorted to wallpaper to feed

their presses. Diaries and correspondence were often written on
wrapping paper and even ink became scarce. By 1863, food shortages, due to poor transportation and the Union blockade, became
the chief peril to the Confederacy, according to Jefferson Davis.

As the war dragged on into years, dampening the ardor of many
volunteers, both sides resorted to conscription. The Confederacy
needed to hold in the army the men already there. It also had to
keep trained men in the shops, factories, and on the plantations.
Therefore, the Act of 1862 drafted only those able-bodied men who
did not already have essential civilian duties. However, the exemption of large planters, overseers, petty officeholders, and those
able to pay for substitutes, as well as highly specialized men, angered
the poorer classes. In North Carolina, W. W. Holden, editor of the
Standard, charged that this was a "rich man's war and a poor man's
fight" serving the wealthy slaveholders. Partly as a result of the
rising resentment, desertion soared with almost 200,000 absent without leave by the time of Lee's surrender.

A year after the Confederacy began conscription, the Lincoln
government followed with the Act of 1863. The chief purpose was
to stimulate state recruiting by the threat of a draft. Here again
exemption could be won by furnishing a substitute or by paying
the government $300. As a result, there were 120,000 substitutes
out of the 170,000 men drafted under the several draft laws. Among
the distinguished men to offer proxies were the young James G.
Blaine, who almost became president, and the still younger Grover
Cleveland, who did. John D. Rockefeller preferred his promising
mercantile career in Cleveland to war, though he conscientiously
lavished attentions upon the family of his substitute. Professor
Muzzey points out that this practice was then considered perfectly honorable, but the Civil War laborer resented it nevertheless.

In New York city, where the Irish longshoreman was already incensed at the employers' practice of importing Negroes as strikebreakers, the draft led to rioting. Mobs attacked Negroes, who were
held to be the cause of the war as well as economic competitors.
On July 13, 1863, a mob overwhelmed the recruiting centers and
sacked the offices of Greeley's *Tribune,* which had urged immediate

emancipation of slaves. After destroying about $500,000 worth of property, the mob clashed with the police and with veterans newly arrived from Gettysburg; before order was restored, they had caused one thousand casualties. To prevent the Irish riots from spreading to other cities, Catholic priests denounced this violence and saved Negro churches from being burnt. Archbishop Hughes, who had urged conscription as a quick method to end the war, was embarrassed by Irish critics, but he defended himself by explaining that he, too, was opposed to discrimination in favor of the rich in the operation of the draft.

States paid ever higher bounties to men who would enlist, thereby encouraging a class of "bounty jumpers" who thrived by alternately enlisting and deserting. Here, as in the South, the notion grew that this was a rich man's war. In both sections, conscientious objectors demanded exemption. Generally speaking, religious pacifists were given exemption upon the payment of a commutation fee, but some states, particularly those in the South, were adamant toward extreme Quakers who would neither pay the fee nor serve as army nurses and attendants.

2

The impossible Confederate task of improvising a nation and a war at the same time caused intense suffering at the front. Rich as the South was in foodstuffs, her worn-out railroads and wagon equipment forced the curtailment of rations in 1862 especially during active campaigns. Living on a diet of salt meat—provided there was salt—dry corn or flour, the soldiers showed emaciation and suffered from scurvy. Those with a little money could get dry fruits and even cake from the rascally sutlers at extortionate prices; others might rifle the well-stocked kits of dead Yankees for real coffee, almost nonexistent in Lee's armies, and crackers. As the war progressed, the bright uniforms of the volunteers became dull and tattered except for the fortunate minority whom the Confederacy, the states, or relatives were able to supply. Lacking shoes, thousands went barefoot even in winter, their footprints stained with blood; others managed to bind up their feet with scraps of leather or with rags. Ignorant of sanitation the backward men of the hills polluted the camps with the crudest of latrines or perhaps dispensed with these altogether. Poor food, tainted streams, filth, and aggressive insects, as well as exposure killed tens of thousands as dysentery, diarrhea, pneumonia, and malaria took their toll. The Gray-clad soldiers—and the Blue, too—suffered severely from venereal diseases as camp-followers and town prostitutes plied their trade.

This improvised war meant needless suffering for prisoners on both sides; tragic incidents grew into exaggerated atrocity stories and embittered both sections for years after the war ended. In the Confederacy, where soldiers were on short rations and remained ill clad, the lot of the Union prisoners entitled by the usages of war to the same rations as their captors was horrible indeed. Especially bad were Libby Prison at Richmond and the huge prison stockade at Andersonville, Georgia. Union prisoners afterwards testified that they had been starved at Libby; wild stories spread that doctors had injected syphilis into prisoners and that guards shot men at the windows. At bleak, isolated Andersonville, where authorities operated for long periods without funds or supplies, almost 30,000 Union soldiers were crowded into crude barracks intended for a third of that number; many died of pulmonary ailments in those exposed conditions and others starved on the meager Confederate ration. In the imagination of the prisoners and the North, Captain Henry Wirz who headed Andersonville was a sadistic monster who broke the spirit of the prisoners in his stinking, malarial camp, murdered many in cold blood, and systematically planned the tortures of prisoners, throwing their corpses to his dogs. After the war he was tried in an angry partisan atmosphere and hanged. In Yankee prisons, too, Southern soldiers, unaccustomed to the icy winds of the Great Lakes, died in large numbers from exposure and some Union officers thought they were but the agents of divine retribution for Libby and Andersonville by showing calculated neglect toward Johnny Reb.

Although Yankees and Rebs were well supplied with hatreds against each other, a surprising amount of fraternizing went on, much to the annoyance of officers. The war began at Fort Sumter

with the most chivalric courtesies such as a Confederate gift of
cigars and claret to Major Robert Anderson before the batteries
opened their fire to smash the Union fort into ruins; this attitude
changed soon afterward. Pickets and other enlisted men of both
sides often became intimate, exchanged pictures of sweethearts,
engaged in petty barter, and even invited each other to parties.
Wiley tells of informal truces declared so that each might gather
blackberries, and he describes those enjoyable interludes when
the enemies competed with rival bands instead of cannon-shot and
ended by joining together feelingly in "Home, Sweet Home."

3

Grant's armies had far more effective civilian aid than did Lee's.
Although the United States had not yet sought the help of the
Red Cross, which came into existence during the war, numerous
federal and civilian agencies ministered to the sick and wounded.
The British Sanitary Commission, an outgrowth of the recent
Crimean War, was closely studied by Americans. The most active
agency to promote war relief was the Women's Central Relief
Association of New York, the predecessor of the United States
Sanitary Commission. To meet the desperate disease-breeding conditions in the camps, the Union government created this Commission, but left its financing largely to private groups. Fortunately,
these agencies collected over $7,000,000 in cash and twice as much
in gifts and services from benevolent sources. About 500 agents
were sent out by the executive chairman, Frederick Law Olmsted,
to distribute food, clothing, health pamphlets, and other gifts to
the boys in blue. They cooperated with the Medical Bureau,
helped the men make out official papers, prepared Thanksgiving
dinners, and set up numerous soldiers' homes.

The lessons learned in sanitary science, despite the prevailing
ignorance of modern principles of disease transmission, were to
influence the postwar movement in public health, as Professor
Howard D. Kramer has suggested. However, the war actually
arrested the organization of the first American public health asso-

ciation. This had been projected shortly before the war began by a Boston convention of leaders who had been active in studying urban problems such as housing, food supplies, drugs, and refuse disposal. One can easily surmise the staggering total of needless deaths due to the crude medical techniques of that day. One Civil War surgeon, who was to live long enough to watch modern sterilization methods replace ancient practices, later recalled:

> We operated in our old blood-stained and often pus-stained coats... We used undisinfected instruments from undisinfected plush cases, and still worse, used marine sponges which had been used in prior pus cases and had been only washed in tap water. If a sponge or an instrument fell on the floor it was washed and squeezed in a basin of tap water and used as if it were clean.

Another surgeon afterwards estimated that "it was seven times safer to fight all through the three days of Gettysburg than to have an arm or leg cut off... with the septic surgery then practiced." A minor operation or even a slight wound was often the prelude to lockjaw. Hospital gangrene carried off entire wards. Doctors seemed helpless to stop heavy fatalities from diarrhea, dysentery, and malaria. Many of the doctors never saw a thermometer or a hypodermic syringe during the war and pulse-taking had gone into disfavor at this time.

Standards of precision in medicine had declined in the antebellum era due to the cheapening of medical education resulting from the overwhelming demand of a fast-growing population for doctors. Anyone could get his M.D. by simply attending a winter course of lectures on medicine. As for mental cases, these usually seemed insoluble for Civil War doctors; many of them disposed of such patients by sending them to the pioneer neurologist, Dr. S. Weir Mitchell, who was in charge of a Union base hospital at Philadelphia. Mitchell's special ward for nerve injuries expanded into a psychiatric clinic. A disciple of Benjamin Rush, who had frequently caught glimpses of twentieth-century psychiatric theories in his bold speculation and experiment, Mitchell had embarked upon a significant career in mental hygiene, which he was later to combine successfully with his writings in the psychiatric novel. Eventually, the discoveries and errors of the medical profession during the Civil War were to be gathered together meticulously for the benefit of the next generation in the seven-volume *Medical and Surgical History of the War of the Rebellion* (1870-88).

One of the most creative aspects of the Civil War was the rise of professional nursing, particularly in the North, and its influence upon the advance of women in society. Florence Nightingale, English founder of professional nursing, inspired the women of this era by her heroism and administrative ability in mitigating the horrors of the Crimean War, demonstrating that women are not too delicate to play a major role in wartime. In previous American wars untrained men and an occasional elderly lady did the nursing, leaving behind an unedifying record of indifference or ignorance. But the advance of women to a fuller participation in a man-made world was hampered during the antebellum era by the tendency to elevate Eve from a snare of Satan to a lofty uncomfortable position upon a pedestal. This situation was steadily challenged by the growing implications of the Industrial Revolution, which opened new doors of activity to women. When the Civil War came and the most annihilative battles in American history began, Lincoln and his advisers were ready to try new methods and solutions such as organized nursing.

The elderly Dorothea Dix, internationally famous for her crusade in behalf of the mentally ill, and long experienced in hospital administration, accepted in 1861 the post of superintendent of United States Army Nurses. In her determination to avoid scandal or discredit to women in war service, she hit upon the desperate expedient of outlawing Cupid. She advertised for women over thirty and added specifically, "All nurses are required to be plain looking women. Their dresses must be brown or black, with no bows, no curls, no jewelry, and no hoop skirts." But many nurses did find husbands despite her rules. Dr. Victor Robinson concludes humorously regarding the Dix plan to foil romance, "As an ex-schoolteacher, who had once taught Greek mythology, Miss Dix should have remembered the connection between Mars and Venus." She tended to be unduly rigid in her views, even seeming a bit queer to many nurses, and showed obvious prejudices in her contacts with Catholic sisters (about 600 nuns did army nursing); but she was motherly in her devotion to the hospitalized soldiers. If her patients lacked anything, she would frighten the petty bureaucrats into providing what was necessary; on occasion she would commandeer food from the well-stocked tables of the officers; and she was there to stop any brutal treatment of her charges.

One of her subordinates, Louisa May Alcott, called her, "Our Florence Nightingale." Miss Alcott herself, after enduring six weeks of contagion and hardship in an army hospital, finally came down with pneumonia, which ended her nursing career. "I spent my shining hours," wrote this gifted daughter of Bronson Alcott, "washing faces, serving rations, giving medicine, and sitting in a very hard chair, with pneumonia on one side, diphtheria on the other, two typhoids opposite and a dozen dilapidated patriots hopping, lying, and lounging about." Nurses had to cope with endless rows of bedridden patients and to work at night by candlelight when army lanterns were not available. The things they had to witness and the intimate functions they had to perform should have ended forever the stereotype of the delicate female.

An important phase of Dorothea Dix's work was the training of nurses, in itself a novel and pioneer activity, for in those days there were only practical nurses at best, not scientifically-trained ones in the modern sense. To help her she had the able assistance of Dr. Elizabeth Blackwell, the first American woman to earn a medical degree. Dr. Blackwell had stubbornly persisted despite male ridicule in her efforts to get into a medical school and had gained her hospital experience in Paris and London. Aided by New York Quakers and encouraged by Florence Nightingale, she and her sister Emily (also an M.D.) founded the New York Infirmary for Women and Children partly to give clinical experience to women interested professionally in medicine. When the war broke out, she tried to get a post with the Medical Bureau but was repulsed. Thereupon, she made Bellevue Hospital a training center for nurses where an intensive four-week course prepared women for service in military hospitals.

The future founder of the American Red Cross, Clara Barton, also was a major figure in the story behind the lines. Like Dorothea Dix and Elizabeth Blackwell, she had more than an ordinary amount of determination; like Miss Dix, she was a former New England schoolteacher who found a psychological outlet only in assuming vast social burdens. In 1854, she had been appointed to a clerkship in the Patent Office, perhaps the first time that a government position had been held by a woman. During the war, she waited for no one to assign her a role, but began independently to direct large-scale war relief operations, showing genuine ability in improvising agencies capable of furnishing huge quantities of supplies to the army and the hospitals. On occasion, she also did personal nursing. Within a short time, her remarkable efforts came to the attention of the public and she won the plaudits of the nation.

Army regulations restricted the number of women in nursing to one for every two male nurses, but nevertheless about 2000 women were appointed in this field. Male nurses accounted for most of the nursing work done. Government bureaus urged their clerks to volunteer as nurses. Best remembered of them is Walt Whitman, who impaired his health while nursing both Northern and Southern soldiers for many months in the hospitals of Washington.

In the South, where the chivalrous tradition was stronger than in the commercial-industrial North, women encountered greater difficulties and prejudices in volunteering as nurses for the soldiers, but hundreds served nevertheless. Aristocratic Southern matrons and belles were encouraged by the example of the English women of their class who had bravely undertaken army nursing regardless of gossip or ridicule. They did much to help meet the critical shortage of medicines and drugs like quinine and chloroform. Some of the more daring women even smuggled large quantities of precious supplies through enemy lines by concealing them in their capacious hoop skirts—this garment had been incredibly expanded by the fashion designers of Europe during the sixties. Union officers soon put a stop to this trick by hiring Yankee women to conduct a careful search of suspects. Wealthy plantation houses were converted into hospitals and numerous wayside hospitals along the military highways provided rest, care, and smiling nurses to cheer up tired Johnny Reb. Here, as in the North, Catholic religious orders, like the Sisters of Charity, sent nuns in their gray garb and white bonnets to serve men of all faiths—even those who believed that these nurses were sinister agents of the Pope. Nursing volunteers also came from mothers who wished to be near their sons or wives who wanted to share the lot of their soldier husbands.

4

Both sides were equally solicitous in looking after the spiritual life of the soldiers. The wide distribution of bibles and religious tracts was encouraged by both Blue and Gray generals. Southern men, many of them products of revivals, tended to remain orthodox despite camp temptations. When the war turned against them and death seemed very close, as Bell Wiley relates, the Confederate armies were swept by large-scale revivals, though without the extravagances of the jerks or the hysterical frenzies of the camp meetings. About 150,000 men professed themselves converted to religion.

Although the Union armies included far larger contingents of unorthodox men, they, too, welcomed the Bibles and tracts of the church organizations. Out of the interdenominational Young Men's Christian Association, which had been born in London in 1844 and carried over to Boston in 1851, grew the United States Christian Commission. Young Dwight L. Moody was already prominent in the Protestant evangelical organizations and was destined to become an internationally famous evangelist despite the fact that he was a layman. His Chicago branch of the Y.M.C.A. affiliated itself with the Christian Commission and he himself actively spread the gospel and supervised the distribution of books and tracts among the soldiers. Novels, magazines, and other secular reading matter were of course in heavy demand and these, too, were provided by the Commission.

The role of the Catholic Church during the Civil War is significant, though it could not share the Protestant evangelical activities of the U. S. Christian Commission. Catholic newspapers complained that in the system of chaplains set up in both Union and Confederate armies, the representatives of their faith were disproportionately small. In 1860, there were about 3,000,000 Catholics in America, totalling one-tenth of the population. Three-quarters of their communicants were in the North and every Southern bishop was born outside the Confederacy. Under such conditions, differences within the American Catholic Church did not culminate in the schisms that had rent the Baptist, Methodist, and Presbyterian sects.

During the antebellum era, Catholic leaders had been cool toward the utopian and humanitarian movement because of the underlying rationalist, secularist, and anti-clerical philosophy of so many of the American reformers. None could help knowing that the liberal family of Harriet Beecher Stowe was militantly anti-Catholic. While Catholics accepted the papal condemnation of the slave trade (which did not include domestic slavery), they divided on the question of the sinfulness of slaveholding. Most of the Catholic press, according to Father Blied and others, seems to have denounced abolition as an incendiary appeal to race war or as inexpedient under existing conditions. Irishmen, who made up at least half of the Catholic population, resented the economic competition of Negroes for manual jobs and feared the economic consequences of abolition on their future. They had their outspoken organ in the *Boston Pilot,* which emphasized these ideas. In the South, many French Catholics, mindful of the fate of the Church during the French Revolution and under French liberal legislation, leaned heavily upon the authoritarian philosophy of Bonald and De Maistre. The antislavery movement and other liberal reforms were therefore suspect to them.

Yet as Father Blied had shown in his book, *Catholics and the Civil War,* there was considerable independence of political opinion within the American Catholic Church. Once the war began, Archbishop Hughes of New York, as we have seen, called for conscription and a united support of the Union. Lincoln even invited him to go as an informal ambassador of good will to France; there, the archbishop tried to reassure Louis Napoleon and the conservative French Catholics of the justice and sincerity of the Union cause. At the same time, the Confederacy had its ardent Catholic spokesman in the Bishop of Charleston, Patrick N. Lynch. He, too, was sent abroad to act as an ambassador at large; in this capacity, he eloquently defended secession and the Confederacy. However, Pope Pius IX had already revealed his private opinion to the American minister when he stated that he could not "as a Christian and the head of the Catholic Church lend any sanction or countenance to the system of African slavery." Bishop Lynch eventually suffered an official ecclesiastical rebuke and later altered his ways. Other American Catholic churchmen differed considerably over the merits of the struggle but tended to steer a cautious course between the political reefs of secession and outright abolition. The Catholic editor and lay convert, Orestes Brownson, urged a stronger pro-Union stand among Catholics and precipitated a violent controversy by his charges against the Catholic press.

5

Of all conflicts, civil wars in which the enemy is within the gates put the greatest strain upon civil liberties. Not all rebels lived in Dixie and thousands of Union sympathizers appeared in eastern Tennessee, western Virginia, and in other Southern states. A common heritage of language and tradition did not soften appreciably the virulence of war hatreds. On either side, mobs and guerrillas operated on a scale unheard of since the American Revolution, intimidating editors who criticized local ideas of patriotism and loyalty. Genuine treason and deliberately instilled defeatism plagued both Lincoln and Davis. The most serious Union problem of coping with potential Fifth Columns lay in the divided loyalty of the Southerners who had settled since pioneer days in the lower counties of the Middlewestern states. Professor Wood Gray writes in *The Hidden Civil War*, "Perhaps about forty per cent of the midwesterners of 1860 were of Southern blood, forty per cent Northeastern, and

twenty per cent of foreign birth or parentage." The Mississippi and
the Ohio rivers had linked the Old Northwest and the South through
trade and personal contacts; this influence had only recently been
countered by the numerous East-West canals and railroads reinforcing the Great Lakes as a geographic bond of union. In New York
city, Mayor Fernando Wood echoed the sentiment of many proslavery residents by proposing that the city secede from the Union.

Within an amorphous "peace party" in the North were men of sincerity as well as traitors. Unionists lumped these people together as
Copperheads, including many harmless Democratic critics of the
administration as well as secessionist sympathizers. The Copperheads of the Middlewest were associated with the revival of the
subversive and secret Knights of the Golden Circle, which had
originated in 1854 as part of a Southern imperialist plot to seize
Mexico and convert it into a huge slave empire. During the Civil
War, the Knights were charged with promoting defeatism, discouraging Union recruiting, and interfering with military operations. Quite a few Democratic newspapers of Illinois, Indiana, and
Ohio ridiculed Union claims of victory and campaigned for the
exclusion of free Negroes from their states by stressing alleged
crimes of rape and murder by the blacks. They attacked emancipation as a dangerous folly that invited the wholesale economic
competition of the Negro freedmen with the white laborers. Lincoln was vilified as a coarse buffoon and as a conscienceless despot.
Many of these newspapers were curbed by angry mobs and bands
of soldiers off duty. In 1861, pro-Union mobs from San Francisco
to New York invaded Democratic newspaper offices and destroyed
the presses and furniture; occasionally, they lynched a suspected
secessionist. In the *New York Herald,* in 1861, the cynical James
Gordon Bennett defended the South's "right of revolution," but
after a mob visited him, he reversed his editorial policies on the war.

The governments on both sides struck back at disloyal elements
and even encouraged arbitrary arrests of suspects without allowing
them trial. Lincoln, later supported by Congress, though challenged
by Chief Justice Taney, took the drastic step of suspending the writ
of habeas corpus within a wide area outside as well as within the

war lines. This ancient writ, which had traditionally protected the individual from arbitrary arrest by assuring an immediate trial, was also suspended by Davis and the Confederate Congress, especially in regard to the disaffected Virginia counties and key cities like Richmond. As the Union cause advanced, Southern authorities imposed a far stricter censorship of the press than did the North. Reporters were excluded from Confederate lines and too little besides Confederate victories was permitted to reach newspapers. In the North, the Postmaster General undoubtedly kept many newspaper editors in line by canceling the mailing privileges of the most recalcitrant newspapers. The United States Senate so far reflected the war spirit as to expel a veteran member, Jesse Bright of Indiana, for alleged treasonable correspondence with Davis—actually only a friendly but pro-Union note to his old college mate. This instance was the first case of expulsion of a member in the entire history of the Senate.

The suppression of Wilbur F. Storey's *Chicago Times* aroused even loyal editors to criticize the civil rights policy of the Lincoln administration. The highly individualistic Storey had been pro-Union until the Emancipation Proclamation converted the struggle into a conflict over slavery. Thereafter, he had violently attacked Lincoln and even when mobs threatened he persisted, adding the precaution of appearing fully armed. Acting independently, General Burnside seized the *Times* and suspended its operations. So angry was the outcry of Horace Greeley and other pro-Union editors that Lincoln quickly rescinded the order.

Loyal editors, confident of their intuitive ability as military strategists, also harassed the administration by making political issues of strategic problems best left to the experts. Greeley's slogan of "On to Richmond!" culminated miserably in the Bull Run disaster. Samuel Bowles of the *Springfield Republican* kept up a lively criticism of Lincoln's conduct of the war. Even Joseph Medill, whose *Chicago Tribune* was an "original" Lincoln paper and generally supported the administration, could be a very distressing human gadfly on occasion, especially in urging radical policies toward the South such as the confiscation of Southern property. Medill was influential enough in a newspaper campaign to enable the soldiers at the front to cast their ballots in the election of 1864.

The Protestant press in the North, as Dr. C. F. Dunham shows, tended to be fervently pro-Union and antislavery. Southern church secessions of the 1840's and 1850's had left the Northern churches more united in their antislavery attitude. While Southern propagandists were emphasizing the distinction between fanatical Puritans and gentlemanly Cavaliers, many Northern ministers reversed this argument in their own favor. One Baptist minister, for example, argued:

> The Cavalier brought with him those ideas of proscription and caste which had led him to battle from the time of the Norman Conquest for aristocracy and absolutism. The Puritan brought with him those ideas of individual freedom and equality which . . . contained the germs of Republican life . . .

Most influential of all clerical writings was the short story, "The Man Without a Country," written by a Unitarian minister, Edward Everett Hale, and published in the *Atlantic Monthly* of December, 1863. Hale was proud of the fact that his father, a leading Boston newspaper editor, was the nephew of the Revolutionary patriot, Nathan Hale. Like other Boston intellectuals he had been active in the antislavery cause and in other reform campaigns. His largely fictional story dealt with the officer, Philip Nolan, who had bitterly damned the United States and said that he never wished to see it again—a desire that was fulfilled only too well during the isolated life that he thenceforth lived as a prisoner on a ship. Nolan's plight aroused a genuine fervor of renewed patriotism in the North. The story that was intended to influence the election of 1864 was to inspire later generations of schoolchildren as well.

6

The Negro was far from passive in a war that meant so much to him and his children. For a while, Southern Negroes tended to accept the Confederate explanation that the South was fighting solely against Yankee subjugation. The Southern press publicized in 1861 the loyalty of the slaves and the generous services of free Negroes in building fortifications. At first, several Negro regiments served in state forces, but these did little more than parade. Once the Emancipation Proclamation made it clear that freedom was the prize of a Union victory, thousands of slaves fled to the North. Insurrections flared up, especially in Mississippi, compelling white patrols to be more zealous than ever. Slaves plotted with Union troops, burnt strategic towns and villages, spied upon Confederate positions, fought as guerrillas behind the lines, or escaped to fight as Union soldiers. James Woodson, father of the noted historian, Dr. Carter G. Woodson, deserted his hard Virginia master to serve with Sheridan.

Over 186,000 Negroes were mustered into the Union armies and, despite white prejudices that confined most of the blacks to menial posts, many did fight on the battlefield. Nothing incensed the Rebels more than to face armed Negroes whom they sometimes refused to treat as prisoners when they captured them. To stop the killing or enslaving of captured Negro soldiers, federal officers threatened reprisals upon Confederate troops and thus ended most of the abuses. At Milliken's Bend, Louisiana, where Negro troops fought during 1863 in a battle of exceptional bitterness and ferocity against the Confederates, the official report sent to Grant stated, "Three fourths of the African troops that were slain were found dead in the ditch where they were ordered to make their stand."

Before the war ended, the Confederacy authorized the arming of 300,000 slaves in behalf of the South, but too few masters were yet willing to offer emancipation as a price for this service and little came of the plan. While innumerable personal servants showed a pathetic devotion to kindly masters even to the end, the Southern Negro was usually awake to the hope of freedom and was determined to take an active role in this great adventure. In Union-held areas, federal agencies for the freedmen tried to supply food, employment, and education. The wartime labor shortage in the North gave the Negroes in that section new economic opportunities despite the fact that prejudiced politicians in Illinois and Indiana tried to keep colored people out. The North was not prepared for social equality, little was done to adjust the Negro to Northern city life, and ignorant New York mobs attacked Negro workers as competitors for their jobs.

7

Behind the lines, civilian leaders marshaled every resource at their command, for modern wars had already become conflicts between rival home fronts as well as armies. The war planners were absorbed in developing stimulants for production and in gathering revenues through taxes, fiat money issues, and requisitions for goods. Southern belles left their seminaries to teach or to work at tasks hitherto held by men. In the North, where feminism had made far greater strides, thousands of women invaded the factories, shops, and offices and, as we have seen, made professional nursing into a career. On both sides, women took over the management and heavy labor of the farms while the men were in the army; this was often the sole alternative to the loss of crops. Overburdened with cotton supplies in the South, Davis stimulated the production of food crops as everyday necessities through his policy of exemptions for valuable civilian workers in field and factory.

Precious government contracts and the labor shortage accelerated the progress of mechanization in the North. Whereas 20,000 mowers were manufactured in 1861, 70,000 were made in 1864. McCormick's reapers and other machines were not too expensive for short-handed farmers enriched by high prices and war demands. Thus it happened that the loyal states, which had produced 138,000,000 bushels of wheat out of a national output of 173,000,000 in 1859, even exceeded that national total by 1862. The Homestead Act of 1862—which excluded Confederates from its benefits—gave away 2,500,000 acres to 20,000 families in two and a half years, thus enlarging the food output in wartime. Besides, the Illinois Central Railroad, a beneficiary of government land grants, sold excellent farm lands to 13,000 families. Even during wartime the Union astonished the world by exporting wheat and feeding hard-pressed Britain. "King Corn" it was said, had dethroned King Cotton. The sewing machines of Elias Howe and his rivals, encouraged by unprecedented orders for clothes, particularly government uniforms, revolutionized the textile business; federal contractors, however, continued to send most of their orders to private homes where the needle still reigned supreme. A man's shirt, which required almost fourteen and a half hours when made by hand, took no more than an hour and a quarter by machine. The principle of the sewing machine, as modified by Gordon McKay, led to the mechanization of shoe manufacturing. One man could now sew several hundred shoes a day by machine instead of the few he managed to finish by hand. Once steam power was added, the shoe factory displaced the numerous picturesque but inefficient cobbler's shops along the roads. Other industrial processes shared this new rapid momentum toward mechanization. Materials in short supply were stimulated by high prices and new mineral resources such as the copper and iron from the rich Lake Superior region. The discovery of oil at Titusville, Pennsylvania, in 1859 led to a major Civil War industry that furnished a cheap illuminant in kerosene; countless homes were cheered during the long evenings by the new "coal oil" lamps.

With the closing of the Mississippi by war, Chicago leaped forward in importance as the key city for the Northeast, thanks to railroad and lake steamer advantages. The meat-packing business almost tripled during the war years as a dozen important packing houses came into existence. At this time the huge Union Stock Yards, the most extensive in the world, were built covering three hundred acres and divided into pens for 10,000 cattle and 100,000 hogs, costing altogether $1,500,000. After the war, when the Texas cattle began to reach Chicago packers, the city's eminence as "hog-butcher of the world" soared even higher. The inevitable price for this distinction was an animal stench that suffocated the citizens and an aggregation of filth that poured into the river and the lake, polluting the water supply.

After an initial setback from the loss of Southern markets and the default of $300,000,000 in debts owed by Southerners, Northern business prospered. Bankers were harassed, it is true, by the wave of counterfeiting that accompanied the wartime confusion of dealing with 12,000 different kinds of banknotes. The ups and downs of Union campaigns affected the value of money and led to the depreciation of federal greenbacks. The greatest achievement of any banker was the sensational success of Jay Cooke of Philadelphia in floating successive federal bond issues directly to the people instead of dealing exclusively with the large banks. Employing an army of agents, bankers, brokers, and publicity men, he circularized the nation with a fanfare unprecedented in the sober annals of finance.

Labor, despite full employment, lost in real wages as inflation became steadily worse, recovering only in part after 1863. Hundreds of strikes, though usually of short duration, broke out and wartime conditions spurred on unionization. Strikers paraded with banners and bands, picketed employers, and blacklisted "scabs." Employers retaliated with lockouts at strategic times and often displaced their men with immigrants whom they hired through the offices of the American Emigrant Company. Labor resentments against Negro strikebreakers and the one-sided operation of the draft have already been noted. While wages for men never caught up with rising prices, the plight of working women was far worse. Taxes imposed on everything imaginable injured labor's income. The prewar trend toward national unions for single trades was accelerated, for these organizations afforded more adequate sickness and death benefits, served as employment agencies, and assisted traveling members. After the Civil War these national unions were to use their combined strength in collective bargaining with large corporations.

Injurious to morale, both North and South, were the profiteering extortions of speculators, blockade runners, sutlers, and corrupt contractors. While patriotic Southerners tried to cheer up the community with ascetic "starvation parties," the newly-rich classes did not hesitate to hold real parties and balls where all the scarce commodities suddenly appeared in abundance. In the North, where unscrupulous manufacturers and merchants sold shoddy uniforms and shoes to the government, the "shoddy aristocracy" thronged Saratoga and other watering places, displaying their fashionable clothes, gambling on the races, and drinking the most expensive wines. The term "shoddy" arose from the practice of certain manufacturers of pressing together rags of all hues into a semblance of wool felt that fell apart in the first real shower or revealed its original color after exposure for some time in the sunshine.

8

While the Civil War absorbed the fratricidal hates of the older states, the trans-Mississippi West was not content to remain a spectator. Not only were Texas, Louisiana, and Arkansas partners in the Confederate cause, but Missouri was torn between adherents of both sides and in the Far West a Texas-inspired plot took shape for a Confederate coalition of New Mexico, Arizona, and Southern California. Memories of "Bloody Kansas" of John Brown's day frightened the Middle Border as William C. Quantrell, an Ohio schoolteacher who had turned desperado, and his Confederate guerrillas sacked Lawrence in 1863 for the second time in its history, murdering almost two hundred people. Fighting and robbing on Quantrell's side, until Union men dispatched that guerrilla chief was a fifteen-year-old boy, Jesse James of Clay County, Missouri, who had been an informer against federal troops until he had joined the guerrillas. After the war the infamous Jesse James Band became outlaws, robbing railroads and banks until Jesse was killed in 1882; he was revered as a kind of Robin Hood in the ballads and dime novels perpetuating his memory.

Distinctions between the Blue and the Gray grew vague as Kansans conspired to rustle hundreds of thousands of cattle in Indian Territory, and brigands thrived on both sides. Most of the slaveholding Five Civilized Tribes of that territory—Cherokee, Creek, Choctaw, and Seminole—joined the Confederacy. Unionist sympathizers among the Creek and Cherokee left for Kansas. In Southern California, where the landowning and cattle-herding barons had long fought the power of the Northern counties with their mining, commercial, and diversified farming interests, secessionists banded together in local chapters of the Knights of the Golden Circle or the Knights of the Columbian Star. In Colorado Territory, Union troops cowed secessionists and kept an invading Confederate army from Texas from advancing into New Mexico.

For the time being war halted all plans for a transcontinental railroad, though it eliminated the hope of the South that the first projected road would be a Southern one. It also delayed the prewar promise of a prosperous cattle industry, for Union control of the Mississippi cut off the Confederate outlet for Texas cattle. There remained, regardless of war, the continued westward advance of the farmers, especially those bound for Kansas and Nebraska homes, and the exciting, if ephemeral, empire of the miners. The Homestead Act of 1862, passed by Congress after its secessionist opponents withdrew, excluded Confederates and helped to give New England institutions a stronger grip on the West than ever. In the years to come, however, railroad land grants were to give Southerners a second chance to become western farmers by selling relatively good land to them regardless of their rebel taint. Even in these years thousands of Southern veterans—and many a Yankee deserter or draft-evader, too—moved into the Great Plains or to the Pacific Coast. Pemberton's army of 30,000, which surrendered to Grant at Vicksburg, were released on a parole forbidding them to take up arms for the South again unless exchanged. For these men the new Northwest with its rich mines meant fresh opportunities to forget the ache of failure and futility.

In 1859, the Pikes Peak gold rush had attracted many thousands of eager prospectors and over-sanguine city builders. Across the Overland and Santa Fe trails came long trains of prairie schooners jauntily marked "Pikes Peak or Bust" and Horace Greeley arrived by the new Leavenworth and Pikes Peak stages to report enthusiastically on the cities springing up in the wilderness and on the heroism of the gold-seekers. Despite continual disappointments at Pikes Peak, which led disgruntled prospectors to chalk up on their returning wagons, "Busted, by Gosh!", riches came to others in the Gregory Lode near Central City, Colorado.

By 1861, the newcomers had persuaded Congress to give Colorado separate territorial status. This process of self-government, regardless of primitive conditions, led one Denver journalist to write: "Congregate a hundred Americans anywhere beyond the settlements and they immediately lay out a city, frame a state constitution and apply for admission into the Union, while twenty five of them become candidates for the United States Senate." Tough Denver, where every fifth building was a saloon and every tenth one a gambling hall, had more than its quota of loose women, outlaws, and guerrillas in a local extension of the Civil War that ended only after the secessionists were expelled. As a teeming center for mining supplies and adventurous social life, Denver flourished in its unsteady fashion.

Mountainous and desert Nevada, whose gold had been discovered almost at the same time as California's riches, actually won statehood in 1864, profiting by Lincoln's need for another state to ratify the Thirteenth Amendment abolishing slavery. Forty-niners who had neglected the California gold rush in the hope of finding more gold in Nevada awakened in 1859 to learn that their fabulously rich Comstock lode assayed over $4700 in gold and silver per ton, of which almost $3200 was in silver. The "blue stuff," which had been considered a hindrance to gold mining, turned out to be largely silver. Among the noteworthy fortunes won here was that of the prospector George Hearst, father of the journalist, William Randolph Hearst. This boom at Virginia City helped create the millionaires of Nob Hill, San Francisco, and made that California city more powerful than ever. By the end of the Civil War, Nevada had produced $43,000,000 in precious metals—a substantial gift to the Union cause.

While Grant faced Lee in Virginia, eager gold and silver miners were founding Helena at Last Chance Gulch, making Montana a separate territory in 1864. By the end of the war the peak of Montana mining had been reached with $18,000,000 mined in 1865. Idaho had a similar history, as did the Dakotas. Elsewhere prospectors made their exciting strikes, disregarding the Indian titles that still blanketed so much of the Far West. Although mining was carried on only from transient tent towns or shanty settlements, it was nonetheless disturbing as a disruptive force on the earlier life of

the Great Plains. At first, placer mining, which searched for par-
ticles of the precious metals washed up from the streams, was the
chief method, but it provided work only in warm weather; once
the source or lode was discovered, expensive year-round excavating
with machinery was required; at this point the corporation stepped
in and mining became an increasingly impersonal business.

In the early mining town, life moved on at a dizzy pace marked
by fabulous price inflation as well as by adventure, with gambling
houses, saloons, and painted ladies of the dance halls draining off
the surplus money. Dan Rice's circus made the rounds among these
towns even in the war years and entertainers of all kinds, from
phrenologists and ventriloquists to lecturers and actors, were usually
certain of an audience. With pistols almost a conventional part of
the attire, life was lived dangerously and men frequently died with
their boots on—and were buried without coffins in bleak mine regions where few trees grew. As in earlier frontier settlements, out-
lawry was rife and vigilante justice common among a population
heavily drawn from the most adventurous souls, including not a
few professional cutthroats, thieves, and reckless debtors. A peculiar
and notorious variant of frontier criminal was Henry Plummer, a
sheriff of Virginia City, Montana, who organized a gang of stage-
coach thieves as his deputies and murdered over a hundred travelers to conceal his thefts. By 1865, however, Montana vigilantes
trapped these "road agents" and hanged Plummer together with
nearly all of his accomplices.

The thriving mineral empire and the increasing importance of the
Far West led Congress to subsidize a transcontinental stage-coach
system to carry the mail as well as passenger traffic. In 1858, John
Butterfield's Overland Mail coaches crossed the plains, beginning
at St. Louis or Memphis, going to El Paso, and finally connecting
with Los Angeles and San Francisco. This trip was broken by stops
at stations some ten or fifteen miles apart and occasionally was enlivened by Indian attacks or holdups by road agents. Samuel
Clemens, soon to be renowned as Mark Twain, traveled with his
brother Orion by steamboat from St. Louis up the Missouri and then
by Overland stage coach to Nevada where Orion had been ap-

pointed secretary of the territory. Armed with Colt revolvers, they watched apprehensively for Indians, being worried over the tell-tale bullet holes in the stage curtains. They escaped the homicidal toughs of the plains, like the notorious Slade, and even survived the lethal greasy meals of bacon and "slumgullion" served at the un-heated adobe stage stations. The passengers amused themselves by shooting at jackrabbits, gaped at the unbelievable speed of the phantom pony express riders, and accumulated a stock of jokes about Mormon polygamy during the stop at Salt Lake City—later embellished and retold in Twain's *Roughing It.*

The transcontinental express and mail businesses were combined and expanded by Ben Holladay, "the Napoleon of the Plains," who covered over 3300 miles of stage lines, using some 700 men and over 1000 horses and mules by the time the war ended. He sold his holdings in 1866 to Wells, Fargo and Company, in time to escape the competition of the newly installed telegraph. For the heavy over-land freighting needed by the Union Army as well as by large commercial firms, the chief concern was Russell, Majors, and Wad-dell. Their numerous warehouses, huge wagons, 6000 teamsters, and many thousands of oxen testified to the extent of this early transportation business. Serving this firm was the half-legendary William Cody—"Buffalo Bill"—who was at various times a pony express rider and a wagon boss.

Russell, Majors, and Waddell introduced the famous Pony Ex-press in 1860 to expedite messages. These fast horses were ridden by light men who carried small packages of mail written on thin paper along a relay route, changing horses at each twenty-mile sta-tion until relieved by other riders. Wild Indians, piercing blizzards, and sudden illness failed to interrupt the service. While Butterfield's stage line could deliver messages from the Missouri frontier to the Pacific in twenty-five days, the Pony Express riders did it in ten and could boast of delivering Lincoln's first inaugural address in seven days and seventeen hours.

This bizarre episode in transportation history quickly came to an end, for its excessive costs made the Pony Express an ephemeral adventure. On October 24, 1861, the transcontinental telegraph was completed after being subsidized by the Treasury and contracted for by the head of the Western Union Telegraph Company, Hiram Sibley of New York. Buffaloes rubbed against the poles and knocked them down; angry Indians tore down the wires, and not a few westerners joined in the demolition, thinking that the wires were very convenient for wrapping and other purposes. Soldiers had to patrol the line while telegraph operators kept a vigil over each connection. Thus East and West were united at a time when North and South were battling one another. The penetration of the Great Plains advanced another major step.

Such sensational speed in conquering the plains, the mountains, and the deserts inevitably brought on clashes with the Indians. Disregarding the U.S.-Indian treaties, newcomers killed off the buffalo and smaller game and not only violated promises of protection, but even drove off and abused the Indian inhabitants. Hundreds of battles and skirmishes were fought against a desperate foe and both sides resorted to cold-blooded slaughter, mutilation, and trickery. Assimilationist Indians—"farmers" as they were called in the Missouri Valley—lost their influence among tribesmen to the traditionalists—the "blanket Indians"—as the evidence of the white man's greed and irresponsibility mounted. The conflicting policies of the War and Interior departments, one bent on subduing the Indian, the other on protecting him, confused and angered the Indians. White outlaws robbed the redmen with impunity and traders often did the same thing. In California, the various tribes had been thoroughly debauched, driven from their lands, reduced to beggary, and put on the road to extinction.

Elusive Apaches of New Mexico and Arizona, familiar with the endless canyons and isolated mountain hide-outs, raided white settlements and held off American and Mexican troops. The Navajo of the Southwest struck repeatedly until 7000 of them were forced to surrender in a New Mexican canyon to Kit Carson's troops. Similar uprisings broke out in Utah, Colorado territory, and especially among the Sioux in Minnesota. The Siouan tribes proved a dogged foe in the Minnesota River valley, in the Dakotas, in Montana, and in Wyoming territory.

In their turn, federal generals, angered by the Indian guerrilla tactics and attacks upon the settlements, tolerated or even encouraged vicious retaliation. The worst example was the Sand Creek Massacre of 1864 in southeast Colorado, an incident provoked by Colonel J. M. Chivington. His men, according to considerable (though not uncontested) testimony, murdered four or five hundred Cheyenne men, women, and children, mostly defenseless people, butchering them in barbaric style, destroying the lodges, and seizing their livestock. The Sand Creek Massacre incited the Cheyenne, Arapaho, and Sioux (Dakota) to savage retaliations, killing, and robbing settlers, and even smashing military detachments sent against them. Years were to elapse before the last of these Indian wars ended. Lincoln, appalled by the repetition of Indian uprisings, asked Congress for a new Indian policy to insure the welfare of the tribes as well as the safety of the whites. But this had to wait until the Civil War was long over.

9

"This war has brought the levity of the American character out in bold relief," wrote the strait-laced correspondent of the London *Times* in November, 1863, shocked at the perpetual round of amusements on both sides of the Mason and Dixon line. In the North, where opportunities were especially great, merchants and lawyers tasted pleasures only dimly known in piping times of peace. Horseracing, which had been almost surrendered to the border states and the deep South, revived on a large scale around Chicago, Boston, St. Louis, and elsewhere, with fancy purses at stake. Grand opera, including German, Italian, and English varieties, reported its most brilliant season in 1863-64. Gounod's *Faust* made its debut in an era when its "Soldier's Chorus" could thrill martial Americans.

Negro minstrel shows drew larger crowds than ever. According to Fite, "Twenty-five negro troupes toured the country in the season of 1864, all playing to crowded houses." Barnum's dwarf, General Tom Thumb, shone in the presence of a distinguished crowd at his well-publicized wedding. Traveling circuses, Irish prize fighters, billiard or chess championship matches, all had their full share of spectators. Several champion chess matches were even carried on by telegraph. In the colleges, boating continued its prewar vogue and a new game, baseball, was gaining ground. Serving in the Union armies was General Abner Doubleday, who was credited with originating the rules and the diamond-shaped playing field for baseball at Cooperstown, New York, in 1839. However, this claim has been effectively challenged by those who have traced the easily recognized antecedents of the game to at least eighteenth-century English and colonial American times. Oliver Wendell Holmes (Harvard, Class of 1829) recalled his college days when he had played baseball frequently. By the Civil War, baseball had evolved considerably from the old English children's game of "Rounders" and that variation known as "New York baseball" won the ascendancy through being played by Union soldiers from New York and New Jersey during the leisure hours between active assignments. Just before the war, New York city had a National Association of Baseball Players consisting of sixteen clubs and operating according to well-defined rules. While the war discouraged civilian players outside of the colleges, the Union armies kept the awakening American enthusiasm for baseball at a high level. Nor did the war interfere with a new English game, croquet, which arrived during the late fifties and assumed the proportion of a popular craze. Ice-skating seemed more popular than ever during the winter season and the less-athletic devoted themselves to a rising hobby of collecting photographs in neatly arrayed albums.

The stage fairly outdid itself in brilliance during the war years, though its history was to be tragically allied with the assassination of President Lincoln. On the fatal night of April 14, 1865, while the nation was jubilantly celebrating the end of the war, Lincoln decided to relax by going to Ford's Theatre to see Laura Keene, the versatile comedienne, in *Our American Cousin,* a play that the management claimed had run for one thousand nights. Here he was murdered in his box by the half-crazed actor, John Wilkes Booth. This was the son of the erratic genius of the stage, Junius Brutus Booth, and the brother of the talented actor, Edwin Booth. John him-

self was a Shakespearean interpreter of distinction and had successfully toured the South and the Northwest in 1861, impressing
audiences with the realism of his Romeo and his Anthony. A theatrical critic who knew the family well observed, "John has more of the
old man's power in one performance than Edwin can show in a
year." Alone of his family, he had turned into a proslavery fire-eater
and relished the real-life role he played in the Virginia militia in
arresting and executing John Brown. Once before, in 1864, he had
plotted to kill Lincoln.

The man who could draw crowded playhouses better than any
other actor was Edwin Forrest, who emulated the passionate style
of the noted English star, Edmund Kean. His athletic figure and
stentorian vigor of expression won him the admiring shouts of the
galleries. Long a stormy petrel of the American stage, he sent his
notorious claques to hiss down rivals and added to his publicity by
a sensational divorce suit. So devoted were his wartime audiences
that he earned $20,000 in gold for thirty-five performances in San
Francisco and by 1866 was earning $2500 a night in Chicago.

The Civil War, perhaps in larger measure than is true of other
conflicts, was fought with songs as well as lethal weapons. Publishers reaped fortunes from best-selling songbooks. The South had
its "Marseillaise" in "Maryland! My Maryland!" written by a Balti-
more-born college professor, James Ryder Randall, after reading
of the attacks upon Union troops by many pro-Southern citizens
of his native city. The Cary sisters of Baltimore set the words to a
college tune adapted from "Tannenbaum, O Tannenbaum." One
of the greatest prizes of the musical duel, "Dixie," with new bellicose words by Albert Pike, went to the South, though its author,
Dan Emmett, had written it in 1859 for Bryant's Minstrels in New
York as a "walk-around." Next to these favorites among the new
songs was "The Bonny Blue Flag," written by an English-born
comedian, Harry Macarthy, who was serving in a Confederate regi-
ment in New Orleans.

In the North, Julia Ward Howe, liberal reformer, decided that
the words to a current soldier's tune, "John Brown's Body Lies
A-mouldering in the Grave," with its crudity about hanging Jeff

Davis to a sour apple tree (not to mention the bawdy parodies on this theme) was unworthy of the fine Methodist hymn, "Say, Brothers, Will You Meet Us?" Thereupon, she sat down to write the words of "The Battle Hymn of the Republic," beginning with the fervent prayer, "Mine eyes have seen the glory of the coming of the Lord." How these stirring words, originally published in the *Atlantic Monthly* of February, 1862, swept the country has often been told. Enthusiastic honors fell to Mrs. Howe on a scale unbelievable to the author at the time she composed this national hymn.

The nostalgic song, "We Are Tenting Tonight on the Old Camp Ground," was too good to keep north of the Mason and Dixon line, for Johnny Reb sang it heartily, too, and shared its sentiment of homesickness and war-weariness. However, no true Confederate cared to steal the song, "Marching through Georgia," written by Henry Clay Work, author of innumerable catchy tunes for all occasions, to express the jubilation of the North at impending victory. This triumphant music kept Southern resentment alive at Sherman's deliberate destruction of a wide swathe of Georgia's richest fields and homes. One of the first American generals to develop the concept of total war, Sherman justified his acts by insisting that Southern civilians were actually guerrillas and saboteurs and therefore must be treated as enemy soldiers. Scores of sentimental songs about home and mother enjoyed lasting popularity: "Just before the Battle, Mother," which the Rebels also found suitable, "When Will My Darling Boy Return?" and "When This Cruel War Is Over." But the old songs were those most often sung, the familiar hymns of the village and the nostalgic themes of peacetime like "Annie Laurie" and "Home, Sweet Home."

Poets found an immense vogue for war lyrics. Longfellow complained that his fellow-craftsmen could think of nothing but war themes. Most of the Civil War poetry proved ephemeral, though Walt Whitman left a haunting sense of beauty and anguish in his Lincoln memoriam, "When Lilacs Last in the Dooryard Bloomed." The plain citizen preferred his metrical expression of grief, "O Captain! My Captain!" and schoolchildren were to perpetuate its memory. However, these were actually postwar poems. The Quaker poet, Whittier, wrote the most defiant war poem of all in "Barbara Frietchie," whose literary inconsequence was overlooked because of the unique patriotic sentiment of an old lady who shamed the Confederates by stubbornly holding up the Stars and Stripes at the risk of being shot. After the war, Whittier was to find a better theme in "Snowbound," a winter idyll of New England filled with a deep sense of peace and a love of nature. But the war poems of Emerson, Melville, Bret Harte, and Oliver Wendell Holmes were to be largely forgotten.

The Confederacy was honored with the finest poetry that Dixieland had yet produced. Her best poets knew the sacrifices and sufferings of army life and drew their themes from the heat and emotions of battle. Henry Timrod, "the laureate of the Confederacy," gave his stillborn nation its noblest apostrophe in "Ethnogenesis." This poem was one of the very few genuine Southern poems that depicted the actual Southland instead of giving vague idealizations of it in descriptions that could fit almost any country. Although he briefly condemned the fanaticism, the hypocrisy, and the unorthodoxy of the North, he devoted his poem largely to the beauty of his native Southland. Even more indigenous was his poem, "The Cotton Boll," which dealt even more convincingly with the Southern environment, the cotton fields, the pine forests, and the mountains. While he begged the Lord to bring the "Goth" to his knees, he also prayed that the Confederate States would "revive the half-dead dream of universal peace." Timrod, leaving the army after contracting tuberculosis, lived on to endure the final humiliation of defeat and the destruction of his home and livelihood with the wartime burning of Columbia, South Carolina. His fellow Carolinian poet, Paul Hamilton Hayne, carried on the indigenous lyrical spirit awakened during the war. Hayne's best poem, "The Battle of Charleston Harbor," expressed a deep love for his native city.

Amid the tragedy of war, there was still room for comedy and humor. Lincoln, himself, kept his mental balance by giving play to his keen frontier sense of humor, as has been so often noted. His serious-minded cabinet could not understand his habit of telling humorous stories at critical times, especially his reading aloud of Artemus Ward's jokes just before discussing the Emancipation Proclamation. Charles Farrar Browne, a columnist for the *Cleveland Plain Dealer*, had in 1862 just sold 40,000 copies of his humorous and ardently pro-Union work, *Artemus Ward: His Book*. With marked success, he mixed puns, rustic dialect, crude spelling, and utter incongruities. On the lecture platform, where he chose subjects that had nothing to do with his talk, he kept a "dead pan" expression while retailing hilarious nonsense. A San Francisco theater manager wired him, "What will you take for forty nights in California." He replied, "Brandy and water." Socially conservative, he followed the conventional line of poking fun at women's rights and utopian community experiments. He pictured several masculine-looking suffragettes of the "Bunkumville Female Reformin & Wimen's Rite Associashun" trying to enter his show (he took the role of a showman) without paying and asking imperiously if he knew who they were. "My impreshun is," sed I, "from a kersery view, that you air females." In his half-serious moralistic argument, he paid his homage to womankind, "The female woman is one of the greatest institooshuns of which this land can boste;" but, he concluded triumphantly, "when you undertake to play the man, you play the devil and air an emfatic noosance."

Although twentieth-century tastes can scarcely relish the witticisms of Orpheus C. Kerr and Josh Billings, both convulsed Civil War audiences. Robert H. Newell's "Orpheus C. Kerr" papers—the name is apparently a mouthing of "office seeker"—were written in the form of Washington correspondence and attempted a comic commentary upon the direction of the war, including Dickens-style dialogue, parodies, and sentimental poems. Henry Wheeler Shaw, a proverbial rolling stone, gathered a good deal of moss after Artemus Ward helped him publish *Josh Billings: His Sayings*, which was Yankee humor ornamented with fanciful misspellings. In his *Essa on the Muel*, he began, "The mule is haf hoss and haf Jackass, and then kums to a full stop, natur diskovering her mistake." In "Josh Billings' Aphorisms" were some mild efforts at homely humor:

Mankind love misterys, a hole in the ground excits more wonder than a star up in heaven.

I often hear affekshunate husbands kall their wifes "Mi Duck"—i wunder if this aint a sli delusion tew their big bills?

10

The inner world of creative ideas and intellectual life was neglected during the war, though the amassed wealth of Northern businessmen made possible an unusual expansion of educational and scientific institutions. Vassar College, with $400,000 from a wealthy brewer of that name, and the Massachusetts Institute of Technology, with generous state funds, dedicated their buildings in wartime. The early multimillionaire, Ezra Cornell, whose $5,000,-000 fortune grew out of his profits as an associate of Morse in founding the telegraph and as the largest stockholder of the Western Union Telegraph Company, established Cornell University at Ithaca, New York, in 1865. He endowed it with $500,000 and a gift of 300 acres of land. Yale received heavy endowments to build the noted Sheffield Scientific School and Harvard also did well in financing the Lawrence Scientific School.

Even more significant was the passage in 1862 of the Morrill Land Grant College Act, which gave the states 30,000 acres of public land for each senator and representative in Congress. The proceeds were to be used for state colleges "without excluding scientific and other practical studies, and including military tactics, to teach such branches of learning as are related to agriculture and the mechanic arts." This meant that something more ambitious than mere "cow colleges" was intended by Congress. Eventually, 13,000,000 acres of public land were to be given away under this Act for agricultural, industrial, and general education. While Northern colleges declined in enrollment and Southern colleges sometimes collapsed entirely, the elementary schools expanded despite teacher shortages. The new high school movement in the North was retarded by the withdrawal of many boys for military service, industry, or farm work. Instruction suffered from war propaganda. Wiley notes a Southern textbook that poses this relevant problem, "If one Confederate can whip 7 Yankees, how many soldiers can whip 49 Yankees?"

Scientists too often were compelled to divert their energies to war assignments. Joseph Le Conte, the geologist, busied himself in trying to solve the acute Confederate shortage of munitions and medicines. Matthew F. Maury was experimenting in Richmond with a submarine electrical torpedo. Louis Agassiz concentrated on applied science at the expense of theoretical problems. Scientific societies decided to suspend meetings or occupied themselves with war researches. Literary men, as already noted, responded heavily to war themes. Even the pacific Emerson lost his poise sufficiently to praise war in the abstract:

War is a realist, shatters everything flimsy and shifty, sets aside all false issues, and breaks through all that is not real as itself; ... like its own cannonade, comes crushing in through party walls that have stood fifty or sixty years as if they were solid.

Most lasting in the world of letters and ideas was the magnificent prose of Abraham Lincoln. His Gettysburg address, a miracle of brevity and depth, gave future democrats a fighting faith based on the ideal of human equality. Even his political speeches and his inaugural addresses had the quality of intimacy and a kindly appeal to reasonableness. Though his Whiggish notions of the indestructible Union were partly those of the conservatives, Marshall and Webster, he conceived of the Union as an instrument of beneficent change in behalf of the common man. His early social heritage had left him with doubts regarding social equality between the races and with lukewarmness toward immediate emancipation, but his humane inclinations led him, like Jefferson, gradually to discard earlier prejudices as his education unfolded. In his Second Inaugural Address of March 4, 1865, he spoke openly of a war to the death against slavery:

Fondly do we hope, fervently do we pray, that this mighty scourge of war may speedily pass away. Yet, if God wills that it continue until all the wealth piled by the bondman's two-hundred and fifty years of

unrequited toil shall be sunk, and until every drop of blood drawn with
the lash shall be paid by another drawn with the sword, as was said
three thousand years ago, so still it must be said, that the judgments of
the Lord are true and righteous altogether.

Many Americans were to recall far more readily the plea, in the
next sentence he spoke, for the reconstituting of American nationality in the spirit of the Sermon on the Mount:

With malice toward none; with charity for all; with firmness in the
right, as God gives us to see the right, let us strive on to finish the work
we are in; to bind up the nation's wounds; to care for him who shall
have borne the battle, and for his widow and his orphan—to do all which
may achieve and cherish a just and lasting peace among ourselves and
with all nations.

To keep America "one and inseparable" cost over 359,000 Union
lives and almost 134,000 Confederate slain. The freedom of 4,000,-
000 slaves cost the planters four billions in the capital these slaves
represented. Unlike the lucky British West Indies slaveholders,
who had been compensated for emancipation, the planters of Dixieland received absolutely nothing, bearing this loss together with
the dissipation of the millions they had futilely poured into Confederate bonds, war taxes, and other such costs. The race problem
and racial prejudices remained as did the poverty of the Southern
white masses; and the freedmen had yet to undergo a stage of
peonage before genuine citizenship could be won. But the national
humiliation of slavery was ended and millions of Negroes soon
became American citizens after a naturalization period of over two
centuries.

At Washington, the wartime transfer of political power to Northern merchants, industrialists, and farmers—the broad Republican
coalition of 1860 and 1864—meant that American nationality would
be bound up with a liberal middle-class program hitherto thwarted
by the planters. Already a Homestead Act, a Land Grant College
Act, a moderate tariff law, and a transcontinental railroad charter
had been voted. North and West united to create the greatest industrial era in American history, even before the "road to reunion"

with the South had been discovered. The war settled the unfinished business left by the American Revolution, for it redefined the constitutional terms upon which all sections and classes were to cooperate. The terms were those that the Industrial Revolution had made inevitable—the leadership of the industrial middle class.

Since the Jamestown colony and the Plymouth Rock landing, America had made great strides from a colonial status that was political, economic, and cultural, but the process was not yet complete. Industrially, America had become a serious competitor of England and France for world markets but the vast underdeveloped resources at home continued to act as a magnet for foreign and domestic capital. Agriculture, fed by a huge reservoir of vacant lands, absorbed most of American labor, although the pattern of farm mechanization was beginning to emerge, especially during the Civil War. Culturally, especially in the arts, the colonial status continued and literary geniuses like Whitman and Melville were grossly underrated both at home and abroad, even though Europeans had ceased to repeat Sidney Smith's rhetorical question of 1820, "Who reads an American book?" An expanding economy had created a wealthy class of patrons like Cornell and Vassar, and there was considerable mass patronage of the arts and sciences, but the colonial psychology led Americans to overlook talented native painters, musicians, and novelists for Europeans with more impressive reputations. While European visitors criticized the provincial character of a dollar-worshipping society as revealed in the mass patronage given to mere spectacles like those of Barnum or to mechanical inventions like the daguerreotype, the new western European cities born of the Industrial Revolution—and many peasant communities, too—showed similar affinities for the practical and the applied. American cultural colonialism, despite the frontier and rural life, did not spring from primitive roots, for its inhabitants were the direct heirs of a rich European tradition.

One acute English observer, Edward Dicey, wrote that Americans "value the possession of the 'almighty dollar' rather as a proof of success in life than as an end of existence." In a nation without an aristocracy or a learned leisure class, status was often determined by the ability to earn large sums. It is unnecessary to fall back upon the Calvinist heritage that stressed the gospel of success as evidence of salvation in order to explain the significance of status even in a democratic society. A secondary feature of status in America was spending, even to the extent of profligacy, a practice curiously similar to the potlatch of the Pacific Northwest tribes. So eager were Americans to squander their money that family accumulations were relatively few and numerous wealthy families were reduced to modest conditions in one or two generations. Two Hungarian liberals, Francis and Theresa Pulszky, stressed the generosity of Americans, especially their huge contributions for churches, hospitals, colleges, libraries, and charitable institutions. A Polish visitor was enchanted to hear over and over again the hospitable American phrase, "Help Yourself!" Frontier generosity and the bankrupting nature of Southern hospitality have already been noted.

Educated foreign visitors complained that Americans were voluble but monotonous. "I believe that this monotony in the tone of American talk and opinion," wrote Dicey, "arises from the universal diffusion of education. Everybody is educated up to a certain point, and very few are educated above it." Still travelers conceded the avid thirst of Americans for information, if not for abstract thought. As for the boastfulness attributed to "Brother Jonathan," he made no secret of his belief that America was a success as compared to "effete" Europe and he angrily resented the slurs of Dickens, Frances Trollope, and Carlyle. His continental resources led him to waste his forests and butcher his soil in a way that shocked visitors from less favored lands. There was little inducement for conservation, though every incentive existed in this land of plenty to conserve the relatively scarce labor supply. Hence Connecticut Yankees like Eli Whitney prepared the way for the truly American tradition of mass production in a country that had been only lightly touched by traditional guild restrictions.

Captain Frederick Marryat of England and other foreign observers poked fun at American prudishness and sex inhibitions—though they could have made similar judgments of the Anglo-Canadians and much of the Victorian world of western Europe. Marryat told the story of how he offended an American woman by saying "legs" instead of "limbs" and of the girls' seminary where piano "limbs" were dressed "in modest little trousers, with frills at the bottom of them!" However, this tale of piano pantalettes is said to have been manufactured by a mischievous American who retailed it to the credulous Marryat. Noah Webster, "schoolmaster to America," had done much to purge the American language of robust Anglo-Saxon words. Undoubtedly American sex inhibitions—insofar as they were at all unique—owed a good deal to the numerous dissenting sects, like Walther's "puritanical" German Lutherans and the evangelical cults among the Methodists and Baptists; one need not go back to the alleged Puritan origin for this trait.

American middle-class reticence on sex matters was also related to the high status of women in a frontier society where their relative scarcity and economic opportunities made them more difficult to please in courtship. While the South enjoyed a latter-day chivalry with roots deep in feudal times, the North, too, had its ritual of courtesies due to women. Everywhere, seduction and breach of promise suits were apt to be prejudiced in the woman's favor. Here one addressed a mixed audience as "Ladies and Gentlemen" instead of the traditional "Gentlemen and Ladies." Women traveled alone without losing caste and their daughters dispensed with chaperons (even if they belonged to the well-to-do class). While the Industrial Revolution was emancipating western European women as well as their American sisters, the American woman was definitely ahead in status—though the chivalry accorded her concealed the fact that she, too, was denied very vital liberties in the spheres of her person, her property, her marital rights, and her choice of livelihood.

Among those things distinctive of antebellum America was its unique role as the cultural and economic laboratory of Europe, where the dreams of European as well as American innovators and rebels might be lived or at least tested. Religious and economic dissenters from Great Britain, France, Germany, and Scandinavia had found wish-fulfillment in thriving communities and had evolved a practical formula for getting along without recurrent struggles and suspicions. Even the huge Catholic influx into a land of militant

Protestants produced only temporary violence and, as it turned out, even strengthened the principle of separation of church and state. The utopian ideas of Roger Williams, William Penn, and Étienne Cabet had been tested on New World soil; Tocqueville and Beaumont had studied penal theories as they operated in a new country, using these observations as a basis for French reforms. Although feudal lords had also attempted to experiment with an American variety of a stratified feudal society, they had been rebuffed by frontier conditions that favored equality of opportunity rather than fixed status. In the sciences, naturalized Americans from Alexander Wilson and Audubon to Louis Agassiz found the American forests a laboratory in a very literal sense. Out of such rich intercultural contacts, American nationality had emerged, not only the product of the usable past of England and to a lesser extent of the Continent and Africa, but also the creature of the liberating forces of its own land and people.

Freedom, in the sense of middle-class liberalism, had made revolutionary gains on both sides of the Atlantic. America owed much to English liberalism as it was formulated during and after the Puritan revolution. To the liberalism of Milton and Locke were later added religious tolerance and the social awareness implied in the rise of English trade unionism, abolitionism, and factory reform. The world of Roger Williams had been half-medieval in its adherence to political controls over economic life, but it had long watched the development of large-scale private enterprise and the capitalist spirit. The liberal doctrine of buying in the cheapest market and selling in the dearest had troubled John Cotton and other colonials who could not reconcile themselves to the ethics of *laissez-faire*. Even with the progress of liberal economic doctrines in the eighteenth century, the generation of Franklin and Jefferson were too bound up with traditional religious and ethical concepts regarding the nature of man and his role in the community to yield to the notion that economic forces must be given unrestricted play. The statute books and the courts, well into the mid-nineteenth century, revealed a sharp distrust of unregulated economic life. The innumerable utopian experiments, mass education, abolitionism, and trade unionism in the era of Jackson and Lincoln revealed the same ethical belief that cooperation rather than reliance upon blind economic determinism would best preserve the values of democratic individualism.

Imported liberal theories were modified by an increasingly exalted concept of the nature of man. The sinful man of Milton's *Paradise Lost*, so familiar to Calvinist theology, became a more secular and reasonable person in the eighteenth century; but, as Madison, Hamilton, and Jay insisted, he was a creature of self-interest who had to be kept in restraint by political checks and balances. By the time of Horace Mann and Ralph Waldo Emerson, the enthusiastic environmentalists taught that man, given a proper education, was plastic psychologically and responsive to the highest motivations. To Emerson, the thinking man was part and parcel of God—not merely a degraded son of Adam. The crusade against slavery, in which many Southerners had been leaders until the 1830's, was in large part an expression of the idealism that stemmed from the concept of Emerson, Whitman, and Thoreau regarding man's dignity. This ethical tradition harked back to the religious idealism of Roger Williams and the great ethical teachers of the past.

Select Bibliography

· 1 ·

THE ENGLAND OF ROGER WILLIAMS

On the controversial origins of modern capitalism, the most balanced analysis appears in Richard H. Tawney, *Religion and the Rise of Capitalism* (Harcourt, Brace, 1926); the influence of John Calvin is even more heavily stressed in Max Weber, *The Protestant Ethic and the Spirit of Capitalism* (Allen and Unwin, 1930). Hector M. Robertson offers a sharp historical critique of the Weber thesis in *Aspects of the Rise of Economic Individualism* (Cambridge University, 1935).

The meaning and historical ramifications of liberalism are developed convincingly in Harold J. Laski, *The Rise of European Liberalism* (Allen and Unwin, 1936), and in J. S. Schapiro, *Liberalism and the Challenge of Fascism* (McGraw-Hill, 1949), chapters 1 and 2. Other concepts relevant here are discussed in Roscoe Pound, "Common Law," *Encyclopedia of the Social Sciences;* B. Groethuysen, "Renaissance," *ibid.;* H. R. Niebuhr, "Reformation," *ibid.;* G. de Ruggiero, "Religious Freedom," *ibid.* An excellent handbook for the intellectual history of modern Europe is John H. Randall, Jr., *Making of the Modern Mind* (Houghton Mifflin, 1940).

For the background of the Roger Williams theme used in this chapter, see S. H. Brockunier, *The Irrepressible Democrat: Roger Williams* (Ronald Press, 1940). The most useful single volume dealing with all phases of this chapter is Godfrey Davies, *The Early Stuarts, 1603-1660* (Oxford, 1937). Percy A. Scholes explodes the myth that the Puritans hated music and esthetics in *The Puritans and Music In England and New England* (Oxford, 1934). Other relevant aspects are dealt with in G. M. Trevelyan, *English Social History* (Longmans, Green, 1946); C. M. Andrews, *The Colonial Period of American History* (Yale, 1933), I; Marshall M. Knappen, *Tudor Puritanism* (University of Chicago, 1939); L. B. Wright, *Middle-class Culture in Elizabethan England* (University of North Carolina, 1935); David M. Robb and J. J. Gar·

577

rison, *Art in the Western World* (Harper, 1942, rev.); and Curtis P. Nettels, *The Roots of American Civilization* (Crofts, 1939).

• 2 •

THE NEW ENGLAND OF ROGER WILLIAMS

Foremost among the scholars who have revised the unfavorable stereotype of the Puritans left by their enemies are: Samuel Morison, *The Puritan Pronaos: Studies in the Intellectual Life of New England in the Seventeenth Century* (Oxford Press, 1936) and his *Builders of the Bay Colony* (Houghton Mifflin, 1930) ; Perry Miller, *The New England Mind* (Macmillan, 1939), which contains ideas much more simply summarized in the introduction to P. Miller and T. H. Johnson, *The Puritans* (American Book, 1938); Ralph B. Perry, *Puritanism and Democracy* (Vanguard, 1945), a very sympathetic essay; Herbert W. Schneider, *A History of American Philosophy* (Columbia, 1946); and P. A. Scholes, *The Puritans and Music*...cited.

The best among the other specialized studies of Puritan life and thought include: Kenneth Murdock, *Increase Mather* (Harvard, 1925); Richard B. Morris, *Government and Labor in the Early American Colonies* (Columbia, 1946) and his very original *Studies in the History of American Law* (Columbia, 1930); Marcus W. Jernegan, *Laboring and Dependent Classes in Colonial America, 1607-1783* (University of Chicago, 1931); Lorenzo J. Green, *The Negro in Colonial New England, 1620-1776* (Columbia, 1942), which shows how startlingly alike were the reactions of slaveholding New England and of the antebellum South; George F. Willison, *Saints and Strangers* (Reynal and Hitchcock, 1945), easily the most fascinating account of life among the Pilgrims; George F. Dow, *Everyday Life in the Massachusetts Bay Colony* (Society for the Preservation of New England Antiquities, Boston, 1935); Thomas F. Wright, *Literary Culture in Early New England, 1620-1730* (Yale, 1920), which contains invaluable lists of Puritan-owned books as revealed by inventories; and E. P. Cubberley, *Public Education in the United States* (Houghton Mifflin, 1934), still the most informative single volume, though weak on interpretation. Vernon L. Parrington has written the most provocative interpretation of the economic assumptions underlying American thought, though his section on the Puritans has been severely shaken by the revisionists, *The Colonial Mind, 1620-*

1800: Main Currents in American Thought (Harcourt, Brace, 1927), vol. 1. Most useful in social history among the basic first-hand accounts are William T. Davis (ed.), *Bradford's History of Plymouth Plantation, 1606-1646* (Scribner, 1908), *Winthrop's Journal* (1630-1649) (Scribner, 1908), 2 vols., and *Winthrop Papers* (Massachusetts Historical Society, 1929-1947), 5 vols.

· 3 ·

FEUDALISM AND THE FRONTIER IN FITZHUGH'S VIRGINIA: THE SEVENTEENTH CENTURY

The numerous works of Philip A. Bruce on Virginia, while encyclopedic rather than analytical and modified by subsequent studies of others, must still be consulted for many social and economic aspects, particularly his *Economic History of Virginia in the Seventeenth Century* (Macmillan, 1907), 2 vols., *Institutional History of Virginia in the Seventeenth Century* (Putnam, 1910), 2 vols., and *The Virginia Plutarch* (University of North Carolina, 1929). Fundamental aspects of the Bruce presentation have been revised by Thomas J. Wertenbaker, who has stressed the basic fact that the overwhelming majority of Southerners were small farmers, not aristocrats, and that their culture reflected this situation; see his *The Planters of Colonial Virginia* (Princeton, 1922), *Torchbearer of the Revolution* (Princeton, 1940), dealing with Nathaniel Bacon, and *The Old South: The Founding of American Civilization* (Scribner, 1942). Between the emphasis of Bruce on the aristocratic heritage and that of Wertenbaker on the democratic rural aspect of the South is the imaginative interpretation of Louis B. Wright, who shows the role of an elite of about one hundred families in the affairs of Virginia, *The First Gentleman of Virginia* (Huntington Library, 1940). Most recently, Wesley F. Craven has challenged the Wertenbaker interpretation of Bacon's Rebellion as a democratic revolution forecasting the ultimate break with England; he has also drawn one of the best pictures of the Virginia-Maryland county court system with all its oligarchic manifestations, *The Southern Colonies in the Seventeenth Century* (Baton Rouge, 1948).

Fundamental for any interpretation of the Old South is Avery O. Craven, *Soil Exhaustion as a Factor in the Agricultural History of Virginia and Maryland, 1607-1860* (University of Illinois, 1926); very informative is Lewis C. Gray, *History of Agriculture in the Southern United States to 1860* (Washington, 1933). Herbert I. Priestley, *The Coming of the White Man, 1492-1848* (Macmillan, 1929), covers the various immigrant groups for this era; in this same series of A. M. Schlesinger and D. R. Fox, "History of American Life Series" is T. J. Wertenbaker's *The First Americans* (Macmillan, 1927). Melville J. Herskovits maintains a significant thesis that Africanisms have influenced American culture far more than is yet conceded in *The Myth of the Negro Past* (Harper, 1941). Excellent brief explanations of feudal borrowings appear in R. B. Morris, "Entail," in *Encyclopedia of the Social Sciences* and Carl Brinkman, "Primogeniture," *ibid.* See also Andrews, Morris, Cubberley, Nettels, and Robb-Garrison.

· 4 ·

FEUDAL EXPERIMENTS AMONG VIRGINIA'S NEIGHBORS

Ellis L. Raesly has unlocked hitherto unused Dutch sources to provide the delightfully fresh picture of life in Peter Stuyvesant's times, *Portrait of New Netherlands* (Columbia, 1945). A most revealing contemporary source is B. B. James and J. F. Jameson (eds.), *Journal of Jasper Dunckaerts 1679-1680* (Scribner, 1913), dealing with a keen Dutch observer. The standard work on the colony is A. C. Flick, *History of the State of New York* (Columbia, 1933), vol. 2. Considerable social history in a simple narrative form appears in Alice M. Earle, *Colonial Days in Old New York* (Scribner, 1912), and her *Home Life in Colonial Days* (Macmillan, 1902).

The confusion between Finns and Swedes in the story of Delaware has been clarified by John H. Wuorinen, *The Finns on the Delaware, 1638-1655* (Columbia, 1938). Ponderously detailed is Amandus Johnson, *The Swedish Settlements on the Delaware, 1638-1644* (Appleton, 1911), 2 vols. Pennsylvania's social history has many excellent studies: Ralph Wood has edited some splendid essays in *The Pennsylvania Germans* (Princeton, 1942). This colony is heavily represented in T. J. Wertenbaker, *The Founding of American Civilization: The Middle Colonies* (Scribner, 1938). Other special works relevant for Pennsylvania are Elbert Russell, *The History of Quakerism* (Macmillan, 1942), Edward C. O. Beatty, *William Penn as Social Philosopher* (Columbia, 1939), and W. F. Dunaway, *A History of Pennsylvania* (Prentice-Hall, 1935).

All the colonies are dealt with from a special angle in Joseph Dorfman, *The Economic Mind in American Civilization* (Viking, 1946), I; Seymour Dunbar, *A History of Travel in America* (Bobbs-Merrill, 1915); and Arthur W. Calhoun, *A Social History of the American Family* (Arthur H. Clark, 1917-1919), I, written by a sociologist with a wealth of historical data, but necessarily modified by newer monographs by historians. See also Parrington, W. F. Craven, A. O. Craven, Gray, Andrews, Morris, Priestley, and Robb-Garrison.

· 5 ·

TOWN AND COUNTRY IN THE AGE OF FRANKLIN (1760-1763)

The dominant role of colonial towns and the merchant class in a rural society is convincingly presented in Carl and Jessica Bridenbaugh, *Rebels and Gentlemen: Philadelphia in the Age of Franklin* (Reynal and Hitchcock, 1942), and in Carl Bridenbaugh's more inclusive, *Cities in the Wilderness: The First Century of Urban Life in America, 1625-1742* (Ronald Press, 1938). There is considerable social history in Carl Van Doren's excellent *Benjamin Franklin* (Viking, 1938) and his edition of *Benjamin Franklin's Autobiographical Writings* (Viking, 1945).

A comprehensive one-volume survey of the social history of this era is attempted in James T. Adams, *Provincial Society, 1690-1763* (Macmillan, 1927). Very useful for economic history are William B. Weeden, *Economic and Social History of New England, 1620-1789* (Houghton Mifflin, 1890), 2 vols., Richardson Wright, *Hawkers and Walkers in Early America* (Lippincott, 1927). Other useful books in this field are Dixon Wecter, *The Saga of American Society: A Record of Social Aspirations, 1607-1937* (Scribner, 1937); Mary Benson, *Women in Eighteenth-century America* (Columbia, 1935); Foster R. Dulles, *America Learns to Play: A History of Popular Recreation, 1607-1940* (Appleton-Century, 1940); Arthur Hornblow, *A History of the Theatre in America* (Lippincott, 1919). See also among previously cited works, Nettels, Calhoun, A. M. Earle, Dunbar, and R. B. Morris' *Government and Labor in Early America*, and Monica Kiefer, *American Children through Their Books, 1700-1835* (University of Pennsylvania, 1948), a social history investigating the changing status of children.

· 6 ·

THE ENLIGHTENMENT AND THE GREAT AWAKENING (1700-1763)

On the concepts of the Enlightenment, see Ernst Cassirir, "Enlightenment," in *Encyclopedia of the Social Sciences* and Carl Becker, "Progress," *ibid.* Rationalism is dealt with in Herbert W. Morais, *Deism in Eighteenth-century America* (Columbia, 1934). Max Savelle has written a comprehensive and thoughtful cultural history of the American Enlightenment in *Seeds of Liberty: The Genesis of the American Mind* (Knopf, 1948). Scientific life is discussed in Frederick P. Bowes, *The Culture of Early Charleston* (University of North Carolina, 1942); Henry B. Shafer, *The American Medical Profession, 1733-1850* (Columbia, 1936); Francis R. Packard, *History of Medicine in the United States* (Hoerber, 1931); and, for invention, see Roger Burlingame, *March of the Iron Men* (Scribner, 1940). Splendid university histories include Samuel E. Morison, *Three Centuries of Harvard* (Harvard, 1936); Thomas J. Wertenbaker, *Princeton, 1746-1896* (Princeton, 1946); and Edwin Oviatt, *The Beginnings of Yale, 1701-1726* (Yale, 1916). For literature, see Parrington, cited; Louis B. Wright and Marion Tilling (eds.), *The Secret Diary of William Byrd of Westover, 1709-1712* (Dietz Press, 1941); Frank L. Mott, *American Journalism* (Macmillan, 1950); Carl Van Doren (ed.), *The Cambridge History of American Literature* (Macmillan, 1917, 3 vols.; single volume edition, 1945).

The Great Awakening can best be followed in William Sweet, *Religion in Colonial America* (Scribner, 1943); Ola Elizabeth Winslow, *Jonathan Edwards* (Macmillan, 1940); Perry Miller, *Jonathan Edwards* (William Sloane, 1949), the most analytical biography; C. H. Faust and T. H. Johnson, *Jonathan Edwards* (American Book, 1935), which is a combination of biography and relevant selections; and Parrington, *op cit.* For art, the most satisfactory general treatment is Oliver Larkin, *Art and Life in America* (Rinehart, 1949); architecture is best handled in Fiske Kimball, *American Architecture* (Bobbs-Merrill, 1928); and T. E. Tallmadge, *The Story of Architecture in America* (Norton, 1936). For other aspects, see Livingston Rutherford, *John Peter Zenger* (Dodd, Mead, 1904); Stuart G. Noble, *A History of American Education* and Cubberley, previously cited.

· 7 ·

THE REVOLUTIONARY ERA OF HANCOCK AND JEFFERSON
(1763-1789)

The most convenient summary for the social-economic history of this period is Evarts B. Greene, *The Revolutionary Generation, 1763-1790* (Macmillan, 1943). For the role of the merchants in the Revolution, see A. M. Schlesinger, *The Colonial Merchants and the American Revolution, 1763-1776* (Longmans, Green, 1918); W. T. Baxter, *The House of Hancock, 1724-1775* (Harvard, 1945); which is an expert study of economic factors in history; Herbert S. Allen, *John Hancock, Patriot in Purple* (Macmillan, 1948), a popular, highly informative account of the man and his role in business as well as politics. Constitutional and religious aspects are dealt with in Charles H. McIlwain, *The American Revolution: A Constitutional Interpretation* (Macmillan, 1923); Carl Becker, *The Declaration of Independence* (Knopf, 1942); Alice M. Baldwin, *The New England Clergy and the American Revolution* (Duke, 1928); Philip Davidson, *Propaganda and the American Revolution* (University of North Carolina, 1941). For still other aspects, there are C. H. Van Tyne, *The Loyalists in the American Revolution* (Macmillan, 1902); Allan Nevins, *The American States during and after the Revolution* (Macmillan, 1927); W. C. Abbott, *New York and the American Revolution* (Scribner, 1929); Oscar T. Barck, Jr., *New York City during the War for Independence* (Columbia, 1931); C. H. Sherrill, *French Memories of Eighteenth-century America* (Scribner, 1915).

The literature on Jefferson is growing rapidly. What may well stand indefinitely as the best biography is Dumas Malone, *Jefferson, the Virginian* (Little, Brown, 1948), of which the second volume is soon expected. Adrienne Koch has written a well-rounded study in *The Philosophy of Thomas Jefferson* (Columbia, 1943) and presented the general student with a convenient source handbook in *The Life and Selected Writings of Thomas Jefferson* (Modern Library, 1944). Harry H. Clark's *Thomas Paine* (American Book, 1944) offers a good brief biographic essay and selected writings of Paine. Carleton J. H. Hayes, who has conducted many seminars on nationalism, summarizes his position in "Nationalism," *Encyclopedia of the Social Sciences*. A careful historical analysis appears in Hans Kohn's *The Idea of Nationalism* (Macmillan, 1944), pp. 263-325.

A good deal of the history of medical science during this era may be gleaned from Nathan G. Goodman, *Benjamin Rush* (University of Pennsylvania, 1934), and Richard Shryock, *The Development of Modern Medicine* (University of Pennsylvania, 1936). A fascinating, excellent biographic approach to art history may be obtained from James T. Flexner, *America's Old Masters* (Viking, 1939). A highly useful quantitative as well as historical view of "best sellers" is given in Frank L. Mott, *Golden Multitudes* (Macmillan, 1947). For literature, see Parrington, *op. cit.*, the *Cambridge History of American Literature*, and Spiller.

On the Constitution, see the provocative thesis of Charles Beard, *An Economic Interpretation of the Constitution* (Macmillan, 1913); compare this with Andrew C. McLaughlin, *Constitutional History of the United States* (Appleton, 1935).

On other phases dealt with in this chapter, see previous citations.

· 8 ·

THE OLD SOUTH AND THE NEW WEST IN JEFFERSON'S DAY
(1789-1830)

Despite recent attacks on Frederick J. Turner and his frontier theories, much remains in his work that is pertinent to understanding American social history. The most convenient introduction to this controversy is found in George R. Taylor (ed.), *The Turner Thesis* (D. C. Heath, 1949), which includes articles by B. F. Wright, Jr., F. A. Shannon, L. M. Hacker, G. W. Pierson, C. J. H. Hayes, and Avery O. Craven; the famous Turner essay on "The Significance of the Frontier in American History" is reproduced. F. J. Turner, *Rise of the New West* (Harper, 1906), covers part of this period, using the sectional approach to American history. A good history of our land policy is Roy M. Robbins, *Our Landed Heritage* (Princeton, 1942). The Franco-American melting pot in Upper Louisiana is analyzed in Harvey Wish, "The French of Old Missouri, 1804-1821," *Mid-America*, XXIII (1941), 167-89. Other highly relevant accounts on western history are P. W. Bidwell and J. I. Falconer, *History of Agriculture in the Northern United States, 1620-1860* (Washington, D.C., 1925); Milo M. Quaife and Sidney Glazer, *Michigan* (Prentice-Hall, 1948); John D. Barnhart, "The Southern Influence in the Formation of Illinois," *Journal of the Illinois State Historical Society*, XXXII (Sept., 1939).

Among the very useful first-hand accounts of western history are Timothy Flint, *Recollections of the Last Ten Years* (Knopf ed., 1932); W. W. Sweet (ed.), *Religion on the American Frontier: The Presbyterians, 1783-1840* (Harper, 1936); Rufus Babcock, *Memoir of John Mason Peck* (Philadelphia, 1899); Hugh H. Brackenridge, *Views of Louisiana* (Pittsburgh, 1814); Allan Nevins, *American Social History . . .*, cited; Daniel Drake, *Pioneer Life in Kentucky, 1785-1800* (Henry Schuman, 1948); Isaac Weld, *Travels through the States of North America . . . 1795, 1796 and 1797* (London, 1799), 2 vols.; and Oscar Handlin (ed.), *This Was America* (Harvard, 1949).

The literature on the Old South is voluminous; those books especially useful on social history are U. B. Phillips, *Life and Labor in the Old South* (Little, Brown, 1929); Everett Dick, *The Dixie Frontier* (Knopf, 1948), which is especially valuable; Eugene T. Mudge, *The Social Philosophy of John Taylor of Caroline* (Columbia, 1939); Avery O. Craven, *Edmund Ruffin, Southerner* (Appleton, 1932); Dumas Malone, *Thomas Cooper* (Yale, 1926). Thomas D. Clark has blended humor with sound social history in his *Pills, Petticoats, and Plows: The Southern Country Store* (Bobbs-Merrill, 1944) and his *The Rampaging Frontier: Manners and Humors of Pioneer Days in the South and the Middle West* (Bobbs-Merrill, 1939). Clement Eaton has written an informative and provocative synthesis in *A History of the Old South* (Macmillan, 1949).

· 9 ·

THE NORTHEAST: BUSINESS AND SOCIETY UNDER THE ASTORS AND THE LOWELLS (1789-1830)

The most convenient general survey is in John A. Krout and D. R. Fox, *The Completion of Independence, 1790-1830* (Macmillan, 1944). The national shift from commerce to industry can be followed in Kenneth W. Porter, *John Jacob Astor* (Harvard, 1930); John B. McMaster, *Stephen Girard* (Lippincott, 1918); A. H. Cole, *The American Wool Manufacture* (Harvard, 1926), 2 vols.; and Robert G. Albion, *The Rise of New York Port, 1815-1860* (Scribner, 1939); see also the articles on Francis C. Lowell, Nathan Appleton, and Eli Whitney in the *Dictionary of American Biography*. An excellent basic article is Herbert Heaton's "Industrial Revolution," *Encyclopedia of the Social Sciences*.

The rise of trade unionism can be followed in John R. Commons *et al,*

Documentary History of American Industrial Society (Arthur H. Clark, 1910-1911), 11 vols.; Commons *et al., History of Labour in the United States* (Macmillan, 1918), I; Selig Perlman, *A History of Trade Unionism in the United States* (Macmillan, 1923); an interesting over-all labor history intended for the layman is Foster R. Dulles, *Labor in America* (Crowell, 1949). A special phase of the labor-capital picture is in Samuel Reznick, "The Depression of 1819-1822: A Social History," *American Historical Review,* XXXIX (Oct., 1933).

For transportation history, see B. H. Meyer (ed.), *History of Transportation in the United States before 1860* (Washington, 1917); Philip D. Jordan, *The National Road* (Bobbs-Merrill, 1948); and Archer B. Hulbert, *Paths of Inland Commerce* (Yale, Chronicles Series, 1920). Relevant social history for this era appears in Anne H. Wharton, *Social Life in the Early Republic* (Lippincott, 1903), somewhat superficial, but still useful; David M. Ludlum, *Social Ferment in Vermont, 1791-1850* (Columbia, 1939); Jennie Holliman, *American Sports, 1785-1835* (Duke, 1931); the various source selections in Henry S. Commager (ed.), *America in Perspective* (Random House, 1947); and Allan Nevins (ed.), *America through British Eyes* (Oxford, 1948). An excellent new edition of a classic account of the eastern cities is Kenneth and Anna M. Roberts (eds.), *Moreau de St. Mery's American Journey (1793-1798),* (Doubleday, 1947).

· 10 ·

CULTURE IN THE EAST: FROM FRENCH CLASSICISM TO GERMAN ROMANTICISM (1789-1830)

Professor G. A. Borgese has given a good deal of concreteness to the nebulous term, "romanticism," in his excellent article on the subject in the *Encyclopedia of Social Sciences.* For the French classical pattern, see Howard M. Jones, *America and French Culture, 1750-1848* (University of North Carolina, 1927). A good deal of social as well as literary history can be gleaned from the charming pages of Van Wyck Brooks, *The World of Washington Irving* (Dutton, 1944). Other specialized works on literature for this era are: Leon Howard, *The Connecticut Wits* (University of Chicago, 1942); Herbert R. Brown, *The Sentimental Novel in America, 1789-1860* (Duke, 1940); C. E. Cunningham, *Timothy Dwight* (Macmillan, 1942); Robert E. Spiller, *James Fenimore Cooper*

(American Book, 1936), which contains a brief biography, notes, and selections; Harry Warfel, *Noah Webster, Schoolmaster to America* (Macmillan, 1936), and Erwin C. Shoemaker, *Noah Webster* (Columbia, 1936), both of which deserve to be read carefully for the light they cast on American cultural nationalism. Vernon Parrington, *The Romantic Revolution in America;* vol. 2 of *Main Currents in American Thought* (Harcourt, Brace, 1930), deals with political theorists as well as literary figures. On the legal and constitutional aspects, see John T. Horton, *James Kent: A Study in Conservatism* (Appleton, 1939); A. J. Beveridge, *John Marshall* (Houghton, Mifflin, 1916-1919), 4 vols.; William R. Leslie, "The Influence of Joseph Story's Theory of the Conflict of Laws on Constitutional Nationalism," *Mississippi Valley Historical Review,* XXXV (1948), 203-20.

On music, see John Tasker Howard, *Our American Music* (Crowell, 1939), and Sigmund Spaeth, *A History of Popular Music* (Random House, 1948). For the arts see Talbot Hamlin's splendid volume, *Greek Revival Architecture in America* (Oxford, 1944), and the first-hand views of Benjamin H. Latrobe on contemporary architecture and incidentally American life in its wider phases, *The Journal of Latrobe* (Appleton, 1905). Oliver Larkin, *Art and Life in America,* cited, offers the most recent judgments on the arts. For a good picture of New England religious orthodoxy, see James K. Morse, *Jedidiah Morse* (Columbia, 1939). On journalism, see Frank Mott, *American Journalism,* cited, and W. G. Bleyer, *Main Currents in the History of American Journalism* (Houghton Mifflin, 1927).

· 11 ·

THE MELTING POT OF CARL SCHURZ' DAY (1830-1861)

There are invaluable contemporary accounts of immigration in Edith Abbott (ed.), *Historical Aspects of the Immigration Problem: Select Documents* (University of Chicago, 1926), which covers practically every major group. For the Irish wave, the best books are W. F. Adams, *Ireland and Irish Emigration to the New World from 1815 to the Famine* (Yale, 1933), and Oscar Handlin, *Boston's Immigrants, 1790-1865: A Study in Acculturation* (Harvard, 1941). Allied with the Irish immigration story is the Catholic-Protestant clash of this era as told most objectively by Ray Billington, *The Protestant Crusade, 1800-1861* (Macmillan,

1938), and, from a Catholic viewpoint, by Theodore Maynard, *Story of American Catholicism* (Macmillan, 1941).

The German-American has attracted the greatest number of historians among the foreign groups. A. B. Faust has written the most encyclopedic, sometimes unreliable, but often suggestive survey of the subject in *The German Element in the United States* (Houghton Mifflin, 1909), 2 vols. Carl Wittke has been a host in himself in interpreting the German-American of this period from a scientific point of view, notably in *Against the Current: The Life of Karl Heinzen* (University of Chicago, 1945), *Wilhelm Weitling, Utopian Communist* (Louisiana State University, 1950), and his forthcoming, *The German Forty-Eighters in America;* his very useful general summary of immigrant history is *We Who Built America* (Prentice-Hall, 1939), which deals with all groups except the English. John A. Hawgood has emphasized the nationalist spirit of so many of the German-American immigrant projects in *The Tragedy of German-America* (Putnam, 1940). An excellent biography that tells much about the German-American is Frank Friedel, *Francis Lieber* (Louisiana State University, 1948).

The Scandinavians are now very well represented in historical literature. Theodore C. Blegen has written authoritatively in *The Norwegian Migration to America, 1825-1860* (Norwegian American Historical Association, Northfield, Minn., 1930) and entertainingly on the same subject in *Grass Roots History* (University of Minnesota, 1947); Adolph B. Benson and Naboth Hedin have edited considerable first-hand material in *The Swedes in America, 1638-1938* (Yale, 1938); and K. C. Babcock discusses the entire subject in *The Scandinavian Element in the United States* (University of Illinois, 1914). On other groups see, Mary R. Coolidge, *Chinese Immigration* (Holt, 1909); Lee J. Levinger, *A History of the Jews of the United States* (Union of American Hebrew Congregations, Cincinnati, 1935); Marcus Lee Hansen, *The Atlantic Migration, 1607-1860,* which covers the major groups in a brilliant synthesis with considerable emphasis on the European setting. There is much about the immigrant in American culture in the essays edited by David F. Bowers, *Foreign Influences in American Life* (Princeton, 1944). A good standard history is George M. Stephenson, *A History of American Immigration* (Ginn, 1926).

· 12 ·

THE WEST OF JACKSON AND FRANCIS PARKMAN (1830-1861)

The most extensive first-hand sources on the West are in Reuben G. Thwaites (ed.), *Early Western Travels, 1748-1846* (Cleveland, 1904-1906), 32 vols. The Parkman theme of this chapter can be followed from Francis Parkman, *The Oregon Trail* (Little, Brown, 1910); Mason Wade (ed.), *The Journals of Francis Parkman* (Harper, 1947) and his *Francis Parkman, Heroic Historian* (Viking, 1942). This period is partly covered by the sectional analysis in Avery O. Craven (ed.), Frederick J. Turner's *The United States, 1830-1850* (Holt, 1935). Ray Billington's *Westward Expansion* (Macmillan, 1949) is one of the most useful general histories of the West.

For the Mississippi Valley, the most reliable and readable studies are: Francis P. Weisenburger, *The Passing of the Frontier: The History of Ohio* (Ohio State, 1941); Bayrd Still, *Milwaukee* (State Historical Society, Wisconsin, 1948); R. G. Thwaites, *Wisconsin* (Houghton Mifflin, 1908); T. C. Pease, *Illinois: The Frontier State, 1818-1848* (McClurg, 1922); Bessie L. Pierce, *A History of Chicago* (Knopf, 1937-1940), 2 vols.; B. L. Pierce (ed.), *As Others See Chicago: Impressions of Visitors, 1673-1933* (University of Chicago, 1933); Cyrenus Cole, *A History of the People of Iowa* (Torch Press, 1921); John G. Fletcher, *Arkansas* (University of North Carolina, 1947); William R. Hogan, *The Texas Republic* (University of Oklahoma, 1946); Rupert N. Richardson, *Texas* (Prentice-Hall, 1943); Marquis James, *The Raven: Sam Houston* (Bobbs-Merrill, 1929); William J. Petersen, *Steamboating on the Upper Mississippi* (State Historical Society of Iowa, 1937); Mark Twain's classic on steamboat life, *Life on the Mississippi* (Bantam Books, 1945); and Bruce Nelson's *Land of the Dacotahs* (University of Minnesota, 1946), which is both fascinating and informative reading on the upper Missouri Valley.

The Great Plains and the Far West have an enormous literature: Sidney Warren, *Farthest Frontier: the Pacific Northwest* (Macmillan, 1949); Oscar Winther, *The Great Northwest* (Knopf, 1947); G. W. Fuller, *History of the Pacific Northwest* (Knopf, 1931); Jay Monaghan, *The Overland Trail* (Bobbs-Merrill, 1947); John F. McDermott (ed.), *The Western Journals of Washington Irving* (University of Oklahoma,

1944); R. L. Duffus, *The Santa Fe Trail* (Longmans, Green, 1930); Maurice S. Sullivan, *The Life of Jedidiah Smith* (Santa Ana, 1937); Stanley Vestal, *Jim Bridger: Mountain Man* (Morrow, 1946); Everett Dick, *Vanguards of the Frontier* (Appleton, 1941), which is especially valuable for social history; Bernard De Voto, *The Year of Decision, 1846* (Little, Brown, 1943); Grant H. Smith, *History of the Comstock Lode* (University of Nevada, 1943); Hiram M. Chittenden, *The American Fur Trade in the Far West* (Harper, 1902), 3 vols., the standard account; H. E. Bolton *The Spanish Borderlands* (Yale, 1921); Alfred B. Thomas, *After Coronado* (University of Oklahoma, 1935), covering the early Spanish advance.

On the California story, the leading accounts useful for the social and economic aspects are: Robert G. Cleland, *From Wilderness to Empire* (Knopf, 1944) and his *The Cattle on a Thousand Hills: Southern California, 1850-1870* (Huntington Library, 1941); John W. Caughey, *California* (Prentice-Hall, 1940); Carey McWilliams, *Southern California Country* (Duell, Sloan, 1946); Richard H. Dana, Jr., *Two Years before the Mast* (Macmillan, 1911), a classic first-hand account of the New England trade with California; J. P. Zollenger, *Sutter* (Oxford, 1939); H. E. Bolton, *Outpost of Empire* (Knopf, 1931), which deals with San Francisco.

For the story of the Indian, the convenient summary is Clark Wissler, *Indians of the United States* (Doubleday, 1940). Other historical aspects relevant to this chapter are Grant Foreman, *The Last Trek of the Indians* (University of Chicago, 1946), also his *Indian Removal: The Emigration of the Five Civilized Tribes of Indians* (University of Oklahoma, 1932). Among the leading anthropological accounts are: Paul Radin, *The American Indian* (Liveright, 1934); A. L. Kroeber, *Cultural and Natural Areas of Native North America* (University of California, 1939); C. Kluckholn and D. C. Leighton *The Navaho* (Harvard, 1946); and Ralph Linton (ed.), *Acculturation in Seven American Indian Tribes* Appleton-Century, 1940).

· 13 ·

CULT OF THE COMMON MAN: HORACE GREELEY'S ERA
(1830-1861)

The convenient survey of the social-economic phases of this period is Carl Fish, *The Rise of the Common Man, 1830-1850* (Macmillan, 1929). For the controversial Jackson wage-earner factor, see Arthur M. Schlesinger, Jr., *The Age of Jackson* (Little, Brown, 1947), a Pulitzer prize winner; Joseph Dorfman, "The Jackson Wage-Earner Thesis," *American Historical Review,* LIV (1949), 296-306; also Dorfman's *The Economic Mind in American Civilization,* II cited; Richard Morris, "Andrew Jackson, Strikebreaker," *American Historical Review,* LIV (1949), 54-68. For other labor phases, see Helen S. Zahler, *Eastern Workingmen and National Land Policy, 1829-1862* (Columbia, 1941); Norman Ware, *The Industrial Worker, 1840-1860* (Houghton Mifflin, 1924); and, among those previously cited, J. R. Commons *et al., Documentary History of American Industrial Society,* and, by the same author, *A History of Labour in the United States,* also Dulles, *Labor in America,* cited, Selig Perlman, *A History of Trade Unionism . . . ,* cited.

For the industrial aspects, see Leland D. Baldwin, *Pittsburgh* (University of Pittsburgh, 1937); Paul W. Gates, *The Illinois Central Railroad and Its Colonization Work* (Harvard, 1934); Blake McKelvey, *Rochester, the Water-Power City, 1812-1854* (Harvard, 1945); A. H. Cole, *The American Wool Manufacture,* cited; R. G. Albion, *The Rise of New York Port,* cited; K. W. Porter, *John J. Astor,* cited. Grace Lee Nute, *Lake Superior* (Bobbs-Merrill, 1944); Arthur Pound, *Lake Ontario* (Bobbs-Merrill, 1945).

The most fascinating discussion of the various "Utopias" is Alice F. Tyler, *Freedom's Ferment* (University of Minnesota, 1944). Other valuable books and articles on the subject are M. F. Melcher, *The Shaker Adventure* (Princeton, 1941); D. W. Douglas and K. D. Lumpkin, "Communistic Settlements," *Encyclopedia of the Social Sciences;* Fawn Brodie, *No Man Knows My History: the Life of Joseph Smith* (Knopf, 1945). Very useful for other reforms are: Horace Greeley, *Recollections of a Varied Life* (Treat, N. Y., 1872); G. W. Pierson, *Tocqueville and Beaumont in America* (Oxford University, 1938); Alexis de Tocqueville, *Democracy in America* (Knopf, 1945), 2 vols., a brilliant effort to interpret the American psychology; Merle Curti, *The American Peace Crusade, 1815-1861* (Duke, 1929); Curti, *The Learned Blacksmith* (Wilson-Erickson, 1937), Elihu Burritt's account of the peace movement; J. A. Krout, *The Origins of Prohibition* (Knopf, 1925). The antislavery emphasis has shifted regionally from New England to the Middle West since the publication of Gilbert H. Barnes's *The Anti-Slavery Impulse, 1830-1844* (Appleton-Century, 1933), which stresses the role of Theodore Weld rather than of Garrison, and Dwight L. Dumond's *Antislavery Origins of the Civil War* (Oxford, 1939); also of value is G. H. Barnes and D. L. Dumond (eds.), *Letters of Theodore D. Weld, Angelina Grimke Weld and Sarah Grimke, 1822-1844* (Appleton-Century, 1934), 2 vols.; much on the movement can be gleaned from Henry S. Commager, *Theodore Parker* (Little, Brown, 1936), and Ralph Harlow, *Gerrit Smith, Philanthropist and Reformer* (Holt, 1939); and from Philip S. Foner, *Business and Slavery: New York Merchants and the Irrepressible Conflict* (University of North Carolina, 1941).

Among the useful first-hand accounts of contemporary society are: Charles Mackay, *Life and Liberty in America* (Harper, 1859); Alexis de Tocqueville, *Democracy in America* (Knopf, 1945), 2 vols., widely considered the most brilliant analysis of the American outlook; Charles Dickens, *American Notes* (Macmillan, 1893), an obviously biased account, but valuable for the skillful pen pictures of contemporary towns; Thomas Hamilton, *Men and Manners in America* (Carey, Lea, Philadelphia, 1833); Francis J. Grund, *Aristocracy in America* (London, 1839), 2 vols.; Alexander Mackay, *The Western World* (London, 1849).

· 14 ·

THE AMERICAN RENAISSANCE OF MANN AND EMERSON: HIGH TIDE OF ROMANTICISM (1830-1861)

Much more than the chapter title is due F. O. Matthiessen, *American Renaissance: Art and Expression in the Age of Emerson and Whitman* (Oxford, 1941), which deals with the esthetic aspects of literature. George Boas has thrown a good deal of light on an abused term in his edition of *Romanticism in America* (Johns Hopkins, 1940). The literary history for this era can be derived in considerable detail from V. L. Parrington, *Main Currents in American Thought,* II; Spiller *et al., Literary History of the United States,* II; Van Wyck Brooks, *The Flowering of New England, 1815-1865* (Dutton, 1936); S. I. Hayakawa and H. M. Jones, *Oliver Wendell Holmes* (American Book, 1939), an excellent biographic essay and copious selections; Constance Rourke, *American Humor* (Harcourt, Brace, 1931). None of these books, of course, is a substitute for the first-hand reading into substantial portions of Emerson's essays, Melville's novels, Whitman's poetry, etc.

For journalism, the best works are those of Frank L. Mott, *A History of American Magazines, 1741-1850* (Appleton, 1930), 3 vols., and his *American Journalism,* cited. Among the useful works on the historians are C. P. Higby and B. T. Schantz, *John L. Motley* (American Book, 1939), biographic essays and selections; Russell Nye, *George Bancroft* (Knopf, 1944); Mason Wade, *Parkman*, cited. On sociological thought, see L. L. Bernard, *Origins of American Sociology* (Crowell, 1943), and Harvey Wish, "Stephen P. Andrews, American Pioneer Sociologist," *Social Forces*, XIX (1941), pp. 447-82. For political theory, there are Richard Hofstadter, *The American Political Tradition and the Men Who Made It* (Knopf, 1948); Carl B. Swisher, *Roger B. Taney* (Macmillan, 1935); Benjamin F. Wright, Jr., *The American Interpretation of Natural Law* (Harvard, 1931), and his *The Growth of American Constitutional Law* (Reynal and Hitchcock, 1942); Ralph Gabriel, *The Course of American Democratic Thought*, cited.

Merle Curti's *The Growth of American Thought* (Harper, 1943) may be consulted profitably on almost every phase of intellectual history, literary, scientific, popular reading tastes, etc. His *The Social Ideas of American Educators* (Scribner, 1935) is a contribution to the philosophy and underlying assumptions of American education. Other worth-while books on the subject are: Morison, *Three Centuries of Harvard*, cited; A. C. Cole, *Mount Holyoke* (Yale, 1940); Robert S. Fletcher, *History of Oberlin College* (Oberlin, 1943); John A. Walz, *German Influences in American Education and Culture* (Carl Schurz Memorial Foundation, 1936), a very brief, but highly informative discussion. For the lyceum movement, see "Josiah Holbrook," *Dictionary of American Biography* (Scribner, 1928-1932); for the common school revival, see "Horace Mann," *ibid.*

On the contemporary musical scene, John T. Howard has written *Stephen Foster, America's Troubadour* (Crowell, 1934), and *Our American Music*, cited; R. Walters, *Stephen Foster* (Princeton, 1936); Carl Wittke, *Tambo and Bones: A History of the American Minstrel Stage* (Duke, 1930); Philip Jordan, *Singin' Yankees* (University of Minnesota, 1946), which deals with a troupe of American entertainers. For art, there is much in the biography of F. Carlton Mabee, Jr., *American Leonardo: A Life of Samuel F. B. Morse* (Knopf, 1943); Lorado Taft, *A History of American Sculpture* (Macmillan, rev. ed., 1930); Oliver Larkin, *Art and Life in America*, cited.

Unusually successful in integrating science with the social milieu is Dirk J. Struik, *Yankee Science in the Making* (Little, Brown, 1948); very fascinating and integrative also is Bernard Jaffe, *Men of Science in America* (Simon & Schuster, 1944). Mabee's biography of Morse, cited above, has a good deal of scientific history. There are a number of valuable first-hand observations of scientific as well as social value in the record of the famous English scientist, Charles Lyell, *Travels in America in the Years 1841-1842* (Wiley and Putnam, 1845), 2 vols.

· 15 ·

THE ANTEBELLUM SOUTH: FROM JEFFERSON TO JEFFERSON DAVIS (1830-1861)

The most convenient general work on social and economic history is Arthur C. Cole, *The Irrepressible Conflict* (Macmillan, 1934); for the South alone, the best-rounded story is that of Clement Eaton, *A History of the Old South* (Macmillan, 1949); also useful is Francis B. Simkins, *The South, Old and New* (Knopf, 1947). There is much social history in Allan Nevins, *Ordeal of the Union* (Scribner, 1947), 2 vols., two in preparation.

On slavery, the standard work has been U. B. Phillips, *American Negro Slavery* (Appleton, 1918); much of this story has been revised in John Hope Franklin, *From Slavery to Freedom* (Knopf, 1947). Challenging the historians who have minimized the role of slave insurrections is Herbert Aptheker, *American Negro Slave Revolts* (Columbia, 1943); the psychology of a single slave insurrection incident is analyzed in Harvey Wish, "The Slave Insurrection Panic of 1856," *Journal of Southern History*, V (1939), 206-22. The same writer has examined the non-slaveholders' stake in slavery in "The Revival of the African Slave Trade in the United States, 1856-1860," *Mississippi Valley Historical Review*, XXVII (1941), 569-88. A useful source is Carter G. Woodson (ed.), *The Mind of the Negro as Reflected in Letters, 1800-1860* (Association for the Study of Negro Life and History, Washington, 1926).

Economic, geographic, and social factors are dealt with in E. M. Coulter, *Georgia: A Short History* (University of North Carolina, 1947); Joseph C. Roberts, *The Story of Tobacco in America* (Knopf, 1949); Minnie C. Boyd, *Alabama in the Fifties* (Columbia, 1931); Charles Sydnor, *The Development of Southern Sectionalism, 1819-1848* (Louisiana State University, 1948); R. B. Vance, *Human Geography of the South* (University of North Carolina, 1932); Kathleen Bruce, *Virginia Iron Manufactures in the Slave Era* (Century, 1930); J. D. B. De Bow, *The Industrial Resources of the Southern and Western States* (New Orleans, 1852), largely contemporary data, news reports, letters, etc.

On the social classes of the South, a very recent attempt to shift the emphasis from the planter to the yeomanry is Frank Owsley, *The Plain Folks of the Old South* (Louisiana State University, 1949). Clarifying the definition of "poor white" from a social and literary viewpoint is Shields McIlwaine, *The Southern Poor White from Lubberland to Tobacco Road* (University of Oklahoma, 1939); Paul Buck, "The Poor White in the Antebellum South," *American Historical Review*, XXXI (1925), 41-54. Among the better first-hand views of the class structure are F. L. Olmsted, *The Cotton Kingdom* (N. Y., 1861), 2 vols.; A. B. Longstreet, *Georgia Scenes* (Harper, 1897); J. G. Baldwin, *The Flush Times of Alabama and Mississippi* (N. Y., 1853); Susan D. Smedes, *Memorials of a Southern Planter* (N. Y., 1890). On the plantation, see T. P. Abernethy, *From Frontier to Plantation in Tennessee* (University of North Carolina, 1930). For other phases, see Shields McIlwaine, *Memphis Down in Dixie* (Dutton, 1948); G. M. Capers, Jr., *The Biography of a River Town, Memphis* (University of North Carolina, 1939); Jesse T. Carpenter, *The South as a Conscious Minority* (New York University, 1930); R. R. Russel, *Economic Aspects of Southern Sectionalism, 1840-1861* (University of Illinois, 1924); Avery O. Craven, *The Coming of the Civil War* (Scribner, 1942); R. H. Taylor, *Antebellum South Carolina: A Social and Cultural History* (University of North Carolina, 1942). Extremely valuable for many aspects of cultural, social, and economic history is W. T. Couch (ed.), *Culture in the South* (University of North Carolina, 1935).

· 16 ·

INTELLECTUAL TRENDS IN SOUTHERN NATIONALISM (1830-1861)

The proslavery literature and Southern nationalism are discussed in Jay B. Hubbell, "Literary Nationalism in the Old South," *American Studies in Honor of William K. Boyd,* ed. by D. K. Jackson (Duke, 1940); William S. Jenkins, *Proslavery Thought in the Old South* (University of North Carolina, 1935); Clement Eaton, *Freedom of Thought in the Old South* (Duke, 1940); Harvey Wish, *George Fitzhugh, Propagandist of the Old South* (Louisiana State University, 1944); and, for a contemporary view, Hinton R. Helper, *The Impending Crisis* (A. B. Burdick, N. Y., 1860).

On Southern literature, the quarrel over the role of Walter Scott in the

South can be followed in George H. Orians, *The Influence of Walter Scott on America and American Culture before 1860* (University of Illinois, 1929), and in his "Walter Scott, Mark Twain, and the Civil War," *South Atlantic Quarterly*, XL (1941), 342-59, both of which deny that Scott revolutionized Southern thought; along similar lines, see Grace C. Landrum, "Sir Walter Scott and His Literary Rivals in the Old South," *American Literature*, II (1930), 256-76. Far more inclined to credit the Scott thesis is Rollin G. Osterweis, *Romanticism and Nationalism in the Old South* (Yale, 1949). Much of the Southern literary scene can be learned from W. P. Trent, *William Gilmore Simms* (Houghton Mifflin, 1892); Robert E. Spiller *et al., Literary History of the United States,* cited; Gregory Paine, *Southern Prose Writers* (American Book, 1947), which contains biographical essays and large selections from the leading writers; V. L. Parrington, *Main Currents in American Thought*, II, cited; *Cambridge History of American Literature,* II, cited.

For other intellectual aspects, see Thomas C. Johnson, *Scientific Interests in the Old South* (Appleton, 1936); W. J. Cash, *The Mind of the South* (Knopf, 1941), a brilliant discussion; Harvey Wish, "George F. Holmes and the Genesis of American Sociology," *American Journal of Sociology*, XLVI (1941), 698-707, and his "Aristotle, Plato, and the Mason-Dixon Line," *Journal of the History of Ideas*, X (1949), 254-66; and for a first-hand view, see Frances A. Kemble, *Fanny Kemble: Records of Later Life* (Holt, 1882). See the bibliography for Chapter 14 for many relevant books.

· 17 ·

CIVIL WAR: TRIUMPH OF AMERICAN NATIONALITY

The most informative behind-the-lines story is told by Emerson D. Fite, *Social and Industrial Conditions in the North during the Civil War* (Macmillan, 1910), and by A. C. Cole, *The Irrepressible Conflict, 1850-1865,* cited. The latter has also written *The Era of the Civil War* (Mc-Clurg, 1922), dealing with wartime Illinois. Also very relevant for the Union side are Earle D. Ross, *Democracy's College: The Land Grant Movement* (Iowa State College, 1942); W. C. Ford (ed)., *A Cycle of Adams Letters, 1861-1866* (Houghton Mifflin, 1920); and the articles on John Wilkes Booth, Charles F. Browne, Ezra Cornell, and Julia Ward Howe in the *Dictionary of American Biography.*

Especially useful for the Confederacy are: Bell I. Wiley, *The Life of*

Johnny Reb (Bobbs-Merrill, 1943), and his *Southern Negroes, 1861-1865* (Yale, 1938); along the same line, showing the active role of the Negro in behalf of his own freedom is Harvey Wish, "Slave Disloyalty under the Confederacy," *Journal of Negro History* (1938), 435-50. Among the best first-hand accounts are Mary B. Chesnut, *Dixie War Diary* (Houghton Mifflin, 1949), edited by Ben Ames Williams, making available the complete diary for the first time; Sarah A. Pryor, *Reminiscences of Peace and War* (Macmillan, 1905); J. B. Jones, *A Rebel War Clerk's Diary* (Houghton Mifflin, 1913); Sarah M. Dawson, *A Confederate Girl's Diary* (Houghton Mifflin, 1913).

On western history, see J. V. Frederick, *Ben Holladay* (Glendale, 1940), for the expressing activities on the Great Plains; Le Roy Hafen, *The Overland Mail, 1849-1869* (A. H. Clark, 1926); G. D. Lyman, *The Saga of the Comstock Lode* (Scribner, 1934); Robert L. Thompson, *Wiring a Continent* (Princeton, 1947); Le Roy Hafen and Carl Rister, *Western America* (Prentice-Hall, 1941). See the detailed western bibliography on Chapter 12.

An authoritative explanation of the role of the Catholic church during the Civil War is given by a priest in Benjamin J. Blied, *Catholics and the Civil War* (Milwaukee, 1945), and in a doctoral thesis by Rena M. Andrews, *Archbishop Hughes and the Civil War* (University of Chicago, 1935). A rather critical view of the Protestant clergy is taken in the doctoral thesis of Chester F. Dunham, *The Attitude of the Northern Clergy toward the South, 1860-1865* (Gray Company, Toledo, Ohio, 1942). The most fascinating and detailed accounts of war nursing are those of Helen E. Marshall, *Dorothea Dix* (University of North Carolina, 1937), and Victor Robinson, *White Caps: The Story of Nursing* (Lippincott, 1946); for the broader public health movement, see Richard H. Shryock, *The Development of Modern Medicine* (Knopf, 1947), and Howard D. Kramer, "Effect of the Civil War on the Public Health Movement," *Mississippi Valley Historical Review*, XXXV (1948), 449-62. William B. Hesseltine explodes the myth of Libby Prison and Andersonville in *Civil War Prisons* (Ohio State University, 1930). A hitherto unknown aspect of the war is briefly discussed in Edward N. Wright, *Conscientious Objectors in the Civil War* (University of Pennsylvania, 1931).

Index